CHARLES MACKLIN
by Opie

A

BIOGRAPHICAL

DICTIONARY

OF

ACTORS, ACTRESSES, MUSICIANS, DANCERS,

MANAGERS & OTHER STAGE PERSONNEL

IN LONDON, 1660–1800

Volume 10: M'Intosh *to* Nash

by

PHILIP H. HIGHFILL, JR., KALMAN A. BURNIM

and

EDWARD A. LANGHANS

SOUTHERN ILLINOIS UNIVERSITY PRESS

CARBONDALE AND EDWARDSVILLE

Publication of this work was made possible in part through a grant from the National Endowment for the Humanities

Library of Congress Cataloging in Publication Data
(Revised for volume 10)

Highfill, Philip H.
   A biographical dictionary of actors, actresses, musicians, dancers, managers & other stage personnel in London, 1660–1800.

   Includes bibliographical references.
   CONTENTS: v. 1. Abaco to Belfille. —v. 2. Belfort to Byzand. —[etc.]—v. 10. M'Intosh to Nash.
   1. Performing arts—England—London—Biography.
I. Burnim, Kalman A., joint author. II. Langhans,
Edward A., joint author. III. Title.
PN2597.H5   790.2'092'2 [B]   71–157068
ISBN 0–8093–1130–5 (v. 10)

List of Illustrations

SCENES AND MACHINES

Volume 10

M'Intosh *to* Nash

M'Intosh. *See* MACKINTOSH.

Mackarel, Betty ₍*fl.* 1674–1704?₎, actress.

When *The Mock Tempest* was presented at Drury Lane Theatre, perhaps in the late spring of 1674 and certainly on 19 November of that year, Betty Mackarel rose from the rank of orange girl to that of actress. (Her real name is not known; "Mackarel" was a cant term for bawd or procuress.) With Joe Haines she spoke the introduction to the work, and the dialogue took full advantage of her impudence, bawdy behavior, and statuesque beauty. Haines called her Ariel, and she was probably in breeches:

Here's Betty———Now rail if you dare:
Speak to 'em Betty———ha! asham'd, alas poor
    Girl,
Whisper me!—Oh I'le tell 'em—Gentlemen! she
    says,
Y' are grown so wild she could not stay among ye,
And yet her tender heart is loath to wrong ye.
Spare 'em not,
Whom kindness cannot stir, but stripes may move.
    Bet. *O Mr Hains! I've often felt their Love.*
    Ha. *Poh, felt a Pudding that has taken vent,*
Their love cools faster, and as soon is spent.
Think of thy high calling Betty, now th'art here,
They gaze and wish, but cannot reach thy Sphere,
Though ev'ry one could squeeze thy Orange there.
    Bet. *Why this to me, Mr. Haines (d'ee conceive*
        me) why to me?
    Ha. *Ay, why this to Betty?*
O Virtue, Virtue! vainly art thou sought,
If such as Betty must be counted naught:
Examine your Consciences Gentlemen!
When urg'd with heat of love, and hotter Wine,
How have you begg'd, to gain your lewd design:
Betty, dear, dear, dear Betty,
I'le spend five Guinnyes on thee, if thou'st go:
And then they shake their (d'ee conceive me) Betty
        is't notso, their yellow Boyes.
    Bet. *Fie Mr. Hains, y'are very rude (d'ee con-*
        ceive me)
    Ha. *Then speak your self.*
    Bet. *Gentlemen! you know what I know.*
                If y'are severe, all shall out
        by this light:
                But if you will be kind, I'le
        still be right.
    Ha. *So that's well—make thy Cursy*
Betty.
Now go in Child, I have something to say to these
    Gentlemen in private.
                        {Exit Betty.

How much more acting Betty did is not known; she may well have played bit parts for the King's Company while also serving as an orange girl.

The satirist Robert Gould pictured the wits in the pit

hot at repartee with Orange Betty,
Who tho not blest with halfe a grain of sense,
To leaven her whole lump of impudence,
Aided with that she allways is too hard
For the vain things & bests them from their guard.

Phillips's *History of Don Quixote* in 1687 described her as "the gyantess Betty-Makarela," and Etherege in 1686 called her "handsom." She became the mistress of Sir Thomas Armstrong, and in "Sir Thomas Armstrong's Last Farewell" in *Poems on Affairs of State* in 1684 she was cited as "Bess Mackrell." At the end of that poem the satirist wrote: "Sweet Betty, farewell: 'twas for thee I abjured / My lady and children this fourteen long years." In "To Mr. Julian" in the *State* poems in 1704 is the line, "May Betty Mackrel cease to be a whore."

Mackarnea, Mr ₍*fl.* 1748₎, actor.
On 24 August 1748 at Bartholomew Fair a Mr Mackarnea played Lord Worthy in *The Unnatural Parents*; he was replaced in the part when the work was given again (as *The Fair Maid of the West*) at Southwark Fair on 7 September. Probably he was the "Mackennea" who acted the Uncle in *The London Merchant* at James Street on 31 October 1748.

Mackennea. *See* MACKARNEA.

Mackenzie, Mr ₍*fl.* 1723–1741?₎, actor.
A Mr Mackenzie shared a benefit with two others at Lincoln's Inn Fields on 14 May 1723; the gross receipts were £93 15s. 6d. The following year he shared £80 14s. with two actresses. That might suggest that Mackenzie was an actor, but no roles are known for him. A Mackenzie was the Captain of the Guard in *The Siege of Troy* at Lee's Southwark Fair booth in September 1734, and at the same fair in 1736 Mackenzie played Roger in *The Innocent Wife*. The same man, perhaps, was the Mackenzie who acted Chant in *Kouli Kan* at Bartholomew Fair on 22 August 1741.

Mackeral. *See* MACKAREL.

Mackintosh, John *1767–1844, bassoonist, violinist.*

According to the information collected by the Royal Society of Musicians when John Mackintosh was considered for membership, he was born on 6 February 1767, the son of Angus and Margaret Mackintosh of the parish of St Margaret, Westminster. He was christened at the parish church on 22 February. Nothing is known of his early training, but by 1794, when Doane's *Musical Directory* came out, Mackintosh had established himself in London as a bassoonist. He belonged to the New Musical Fund, played at the Apollo Gardens, and participated in the Handel concerts at Westminster Abbey. His address was No 29, St Martin's Street, Leicester Square.

On 6 April 1794 Mackintosh was recommended for membership in the Royal Society of Musicians by Samuel Okell, who reported that John was a violinist as well as a bassoonist, played first bassoon at Salomon's concerts and in the Drury Lane band, and had a wife and two children, Elizabeth, nearly seven years old, and John William, nearly two. Mackintosh was elected unanimously on 6 July. Beginning in 1795 he played bassoon regularly in the May concerts at St Paul's sponsored by the Society, and in 1798, 1799, and 1800 he played in the oratorios at Covent Garden for 10s. 6d. nightly. By 1800 he was a Governor of the Royal Society of Musicians, and in later years he served on the Court of Assistants and the House Committee.

On 11 November 1837 John Mackintosh wrote his will. He was then living at Belmont House, Vauxhall, Surrey (in 1805, when his son Alphonso was born, he had been living in the parish of St Mary, Lambeth). To his wife Mariana he left his freehold property in the Market Place in Kingston, all of his household goods, and a £250 annuity. His sons Thomas James and Alphonso were residuary legatees of those bequests. Mackintosh left £15 to his daughter-in-law, the widow of his late son John William, and £10 to her brother John. To Jane, the widow of Mackintosh's late son James Jeremiah, he left £10, and to his two nieces, daughters of the late William Smith of Greenwich, he bequeathed £15 each. John Mackin-

tosh died on 23 March 1844, and his widow proved his will on 8 June.

Grove in the entry on the bassoon says that Mackintosh was famous as one of the finest performers of his day and celebrated "for the excellence of his tone and style," but in Mackintosh's own entry it is stated that he had a "full, rich and powerful but somewhat coarse tone." His son Alphonso Mackintosh (Grove [5th edition] calls him Alphonse, but the Royal Society of Musicians' records regularly cite him as Alphonso) was a pianist and violinist who performed at Vauxhall and became a member of the Society. He died in 1862, leaving his wife in poor circumstances. John William Mackintosh was also a musician and a member of the Society, but we have found no details of his career. In any case, our subject's sons did not perform in the eighteenth century. John Mackintosh seems not to have been related to the temperamental Scottish violinist Robert "Red Bob" Mackintosh (1745–1807), who apparently did not perform in London.

Mackland. *See* MACLOUD.

Macklean. *See* MACKLIN.

Macklin, Charles *1699–1777, actor, dancer, singer, manager, playwright.*

Charles Macklin was probably born in the parish of Culdaff, County Donegal, Ireland, in 1699, one of two children of Terence Melaghlin (or McLaughlin) and his wife, née Agnes Flanagan. Undocumented claims in contemporary lives of the actor that Macklin sprang from more aristocratic stock were weighed and found wanting by William Appleton in *Charles Macklin an Actor's Life* (1960), which contributes substantially to the present account.

However, the story told by one of those early biographers—James T. Kirkman, in *Memoirs of the Life of Charles Macklin* (1799)—that the actor's widowed mother married a Dublin tavern-keeper, Luke O'Meally, appears to be veritable. O'Meally sent the boy to a boarding school at Island Bridge which was kept by a Scot named Nicolson. Charles is supposed to have astonished his schoolfellows by giving a creditable portrayal of the melting Monimia in a school production of Otway's tragedy *The Orphan*, despite the drawbacks of his blocky physique and rugged countenance. Kirkman

Courtesy of the National Gallery of Ireland

CHARLES MACKLIN, as Shylock
by Zoffany

and another early memorialist—William Cooke, in *Memoirs of Charles Macklin* (1804)—agree on the story that a Mrs Pilkington, who had coached Macklin for his performance, took him into her household for further instruction.

Among the few other credible assertions by early biographers and pamphleteers are those that he was for a time employed as a scout at Trinity College, Dublin, and that he found his first London employment as a waiter in a coffee house in Lincoln's Inn Fields which was kept by a relative. Evidently that service came just before he began a long apprenticeship as a performer at Bristol and with country companies in Wales and the Midlands.

Macklin may have made an early London stage appearance, around 1720, as a harlequin with strollers at Hockley-in-the-Hole near Clerkenwell Green; and sometime before 1725 he was probably playing at Richmond. But his most conservative early biographer, Francis Congreve, in *Authentic Memoirs of the Late Charles Macklin* (1798), declared that he first appeared in London at Lincoln's Inn Fields Theatre in 1725, as Alcandor in Dryden and Lee's *Oedipus*. No known surviving playbill confirms that performance, however, or his presence in or

around London before 24 September 1730, when he played Sir Charles Freeman in *The Beaux' Stratagem* at Lee and Harper's booth on the Bowling Green, Southwark, in the time of Bartholomew Fair. On that bill his name was spelled "Macklin." The 1731 edition of Fielding's *Coffee-House Politician* entered his name as "Maclean" opposite Poser (not "Porer" as in *The London Stage*) and Brazencourt. He had doubled in the parts at Lincoln's Inn Fields on 4 December 1730, but the roles were too small to appear in the playbill.

On 5 April 1731 "Mecklin, from Lincoln's Inn Fields, being the first Time of his appearing on this Stage" was advertised for Tattle in *Love for Love* with Odell's company at Goodman's Fields Theatre. On 19 April he played Tinsel in *The Drummer* there and closed out his season on 28 April as Marquis in *The Gamester*. Very likely he returned then to the provinces. The theatrical annalist James Winston recorded in *The Theatric Tourist* (1805) that Macklin was playing at Portsmouth in 1732. Sybil Rosenfeld in *Strolling Players and Drama in the Provinces* proposed that he was "trying his strength" in the Bath company early in the 1730s.

He may have been a familiar figure on provincial stages in the south and west of England. But he found no firm foothold in London until the season of 1733–34, when Theophilus Cibber led a sudden revolt against the management of the amateurish Drury Lane patentee John Highmore. A number of first-line actors seceded from the Drury Lane Company and set up for themselves at the Haymarket Theatre. The desperate Highmore began to pick up actors where he could, and Macklin was one of his recruits.

The opportunity for London employment had perhaps been brought to Macklin's attention by one of the seceders, Mrs Ann Purvor Grace, a widow whom he had probably met when they were both playing in the west and who had since 1727–28 served at Drury Lane with fair regularity. Macklin and Mrs Grace had for some time lived together, and according to Kirkman their daughter Maria had been born in 1733 at Portsmouth. Their liaison seems not to have been generally known in London—at least it is obvious that Highmore knew nothing of it or he would scarcely have hired Macklin. Mrs Grace would not be acknowledged in the bills as "Mrs Macklin" until 1739, and Macklin never married her.

His name ("Mechlin") was seen first on a Drury Lane bill on 31 October 1733, as Brazen in *The Recruiting Officer*. He was for four months steadily employed there in a variety of comedy roles, some of which had belonged to Theophilus Cibber: Whisper in *The Busy Body*, Clodio in *Love Makes a Man*, Teague in *The Committee*, Wimble in *The Cornish Squire*, the original Bluff in Fielding's farce *The Intriguing Chambermaid*, Marplay Jr in *The Author's Farce*, and on 11 March both Jack Stocks in *The Lottery* and Brass in *The Confederacy*. On 2 February Highmore sold his share of the patent. The seceders returned from the Haymarket on 12 March, and Macklin became supernumerary. But he had made a distinct impression on London audiences and was consequently invited to perform Marquis in *The Country House* for Cibber's benefit on 30 March and Foppington in *The Careless Husband* for Roger Bridgwater's benefit on 23 April. Between 9 and 29 April he joined some other dispossessed actors at the Haymarket, introducing Henry Fielding's new farce *Don Quixote in England*. He played Squire Badger. On 3 May, "At the particular Desire of several Persons of Quality," he repeated Brass, for his own benefit at Lincoln's Inn Fields. On 27 May, for Hewson's benefit at the Haymarket, he was invited to play Prince Hal in *1 Henry IV*.

Macklin was somewhere in the provinces again in the summer of 1734. According to Kirkman's uncertain chronology, he may have been at Chester and Bristol and on tour in Wales. A surviving playbill shows him to have been at Portsmouth on 15 August. In the fall he signed articles at Drury Lane and joined the regular company. On 24 September he assumed Poins in *1 Henry IV* and on 26 September Abel in *The Committee*. On 7 October he was borrowed by a pickup company at the Haymarket to play Ben in *Love for Love* "at the desire of Tomo Chachi, Micho or King of the Indians of Yamacraw, Senauki his Queen, Prince John Tooanahowi, and the rest of the Indians."

Thereafter that season he was seen as Ramilie in *The Miser*, Davy in *The Mock Doctor*, Mustacho in an adaptation of *The Tempest*, Sancho in *Love Makes a Man*, Clincher Jr in *The Constant Couple*, a Citizen in *Julius Caesar*, Strut in *The Double Gallant*, the original Wormwood in Fielding's farce *The Old Man Taught Wisdom*, Petulant in *The Way of the World*, the Undertaker in John Kelly's "New Tragi-Comi-Farcical Operatical Grotesque Pantomime" *The Plot*, the original Manly in James Worsdale's farce *A Cure for a Scold*, and the original Snip in Coffey's "Ballad Farce" *The Merry Cobler*. Though some of those were respectable roles, others were trifling, and a few, like Petulant, did not suit Macklin's genius at all. But he had shown himself willing to take up any acting assignment and was settling into the company both as an actor and as an aide to Fleetwood the manager.

On 10 May 1735 Macklin was to have acted Sancho in Fabian's new farce *Trick for Trick*. But on that date he suddenly found himself acting not a minor role in a theatrical farce but a principal role in a real tragedy. Before he could reach the stage that evening the ungovernable temper which plagued him all his life had caused him to kill a fellow actor, Thomas Hallam. Macklin's biographer Kirkman quotes the testimony of Thomas Arne, a numberer at the theatre, about the sorry affair as related at Macklin's trial:

The play was almost done, and they were making preparations for the entertainment, when the prisoner came into the scene-room and sat down next me and high words arose between him and the deceased about a *stock wig*, for a disguise in the entertainment. The prisoner had played in the *wig* the night before: and now the deceased had got it.—"D——n you for a rogue," says the prisoner, *"what business have you with my wig."*—*"I am not more a rogue than yourself,"* says the deceased; "it's a *stock wig*, and I have as much right to it as you have." Some of the players coming in—they desired the deceased to fetch the wig, and give it to the prisoner, which he did, and then said to him, "Here is *your* wig; I have got one that I like *better*." The prisoner, sitting by me, took the wig, and began to comb it out, and all seemed to be quiet for about half a quarter of an hour: but the prisoner began to grumble again, and said to the deceased "G—d d——n you for a blackguard, scrub, rascal, how durst you have the impudence to take *this* wig?" The deceased answered "I am no more a rascal than yourself." Upon which the prisoner started up out of his chair, and, with a stick in his hand, made a longe at the deceased, and thrust the stick into his left eye; and, pulling it back again, looked pale, turned on his heel, and, in a passion, threw the stick into the fire— "G—d d——n it," says he; and, turning about again on his heel, he sat down.

5 MACKLIN

The deceased clapped his hand to his eye, and said it was gone through his head. He was going to sink; but they set him in a chair. The prisoner came to him, and, leaning upon his left arm, put his hand to his eye. "Lord," cried the deceased, "it is out."—"No," says the prisoner, "I feel the ball roll under my hand." Young *Mr. Cibber* came in, and immediately sent for *Mr. Coldham*, the surgeon.

Testifying in his defense, Macklin added a bizarre detail: "[Hallam] sat down, and said to Mr. Arne's son (who was dressed in woman's cloaths) 'Whip up your clothes, you little b——h, and urine in my eye,' But he could not; so I did." The stick had penetrated Hallam's brain; he died at six o'clock the next morning. Macklin fled, returned and gave himself up, and was indicted for wilfull murder on 13 May. He spent an anxious seven months until he came to trial on 12 December. He was convicted of manslaughter and sentenced to be burned in the hand, a sentence which was executed with a cold iron.

The grisly occurrence did no permanent harm to Macklin's career, though it marred his reputation. Six weeks after his trial he was back at Drury Lane, rehearsing his old part of Ramilie in *The Miser*, which he played before an appreciative house on 31 January 1736. He rounded out the season with the addition to his repertoire of Appletree in *The Recruiting Officer*, the original Cheatly in Connolly's comedy *The Connoisseur*, Snap in *Love's Last Shift*, and Robin in *The Contrivances*. On 13 April he and the actors Robert Turbutt of Drury Lane and Peter Bardin of Goodman's Fields were the beneficiaries of a performance at Lincoln's Inn Fields during which Macklin played for the first time one of the Carriers in *1 Henry IV*. He returned to the Kentish circuit for the summer of 1736.

In the 1736–37 season Macklin added two roles which were to become special favorites with him and with his audiences, Peachum in *The Beggar's Opera* and Razor in *The Provok'd Wife*. He also learned Lory in *The Relapse*, Peter Nettle in *The What D'Ye Call It*, the Beggar in *Phebe*, Young Cash in *The Wife's Relief*, Finder in *The Double Gallant*, the Boor Servant in *The Burgomaster Trick'd*, Subtleman in *The Twin Rivals*, Osric (while he doubled as a Gravedigger) in *Hamlet*, Francis in *1 Henry IV*, Pierot in *Poor Pierot Married*, Jeffery in *The Amorous Widow*, Cleon in *Timon of Athens*, Sir Hugh in *The Merry Wives of Windsor*, a Sailor in *The Tempest*, some role unspecified in *Eurydice*, and Basset in *The Provok'd Husband*.

Macklin's extensive service in country companies which could afford few specialists had made him a theatrical jack-of-all-trades. Kirkman testified that

Sometimes he was an architect, and knocked up the stage and seats in a barn; sometimes he wrote an opening Prologue, or a parting Epilogue, for the company; at others, he wrote a song, complimentary and adulatory to the village he happened to play in, which he always adapted to some sprightly air, and sung himself; and he often was champion, and stood forward to repress the persons who were accustomed to intrude upon, and be rude to actors.

Such experiences made him triply attractive to the amateur patentee of Drury Lane, Charles Fleetwood, who not only began to thrust directorial tasks upon him and to promote larger roles for him but increasingly relied upon his companionship on forays into the gambling clubs and taverns in which Fleetwood was busily squandering a large patrimony. Macklin's status as the patentee's favorite did nothing, of

The National Theatre

CHARLES MACKLIN, as Shylock
by Zoffany

course, to endear him to the other members of the company, even though he seems to have tried to make himself acceptable by exceptional service. For instance, on 13 September 1737, when *The Conscious Lovers* played, the prompter entered in his diary: "Mr Cibber ill at Kingston, Tom read by Mr Machlin [*sic*] hiss'd when he first came on; but was applauded at last having read it tolerably well." British Library MS Egerton 2320 informs us that on another night, when *1 Henry IV* played and Macklin was Francis, "Harper was ill Macklin did ye carrier for him."

Still, friction with some of the older players grew. He was guilty of inventing bits of naturalistic business which upset traditionalists and distracted attention from their stately movement and pompous declamation. James Quin, the acknowledged male star of the company, some seven years senior to Macklin, attempted to curb the younger Irishman's exuberance and ignited a long-burning feud. In the season of 1737–38, on an evening when he played a new part, Jerry Blackacre in *The Plain Dealer*, Macklin inserted comic business which Quin thought drew attention from his ponderous recital of Manly, the leading role. As Macklin reconstructed the sequence of events long afterward, Quin, after repeatedly and imperiously ordering him between scenes to desist, became enraged and hurled a piece of apple in Macklin's face. The younger man pushed Quin into a chair and, before an astonished crowd of gentlemen in the green room, began to beat him. Quin's face was swollen so severely that he could not go back on. He immediately challenged Macklin. The quarrel was defused for the time by Fleetwood, who wished to see neither of his valuable properties damaged. That was perhaps fortunate for Macklin, for Quin had already killed two men in duels. But the animosity between the combatants smoldered on for years.

Theophilus Cibber's flight to France to escape his creditors in April 1738 and his subsequent defection to Covent Garden again left Macklin in possession of his roles. Macklin was earning permanent possession of still others with earnest study and intelligent innovation. In 1737–38 he added Jeremy in *Love for Love*, the Morocco Servant in *The Fall of Phaeton*, Beau Mordecai in *The Harlot's Progress*, Cutbeard in *The Silent Woman*, Face in *The Alche-*

mist, Quaint in *Aesop*, Pierrot in *Harlequin Grand Volgi* ("I was a great pantomime boy in those days," he would boast to his companions at the Rainbow Coffee House in 1787), the Orange Woman in *The Man of Mode*, Scrub in *The Beaux' Stratagem*, Froth in *The Double Dealer*, the title role in *The Man of Taste*, Roxana in *The Rival Queens*, and Clodio in *Love Makes a Man*.

In 1738–39 his repertoire continued to expand: Coupée in *An Old Man Taught Wisdom*, Foigard in *The Beaux' Stratagem*, Butler in *The Drummer*, Setter in *The Old Bachelor*, Teague in *The Twin Rivals*, a Witch in *Macbeth*, the original Slouch in the anonymous "Pantomime Entertainment" *Robin Goodfellow*, Sir Polidorus in *Aesop*, Trappanti in *She Wou'd and She Wou'd Not*, Numps in *The Tender Husband*, the Mad Welshman in *The Pilgrim*, Squib in *Tunbridge Walks*, Sir Philip in *A Bold Stroke for a Wife*, Choleric in *Love Makes a Man*, Moody in *The Provok'd Husband*, Ben in *Love for Love*, Old Mirabel in *The Inconstant*, the title role in *The Mock Doctor*, and Sir Fopling in *The Man of Mode*.

Macklin and Ann Grace and their seven-year-old daughter Maria had taken up residence by 1738 at No 12, Wild Court, Covent Garden, where they were to maintain residence for five years. On 23 November 1739 "Mrs Grace" was printed for the last time in a Drury Lane bill, and on 8 December "Mrs Macklin" began playing her parts. No record of a marriage has ever been found.

Macklin continued to expand his repertoire in 1739–40, adding Sir Novelty Fashion in *Love's Last Shift*, Sir John in *The Silent Woman*, the original Mercury in James Miller's "Dramatic Fable" *A Hospital for Fools*, Bullock in *The Recruiting Officer*, the original Lieutenant Meanwell in Edward Phillips's farce *Britons Strike Home*, Trincalo in *The Tempest*, Jacomo in *Don John*, Lovegold in *The Miser*, Sir William in *The Squire of Alsatia*, Tom in *The Conscious Lovers*, Trim in *The Funeral*, the original Sir John Linger in the anonymous afterpiece *Polite Conversation*, and Sir Jasper in *The Country Wife*.

More important than any of those parts in its influence on his future was Macklin's assumption, at a special benefit given at Drury Lane for the Goodman's Fields manager Henry Giffard, of the modest role of the Drunken man in the "new Dramatic Satire" *Lethe: or,*

Esop in the Shades on 15 April 1740. For the author of the piece was a young London vintner, Giffard's friend David Garrick. From that period of rehearsal began an intimacy, warm and then troubled, of considerable significance for the British theatre.

But during that season violence had again touched Macklin's career. Miller's afterpiece *A Hospital for Fools*, with Macklin in the lead, was rejected by a riotous audience on 15 November 1739. A far worse riot occurred on 23 January 1740. Macklin himself left an amusing account of it which was published in the "Macklinana" feature of the *Monthly Mirror* in 1798. Following a performance of *Hamlet*, the ballerina Mme Chateauneuf and the ballet master Denoyer were scheduled for the third time—and for the third time failed to appear—to dance in the new pantomime *The Fortune Tellers*. Macklin "made an apology for Denoyer, but was hissed by the audience, who were in a great rage, created by the Calveshead Club," including "Lord Boyne, his brother, Captain Hamilton, and Lord————, who went out of his mind afterward." The rioters attacked the stage:

They made a gang-way out of the pit, with the benches of it, over the orchestra; Macklin got up to the thunder-loft, and ordered the servants of the theatre to make the stage dark, to open the traps, to let loose hell, to roll the thunder, and to flash the lightning; this he did with a stentorophon, which frightened the audience much.

This manoeuvre hindered the rioters for a long time from coming on the stage: various incidents arose, during this riot, which lasted till twelve at night; . . . they . . . cut all the scenes; Macklin saved himself by creeping under the world, which was shewn in the last scene of the pantomime of the night.

The rioters abused many persons, among them one whom they took to be a dancer but who was really a famous duellist, Dick Surrige. His reputation Macklin and the managers took care to spread and inflate in ensuing days, to the great discomfiture of the rioters, who speedily came to heel and paid damages.

The theatrical season of 1740–41 was the most significant single season in Macklin's career. In contrast to the five seasons immediately preceding, he studied only half a dozen new roles. But with one of them he created a sensation and effected a revolution in the interpre-

tation of one of Shakespeare's most controversial characters. The character was, of course, Shylock. The traditional presentation, in the revised version of the play by George Granville, Lord Lansdowne, which had held the stage since 1701, had been broadly comic. Macklin nourished a different conception, fierce, bold, and harsh. His preparation included a thoughtful immersion in Josephus's *History of the Jews* and—as his commonplace book shows—in the Old Testament: "Jewes Their history an instance of human incertainty—from the Creation to the Flood—in Egypt leaving it—robbing their masters, mutinying—Jericho—wilderness—murder of the Innocents—captivity—lion's den—Shadrack, Meshack, Abednigo, Babel. go thro the history of it—act the great characters."

Some outward aspects of the character, which English audiences had been accustomed to see from the time of Richard Burbage onward, were retained by Macklin—both the "Jewish" hooked nose and red hair which descended from the conventional iconography and the general costume effects of the *pantalone*, the old Venetian with the young daughter, who came from the *commedia dell' arte*. To these traditonal features of costume Macklin added a short red beard and a red hat which he had found from his researches Venetian Jews still wore.

Macklin revealed none of his ideas to Fleetwood, the hostile Quin, or the rest of the actors. He ran through his rehearsals in perfunctory fashion, giving no indication of his intentions as to rhetorical style, stage business, or dressing the role. The first performance was on 14 February 1741 before a crowded house which had been assured by the playbill that the version about to be seen had been "Written by Shakespeare." The claim was to some considerable degree true, though Portia had lost two suitors and much dialogue, and Lorenzo and Jessica had gained several songs by T. A. Arne. But Shylock's part of the text was left nearly whole.

William Cooke's *Memoirs* purport to preserve Macklin's recollections of the performance:

The two front rows of the pit, as usual, were full of critics, "Who, Sir, (said the veteran) I eyed through the slit of the curtain, and was glad to see there, as I wished, in such a cause, to be tried by a *special Jury*. When I made my appearance in the green-room, dressed for the part, with my red hat

The Tate Gallery

MICHAEL DYER as Gratiano, CHARLES MACKLIN as Shylock, MARIA MACKLIN as Portia, MAT-
THEW CLARKE as Antonio, and ROBERT BENSLEY as Bassanio: the Trial Scene in *The Merchant of
Venice*

by Zoffany

on my head, my piqued beard, loose black gown,
&c. and with a confidence which I never before
assumed, the performers all stared at one another,
and evidently with a stare of disappointment. Well,
Sir, hitherto, all was right—till the last bell rung—
then, I confess, my heart began to beat a little:
however, I mustered up all the courage I could,
and, recommending my cause to Providence, threw
myself boldly on the stage, and was received by
one of the loudest thunders of applause I ever before experienced.

"The opening scenes being rather tame and level,
I could not expect much applause; but I found myself well listened to—I could hear distinctly, in the
pit, the words 'Very well—very well, indeed! This
man seems to know what he is about,' &c. &c.
These encomiums warmed me, but did not overset
me—I knew where I should have the pull, which
was in the third act, and reserved myself accord-

ingly. At this period I threw out all my fire; and
as the contrasted passions of joy for the Merchant's
losses, and grief for the elopement of Jessica, open
a fine field for the actor's powers, I had the good
fortune to please beyond my warmest expectations—The whole house was in an uproar of applause—and I was obliged to pause between the
speeches, to give it vent, so as to be heard. When
I went behind the scenes after this act, the Manager met me, and complimented me very highly
on my performance, and significantly added,
'Macklin, you was right at last.' My brethren in
the green-room joined in this eulogium, but with
different views—He was thinking of the increase
of his treasury—they only for saving appearances—wishing at the same time that I had broke
my neck in the attempt. The *trial scene* wound up
the fulness of my reputation: here I was well listened to; and here I made such a silent yet forcible

impression on my audience, that I retired from this great attempt most perfectly satisfied.

"On my return to the green-room, after the play was over, it was crowded with nobility and critics, who all complimented me in the warmest and most unbounded manner; and the situation I felt myself in, I must confess, was one of the most flattering and intoxicating of my whole life. No money, no title, could purchase what I felt: And let no man tell me after this, what Fame will not inspire a man to do, and how far the attainment of it will not remunerate his greatest labours. By G–d, Sir, though I was not worth fifty pounds in the world at that time, yet, let me tell you, I was *Charles the Great* for that night."

The German traveler Georg C. Lichtenberg was able to recall exactly, more than 30 years later, Macklin's entrance onto the stage that evening (the translation is from his *Letters* edited by M. L. Mare and W. H. Quarrell):

Imagine a rather stout man with a coarse yellow face and a nose generously fashioned in all three dimensions, and a long double chin, and a mouth so carved by nature that the knife appears to have slit him right up to the ears, on one side at least, I thought. He wears a long black gown, long wide trousers, and a red tricorne. . . . The first word he utters, when he comes to the stage, are slowly and impressively spoken: "Three thousand ducats." The double "th" and the two sibilants, especially the second after the "t," which Macklin lisps as lickerishly as if he were savoring the ducats and all that they would buy, make so deep an impression in the man's favour that nothing can destroy it. Three such words uttered thus at the outset give the keynote of the whole character.

Francis Gentleman the actor-critic, who, after seeing the part performed, became Macklin's nearly constant advocate, summed up his admiration in *The Dramatic Censor* (1770):

there is no doubt but Mr. MACKLIN looks the part as much better than any other person as he plays it; in the level scenes his voice is most happily suited to that sententious gloominess of expression the author intended; which, with a sullen solemnity of deportment, marks the character strongly; in his malevolence there is a forceful and terrifying ferocity. . . .

Lichtenberg described Macklin's rushing on at the beginning of that scene "hatless, with disordered hair, some locks a finger long standing on end, as if raised by a breath of wind from the gallows, so distracted was his demeanour.

Both his hands are clenched, and his movements abrupt and convulsive. To see a deceiver, who is usually calm and resolute, in such a state of agitation is terrible."

Despite the woeful miscasting of several of the other players, notably the comical Kitty Clive as Portia, Macklin's acting kept the play on the boards for 11 successive nights, after which he was given two days' rest before another run of four performances. He played the part some 20 times, including the night of his benefit, before season's end. All the town rushed to see him. The Prince and Princess of Wales

Courtesy of the National Gallery of Ireland

CHARLES MACKLIN, as Sir Pertinax Macsycophant

by De Wilde

commanded it on the fourth and again on the sixteenth night and "their Royal Hignesses the Duke [of Cumberland] and the Princesses Amelia, Caroline and Louisa" on the fifteenth. Their father George II saw Macklin play only after he had long established his fame in the character. Reportedly he tossed and turned sleeplessly after viewing the horrifying portrayal; and when Sir Robert Walpole complained that Parliament might not pass a certain Whiggish measure, the monarch suggested, "What do you think of sending them to the theatre to see that Irishman play Shylock?" Soon was heard on every hand the couplet, dubiously attributed to Pope: "This is the Jew/ That Shakespeare drew."

There were a few dissenters, for Macklin's personality assured that he would never be without enemies. They were mostly prudently anonymous. The author of *A Clear Stage and No Favour: Or, Tragedy and Comedy at War* (1742) invited his readers to

> *Mark one who tragical struts up and down,*
> *And* rolls *the words as Sysiphus his Stone:*
> *His lab'ring Arms, unequal to the Weight,*
> *Heave like a Porter's when at Billingsgate*

as he acts the Jew. And the author of *A Guide to the Stage* remained still unconverted in 1750. Macklin as Shylock had "the looks of a Judas, and the howl of a Hyena"; he was "an ambitious player, who aims at reputation by outheroding Herod." But most who saw him, though shaken by his savage power, felt that he had in the portrayal turned his back on the fustian and posturing of the Quin persuasion. Until he left the stage, no one could deny him pre-eminence in the role, even after powerful and different portrayals mounted by John Henderson and John Philip Kemble and, indeed, until Edmund Kean's version in 1814. The conception ranked in power with Garrick's Richard III and Kemble's Coriolanus and surpassed both in its eventual influence over acting style.

The preparation of his *coup* with Shylock had left Macklin little leisure to prepare other new roles in 1740–41, but several were significant: Fondlewife in *The Old Bachelor*, Higgen in *The Royal Merchant*, Macahone in *The Strollers*, and Malvolio in *Twelfth Night*. He also indulged his fondness for being a "pantomime boy" as a Clown in *Harlequin Shipwrecked*. At the end of his season he and his wife and daughter Maria

left London for a summer with John Hippisley's company at the Jacob's Wells Theatre, Bristol. They remained there from 8 June through 2 September.

Macklin returned to Drury Lane for the season 1741–42, in which he again emphasized comedy and farce, adding to his list the Old Woman in *Rule a Wife and Have a Wife*, Sir Paul in *The Double Dealer*, Rigdumfunnidos in *Chrononhotonthologos*, Dollalolla in *Tom Thumb*, the original Zorobabel in Fielding's new farce *Miss Lucy in Town*, Dromio of Syracuse in *The Comedy of Errors*, and one of his most memorable Shakespearean roles, Touchstone in *As You Like It*.

David Garrick had now signed a contract with Drury Lane for the 1742–43 season and had left Goodman's Fields to join Drury Lane for the last three months of the 1741–42 campaign. He had essayed King Lear for the first time before leaving Goodman's Fields, on 11 March, and it had been fairly coldly received, especially compared to his previous triumph as Richard III. Macklin had been frank in his criticism. Garrick, he said, did not make Lear sufficiently infirm, had sometimes lacked dignity, had cursed Goneril too temperately. Macklin had set about coaching the younger actor in the part, and by the time Garrick acted it at Drury Lane, on 28 May, it was on its way to assuming the pre-eminent place in his repertoire which it finally took.

Macklin was justifiably proud of his part in the transformation. Cooke reported his generous praise of his pupil:

> The curse [Macklin now] particularly admired; he said it exceeded all his imagination, and had

Folger Shakespeare Library

"Covent Garden all in an Uproar," 1773

such an effect, that it seemed to electrify the audience with horror. The words "Kill-kill-kill" echoed all the revenge of the frantic king; whilst he exhibited such a scene of the pathetic on discovering his daughter Cordelia, as drew tears of commiseration from the whole house.

"In fact," said Macklin, "The little dog made it a chef d'oeuvre."

The friendship continued to thrive when in the fall Garrick returned to London after a summer in Dublin with Peg Woffington, and the pair reportedly moved into the house occupied by the Macklins, Robert Wilks's former residence at No 5, Bow Street, Covent Garden. The rumours of a *ménage à trois* (and the establishment of an histrionic academy by its members) handed on by Cooke and others may be set aside as unproved and inherently unlikely. But Macklin was teaching acting to pupils other than Garrick, and one of his apter scholars was his own daughter Maria, who made her London debut in the traditional introductory role for children, the Duke of York in *Richard III*, on 20 December 1742.

Apparently the avuncular relationship of Macklin to Garrick—there was a twenty-year difference in ages—changed gradually over the 1742–43 season into a friendship between equals. Macklin's roles frequently supported Garrick's. When Macklin played for the first time Noll Bluff in *The Old Bachelor*, Garrick was Fondlewife; when Henry Fielding's comedy *The Wedding Day* was introduced, Garrick was the original Millamour, and Macklin (who also wrote and spoke the prologue) was Stedfast; in *Jane Shore* that season Garrick played Hastings and Macklin the Duke of Gloucester, both for the first time. Macklin also added to his repertoire that season Marplot in *The Busy Body*.

Perhaps Garrick and Macklin could not have remained cronies even under the best of conditions. But conditions at Drury Lane, never ideal, had steadily worsened until, in May 1743, the actors revolted again over unpaid salaries and wretched conditions backstage, with Garrick and Macklin leading them out of the theatre. Any such desperate gamble for independence was foredoomed to failure by the Licensing Act of 1737 and Macklin, at least, should have known it. The players' petition to the Lord Chamberlain to be allowed to form their own company was indignantly refused. The dissidents then had nowhere to go in London but

back to Drury Lane. They urged Garrick to make the least humiliating terms he could for their capitulation. Fleetwood signified his willingness to receive everyone back into the fold—everyone but Macklin, whom he had stood by during the Hallam affair and whom, consequently, he now saw as an ingrate. But as Thomas Davies explained, the actors had signed a "formal agreement, by which they obliged themselves not to accede to any terms which might be proposed to them by the patentee without the consent of all the subscribers," and Macklin angrily refused to give his consent to any arrangement which would leave him odd-man-out.

Inevitably, Garrick had to side with the majority of the jobless performers. He tried to appease Fleetwood by offering to cut £100 from his own salary if Macklin could be re-hired; Fleetwood refused. Garrick offered to pay Macklin £3 a week; Macklin proudly spurned the offer. Pamphlet warfare ensued. Dr William Barrowby led a mob of Macklin's adherents, who pelted Garrick off the stage. Fleetwood and Garrick quelled a second attempt at intimidation by filling the pit with pugilists armed with clubs. Order gradually returned, but Macklin was to act no more at Drury Lane while Fleetwood held the patent. Though the difference between the actors was eventually mediated, and though they acted together peaceably, Macklin's distaste for his former friend grew inveterate over the years, as passages in his commonplace book show.

Unable for the moment to secure employment in the patent houses, Macklin resolved to form his own company from among young pupils trained to act according to his theories. Macklin hired the Haymarket Theatre and, employing an oft-attempted evasion of the Licensing Act, advertised for 6 February 1744 "A Concert of Musick," for which the audience would pay and after which would "be acted Gratis the Tragedy" *Othello*. Macklin played Iago. In the title role and making his first appearance as an actor was the wit and author Samuel Foote, who would in future years become renowned as a comedian, mimic, and manager. Macklin's company—if it can be called such—gave 14 scattered performances from 6 February through 10 July. Thirty-five people were concerned from first to last in presenting six mainpieces and a variety of afterpieces and musical turns. The company was stiffened several times with experienced performers like Henry Vaughan and old "Dagger" Marr. But most roles were attempted by young folk who were seen once or twice and never again in London. Macklin himself acted with his tyros and added to his repertoire Loveless in *The Relapse*.

The Haymarket experience cannot have been a great financial success. Macklin and his wife acted on the Kentish circuit in the summer of 1744, but that employment meant bare subsistence. The measure of the family's desperation can be understood from the letter which Macklin, choking down his pride, sent to Fleetwood on 2 November 1744, begging forgiveness and reinstatement:

> Consider, sir, I have been in Purgatory fourteen long, long months; . . . Consider, sir, you have a Family yourself, let that give you some feeling of my condition—had your hard treatment . . . affected only myself . . . I should not have sunk into the meanness of repeated supplications—. . . .
>
> You must imagine, sir, that by this time I am in no small distress, and distress, they say, even in an Enemie, will excite Humanity. . . .
>
> Whatever could be suggested on my part to conciliate an agreement has been put in Practise. I have been silent, Patient, & Repentant. I have beside in several letters made an humble tender of my services. . . .

Macklin might have spared himself the humiliation. Fleetwood would shortly sell his patent to the bankers Richard Green and Norton Amber. By 19 December 1744 Macklin had returned to Drury Lane and to Shylock. For his reinstatement he had prepared a prologue:

> *From scheming, fretting, famine, and despair,*
> *Behold to grace restored an exil'd player;*
> *Your sanction yet his fortune must complete,*
> *And give him privilege to laugh—and eat.*
> *No revolution plots are mine again;*
> *You see, thank heaven! the quietest of men:*
> *I pray that all domestic feuds may cease;*
> *And beggar'd by war, solicit peace.*
> *When urg'd by wrongs, and prompted to rebel,*
> *I fought for freedom, and for freedom fell.*
> . . . .
> *Once warn'd, I meddle not with state affairs,*
> *But play my part, retire, and say my prayers.*

—and fourteen lines more of uncharacteristic humility.

During that season Macklin displayed a variety of his old parts of all sizes and added Sir Francis Wronghead in *The Provok'd Husband*, Gomez in *The Spanish Fryar*, and a notable Pandulph in the revival of *King John*. On the last day of the Covent Garden season, 29 May, he and Mrs Macklin crossed over to that house to play Mr and Mrs Peachum in *The Beggar's Opera* for the benefit of Kitty Clive's brother, James Raftor.

The alarums of the Jacobite rebellion depressed theatrical business in 1745–46 despite several attempts to capitalize on the news from the north by reviving old "patriotic" plays or writing new ones. Macklin in great haste tinkered up a "loyal" tragedy, *Henry VII; Or, The Popish Imposter*. Acted on 18 January 1746, it was a most dismal failure, though it was kept faintly alive through the third, or author's, night. Macklin played a principal role, the Earl of Huntley. Mrs Cibber wrote to Garrick (who, luckily for him, had not been concerned in the fiasco), "It was entirely new-dressed, and no expense saved in the clothes. I shall say nothing of the piece, because you may read it; but be as vain as you will about your playing Bayes, you never made an audience laugh more than Henry VII has done."

Though considerably daunted by the death of his tragedy, Macklin continued to aspire to success as a playwright. He went to work immediately on a two-act farce, a reworking of Regnard's *Le Légataire Universel*, which he called *Will and No Will; Or, A Bone for Lawyers*. It was produced as the afterpiece for his benefit on 23 April 1746. The mainpiece of the evening featured Peg Woffington as the Female Officer in *The Humours of the Army*, which was revived after 30 years and in which Macklin played Captain Cadwallader. He also wrote and read a lengthy comic prologue on that occasion. Other new roles for him that season were Humphrey in *The Tender Husband*, Stephano in *The Tempest*, and Storm in the revival after 43 years of Steele's *Lying Lover*. He and Mrs Macklin again strolled through Kent in the summer of 1746.

Macklin was relieved of Garrick's irritating presence in the season of 1746–47 when Rich hired Garrick at Covent Garden. To take his place at Drury Lane, the manager James Lacy brought from Dublin the brilliant Irish tragedian Spranger Barry, with whom Macklin began a lasting friendship. His dislike of Garrick did not prevent Macklin from feeling indignation at the picayune objections some critical scribblers were leveling at Dr Benjamin Hoadly's popular new comedy *The Suspicious Husband*, in which Garrick was starring as Ranger. Moreover, Macklin had not exercised his combative spirit for some time; so he satirized the petty censors in his one-act farce *The New Play Criticiz'd; or, The Plague of Envy*, produced for his benefit on 24 March 1747. Which of the "Principal Characters" Macklin himself played is uncertain; probably it was the downright, commonsense critic, Heartly. His only other new characters that season were Trapum in *Marry or Do Worse* and Bramble in *The Fine Lady's Airs*. In June, Macklin and Mrs Macklin joined their friends the brothers Luke and Isaac Sparks, forming a company to play a summer engagement at the White Swan in Norwich.

In 1747, David Garrick formed his partnership with James Lacy in the ownership and management at Drury Lane Theatre. They opened on 15 September with the famous prologue by Samuel Johnson—and with Macklin as Shylock. Macklin appeared in that or other parts on 24 of the first 25 nights of the new season and he was almost as busy throughout its length, giving the new patentees his utmost in cooperation. He studied six new characters—Sir Gilbert Wrangle in *The Refusal*, Pandolfo in *Albumazar*, Flash in *Miss in Her Teens*, Strictland in *The Suspicious Husband*, Fluellen in *Henry V*, and the original Faddle in Edward Moore's comedy *The Foundling*. The itch for recognition as a playwright seduced Macklin to another pair of literary indiscretions. For his wife's benefit, on 28 April 1748, he inexpertly adapted John Ford's *The Lover's Melancholy* and penned the unattractive farce *The Fortune Hunters*. Despite Macklin's elaborate puffery in the *General Advertiser*, his dramas drew a house which yielded his wife only £33 after charges.

Macklin again grew restless. Lured by Thomas Sheridan's promise of £800 per season for their joint efforts, the Macklins packed up and sailed for Dublin. Their engagement was for the two seasons 1748–49 and 1749–50; but before the end of March 1750, Macklin and Sheridan had assembled so many grievances that the Macklins were dismissed from the Smock Alley company, unpaid. Macklin

sued Sheridan for £800, recovered £300, and came disgruntled back to England. He gathered a small company, including one of the Sparkses and one of the Palmers, and performed during the spring at Chester. In the summer, Macklin signed articles for himself and his wife with John Rich at Covent Garden. Probably at some time between 1748 and 1750 the Macklins' second child, John, had been born, perhaps at Dublin.

The Macklins made their first appearances at Covent Garden on 24 September 1750, he as Lovegold and she as Lappet in *The Miser*. He added to his list of parts Mercutio in *Romeo and Juliet*, Polonius in *Hamlet*, Vellum in *The Drummer*, Manuel in *She Wou'd and She Wou'd Not*, Sir Oliver Cockwood in *She Wou'd If She Cou'd*, Leontine in *Theodosius*, and Sir Wilful in *The Way of the World*. On 7 March 1751 the talented and dissolute Sir Francis Delaval, with his mistress, his brother, and a group of aristocratic amateurs put on a performance of *Othello* before a fascinated crowd of the *haut monde* at Drury Lane. Macklin had coached them individually and had supervised their rehearsals. Sybil Rosenfeld, who in *Temples of Thespis* describes the preparations and the performance in detail, declares that 1,000 people saw the play but that 20,000 had sought tickets. The House of Commons adjourned two hours early to accommodate members who wished to be present. The amateurs acted with spirit and with a degree of competence sufficient to bring praise to them and to Macklin from some of the most influential members of society. It was all an excellent advertisement for Macklin as a teacher of acting and elocution, which he was off and on for the rest of his life. He had continued the careful instruction of his daughter Maria, now 19, and at his benefit on 10 April 1751 she played her first adult part, Athenais in *Theodosius*.

The season of 1751–52 at Covent Garden went off tranquilly enough for Macklin. He studied only four new parts, Plyant in *The Double Dealer*, Barnaby Brittle in *The Amorous Widow*, Lopez in *The False Friend*, and Lopez in *The Mistake*; and though he performed Shylock half a dozen times as expected and continued to draw with Iago, the number of his appearances was far fewer than in previous seasons. For his 8 April 1752 benefit he wrote a "New Dramatic Satire" in two acts, *Covent*

Garden Theatre; or, Pasquin Turn'd Drawcansir.
The piece was feeble as satire and pale as farce.
It was never repeated. But the night was otherwise notable: young Maria drew critical applause for her first role in comedy, Lady Townly
in *The Provok'd Husband.*

There were many signs now that Macklin,
after more than 35 years in the theatre, was
wearied by its demands. His dramaturgy had
been rejected and he was at odds with the
principal managers, both in England and Ireland. In 1752–53 he acted only some 25 times
and added only four new roles: Renault in
Venice Preserv'd, the Mad Englishman in *The
Pilgrim*, Sciolto in *The Fair Penitent* (with Maria
as Calista, her "fourth appearance on any stage"),
for his benefit, and the title role in Samuel
Foote's new comedy *The Englishman in Paris.*
But Foote was dissatisfied. He wrote to Delaval
that the play was "damnably acted" and
"Macklin miserably imperfect in the words and
in the character (O stain to Comedy). You
might have seen what I mean,—an English
Buck, by the power of dulness instantaneously
transformed into an Irish chairman." All occasions seemed to inform against Macklin. It
was time for him to try something new.

In the eighteenth century the relationship
between the various applications of oratory—
parliamentary eloquence, pulpit persuasion,
school declamation—and acting was obvious
and acknowledged. Many actors, in addition
to or in conjunction with lessons in acting,
provided tutelage in "elocution." Fledgling
performers attended "spouting clubs" and mature ones frequented debating societies. Macklin had long been a teacher and theorist of
acting and oratory and a participant at the
forensic coffee houses and debating societies,
some of which had radical reputations. William Kenrick, in a note to his *Pasquinade* (1753),
called Macklin "a famous player, and author,
particularly celebrated for his harangues on
religious subjects, at the oratory of the *Robin-
hood*," a society of political disputants, some of
them with seditious ideas. For several years
Macklin had talked of founding an academy of
oratory and had also spoken of establishing a
coffee house to be frequented by authors and
actors. In September 1753 he took steps to put
both plans into effect.

Leasing chambers under the Great Piazza of
Covent Garden from the Duke of Bedford for

£45 a year, Macklin contracted with the builder
John Tinkler to refurbish the apartment for "a
Magnificent Coffee-Room & a School of Oratory." In a prologue spoken at a special benefit
given him at Drury Lane on 20 December
1753, Macklin slyly reminded the audience of
his pending project; and all that winter he
artfully stimulated tavern talk about his plans,
until the rooms were at last ready, in March
1754, for the grand opening of his coffee house.
There Macklin, in formal attire, presided in
person over the elaborate meals, which were
conducted with great decorum and style. At
first he drew heavy patronage. But Macklin
found that, to the original outlay of some
£1200, he was obliged to add £700 for the
improvement of the space above his dining
room before he could complete his scheme by
opening his forensic enterprise, "The British
Inquisition." He advertised:

This Institution is upon the plan of the ancient
Greek, Roman, and Modern French and Italian Societies of liberal investigation. Such subjects in Arts,
Sciences, Literature, Criticism, Philosophy, History, Politics, and Morality, as shall be found useful and entertaining to society, will there be lec-
tured upon and freely debated; particularly Mr.
Macklin intends to lecture upon the Comedy of the
Ancients, the use of their masks and flutes, their
mimes and pantomimes, and the use and abuse of
the Stage. He will likewise lecture upon the rise
and progress of the modern Theatres, and make a
comparison between them and those of Greece and
Rome, and between each other; and he purposes to
lecture also upon each of Shakespeare's Plays; to
consider the original stories from whence they are
taken; the artificial or inartificial use, according to
the laws of the drama, that Shakespeare has made
of them; his fable, moral character, passions, manners will likewise be criticized, and how his capital
characters have been acted heretofore, are acted,
and ought to be acted. And as the design of this
inquiry is to endeavour at an acquisition of truth
in matters of taste, particularly theatrical, the lecture being ended, any gentleman may offer his
thoughts upon the subject.

But the subjects for disquisition and dispu-
tation gradually became less elevated and more
miscellaneous—ranging downward from the
painful consequences of immorality, the depraved taste of the age (as in bear-baiting and
pantomimes), and the arguments for Protes-
tantism, to the kidnapping of Elizabeth Can-
ning and "the ingenious nation of the Pyg-

mies." Macklin's quondam pupil and friend the gadfly Samuel Foote could not resist attending to interrupt Macklin's discourse with barbed witticisms.

Foote also set up a burlesque counter-attraction at the Haymarket, a series of comic lectures called *A Writ of Enquiry . . . On the Inquisitor General*, in which he artfully mimicked Macklin. His lectures soon outdrew Macklin's oratory in the Piazza. Macklin began to attack Foote personally in his orations. Foote published *An Epistle from Tully in the Shades to Orator MA*****N*. In reference to a brothel located at the other end of the Piazza, "Tully" questioned "whether an Academy for Moral Lectures carried on in one End of a House, is more likely to make Converts, than one for Fornication in the other." Stung, Macklin retorted hotly with his own pamphlet, *M——ckl——n's Answer to Tully*. Macklin was also mocked in *The Connoisseur*, by George Colman and Bonnell Thornton, as "the Martin Luther of the age (as he frequently calls himself), the great Orator Macklin." They, too, observed ironically that "our rakes and bloods, who had been used to frequent Covent Garden merely for the sake of whoring and drinking, now resort thither for reason and argument; and the Piazza begins to vie with the ancient Portico, where Socrates disputed."

But the satirical attacks disturbed Macklin far less than the fact that custom at his ordinary and oratory had dwindled disastrously. On 25 January 1755 he pleaded bankruptcy and was so posted in the *Gentleman's Magazine* for February: "Charles Macklin, of St. Paul, Cov. Garden, vintner." He had to fall back on the earnings of his wife Ann and his daughter Maria. For Maria's Drury Lane benefit on 29 March 1756 he translated ("from the French" said the playbill) *A Will and No Will; or, a New Case for the Lawyers*.

We know virtually nothing else of Macklin's activities for the three years from January 1755 through early 1757. In 1756 he was attacked by "Peter Pounce" (Richard Lewis) in *The Robin-Hood Society with Notes Variorum* as a constant member of that "low" and "vicious" fellowship and especially for his bitter sallies at those meetings against David Garrick. William Cooke stated that, at about that period, three times a week from 10 o'clock to 12 noon, he interviewed aspirants to the stage, a statement which

probably means that he had continued to offer lessons in acting.

Macklin's friend Spranger Barry had caught the managerial disease, and in 1758 the pair began to negotiate with the owners of the Crow Street Music Hall in Dublin, with a view to establishing a new theatre on that site, by popular subscription. The planned partnership came to naught, but the possibility of its success excited the jealous fury of Macklin's old adversary Thomas Sheridan and precipitated still another paper war, first between Sheridan and Macklin, later between Macklin and Barry. Earnest attempts by Macklin during 1758 to find employment with Barry (who had opened Crow Street in partnership with Henry Woodward) were fruitless. For a time that year Macklin acted as a sort of theatrical agent, trying to find players for Benjamin Victor, who had been deputed by Sheridan to manage Crow Street.

An offer from Victor to hire Macklin and Maria on a sharing arrangement for 1758–59 had to be refused because of the serious illness of Mrs Macklin, which resulted in her death on 28 December 1758. Macklin did not long remain celibate. A young servant in his household, Elizabeth Jones, soon took Ann Grace Macklin's place. Though Kirkman states that they were married on 10 September 1759, the marriage register at St Paul, Covent Garden, shows that the formal union did not take place until 13 February 1778, 19 years later.

Macklin, unable to find steady theatrical work, turned his attention again to writing in the fall of 1758 and by the fall of 1759 was trying to peddle his new comedy *Love à-la-Mode* to Garrick at Drury Lane. Two stories of the genesis of the play handed down by contemporaries hold interest. Likely, both the one told by William Cooke and the one passed on by James Boswell have some elements of truth. Cooke wrote that Sir Callaghan O'Brallaghan, the play's hero, was modeled on an agreeable Irishman who had served as an officer in the Prussian Army and whom Macklin and Barry had met in a Convent Garden tavern in 1758. Boswell entered in his journal in 1781 an account of an evening he and Tom Davies had spent with the aged Macklin: "He told us as we walked to the Shakespeare [Tavern] that his 'Love Alamode' was first thought of at his house or Lodgings in Great Russel Street, (to which he pointed,) Sir John Irwin, Dean Marli, and somebody else whom he named, present."

Whatever the circumstances of its conception, the play was to prove the best investment of time that Macklin ever made, excepting only the weeks he had spent perfecting Shylock. It was the passport with which, after the six seasons of his latest exile, he was again re-admitted to Drury Lane Theatre. *The London Stage* prints the rather complicated "Memorandum of Agreement relating to Mr Macklin's Farce" in which the wary Garrick stipulated conditions of its production. Boiled down, they meant simply that the play had to succeed substantially (at least £100 to the management each night) or would be summarily jerked from the stage. Macklin was to have had the usual author's sixth night—all proceeds after house charges of £63—and that was to have been the end of the transaction, apparently.

But Macklin was canny enough to sell his own services as the performer of one of the chief characters along with the work (which at the insistence of Arthur Murphy and William Chetwynd was reduced from a five-act comedy to a two-act farce). On 12 December 1759, with Macklin playing the comic Scot Sir Archy Macsarcasm, *Love à-la-Mode* "went off very greatly," according to the notebook of Richard Cross the prompter. The mainpiece of the evening was *The Merchant of Venice*, in which Macklin worked his old spell with Shylock. The farce was repeated some 20 times during the remainder of that season and, despite some grumpy comment from sensitive Scots, it became a permanent feature of the repertory. And Macklin remained on the payroll for the remainder of the season.

Love à-la-Mode was Macklin's favorite; he had guarded it jealously against possible piracy during rehearsal and he continued to threaten managers who gave unauthorized performances of it, both in England and Ireland. He severely scolded actors who wandered away from his conception of the roles. The work's success somewhat restored his confidence in his ability as a playwright. But he was still not very comfortable working for Garrick and he had never cared for Garrick's co-proprietor James Lacy. At season's end he resigned from the company.

In 1760–61, Macklin signed himself and Maria again onto Rich's roster, both the actor and the manager evidently expecting a continuation at Covent Garden of the previous season's successes. But Macklin performed only on a few nights, and his new comedy *The Married Libertine*, in which he assumed the leading role, Lord Belville, and Maria the heroine, Angelica, was violently condemned by the audience at its only performance, on 28 January 1761.

Once again, Macklin sailed for Ireland, where Barry offered him £600 (English) a season to act at Crow Street and sweetened the offer by promising him half the profits when any farce of his should be performed. Macklin wrote Frank Delaval exultantly that his Shylock had attracted "in three nights about 450" and that *Love à-la-Mode* was "in much higher reputation than ever it was in London." He had, he said, "a player's and an author's *summum bonum*, full houses and applause," and was living "retired, quite sequestrated, and deep in the buskin," working at odd hours on his next comedy, *The True Born Irishman*. That work was acted, after uncomfortable delays, on 14 May 1761.

But Spranger Barry and his managerial partner Henry Woodward were now at daggers' points over theatrical expenditures, and in the summer of 1761 Woodward decamped for London. Macklin was requested, and agreed, to decide the fair purchase price for Woodward's share of the property at Crow Street. He arrived at the sum of £3800. Macklin signed again at Crow Street with Barry in 1761–62 and 1762–63 (surviving bills show him also at Cork on 27 August and 8 October 1761 and 29 March 1762). His Dublin sojourn was further enlivened by his lawsuit against Henry Mossop, John Johnson, and Matthew Williamson, proprietors of the Crow Street Theater, early in 1763, because of their threat to act several of his farces without any compensation to him.

Macklin was scribbling again and hoped not only to supply Dublin but Drury Lane as well. He was, for the time, disappointed in both. Though he worked hard to revise Charles Shadwell's *The Humours of the Army* (called by Macklin *The Female Captain*) for Barry's production, it was abandoned in February 1763 after being announced as in rehearsal. Disgruntled, Macklin went off to London, as he did every spring, to act for Maria's Covent Garden benefit. On 12 April he played Sir Gilbert in *The Refusal* and Sir Archy in *Love à-la-Mode*. He repeated Sir Archy on 20 April. While in London, on 28 April, he presented to Garrick several alternative proposals for a new engagement at Drury Lane (preserved in the Forster Collection at the Victoria and Albert Museum). He would engage to act from October to Christmas or from Christmas "to the Benefits" in March or from October on through to the beginning of the benefits. But he must be allowed to go to Ireland during some time of the season, if only for awhile. He would write farces for the exclusive production of the house, but the property of his plays should be invested in himself alone. Garrick evidently expressed no interest, and Macklin returned in the fall to Dublin, acting at Crow Street until the season's end in July 1763.

Henry Mossop, manager at the rival Smock Alley Theatre, now offered Macklin two nights a week, October to April, and, ignoring their past differences, Macklin accepted for the 1763–64 season. He went at once to work on a revision of *Philaster*, which he called *The Lover's Melancholy*, but that also was found unsuitable after a few days of rehearsal. Macklin's bruised feelings were salved by the warm reception given his comedy *The True Born Scotchman* when it was acted for the first time on 10 July 1764, at Smock Alley. It would later be known, in a re-worked version, as *The Man of the World* and was his most artistic and popularly successful work. Yet, by season's end, in mid-August, Macklin had once more quarreled with Mossop, over salary arrears.

When Macklin returned from a jaunt to England in October 1764, it was to Barry and Crow Street. There he acted his usual repertoire in 1764–65, helped in the stage direction of the theatre, and turned out a Christmas trifle called *The Whim*, the text of which has been lost. He remained at Crow Street two additional winter seasons, 1765–66 and 1766–67.

Macklin concluded an agreement with Colman at Covent Garden to act 20 times during the winter of 1767–68 for £400 and a benefit. But he appeared only 16 times—though to gratifying houses—and always either as Shylock or Sir Archy (often both in a night), ex-

cept for 5 December, when he startled the audience with Iago for the "first time in 12 years," and on 28 November 1767. On the latter date he persuaded the managers to put on his afterpiece *The Irish Fine Lady* (which had been given as *The True Born Irishman* at Dublin) with himself as Murrough O'Dogherty and Maria as Mrs O'Dogherty. It failed utterly with the London playgoers and was withdrawn after one night. As Macklin's biographer Cooke explained: "Its curious idiom, half-brogue, and half Cockney, puzzled the audience, as did its highly topical Irish allusions. With his usual candor, Macklin observed: 'I believe the audience are right. . . . There's a geography in humor as well as in morals, which I had not previously considered.'" Another early biographer, Kirkman, asserted that Macklin came before the curtain "courageously" to admit: "Ladies and Gentlemen, I am very sensible that there are several passages in this play which deserve to be probated and I assure you that they shall never offend your ears again." The promise was applauded.

Macklin's whereabouts during the winter seasons of 1768–69 and 1769–70 are unknown. He was probably in Dublin, but he returned to London, as his faithful practice was, in time for his daughter's benefits at Covent Garden on 1 April 1769 and 5 April 1770. He managed to wound Garrick's *amour propre* in the fall of 1769, after the Stratford Jubilee, by offering a blunt critique of Garrick's cherished confection, the Jubilee *Ode to Shakespeare*. The draft of Garrick's long, detailed, defensive reply is in the Forster Collection (it has been printed by James Boaden and by Little and Kahrl in the Garrick *Letters*). Garrick endorsed his draft: "I might have spent my time better than supporting a foolish business against a very foolish Man."

On 12 October 1770 Macklin wrote to George Colman from James Street, Covent Garden, offering his services as actor "on the same footing on which other actors usually engage" and the use of *Love à-la-Mode*. An undated reply in Colman's *Posthumous Letters* refuses the offer but assures Macklin of an engagement of 20 nights, scattered through the season, plus a benefit and profits from any farces he should write. Macklin, in a letter of 16 October, argues that his presence regularly

would increase house receipts, and offers to
buy the house for £180 on each of as many
nights as he will act. But Colman was ada-
mant, for he disliked the thought of the explo-
sive Macklin constantly in his theatre.

Macklin bulks large and formidable in the
transcript (British Library Add MS 33,218) of
the depositions given by various theatre people
preparatory to the sensational trial for the control of Covent Garden Theatre in 1770. The
contest was between the elder George Colman
and the Harris-Rutherford-Powell faction.
Macklin's testimony was balefully hostile to
Colman and it was transparently inspired by
Colman's refusal to rehire him in 1768. But it
contained some extremely valuable evidence
about theatrical practices, from very early in
the century onward.

The winter season of 1770–71 found Macklin for the first time at the little Capel Street
Theatre in Dublin, which had been leased by
William Dawson and Robert Mahon. There he
began well—being allowed to add some of his
pupils to the roster—but as usual he ended in
strife, directing thunderbolts against the managers because of slow payment of his salary.
The months immediately following were hard.
Macklin's friend Frank Delaval died, his wife
was ill, his own health was poor, and he was
angered by the provincial manager James
Whitley, who performed *Love à-la-Mode* without permission. Though he was allowed no
regular articles, he played at Covent Garden
three times in April and once in May 1771.
After engagements in the Midlands in the
summer, he returned to Covent Garden in the
fall to act Shylock, but on only six nights.

A failed plan to enter into a managerial
partnership with Dawson at Smock Alley left
Macklin bitter and frustrated. Letters from
Dawson in Dublin to Macklin in London, dated
March 1771 and May 1772, show that Macklin was busily sounding out actors for the venture. Macklin played at Limerick on 13 March
1772, according to a surviving bill. Shortly
thereafter a shipwreck on the Irish coast drowned
many of his books and some important manuscripts, including one on the "Science of Acting." A letter in the Harvard Theatre Collection dated 23 March 1772, from Maria in
London to her father at Crow Street, inquires
anxiously about his health and hopes that he
will be able to play for her April benefit. For

the first time in years he could not go. He was
still recovering from illness at his lodgings at
"Mr Dunn's, Mantua Maker, Bolton St, Dublin" when Maria wrote again on 6 May 1772:
"I sincerely lament the loss of your most valuable Library, it was indeed a dreadful Stroke.
Yet I had rather all the Books in the World
had been lost sooner than you shou'd have
suffer'd such an Illness or have ventur'd down
to the Wreck in such Weather." She described
the difficulties she had been under in trying to
organize a benefit without him and lamented
her meagre profit of £62 4s.

Macklin was now at least 73 years old. He
may have been frightened into a consideration
of his mortality by the serious illness of the
spring, for on 16 December he signed a power
of attorney (now in the Harvard Theatre Collection) to his wife. It enabled her to "sell or
assign his estate and interest in his dwelling
house in Saint Martins Court near Leicester
Fields in the City of London for such sum . . .
as she thinks proper, and to give the deed and
receive the money thereof." She was now also
empowered to settle his accounts and manage
his premises in England.

Despite his shuttlecock progression from
Dublin to London and back and his excursions
to the Irish and English provinces, the greater
part of Macklin's time during the late sixties
and early seventies was spent in Dublin; and
there, in addition to acting, he apparently carried on a thriving business in coaching players,
some of them already relatively experienced,
like Miss Younge and Ann Catley, but most of
them youngsters like Henrietta Leeson (with
whom he became deeply but fruitlessly infa-
tuated). But Macklin could never turn his back
permanently on London, and in December 1772
he began to court Colman again. After inter-
minable haggling the two came to a fragile,
tentative, and entirely tacit agreement. Again,
the wily Colman evaded Macklin's terms, and
no articles were signed, but it was understood
that Macklin would perform for Covent Garden in 1773–74 and would undertake some
new roles. Richard III, Lear, and Macbeth were
discussed. Macklin finally settled on Macbeth
for the main thrust of his novelty that season.

As his notes on the production preserved in
the Harvard Theatre Collection show, Macklin
prepared his presentation of Macbeth the character with the same thoughtful intensity that

he had given Shylock 32 years before. Though
he was forced to modify some of his ideas of an
"authentic" and "ancient" Scottish stage-setting
by the weight of custom and the grumbling
opposition of other actors, Macklin's production began to take shape as the freshest conception of the play seen in many years. William
Cooke noted:

Macbeth used to be dressed in a suit of scarlet
and gold, a tail wig, etc., in every respect like a
modern military officer. Garrick always played it
in this manner. Macklin, however, . . . saw the
absurdity of exhibiting a Scotch character, existing
many years before the Norman Conquest, in this
manner, and therefore very properly abandoned it
for the old Caledonian habit. He shewed the same
attention to the subordinate characters as well as
to the scenes, decorations, music, and other incidental parts of the performance.

Just what Macklin's conception of "the old
Caledonian habit" was is difficult to determine
now. An engraving published by M. Darly (No
18 in the list of portraits below) depicts him
in tartan stockings, with a sword, wearing a
Balmoral bonnet. An engraving in the *London
Magazine* (No 19 below) shows him in cloak,
breeches, and buskins. Though those are caricatures, probably he wore something like the
costumes, in different scenes, and perhaps a
kilt in still another, for it is traditional that he
established that garment for the role. But it
also generated still another of those bitter broils
which periodically punctuated Macklin's career. Mrs Macklin, seated with a friend in the
gallery, had heard some hissing and had heat-
edly accused the actor Samuel Reddish and
James Sparks, son of the actor Luke Sparks,
who were seated near her. Macklin believed
the charge and publicized it in the newspapers.
On 30 October, Reddish stood in the gallery
and momentarily disrupted the second performance of *Macbeth* by attempting to deny the
allegation. On the fourth night there was a
small riot against Macklin, led by John James
and Ralph Aldus, friends of the actor William
"Gentleman" Smith, who were resentful that
Macklin had assumed some of Smith's roles.
James Sparks, with the help of his brother-in-
law the master tailor Thomas Leigh, collected
a parcel of idle tailors, primed them with drink
and inflammatory oratory, and paid their way
into the theatre on 18 November to halt the
performance of Macklin in *The Merchant of Ven-*

Harvard Theatre Collection

"Shylock turn'd Macbeth"

artist unknown

ice. The demand that Macklin come on stage
and kneel in submission was, predictably, ignored. That refusal sparked another riot, with
damage to the playhouse. In the end, intimi-
dated by the tailors' faction, George Colman
the patentee discharged Macklin from Covent
Garden.

Macklin determined to seek a prosecution of
six of the rioters for "conspiracy to deprive him
of his livelihood." Many months were spent
seeking an indictment, in negotiations over
out-of-court settlement, and collection of affidavits. Finally, on 24 February 1775, five of
the rioters—Clark, Aldus, Leigh, James, and
Miles—were tried before Justice Aston and a
select jury, who found them guilty. On 11 May
the defendants appeared for sentencing before
Lord Chief Justice Mansfield in the Court of
the King's Bench. Mansfield suggested that
arbitration over damages to the theatre should
be possible still and, threatening the defend-

ants with jail and fines, reminded them that Macklin could still sue. Macklin rose to deny that either money or revenge was his object and proposed that the defendants pay his legal expenses, take tickets worth £100 for his daughter's benefit and the like number for his own, plus a third £100 in tickets to indemnify the theatre management for losses. The proposal was accepted. Lord Mansfield addressed Macklin with a speech complimenting his magnanimity, and the "honourable complexion and singular moderation" of his proposal, assuring him that, "You will do more good by this, in the eyes of the public, than if you had received all the money you had a right to receive." The Justice concluded, "You have met with great applause today. You never acted better." Throughout the whole contention Macklin had believed that, somehow, David Garrick was at the bottom of the conspiracy. Several of the pamphlets generated by the controversy were probably by Macklin.

In March and April 1774, letters from West Digges the Edinburgh manager (now in the Garrick Club and Harvard Theatre Collection) sought to entice Macklin northward with an offer of £25 per week, assuring him that the sum was £10 more than Macklin's old rival Henry Woodward was making. But, so far as is known, Macklin stuck stubbornly in London until he humbled his riotous adversaries. He returned to the Covent Garden stage to play Shylock and Sir Archy on 18 May 1775, for Maria's benefit, a week after the end of the trial. It was his first appearance there since his dismissal on 18 November 1773. On 25 May he played Richard III for the first time, with Maria as Lady Ann, and repeated the part for his benefit on 1 June, the last evening of the season, when Mrs Hopkins favored him by crossing over from Drury Lane to play Queen Margaret. From 12 June through 28 July 1775 Macklin was in Younger's company at the King Street Theatre, Birmingham, and later was at Liverpool.

Plagued by ill health in the 1775–76 season Macklin played at Covent Garden only five times. His zest for combat had not diminished, however. He had obtained satisfaction from the rioters, but his courtroom scene of abnegation had cost him money. George Colman had dismissed him abruptly and, he felt, without just cause. Though Colman had sev-

ered his connection with Covent Garden Theatre on 26 May 1774, Macklin, weekly during each theatrical season since his dismissal, had delivered the same message to Colman's house, signifying his willingness to play and demanding his salary. In 1776 he began to file a series of complaints in Chancery, but his efforts to find witnesses to Colman's ill-treatment met with little success. (The suit would drag on for years until, in 1784, it was finally settled by a compromise once again engineered by Lord Mansfield, which gained for Macklin £500, half the sum in contention.)

Macklin continued to act at Covent Garden for another decade, but his appearances were few and on widely separated evenings: about eight times in the fall of 1777 and not at all the season following; and though the playbill of 23 February 1779 announced that he would play Shylock and Sir Pertinax on 25 February, the performance was "obliged to be postponed" by his "being taken ill." He had seven appearances in 1779–80, 14 in 1780–81, a dozen in 1781–82, eight in 1782–83, seven in 1783–84, but only six in 1784–85. He was well paid, if infrequently. The Covent Garden account book in the British Library shows on 12 February 1784: "Paid Macklin for 4 Nights Performance £126." But he was growing increasingly deaf and forgetful. The *Public Advertiser* on 5 February 1784 reported that even when he played Sir Pertinax "if [he] once loses the Catch Word he is gone irretrievably." When some apprentices, admitted for half price at the end of Act III, came into the pit and were boisterous, "Macklin stopped; he lost himself. . . . He came to the Side of the Stage, and stooping down to the Talkers, said, 'Gentlemen, I must beg you to be silent; my Hearing and Recollection are not so perfect as they were; I cannot proceed for your talking.'"

Macklin began to feel again the powerful old urge to hear the applause of Irishmen. On 5 May 1785 he began an engagement at Smock Alley under Richard Daly's management, at the salary of £50 (English) per week. Mrs Macklin remained in England, but Macklin was accompanied by his son John. That aging young man—now somewhere around 35— had been an exasperation to his father most of his life and continued to be so. Macklin, at some cost of time and money, had obtained for him an appointment as a writer in the East

India Company and had sent him out to India in 1769. John had shortly returned penniless and in disgrace, followed by rumors of dueling and gambling. Admitted to the Middle Temple in 1775, before long he had sold his law books to support his gambling habit. Macklin procured him a commission in the Royal Artillery, and he was at once caught up in the American War. He returned from America, again under cloudy rumors. In Ireland, John's public behavior was as dissolute as ever, and to his father he was insulting. Macklin sent him home. "I gave him seven guineas," Macklin wrote his wife Bess, "to bear his charges to London—I suppose he might spend on the road four or five, so he has two or three left for his evening drams . . . well, as you say, God mend him—for we cannot."

But in all other respects, both socially and professionally, Macklin got so much satisfaction from the excursion as almost to forget that he was 86 years old. Toward the end of his engagement he was reminded of his age, for he began again to drop his lines. At his benefit, in August, he was obliged to leave the stage after the first act and allow George Dawson to step into the part of Sir Pertinax. At the end of that month he sailed for England. Though he had complained of chills and fever during the final weeks in Dublin, he revived after a few weeks' rest and entered on an engagement at Manchester from 26 September through 28 October 1785. It is uncertain how many times he played.

In the spring of 1786 Macklin performed at Covent Garden twice in February and twice in March. In the spring of 1787 he appeared only at his own benefit on 5 May, when a generous public response brought total receipts to £335. On that evening his old pupil Miss Ambrose came out of retirement to substitute for Mrs Morton, absent from a leading role because of illness. Macklin's own "indisposition" again deferred his Shylock on 20 December 1787. He dropped down to three performances that season. He attempted only three again in 1788–89, and from one of them, when he played Sir Pertinax on 26 November, he had to withdraw in confusion. Announced to play Shylock on 10 February 1789, he was unable to come to the theatre.

At Covent Garden on 7 May 1789, in a performance for his benefit, Macklin mounted

Harvard Theatre Collection

MACKLIN'S residence in Tavistock Street

the stage for the last time. William Cooke gave an account of the melancholy event:

> When Macklin had dressed himself for the part, which he did with his usual accuracy, he went into the Green Room, but with such a "lack-lustre looking eye" as plainly indicated his inability to perform; and coming up to . . . Mrs. Pope, said, "My dear, are you to play tonight?" "Good God! to be sure I am, Sir. Why, don't you see I am dressed for Portia?" "Ah! Very true; I had forgot. But who is to play Shylock?" The imbecile tone of his voice and the inanity of the look, with which the last question was asked, caused a melancholy sensation in all who heard it. At last Mrs. Pope, rousing herself, said, "Why you, to be sure; are you not dressed for the part?" He then seemed to recollect himself, and, putting his hand to his forehead pathetically exclaimed, "God help me—my memory, I am afraid, has left me."

He began to perform, but after a few speeches left the stage. Thomas Ryder, alerted for that contingency, stepped into the part and finished the evening.

Harvard Theatre Collection

CHARLES MACKLIN, at age 97

artist unknown

Macklin lived on in his house at No 6, Tavistock Row, whence he had moved in 1788, sustained partly by his savings and partly by the aid of friends like Arthur Murphy, who saw a subscription edition of *The Man of the World* and *Love à-la-Mode* through the press, enabling an annuity worth £200 to be assured. Macklin continued his accustomed rounds, to the Antelope Tavern, to his place in the front row of the pit at Covent Garden, growing ever more peremptory and more eccentric. The underlying strength of his constitution, which had borne him up stiffly through so much hardship, accident, and disease, had begun at last to give way. The *Monthly Mirror* for February 1796 reported that "Macklin, the father of the stage, has, for several years past, slept in an arm-chair, fearful of being suffocated if he went to bed."

Macklin died on the morning of 11 July 1797, at age 98, at his house in Tavistock Row. He was buried at St Paul, Covent Garden, "in the vault close to the north gate of the churchyard," attended by a small group of friends, among whom were several fellow actors, according to the account in the *Monthly Mirror* for August. The *Monthly Visitor*, in the summer of 1797, added that he had been buried beside his brother and that prayers had been read by the Reverend Mr Ambrose, who had been Macklin's pupil.

Charles Macklin was on the stage for nearly 70 years. His career began while the traditions of Betterton and Booth were still alive. It continued through the successive eras of James Quin and David Garrick and lasted until the heyday of John Philip Kemble and Mrs Siddons. No actor could have kept to one unchanging "style" over such a span of time and subject to so many powerful influences, and surely Macklin did not. But the main features of the style which he would eventually develop became apparent early, when, as he said, he refused to deliver speeches "in the hoity-toity tone" of Quin, because his aim was to speak "familiar." The "natural" acting of Macklin seemed to Quin's generation to lack dignified artifice. It apparently neglected the studied gesture and ponderous periods which often made Quin's tragedy seem more like declamation than acting. Very likely the origin of Macklin's rebellion lay in the four-square bluntness of his personality and not in any theoretical notions. But in time instinct and thought merged into a considered method. Finally, Thomas Davies could write that Macklin "was the only player I ever heard of that made acting a science."

It is sometimes forgotten that Macklin had been acting for perhaps as long as 20 years before he shocked theatrical society, the critics, and the public with his conception of Shylock. Ten years after that revelation John Hill wrote in *The Actor* (1750):

There was a time indeed when everything in tragedy, if it was but the delivering a common message, was spoken in high heroics; but of late years this absurdity has been in great measure banish'd from the English, as well as from the French stage. The French owe this rational improvement in their tragedy to Baron and Madam Couvreur, and we to that excellent player Mr. Macklin: the pains he took while entrusted with the care of the actors at Drury-Lane, and the attention which the success of those pains acquir'd him from the now greatest actors of the English theatre, have founded for us a new method of the delivering tragedy from the first rate actors, and banish'd the bombast that us'd to wound our ears continually from the mouths of the subordinate ones, who were eternally aiming to mimic the majesty that the principal performers employ'd on scenes that were of the utmost consequence, in the delivery of the most simple and familiar phrases. . . .

Yet James Boaden, who "paid much attention to Macklin's performances, and personally knew him," was convinced that Macklin had inherited much from "the old school" (presumably that of Betterton and Booth) and that "that school taught what was truth and nature." Boaden recalled:

His action was essentially manly—there was nothing of trick about it. His delivery was more level than modern speaking, but certainly more weighty, direct and emphatic. His features were rigid, his eye cold and colourless; yet the earnestness of his manner, and the sterling sense of his address, produced an effect in Shylock, that has remained to the present hour unrivalled. . . . If this perfection be true of him, when speaking the language of Shakespeare, it is equally so, when he gave utterance to his own. . . . His performance of the *two true born Scotsmen* [in his *Love à-la-Mode* and *Man of the World*] was so perfect, as though he had been created expressly to keep up the prejudice against Scotland. . . . Macklin could inveigle as well as subdue; and modulated his voice, almost to his last year, with amazing skill. . . .

It has been commonly considered that Garrick introduced a mighty change in stage delivery: that actors had never, until his time, been natural. . . . [But Macklin] abhorred all trick, all start and ingenious attitude; and his attacks upon Mr. Garrick were always directed to the restless abundance of his action and his gestures, by which, he said, rather than by the fair business of the character, he caught and detained all attention to himself. . . .

Macklin's salutary influence on younger actors—including Garrick—seems to have been recognized in his own time. We have seen how he coached Garrick's Lear into success. Hill thought that he was similarly responsible for refining Iago. In Iago's sly soliloquy about tricking Cassio ("If I can fasten but one cup upon him"), "Mr Macklin first set an example which has been followed by Mr. Garrick, of delivering plainly and without ornament, a speech in which we have been us'd to see a world of unnatural contortion of face and absurd bye-play."

Macklin is entitled to rank, with Garrick, as one of the two most "revolutionary" performers between Betterton and Kean. He lacked the range and flexibility, the appearance and the voice, of Garrick. And some critics complained that he infused some of Shylock into all of his characters. But they should have noted instead how well he overcame, in those other characters, the physical and psychical attributes which had been assets in Shylock. Francis Gentleman, in *The Dramatic Censor* (1770), took note of the handicaps Macklin had to overcome to play Mercutio, though the character was "extremely well received" in the end: "[A] saturnine cast of countenance, sententious utterance, hollow toned voice, and heaviness of deportment, ill suited the whimsical Mercutio . . . however the author's sense was critically observed in this, as well as all other characters by the theatrical Nestor. . . ." Though Macklin "never had, in voice, figure, or features, much capability for the fop cast, yet [he] struck out some things in Faddle [in Moore's *The Foundling*], which we have not seen any body equal; particularly marking the obsequious knave all through." His was far the best Polonius because it "shewed oddity, grafted upon the man of sense." His Peachum "stood, in our opinion, foremost" and he excelled in Sir Francis Wronghead in *The Provok'd Husband* because he "filled the author's ideas . . . and conveyed them to the audience admirably; consequential stupidity sat well painted on his countenance, and wrought laughable effects without the paltry resource of grimace."

A few critics remained hostile, like the severe Charles Churchill, who wrote in his *Rosciad*:

> Macklin, who largely deals in half-formed sounds,
> Who wantonly transgresses nature's bounds,
> Whose acting's hard, affected, and constrained,
> Whose features, as each other they disdained,
> At variance set, inflexible and coarse,
> Ne'er knew the workings of united force,
> Ne'er kindly soften to each other's aid,
> Nor show the mingled powers of light and shade.

But to most, like "Anthony Pasquin," who gave him 82 lines of adulatory verse in *The Pin Basket. To the Children of Thespis* (1796), he was "Like the Eddystone pillar," for "his excellence braves / The rude dashing foam of the critical waves." "In blood thirsty SHYLOCK, sublimely infernal, / He bares ghastly Vice, and exposes the kernel." "So perfect the Actor can damn and dissemble, / Could Shakespeare behold him, e'en Shakespeare would tremble." For Pasquin also he was the Nestor of the stage, as he was for Francis Gentleman and the anonymous writers of *A Trip to Parnassus* (1788) and *The Mirror* (1790).

It seems certain that Macklin had a large influence in ushering onto the British stage a more naturalistic style of acting—in London, in Dublin, and in the English and Irish provinces—both by the example of his performance and by his teaching inside the theatre and in his "school." His known "private" pupils included, besides his daughter Maria, Ann Catley, Mrs Belfille, John Hill, Miss Minors, probably both of the Misses Ambrose, Miss Jackson, and Miss Leeson. But there were certainly many more. He was a stern taskmaster, and his "harsh manners" forced a few of his students from his tutelage, as they did the 18-year-old Miss Cleland, according to the *Secret History of the Green Room* (1804).

One of his pupils, John Hill, left a description of his methods:

In Macklin's garden there were three long parallel walks, and his method of exercising the voice was thus. His two young pupils with back boards (such as they use in boarding-schools) walked firmly, slow, and well, up and down the two side walks; Macklin himself paraded the centre walk; at the end of every twelve paces he made them stop; and turning gracefully, the young actor called out across the walk, "How do you do, Miss Ambrose?" She answered, "Very well, I thank you, Mr. Glenville." They then took a few more paces, and the next question was, "Do you not think it is a very fine day, Mr. Glenville?" "A very fine day, indeed, Miss Ambrose," was the answer. Their walk continued; and then, "How do you do, Mr. Glenville?" "Pretty well, I thank you, Miss Ambrose." And this exercise continued for an hour or so. . . . Such was Macklin's method of training the management of the voice; if too high, too low, a wrong accent, or a faulty inflection, he . . . made them repeat the words twenty times till all was right. It was his manner to check all the cant and cadence of tragedy; he would bid his pupil first speak the passage as he would in common life . . . and then giving them more force, but preserving the same accent, to deliver them on the stage. . . . and with nothing more than this attention to what is natural, he produced, out of the most ignorant persons, players that surprised everybody. . . .

Except for the probably apocryphal story of a ménage à trois with Peg Woffington and Garrick, Macklin was the subject of no scandalous gossip. Though he almost certainly never formally married Ann Grace, they lived together in apparent harmony until her death. Surviving correspondence between him and his second wife Elizabeth Jones Macklin shows them as an affectionate and loyal couple. The *Monthly Visitor* writer reported that Macklin left the reputation of a "fond husband and affectionate father. And whatever were the petulancies of his temper, his affections were on the side of virtue." He was fiercely protective of his daughter. A story was told by his biographer Cooke that a baronet called at Macklin's house while he was at breakfast and offered to settle large sums upon both him and Maria if she would consent to be the baronet's mistress. The enraged Macklin, knife upraised, chased the dastard downstairs. The episode was commemorated in a satirical print, "Mr Macklin and the Amorous Baronet."

Certainly Macklin carefully nurtured Maria's talent and assiduously promoted her interests in the theatre. But it has been repeatedly suggested that the determined assertiveness of his personality damaged his children emotionally and was to some extent responsible for John's waywardness and Maria's failure to marry. That charge has probably been overstated and must remain unproved. Yet apparently Maria did have a difficult time both living with him and freeing herself from his household and his control. Her letters show both her love for him and her emotional dependence on his direction. Evidently she also began, late in her career, to resent his imposition of certain interpretations on her roles. She died in 1781, to Macklin's lasting sorrow. The old actor also strove earnestly to advance the fortunes of his wastrel son John, to no lasting effect. John died in 1790.

Charles Macklin's wife Elizabeth survived him by 11 years. Macklin had hoped to leave her in comfortable circumstances. A letter dated 14 April 1785, quoted in a clipping in the Harvard Theatre Collection, from Macklin to his banker Thomas Coutts, reads: "Whatever property I have in this life, I have, by will, bequeathed to my wife Elizabeth Macklin, and were it as great as any subject in this realm enjoys, her affection, order, sobriety, and good morals, as a wife, a mother, and a friend and neighbour, she would deserve it. Therefore I hope, that you will, upon my decease, pay her whatever balance you may have in my favour. . . ."

But by the time of his death there was little but the sentiment left for her comfort. She received aid from the Covent Garden Fund established for the relief of superannuated players; and in June 1805 John Philip Kemble granted her a benefit at Drury Lane Theatre which realized about £400. The money was invested, the interest to be for her use. In April 1806 Mrs Macklin made her will, leaving to "The Theatrical ffund Established for the relief of decayed performers who have belonged to the Theatre Royal in Covent Garden London the interest for ever of three hundred Pounds now invested in my name in the public ffunds of the Bank of England termed Navy 5 per cent Annuities" provided that the managers of the Fund should undertake to keep constantly polished and in good repair "the monumental slab erected to the memory of my late husband Charles Macklin Comedian which is now placed against the South Wall withinside the Parish Church of Saint Paul Covent Garden." If ever destroyed, it should be replaced, so that it might "be preserved to the end of time. . . ."

Macklin constantly affected the writer-scholar and, indeed, had acquired considerable learning of the sort given by random reading over many years. But he was, ironically, persistently taunted by enemies, even after he achieved a degree of professional success, with being an ignorant boor and even with having been completely illiterate until his early twenties. The charge seems ridiculous on its face, for with actors there is a presumption of literacy. Besides, his attendance at the school at Island Bridge seems well documented. But strangely, the assertion seems even to have been passed along by Dr Samuel Johnson, with whom Macklin was acquainted. The entry for 1761 in Bishop Percy's pocket diary (BL MS 32,336)—a date on which Percy, Johnson, Johnson's blind charge Miss Williams, and Macklin took tea together—reads: "Johnson says Maclin . . . was 2 or 3 & 20 before he learnt to read."

Dr Johnson made a deep impression on Macklin, who, it was said, began to imitate some of his mannerisms. On one or two occa-

sions when Macklin presumed to be disputatious Johnson found it easy to demolish him. But he had a good opinion of Macklin's understanding. Boswell, who found the actor fascinating, made light of his learning while defending his veracity in a letter to Edmond Malone on 18 January 1781. Boswell had just been reading Malone's attack on Macklin's assertion, in a letter to the *General Advertiser* back in April 1748, that he had read a seventeenth-century pamphlet entitled *Old Ben's Light Heart made heavy by Young John's Melancholy Lover*. Malone had asserted that "excerpts" which Macklin had purported to give had been fabricated. But Boswell defended "poor Charles, who unquestionably could not *himself* be the authour of the statement for which more reading than he has, nor of the verses for which more genius than he has, is requisite."

Boswell's patronizing assertion may have been no sounder than his grammar. Leaving aside Macklin's pamphleteering and his successful comedies (a genre perhaps beyond Boswell's abilities), the evidence of the actor's intellectual interests lies in the *Catalogue of the Library of the Late Mr. Charles Macklin, Comedian Deceased*, published before the auction of his books and manuscripts on 21–25 November 1797. It lists 1117 items, representing history, poetry, fiction, drama, travel, philosophy, and religion, in several languages.

Portraits of Charles Macklin include:

1. By William Beechey. Location unknown. Engraving by W. Ridley, published as a plate to *Monthly Mirror*, 1796.

2. By John Opie, c. 1792. Half-length, seated at a table. In the National Portrait Gallery (No 1319). Presumably the portrait painted for the Reverend Edward Clarke (1769–1822). This portrait was probably the one sold at Christie's in March 1856, bought by Mr Hermann for John Green of Covent Garden. It was sold at Christie's again on 22 July 1871. The National Portrait Gallery bought it from James McCulloch in 1902. A version is in the Garrick Club (No 16). Engraving by J. Condé as a plate to Murphy's edition of Macklin's works, published by J. Bell, 1792. Other engravings by J. Freeman, published by Longman & Co, 1806; by J. Hopwood, published as a plate to Doran's *Annals of the English Stage*, 1888; and by unknown engraver, undated.

3. Engraved portrait by J. Corner, after J. C.

Lochée, 1784. Published as a plate to *European Magazine*, 1787. It is a copy of the portrait by Lochée on a Wedgwood medallion owned by Macklin. The medallion is in the Wedgwood Museum, Barleston, Stoke-on-Trent. Copies were engraved by D. Edwin as a plate to *The Mirror of Taste*, 1811; by J. Rogers as a plate to Oxberry's *Dramatic Biography*, 1827; and, in reverse, by W. Ridley as plates to Kirkman's *Memoirs of the Life of Charles Macklin*, 1799, and to William Cooke's *Memoirs of Charles Macklin*, 1804.

4. Engraved portrait by Heath. Published as a plate to *British Theatre*, Dublin, 1793.

5. Engraved portrait by J. Wright, after C. Hayter. Published by Darling & Thompson, 1794. A copy was engraved by W. Read as a plate to Ryan's *Dramatic Table Talk*, 1825.

6. By unknown artist, 1789. Original pastel in the Picture Post Library. Made just before Macklin's retirement. Reproduced in Mander and Mitchenson's *A Picture History of the British Stage* (pl 107).

7. By unknown artist. Pen drawing in a Folger Library commonplace book.

8. By unknown engraver. Published as a plate to *Hibernian Magazine*, February 1771.

9. By unknown engraver. Macklin at 97, standing, holding cane. Published as a plate to Congreve's *Memoirs of Macklin*, 1798.

10. Speaking his farewell prologue to *The Refusal* in 1753. Engraving by Walker, after D. Dodd. Published by Fielding & Walker, 1779.

11. As Squire Badger in *Don Quixote in England*. By unknown engraver. Published by J. Wenman, 1777.

12. As Sir Francis Wronghead, with John Dunstall as John Moody, in *The Provok'd Husband*. Engraving by Reading, after Dodd, for *New English Theatre*, 1766. Reproduced in this dictionary, volume 4, p. 597.

13. As Sir Gilbert Wrangle in *The Refusal*. Colored drawing by J. Roberts. In the British Museum. Engraving by Thornthwaite for *Bell's British Theatre*, 1777.

14. As Sir Gilbert Wrangle in *The Refusal*. Engraving by Thornthwaite, after Samuel De Wilde, for *Bell's British Theatre*, 1792.

15. As Sir Pertinax Macsycophant in *The Man of the World*. Oil by De Wilde. In the National Gallery of Ireland, bought in 1881. Probably the painting sold at Christie's in 1871

from John Green's collection. A similar version by De Wilde is in the Garrick Club (No 476). Engraving by R. H. Cromek, for *Bell's British Theatre*, 1795. A copy by an unknown engraver was published by G. Cawthorne, 1795.

16. As Sir Pertinax Macsycophant. Engraving by W. Gardiner, after S. Harding. Published by E. Harding, 1786.

17. As a Witch, with John Williams as another Witch and John Henderson as Macbeth, in *Macbeth*. Painting by George Romney, 1780, location of original unknown. Copies are in the Garrick Club (No 435) and the Folger Shakespeare Library. For additional details on the paintings and engraved versions see the iconography for John Henderson in this dictionary, vol 7, p. 262.

18. As Macbeth. By unknown engraver ("Old Envy sculp., after Young Vanity invt"). Titled "Shylock Turnd Macbeth," published by M. Darly on 5 November 1773. Caricature of Macklin's appearance in Scottish dress. A copy in reverse was also issued.

19. As Macbeth. By unknown engraver. Published as a plate to *London Magazine*, 1773.

20. As Macbeth, standing, right foot on step. By unknown engraver. A copy in reverse was also issued.

21. As Shylock, with Maria Macklin as Portia, in *The Merchant of Venice*. By Edward Alcock. This portrait, once in the collection of Lincoln Kirstein, was owned by the American Shakespeare Theatre, Stratford, Connecticut, until 1975, when it was acquired by the Yale Center for British Art. The figures of Shylock and Portia have been tentatively identified as Macklin and his daughter Maria. See Geoffrey Ashton, *Shakespeare and British Art* (catalogue of exhibition at Yale Center for British Art, 1981). A similar picture, probably also by Alcock, is in a private collection in New York.

22. As Shylock, holding knife and scales. Engraving by N. C. Goodnight, undated. A copy, in another edition, was also issued.

23. As Shylock, holding knife and scales. Engraving by J. Lodge, published by T. Wright, 1775.

24. As Shylock, with Elizabeth Pope as Portia. Engraving by William Nutter, after John Boyne. Published by W. Yolland, 1790.

25. As Shylock, holding knife and scales. India ink drawing by Thomas Parkinson. In the British Museum. Engraving by C. Gri-

gnion, published as a plate to Bell's *Shakespeare*, 1775.

26. As Shylock. Drawing by J. H. Ramberg. In the British Museum. Engraving by T. Cooke, published by J. Bell, 1785.

27. As Shylock, with Michael Dyer as Gratiano. Engraving by T. B. Simonet, after P. J. De Loutherbourg.

28. As Shylock, with Maria Macklin as Portia, Matthew Clarke as Antonio, Michael Dyer as Gratiano, David Morris as the Duke, Jane Lessingham as Nerissa, and others, in the trial scene. By Johann Zoffany, c. 1768, unfinished. In the Tate Gallery. Once in the collection of the Marquis of Lansdowne. For the provenance and a detailed discussion of this painting and the Nos 29, 30, and 31, below, see Mander and Mitchenson, *The Artist and the Theatre* (1955).

29. As Shylock, solo figure from Zoffany's painting of trial scene (above, No 28). Engraving by John Smith, published in Robert Sayer's edition of *Dramatic Characters, or Different Portraits of the English Stage*.

30. As Shylock. By John Zoffany. Full-length, with arms extended. Once in the collection of Sir George Beaumont, at Coleorton Hall, Leicestershire. It was bought at Sotheby's on 30 June 1948 by Somerset Maugham, who bequeathed it to the National Theatre, where it now hangs.

31. As Shylock. By Johann Zoffany. Head and shoulders, oil, study for No 30, above. In the National Gallery of Ireland, purchased at Christie's in 1888.

32. As Shylock, with Michael Stoppelaer as Tubal. Said to be by Johann Zoffany, but possibly by Charles or Herbert Stoppelaer. In 1955 in the possession of the family of the late Sir Herbert Hughes-Stanton.

33. As Shylock, with Michael Stoppelaer as Tubal. By Herbert or Charles Stoppelaer. Reported to be in the possession of the American Shakespeare Theatre, Stratford, Connecticut. Perhaps the same as No 32, above.

34. As Shylock. By unknown artist. On a delftware tile. Example in the City of Manchester Art Gallery.

35. As Shylock, sharpening knife on ground. By unknown engraver. Published by Wenman, 1777.

36. Satirical Print: "Roscius in Triumph, or the Downfall of Shylock alias Mackbeth." By unknown engraver, in the *Macaroni Magazine*, 1773. Macklin, dressed as Shylock, lies on his back, at the foot of Comedy and Tragedy, which figures support Garrick on their shoulders. Explained in the *Catalogue of Political and Personal Satires in the British Museum* (No 5203).

37. Satirical Print: Macklin as Shylock, carrying Shakespeare on his shoulders, below title "Immortal Shakespear! Child of Heaven & Fire, The more we sink him rises still the higher."

38. Satirical Print: Broadside, "Covent Garden in an Uproar: Or the Town robbed of its Liberty. Being a True and Particular Account of Macklin's Defeat by a Party of Players." Macklin with 15 other actors on stage.

39. Satirical print: "The Theatrical Contest," published 24 October 1743 by G. Foster. Reproduced in this dictionary, vol 5, p. 300; the print is explained in the *Catalogue of Political and Personal Satires in the British Museum* (No 2599).

40. Caricature: "Sir Archy McSarcasm—in the Character of Macbeth." By unknown engraver.

41. Caricature: "Mr. Macklin and the Amorous Baronet." Macklin threatening the Baronet with a knife. By unknown engraver.

Macklin, Mrs Charles the first, Ann [née Grace Purvor?] sometime stage name Mrs Grace *d. 1758, actress, dancer, singer.*

The origins of the first Mrs Charles Macklin are obscure. Not even her maiden name can be truly ascertained. William Cooke, in some ways the most reliable of the early memorialists of her famous husband, declared that she was born Grace Purvor. But perhaps she was Ann Grace Purvor, for she was later known as Mrs Ann Macklin. James Kirkman, another biographer of Charles Macklin, thought her to have been a widow when she "married" Macklin. It may be, then, that her first husband was named Grace, the name under which she for a long time acted. Or she may have been just such a "widow" as she became a "wife" when she met and consorted with Macklin. For it appears that she never formally married him.

She first appeared to London notice as a dancer at Lincoln's Inn Fields Theatre on 26 April 1721. (Our entry for Mrs Grace in volume 6 of this *Dictionary* failed to associate her with Macklin and was thus in error.) She was very likely the Mrs Grace who acted at Smock Alley Theatre in Dublin from the season of 1721–22 through that of 1725–26, where the surviving playbills show her acting, in 1721–22, Jenny in *Love for Love* and Eugenia in *The Rival Generals*; in 1722–23, Dolly in *The Deceit* and Teresa in *The Spanish Fryar*; in 1723–24, Miss Flirt in *A Wife and No Wife*; in 1724–25, Penelope in *Tunbridge Walks*, Prudence in *The Amorous Widow*, and Situp in *The Double Gallant*; and in 1725–26, Constance Holdup in *The Northern Lass* and Panura in *The Island Princess*. In the summer of 1726 she joined the company at Lincoln's Inn Fields Theatre in London. On 5 July she played Belinda in *Tunbridge Walks*, advertised as from "Dublin, being the first Time of her Appearance on this Stage." Thereafter that summer she played Carolina in *Epsom Wells*, Lady Wealthy in *The Gamester*, Elenora in *The Spanish Wives*, and Lucy in *The Wits*. She apparently then retreated to Ireland.

But by 16 September 1727 Mrs Grace was in London again. For on that date she acted Goneril in *King Lear* at Drury Lane. The only other part known for her that season is Myrtilla in *The Provok'd Husband* on 10 January 1728, and she may not have been a member of the regular company. She was absent from London notices in the first half of the 1728–29 season but resumed at Drury Lane on 11 January, as Goneril, and followed that part with several new ones (some of which she may have acted in Ireland): the Widow in *The Scornful Lady*, Altea in *Rule a Wife and Have a Wife*, Peggy in *The Village Opera*, Cephisa in *The Distrest Mother*, Lady Townly in *The Man of Mode*, Lucy in *Wit Without Money*, Lettice in *The School Boy*, and Mrs Squeamish in *The Country Wife*.

Mrs Grace remained at Drury Lane in the winter seasons constantly for the following five years, pursuing for the most part a line of comic eccentrics but varying that with an occasional ingénue. In the summers she was often to be found acting at suburban Richmond or at one of the London fairs.

At Drury Lane in 1729–30 she added to her list Theodosia in *The Lancashire Witches*, Gazett in *She Wou'd If She Cou'd*, a Wife in *The Comical Distresses of Pierot*, Mrs Haughty in *The Humours of Oxford*, Dolly in *The Chambermaid*, and Jenny in *Patie and Peggy*. At Richmond she added Isabinda in *The Busy Body*, Elvira in *The Spanish Fryar*, and Lady Grace in *The Provok'd*

Husband. She was in the company at Richmond in June. At the Oates-Fielding booths at Bartholomew Fair in August and at Southwark Fair in September she played Caelia in *The Generous Free-Mason*.

At Drury Lane in 1730–31 Mrs Grace added Lady Hazard in *Greenwich Park*, the Barmaid in *The Fair Quaker of Deal*, Scentwell in *The Busy Body*, the original Euriale in Charles Johnson's tragedy *Medea*, Aurora in *Cephalus and Procris*, a Beggar Woman in *The Jovial Crew*, Flora in *Hob*, and Angelica in *The Constant Couple*. At Richmond that summer she was, for the first time, Mrs Page in *The Merry Wives of Windsor*; and at the Fielding-Hippisley-Hall booth at Bartholomew Fair she played Isabella in *The Emperor of China*. At Drury Lane in 1731–32 she added Lady Loverule in *The Devil to Pay*, Mrs Centaure in *The Silent Woman*, a Lady in Aaron Hill's new (speedily rejected) tragedy *Athelwold*, Cleone in Petiplace Bellers's poor melodrama *Injur'd Innocence*, Lady Lurewell in *The Devil to Pay*, some part unspecified in Charles Johnson's new ballad opera *The Ephesian Matron*, and Lucinda in *The Comical Revenge*. At Richmond in June she was Kitty in *The What D'Ye Call It* and Hillaria in *Love's Last Shift*. In August she was with Hippisley and Hall at Bartholomew Fair, playing some unspecified role in *The Envious Statesman*.

In 1732–33, Mrs Grace studied the original Keeper's Wife in Charles Johnson's wretched *Caelia* and added to her list Jenny in *The Beggar's Opera*, Wishwell in *The Double Gallant*, a Shepherdess in *The Judgment of Paris*, the original Mrs Wisely in Henry Fielding's comedy *The Miser*, a part in a new anonymous farce *The Mock Officer*, Lucy in *The Old Bachelor*, the original Daphne in Theophilus Cibber's *Damon and Daphne*, and Prudence in *The Amorous Widow*.

Evidently by 1732 Ann Grace and Macklin had lived together for some time. According to James T. Kirkman, Mrs Grace's daughter Maria by Charles Macklin was born some time in 1733. The Master Grace who had put on black-face on 31 March 1733 for the little Negro Pompey in Theophilus Cibber's new afterpiece *The Harlot's Progress*, in which Mrs Grace played Jenny, was also more than likely her child, though almost certainly not Macklin's. Perhaps the birth of Master Grace had been the cause of her assumption, in 1721, of "Mrs Grace." The child may have died soon after his several stage appearances in the after-piece, for he was not heard of again.

Mrs Grace played Selima in the droll *Tamerlane* in the Cibber-Griffin-Bullock-Hallam booth at Bartholomew Fair on 23 August 1733 and a month later joined the group of seceders from the Drury Lane Company who followed Theophilus Cibber to the Haymarket. There on 26 September she added two new parts, Mrs Foresight in *Love for Love* and Lady Loverule in *The Devil to Pay*, as the "Company of Comedians of his Majesty's Revels"—so-called—opened its season. In mid-March 1734 the rebels returned to Drury Lane. Despite the interruptions, Mrs Grace figured in some 75 nights that season and added several other characters to her repertoire: Angelina in *Love Makes a Man*, Mrs Clerimont in *The Tender Husband*, Patch in *The Busy Body*, Lady Grave-airs in *The Careless Husband*, Lady Dainty in *The Double Gallant*, Melinda in *The Recruiting Officer*, Desdemona in *Othello*, Dame Pliant in *The Alchemist*, Tattleaid in *The Funeral*, and Mrs Barnard in *The Country House*.

Charles Macklin had come to Drury Lane from the provinces in October 1733, recruited by the manager Highmore to fill the gap left by the departure of Theophilus Cibber. He was dismissed at Cibber's return in March 1734. He went on tour in the south of England and Wales in the summer and was probably accompanied by Mrs Grace. In the fall, both she and Macklin were regulars of the Drury Lane company, where in subsequent years they were frequently to be seen in the same bill. From this period they were also sharing lodgings in Bow Street.

Mrs Grace played much less frequently in 1734–35 and 1735–36 than thitherto, a diminution which may be attributed in 1734–35 to the care of her young daughter. In 1735–36 it was certainly in part due to the protracted anxiety over the fate of Charles Macklin, who had killed his fellow-actor Thomas Hallam in the Drury Lane Theatre on 10 May 1735 and who was not brought to trial until 12 December. He was convicted and sentenced to be burned in the hand, a sentence which was carried out with a cold iron. In 1734–35 Mrs Grace learned only one new part—Mrs Sledge in Charles Coffey's new "ballad farce" *The Devil to Pay*—and the following season nothing new at all. In 1736–37 she was Wheedle in *The*

Miser, Mrs Otter in *The Silent Woman*, Anne in *Love's Last Shift*, and Florella in *The Orphan*. In 1737–38, she learned Ruth in *The Squire of Alsatia*, Mrs Slammekin in *The Beggar's Opera*, Mrs Fruitful in *Aesop*, Lady Laycock in *The Amorous Widow*, Mrs Quickly in *The Merry Wives of Windsor*, Lady Wishfort in *The Way of the World*, and Lady Henpeck in *The Man of Taste*. In 1738–39, Mrs Grace added Flora in *She Wou'd and She Wou'd Not*, Mrs Prim in *A Bold Stroke for a Wife*, Mrs Hartshorn in *The Lady's Last Stake*, and Parley in *The Constant Couple*.

By about 1738, Macklin, Mrs Grace, and their daughter Maria had moved into a house at No 12, Wild Court, Covent Garden. Macklin was expanding in artistic power and popularity. He was about to launch his ambitious project to change the nature of Shylock and he was deliberating several literary schemes. He craved respectability. Besides, despite his violent and contentious nature, he was at bottom a solidly domestic man, fond of his home and family. He decided in the middle of the season of 1739–40 to acknowledge his spouse publicly. On 23 November 1740, the playbill carried her as "Mrs Grace." On 8 December she was "Mrs Macklin." That season she added Mrs Mixum in *A Match in Newgate*, the Landlady in *The Chances*, Diana Trapes in *The Beggar's Opera*, Mrs Tipkin in *The Tender Husband*, Mrs Prim in *A Bold Stroke for a Wife*, Mrs Amlet in *The Confederacy*, and Mrs Day in *The Committee*.

Charles Macklin's growing worth to Drury Lane certainly aided Mrs Macklin's advancement. But she had developed a respectable repertoire before he became prominent and season by season she continued to acquire good roles in her line. In 1740–41 she played many of her old ones plus the Widow Lackit in *Oroonoko*, Mademoiselle in *The Provok'd Wife*, Maria in *Twelfth Night*, Lucy in *The Country Wife*, and Mrs Peachum in *The Beggar's Opera*. In the summer of 1741 all three Macklins were at the Jacob's Wells Theatre, Bristol. In 1741–42 Mrs Macklin's new roles were Flareit in *Love's Last Shift*, Poundage in *The Provok'd Husband*, the Lady Abbess in *The Comedy of Errors*, and Mrs Haycock in *Miss Lucy in Town*; and in 1742–43, the original Mrs Useful in Fielding's scandalous comedy *The Wedding Day* and Mrs Frail in *Love for Love*.

But Mrs Macklin's fortunes were now tied firmly to those of her husband. She followed him out of the theatre when he and David Garrick led a revolt against the management of Charles Fleetwood at Drury Lane. When that insurrection collapsed, Fleetwood forgave all the rebels except Macklin, whom he had helped survive the Hallam affair and whose rebellion he therefore had regarded with a special detestation. Both Macklins were out of work for months. The desperate Charles rehearsed a motley group of his young student actors and some unemployed veterans for a series of performances at the Haymarket from 6 February through 10 July 1744. The experience was dismal for the Macklins, but at least it gave Ann the opportunity to add to her list Berinthia in *The Relapse*, Dorcas in *The Mock Doctor*, Mrs Sullen in *The Stratagem*, and the Queen in *Hamlet*.

The elder Macklins went strolling through Kent in the summer of 1744. Fortunately for the family, Fleetwood sold the Drury Lane patent in the fall, and the new patentees allowed Macklin to return to the theatre on 19 December. But for some reason, Ann Macklin was kept idle until 7 March 1745 when for the first time she played Emilia in a performance which featured Garrick's first attempt at Othello. Macklin was Iago.

In the season of 1745–46, Mrs Macklin shared acclaim for the successful revival after 30 years of Cibber's old comedy *The Non-Juror*, playing Lady Woodvil. She was concerned in three other resuscitations that season: as Lady Dorimen in Lansdowne's *The She Gallants*, brought back after 50 years for her husband's benefit night; as Lady Bloodmore in Charles Shadwell's *The Humours of the Army*, which had not been performed for 33 years; and as Abigail in Beaumont and Fletcher's *The Scornful Lady*, revived after a decade for the benefit of the Macklins' old friend Peg Woffington. Again, at the end of the season, Mr and Mrs Macklin made their professional rounds in Kent.

In the season of 1746–47, Ann appeared only 23 times—fewer than half the number in the previous season—but nevertheless performed four new parts: Lady Wrangle, in the revival after 25 years of Cibber's *The Refusal*, Hob's Mother in *Flora*, Mademoiselle in *The Artful Husband*, and Lady Macbeth. That last attempt was doubtless an experiment, and not a very hopeful one. Spranger Barry, a close friend of the Macklins, was new both at Drury

Lane and in the part of Macbeth and had certainly exerted his influence to cast Mrs Macklin as his co-star. But the audiences did not take to his Macbeth, and evidently they cared even less for Ann Macklin's effort, for by the third night "Mrs Furnival from Dublin" had replaced her in the role.

The Macklins played briefly during the summer of 1747 at the White Swan in Norwich. In 1747–48, Mrs Macklin returned to her usual round of comedy and added to her now-sizeable repertoire the Hostess in *Henry V*, Lady Darling in *The Constant Couple*, Lady Manlove in *The School Boy*, and Mrs Sealand in *The Conscious Lovers*. Probably at some time between 1748 and 1750 the Macklins' second child, John, was born.

In the spring of 1748, Thomas Sheridan, manager of Smock Alley Theatre in Dublin, came to London and recruited the Macklins for the 1748–49 and 1749–50 seasons. Mrs Macklin's first appearance was as Lady Pliant in *The Double Dealer*. Thereafter that season she and her husband played a full range of their favorite parts. But by the beginning of the second season, in September of 1749, Sheridan and Macklin had clashed over coveted roles and precedence in the billing. By March 1750 they were hardly speaking to each other. At some time early that March, Sheridan peremptorily discharged both Macklins. On 23 April 1750 Macklin sued Sheridan for £800, the residue of their salaries for the season. He finally settled for £400 and the Macklins returned to England. At Chester that summer they assembled and led a company composed of players from Drury Lane. In the fall they signed on with John Rich at Covent Garden.

The Macklins made their first appearance at Covent Garden in the same bill, she as Lappet and he as Lovegold in *The Miser*, on 24 September 1750. Early in that season the rival productions of *Romeo and Juliet* mounted by the two patent theatres, starring Garrick and George Ann Bellamy at Drury Lane and Barry and Mrs Cibber at Covent Garden, caused a great hubbub in the town. The rivalry continued for 12 nights, until performers were exhausted and critics had run out of adjectives. Most of the praise went to the representatives of the title characters. But Mrs Macklin, playing the Nurse for the first times, established herself during the run as the best interpreter of the character in her generation. Her only other new roles that season were Lady Cockwood in *She Wou'd If She Cou'd* and Viletta in *She Wou'd and She Wou'd Not.*

Mrs Macklin played fewer than 20 nights in 1751–52 and her only new role was Jacinta in *The Mistake.* She was now probably not in good health. In 1752–53 she acted only 14 times and added only an anonymous part in Foote's new farce *The Englishman in Paris,* for her husband's benefit. She was perhaps caught up in Charles Macklin's new scheme of a coffee house and oratory, for which he temporarily resigned from acting at the end of the 1752–53 season. She was absent from the stage in 1753–54, except for a single appearance at the special benefit given Macklin at Drury Lane on 20 December 1753 so that he might, in a "farewell epilogue," tout his new elocutionary enterprise.

But by January 1755 Macklin was bankrupt, and the support of the family devolved upon Ann and her daughter Maria, now rising into prominence. When Mrs Macklin returned to work it was once again at Drury Lane, under the management of Garrick. But she played only five times in 1754–55 and had no new roles. She was a little more active in 1755–56, with 14 appearances, and much more in 1756–57, with 29. In the latter season she added only Bromia in *Amphitryon.* In 1757–58, she acted 10 times—the Nurse, Mrs Quickly, and others of her old favorites.

She began the season of 1758–59 with her health so poor that Charles and Maria refused a good opportunity of employment in Ireland in order to remain with her. After seven attempts in September and October she became too ill to take the stage again. She died on 28 December 1758 and was buried at St Paul, Covent Garden, three days later.

Kirkman described Mrs Macklin as "rather below the middle size, but extremely well-formed; she had no pretensions to beauty, but her countenance was uncommonly expressive." She was not a star of the first magnitude but she was more than a satellite of her husband. She supported him loyally in his scrapes and broils and probably also gave him considerable professional aid. For she had been trained in the same rough school of provincial strolling as Macklin had and she may have preceded him in the profession. The old prompter W. R.

Chetwood was able to say in 1749 that she ranked with the best in her line and "in some Articles, lead[s] the Way." She "never sets up for a Heroine" and "knows the Power of her Talents," he observed. "In my Theatrical Course of above thirty Years, I have not seen her Equal in many Parts." He cited the Widow Blackacre, Mrs Day, Widow Lackit, Lady Pliant, Mrs Amlet, and Lady Wishfort. *The Present State of the Stage* (1753) declared that she gave "infinite pleasure" in Lady Wrangle and Lady Wronghead.

Francis Gentleman, who had seen her act both in the provinces and in London, praised her 12 years after her death, in *The Dramatic Censor* (1770). She had "most admirably represented" Lady Capulet. Her Mistress Quickly was excellent in both parts of *Henry IV* and in *Henry V.* Her "description of Falstaff's dying was inimitable." Lady Wronghead, in *The Provok'd Husband,* that "bounce about, clumsey imitation of polite life," had "never appeared more diverting" than in Mrs Macklin's representation. She was superior to everyone in "petulant bustling affectation." Tom Davies, in his *Memoirs of the Life of David Garrick, Esq.* (1780), singled out for praise, in addition to all those, her widow Abigail in *The Scornful Lady* and her Landlady in *The Chances.*

Macklin, Maria   *c. 1733–1781, actress, singer, dancer, instrumentalist.*

Maria Macklin was born to Ann Purvor Grace and Charles Macklin about 1733, according to James T. Kirkman, an early biographer of her father. Mrs Grace became "Mrs Macklin," at least in the London playbills, in 1740 but she almost certainly never married Macklin, with whom she continued to live until her death in 1758.

Throughout her formative years Maria was under the assiduous tutelage of her talented father, who applied to her, as to all his pupils, his theories of "natural" acting. In the words of the *Theatrical Review* (1758), "Momus was her forster-father [*sic*], Melpomene her nurse, and the stage her cradle." She was an apt learner. Her "first appearance on any stage" was at Drury Lane Theatre on 20 December 1742, as the little Duke of York in *Richard III,* the role chosen for the professional debut of many children. She played it half a dozen times that season and then she was withdrawn from the

MARIA MACKLIN, as Helena

engraving by Grignion, after Roberts

the White Swan Inn. She did not act at all during the season of 1747–48, although her parents were busy at Drury Lane. When they left London in the fall of 1748 for two winter seasons at the Smock Alley Theatre in Dublin, Maria went along. There is no record of her acting in Dublin. But she does seem to have performed in the company her parents assembled for a summer season at Chester in 1750.

The elder Macklins signed articles with Rich at Covent Garden for 1750–51. Maria did not belong to the company, but on 10 April 1751, on the occasion of Charles Macklin's benefit, she made her first adult London appearance, as Athenais in *Theodosius*. On 24 April she played Brass in *The City Wives Confederacy* for Leveridge's benefit. Maria was now about 18, by which age, wrote the author of *Theatrical Biography* (1772), her father had

had her instructed in all those branches of polite education that entitle a woman to the first circles of life: at a very early age she could speak French fluently, for which she took a trip to the continent. He next had her instructed in Italian, nor was she less deficient in music, drawing, and a perfect knowledge of the *belles lettres*, so that at the age of eighteen Miss Macklin was said to be one of the most accomplished women in England.

When Maria was next seen at Covent Garden she was in the title role of *Jane Shore*, on 25 October 1751, with the illustrious Susanna Maria Cibber playing Alicia and the golden-voiced Spranger Barry playing Hastings. The author of *Inspector No. 207* in the *Daily Advertiser and Literary Gazette* for 30 October (quoted in *The London Stage*) reported his satisfaction with the two older actors and continued:

Great as I had declared my expectations for Miss Macklin, she surpassed them; particularly on the second night. On the former, indeed, in the first and in part of the second act, her embarrassment was insuperable, and I cannot sufficiently admire and applaud the Candour of the Audience on the distressed Occasion! In my judgment, never were two parts better adapted to the persons and powers of the performers, than those . . . to Mrs Cibber and Miss Macklin.

Evidently her father thought her still not ready for a London career, despite her third-act recovery. She was tested again at Macklin's benefit on 8 April 1752, when she played Lady

stage for more instruction. Sybil Rosenfeld found her with her parents in a summer company in Kent in the summer of 1744.

Maria returned to Drury Lane on 1 February 1745 in the thin role of the Page in *The Orphan*. She was then given her first substantial part, Prince Arthur in a new production of *King John* supervised by David Garrick, who took the title role. It had a run of eight performances between 2 February and 2 March. In 1745–46 Maria repeated the Page and the Duke of York and added to her repertoire Tom Thumb in *The Tragedy of Tragedies*. She performed nine times that season and in the summer accompanied her parents on the Kentish circuit again.

Maria played again at Drury Lane in the 1746–47 season but on only four nights and she added to her list of characters only the Boy in *The Contrivances*. Presumably she accompanied her father and mother on their excursion to Norwich in the summer of 1747 and she may have acted there with their company at

Harvard Theatre Collection

MARIA MACKLIN, as Camillo

engraving by Thornthwaite, after Roberts

Townly in *The Provok'd Husband* to Barry's suave Townly. She was received with plaudits in that part also, and it was later one of her best. There followed another year of instruction until, on 24 March 1753, she was once more given a starring role, Calista in *The Fair Penitent*; that same night she introduced Lucinda in Samuel Foote's new farce *The Englishman in Paris*. (She was then advertised incorrectly as making her fourth appearance on any stage.) Macklin's friend John Delaval wrote to his brother Frank that she had "danced a minuet, played on a 'pandola,' and accompanied it with an Italian song, all of which she performed with much elegance." Cross, the prompter at the other house, wrote in his diary that "All went well." And so it must have done for Maria. She was allowed her first benefit performance on 24 April following. For that occasion Mrs Cibber graciously relinquished to Maria her usual role of Monimia in *The Orphan*.

After these early appearances the anony-

mous author of *The Present State of the Stage in Great Britain and Ireland* (published in March 1753) came down emphatically in her favor:

Her Figure is a very good one; her Eye strong, piercing, and significant; her Voice clear, melodious, and intelligible; her Deportment easy, and her Action happily just. She has every Qualification requisite in a great Actress, but Practice. In Theory I dare say she is very near capital; and as I wish well to the Stage, I am impatient to see her properly brought forward; for I am convinced she, who on her first Appearance rose so near to Perfection, must prove, in some Time, one of the Theatre's greatest Boasts, and her own Merits, will secure her encouragement.

That might be suspected a puff inspired by her father, except that private and disinterested voices were also raised in her praise. The actor and manager West Digges, writing to the actress Sarah Ward on 16 July 1753, thought that

Miss Macklin is the only solid dependence Rich has; the world talks much in her favour. I hear such encomiums on her accomplishments as appear almost romantic; but I hear them also from men of knowledge and integrity. She moves gracefully, speaks articulately, sings agreeably, and Mrs Garrick admires her dancing; you know she is an indisputable judge. I hear that Lady Townley never pleased more than in her playing it; they tell me she showed the true spirit of Comedy, and never let the actress appear before the woman of distinction through the whole character. Depend on it she'll make a great figure.

In the fall of 1753 Maria joined David Garrick's Drury Lane company, bringing along with her for her debut on 20 October her successful part in *The Englishman in Paris* and also its author Foote (who now played Buck in his farce because he had thought Maria's father clumsy in the role). Cross wrote in his prompter's diary: "went off tol: ye Girl was lik'd— she sung in ye Character Aly Croky—fine,— & danc'd a Minuet—well." Maria rounded off the evening speaking an "Original Epilogue." The farce was received with enthusiasm then and each time it was revived throughout the season. Maria added to her repertoire that season Charlotte in *The Refusal*, Miss Prue in *Love for Love*, the original Ilyssus in William Whitehead's tragedy *Creusa, Queen of Athens* (which, wrote Cross, was received with "Great Applause"), and Sylvia in *The Recruiting Officer*, in which she could display her figure to advantage. Observed the *Gray's Inn Journal* for 16 February 1754: "Miss Macklin is admirable in . . . Sylvia. . . . In Woman's Attire she is beautiful, [but] the Petticoat laid [aside], she is the very *Form of Beauty*. I do not remember to have seen any Actress wear the Breeches with so good a Grace. . . ."

Though her father and mother had forsaken Drury Lane for Charles Macklin's doomed attempt to establish an oratorical coffee house, Maria had found a secure place to display her talents for the following six seasons.

In 1754–55, she added to the fast-expanding list her notable Polly in *The Beggar's Opera*, the First Constantia in *The Chances*, Jacintha in *The Suspicious Husband*, Rosalind in *As You Like It*, the original Irene in John Brown's tragedy *Barbarossa*, and the Widow Lackit (which had been her mother's role) in *Oroonoko*. When her benefit night came around on 22 March, subscribers could be sent for tickets to "Miss Macklin's, Russel St. next door to Tom's Coffee House." She played on that evening for the second time—the first had been on 25 January—her excellent Almeria in *The Mourning Bride*, inspiring these verses in the *Public Advertiser*:

> Should Death (for Oh! what power can save
> Our tragic heroine from the grave)
>   At Cibber aim his dart:
> Tears should forever speak my moan,
> For oh! 'tis she, and she alone
>   Can melt the feeling heart.
>
> Britannia spake, when Lo! a Voice
> Britain be happy, and rejoice,
>   That when your Cibber dies
> The Gods have yet in store for thee,
> A Macklin; and in her you'll see
>   Another Cibber rise.

In 1755–56, Maria Macklin first learned Ophelia in *Hamlet*, Helena in *All's Well that Ends Well*, Miss Notable in *The Lady's Last Stake*, Indiana in *The Conscious Lovers*, and Perdita in *The Winter's Tale*. She performed a minuet with the dancer Leviez on her benefit night, a grace-note which became usual with her.

In 1756–57, she added Angelica in *The Gamester*, Damon in *Damon and Phillida*, Violante in *The Wonder*, the original Harriet in

Tobias Smollett's farce *The Reprisal*, Elvira in *The Spanish Fryar*, Anne Lovely in *A Bold Stroke for a Wife*, and Miranda in *The Busy Body*. In 1757–58, she added Penelope in *The Gamesters*, Arabella Zeal in *The Fair Quaker of Deal*, and Bromia in *Amphitryon*. As a special attraction to her benefit, on 18 March, she introduced "an Ode call'd *The Fair Monitor*," in which she accompanied her singing on the harpsichord. The ballet master Noverre assisted her in her minuet.

In 1758–59, Miss Macklin added only Cleone in *The Ambitious Stepmother*, a revival after 30 years which, according to Cross's diary, "went off very Dull." She also acted on considerably fewer nights than she had done in the previous season. That fact may have had something to do with her father's effort that year to conclude a deal in Dublin with Benjamin Victor. But it may also have been due to the illness of Mrs Macklin, which resulted in her death on 28 December 1758. Maria remained one more season with Garrick and Drury Lane, a season in which she added to her repertoire the original Charlotte ("with Prologue") in her father's new farce *Love à-la-Mode* (which, wrote Cross, "went off very greatly"), the original Widow Bellmour in Arthur Murphy's "entertainment" *The Way to Keep Him*, Lady Harriot in a revival of *The Funeral*, Biddy in *The Tender Husband*, Clarinda in *The Double Gallant*, and, for Kitty Clive's benefit, some part unspecified in a new farce, *Every Woman in Her Humour*.

David Garrick had treated Maria with exceptional kindness during her stay at Drury Lane, despite a long-standing resentment which Charles Macklin had maintained against Garrick because of the latter's fancied "desertion" of Macklin when he had been excluded from Drury Lane years before. But apparently Maria, at about 25 years of age, was still under her father's domination. For when he resigned from Drury Lane at the end of the 1759–60 season and went to the management of Rich at Covent Garden, Maria followed. There she opened her campaign on 29 September 1760 as Juliet, advertised as being for the "first time at that theatre in 7 years." She played a number of her established roles that season, but added only Angelica in *The Married Libertine*, a slight farce by her father, and Portia, opposite his Shylock, on her benefit night, 9 April 1761. Her season's salary of £300 was toward the top of the Covent Garden scale, although it was mulcted by £31 16s. 10d. because of the closure of the theatres following the death of King George II on 25 October 1760.

Charles Macklin went off to Ireland in 1761–62, but where his daughter Maria was nobody knows. She disappeared from the Covent Garden roster, but if she accompanied her father and her new stepmother to Ireland the record does not show it. Her health was never robust; perhaps she simply took a rest. When she was reintroduced to Covent Garden audiences, on 22 September 1762—incorrectly billed as appearing there for the first time in two years—she played Juliet and danced a minuet with Signior Maranesi. During the season she added Lady Grace in *The Provok'd Husband*, Desdemona in *Othello*, Lady Betty in *The Careless Husband*, Ethelinda in *The Royal Convert*, Rutland in *The Earl of Essex*, and Hypolita in *She Wou'd and She Wou'd Not*.

Maria Macklin remained at Covent Garden—acting, singing, and dancing and making modest additions to her repertoire—until her retirement at the end of the 1776–77 season. In 1763–64 she added Aura in *The Country Lasses*; in 1764–65, Volumnia in *Coriolanus* and Bizarre in *The Inconstant*; in 1765–66, the original Lady Mary in Elizabeth Griffith's comedy *The Double Mistake*, Camillo in *The Mistake*, Lady Diana Talbot in *Vertue Betray'd*, Charlotte in *Oroonoko*, and Douglas in the revival, after 20 years, of *The Albion Queens*; in 1767–68 (now making £7 per week) the original Clarissa in Isaac Bickerstaffe's comic opera *Lionel and Clarissa*, and Widow Bellmour in *The Way to Keep Him*; in 1769–70, Leonora in *Sir Courtly Nice*; in 1770–71, Lady Alton in *The English Merchant*; in 1774–75, Lady Ann in *Richard III*; and in 1776–77, Lady Wronghead in *The Provok'd Husband*.

Miss Macklin's health had been for some years uncertain. Francis Gentleman had found in 1770 that her "extensive, spirited abilities" were "on the decline." Her relationship with Colman her manager was no longer cordial. She had saved her money. A letter dated 12 March 1777 from Leonard MacNally in London to her father in Dublin reported that Maria was in good spirits, making five guineas a week, and encouraged by her father's promise

to come and play for her benefit in May, but she abruptly retired at the end of the 1776–77 season.

She left her house, No 59, Great Queen Street, Lincoln's Inn Fields, in the theatrical area where she had spent her whole life, and moved to Brompton. There, on 3 July 1781, she died. Her father's biographer Kirkman advanced an explanation for her decline and death:

She went often into breeches, and, by buckling her garter too tightly, a large swelling took place in her knee, which, from motives of delicacy, she would not suffer to be examined, till it had increased to an alarming size. This fleshy excrescence was, however, cut off, and Miss Macklin underwent the operation with great firmness; but she never after regained her former strength.

The will of "Mary Macklin Spinster late of Great Queen Street Lincoln's Inn Fields but now residing at Brumpton" had been signed ("Mary," not "Maria") on 27 May, a week before her death. In it she desired "to be decently interred in the parish of Brumpton," and she left in trust to her executors Sarah Savile Jenkins and John Ritson £2000 in three per cent "Bank Annuities," the income of which was to provide an annuity of £35 for her father and an immediate payment of £50 and an annuity of £35 for her "old and faithful Servant Jane Dewe who has from my Infancy lived with me." Residuary legatees were Sarah Savile Jenkins, Anna Maria Haines, and Mary Blittenberg. Jane Dewe also received her "Wearing Apparel" and "Silver Tea Spoons and Tea Tongs," and Anna Maria Haines her "Silver Plated Coffee Pot," and "Mrs Washbourne of Edmonton" her "Silver Plated Ink Stand."

Maria Macklin was survived by her father, her stepmother, and her brother. For some years she had distanced herself emotionally, in varying degrees, from all of them. She had never felt close to her stepmother, a woman too close to her own age whom she doubtless felt inferior in education and attainments. She had behaved affectionately to her brother John (when he went out to India she sent him a flute, "some music, some drawing materials, some very good prints, and a book of macaronys," she wrote her father). But, though she continued dutiful when he returned in disgrace, his dissolute behavior made him at last a stranger. For, said *Theatrical Biography*, "She was unfashionable enough . . . to be religious . . . for which, no doubt, [she] often underwent the laugh of the green-room; she went to her devotions oftener than she went to rehearsals. . . ."

Maria's relationship to her father had been odd and intricate. Macklin was a faithful husband and a devoted father, but his overbearing and intolerant nature, combined with the fact that he undoubtedly knew his business when it came to acting and the teaching of acting, posed problems for his daughter and pupil. The careful and—by his lights—kind and loving attention which he bestowed on her early education had grown to an over-solicitous and strict control over her professional life. She had finally seized the opportunity given by one of his long absences in Ireland to move out of the parental dwelling. Nevertheless, letters in the Harvard Theatre Collection, from Maria in London to Charles in Dublin, full of gossip of the playhouses and expressing concern for his health and joy for his professional successes, show a warmth in the relationship continuing through the 1770s. During the years he acted in Dublin, Macklin loyally returned to London each spring to play at her benefit. Anecdotes passed on by John Bernard and others point to tension between those two talented and highly emotional people; and no doubt the author of *Theatrical Biography* was correct in his opinion that Macklin "had a temper that made it impossible for any one to live with him in a state of dependence." But the decision by some of Macklin's biographers that he was entirely responsible for what is seen as Maria's unnaturally celibate and reclusive nature seems strained. Indeed, such evidence as we have seems to show that, to the extent that her acting may have been "cold" or "mechanical," it became so after Macklin's influence had diminished.

We have seen the critical enthusiasm with which in 1753 Maria's adult debut in tragedy was greeted. It was matched by popular acclaim as she added other tragedy roles and moved into comedy, her forte. The playwright Henry James Pye (later a lamentable poet laureate) exercised his puny poetic powers in her behalf, anonymously, in *The Rosciad of C—v—nt G—rd—n* in 1762: "But tho' so

well she plays the tragic queen; / She shines superior in the comic scene" for "There beams her sterling wit. . . ." Pye spoke of one of the chief charms of her youth, her figure in "breeches" roles, when "most she charms in the rake's disguise" and "with easy freedom apes the coxcomb's rage, / And struts and swaggers all around the stage." Others, like the critic of the *Macaroni and Savoir Faire Magazine*, in October 1773, admired not only her "elegant figure" but her "taste in music," especially as Polly in *The Beggar's Opera*. That critic also commended her tragedy roles, though they were "but few, and . . . generally confined to the tender cast. . . ."

In her earlier years Maria was constantly compared, always somewhat to her disadvantage, of course, with the incomparable Susanna Maria Cibber. Thomas Wilkes, in *A General View of the Stage* (1759), scolded the managers for not employing her in a wider variety of roles and expressed "hopes, to see her in time a worthy successor" to Mrs Cibber. But, though she became a popular and successful personage, she never achieved that exalted stature. And even at the height of her success she was apparently not for all markets. The playwright Hugh Kelly, in *Thespis* (1767), represented one body of critical opinion:

Through MACKLIN's form such elegance we trace,
Each step is breeding, and each action grace;
Yet, a meer mass of amiable snow,
She never bids us generously glow;
Nor, tho' with sense her periods always roll,
E'er sends an accent nobly to the soul;
But freezes still intensely on the mind,
Politely cold, and languidly refined.

The Dramatic Censor (Francis Gentleman) in 1770 was able to place her first among all the Mirandas in *The Busy Body* that he had seen. He remembered her Sylvia in *The Recruiting Officer* for her "spirit of expression, sensibility of look, delicacy of emphasis, and gentility of deportment," and put her Rosalind high, inferior only to Mrs Barry's, Mrs Pritchard's, and Miss Woffington's. But her Portia, admired by other critics, fell short of his standard. She "speaks the part in an unexceptionable manner, but we deem her rather too petit in person and expression." Two years afterward, in *The Theatres* (operating under the nom de plume

Sir Nicholas Nipclose) Gentleman found that she had "now got beyond her youthful bloom" and disclosed other faults that he had not mentioned before. He now believed that she had "never liked" the stage but had been "fetter'd with a father's rigid laws" and "mechaniz'd instruction"; hence her "Nature" had been "trammell'd" by "dull correctness." Perhaps he had been swayed by Hugh Kelly.

Several songs published "as sung by" Maria Macklin are listed in the *Catalogue of Printed Music in the British Museum*.

Portraits of Maria Macklin include:

1. By James Roberts. Pencil drawing in the Harvard Theatre Collection.

2. As Camillo in *The Mistake*. Engraving by Thornthwaite, after J. Roberts, for *Bell's British Theatre*, 1778.

3. As Helena in *All's Well that Ends Well*. Engraving by C. Grignion, after J. Roberts, for *Bell's Shakespeare*, 1775.

4. As Irene, with Robert Bensley as Barbarossa, in *Barbarossa*. Engraving by J. Caldwall, after E. Edwards. Published by T. Lowndes as a plate for *New English Theatre*.

5. As Portia, with Charles Macklin as Shylock, and other actors, in *The Merchant of Venice*. By Johann Zoffany. In the Tate Gallery. See iconography list for Charles Macklin, No 28.

6. As Portia, with Charles Macklin as Shylock. By Edward Alcock. In the Yale Center for British Art. A similar picture is in a private collection in New York. See iconography list for Charles Macklin, No 21.

Mackloud, Mr ₍*fl. 1798–1799*₎, *pyrotechnist*.

The pyrotechnist Mackloud (or Cloud, McLeod, Macloyd) was regularly cited in the Drury Lane accounts from February 1798 through December 1799. The entries usually just said "for fireworks," but in addition to supplying them Mackloud seems to have been hired by the night (£2 2*s*. was paid to him for four nights in March 1799) to set off the displays. He was, doubtless, the "Mackland" who had exhibited fireworks at Ranelagh Gardens on 18 June 1798.

Maclalan. *See* MACLELAN.

McLane, Mr ₍*fl. 1791*₎, *piper*.

At Covent Garden on 18 May 1791 was offered, within the afterpiece *The Union*, "the *Highland Competition Prize*, exactly as represented annually in the City of Edinburgh, by McLane, McGeorge, McTavish, and several other celebrated Pipers, who will perform several Strathpays [strathspeys], Laments and Pebruchs [pibrochs]."

M'Lane, Miss ₍*fl. 1768*₎, *actress*.

On 19 December 1768 at the Haymarket Theatre, Peggy in *The Gentle Shepherd* was played by Miss M'Lane.

M'Laughlin. *See* MACKLIN.

M'Lauglin. *See* MACKLIN.

Maclean. *See* MACCLEAN *and* MACKLIN.

Mclean, Mr ₍*fl. 1758*₎, *performer?*

Patie and Roger was presented at the Haymarket Theatre on 13 March 1758 for the of McLean and Grant. They were, perhaps, performers.

M'Clean, Mr ₍*fl. 1772*₎, *actor*.

Mr M'Clean played Symon in *The Gentle Shepherd* at the Haymarket Theatre on 21 December 1772.

M'Lean, Niel ₍*fl. 1788*₎, *piper*.

The Sadler's Wells bill for 10 September 1788 advertised "Mr. Niel M'Lean, Piper to the Highland Society in London," who performed on the pipes for that night only.

Maclelan, Henry ₍*fl. 1742–1762*₎, *actor*.

Genest reported that on 28 September 1742 Henry Maclelan made his second appearance on any stage, playing Loveless in *Love's Last Shift* at Drury Lane. *The London Stage* does not note that as his second appearance, and we have not found an earlier citation for Maclelan. On 14 December he played the title role in *Oroonoko*, but only that once, and on 16 May 1743 he acted Loveless again at his shared benefit with two others. The late W. S. Clark's calendar of Dublin performances shows "Henery Maclalan," also "Maclean," acting at the Smock Alley Theatre, Dublin, in 1746–47. He is known to have played Claudio in *Much Ado about Nothing* on 8 December 1746. He signed a petition at the end of February 1747, urging the Lord Lieutenant to reopen the playhouses. Maclelan was at Bath in 1753–54 and made his Norwich debut on 9 February 1756, according to the Norwich *Mercury*, and he apparently performed in that town until 1762.

McLeod. *See* MACKLOUD.

Macloughlan. *See* MACKLIN.

M'Mahon. *See also* MACMAHON *and* MAHON.

M'Mahon, Mr ₁*fl. 1757–1767?*₁,   *actor.*
The Mr M'Mahon who was a member of the Smock Alley troupe in Dublin in 1757–58 and 1760–61 (and very likely other seasons) was probably the M'Mahon who played Durand in *Venice Preserv'd* at the King's Theatre in London on 13 August 1766 with Barry's company. On 12 September he was Charon in *Lethe* and the next day he acted Denis in *As You Like It.* A year later, on 9 September 1767 at the Haymarket Theatre, M'Mahon was added to the cast of *The Orator*—unless that was an error for Mrs Mahon, who was a member of Foote's troupe that month.

MacMahon, Parkyns ₁*fl. 1783–1785*₁, *secretary.*
Parkyns MacMahon served as secretary at the opera house (the King's Theatre) from at least 1783 to 1785. *The Case of the Opera House Disputes, Fairly Stated* (1784) said that MacMahon's position had been specially created and called him "puff master to the trustees." He dispatched bills, received subscriptions, and handled other duties that had formerly belonged to the treasurer. For his services MacMahon received £150. He lived at No 77, Haymarket, next door to the theatre, according to the playbill of 18 June 1785. He was described as an unsavory character who had been a servitor at a convent, then a monk, then a soldier in an Irish brigade before coming to London.

M'Millin, Mr ₁*fl. 1780*₁,   *actor.*
At the Haymarket Theatre on 5 April 1780 Jeffery in *No Wit Like a Woman's* was played by a Mr M'Millin.

McMorland. *See* MORLAND.

M'Nab, Mr ₁*fl. 1785*₁,   *actor.*
Mr M'Nab played Madge in *The Gentle Shepherd* at the Haymarket Theatre on 24 January 1785.

McNamara, Mr ₁*fl. 1776–1777*₁,   *dresser.*
Mr McNamara was a dresser at Drury Lane in the 1776–77 season at a weekly salary of 9s.

MacNeale. *See* MCNEIL.

M'Neil. *See* MACNEIL.

McNeil, Miss. *See* HAWTRY, MRS.

McNeil, Gordon ₁*fl. 1749–1755*₁, *dancer.*
The London Stage lists as dancers at Drury Lane Theatre in 1749–50 a Macclean and a McNeil, but it seems likely that the one reference to the former, on 11 October 1749 as a dancer in *Comus*, is a misprint, and that Gordon McNeil was the Scottish dancer meant. During the season he appeared as a Shepherd in *Acis and Galatea*, was in a *Rural Dance* in *The Chaplet* and a *Dance of Winds* in *The Tempest*, and participated in such entr'acte turns as *Venetian Gardeners*, and *The Savoyard Travellers.* On 20 April 1750 he offered a solo *Fingalian Dance.* The bills at Drury Lane often spelled his name Macneale, and when he appeared on 16 April at the New Wells, London Spa, he was cited as M'Neil. McNeil returned for a second season at Drury Lane and danced in a *New Running Footman's Dance*, offered a comic dance with Mme Camargo in Act IV of *The Way of the World*, participated in *Shepherds*, and probably offered other turns not cited in the bills. His 1750–51 season seems not to have been as busy as his previous one, and after it he left the company.
On 23 September 1751 McNeil made his first appearance at the Smock Alley Theatre in Dublin, hailed as from Drury Lane, and there

he remained through 1754–55, dancing and introducing his students to the Dublin public. With Mrs Woffington he danced a minuet at the end of *The Non-Juror* on 1 February 1752, but most of his performing was not given any specific description in the bills. He was seen as the Captain of Corsairs in the pantomime *The Constant Captives* on 9 April 1752, a role he danced also in the two following seasons. In *Harlequin Ranger* in 1751–52 he was a Savoyard; in 1753–54 he was one of the dancing Witches in *Macbeth*, and in *The Tempest* that season McNeil appeared as one of the Grand Dancing Devils.

On 10 February 1753 *Pue's Occurrences* reported the death of Gordon McNeil's wife Mary on 8 February.

MacOwen. *See* OWENSON, ROBERT.

McPherson, Mr [*fl.* 1770], *actor.*
Mr McPherson played Patie in *The Gentle Shepherd* at the Haymarket Theatre on 19 March 1770. Perhaps related to him was the Mrs MacPherson who performed at the Theatre Royal, Edinburgh, in 1776.

MacPherson, Malcolm [*fl.* 1784–1794], *horn player.*
A Mr McPherson played horn in the Handel Memorial Concerts at Westminster Abbey and the Pantheon in May and June 1784. He was surely Malcolm MacPherson, who was listed in Doane's *Musical Directory* in 1794 as a horn player from Pimlico who had participated in the Abbey performances. MacPherson was a member of the Court of Assistants of the New Musical Fund.

Macquire. *See also* MACGUIRE and REDIGÉ, MME PAULO.

Macquire, Mr [*fl.* 1740], *actor.*
At Yeates's booth at Bartholomew Fair on 23 August 1740 Mr Macquire played Ascalax and his wife played Gawkey's Mother in *Orpheus and the Death of Eurydice.*

Macquire, Mrs [*fl.* 1740], *actress. See* MACQUIRE, MR.

Macquoid, Mr [*fl.* 1788–1794], *scene painter, machinist.*
From 1788 to 1794 Mr Macquoid was an assistant scene painter at Covent Garden Theatre at a salary of 10s. 6d. daily. The accounts, as reported by Sybil Rosenfeld in *Theatre Notebook*, mentioned a Macquoid Junior in 1794, so there evidently were two members of the family employed at the theatre. The elder, apparently, was the one who worked with the machinist Cabanel on the practical small boats for *The Royal Naval Review at Plymouth*, a spectacle staged at Astley's Amphitheatre on 4 September 1789.

Macquoid, Mr [*fl.* 1794], *scene painter.*
See MACQUOID, MR [*fl.* 1788–1794].

Macready, William 1755–1829, *actor, manager.*
William Macready, the father of William Charles Macready the prominent nineteenth-century actor-manager, was born in 1755 in Dublin, the son of William Macready, an upholsterer. Young William early deserted his apprenticeship to his father and began acting in provincial Irish companies. He was at Kilkenny in August 1776. He was acting at Edinburgh in 1776–77, the unfortunate season in which West Digges was jailed for debt and gave over the management.

Macready's wanderings until he reached Capel Street Theatre, Dublin, in the fall of 1782 are unrecorded, but it is likely that they were in Ireland. (Probably he was the "M'Cready" who shared benefit tickets at the Haymarket in London on 27 December 1779.) He joined the Crow Street Theatre, Dublin, late in the 1782–83 season, took a benefit there on 11 March, and went on to Belfast by way of Kilkenny. He played at Smock Alley Theatre in Dublin through the 1783–84 and 1784–85 seasons (though he was recorded in one performance at Cork on 30 September 1784).

By the recommendation of the old trouper Charles Macklin, Macready gained a place in the Manchester company under George Mattocks's management in January 1786. Another newcomer to the company was Christina Ann Birch (1765–1803), a genteel girl, daughter of a Lincolnshire surgeon, and a great-granddaughter of William Frye, president of the Council of Montserrat. Macready and Miss

WILLIAM MACREADY

engraving by Ridley, after Halpin

Birch shared a benefit on 7 April, he playing Bob Acres and she Julia in *The Rivals*. On 17 June 1786 they were married at the Collegiate Church in Manchester.

Macklin's influence extended to Thomas Harris at London, and on 18 September 1786 Macready made his Covent Garden debut as Flutter in *The Belle's Stratagem*. He was to remain at Covent Garden for 11 years, settling comfortably into varied lines of secondary and tertiary characters, producing several afterpieces and fathering five children, three of whom survived and one of whom was William Charles Macready the great tragedian.

Macready's roles at Covent Garden, in the order of assumption were: in 1786–87, Flutter in *The Belle's Stratagem*, Norfolk in *Richard III*, Phocion in *The Grecian Daughter*, Clerimont in *The Double Gallant*, Gratiano in *The Merchant of Venice*, Woodley in *Three Weeks after Marriage*, Florestine in *Richard Coeur de Lion*, Paris in *Romeo and Juliet*, Selim in *The Mourning Bride*,

Octavian in *The Cheats of Scapin*, Sir Walter Blount in *1 Henry IV*, Fenton in *The Merry Wives of Windsor*, Sir Harry Lizard in *Know Your Own Mind*, Courcy in *Eloisa*, Young Gerald in *The Anatomist*, Frederick in *The Wonder*, Euricles in *Mérope*, Count Basset in *The Provok'd Husband*, the Duke in *Rule a Wife and Have a Wife*, Lavinio in *A Duke and No Duke*, Mr Meanright in *Such Things Are*, Leander in *The Mock Doctor*, Surrey in *Henry VIII*, Valentine in *The Intriguing Chambermaid*, one of the Brothers in *Comus*, Borachio in *Much Ado about Nothing*, Phoenix in *The Distrest Mother*, Captain Loveit in *Miss in Her Teens*, Freeman in *High Life below Stairs*, a Frenchman in *Cymbeline*, Captain Manly in *Bonds without Judgment*.

In 1787–88 he added to his repertoire Colonel Raymond in *The Foundling*, Malcolm in *Macbeth*, Cassio in *Othello*, Elliot in *Venice Preserv'd*, Dugard in *The Inconstant*, Elvirus in *Such Things Are*, Octavian in *The Cheats of Scapin*, Clerimont in *The Miser*, Lake in *The Positive Man*, O'Toole in *Tantara Rara! Rogues All*, Don Struttolando in *Omai*, Jack Stanmore in *Oroonoko*, Charles Oakly in *The Jealous Wife*, Colonel Ormsby in *The Romance of an Hour*, Young Meanwell in *Tit for Tat*, Sir George Wealthy in *The Minor*; and, 1788–89, Rodolpho in *Tancred and Sigismunda*, Le Beau in *As You Like It*, Vainlove in *The Old Bachelor*, the Barber in *The Little Hunchback*, Polyperchon in *Alexander the Great*, and Willoughby in *The Dramatist*.

In 1789–90 he added Granada in *The Child of Nature*, Jessamy in *Bon Ton*, Cornwall in *King Lear*, Sir John Melville in *The Clandestine Marriage*, Littlestock in *The Gamesters*, Jack Meggot in *The Suspicious Husband*, the Adjutant in *Love in a Camp*, Wilson in *A Peep behind the Curtain*, Antipholus of Syracuse in *The Comedy of Errors*, Don Felix in *The Female Adventure*, and Young Fashion in *The Man of Quality*; in 1790–91, the Prince in *Romeo and Juliet*, Serjeant Eitherside in *The Man of the World*, Glenalvon in *Douglas*, George Bevil in *Cross Purposes*, Tressel in *Richard III*, Axalla in *Tamerlane*, Charles Gripe in *The Busy Body*, Don Manuel in *Love Makes a Man*, Raleigh in *The Earl of Essex*, Ferdinand in *Two Strings to Your Bow*, the original Muz in *Wild Oats*, the title role in *The Minor*, Paterson in *The Brothers*, Brigadier Moncton in *The Soldier's Festival*, Ormond in *The Dreamer Awake*, Sir Frederick O'Neil in *National Prejudice*, Plausible in *The Union*, Pe-

WILLIAM MACREADY, as Colloony
by De Wilde

truchio in *The Chances*, Squire Snareall in *The Cottage Maid*, and Captain Brazen in *The Recruiting Officer*; in 1791–92, Orasmin in *Zara*, Raleigh in *The Earl of Essex*, the original Muley in *A Day in Turkey*, Ratcliffe in *Jane Shore*, the original Hosier in *The Road to Ruin*, Jack Connor in *The Prisoner at Large*, Dupely in *The Maid of the Oaks*, Colonel Gorget in *The Cozeners*, Erastus in *The Intrigues of a Morning*, and Blandford in *Oroonoko*; and in 1792–93, Mr Colloony in *The Irishman in London*, Villers in *The Belle's Stratagem*, Midge in *Wild Oats*, Fag in *The Rivals*, Captain Forrester in *Hartford Bridge*, Marquis D'Lancy in *Animal Magnetism*, the original Rodan in *Columbus*, Young Marlow in *She Stoops to Conquer*, Garcia in *The Mourning Bride*, Charles Evergreen in *The Invasion*, O'Clabber in *The Reprisal*, and Figaro in *The*

Follies of a Day. In 1793–94 Macready's new roles were Harry in *Wild Oats*, the original Briars in *The World is a Village*, Phoenix in *The Distrest Mother*; in 1794–95, Guiderius in *Cymbeline*, Tibalt in *Romeo and Juliet*, the original Bernardo in *The Mysteries of the Castle*, the original Darnley in *Crotchet Lodge*, the original Lord Edward Spenser in *Windsor Castle*, Demetrius in *Bonduca*, Myrtle in *The Conscious Lovers*, Captain Clifford in *The Irish Mimick*, Lieutenant Selby in *The Bank Note*, La Varenne in *The Battle of Hexham*, and the Duke of Wirtemberg in *The Secret Tribunal*; in 1795–96 Benvolio in *Romeo and Juliet*, an Irish Haymaker in *Rosina*, O'Daub in *The Poor Sailor*, Saunter in *Notoriety*, Sir Henry Harlowe in *The Mysterious Husband*, Wat in *Arrived at Portsmouth*, Sibald in *Days of Yore*, McQuery in *The Way to Get Married*, Page in *The Merry Wives of Windsor*, Patrick in *British Fortitude and Hibernian Friendship*, Lord Lovel in *A New Way to Pay Old Debts*, Antonio in *The Merchant of Venice*, Worth in *The Recruiting Officer*, King Edward in *The Earl of Warwick and Margaret of Anjou*; and in 1796–97 Flam in *The Doldrum*, Pharon in *Mahomet*, Marshal Ferbelin in *Love in a Camp*, Poins in *2 Henry IV*, Orville in *Fortune's Fool*, Captain Savage in *The School for Wives*, the Duke of Tuscany in *A Duke and No Duke*, the original Colonel Careless in *The Honest Thieves*, Marcus in *Cato*, Ferdinand in *Two Strings to Your Bow*, and Tattle in *Love for Love*.

The first season Macready was in London Mrs Macready played at Liverpool. Apparently she was trying to help the family finances, but a Liverpool document at the Folger Library shows that she lost money at her benefit in 8 December 1786, when she took in £34 16s. and paid the house £35 in charges. She seems then to have come to London. She acted no more. But the diligence which Macready showed that first season (playing over 30 characters from September to March), and which he continued to show, assured him and his wife a living for the moment, and his modest pay of £2 per week was to rise: to £2 10s. in 1787–88, £3 the following season, £4 in 1793–94, and £4 10s. 1794–95 through 1796–97. He supplemented income by playing at Crow Street in the summers of 1788, 1790, 1791, 1792 (when he was also briefly at Cork; he seems to have been at Cork also in August and September 1793). He also played at Richmond, Surrey, in October 1788 (Gilliland seems to be in error in giving him a share in the management at Richmond in 1791).

But the total emoluments were apparently insufficient, and Macready "left Covent Garden in consequence of a disagreement about salary," according to the brief account in the 1806 edition of *Authentic Memoirs of the Green Room*. In the summer of 1796 he had responded to an advertisement by the proprietors of the New Theatre in Birmingham, who were looking for a manager. His first summer there produced enough success to encourage him to try a second and to cut his ties to Covent Garden.

In November 1797 Macready gathered a company—Dighton and Mrs Wybrow from Sadler's Wells, Mrs Harlowe from the Haymarket, Holland from the Royal Circus, Delpini from Covent Garden, and others, clowns, straight actors, musicians, and dancers, and began giving variety performances at the Royalty Theatre, Wellclose Square.

The *Monthly Mirror* praised his efforts:

Nothing can exceed the industry of Mr. Macready, in his exertions to produce novelty for the amusement of his friends. Collins's Brush [a monologue performance] has been succeeded by Martinelli's Fantoccini [puppets moved mechanically], and a vast train of new performances. Mrs. Harlowe never appeared to greater advantage than at this theatre—there is a spirit and animation in her burletta performances, which has seldom been equalled. . . . Surely it was unexampled liberality in the manager, so soon after expending a large sum of money in preparing this theatre for public reception, to give the whole profits of one night to the fund at Lloyd's, for the benefit of those brave tars who fell in the engagement between Lord Duncan [Viscount Duncan] and the Dutch fleet [off Camperdown on 11 October].

But his industry and generosity notwithstanding, Macready's Royalty venture, like all previous ones at that house, was doomed for lack of sufficient patronage.

Not so his Birmingham summer theatre. Despite early jealous attacks like *The Dissection of a Bir—g—m Manager* (1796), Macready for a while grew stronger each successive summer. He drew on his wide acquaintance with performers in London to bring in stars to supplement his regulars. Also, as Kathleen Barker and Joseph Macleod have shown in a study of

his promptbooks (*Theatre Notebook*, 4), he paid an extraordinary amount of attention to scenery and lighting. Moreover, he imposed on his resident company a rigorous discipline highly unusual in the provinces. But his success planted the seeds of his failure, for, observing it, his landlord in 1807 doubled the rent of the theatre. That blow came exactly at the beginning of an economic depression and suddenly decreasing attendance. Macready resigned the Birmingham managership.

There was another complication: the Birmingham company had also toured to Manchester for a number of years. In 1806 a new theatre was erecting there. Macready rented it before it was finished, for £1600. Mrs Siddons persuaded her friend the Irish fencing master Galindo to subscribe £3500 to the theatre for decorations and equipment. Houses were thin. The enterprise faltered. Galindo withdrew support and demanded immediate payment. Macready was forced to sell all his household furniture, and a reluctant young William Charles Macready came home from Rugby to assist, beginning one of the most illustrious stage careers in British history. But no expedient could stave off bankruptcy, and for a while Macready was imprisoned for debt.

William Macready never regained his former prosperity, but he had continued to act in his companies at Birmingham, Leicester, Sheffield, and Manchester (and in the winter of 1800 at Dublin and Edinburgh), and he went on acting and managing after the 1809 debacle. He was of the Crow Street, Dublin, company in 1814–15. He is described in the Larpent licensing notebook at the Huntington Library as the manager of "Theatre Royal Newcastle upon Tyne" as of 6 May 1816. He was bankrupt again at Whitehaven (and circuit) in 1817 but bounced straight up to the management of the Bristol company (and a side-venture in the summers, at Swansea) in 1819. (His indefatigable labor in these companies, presiding over every sort of theatrical offering from opera to pugilism, from Ducrow's stud of horses to the most elegant of serious actors, has been well detailed by Kathleen Barker in *The Theatre Royal Bristol* [1974] and Cecil Price in *The English Theatre in Wales* [1948].)

Macready's natural qualifications as an actor were meagre, but he worked diligently and rather successfully to improve them over the years. He had nothing like the mesmerizing presence of his son, nor (unlike his son) did he enjoy immediate acceptance. At his Covent Garden debut in 1786 one newspaper critic had thought that "his person and features, though neither strikingly elegant or expressive, qualify him for the representation of a variety of comic characters." And as his early repertoire shows variety was his mainstay. Critics resisted him in tragedy. A writer in the *Biographical and Imperial Magazine* for January 1790, thought him "decent" as William in the comedy *The Way to Keep Him* but believed that "The Bastard [Edmund in *King Lear*] ought not to be given to such a player as Macready." His fellow-performer F. G. Waldron, writing (but anonymously) in *Candid and Impartial Strictures on the Performers* in 1795, damned with the faintest of praise: "A useful actor, frequently pushed beyond what his powers are capable of supporting," adding that "He has a most insufferable roll in his deportment."

The *Monthly Mirror*, his constant advocate, gave the most complete and balanced assessment, in 1800, when his career was well-advanced, and he was playing a round of a dozen parts in Edinburgh:

The gentleman possesses a handsome, though rather a heavy figure; his manner is easy; and his countenance, though not remarkable for expression, is by no means devoid of it. He counterfeits well, the silly, conceited look, and the flippancy of expression, which are suited to the cast of coxcombs, and he appears to great advantage in the parts of Tinsel and Clodio. He is likewise a respectable actor in the whimsical, bustling characters, which make the most conspicuous figure in many comedies, particularly in Marplot and Tangent. He is, neither endowed, however, with that variety in action and deportment, nor with those little elegancies and graces of manner, which are necessary to constitute an actor for genteel comedy. These deficiencies are glaring in his performance of Young Mirabel, Archer, and Young Marlowe. In tragedy he is still more defective; the monotony of his voice is but ill calculated for declamation, and he has frequent breaks in his utterance, and ill-tuned pauses, which are extremely offensive. Still, however, good sense, and his perfect acquaintance with stage business, render him a decent actor in almost all his characters.

As a manager, Macready's obvious integrity and fair dealing drew general praise, except for *The Dissection* of 1796 (of which its reviewer in the *Monthly Mirror* said "The whole matter is libellous, but too despicable for any legal notice") and a spleenful and unfair Manchester paragrapher in 1807. Michael Kelly, the singer and composer, "ever found" him "in theatrical business . . . honest, upright, obliging, clever, and friendly, and in all his dealings, whether Fate smiled or frowned, a man of punctuality and rectitude."

Macready's first wife, Christina, died at Sheffield on 3 December 1803, according to the *Gentleman's Magazine* for that month. On 26 November 1821, at Whitehaven, he married his handsome mistress, the actress Sarah Desmond (who died on 8 March 1853 at 63). She was a leading light in his company for many years.

During the summer of 1828 Macready became ill and made his will on 12 July. He died at Bristol on 9 April 1829 and was buried in Bristol Cathedral. His will was proved at London on 19 September 1829 and administration granted to his widow. It provided, rather puzzlingly, to Macready's sister Olivia Robinson two houses "nearly opposite Ranelagh being a ffreehold purchased by my father Wm Mc Ready late of Bride St. Dublin which at his decease became my property and from calamitous circumstances occurring to me at New Castle upon Tyne I was compelled to sell and dispose of it to my said sister Olivia Robinson for a sum of money which she paid me." He had "only his blessings" to bestow on his four children by his first wife: "vizt. William Charles McCready, Letitia Margaret McCready, Elinor Matilda McCready and Edward Neville McCready being of age & having the means of providing amply for themselves thro' means of the very heavy and expensive education I bestowed on them." His "circumstances" were limited. (He had sent both of his sons to Rugby. The acting career of William Charles has been the subject of many accounts. For Edward, born in 1798, William Charles purchased a commission in the army. He rose to the rank of Major. Letitia Margaret, born in 1794, did not marry and was her actor-brother's constant companion and sage counsel until her death in 1858. The fate of Elinor Matilda we do not know, nor that of another daughter, Olivia, though apparently she died young.)

To Sarah his widow, their daughter Mazarina Emily Macready "and the boy known by the name of George William McCready"—either an adoptive son, a son of Sarah's by someone else, or Macready's illegitimate offspring— Macready left all "right and interest in Theatre Royal Bristol" and the theatres in Swansea and Cardiff, with all "scenery, wardrobe, music books, looking glasses, properties & every article belonging to me in these, private wardrobe, linens, plate, pictures . . . together with whatever the Suit in Chancery pending in Dublin Courts may produce. . . ."

William Macready is credited by Nicoll with three plays, the farce *The Village Lawyer* (Haymarket, 1787) published in 1795; the farce *The Irishman in London; or, The Happy African* (Covent Garden, 1792) published in 1793; and the comedy *The Bank Note; or, Lessons for Ladies* (Covent Garden, 1795), published in 1795.

A portrait of William Macready engraved by W. Ridley, after Halpin, was published as a plate to Parsons's *Minor Theatre* in 1794. A picture by Samuel De Wilde, in black and red chalks with watercolor, signed and dated 20 October 1805, of Macready as Colloony in his *The Irishman in London* is in the British Museum. A pencil and watercolor sketch by De Wilde of Macready as Colloony, dated the same day, is owned by Edith Holding and was exhibited at the Northampton Central Art Gallery in 1971.

Macswiney, Macswinny, Mcswinney. *See* SWINEY.

McTavish, Mr ₁*fl. 1791*₁, *piper.*
Mr McTavish was one of the "celebrated Pipers, who will perform several Strathpays [strathspeys], Laments and Pebruchs [pibrochs], at Covent Garden Theatre on 18 May 1791 as part of the "*Highland Competition Prize,* exactly as represented annually in the City of Edinburgh. . . ."

"Macularius, Martinus." *See* SMART, CHRISTOPHER.

Maculla. *See* MACCULA.

Macy, Mr ₁*fl. 1795*₁, *horse trainer?*
A cryptic note in the Drury Lane accounts on 23 March 1795 directed that a Mr Macy be paid £4 4s. for horses. It is not certain that Macy was a theatre employee, but he may have handled the horses for the spectacular procession in *Alexander the Great,* which had opened on 12 February and had long been in rehearsal.

"Mad Fiddler, The." *See* MESSING, FREDERICK JAMES.

Madan, Miss. *See* HEARD, MRS WILLIAM.

Madden. *See also* MADDIN.

Madden, Ann. *See* HEARD, MRS WILLIAM.

Maddin, Mr ₁*fl. 1770?–1781*₁, *actor.*
Mr Maddin acted Pamphlet in *Love and a Bottle* at the Haymarket Theatre on 26 March 1781. In that performance, Miss Maddin, no doubt his daughter, played Pindress. Maddin may have been the "Madden" who performed at Cork in August 1770 and at Kingston, Jamaica, in September 1780.

Maddin, Miss ₁*fl. 1781*₁, *actress. See* MADDIN, MR.

Maddocks. *See also* MADDOX and MATTOCKS.

Maddocks, Mr ₁*fl. 1714–1716*₁, *actor.*
In the summer of 1714 a troupe called "the Duke of Southampton and Cleaveland's Servants" performed at Richmond, Surrey. Among the 14 players was one "Madox," who took the part of Eumillius in Benjamin Griffin's *Injured Virtue,* according to the cast in the edition of 1714 (*recte* 1715). On 1 November 1714 the same company repeated the play at the King's Arms Tavern, Southwark.

"Maddocks" (evidently the preferred spelling) seems to have acted a Captain of the Guards, a minor part in Nicholas Rowe's *Lady Jane Gray* when it was presented for the first time at Drury Lane Theatre on 20 April 1715 (though again the cast is derived from the editon of that year). In Mrs Mynn's establishment "At the Queen's Arm [*sic*] Tavern near the Marshalsea Gate" at the time of Southwark Fair, on 5 September 1715, "on a small Stage" "Maddox" presented "The Droll of Bateman."

He must have been active at Drury Lane in the 1715–16 season, for on 8 June 1716 "Maddocks" shared a benefit with Weller and Boman Jr. Nothing further is known of him.

Maddocks, Master. *See* MADDOCKS, WALTER HENRY.

Maddocks, James. *See* MADDOCKS, WALTER.

Maddocks, Walter *d. 1823, actor, singer.*
Details of the early life of Walter Maddocks (occasionally Maddox) were furnished by short accounts in *The Secret History of the Green Rooms* (1790) and *Authentic Memoirs of the Green Room* (1799), which agree that he was born in Chester, that he was later a schoolmaster there, and that he made his acting debut at Norwich. (Neither account furnishes a first name, and the Maddocks who was at Norwich in 1782–83 and 1783–84 was called "Jas Maddocks" in the Norwich Committee Books when he was discharged on 29 April 1784. But the Maddocks we follow was carried as "W." Maddocks in later Drury Lane documents and signed himself "Walter" on an actors' petition of 1810.) Only two of his Norwich roles are known: the First Gentleman in *The Belle's Stratagem* (with the Norwich company at Stourbridge Fair on 3 October 1782) and Freeburg in *The Fair American* on 12 February 1783.

From Norwich, Maddocks went to the theatres at Liverpool, Manchester, and Birmingham, playing in the provinces for five years more before being called to Drury Lane to replace Chaplin, who had suddenly died, in 1789. The Drury Lane Fund Book notes his original subscription of 10s. 6d. in 1789, and the account book states his salary as £2 per week. In 1794 he lived at No 10, Brownlow Street, Longacre.

Maddocks settled in with the Drury Lane company for the following three decades as tenor chorus singer and minor actor, walking on dozens of times each season in comedy, farce, opera, melodrama, and pantomime (rarely in tragedy) in an endless procession of nameless beggars and bailiffs, shepherds and soldiers, peasants, citizens, daemons, lawyers, priests, and watchmen. A dozen times a season, more or less, he was thrust on in named parts scarcely larger or was allowed a tertiary or even a secondary character. A list of his roles follows, in order of assumption: In 1789–90, Wat in *All the World's a Stage*, the Archbishop of Canterbury in *Henry V*, Wheatear in *Belphegor*, Captain Driver in *Oroonoko*, Antonio in *The Two Gentlemen of Verona*, Sternhold in *The Deaf Lover*, Alguazile in *She Wou'd and She Wou'd Not*, Mittimus in *Mordecai's Beard*, Dr Camphire in *The College of Physicians*, Easy in *The Quaker*, and Catchpole in *The Apprentice*; in 1790–91, Gasconade in *Harlequin's Invasion*, the Lawyer's Clerk in *Better Late than Never*; in 1791–92, Darby in *Jane Shore*, Solitaire in *The Englishman in Paris*, Wealthy in *The Minor*, Biondello in *Catherine and Petruchio*, and Matthew in *Richard Coeur de Lion*; in 1792–93, the Doctor in *Macbeth*, Bruin in *The Mayor of Garratt*, Buckram in *Love for Love*, Snake in *The School for Scandal*, and Scruple in *The Recruiting Officer*; in 1793–94 (at the Haymarket), Sir Charles Marlow in *She Stoops to Conquer*, Goodwill in *The Virgin Unmask'd*, Clip in *The Confederacy*, Dapper in *The Citizen*, Simon Pure in *A Bold Stroke for a Wife*, Don Alvarez in *The Constant Couple*, Kilderkin in *A Flitch of Bacon*, Robert in *The Haunted Tower*, the Earl of Mercia in *Peeping Tom*, Chagrin in *All in Good Humour*, Jones in *The Box-Lobby Challenge*, Bates in *The Irish Widow*, the Lord Chancellor in *Henry VIII*, Sir Matthew Medley in *My Grandmother*, Saunders in *The Jew*, and Gregory in *Catherine and Petruchio*; and in 1794–95, Pirro in *Emilia Galotti*, Vindicius in *The Roman Father*, Thomas in *Measure for Measure*, Rowley in *The School for Scandal*, Arsites in *Alexander the Great*, Seville in *The Child of Nature*, and Chignon in *The Heiress*.

In 1795–96 Maddocks added to his repertoire Flint in *The Adopted Child*, Harry in *The Dependent*, the Notary in *The Spanish Barber*, Bolus in *The Suicide*, Splitcause in *The Plain Dealer*, Walter in *The Iron Chest*, Friar John in *Romeo and Juliet*, and Rusticus in *The Roman Actor*; in 1796–97, William in *The Country Girl*, the Lord Mayor in *Richard III*, Poundage in *The Provok'd Husband*, Tubal in *The Merchant of Venice*, Sampson in *Isabella*, Bazil in *The Follies of a Day*, Haly in *Tamerlane*, Gonzalez in *The Tempest*, Philario in *Cymbeline*, and the Duke of Venice in *Othello*; in 1797–98, Oliver in *The Children of the Wood*, Duke Frederick in *As You Like It*, Copsley in *The Will*, Easy in *The Quaker*, Thybolt in *The Count of Narbonne*,

Ritornello in *The Critic*, and Caddy in *The Prize*; in 1798–99, Manuel in *The Revenge*, Francisco in *The Outlaws*, Ben Budge in *The Beggar's Opera*, Silvertongue in *The Belle's Stratagem*, Plodwell in *First Faults*, and Justice Guttle in *The Lying Valet*; and in 1799–1800, Serjeant Flower in *The Clandestine Marriage*, Sir Jasper in *The Mock Doctor*, and Mr Milden in *The Wedding Day*.

A surviving casting book of about 1815–16 in the Folger Library adds the following roles to Maddocks's repertoire in the nineteenth century: Augustine in *The Duenna*, the Friar in *Much Ado about Nothing*, the Cook in *Turn Out*, Campillo in *The Honey Moon*, Pinch in *Three and the Deuce*, Corregidor in *She Wou'd and She Wou'd Not*, Stukely in *The West Indian*, Justice Day in *The Honest Thieves*, Lord Fitzbalaam in *John Bull*, the Hair Dresser in *Of Age Tomorrow*, Gagger in *Fontainebleau*, Hugo in *The Haunted Tower*, Snapall in *Hole in the Wall*, Don Sancho in *Two Strings to Your Bow*, Stubble in *The Farmer*, Tap in *The School for Prejudice*, Iman in *The Ninth Statue*, Ross in *Richard II*, Allan in *The Family Legend*, Margin in *The World*, and the Lieutenant of the Tower [Brakenbury] in *Richard III*. He also continued to play numbers of officers, mountebanks, landlords, waiters, coachmen, and gamekeepers, for he seemingly brought something especially bright to these "small" characters which were so important to the soft farce and melodrama of the turn of the century. His salary seems never to have climbed above £2 per week, and he always shared benefit tickets with several others. But he may have found employment singing in the public pleasure gardens.

Very little more than his roles is known of Maddocks in London. He was married to an actress who made the provincial rounds with him and who came on the Drury Lane stage in 1795. She remained with the company through 1817–18, at least, and he collected her weekly salary of £1 10s. along with his own £2.

Strangely, for an actor so humble, Maddocks was a trustee of the Drury Lane Fund in 1806, and its secretary in 1810–11. In 1810 he was one of a number of actors signing a petition to the King for a patent for a third theatre to present nonmusical drama in London. He died on 25 March 1823, according to James Winston's diary.

Walter James Maddocks the musician, who was in the Drury Lane band early in the nineteenth century, was doubtless a relative and was probably a son.

Walter Maddocks perhaps was pictured with other actors in a scene from *All the World's a Stage*, painted by Samual De Wilde. That picture, now at the National Theatre, London, is reproduced in volume 5 of this dictionary. In *The Artist and the Theatre* Mander and Mitchenson suggest that the figure shown on the left of the canvas, behind and between two other figures, was either Maddocks as Wat or John Purser as Cymon.

Maddocks, Mrs Walter *d. 1834, actress.*

Mrs Walter Maddocks and her husband were with the Norwich Company when, on 3 October 1782, it came to a temporary theatre at "Stirbich" (Stourbridge) Fair near Cambridge. Mrs Maddocks played Kitty in *The Belle's Stratagem*. One other role by Mrs Maddocks while she was with that company has been preserved: Miss Melcomb in *The Fair American* at Norwich on 12 February 1783.

The Maddockses left Norwich in April 1784. Presumably Mrs Maddocks accompanied her husband when he went to Liverpool. She, at least, was at "the new Theatre, Hanley" from 24 September 1787 until May 1788. They were together in 1788–89 at Manchester and she remained there in 1789–90, when he was called to Drury Lane. She assisted the amateurs at Lord Barrymore's Wargrave Theatre in 1791.

How long the couple were separated by their several employments is not known. Mrs Maddocks did not appear at Drury Lane until 27 October 1794, when she was one of many singing in the chorus of the musical spectacle *The Pirates*. The piece was many times repeated that season, as was *The Cherokee*, for which Mrs Maddocks also assisted in the chorus. She was given her first named role at Drury Lane on 6 January 1795, when she stepped in for the absent Mrs Booth to play Mrs Coupler in *A Trip to Scarborough*, and thereafter her professional life fell into a pattern not much different from that of her husband—chorus singing constantly, but named parts once in awhile.

Her other roles, in order and by season, until 1800 were: in 1794–95, Mrs Peachum in *The Beggar's Opera*, Mrs Overdone in *Measure for Measure*, Dame Dunckley in *The Wheel of Fortune*, Hob's Mother in *Hob in the Well*, and the Nurse in *The Chances*; in 1795–96, Dame Dawkins in *The Dependent* (a comedy by Richard Cumberland which played only once), Winifred in *The Children in the Wood*, the Nurse in *Isabella*, Miss Pickle in *The Spoil'd Child*; in 1796–97, Dorcas in *Richard Coeur de Lion*, Mrs Hamford in *The Wedding Day*, Mrs Matadore in *The Humourist*, Deborah in *The Will*, Margaret in *The Deserter*, Trusty in *The Clandestine Marriage*, Maud in *The Haunted Tower*, and Cicily in *The Quaker*; in 1798–99, Margery in *The Spoil'd Child*; and in 1799–1800, Suky Tawdry in *The Beggar's Opera* and Marchioness Merida in *The Child of Nature*.

A Drury Lane casting list of around 1815, now in the Folger Library, adds a few more characters to her repertoire: the Cook in *High Life below Stairs*, Mrs Honeymouth in *Hit or Miss*, Victoria in *Rule a Wife and Have a Wife*, Mrs Motherly in *The Provok'd Husband*, Furnish in *The Way to Keep Him*, Anne in *The Birth Day*, Dame Rawbold in *The Iron Chest*, Rachel in *The School for Prejudice*, Lady Bountiful in *The Beaux' Stratagem*, Mrs Goodison in *The Jew*, and a Witch in *Macbeth*.

Mrs Maddocks's salary was £1 10s. per week, which her husband collected for her, along with his own. She apparently remained in the Drury Lane company through 1816–17. She died in 1834, according to a notation in the Drury Lane Fund Book at the Folger Library.

Very likely Walter Henry Maddocks the musician was the son of Walter and Mrs Maddocks.

Maddocks, Walter Henry *b. 1788, singer?, violinist.*

A Master Maddocks was carried on the list of people in the chorus at Drury Lane Theatre on 10 June and also on the end-of-season company list in July 1800. Inasmuch as Walter Maddox and his wife were both in the chorus that season (and for many years before and after), it is probable that our subject was their son.

It is also probable that their son was the Walter Henry Maddocks who was "recommended by Mr Cobham as a proper person to be a member" of the Royal Society of Musicians on 6 June 1813 and was elected unanimously on 5 September 1813. A Mr Maddocks played second violin in the Haymarket band at £1 10s. per week in 1815, 1816, and 1817. In the 1815–16 and 1816–17 seasons he was in the band at Drury Lane at £1 16s. per week.

In 1818 and 1819 Maddocks was listed in the Minute Books as a Governor of the Royal Society of Music. On 3 July 1836 he was granted £10 medical relief to "go to the seaside." On 4 September he was granted a "fuel allowance" and was said to be 48 years old. On 2 July 1837 his wife was ill and requesting funds. On 2 September 1838 it was reported to the Society that Maddocks "was going to Canterbury for a change of air for his health." His wife had died by 2 April 1839, when Walter Henry Maddocks was granted £8 for her funeral and notified that his allowance had been reduced to £4 per month.

Maddox. *See also* MADDOCKS *and* MATTOCKS.

Maddox, Mr ₁*fl. 1783–1785*₁, *boxkeeper and lobby-keeper.*

A list of persons serving at the King's Theatre in 1783, now at the British Library, calls Mr Maddox a boxkeeper. A similar list in the Lord Chamberlain's accounts sets him down as a "box and lobby keeper" in the 1784–85 season.

Maddox, Anthony *d. 1758, dancer, equilibrist, instrumentalist.*

Anthony Maddox the wire dancer came into sudden popularity at Sadler's Wells in 1751. By August that year David Garrick had been alarmed by the proposal of his managerial partner James Lacy that Maddox's equilibres be exhibited on the stage of Drury Lane Theatre. Garrick wrote to Draper 17 August: "I cannot possibly agree to such a prostitution upon any account; and nothing but downright starving would induce me to bring such defilement and abomination into the *house of William Shakespeare*."

John Rich at Covent Garden had no such scruples. Cross, the Drury Lane prompter, noted in his diary that on that night, 2 November 1752, "Mr Maddox ye Ballance Master" was at the other house in a revival of Rich's old afterpiece *The Fair*. The *Gentleman's Magazine* for November 1752 reported what ensued:

The Town had been allured to Covent Garden by a wire dancer and some strange animals, which

by B. Cole in the *New Universal Magazine* in the spring of 1753 described both graphically and verbally the activity of "Mr. Anthony Maddox, who is allow'd to excel all the masters in the art of ballancing and dexterity of the human body, that ever appear'd on the stage at home or abroad." The plate featured a central portrait surrounded by 12 smaller, numbered, figures:

At No. 1. He tosses 6 balls with such dexterity, that he catches them all alternately, without letting one of 'em drop to the ground, and that with surprizing activity.
2. He ballanceth his hat upon his chin.
3. He ballanceth a sword with its point on the edge of a wine-glass.
4. He at the same time plays a violin.
5. He lies extended on his back up-on a small wire.
6. He ballanceth a coach-wheel on his chin.
7. He standeth upon his head upon the wire.
8. He ballanceth a chair on his chin.
9. He ballanceth seven pipes, one in another: And
10. Blows a trumpet on the wire.
11. Ballanceth several wine-glasses full, on the wire.
12. Ballanceth two pipes across a hoop, on the wire.
13. Tosseth a straw from his foot to his nose.

By permission of the British Library Board

ANTHONY MADDOX

engraving by Houston, after King

the manager brought together from Sadler's Wells and the Fair. Mr Garrick ridiculed this perversion of theatrical entertainment, by exhibiting a mock entertainment of the same kind. At this the town was offended, and a party went one evening determined to damn it; a person of some distinction [Fitzpatrick] who was very busy in this laudable attempt threw an apple at Woodward and hit him. Woodward resented the blow by some words, which, by the gentleman's account, implied a challenge, but by Woodward's no such thing. Woodward's account is confirm'd by the affidavits of many; that of the gentleman only by his own, though the box in which he sat was full. The *Inspector* espoused the cause of the Gentleman; and the *Covent Garden Journalist* of the comedian.

The Fair, with Maddox, was repeated 28 times in a row, the last night being one by command of the Prince of Wales.

Early in December Maddox left London for an engagement at Smock Alley, Dublin, where, on 1 January 1753, "surprizing equilibres on the wire by the celebrated Mr Maddox" from Covent Garden were advertised as his first performances in Ireland. A copperplate engraving

Maddox was at Simpson's Theatre in Bath on 8 December 1753. He went from there to Bristol. His appearance there on 3 January 1754 was advertised as "positively the last Time of his performing in the West of England." He had added refinements to his act: he would "sound a Trumpet and play on the Violin at the same time, in full Swing."

Also he stands on his Head in full Swing, and discharges a Brace of Pistols at the same Time. ——☞ Mr. Maddox will provide a good Band of Musick; and after the Wire, he will ballance a Straw on his Face, and shift it from all Parts thereof; from thence to his Foot, and kicks it to a considerable Height, catching it again on his Face. The whole to conclude with a Hornpipe in Taste, by Mr. Maddox.

Maddox prospered. A notice in the *Evening Advertiser* for 12 December 1754 asserted that he had "had the prudence . . . to lay by 6000 *l*. and thereby has enabled himself to retire from so hazardous an occupation." But he returned from his retirement to perform at Sadler's Wells again in 1756. In the fall of 1757 he was perhaps mixed up in Christopher Smart's whimsical *Medleys* at the Haymarket. He certainly joined these foolishments when Theoph-

By permission of the British Library Board

ANTHONY MADDOX
engraving by Cole

ilus Cibber took them over later in the fall,
conducting them as "*Impromptu Faragolios*."

On 27 October 1758 Maddox accompanied
Cibber and other performers aboard the *Dublin
Trader* (the *Dublin Merchant*, in the Digges-
Ward correspondence) and sailed from Park-
gate. The overloaded vessel struck a sandbar
not far out, and some of the 60 passengers
turned back in small boats. But Maddox and
Cibber remained. The ship was caught in a
sudden storm, driven north past the Isle of
Man, and sank that day off the Scottish coast,
drowning all hands.

The short will of Anthony Maddox "of Ro-
saman Road in the Parish of St James Clerkenwell, gentleman," is probably that of the equilibrist (despite the claim "gentleman"). It was
made on 3 October 1758 seemingly preparatory to the fatal voyage and mindful of the
hazards of St George's Channel. Maddox bequeathed to his wife Elizabeth all his real estate
in Bristol, Devonshire, and elsewhere. To his

brothers James and John and to his sister Elizabeth he left £10 each.

It seems likely that Anthony Maddox was
the father of the wire dancer Michael Maddox
and the son of the Bristol dancing-master James
Maddox. On 8 December 1744 the *Bristol Oracle
and County Intelligencer* remarked the death on
2 December of "James Maddox late an eminent
Teacher of the Art of Dancing in this City,"
and of his wife only 48 hours later, after being
married for 50 years. They were buried in St
Michael's Church. The wife was said to be the
daughter of a Dr Hoyle, physician. John Hack-
ett in his *Select and Remarkable Epitaphs* (1757)
printed 20 lines of execrable sentimental verse
celebrating their "Twice thirty Years in gentle
Wedlock past," and the near-concurrence of
their deaths.

Anthony Maddox's wife Elizabeth may have
acted in Ireland. She had shared benefit tickets
with him at Smock Alley on 6 June 1753. But
she does not seem to have appeared on the
London stage.

In addition to the engraving published in
the *New Universal Magazine* in 1753 (described
above), an engraving of Anthony Maddox by
R. Houston, after T. King, was published by
Smith and Sayer (n.d.); it shows him standing,
holding a straw in his right hand, and with his
left hand on his hip. An engraving by F. Pailthorpe, giving 12 views of him on the slack
rope, was published (n.d.) with a descriptive
caption. A copy of the Pailthorpe engraving,
by an anonymous artist, was published in July
1752. Another anonymous engraving cap-
tioned "The surprising performances of the famous Mr. Maddox on the Slack Wire at Sadler's
Wells, London," depicts him in 19 different
attitudes.

Maddox, Michael   *b. 1747, equilibrist,
magician, dancer, instrumentalist, entrepreneur.*

Michael Maddox was born in England on 14
May 1747, probably the son of the equilibrist
Anthony Maddox. Michael appeared in Russia
as an equilibrist in 1767, according to Marian
Hannah Winter in *The Pre-Romantic Ballet*. We
believe that he must have been the tumbler
and prestidigitator Maddox who supplied most
of the program at the Haymarket Theatre on
10 December 1770, for Anthony Maddox had
died in 1758. Maddox's Haymarket act succeeded capitally so far as his wire-balancing

was concerned. "But his Sleight of Hand and Physical Experiments . . . were not suffered by the Audience to go on, as being thought more proper for a Room than a Theatre," according to a newsclipping in the Burney Collection in the British Library.

The bill for that evening typifies Maddox's repertoire for us:

1. He will swing and walk on the Wire. 2. Balance a Pipe on full Swing, to the Extent of the Wire. 3. A Cross Balance. 4. Takes a long Pipe in his Mouth and places another on the small End whilst on full Swing. 5. Balances an Egg upon a Straw on the Wire. 6. A Double-Cross Balance. 7. Balances a Straw on the Edge of a Glass, and kneels on the Wire. . . . 11. Stands with one Foot on the Wire, balances a Straw upon the Edge of a Glass, and plays on the Fiddle at the same Time. . . . 14. Will set a Table across the Wire, and perform a Table-dance with three Pewter Plates. . . .

and so on. At one point he played a fiddle, a French horn, and a drum simultaneously while swinging on the wire. An interesting aside in the bill assures his audience: "As many have been deterred from going to see performances on the Wire merely from the apparent Danger, Mr. Maddox does not propose having his [wire strung] more than three Feet from the Stage."

Maddox was both a traveler and a man of mysterious business. The Haymarket appearance was "the first Time of his performing in England," and he promised to "perform several Physical Experiments, such as have never been seen in England." A clipping in the A. M. Broadley Collection at Westminster Public Library dated 4 January 1772 suggests:

If Mr. Michael Maddox, who performed last Winter at Mr. Foot's Theatre . . . will go or send to Mr. John Goode, in Lower Grosvenor Street, he may have an Opportunity of hearing that his affairs in Sweden are settled, and to his utmost satisfaction. Also that the important papers he so often wished for is [*sic*] come safe to hand. . . .

N.B. Mr. Maddox, after he left London, performed at Chichester, Southampton, Portsmouth &c. and is supposed now to be Abroad. . . .

Mr Goode requested any person having knowledge of his whereabouts to come forward.

Evidently Maddox had returned to Russia. He there constructed automatons and gave experimental performances in the physical sci-

ences and later concerned himself with inventing and installing theatrical machinery in Moscow. With Prince P. V. Ourassov he managed the Znamenka Theatre, and after it burned helped raise money for the Petrovsky Theatre. In 1805 he was awarded a pension of 3000 rubles for his services to drama.

Madge, Humphrey *d. 1679, instrumentalist.*

Nicholas Hookes's "To Mr. Lilly, Musick-Master in Cambridge," published in *Amanda* in 1653 makes a fleeting reference to a musician named "Magge," probably Humphrey Madge. It is likely that Madge was a Cambridge man. That poem is the earliest reference we have found for him, the next being in connection with Sir William Davenant's historic production at Rutland House in 1656 of *The Siege of Rhodes*; Madge was one of the instrumentalists in that "opera." In the Lord Chamberlain's accounts are numerous warrants citing Madge. On 10 July 1660 he was appointed to the King's Musick as a cornetist and flutist, replacing the deceased Jerome Lanier. His salary was later stated as £40 12s. 8d. But that was only one of his posts, for he also replaced Theophilus Lupo as a violinist and violist at £40 annually. In addition he received, though often not on time, livery allowances of £16 2s. 6d. each year for each of his two positions.

The accounts mentioned Madge over the years in a variety of ways: in September 1661 he was paid £20 for a violin and strings he had purchased; in the summer of 1662 he attended the King at Hampton Court and received 5s. daily for his expenses, and he made similar trips out of London with the King in other years; in 1666 he was cited as still waiting for his livery allowances for 1663 and 1664; as of 1668 his salary as a string player was £58 14s. 2d. yearly, higher than most of his fellows; in March 1671 a difference between him and a George Reason was referred by the Lord Chamberlain to arbitration; and on 29 October 1677 Sir Richard Beach petitioned against Madge for a debt of £500.

There are a few glimpses of Madge outside the court. Pepys heard him play at Dr "Whores" on 7 January 1660, and on 10 March 1660 he told his diary that "Mage" had come to his office "half-foxed and played the fool upon the viallin, that made me weary." He had evidently been a friend of Pepys for some time, and the diarist spoke of Madge frequently. In August 1660 Pepys had dinner with Madge and some other musicians; in June 1661 Madge recommended Goodgroome to Pepys as a singing teacher, and in December 1663 Pepys thoroughly enjoyed a gathering at Lord Sandwich's where Henry Cooke, Madge, and others sang. In addition, as of 24 June 1672 Madge was a Warden of the Corporation of Music, and it is likely that he served that organization before and after that date.

Humphrey Madge died shortly before 22 December 1679, on which date his positions at court were taken by Aleworth and Crouch. We know from the will of John Hingeston, written on 12 December 1683, that Madge had a son, Hingeston's godson, to whom he left a violin. The registers of St Margaret, Westminster, show the baptism of Madge's son William on 1 November 1664. The court accounts reveal that Humphrey Madge's widow Elizabeth received a bounty from King James in 1686 (probably a yearly allowance amounting to £40) and in 1687 and 1688 Madge's daughter Sarah received annual allowances of £40.

Madox. *See* MADDOX.

Maer, Michael ₍*fl.* 1683–1685₎, *trumpeter.*
Michael "Meire" was appointed a trumpeter in the King's Musick on 16 February 1683, replacing the deceased Albion Thompson. "Maer" was one of the trumpeters who marched in the coronation procession with James II on 23 April 1685; the eight trumpeters, wrote Francis Sandford in his history of the event, were "all in rich liveries of crimson velvet, laced with gold and silver, with silver trumpets, having banners of crimson damask fringed about with gold and silver, with strings suitable and richly embroidered." Michael "Maire" was last mentioned in the Lord Chamberlain's accounts on 12 June 1685, when he was reappointed to the King's Musick under James II.

Maffei, Signora ₍*fl.* 1791–1792₎, *singer.*
On 16 April 1791 Signora Maffei replaced Mme Lops as a singer in the *Entertainments of Music and Dancing* offered at the King's Theatre. She sang again in that entertainment on 2 June. In 1792 Haydn cited her in his notebook as "pretty, but not very musical."

Maffet, Mr ₍*fl.* 1796₎, *actor.*
A Mr Maffet played Sir Walter Raleigh in *The Earl of Essex* at the Haymarket Theatre on 27 April 1796.

Magalli, Signor? ₍*fl.* 1760₎, *singer.*
The London Stage lists a Signor Magalli but no Signora as performing at the King's Theatre and at Soho in 1760 (in the company rosters at the beginning of the 1759–60 season), but within the calendar of performances both a Signor and Signora Magalli are cited. At the Great Music Room in Dean Street, Soho, on 14 February 1760, a *Charlottenburg festegiante* was presented, with vocal parts by "Signoras Passerini, Frederick, Tenducci, and Magalli (who never sung in public before except at the Opera)." The first two singers were, indeed, signoras, but Tenducci was a male soprano and Magalli, too, was probably a man. On 25 February at the King's Theatre Signor Magalli sang Mercury in *La Gran Brettagna emula della antica Roma*, and on 31 May, according to a manuscript notation in a Folger copy of *Erginda regina di Livadia*, he sang Tanette in that work.

Magam or **Magan, James.** *See* MIDDLETON, JAMES.

Mage. *See* MADGE.

Magen, James. *See* MIDDLETON, JAMES.

Maget, James ₍*fl.* 1794₎, *performer?*
The Drury Lane Theatre accounts show a payment of £6 6s. to James Maget on 5 May 1794; he may have been a performer.

"Maggoty Johnson." *See* JOHNSON, SAMUEL *d.* 1773.

Magheary, Mr ₍*fl.* 1799–1800₎, *performer.*
The Covent Garden Theatre accounts in 1799–1800 show a salary of £3 weekly for a performer named Magheary. (Perhaps that is

an error for Macartney, who acted at Covent Garden for £3 weekly that season.)

Magnes, Mr ₁*fl. 1729*₁, *harpsichordist.*
Mr Magnes made his first public appearance on 29 July 1729 at Drury Lane Theatre accompanying the violinist Charke and playing a solo voluntary on the harpischord. Magnes was again noticed in the bills at Drury Lane on 9 August.

Magnus, Master ₁*fl. 1697–1700*₁, *singer.*
See MAGNUS, ₁ CLEMENT?₁.

Magnus, ₁ **Clement?**₁ ₁*fl. 1693–1699*₁, *singer.*
A Mr Magnus sang Mercury in *The Rape of Europa* at the Dorset Garden Theatre in the winter of 1693–94, was probably in Christopher Rich's company in 1696–97, sang in *Phaeton* at Drury Lane in March 1698, and was a member of the Drury Lane troupe in 1698–99. Perhaps he was the Magnus mentioned in the registers of St Paul, Covent Garden: Clement and Flower Magnus baptized their daughter Phebe on 8 January 1699, but the child died and was buried the following 21 September. The Mrs Magnus who sang, according to the *Catalogue of Printed Music in the British Museum*, Daniel Purcell's *To Cynthia then our homage pay* in *The World in the Moon* in 1697 (at Dorset Garden) was presumably our subject's wife. "Magnus' Boy," who was cited as a singer in the late years of the century, was Thomas Morgan; he was probably one of Magnus's students.

Magnus, Mrs ₁ **Clement, Flower?**₁ ₁*fl. 1697–1699?*₁, *singer. See* MAGNUS, ₁ CLEMENT?₁.

Magre. *See* DELAMAINE.

Magrini, Mons ₁*fl. 1787*₁, *acrobat.*
Monsieur Magrini performed at the Royal Circus in April 1787 with a "capital Group" of trampoline acrobats.

Maguire. *See* MACGUIRE, MACQUIRE, and REDIGÉ, MME PAOLO.

Mahomed. *See* CARATTA, MAHOMET.

Mahomet. *See* MUSSULMO.

Mahon, Mr ₁*fl. 1766*₁, *actor.*
A Mr Mahon played Denis in *As You Like It* in a performance of Spranger Barry's summer company at the King's Theatre on 13 September 1766.

Mahon, Mrs, later Mrs John Palmer *d. 1807, actress, singer.*
Mrs Mahon was in Tate Wilkinson's company on the York circuit in 1766. She first appeared in London at Covent Garden Theatre on 18 October 1766, as Lucinda in *Love in a Village*, which part she sang in numerous performances until 11 February, when she was replaced by Mrs Mattocks. On 18 November she was part of the cast of the popular *Harlequin Doctor Faustus* and served that pantomime the rest of the season. On 10 January she was the original Bridget in Arthur Murphy's farce *The School for Guardians*, which was a failure. She sustained Amie in *The Jovial Crew* on 29 January 1767 and Chloe (alias Lady Lace) in *The Lottery* on 19 February.

Foote hired Mrs Mahon for his summer company at the Haymarket, and on 5 August she sang the second lead, Lucy, in *The Beggar's Opera*. Sylas Neville wrote in his diary that night, "Mrs Mahon did Lucy with great ease and propriety and has a good deal of expression in her countenance." He returned to see it again on 10 August: "Mrs Mahon's expression and propriety in Lucy is delightful."

Mrs. Mahon played Phyllis in *The Conscious Lovers* "for the first time," according to the playbill, on 14 August, Maria in *The Citizen* ("first time") on 4 September, and, for her last appearance in London, on 21 September, some part unspecified in *Like Master Like Man*.

During the season of 1768 she was at York with Tate Wilkinson's company, playing we know not what, and in the fall of that year left for the Bath company. She did good work for Wilkinson, who in his *Wandering Patentee* extolled "the merits of Mrs. Mahon, who sustained . . . all the leading parts in the operas; she was also, what very seldom occurs, as good an actress as a singer, and played several characters with great propriety, archness and pleasantry."

At Bath, Mrs Mahon met and, by 1772, married, the younger John Palmer, the Bath theatre proprietor (not to be confused with either of the London actors of that name), and retired to a life of wealth and social prominence. For besides being theatre owner at Bath and Bristol and having large commercial interests, Palmer was the contriver of a successful country-wide system of moving the mails for which he was rewarded with additional wealth. He became comptroller-general of the post office and a member of Parliament. But enjoyment of some of those honors was shared by his second wife, a Miss Pratt whom he married on 2 November 1786. Palmer died on 16 August 1818.

But the subject of this memoir must have been the mother of most of the six children whom, according to Palmer's testimony in 1788, he had fathered. The eldest was Charles Palmer, who was born in Weston near Bath on 6 May 1777, was educated at Eton and Oriel College, Oxford, and served with distinction in the Peninsular War. He was also a member of Parliament. Two other sons, John and Edmund, became distinguished naval officers. Edmund married a niece of Lord St Vincent.

Mahon, Master [fl. 1783–1785?], dancer?

A document among the Lord Chamberlain's records at the Public Record Office shows a Master Mahon added to the list at the "Opera House," the King's Theatre in 1783. One payment to him, inordinately large it seems, of £158 is recorded, apparently sometime in 1785. No mention was made of his function. Perhaps he was a dancer.

Mahon, Miss. See also AMBROSE, MRS.

Mahon, Miss, later Mrs Munday [fl. 1776?–1793], singer.

The soprano singer who became Mrs Munday before 1787 was one of the Mahon family of musicians which included (probably) the father and mother as well as the singer James, the instrumentalists John and William, and the singers Sarah (later Mrs John Second), Miss M. (later Mrs John Warton), and the sister who became Mrs Ambrose.

John H. Mee, in The Oldest Music Room in Europe, finds a Miss Mahon "was allowed nine or ten [benefit] concerts [at Oxford in] 1776 and 1787." These were on 14 March 1776, 22

July 1778, 29 April 1779, 27 April 1780, 14 March 1782, 3 December 1783, 18 November 1784, 20 July 1785, 8 December 1785, and 27 April 1787. This was a great indulgence, for with very few exceptions no one except the leader (first violin) and first cello received benefits. But whether that Miss Mahon was the sister who later became Mrs Munday or the one who became Mrs Ambrose is not known, inasmuch as neither first name survives. The singer could have been Miss M. (later Mrs John Warton) only after 1778, when, it is known, she made her debut.

Our subject sang for the first time at Oxford under her married name on 26 January 1792 and, according to Jackson's Oxford Journal again earned "highest applause." In 1793 she sang at London's Ranelagh Gardens, and several songs "as sung by her" were published.

Though Mrs Munday's career is liable to some confusion with those of her sisters, her certain recognition rests on the fact that she was the mother of the brilliant nineteenth-century soprano Eliza Munday who earned fame as Mrs James Salmon.

Mahon, Mrs Gilbert, Gertrude, née Tilson b. 1752, actress, singer.

One of the eminent filles de joies most discussed in the newspaper gossip of the late 1770s was Gertrude Tilson Mahon, called the Bird of Paradise. Lady Morgan (Sydney Owenson) called her a daughter of Lord Limerick. A writer in the London Morning Post for 29 November 1780 asserted that she was the daughter of the Countess of Kerry by one "Buck" Tilson. That seems to be the fact, for when she married the Irish singer and actor Gilbert Mahon at St George, Hanover Square, on 14 December 1770, the register noted that Gertrude Tilson was "a minor" who was married "By license & with the consent of Rt Hon Gertrude, Countess of Kerry, widow, Mother of the Sd. minor." The bridegroom's name was given as "Gilbreath" Mahon, though he seems to have appeared always in the bills as "Gilbert."

Nothing survives to suggest that Gilbert ever sang in London, though his brother Robert Mahon was prominent there as a singing actor. But Gilbert and his wife may have lodged with his brother for awhile, for Robert's address was No 6, Paradise Street, Marylebone, at the time of his benefit in May 1777, and

GERTRUDE MAHON, the Bird of Paradise

artist unknown

she was surprised "in amorous daliance [*sic*] with . . . her red plumed mate" the captain "by the Entree of a Lawyer who in violation of all love's little delicacies served the hero with an action for special damages at the suit of G[ilbert] M[ahon] Esq the lady's husband who had taken this step as a ground work for divorce—The red pigeon flew away in the greatest agitation with the bit of parchment about his neck. . . ." The captain was said to have paid down £500 "on the nail to her husband to prevent a trial at West[minster] Hall" in May. She was said to have deserted the captain (in March) for someone named Kennedy who speedily forsook *her*. She was reported to be pregnant (in April), to have "broke through . . . her cage & perched on the shoulder of Sir J[ohn] L[add], who carried her home to Park Place [also in April], to have returned to the Captain [in May] and by July to have been divorced."

the *Morning Post* derived Gertrude's fanciful sobriquet, the "Bird of Paradise," from the street on which she had lived.

Most of the rest of the information about Mrs Mahon's London activity rests on the dubious testimony of James Winston's jottings and clippings from the *Morning Post*, now in the Folger Library. The writers for the *Post* pursued Gertrude's adulteries relentlessly after her marriage with Mahon ran into rough water, apparently not long after the wedding. On 9 December 1776: "The little Bird of Paradise has at length flown to the Continent with a Military financier nor could the music of the [goldfinches] of her late proprietor (Mr. B—— of Bond Street) [Winston's conjecture: "Birchall?"] restrain her liberty—the amorous B—— is inconsolable for the loss of his faithless warbler." On 25 December 1776: "Yesterday the Bird of Paradise & her amorous Military Associate Capt T——s of the Guards returned from the Continent."

According to the *Post*, on 1 January 1777,

GERTRUDE MAHON, as Fanny

engraving by Thornthwaite, after Roberts

By 1780 Mrs Mahon's notoriety as a woman of the town had made her valuable to Thomas Harris of Covent Garden Theatre as a theatrical curiosity. The *Morning Post* of 27 September 1780 reported that she would "appear next week in Tom Thumb," but she was not named in the cast for that afterpiece on 3 October. "It was whispered at the masquerade at the Pantheon" in December that she would appear as Elvira in *The Spanish Fryar* at Covent Garden on 12 December, and so she did, not disguised at all as "A Lady (1st appearance on any stage)."

Her beauty, her diminutive size, and her reputation could not suffice to keep her in a London theatre, however, for she could not act very well. On 14 February she attempted Lady Bell in *Know Your Own Mind* and on 21 April 1781 she concluded the London theatrical adventure with Lady Townly in *The Provok'd Husband*. The dramatic critics were severe.

In May 1782 she was reported to own two four-wheeled carriages, six horses, and eight domestics. In September it was said that she had spent a long summer season at Margate. In October there was talk of her going back on the stage. In December she was said to be ill, and by February 1783 dangerously so, at her house in Portland Street. The *Morning Post* in March reported that her "late sister, Miss Tylson," had bequeathed her the interest of £6000 besides £3000 outright to her son by Mahon "as soon as he is of age." In May 1784 she was reported selling her house in Portland Street and going to Montpellier in the south of France with a "Mr C—l—t." On her return she took up residence, with elegance, in Argyle Street. But in November she lost her lover to a Mrs Benwell. The next month she embarked from Holyhead for Dublin in a passage of thirty hours "during twenty of which the Captain expected the vessel would go down."

On 28 January 1785 she returned to the stage at Smock Alley in her debut role of Elvira. Her second character was Lady Townly. She had "noble relations" in Ireland and visited them and she lived in high style in a house near College Green. Evidently her tenure at Smock Alley was also short and unsatisfactory.

The rest of her known existence consisted of dual allegiance to the stage and to the life of an expensive courtesan. For long periods the newspapers give glimpses only: In 1790 and 1791 she was at Bath "dead to her former

eminence" and "only alive to epicurism" with her "keeper." By November 1791 she had left Bath and "her house and furniture [had been] bequeathed to the fate of the [auctioneer's] hammer." In December 1792 Mrs Mahon was "at Boulogne, with Mr. Parry." In August 1794 she was at the Margate Theatre. In September and October 1795 she was seen on the Kilkenny stage and on 10 November was at Crow Street, for the first time in 10 years, advertised as "from Liverpool." She returned to Crow Street for the 1796–97 season. Her death date is not known.

A portrait of Mrs Mahon as Fanny in *The Accomplished Maid* was engraved by Thornthwaite, after J. Roberts, as a plate to *Bell's British Theatre*, 1781. Portraits of her titled "The Bird of Paradise" by an unknown engraver were published by C. Bowles in two separate issues. An anonymous engraving of her as the Bird of Paradise, with Colonel Wetwould, was published in the *Hibernian Magazine* for June 1781. Matching portraits titled "Captain Witwou'd and the Bird of Paradise" appeared in the tête-à-tête column of the *Town and Country Magazine*, 1781.

Mahon, James [*fl.* 1779–1792?], *singer, actor, puppeteer?, scene painter?, machinist?*

Persons named Mahon (Mahoon) are numerous and ubiquitous on the stages of the Three Kingdoms, Wales, and America, from the 1730s through the early nineteenth century. It is often hard to distinguish them each from each and their trails are dim and discontinuous. The relationship (if any) between some and others is not understood.

One family of Mahons can, however, be traced. Of James Mahon's father practically nothing is known—though he was probably a musician and certainly Irish and living in Oxford. Mee, in *The Oldest Music Room in Europe*, suggests that the father was employed in the band of music at the Oxford Music Room, and that James's mother was a singer there. The mother's name was Catherine and she died at Salisbury in 1808. James had at least six siblings, all musicians: John, William, Sarah, who became Mrs John Second, Miss M., who became Mrs John Warton, the Miss Mahon who became Mrs Ambrose, and the Miss Mahon who became Mrs Munday.

James Mahon was a favorite and frequent

bass singer at Bath and the Salisbury Festivals. He assisted at the Music Meetings at Wells Cathedral. By 1779 or earlier he was an occasional singer at Vauxhall Gardens. He was a participant in the Handel Memorial Concerts at Westminster Abbey in 1786 and 1787. Winston places him in the chorus at Drury Lane Theatre on 12 March 1790. But he is not on the bill and it is at least conceivable that he was then in Jamaica, for a Mr and Mrs Mahon, both singers, appeared in newspaper notices for performances at Kingston from 1788 until 1792. They were members of a company playing for the benefit of Mr De Salamons, "at Mr Byrns house, by the Beef Market," on 9 August 1788.

In early August 1790 a Mr Mahon was offering "A Miscellaneous Entertainment of Music, Scenery and Machinery, selected from the favorite Entertainments of the Eidophusikon, Fantoccini and Les Outres Chinoises," along with "The much admired scene of the Broken Bridge. The Dialogue and Song by Mr. Mahon," and divers other scenes "in motion" with accompanying songs by Mr and Mrs Mahon, all leading to (or away from) "a Musical Entertainment never performed" in Jamaica "called The Recruiting Serjent . . . Serjent, Mr. Mahon . . . The whole to conclude with a Transparent Likeness of the gallant Lord Rodney, descending from the Clouds, supported by Victory and Britannia, and accompanied by the Brave Admirals and Officers who supported him on the Memorable 12th of April, 1782, with a full Chorus of Rule Britannia."

Several songs were published "as sung by" James Mahon, including one "at Dublin" and one with Miss Satchell at Covent Garden Theatre. Neither his birth nor death dates are known.

Mahon, John c. 1748–1834, clarinettist, violinist, violist, composer.

John Mahon was born about 1748, probably at Oxford. His parents were perhaps musicians at the Oxford Music Room. His siblings were likewise musicians: James, William, Sarah, who became Mrs John Second, Miss M., who became Mrs John Walton, the Miss Mahon who became Mrs Ambrose, and the Miss Mahon who became Mrs Munday.

In the files of the Royal Society of Musicians is a recommendation for his admission dated 6 April 1783 stating that he "is a Single Man—Performs on the Clarinet, violin, Tenor [viola], &c.&c. [and] is about 35 years of age." There is also an extract from the register of St Andrew's Church, Dublin, proving his marriage to Margaret Perry on 30 June 1792.

John Mahon made his debut as clarinettist in the Music Room at Oxford in 1772 and soon afterward began appearing on the concert circuit in London. From 1773 till 1834 he played in virtually all the provincial music festivals. Charles Burney named him among the first violinists for the first Handel Memorial Concerts at Westminster Abbey and the Pantheon in May and June 1784. Either John or his brother William was a member of the pit band at various performances at the Haymarket Theatre in 1772–73 and 1774–75. He was clarinettist for the spring oratorios at Drury Lane Theatre in 1783 and 1784 and at Covent Garden Theatre from 1790 to 1795 and in 1797 and 1800, at the Haymarket Theatre in August 1784, and at the Pantheon in 1790–91.

In 1791, 1817, 1818, and probably other years, Mahon was clarinettist for the opera at the King's Theatre. In 1786 and 1792 he played in the concerts at the Edinburgh Musical Society. Between 1780 and 1810, according to Ita Hogan, in Anglo-Irish Music, 1780–1830, he played concerts in Dublin, Belfast, Cork, and Waterford. He was appointed by the governors of the Royal Society of Musicians to play at the annual benefit concert at St Paul's Cathedral in May of 1794, 1795, and 1797. But on those occasions he played the violin.

Mahon was praised for his virtuoso playing by W. T. Parke, the famous oboist. He composed concertos for the clarinet, four duets for two clarinets, two marches for the Oxford Volunteer Band, and a song with clarinet obbligato, "Hope, thou cheerful rag" for William Shield's The Woodman.

Mahon evidently suffered financial and other misfortunes, as well as ill-health, in his later years. From 5 June 1814 onward the records of the Royal Society of Musicians illustrate his difficulties. On the above date he was "infirm" and requested relief. He was granted £40. On 6 October 1816 he sent word that he'd received a serious wound in his left hand, which would take from two to three months to cure. He was granted £30. Twice in 1817, in 1818, in 1819, 1820, and 1824 he was granted £15 "for relief." He was given £10 for medical aid in 1824, in 1825 £30, in 1826 £5 5s. per month, and in 1827 five guineas.

At some point before 1821 he had moved to Dublin, where he died in January 1834. Mrs Mahon was granted £1 per month survivor's assistance plus £8 for her own eventual funeral expenses. Entries at this time establish the fact that Mrs Mahon had two daughters, one Mrs Mangan (who was granted £12 for paying for her father's funeral) and a younger daughter "in an imbecile condition."

Mahon, Miss M., later Mrs John Warton
[*fl. 1778–1788*], *singer.*

Miss M. Mahon was the daughter of Oxford residents who were probably professional musicians, and the sister of the instrumentalists John and William and the singer James Mahon, and of the singers who became Mrs Ambrose, Mrs Munday, and Mrs Second.

Because the notices of performances rarely furnish first names, it is often impossible to distinguish one sister from the others. Thus, though little is certainly known about her career beyond the fact that she sang first at Oxford Music Room in 1778 and was a principal singer at the Handel Memorial Concerts at Westminster Abbey and the Pantheon in 1784 and at Westminster Abbey in 1787, some of the engagements listed under Mrs Ambrose and Mrs Second may have belonged to her. She appears, however, to have been the youngest sister and to have had a short career.

After Miss M. Mahon's marriage to the Reverend John Warton, son of the scholar, poet, and headmaster of Winchester College, Joseph Warton, she ceased to sing in public.

Mahon, Robert   *1734–1799, actor, singer, manager.*

Robert Mahon was a member of an Irish theatrical family whose origins, members, and movements are only partly determinable. He was certainly the brother of the actor and singer Gilbert Mahon. There was a Mr Mahon in the company at Smock Alley, Dublin, in the 1749–50 season with a son, Master Mahon, who danced and who was probably either Gilbert or Robert. In the 1750–51 season they were joined by a Miss Mahon, also a dancer. Master and Miss performed through the 1749–50 season. Robert Hitchcock in *An Historical View of*

the Irish Stage mentioned a Patrick Mahon who had a prominent part in the original Crow Street cast, in January 1762, of Kane O'Hara's burletta *Midas*. Perhaps Patrick was Robert's father.

Certainly, according to the records compiled by William S. Clark, Robert Mahon was appearing as a dancer at Smock Alley in 1759–60 and at Crow Street Theatre in 1759–60, 1760–61, 1761–62 and from 1763–64 through 1766–67. In most of those seasons he was joined by his wife. Clark traces Mahon also to the Irish provinces: to Cork several times every year from 1760 through 1767, to Kilkenny in 1759, and to Belfast in 1761. A Mrs Mahon of Crow Street Theatre, probably Robert's wife, died at Glasnevin, Ireland, in May 1768.

The Mahon who played Tybalt at the Foregate Street Theatre in Chester on 14 September 1767 was very likely Robert on his way to his engagement for 10s. per week at Covent Garden Theatre in London. There, on 13 October, Macheath in *The Beggar's Opera* was sung by "Mahoon, 1st appearance this kingdom," to Charlotte Pinto's Polly. On 20 October Mahon essayed Giles in *The Maid of the Mill*, on 23 October Chasseur Royal in *The Royal Chace*, on 30 October one of the Bacchanals in *Comus*, on 7 November Shark in *The Oxonian in Town*, on 2 December the Sailor in *Thomas and Sally*, on 14 December Hubert in *The Royal Merchant*, on 25 February 1768 Harman in *Lionel and Clarissa*. He repeated several capital parts and assisted, with other leading singers, in choruses.

Mahon sang and acted at the Haymarket in the summer season of 1768. He was on the Covent Garden roster again in 1768–69 and then returned to Ireland in 1770 to manage with William Dawson a company at the Capel Street Theatre. He acted at the Crow Street Theatre in 1771–72 and 1772–73 and at Smock Alley the next two seasons. In 1775–76 he came back to Covent Garden to serve frequently and usefully for the next four seasons. He was at Liverpool, earning £2 per week, in the summers of 1776 and 1777 and he took "second leads" at Bristol in the summer of 1778.

Ireland called Mahon once again in the fall of 1780 and he spent two successful seasons at Smock Alley before wandering back to Covent

Garden for two more. He retired after the season of 1783–84. The *Hibernian Magazine* for May 1793 stated that he had recently acted one final night at Crow Street after an absence from the stage of 10 years. He died in Dublin toward the end of April 1799, aged 65.

In addition to the roles cited above for his first London season, he added in subsequent years, the following: at the Haymarket in the summer of 1768, the Squire in *Thomas and Sally*, Quaver in *The Virgin Unmask'd*, Meanwell in *The Statesman Foiled*, Friendly in *Hob in the Well*, Damon in *Damon and Phillida*, Pedro in *The Spanish Fryar*, and Paris in *The Judgment of Paris*; at Covent Garden in 1768–69, Moor of Moor Hall in *The Dragon of Wantley*, Caius Lucius in *Cymbeline*, Cornwall in *King Lear*, Essex in *King John*; in 1775–76, Callaghan in *Love à-la-Mode*, Pan in *Midas*, the original Father Paul in Sheridan's new comic opera *The Duenna*, Austria in *King John*, a principal character unspecified in *Prometheus*, Dionysius in *The Grecian Daughter*, and Sir Patrick in *The Irish Widow*; and in 1776–77, Leander in *The Padlock*, the Duke in *Venice Preserv'd*, Mercury in *The Golden Pippin*, Mervin in *The Maid of the Mill*, Prometheus in *Harlequin's Frolicks*, Granger in *The Refusal*, Rimenes in *Artaxerxes*, Caliban in *The Tempest*, Connelly in *The School for Wives*, O'Donnelly in *The Device*, O'Clabber in *The Reprisal*, the original Mars and Pike in Charles Dibdin's burletta *Poor Vulcan!*, an unspecified role in *True Blue*, and Ballad in *The Country Mad-Cap*. In 1778–79 he added a principal singing part in James Messink's new pantomime *The Medley*, the original Beaufort in Frederick Pilon's farce *The Invasion*, the original Watchman in Dibdin's new pantomime *The Touchstone*, one of the Mob in Pilon's new prelude *The Illumination*, Hatchway in *The Fair Quaker*, and the original Platoon in Dibdin's comic opera *The Chelsea Pensioner*; in 1782–83, Noodle in *Tom Thumb*, the Lieutenant of the Tower in *Richard III*, the original Sanguino in John O'Keeffe's *The Castle of Andalusia*, Lenox in *Macbeth*, Douglas in *1 Henry IV*, the Player King in *Hamlet*, the original Sestius in Richard Bentley's tragedy *Philodamus*, the original Another Irishman in Francis Brooke's comic opera *Rosina*, the original Captain in William Cooke's *The Capricious Lady*, Conrade in *Much Ado about Nothing*, Siberto in *The Pilgrim*, and the Sea Captain in *Twelfth Night*; and in 1783–84,

Lieutenant O'Connor in *St. Patrick's Day*, Maurice in *The Positive Man*, Montano in *Othello*, Francisco in *The Chances*, Rapino in *The Castle of Andalusia*, and a Sportsman in O'Keeffe's new afterpiece *Harlequin Rambler*.

The entry for Robert Mahon in *The Thespian Dictionary* (1805) which says that "He went abroad, and married a West Indian lady," confuses him with some other Mahon.

Mahon, Sarah. *See* SECOND, MRS JOHN.

Mahon, William   *c.1750–1816, clarinettist, violinist, oboist.*

William Mahon was born about 1750, probably at Salisbury, a member of a family of musicians of probable Irish origin. His parents were very likely musicians performing at the Oxford Music Room, where he made his own debut as an oboist. His siblings were James, a singer; John, the esteemed clarinettist; Sarah, a singer, who became Mrs John Second; Miss M., a singer, who married John Warton; the Miss Mahon, a singer, who became Mrs Munday; and the Miss Mahon, also a singer, who became Mrs Ambrose.

William's career is at some points hard or impossible to distinguish from that of his brother John. One of the two (probably John) figured as clarinettist at the Haymarket Theatre in 1772–73 and 1774–75. *Felix Farley's Bristol Journal* of 27 November 1773 noted that "Mr. Mahon, the Performer on the Clarionet," was engaged to play a series of subscription concerts led by Shaw in the Great Room in Prince's Street, Bristol. Almost certainly William was one of the players in the performance of François Joseph Gossec's "Symphony with Clarinets" performed at the Oxford Music Room on 21 February 1774. He (or John) was the "Mahoon" playing a concerto on the clarinet at a performance of Dr Samuel J. Arnold's oratorio *Resurrection* at the Pantheon on 4 April 1774.

Like his brother John, William was a versatile musician. He played the viola in the Handel Memorial Concerts at Westminster Abbey and the Pantheon in 1784 and again at the Abbey in 1786. For thirty years he was violinist and leader of the festival orchestra at Salisbury. He was not a member of the Royal Society of Musicians, as John was, but subscribed to the New Musical Fund and is on surviving lists of 1795, 1805, and 1815. Doane's *Musical Directory* (1794) suggests that he played in oratorios at Drury Lane, but the only oratorio bill surviving in which he figured was that of 11 March 1791 for Covent Garden Theatre. One Mahon played violin, the other clarinet, at subscription concerts in Bristol's Assembly Rooms in November 1791. Doane says that he played also at Ranelagh Gardens. Doubtless he played with effect at many places now unrecorded, for in his obituary the *Gentleman's Magazine* stated that he was "esteemed the first performer on the clarinet in England." He was living at No 11, Margaret Street, Cavendish Square, in 1794. He died in Salisbury on 3 May 1816.

Mahoney, Mr [*fl. 1798–1800*], *watchman.*

One Mahoney was engaged as a watchman at Drury Lane Theatre in the seasons of 1798–99 and 1799–1800.

Maicia. *See* MALIZIA.

Maillard, [François?], **stage name of Mons Cavé** [*fl. 1711–1726*], *actor, dancer.*

Monsieur Cavé, called Maillard, was, according to Marian Hannah Winter in *The Pre-Romantic Ballet*, a Scaramouch in Nivelon's troupe at the Saint-Germain fair in 1711. She gives his name as François Maillard and identifies the columbine in that company as Mlle Maillard; Fuchs in his *Lexique* has Maillard's wife down as the columbine. Fuchs lists Maillard as a member of Beaune's company from 1712 to 1716, after which he toured the provinces from 1718 to 1720, returning to the fair in 1721. François Maillard was at the Hague in 1722–23.

Though Fuchs makes no mention of a Maillard appearing in London, it is certain that an actor of that name was the scaramouch in the French troupe that played at the Haymarket Theatre from 24 March to 11 May 1726. We cannot be certain that he was François. Maillard was in *Arlequin major ridicule chasseur et docteur chinoix* and *Octave dragon*, for on 3 May those works had to be canceled due to his illness. On 9 May he was one of four harlequins in an entr'acte turn.

Maillard's wife, according to Fuchs, performed in the French provinces in Dolet's company for eight years and married Maillard at Bésançon. She acted in the provinces with Baron, Baxter, and Sorin and died in 1721. Winter has it that Mlle Maillard (presumably our subject's daughter) was "well known in London," but we have found no record of her performing there.

Maillardet, Henri [*fl. 1783–1800*], *exhibitor.*

Henri Maillardet was a Swiss clockmaker who was manager of the London branch of a Geneva firm from 1783 to about 1790, according to Richard Altick's *The Shows of London*. He made and exhibited a harpischord-playing automaton called "The Musical Lady." An organ mechanism with registers and bellows made the figure bow to the audience as she sat at the keyboard, look at the notes of music, heave her bosom, express anxiety with her moving eyes, beat time with her feet, and touch the keys with her fingers. She played some 16 to 18 melodies, and at the end of her recital she rose and bowed. Maillardet also exhibited an automaton writer-draftsman and a magician.

By March 1800, as the *Monthly Mirror* tells us, Maillardet was exhibiting at Spring Gardens:

WE are much gratified in saying, that the proprietor and inventor of the interesting curiosities contained in this elegant room, has had, during the late fine weather, his full portion of fashionables.

By means of a glass instrument, furnished with a patent lamp, all the effect of sun-light, is now thrown on the brilliant and varied coating of his preserved *natural* insect—the beautiful and curious native of a foreign kingdom.

Main, Richard de la [*fl. 1720*], *violist.*

Pepusch listed Richard de la Main as a "violino tenore" who played at Cannons in 1720 for £5 per quarter.

Maine, John [*fl. 1721–1730*], *gallery keeper.*

John Maine, the first gallery keeper at Lincoln's Inn Fields, was noticed regularly in the benefit bills from 6 June 1721 to 1 June 1730. He ordinarily shared his benefits with two others, and the gross income usually ran over £100. At his last benefit the receipts came to a healthy £167 4s. The accounts are not clear about Maine's salary; on 16 September 1726, he, with Naylor, was paid 10s. for three days, but one cannot tell if they split the money or if each received 10s. Though usually cited as a gallery keeper, Maine was sometimes referred to as the gallery doorkeeper.

Maiorano, Gaetano. *See* CAFFARELLI.

Maire. *See* MAER.

Maisia. *See* MALIZIA.

Maitland, Mr [*fl.* 1720], *house servant?*
Mr Maitland shared a benefit with three others at Lincoln's Inn Fields Theatre on 2 June 1720. He was probably one of the house servants, as were others on the benefit list.

Maiy, Camillo [*fl.* 1796], *acrobat.*
Camillo Maiy was listed in the Sadler's Wells bill of 5 April 1796 as "an astonishing little Boy." The bill of 16 May cited him as a member of Concetto Coco's troupe of Sicilian acrobats, but the advertisement did not describe what Maiy did.

Majo. *See* DE MAJO.

Major, Miss [*fl.* 1745–1747], *actress.*
Miss Major appeared as Trusty in *The Provok'd Husband* at Goodman's Fields Theatre on 4 November 1745 and returned there on 10 February 1747 to act Kitty in *The Lying Valet* and Edging in *The Careless Husband*. The bill on 20 February was reported differently in two papers: the *General Advertiser* said Miss Moreau played Kitty that date, but the *Daily Advertiser* said Miss Major repeated the role.

Major, Joseph 1771–1829, *violinist, violist, pianist, organist.*
According to testimony presented to the Royal Society of Musicians, Joseph Major was born at No 20, St Martin le Grand, in the parish of St Ann Aldersgate, on 23 December 1771, the son of Samuel Major, music publisher, and his wife Amy, the daughter of Joseph Stenson of Derby. Joseph's father was a musician and had a music shop at his home, No 35, Duke Street, West Smithfield, Lon-

By permission of the Trustees of the British Museum
JOSEPH MAJOR
engraving by Godby, after Engleheart

don, and doubtless had a hand in Joseph's musical training. By 16 February 1790 Joseph had already established himself as a performer: on that date he played a sonata on the pianoforte at a concert at Paul's Head Tavern, Cateaton Street.

Doane's *Musical Directory* of 1794 listed Major as Joseph Junior (though we know of no Joseph Senior) and stated that he was an organist and violist, a member of the Amicable Society, the organist of Knightsbridge Chapel, and a participant in the Handelian concerts at Westminster Abbey. His address was given as that of his father Samuel. On 4 May of that year Joseph Major was proposed for membership in the Royal Society of Musicians. He was described as a violist and still single. He ran two schools and had other business which, he said, had brought him £200 annually the two preceding years and was increasing. Major was admitted to the Society in September 1794 and, beginning May 1795, participated in the annual St Paul's Concert as a violist, or sometimes as a violinist. He served the Society as a Governor from 1797.

Major continued active at least through 1806,

and we know that on 27 March 1800 at Mrs Franklin's Concert at Willis's Rooms he accompanied his friend Incledon in a song that "was loudly and deservedly encored." The biography of John Bannister by Adolphus notes that Major was a long-time friend of Bannister, who said on 20 December 1828, "Major, whom I saw today, is dangerously afflicted with dropsy. He is of the opinion that he shall never quit his house more. He has dined with me on Christmas-day for thirty-eight years." Major died soon after that, evidently in 1829.

Adolphus described Major as a person universally liked, a pianist, frequent accompanist of Incledon, and a composer of "many good melodies." Oddly, Adolphus said that Major had pursued the "bent of his genius" against his family's wishes.

In the British Museum is an undated proof engraving by J. Godby, after P. Engleheart, of Joseph Major.

Major, Samuel [fl. 1771–1825], violoncellist, violist.

Samuel Major was the father of the musician Joseph Major, who was born at No 20, St Martin le Grand, in the parish of St Ann, Aldersgate, on 23 December 1771. That is the earliest record we have of Samuel. Sometime before that, presumably, he had married Amy Stenson, daughter of the bookseller Joseph Stenson of Derby. By about 1778 the Majors were living at No 35, Duke Street, West Smithfield, London, where Samuel ran a music publishing and selling business. Doane's *Musical Directory* of 1794 listed Samuel as a violoncellist and violist (tenor) and a member of the Cecilian Society. The *Monthly Mirror* reported in January 1800 that Mrs Major had died. The date of Samuel Major's death is not known, but Humphries and Smith's *Music Publishing in the British Isles* lists Major as still active as a music seller in 1825.

Samuel Major was very likely related in some way to a number of others of that name with musical interests. A Robert Major had been a wind instrumentalist in the King's Music in 1625; Richard Major was a music engraver at No 10, Broad Street, Bristol, in 1811; an R. Major was a music publisher at No 43, Bedford Street, the Strand, from about 1800 to 1818 and at No 7, High Holborn, in 1820;

and a William Major had a printing shop and sold music at St John's Steps, Bristol, in 1819.

Majorano or Majorno. *See* CAFFARELLI.

Malchair, Johann Baptist 1730–1812, violinist, singer, composer.

The *New Grove* says that Johann Baptist Malchair (or Malscher) was born in Cologne and was christened on 15 January 1730. He was the son of a watchmaker. Malchair was a chorister in Cologne until 1750, when he went to Nancy. In 1754 he came to England, and in London he taught music and drawing, was a violinist, and promoted concerts. He lived for a while in Lewes, Bristol, and Hereford and by 1759 had settled in Oxford, where the following year he was appointed leader of the band at the Oxford Music Room, a post he held for 33 years. In 1760 Malchair married Elizabeth Jenner of Oxford, who died on 14 August 1773.

Malchair became a close friend of the organist William Crotch, organist of Christ Church from 1790. Malchair was a collector of national melodies, aided Crotch in his *Specimens of Various Styles of Music*, and brought him tunes to write down. Malchair was a skillful artist and made many drawings in and around Oxford. In the 1790s his sight began to fail him. He broke his shin against a wheelbarrow in 1799 and twice fell down stairs at his house. Malchair died in Oxford on 12 December 1812.

Male, Mrs [fl. 1735], actress.

Mrs Male played the title role in *Jane Shore* and Colombine in *The Carnival* on 17 September 1735 at the Haymarket Theatre and Maria in *George Barnwell* at York Buildings the following 1 October.

Male, Miss [fl. 1736–1737], actress.

Miss Male was a Nymph of the Chace in *The Royal Chace* at Covent Garden Theatre on 23 January 1736. The following 16 April she played Ophelia in *Hamlet* at Lincoln's Inn Fields, and then a month later she was Lettice in *The Intriguing Chambermaid* at Covent Garden. During the 1736–37 season at Covent Garden she was seen as Delia in *Theodosius*, Elvira in *The Spanish Fryar*, and Phillida in *Damon and Phillida*.

Male, George *d. 1815, dancer, actor, machinist, contriver of pantomimes.*

On 26 November 1796 George Male made his first stage appearance as Friday (a harlequin character) in *Robinson Crusoe* at Drury Lane. He repeated that role many times that winter and added Tamuri in *Lodoiska*. In 1797–98 he was seen as Ralph in *Catherine and Petruchio* and a Male Slave in *Blue-Beard*, a bit part which kept him occupied until December 1798 of the following season. He danced in *The Captive of Spilburg* in November of 1798. Male was also a harlequin at Sadler's Wells in 1797 and 1798. The Drury Lane accounts show that Male (or Mayle) was paid £2 weekly through the 1808–9 season and in 1807 danced at the Haymarket; yet an entry in the accounts for 1804–1806 listed him at £6 weekly at Drury Lane. That higher amount may have been pay for serving as a pantomime contriver, which James De Castro, in his *Memoirs*, says Male was. We know that in 1807 he helped on either the machines or decorations for the pantomime *Furibond*.

Beginning as early as 29 May 1800, Male was active at the Royal Circus; on that date he danced Harlequin in *Harlequin Highlander*, a serio-comic Scotch pantomime. On 11 April 1803 the Royal Circus bill said that Male, along with Honour and Collet, was responsible for the machinery and pantomimical tricks for *The Rival Statues*, and later that month Male danced in *Louisa of Lombardy*, a musical spectacle. That November he was the Lawyer in *The Black Forest* and Captain Courtwell in the burletta *Flats and Sharps*. In May and June 1804 he was in *The Wild Girl* and appeared as Old Robin in *Haste to the Wedding*. According to Wewitzer, George Male died in July 1815.

Malizia, Signora [*fl. 1783–1786*], *dog trainer. See* MALIZIA, MICHAEL.

Malizia, John [*fl. 1783–1786*], *dog trainer. See* MALIZIA, MICHAEL.

Malizia, Michael [*fl. 1783–1786*], *dog trainer.*

On 7 (April?) 1783, apparently at Astley's Amphitheatre, Signor and Signora "Maisia" gave an exhibition of dancing dogs "from France & Italy" which concluded with a "variety of Dogs dressed en militaire; & Two inimitable Bull Dogs. . . ." That clipping is augmented by another from May 1785 which describes an English bull dog who grabbed a rope in his mouth and was drawn up in the air: "rather than quit his hold, [he] suffers himself to be drawn 30 ft. high, whilst the machine is surrounded with Fireworks, representing a heavy discharge of small arms & artillery."

Other notices from 1785 described some of the other feats of activity the "Maicias" had taught their dogs: two dogs acted as chairmen and carried a monkey to a masquerade; two dogs carried milk pails on yokes; a company of dogs carried a basket of grapes from a vineyard, accompanied by a Savoyard with a magic table; a dog imitated a lady of quality in her equipage, attended by other dogs in elegant liveries; a dog performed a spin; a dog walked on any two of his legs; two dogs imitated a tumbler and his attendant clown; and a dog dressed in a Spanish habit took another dog to a boarding school. The dogs performed frequently at Astley's through 4 September 1786.

Surely the trainers in question were the ones cited in the Bristol papers on 29 July 1786: "Michael Malizia, John Malizia, and Bernard Franket, all Neapolitans" were taken up as they were parading the streets of Bristol with dancing dogs. They were cited as vagrants and flogged at St Peter's Hospital. The bills at Astley's in London coincidentally show a gap in the exhibitions of dancing dogs there from 24 July to 4 September 1786. It is not possible to determine from the evidence collected whether Signora Malizia was the wife of John or Michael.

Mall. *See* MELL.

Mallet, John *d. 1798, bassoonist, bass player?*

In May and June 1784 John Mallet played bassoon in the Handel Memorial Concerts at Westminster Abbey and the Pantheon. As a member of the Royal Society of Musicians he participated similarly in the St Paul's Concerts in May 1785, 1789, 1791, and 1792. But in August of the last year he petitioned the Society for financial aid because of his poor state of health, and thereafter he participated no further in their concerts. The Society granted him an allowance of four guineas a month. By 6 July 1794 Mallet informed the Society that he had procured an engagement with a regiment that allowed him to relinquish his claim. Doane's *Musical Directory* of 1794 lists no regimental playing for Mallet, but Doane did state that Mallet was a bassoonist and a bass (player? singer?) who performed at the Royal Circus and at Covent Garden in the oratorios.

When his engagement with the regiment ended in October 1794 Mallet applied again for an allowance, and the Royal Society of Musicians reinstated his four guineas monthly. When on 4 February 1798 the Society was informed by Mary Mallet that her husband John had died, she was given £8 for funeral expenses. In May 1807 Mary told the Society that she had been confined for some months due to a severe hurt; she was granted one guinea. By March 1822 she was over 60 and received a grant of £2 16s. (monthly?). She died shortly before 7 November 1830, when the Society paid for her funeral.

Mallin, ₁Edward?₁ ₁*fl.* 1720?–1744₁, *actor.*

A Mr Mallin (or Mallen, Mollin) played Polonius in *Hamlet* at the Haymarket Theatre on 29 June 1744 and two subsequent performances. Possibly he was the Edward "Mallan" who was cited several times in the registers of St Paul, Covent Garden. Margaret the daughter of Edward and Sarah Mallan was christened on 17 April 1720. Their son John was christened on 8 October 1721 and buried on 6 May 1722; their daughter Mary was christened on 5 May 1723 and buried the following 19 June; and a second John was christened on 22 March 1725 and buried two days later. Edward's wife Sarah was buried on 24 April 1726.

Malloin, Miss ₁*fl.* 1728₁, *actress, dancer.*

Miss Malloin played Gypsy in *The Rivals*, "A Dramatick Entertainment of Dancing in Grotesque Characters" presented by Mme Violante at the Haymarket Theatre on 21 February 1728. A Mr Millon was also in the cast, and it is likely that one of the two names was incorrectly spelled in the bill.

Malmes, Mr ₁*fl.* 1784₁, *singer.*

Mr Malmes sang tenor in the Handel Memorial Concerts at Westminster Abbey and the Pantheon in May and June 1784.

Malone. *See also* MELLON.

Malone, Mr ₁*fl.* 1732–1750₁, *actor, booth operator.*

On 4 August 1732 Mr Malone played Hellebore in *The Mock Doctor* and a Carrier in *The Metamorphosis of Harlequin* at the booth in Cherry Tree Garden, near the Mote, at Tottenham Court. Malone was not cited again in London bills until 4 August 1741, when at Middleton's booth at Tottenham Court he acted Don Drub in *The Rival Queens*. Two years later to the day he played Noailles, and his wife acted the title role, in *The Glorious Queen of Hungary* at a Tottenham Court booth operated by Malone, Daniels, and James. They acted in it again at Bartholomew Fair on 23 August.

At Southwark Fair on 8 September 1743 Malone was Westford in *The Blind Beggar of Bethnal Green*. He was Mat in *The Beggar's Opera* on 30 December 1745 at the New Wells, Clerkenwell. Malone played Peachum in *The Beggar's Opera* at Hickford's Music Room in Panton Street on 10 March 1746, and on the fourteenth he was granted a benefit there. On 8 September at Southwark Fair he was Don John in *The Fate of Villainy*. At the New Wells he acted Perriwinkle in *A Bold Stroke for a Wife* on 26 December 1748, and three days later there he played Thorogood in *The London Merchant*.

At Southwark on 9 January 1749 he was Ballance in *The Recruiting Officer*; at Goodman's Fields on 27 February he played Day in *The Committee*; and on 23 August he acted Sir Thomas Rash in *The Adventures of Sir Lubberly Lackbrains* at Bartholomew Fair. Malone's last notice seems to have been on 7 September 1750, when he appeared as Zekel in *Jephtha's Rash Vow* at Southwark Fair.

Malone, Mrs ₁*fl.* 1743₁, *actress. See* MALONE, MR ₁*fl.* 1732–1750₁.

Malscher. *See also* MALCHAIR.

Malter, Mons ₁*fl.* 1733–1750₁, *dancer, actor.*

The Monsieur Malter (sometimes Maltere) who danced on the London stage between 1733 and 1750 was a member of a family of dancers from Lyon that performed all over Europe. Some details on the family are provided in

Lexique des troupes de comédiens au XVIIIe siècle by Fuchs, who concludes that while the Malters were certainly numerous it is impossible to establish precise relationships. "Malter l'anglais" was perhaps the same dancer sometimes called "Malter l'oiseau"; he was the brother of François-Duval Malter, *maître de ballet* of the Paris Opéra at mid-century.

When Malter was brought to London by Marie Sallé in 1733 he was a relatively unknown figure compared to several Malters who were esteemed performers at the Opéra. Mlle Sallé left Paris over petty disagreements at the Opéra; David Dumoulain, her regular partner in their celebrated pas de deux, remained, so she was required to seek another. The Paris press sneered: "Mlle Sallé is creating her Dumoulain out of a little Malter, whom she is taking with her to London. This Malter is known only in the provinces, where he has preferred to be in the first rank instead of one among many here."

Announced as "newly arrived," Malter and Mlle Sallé appeared at Covent Garden Theatre on 8 November 1733, and they quickly became a popular team, dancing regularly throughout the season. Among the character dances and ballets they presented were *A French Sailor and his Lass*, *The Nassau*, *Shepherd and Shepherdess*, *Pigmalion*, and *Apollo and Daphne*. For his benefit on 17 April 1734, he offered a harlequin dance and performed *Pigmalion* with his partner. At that time both lodged at Mr Grignon's, a watchmaker in Russell Street, Covent Garden.

The following season Malter returned to London as a member of the company of French-speaking comedians brought by Francisque to play at the Haymarket Theatre four times a week from 26 October 1734 through 3 June 1735. With Malter that time was Mme Malter, presumably his wife. He acted L'Exempt in *Tartuffe* on 20 November, Gallomier in *Le Joueur* on 13 December, and the Apothecary in *Le Malade imaginaire* on 23 December. He played Pierrot in *Arlequin Balourd* and danced Dame Jigogne in a new chaconne on 27 December. His other assignments during the French company's tenure included Pierrot in *La Fille capitain et Arlequin son sergeant*, the Bridegroom (with Mme Malter the Bride) in *Le Festin de Pierre*, Pierrot in *La Fausse coquette*, and Lubin in *George Dandin*. He also played Pierrot in

L'Embarras de richesses when the company performed at Goodman's Fields Theatre on 23 May 1735.

In 1740–41 a Mons Malter (presumably l'anglais) was again in London, this time at Drury Lane Theatre, where he and "Mlle" Malter, (presumably Madame Malter) "lately arrived from the Opera in Paris," made their debuts in a *Grand Ballet* on 3 November 1740. Throughout the season they appeared in numerous specialty dances. For their benefit on 9 April 1741, when tickets were available at their lodgings with Mr Farnel in Bridges Street, they performed a *Sailor's Dance*, an *Indian Dance* ("never in England before") and *La Rose Borée et Ziphirs*.

Their names were absent from London playbills for a decade, until 1749–50, when they returned to Drury Lane, this time with a dancing son. On 6 January 1750 Malter's name was added to the salary list and he was paid £5 10s. for the previous 11 days. The elder Malter's name appeared in the bills infrequently that season, and perhaps the payments were being made to him for the work of his son and his pupils, the Misses Forcade, who made their London debuts on 19 December 1749 in dances called *The Swedish Gardeners* and *The Wooden Shoe*. The prompter Cross entered in his diary next day: "Maltere's children first danc'd (well)." The children were seen in these dances throughout the season, including their benefit night, 1 May 1750.

These Malters seem to have left London after the 1749–50 season to resume their continental activities. (It is unlikely that either the father or the son was the Malter who performed at the Royalty Theatre 37 years later.)

In her *Pre-Romantic Ballet*, Winter indicates that a daughter of the English Malter married the Dutch dancer Frederic Sluyter, known as Sieur Frédéric, whose children Caroline and Charlotte Frédéric also performed in Holland.

Malter, Mons [*fl.* 1787–1790], *dancer, choreographer.*

A Mons Malter, no doubt a member of a French family of dancers noted by Fuchs in his *Lexique des troupes de comédiens au XVIIIe siècle*, danced and composed dances at Palmer's Royalty Theatre in 1787–88. On 3 July 1787 he performed his dance *The Triumph of Cupid* with Mme Constance and was seen in the chorus of such pieces as *Harlequin Mungo* in November. He also composed the dances for *The Deserter of Naples*, a pantomime directed by Delpini which had at least 39 performances that season. In the summer of 1790 Malter was working at Hughes's Royal Circus; he danced his own creation, *Punch's Wedding*, on 3 July and with Miss Hamoir appeared in *A Dance of Savages* on 12 August.

Malter, Mme ₁*fl. 1740–1750*₁, *dancer.* *See* **MALTER, MONS** ₁*fl. 1733–1750*₁.

Malter, Master ₁*fl. 1749–1750*₁, *dancer.* *See* **MALTER, MONS** ₁*fl. 1733–1750*₁.

Malter, Mlle. *See* **MALTER, MONS** ₁*fl. 1733–1750*₁.

Malton, Thomas *1748–1804, scene painter, architectural draughtsman.*

Thomas Malton was born in 1748, probably in London, the eldest son of the architectural draughtsman and writer on geometry Thomas Malton the elder (1726–1801), who is noticed in *The Dictionary of National Biography*. His father, originally an upholsterer in the Strand, exhibited drawings at the Free Society of Artists in 1761 and at the Incorporated Society of Artists in 1766 and 1768 and also sent drawings to the Royal Academy. In 1774 the elder Malton published *The Royal Road to Geometry* and in 1775 *A Compleat Treatise on Perspective in Theory and Practice, on the Principles of Dr. Brook Taylor*. A younger brother, James Malton (d. 1803), also noticed in *The Dictionary of National Biography*, followed the father's profession, publishing treatises on perspective and drawing.

Young Thomas Malton learned his skills from his father, whom he accompanied to Dublin in 1769. In Dublin he also worked for three years in the architectural offices of James Gandon, until he was dismissed for irregular attendance. He returned to London in 1773 to enter the Royal Academy school. Malton conducted his main professional activities in London (except for a brief stay at Bath in 1780), residing in Conduit Street from 1783 to 1789 and sub-

THOMAS MALTON
engraving by Barney, after Stuart

sequently in Great Titchfield Street from 1791 to 1796 and then in Longacre. In 1774 he received a premium from the Society of Arts and a silver medal from the Royal Academy; he received in 1782 a gold medal from the Royal Academy for a design of a theatre. He became a regular exhibitor at the Royal Academy, chiefly of tinted scenes in India ink of London streets and buildings, which because of accuracy of detail retain great value as topographical records.

In 1786 Malton decorated the Rotunda at Vauxhall Gardens with a large transparent painting of a large hall through which was viewed the perspective of a garden. His publications include drawings for Watts's *Seats of the Nobility and Gentry* (1779) and his own chief work, *A Picturesque Tour through the Cites of London and Westminster* (1792), illustrated with 100 aquatint plates. Among his pupils in the evening drawing classes he offered at his Conduit Street residence was Joseph M. W. Turner, who later often claimed "My real master was Tom Malton."

Between January 1780 and December 1781 Malton received payments (totaling £77 14s. in 1780–81 and £60 18s. in 1781–82) for painting scenes at Drury Lane Theatre, where De Loutherbourg was chief designer. In 1782 he received £8 from Tate Wilkinson at York for painting a scene of Portia's palace. In 1790–91 he worked at Covent Garden Theatre, earning £90 and painting scenery with Richards, Carver, Hodgins, Pugh, and W. Hamilton for *The Picture of Paris*, a new pantomime afterpiece concocted by Charles Bonnor and Robert Merry.

In January 1793 Malton very skillfully painted a palace scene for the Margravine of Anspach's private theatre in Brandenburgh House. His efforts at Covent Garden Theatre in 1793–94 included, with Richards, Hodgins, and others, an elaborate thirteen-scene production of James Wild's pantomime *Harlequin and Faustus* on 19 December 1793. One of the scenes specifically credited to Malton's design and execution was a representation of the scaffolding prepared for the building of the new Drury Lane Theatre as it appeared in July and which changed to a view of that theatre as it would appear when completed. The press reported that this scene "does infinite credit to the architectural talents of that ingenious artist, who is to have the entire management of that particular department of scenery at the Theatre he has thus given so correct a view of."

When Kemble's new Drury Lane opened toward the end of that season, Malton was employed with Capon, Greenwood, and others on the scenes for *Macbeth*, the first dramatic offering, on 21 April 1794; and with Greenwood, Luppino, and Demaria he prepared the premiere of Kemble's *Lodoiska* on 9 June. Account books now at the Folger Shakespeare Library indicate that he received periodic payments from Drury Lane between 19 March and 25 June 1794 totaling about £163 10s. In 1794–95 he received £174 19s. and in 1795–96 £128, but he seems not to have been one of the major painters there during those years.

After 1796 Malton's work for the stage seems to have ceased. Sybil Rosenfeld points out that at a time when landscape scenery was preeminent, "he was an architectural painter who concentrated on perspective." In his *London Theatres* (1795), Thomas Bellamy praised

Judicious MALTON! *Thy receding scene,*
Of architectural beauty so deceives
The eye of Admiration, that we ask—
"Is this majestic view, unreal *all?"*

Malton died in Longacre of a "putrid fever" on 7 March 1804, leaving a widow and six children. In his will made on 12 August 1799 and proved at London on 6 April 1804, he left his unspecified estate to his wife, unnamed in the document. One of his children was "a Cadet in India." Another, Charles Malton, was a pupil of Sir John Soane and won the Royal Academy Silver Medal in 1807 but did not work as an architect. Charles's portrait, as a child, was painted by Lawrence and engraved by F. C. Lewis. Regina Clementi Malton (b. 1764), who was the sister of the musician Muzio Clementi and received £200 in his will of 1832, may have been related to Thomas Malton.

At the time of his death he had been working on a series of views of Oxford, some of which had appeared in 1802 and then were reissued with additions in 1810. Gilbert Stuart's portrait of Malton was engraved by W. W. Barney and published by J. P. Thompson in 1806.

Man. *See also* MANN.

Man, Mary [fl. 1661–1667], actress.
The Lord Chamberlain's accounts cited Mary Man as an actress in the King's Company on 27 March 1661. *The London Stage* lists her in the company roster in 1663–64 and 1666–67.

Manage. *See* MENAGE.

Manasier. *See* MANESIÈRE.

"Manchester Roscius, The." *See* COOKE, GEORGE FREDERICK.

Manchip. *See* MANSHIP.

Mancia, Luigi [fl. 1687–1708], singer, instrumentalist, composer.
Luigi Mancia (or Manza) was perhaps born in the province of Venice, according to the *New*

Grove, and may have been the Manza at Hanover in 1687. He may also have been the Manza who composed some music for the *pasticcio Arione*, which was presented in Milan in 1694. In 1695–96 he composed three operas for Rome, and in 1697 he wrote an opera for Hanover. He sang in Berlin in October 1697 and composed operas for the Spanish viceregal theatre in Naples in 1698–99.

Grove does not note that Mancia came to London in 1701, singing at Drury Lane on 31 January 1701. He was advertised as formerly servant to the King of Spain and before his Drury Lane appearance had sung at Hampton Court. In October 1703 Mancia was in Düsseldorf, and in 1707 he returned to London with Charles Montagu, Duke of Manchester, the ambassador extraordinary to Venice. Manchester wrote to Sarah, Duchess of Marlborough, that Mancia had served Queen Sophie Charlotte, spoke French and German, and performed "on all instruments, bassoon, guitar, hautboy, and harpsichord in perfection." Mancia's last operas were performed in 1708.

Mancini, Rosa [*fl.* 1743–1744], *singer.*
On 17 November 1743, after seeing Signora Mancini two days before at the King's Theatre as Lisaura in *Rossana*, Horace Walpole wrote to Horace Mann that "The Rosa Mancini, who is second woman [at the opera], is now old." She sang only one season, appearing as Elvira in *Alphonso*, Clelia in *Rosalinda*, and Barsene in *Alceste*.

Mandet. *See* MAUDET.

"Mandolin Player, The." *See* FELIX, SIGNOR.

Manesière, Louisa, later Mrs James Fishar
d. 1775, dancer.
Signora Louisa Manesière had arrived in London by 31 October 1761, for on that day the treasurer of Covent Garden Theatre advanced her £50 on her salary. She made her first appearance on the English stage at that house on 10 December 1761 dancing with Sodi and Miss Wilford in a new comic ballet *The French Gentleman; or, The Female Metamorphoses*, in the presence of the royal family. That

piece was repeated several times, and on 28 January 1762 she danced Daphne in a revival of *Apollo and Daphne*, which was concluded with a *Grand Ballet* by her and Sodi. With him she danced a new comic ballet called *The Pleasures of Spring* on 12 February. Another new comic dance, *Les Sabotiers*, featuring her, Sodi, Maranesi, and Mlle Capdeville, was performed on 19 April 1762. According to *The London Stage*, in which she is sometimes mistakenly listed as a male dancer, a pay list of 26 November 1761 indicates that Signora Manesière received an approximate salary of £210 for her first season.

Over the next 12 years Signora Manesière continued as a serviceable featured dancer at Covent Garden, performing over that period in a host of specialty numbers and ballets. On 23 October 1762 she appeared with Duquesney in *The Jealous Woodcutter* on the night he made his English debut. In *The Sicilian Peasants* on 24 November 1762 she danced the Man Peasant to Miss Wilford's Woman. On other occasions she performed a hornpipe in male character. Other ballets in which she appeared were *Venus Reveng'd*, *Hymen's Triumph*, *Les Matelots provençals*, *The Village Romps*, *The Gallant Shepherds*, *Rural Love*, *The Lamp Lighters*, and *The Tartars*, to cite but a few. Her salary in 1767–68 was £1 1s. per day. Her provincial engagements included Smock Alley, Dublin, in 1763–64, Sadler's Wells in the summers of 1765, 1766, 1767, and 1769, and Bristol in the summer of 1767.

Illness evidently prevented her appearance at Covent Garden in 1773–74, her last season there, until 15 April 1774, when she performed a minuet and allemande with James Fishar, the Covent Garden ballet-master with whom she had frequently appeared over the years since his debut in January 1764. She had lived with him for some years. During her last illness, according to the prompter Hopkins's diary, they married. On 10 August 1775 the *Morning Chronicle* reported that Mrs Fishar, late Signora Manesière, had died at Guildford on 7 August. She was buried on 13 August 1775 at St Mary's, Guildford, where her full name was recorded in the register.

According to Hopkins she had some property and "was a pattern of neatness and exterior modesty." Her husband was still living at

Guildford in 1780. A dancer named Miss Manasier (later Mrs Weston), who performed at Sadler's Wells from 1808 to 1817 and then at the Coburg, may have been related to Signora Manesière.

Manessier, Elisha [fl. 1784–1805], oboist, flutist.

Elisha Manessier (or Manissire, Menessier) played second oboe in the Handel Memorial Concerts at Westminster Abbey and the Pantheon in May and June 1784. In 1787–88 he was paid £6 for playing in the Concerts of the Academy of Ancient Music. Doane's *Musical Directory* of 1794 listed Manessier as an oboist and flutist who subscribed to the New Musical Fund (he was on the Court of Assistants in 1794 and 1805) and played at Sadler's Wells Theatre as well as in the Ancient Music concerts. His address was given as No 2, Aldersgate Buildings, Goswell Street. On 15 January 1798 at the Haymarket Theatre, Manessier participated in a performance of the *Messiah*.

Manet. *See* MOWAT.

"Mango, Ballard" [fl. 1752–1753], trained monkey?

Signor Ballard's trained animals entertained at the Haymarket Theatre from 11 December 1752 to 10 March 1753 as part of "Mrs Midnight's" (Christopher Smart's) show. On 1 March Ballard advertised that

As my Monkeys and me and my Dogs are promised to go to L'Haye and Vienna after some Days more, the grand Noblemans and Gentlemans of this Nation England do desire me to perform every Night, so me shall do with Mrs. Midnight at the Haymarket Playhouse this Thursday Night. Ballard Mango, my big Monkey, will talk the *Prologue*.

It is possible that "Ballard Mango" was a man, not a "big monkey" (i.e., ape), and that he really spoke a prologue.

Manina, Maria. *See* FLETCHER, MARIA.

Manio, Signora. *See* FLETCHER, MARIA.

Manisier. *See* MANESIÈRE.

Manley, John [fl. 1739], musician.

John Manley was one of the original subscribers to the Royal Society of Musicians when it was established on 28 August 1739.

Manly, Mr [fl. 1742–1743], actor.

At the James Street Theatre a Mr Manly acted Mentor in *Ulysses* on 31 May 1742 and the title part in *Don Sebastian* on 5 January 1743.

Mann, Mrs [fl. 1765–1772], dresser.

A Drury Lane paylist dated 9 February 1765 cites Mrs Mann as one of the women's dressers at a daily salary of 1s. 6d., or 9s. weekly. On 4 June 1767 Mrs "Man" was loaned £2 2s. by the management. She was again paid £2 2s. on 16 June 1772 "on note."

Mann, [Mary?] [fl. 1728–1746], actress, dancer.

For almost 20 years a woman named Mann (sometimes Man) acted and danced in the London theatres, and though she was usually styled Miss Mann, throughout her career she was sometimes called Mrs Mann. To complicate matters further, she was identified in a playbill in 1732 as "Mrs Mary Man," but in a letter to the *Daily Advertiser* in 1737 she signed herself (unless there was a typographical error) "Miss H. Mann." Though there is a possibility that two women were referred to during those years, the evidence seems to point to just one.

Her first notice was on 9 August 1728 at the Haymarket Theatre, when "Mrs Mann" played Teresa in *The Spanish Fryar* (the following 26 October at the same house "Miss Man" played that role). On 24 August at Bartholomew Fair "Mrs Man" acted Gossip Longtongue in *Bateman*. She appeared regularly at the Haymarket in 1728–29, usually called "Miss Mann" but once "Mrs Mann," and since that was the pattern for many of the following years, we will treat her henceforth as Miss Mann. In 1728–29 she appeared as Emilia in *The Metamorphosis*, Teresa in *The Spanish Fryar*, Florella in *The Orphan*, a Servant Maid in *The Lottery*, the Miller's Wife in *The Humours of Harlequin*, an unnamed character in *The Royal Captives*, Lusingo in *Hurlothrumbo*, and Blouze in *The Beggar's Wedding*.

On 8 April 1729 Miss Mann enjoyed a solo benefit; then in August and September she played at Bartholomew and Southwark fairs under Reynolds's management. At the former she had a role in *The Beggar's Wedding* and played her Miller's Wife part in *The Humours of*

Harlequin, and at the latter she was Sally in *Southwark Fair* ("being the first Time of her appearing in Boy's Clothes"—which suggests she was quite young) and, again, the Miller's Wife.

After that she played Melinda in *The Recruiting Officer* at Reynolds's booth in the Half-Moon Inn at Southwark on 23 September and the Miller's Wife again on 29 November at the Haymarket. When the latter work was repeated on 16 January 1730 Miss Mann was replaced by Mrs Martin and for two years she was not mentioned in London bills. On 8 March 1732 she acted Mrs Goodfellow in *Tunbridge Walks* at the Haymarket, and on the following 1 June she played Millwood in *The London Merchant* and spoke a new epilogue for her benefit. It was on that occasion that the bill called her "Mrs Mary Man" and she had been styled "Mrs Mann" in March. But when she joined the Drury Lane company for the 1732–33 season the mixed pattern of Miss (usually) and Mrs (sometimes) prevailed.

She was one of the Milkmaids in *The Country Revels* at Drury Lane on 17 November 1732 and then was seen as Cicely in *Caelia*, Goody Grover in *Betty*, a Pierrot Woman in *Harlequin Restored*, Molly in *The Beggar's Opera*, A Syren and a Gardener's Wife in *Cephalus and Procris*, Tarnish in *The Boarding School*, a Shepherdess in *The Judgment of Paris*, an unnamed character in *The Mock Officer*, a Shepherdess and a Lady of Pleasure in *The Harlot's Progress*, an unnamed character in *Deborah*, and Lucy in *The Livery Rake*. During the season she also appeared as an entr'acte dancer. She turned up at the Haymarket on 26 July 1733 to appear in *The Amorous Lady*, and at Bartholomew Fair she played a Masquerader and a Lady of Pleasure in *Ridotto al' Fresco* and Mrs Trumpery in *Sir John Falstaff*.

Miss Mann joined Theophilus Cibber and his seceding Drury Lane performers at the Haymarket during the first half of the 1733–34 season and there tried out such new roles as Mrs Chat in *The Committee*, Honoria in *Love Makes a Man*, Clara in *Rule a Wife and Have a Wife*, Charlotte in *The Mock Doctor*, Kate in the first and Dol Tearsheet in the second part of *Henry IV*, Situp in *The Double Gallant*, Parly in *The Constant Couple*, Lucy in *The Recruiting Officer*, Damaris in *The Amorous Widow*, Lucy in *Oroonoko*, Foible in *The Way of the World*, Martha in *The Scornful Lady*, Mrs Centaure in *The*

Silent Woman, Maria in *The London Merchant*, and Colombine in *The Burgomaster Trick'd*. The rebel players returned to Drury Lane in March 1734 and Miss Mann played some of her old parts and added Colombine in *Cupid and Psyche*, a Peasant Woman and a Lively Lass in *Britannia*, and Wheedle in *The Miser*.

She went over to Lincoln's Inn Fields on 9 May to play Clara in *Rule a Wife and Have a Wife*, on 23 May to play Lettice in *The School Boy*, and on 29 May to dance *The Whim* with Tench. On 27 May—yet another night when she was not scheduled at Drury Lane—she was at the Haymarket playing Kate in *1 Henry IV* and dancing with Tench. Finally, on 31 May she played Mariana in *The Miser* and danced the *Black Joak* with Smith at the James Street Theatre; that performance had been intended for Lincoln's Inn Fields but was transferred to James Street because the former house was in use. At Bartholomew Fair in August and September Miss Mann played Leonora in *Don John* and Colombine in *The Farrier Nick'd*.

Miss Mann remained at Drury Lane through the 1736–37 season, acting and dancing and expanding her repertoire with such parts as Dainty Fidget in *The Country Wife*, Colombine in *Harlequin Orpheus*, Dol Mavis in *The Silent Woman*, a Hussar in *Colombine Courtezan*, Lucetta in *The Rover*, Lisetta in *The Man of Taste*, Colombine in *The Fall of Phaeton*, Trusty in *The Provok'd Husband*, and Mrs Slammekin in *The Beggar's Opera*. During those seasons she appeared rarely at other playhouses: she was Myrtilla in *The Provok'd Husband* at Lincoln's Inn Fields on 16 July 1735 and then Cleora in *The Tragedy of Tragedies* and the Gingerbread Woman in *Bartholomew Fair* at the same house in August. There on 14 April 1736 she played Kate in *1 Henry IV*. As before, she continued appearing as an entr'acte dancer.

On 21 May 1736 Miss Mann was robbed and beaten in the street. The *Daily Post* reported the incident on 24 May:

On Friday night last about 11 o'clock, one John Smith (with two others not yet taken) assaulted Miss Mann, of Drury Lane Playhouse, in Russel Court & robb'd her of a fine Pocket hankerchief & a velvet Mantle. On Saturday he was committed by Col de Veil to Tothill Fields Bridewell for further examination. Upon Miss Mann's crying out "Thieves" they beat & bruis'd her very unmercifully.

On 29 May the paper reported that "John Smith was last night brought up to Col de Veils house for commital for an assault on Miss Mann [but] contrived to escape from the Keeper though ten or twelve people were in the room & nobody observ'd it till he was got clean off."

The *Daily Advertiser* on 24 October 1737 contained a letter from "Miss H. Mann" declaring her intention to remain on the stage. Whereupon she left the stage, at least in London, until 16 September 1738, when she reappeared at Drury Lane as Kate in *1 Henry IV*. She was not as active in 1738–39 as she had been in earlier seasons, though she continued to appear as a dancer between the acts and in colombine roles in pantomimes such as *Harlequin Grand Volgi*, *Robin Goodfellow*, and *Harlequin Restored*. Then she disappeared again until 23 August 1740, when she was a Milkmaid in *Harlequin Restored* at Bartholomew Fair. She began the 1740–41 season at Drury Lane playing Colombine in *Robin Goodfellow* on 14 October, but she left at the end of the year and did not return until 11 November 1741, when she appeared as Colombine in *The Fortune Tellers*. Colombine in *Harlequin Shipwrecked* occupied her to the end of the month, after which she disappeared once more. In January 1744 at Drury Lane she was Colombine in *Harlequin Grand Volgi* and Colombine in *Colombine Courtezan*; then she spent the remainder of the season playing Harlequin's Wife in *The Amorous Goddess*. Though she began her 1744 appearances calling herself Miss Mann, she quickly changed to Mrs Mann and completed her career so-styled.

At Drury Lane in 1744–45 she appeared in nothing but colombine parts and did no entr'-acte performing. If she worked at Drury Lane in 1745–46 the bills did not reflect it until 25 April 1746, when she shared a benefit with two others and played, for her last recorded appearance, Harlequin's Wife in *The Amorous Goddess*. She gave her address as Brownlow Street, Longacre.

Mannington, Mr [*fl.* 1710], *performer?*
On 20 April 1710 at Drury Lane Theatre a Mr Mannington shared a benefit with Shaw. Perhaps Mannington was a performer.

Mannssier. *See* MANESIÈRE.

Mansa, Signor [*fl.* 1777], *acrobat.*
Signor Mansa participated in an exhibition of "Egyptian Pyramids" at Astley's Amphitheatre on 23 September 1777.

Mansel, Elizabeth, later Mrs Frederick Reynolds *d. 1848, actress.*
Elizabeth Mansel, a native of South Wales, was the sister of the Covent Garden actor Robert Mansel. Her sister married a Mr Mortimer, a Bristol physician. Elizabeth's maternal uncle, Colonel Landeg, had an estate at Brinwillach, Glamorganshire. Frederick Reynolds, whose wife Elizabeth was when he wrote his *Life and Times* in 1826, gave a rather romantic account of her decision to become an actress:

Stage-struck, this young lady abandoned family, friends, and the prospect of a fine fortune . . . and, like a true heroine, without the slightest previous declaration of her intentions, she ordered a post-chaise, and accompanied by her maid, with a light

Harvard Theatre Collection

ELIZABETH MANSEL, as Leonora
engraving by Fittler, after Roberts

heart, and purse almost as light, she left her native land, South Wales, intent on the idea of becoming a Mrs. Siddons, a Mrs. Jordan, or a Miss Farren.

According to Reynolds, a female friend from Bristol joined her on the journey, and Elizabeth had no trouble obtaining an audition at Covent Garden Theatre where she was immediately taken on.

According to the *Authentic Memoirs of the Green Room* (1799) Miss Mansel came to London from Liverpool: "she accompanied by chance Mr. Cooper, who was on the same business, and by chance also, the young candidates took lodgings in the same house." Her companion was the young Thomas Abthorpe Cooper, an identification we failed to make in volume 3 of this dictionary in our notice of Cooper (fl. 1798). Harris, the Covent Garden manager, "granted an appearance" to each. Cooper made his London debut as Hamlet on 1 October 1795. Advertised as "a Young Lady" who was making her "First Appearance on any Stage," Elizabeth acted Sophia in *The Road to Ruin* at Covent Garden Theatre on 8 October 1795. *The European Magazine* of that month identified her as Miss Mansel.

Miss Mansel's debut as Sophia earned her sufficient applause to induce Harris to engage her at £3 per week. The press soon announced that Miss Mansel, now reported to have come from Bristol and to possess a "Beauty very striking," would appear in Frederick Reynolds's new comedy, *Speculation*. That piece had its premiere on 7 November 1795, with Miss Mansel as Cecilia, and both the play and the actress proved successful. In addition to 34 performances as Cecilia, she also played that season Fanny Dickins in *Life's Vagaries*, Anne Page in *The Merry Wives of Windsor*, Julia Faulkner in *The Way to Get Married*, Amelia in the premiere of J. C. Cross's *The Way to Get Un-married* (on 30 March 1796), Julia in *The Mysteries of the Castle*, Margaret in *A New Way to Pay Old Debts*, Emmeline in the premiere of O'Keeffe's *The Doldrum* (on 23 April 1796), Sylvia in *The Recruiting Officer*, and Lady Elizabeth Grey in *The Earl of Warwick and Margaret of Anjou*.

In the summer of 1796 Miss Mansel acted at Birmingham, where she "made a very good benefit . . . and was much liked," according to the *How Do You Do?* of 24 September. That

journal also thought she was "an improving little girl, and deserves every encouragement."

In the fall of 1796 she returned to Covent Garden, where she continued to be engaged through 1798–99 at a constant £3 per week. Among her roles during that period were Rachel in *The Prisoner at Large*, Nerissa in *The Merchant of Venice*, Miss Leeson in *The School for Wives*, Maria in *The London Merchant*, Dorinda in *The Beaux' Stratagem*, and Arabella in *The Honest Thieves* in 1796–97; Birtha in *Percy*, Serina in *The Orphan*, Goneril in *King Lear*, Jacintha in *The Suspicious Husband*, Lucinda in *The Conscious Lovers*, and Maria in *The School for Scandal* in 1797–98; and Ellen in *She Stoops to Conquer* and Emily in *The Jew and the Doctor* in 1798–99. She played again at Birmingham in the summers of 1797 and 1798. In his *Pin Basket to the Children of Thespis* (1797), John Williams wrote of Miss Mansel:

> With a warm, merry heart, and a fair rotund face,
> unsophisticate MANSELL stands up in her place:
> ....
> She is buxom and blandishing, blith{e}, beneficial,
> She is Nature's own wench, but too inartificial.
> In Julia her sentiment oft was undone;
> In Dorinda her manners are loosely put on;
> Though her spinster is rural in compassing marriage,
> She at least should be demi-genteel in her carriage.

On 16 March 1799, Miss Mansel married the prolific dramatist Frederick Reynolds at St Clement Danes. She had acted Caroline Dormer in *The Heir at Law* two nights before. That was her last performance. She retired from the stage after her marriage.

In his *Life and Times*, which was published in 1826, Reynolds mentioned little about his wife beyond some coy remarks on his prenuptial panic and his honeymoon. He died on 16 April 1841 and his wife proved his will that May. According to testimony recorded in a subsequent administration of Reynolds's estate on 12 August 1857, Elizabeth Reynolds had died, intestate, on 5 January 1848, leaving a legal tangle concerning £2750 7s. 2d. which her husband had been holding as trustee for the estate of the actor William Thomas Lewis.

The eldest son of Frederick and Elizabeth Reynolds, Frederick Mansel Reynolds (d. 1850),

Harvard Theatre Collection

ELIZABETH MANSEL, as Angelica
engraving by Wilson, after Graham

Courtesy of the Garrick Club

ROBERT MANSEL, as the Duke in *The Honey Moon*
artist unknown

a literary editor, is noticed in *The Dictionary of National Biography*. A second son, Richard Charles Reynolds, was still alive in 1857.

An engraved portrait by Wilson, after J. Graham, of Miss Mansel as Angelica in *Sir Harry Wildair* was published as a plate to the *British Library* by Cawthorn in 1796. An engraving by J. Fittler, after J. Roberts, of her as Leonora in *The Mistake* was published as a plate to the same series in 1795.

Mansel, Robert *d. 1824, actor.*

Robert Mansel, a native of South Wales, was the brother of the actress, Elizabeth Mansel, who married the dramatist Frederick Reynolds in 1799. Another of Mansel's sisters married a Mr Mortimer, a physician at Bristol. Mansel's maternal uncle, Colonel Landeg, had an estate at Brinwillach, Glamorganshire.

According to the *Authentic Memoirs of the Green Room* (1799), Mansel had given up the army to become an actor in Jones's company in Dublin, where on 3 January 1798 he made his debut at the Fishamble Street Theatre. Supposedly Mansel quarreled with the deputy-manager, Bellamy, who had assigned him a character he refused to play. When Bellamy rejected a challenge to a duel, Mansel quit that theatre.

Announced as from the Theatre Royal, Dublin, Mansel first appeared at Covent Garden Theatre on 19 September 1798 as Young Marlow in *She Stoops to Conquer*. The critic in the *Monthly Mirror* for September did not find him a superior actor but thought he might become a useful one. Mansel failed to convey the idea of the gentleman to the complete satisfaction of the critic, but

he performed, upon the whole, with considerable spirit; and his embarrassment, where the part required it, was amusing and characteristic. His figure is tall and genteel, and his face not devoid of expression; but his deportment is without grace, and his action without elegance: he has acquired an unhappy *lounge* in his walk, which counteracts the pleasing effect of his person, and his utterance is deformed by provincialisms, which *must* be corrected before he can become a favourite with a London audience. The word promise, he pronounces prom*u*s; and women, *wimun*. His voice is full and sonorous, not unlike the Chancellor of the Exchequer's; but it is perhaps too deep for the rapidity of comic dialogue. We must not forget his delivery of the sentiment in the fourth act—it was judicious, tender, and impressive.

Mansel's other roles in his debut season, for which he was paid £3 per week, included Octavio in *Two Strings to Your Bow*, Charles in *The Jew and the Doctor*, Lord Edmond in *The Prisoner at Large*, Polyperchon in *Alexander the Great*, Tressel in *Richard III*, Henry Morland in *The Heir at Law*, Count Cassel in *Lover's Vows*, Armstrong in *The Iron Chest*, and Sir Bertrand in *The Adopted Child*. On 26 February 1799 the Covent Garden proprietors invited him to act Charles Oakly in *The Jealous Wife* at Drury Lane.

In 1799–1800, when his salary was still £3 per week, Mansel added to his repertoire Allen O'Dale in *Robin Hood*, Malcolm in *Macbeth*, the Prince in *Romeo and Juliet*, Seymour in the *Irishman in London*, Captain Manly in *The Honest Thieves*, Ratcliffe in *Jane Shore*, Sir Walter Blount in *Henry IV*, Earl Mercia in *Peeping Tom*, an Officer in the premiere of T. J. Dibdin's *The Hermione* on 5 April 1800, and Caius Lucius in *Cymbeline*.

The remainder of Mansel's career was spent in the provinces. Announced as from Covent Garden, he acted in Belfast in February 1801. He was playing at Edinburgh in April 1807 and in 1807–8. At York and Hull he acted and managed for some years. While on the road from Doncaster to visit his sister Elizabeth and her husband in London, Mansel had a stroke and died at Wansford on 22 October 1824.

In 1814 Mansel had published at Hull *Free Thoughts upon Methodists, actors, and the influence of the stage; with an introductory letter to Mrs. ——, of —— Castle, Glamorganshire, upon the origins of the drama*; an American edition was published in 1826 as *A defense of the drama, containing Mansel's Free thoughts, extracts from the*

most celebrated writers. Mansel's *A Short Struggle for stage or no stage* was published at Sheffield in 1818; it consists of a collection of letters which had appeared in the *Sheffield Mercury* in reply to a sermon preached against the stage by the Reverend Thomas Best, in St James Church, Sheffield.

A pencil and watercolor drawing by an unknown artist, of Mansel as the Duke in *The Honey Moon* is in the Garrick Club.

Mansell, Mary. *See* FARREN, MRS WILLIAM.

Manship, Joseph [*fl.* 1689–1712], violinist.
Joseph Manship (or Manchip, Mansuet) was appointed to the private music of William III on 5 July 1689. Though the Lord Chamberlain's accounts contain no further references to Manship, he was surely the violinist who was active at concerts and at the opera house in the early years of the eighteenth century. He and Dean shared a benefit concert at York Buildings on 26 March 1701; Manship played the violin at a concert at Hampstead Wells on 30 July 1709 and was heard during the 1709–10 season in concerts there, at Godwin's Dancing School, at Stationers' Hall, and at York Buildings.

In 1707–8 at the Queen's Theatre in the Haymarket, Manship earned a daily salary of 8*s.*, according to a document in the Coke papers at Harvard; another document, dating about late December 1707, lists him at £25 per season. He was one of the second "trebles," or violins, and among the lowest-paid members of the opera orchestra. He was still playing there in 1711–12.

Mansiere. *See* MANESIÈRE.

Mansill, Mr [*fl.* 1792], actor.
Mr Mansill played Roderigo in *Othello* at the Haymarket Theatre on 6 February 1792.

Mansoli. *See* MANZUOLI.

Manstead, Mr [*fl.* 1778], actor.
A Mr Manstead played Lurcher in *The Country Lasses* and an unnamed but principal character in *All the World's a Stage* on 29 April 1778 at the Haymarket Theatre.

Mansuet. *See* MANSHIP.

Mantagnana. *See* MONTAGNANA.

Mantelli, Signor [*fl.* 1719], *trumpeter.*
In a concert at York Buildings on 19 December 1719 was featured "A Trumpet Piece by the famous Signior Mantelli."

Manuel, Mrs [*fl.* 1667–1668], *actress, singer.*
Pepys noted in his diary on 12 August 1667 that he had gone "to Mrs. Manuell's the Jew's wife, formerly a player" and been pleased with her singing. He was frequently in company where Mrs Manuel was present and usually commented on her singing ability. On 23 March 1668 he and his friends took a barge trip up the Thames:

a very fine day, and all the way sang; and Mrs. Manuel sings very finely, and is a mighty discreet, sober-carriaged woman, that both my wife and I are mightily taken with her, and sings well, and without importunity or the contrary.

Pepys said nothing further about her having been a player, and we have found no other evidence of her having performed in the theatre.

Manza. *See* MANCIA.

Manziotti, Antonio [*fl.* 1763–1764], *singer.*
At the King's Theatre Antonio Manziotti sang Demetrio in *Cleonice* beginning on 26 November 1763, Aristodemo in *Senocrita* on 21 February 1764, and an unnamed part in the oratorio *Pellegrini* on 5 April. He doubtless sang other roles that were not named in the bills. *The London Stage* incorrectly cites him as "Mazzioti" on 21 February and as "Maziotti" on 5 April 1764.

"Manzoletto," stage name of Angiolo Monanni [*fl.* 1779–1782], *singer.*
"Manzoletto" (Angiolo Monanni) was announced in the *Public Advertiser* of 13 September 1775 as having been engaged as second man at the King's Theatre for the 1775–76 season, though no roles are known for him

until 23 January 1779, when he sang the title role in *Artaserse*. During the remainder of the season Manzoletto sang Azore in *Zemire e Azore* and participated in *L'Olimpiade*. The rest of his stay in England, which lasted until June 1782, brought him out as Gandarte in *Alessandro nell'Indie*, Volunnio in *Quinto Fabio*, Tagliacantoni in *L'arcifanfano*, Idreno in *Rinaldo*, the title role in *Il duca d'Atene*, Fabio in *Mitridate*, Corebo in *Piramo e Tisbe*, Valentiniano in *Ezio*, Don Gastone in *I viaggiatori felici*, Aronte in *Giunio Bruto*, Minteo in *L'eroe cinese*, Giocondo in *La Frascatana*, and some unnamed characters. He went to Dublin, probably in the summer of 1781, for the *Hibernian Magazine* in September 1781 published "Non temer bell' idol mio" as sung by Manzoletto at the Rotunda.

Manzoli. *See* MANZUOLI.

Manzuoli, Giovanni, called "Succianoccioli" *c.* 1720–*c.* 1782, *singer.*
Born about 1720 in Florence, Giovanni Manzuoli (often Manzoli in England) was able by 1748 to command 11,250 lire milanese per season to sing in Milan. He was a male soprano called "Succianoccioli" and sang in Milan again in 1759, 1762, 1766, and 1769, according to Heriot's *Castrati in Opera*. Farinelli engaged him in Madrid in 1749 for 16,000 ducats; in 1755 he sang in Lisbon; and in 1763 he had an engagement in Bologna. Heriot quotes a contemporary comment on Manzuoli's relations with the orchestra in Bologna:

The first *musico*, who is a certain Manzoli, insists on giving the note for the instruments to be tuned; and he legislates for the whole orchestra with a certain little bell of his. But the note he gives is always so flat, that all these players sound like our organ at Santa Lucia.

In 1764–65 Manzuoli sang in London at the King's Theatre and caused a tremendous stir. He was first heard as the title character in *Ezio*, a *pasticcio*, on 24 November 1764. He then sang Farnaspe in *Adriano in Siria*, an unnamed character in *Demofoonte*, and Demitrio in *Antigono*. Dr Burney wrote in some detail about the singer:

The expectations which the great reputation of this performer had excited were so great, that at

Civica Raccolta delle Stampe Achille Bertarelli, Castello Sforzesco, Milan

GIOVANNI MANZUOLI

by Betti

the opening of the theatre in November, with the pasticcio of EZIO, there was such a crowd assembled at all the avenues, that it was with very great difficulty I obtained a place, after waiting two hours at the door. Manzoli's voice was the most powerful and voluminous soprano that had been heard on our stage since the time of Farinelli; and his manner of singing was grand and full of taste and dignity. In this first opera he had three songs, composed by Pescetti, entirely in different styles . . . all of which he executed admirably. The lovers of Music in London were more unanimous in approving his voice and talents than those of any other singer within my memory. The applause was hearty, unequivocal, and free from all suspicion of artificial zeal; it was a universal thunder. His voice alone was commanding from native strength and sweetness; for it seems as if subsequent singers had possessed more art and feeling; and as to execution, he had none. However, he was a good actor, though unwieldy in figure, and not well made in person; neither was he young when he arrived in London; yet the sensations he excited seem to have been more irresistible and universal, than I have ever been witness to in any theatre.

T. A. Arne wrote *L'Olimpiade* for Manzuoli, but it was not a success when it opened on 27 April 1765, though Manzuoli as Magacle did well.

At some point during his English visit Manzuoli was ill; William Havard the actor wrote "An Invocation To Saint Cecilia Upon a dangerous sickness of Mansoli," a manuscript now at the Folger Shakespeare Library. The newspapers, however, failed to report any serious illness.

After leaving England Manzuoli sang in Vienna; in 1768 he was in Florence; and in 1771 he made his final appearances in Milan before retiring to an estate outside Florence. Michael Kelly visited him there, and Manzuoli had fond memories of his success in England. Heriot and the *New Grove* give 1782 as the singer's death, in Florence. The *Enciclopedia dello spettacolo* details Manzuoli's continental career.

Manzuoli's portrait, engraved by G. B. Betti, after Luigi Betti, was published in Florence. A scene depicting him in combat with a minotaur in *Arianna e Teseo* (as performed at the Ducale Teatro in Milan) was engraved by Dal Re, after Fabrizio Galliari, and published in 1762. Manzuoli was also included in a large group of singers engraved by Rainaldi, after a design by Antonio Fedi, published between 1801 and 1807. A detail from that engraving showing Manzuoli with Gaetano Guadagni is reproduced in volume 6 of this dictionary with Guadagni's notice.

Maples. *See* MAPPLES.

Mapleson, James Wheble   *1775–c. 1823, violinist, violist, copyist.*

According to the records of the Royal Society of Musicians, James Wheble Mapleson was born on 4 February 1775 in the parish of St James, Westminster, the son of Benjamin and Elizabeth Mapleson. By the time Doane's *Musical Directory* came out in 1794 James was living at No 7, Air Street, Piccadilly, and had played violin in the Handel Memorial Concerts at Westminster Abbey. He was proposed for membership in the Royal Society of Musicians in January 1798 and elected unanimously the following April. At that time he was described as a violinist, violist, and copyist, employed at Vauxhall Gardens. He was married, but as of 1798 he had no children.

Mapleson played violin at the St Paul's Concerts beginning in May 1798, and from 29 November 1800 (if not earlier) he was on the payroll at Drury Lane Theatre as a music copyist. Drury Lane hired him also as a member of the band from as early as 1801, at a weekly salary of £2 10s., a fee which by 1819–20 had dropped to £2. His copyist's salary per week seems to have been a constant £1 5s.

James Wheble Mapleson died about 1823. On 2 February of that year his widow Mary was granted £12 for Mapleson's funeral expenses plus a widow's pension of two and a half guineas monthly and a guinea each for four of her children: Henry, born on 18 July 1809; Eleanor, 28 July 1810; Emma, 20 February 1814; and Emily, 9 December 1817. The Maplesons had had a son James Henry, born on 1 November 1802 and baptized at St Mary, Lambeth. The other children, being under 14, were considered by the Royal Society to be charges. The Minutes of the Society contain frequent notes concerning the Mapleson offspring. Henry was bound apprentice to a grocer in 1823; Eleanor was bound to a Miss F. M. Kelly in 1824; Emma was bound to a dressmaker in 1829; and Emily was bound to a dressmaker in 1832. The Society helped arrange the apprenticeships, paid the children rewards if they did well, and paid the master and mistresses' bounties. Mrs Mapleson was last mentioned in the Minutes on 2 February 1840, when she was granted £3 for medical aid for an illness which had lasted two months.

The eldest of the Mapleson children, James Henry, became a member of the Royal Society of Musicians in 1835; he was a double bass player and had engagements at Drury Lane and Vauxhall Gardens. He died in 1869, leaving a son, James Henry Mapleson, Junior (1830–1901), who is noticed in the *New Grove Dictionary of Music and Musicians*.

Mapples, John *1752–1802, actor, singer.*
According to the obituary notice of John Mapples in the *Gentleman's Magazine* in November 1802, he was born in 1752, worked as an itinerant actor, retired in 1796, and died in 1802. He was doubtless the Mapples who sang at Manchester in 1783, was on the bill of 15 February at Derby with his wife, performed there again in 1787–88, and was a principal in *The What Is It?* at the Royal Circus in

London on 12 May 1789. That attraction was advertised as "A Tragic-Comic-Pastoral-Musical Piece." Mapples appeared in an unspecified part in *Liberty Triumphant* at the Theatre Royal in Edinburgh in January 1790. His wife appeared in both London and provincial companies to which he apparently did not belong.

Mapples, Mrs John ₁*fl.* 1777–1790₁, *actress, singer.*
Mrs Mapples appeared in Bristol, according to an advertisement of 26 June 1777, hailed as from London, though no records of her appearances in London before that date have been found. Though their careers did not always run parallel, we take her to have been the wife of the London and provincial actor John Mapples.

At the Haymarket Theatre on 9 February 1778 Mrs Mapples sang "The Soldier tir'd of war's alarms" and she reappeared there on 7 September to sing in the *Macbeth* chorus. She was with John Mapples on the Derby bill of 15 February 1787 and she was in Pero's company there in 1788–89. On 12 May 1789 she appeared with her husband in *The What Is It?* at the Royal Circus in London. From December 1789 to March 1790 she acted in Edinburgh at the Theatre Royal, taking unspecified roles in *The Battle of Hexham* and *Liberty Triumphant* and appearing as Huncamunca in *Tom Thumb*, Mrs Motherly in *The Provok'd Husband*, Narcissa in *Inkle and Yarico*, and the singing Witch in *Macbeth*. She was also in Pero's troupe at Derby sometime during the 1789–90 season.

MAQUIRE, MRS. *See* **REDIGÉ, MME PAULO.**

Mara, Giovanni Battista *1744–1808, violoncellist.*
Despite his Italianate name, Giovanni Battista Mara was born in Berlin in 1744, according to his notice in Sainsbury's *Dictionary of Music*. He was the son of Ignaz Mara (d. 1783), a native of Teutschbrod in Bohemia, who served about 1755 as chamber violoncellist to the King of Prussia. When Charles Burney met the younger Mara at Gertrud Schmeling's house in Berlin about 1772, he described him as a young violoncellist "with great ability" who was engaged in Frederick the Great's

concerts. Ignoring the King's protestations, Mlle Schmeling married Mara soon after. The couple eventually escaped Frederick's domination in 1780 by fleeing to Vienna, where they remained for two years. They left Vienna in 1782, traveled by way of Holland and Belgium to Paris, and thence to London, where they arrived in 1784.

Mara was among the violoncellists conducted by Burney in the Handel Memorial Concerts at Westminster Abbey and the Pantheon in May and June 1784. During the next decade or so in London his career amounted to little, and he seems to have lived mainly off his wife's success. He played in the oratorios at the King's Theatre in 1787, at Drury Lane in 1788, at the King's Theatre in 1792, and at Covent Garden in 1796. In his *First London Notebook* Haydn listed Johann Mara among the musical people in the metropolis. In 1794 Doane's *Musical Directory* credited him with performing in the Concerts of the Academy of Ancient Music, the Professional Concerts, and in the grand Handelian events at the Abbey.

Doane also gave Mara's address as No 25, Queen Ann Street, East, the same as his wife's, but by 1796 they were estranged, and she had taken up with the musician Charles Haiman Florio. Mara's marriage to the great soprano Mme Mara had been tempestuous, marred by her promiscuity and his dissoluteness. He did seem to be involved in supervising her contractual affairs at the King's Theatre in 1793, signing letters about her engagement that were printed in the *Morning Herald* on 25 February and in the *Morning Chronicle* on 25 March 1793, when he gave his name as John Battista Mara. Haydn was present at a supper following a concert by Mme Mara at the Hanover Square Rooms on 24 March 1795, during which Mara came raging into the party and had to be turned out by the threats of her lawyer.

Sometime after he played in the Covent Garden oratorios in February and March 1796, Mara left England. In 1799 he was reported living near Berlin "in very low circumstances." In 1801 he was seen at Sondershausen by Gerber, who was quoted by Sainsbury:

he still played an adagio of his own composition so well, that no orchestra need have been ashamed of him; and when, in his allegro, he missed now and then a note, it was not so much the fault of his hand, as of his instrument, which was a bad

one. . . . He conducted himself, during his stay here, like a sedate, well-informed gentlemanly man, nor did he ever show the least symptoms of that inclination to intemperance, which has been the bane of his life. He was, however, in very great distress, notwithstanding his noble-minded wife furnished him, from time to time, with considerable sums of money.

Mara passed his last years in Holland, "playing the fiddle for sailors to dance," suffering from hopeless alcoholism, until he died at Schiedam, near Rotterdam, in the summer of 1808.

He should not be confused with several country actors named Mara who played at Dublin, Liverpool, York, and elsewhere in the 1790s and early 1800s.

Mara, Mme Giovanni Battista, Gertrud Elisabeth, née Schmeling *1749–1833, singer.*

The German soprano Gertrud Elisabeth Schmeling was born at Kassel on 23 February 1749, the daughter of Johann Schmeling, a

Civica Raccolta delle Stampe Achille Bertarelli, Castello Sforzesco, Milan

GERTRUD MARA

engraving by Dal Pian, after Castelli

musician of modest talents who supported himself by repairing instruments. It is said that the child was attracted to the violin by the age of 4 and that at the age of 5, after having received some lessons from her father, she could play duets with him. During those early years she suffered from rickets, a debilitation from which it took many years for her to recover. When she was ten, her father conducted her to Frankfurt to display her virtuosity. There she greatly pleased and attracted a subscription which helped pay for further music training. When her health improved her father arranged some concerts for her in Vienna. Upon the advice of the British ambassador to the Hapsburg court, the child was taken by her father to England.

The Schmelings arrived in London in 1759, and soon the ten-year-old prodigy attracted the attention of several influential patrons, including the Queen, by her playing and singing at private musical parties. The *Enciclopedia dello spettacolo* claims she made her debut with other young singers at the Haymarket Theatre on 23 April 1760, but no performances for that theatre on or about that date are known to us, and no other public appearances during that visit to England are recorded. According to *The Manager's Notebook* (1837–1838), where an extensive but often confused notice is given of her in No XII, she performed at taverns, particularly the Rising Sun in the Strand, "for such rewards as they were pleased to give."

The English ladies persuaded Schmeling to have his daughter abandon the violin and devote her energies to singing. It is said that her first singing lessons were from Pietro Paradies, an Italian composer who enjoyed great business as a teacher in London in the 1750s. Paradies, however, was mainly a teacher of instrumentalists, so the assertion that his indiscretions with Gertrud prompted Schmeling to withdraw his daughter from Paradies's tuition may also be one of the legends by which our soprano's early life is colored.

After the Schmelings returned to Germany, the father was unsuccessful in his bid to obtain a position for his daughter at the Berlin court, supposedly because of Frederick the Great's prejudice against German singers. If that story has any truth in it, one must wonder at the father's presumption in offering for the King's service a performer so untrained and so inex-

perienced. Her promise, however, was recognized by Hiller, who heard her sing at Leipzig and took her into his voice school in that city. In five years with Hiller she acquired a vast knowledge of music and developed a brilliant style of singing. The compass of her voice extended from middle G to E *in alt*. She also became proficient on the harpsichord and played some concertos in public. In 1767 she sang at Dresden in *Talestri* with much success.

In 1771 she was again recommended to Frederick the Great, this time as "the most brilliant singer of the century." Finally consenting to hear her, the monarch was so impressed with her singing of an aria from Graun's *Britannico* that he appointed her for life as court singer at Berlin and Potsdam, with an annual salary reputed to have been 11,250 francs.

As Frederick's prima donna, Mlle Schmeling enjoyed his royal favor for seven years, but the King kept her firmly in hand, allowing her few liberties. Once, it is said, he had soldiers drag her from her bed to the theatre to sing, despite her complaints of illness. Even in these earlier years, she was a headstrong woman who often made decisions about both her artistic life and personal life in fits of temperament. At Berlin about 1772 she married Giovanni Battista Mara, a violoncellist of little talent whom she had met professionally at court concerts. Despite the protests of the King and his warnings about Mara's vicious character, she had persisted in the match, and, eventually, much to her regret, she suffered greatly over her husband's folly and debauchery.

Dr Burney visited her in Berlin prior to her marriage and described her at the age of 23:

She is short, and not handsome, but is far from having anything disagreeable in her countenance; on the contrary, there is a strong expression of good-humour impressed upon it, which renders her address very engaging. Her teeth are irregular, and project too much; yet, altogether, her youth and smiles taken into the account, she is rather agreeable in face and figure. I found that she had preserved her English; indeed she sometimes wanted words, but, having learned it very young, the pronunciation of those which occurred was perfectly correct. She was so obliging as to sing, at my request, very soon after my entrance. She began with a very difficult *aria di bravura*, by Traetta, which I had heard before at Mingotti's. She sang it admirably, and fully answered the great ideas I had formed of her abilities, in everything but her voice, which was a little cloudy, and not quite so powerful as I expected. However, she had a slight cold and cough, and complained of indisposition: but with all this her voice was sweetly toned, and she sang perfectly well in tune. She has an excellent shake, a good expression, and a facility of executing and articulating rapid and difficult divisions, that is astonishing. Her second song was a *larghetto*, by Schwanenburg, of Brunswick, which was very pretty in itself; but she made it truly delightful by her taste and expression. She was by no means lavish of graces, but those she used were perfectly suited to the style of the music and idea of the part. After this she sang an *andante*, in the part which she had to practise for the ensuing carnival, in Graun's *Merope*; and in this she acquitted herself with great taste, expression, and propriety.

When Mme Mara was offered a London engagement at advantageous terms, Frederick refused to release her. And despite her repeated pleas that a change of air was necessary for her declining health, the King continued to prohibit her departure, insisting that she could find rest in one of his own dominions. Several accounts claim that with some difficulty the Maras finally managed to escape to Vienna, and that by some subterfuge the Emperor Joseph II saved them from the extradition demanded by Frederick. More likely, however, Frederick, who had lost his interest in music, had probably become bored with the annoyances Mme Mara generated and had decided to release his prima donna.

Passing through Leipzig and Dresden, Mme Mara arrived at Vienna in 1780, where she sang for two years with some success, though the style in *opera buffa* at the imperial city was being set by Nancy Storace. Mozart had heard Mme Mara in Munich, and on 13 November 1780 he recorded that she "had not the good fortune to please me."

Mme Mara departed Vienna in 1782, and after touring Germany, Holland, and Belgium, she arrived at Paris with a letter of introduction from the Empress to Marie-Antoinette. She scored a memorable triumph in the Concert Spirituel on 19 March 1782, but her rivalry with the celebrated Sga Todi divided Parisian society into factions. The contest gave rise to the oft-repeated pun, occasioned when one neighbor asked another, "Après avoir entendu Madame Mara et la Signora Todi, laquelle est la meilleure," and received the re-

Harvard Theatre Collection

GERTRUD MARA, as Mandane
artist unknown

ply, "C'est Mara"—to which the first retorted "C'est bientôt dit" (C'est bien Todi).

When Giovanni Gallini visited France in 1783 to recruit singers for the opera at London, he must have begun negotiations with Mme Mara. On 12 November 1783 she wrote in French to Dr Burney that if Gallini would agree to pay her £1500 she would accept his conditions; she had also promised Abel that she would come to London for his concerts, but she had not received any more news from him. At any rate, she told Burney, she had refused an engagement at Turin in order to return to England.

That she finally did early in 1784. She made her first professional appearance in London on 29 March 1784 in a concert at the Pantheon managed by Abel. Among her selections were Pugniani's "Alma grand anezzo" and Naumanus's "Vadasi del meo bene." The subscription concerts ran six nights, but a general election was responsible for small audiences, despite the superior qualities of Mme Mara's voice. The Pantheon management granted her permission to sing in the grand Handel Memorial Concerts at the Abbey and the Pantheon between 26 May and 5 June 1784, when a considerable throng heard her. She was particularly affecting in her delivery of "I know my redeemer liveth," and her singing of "O sing unto the Lord" caused Dr Burney to shiver. The grand assembly listened, wrote Burney (who produced the whole event), "not only with pleasure, but extacy and rapture." For the last of the subscription concerts at the Pantheon on 11 June, the advertisements announced that night would be "her last appearance in England, until the next season." She was, however, a soloist at the Oxford Music Room on 19 June 1784.

In 1785 she returned to the Pantheon for 14 concerts at a fee of 1000 guineas and a benefit. She also engaged in the Ancient Concerts. Her reappearance that year in the Handel Memorial Concerts included a *faux pas* which eventually developed into a *cause célèbre*, when she remained seated during the Hallelujah choruses though the royal family and the whole assembly were standing. In June 1785 she sang at the Oxford Music Room meeting and refused to repeat an Italian song when asked for an encore. The next day she was hissed after her first song, and she responded by sitting down during the chorus. Despite assurances to the audience by Dr Hayes that she would stand up during the next chorus, she did not, thus provoking the Vice Chancellor to order her, through Hayes, to do so in the next act. But after her song in that act she left the orchestra; the Vice Chancellor, it was reported, stood in the stunned silence of the theatre to exclaim: "Dr Hayes, Madame Mara's leaving her seat after her last song has given just cause of offence, therefore she cannot sing any more here." The audience would not hear her apology and chaos ensued, obliging her to flee the theatre.

On 30 June she wrote to Hayes to explain that "some years ago, I was afflicted with a pleurisy, which entirely deprived me of the use of my voice, professionally, for a period of seven

Harvard Theatre Collection

GERTRUD MARA
engraving by Hüssner

months," and though she had recovered she still suffered pains in her left leg and in her lungs when walking fast or remaining too long on her feet. She also somewhat untactfully protested that she had not violated any laws nor had she been given any instructions about sitting or standing—"I do not know that it is usual to have particular places assigned to performers, when no part of their duty is to be executed." (Despite the Vice Chancellor's proscription, Mme Mara did return to sing at the Oxford Music Room, in 1799 and a number of times in the first years of the nineteenth century.) A caricature of her at a "Wapping Concert," published in 1786, shows her seated and bears the text:

MADAM MARA . . . begs her Polite Audience will excuse her sitting during the Performance, as she contracted in her infancy a Disorder called Le Genoue Inflexible, or (Stiff Knee) which prevents her standing, even in the most Sacred Pieces of Music—her Enemies call it Pride, but it must appear only malice, when she could not rise before their Majesties; or at the Sacred Name of Jehovah.

In October 1785 she promoted subscription concerts at Willis's Rooms in opposition to those sponsored by Gallini at Hanover Square. Those appearances brought her a reputed profit of £3000. On 29 November 1785 the *Public Advertiser* declared her nothing less than "beyond all comparison the first female singer in the world." She was, however, not the most tractable singer in the world. That month at the Winchester Music Festival she once more refused to repeat a song and then complained that the "Hampshire hogs" had behaved with great rudeness when "they absolutely *grunted* me out of the room." In December of that year some rumors spread of her engagement for the Hanover Square concerts, but that became out of the question when in January 1786 she signed with the opera company.

After spending three weeks recuperating from a cold as Lord Exeter's guest at Burleigh, Mme Mara made her opera debut at the King's Theatre as Dido in *Didone abbandonata* on 14 February 1786. The *Morning Herald* of 15 February was astonished by how she united "the talents of an excellent actress with the merit of the most enchanting singer that ever perhaps came forth on any stage." Though Mount-Edgcumbe disagreed about her acting talent— "she was no actress and had a bad person for the stage"—he declared her singing talent "of the very first order," and "Her voice, clear, sweet, distinct, was sufficiently powerful, though rather thin, and its agility and flexibility rendered her a most excellent bravura singer, in which style she was unrivalled." Burney found her so superior to all other singers in the company that "she seemed a divinity among mortals." To her alone he gave credit for the considerable success of this serious pasticcio. All her songs, in several styles, were "severally encored" every night of the eight the opera ran, something that Burney remembered never "to have happened to any other singer."

Her second role in her debut season was Andromeda in *Perseo* on 21 March 1786, when she was encored in a bravura song. "The amazing extent of her voice," reported the *General Advertiser* next day, "never appeared in a more conspicuous light." Mme Mara also had directed the choruses which accounted "for the uncommon precision with which they were executed." On 6 April she took her benefit, and tickets were available from her at No 24, Henrietta Street, Cavendish Square. On 4 May 1786 she sang the title role in *Virginia*, when Rubinelli made his first appearance in England, as Icilius. She sang with Rubinelli again on 25 May as Armida and Rinaldo in *Armida*, a new serious opera by Mortellari, with whom Mme Mara had some quarrel, to the extent that, according to Burney, all the music except Mara's part was by that composer. Mortellari had declared that she could not sing and she had proclaimed that he could not compose. She also sang in the oratorios performed at the Tottenham Court Music Room on six Fridays during Lent.

Mme Mara's second season at the King's Theatre began with her performance of Cleonice in *Alceste* on 23 December 1786. She sang "Pious orgies" from *Judas Maccabaeus* on 23 February 1787, at Drury Lane, and she also appeared in other oratorios there that season.

Harvard Theatre Collection

GERTRUD MARA, as Armida
engraving by Susemihl, after Jean

She was very successful as Cleopatra in a revival of Handel's *Giulio Cesare in Egitto* at the King's on 1 March 1787. Her other roles there included Dido, Virginia, and, on 1 May 1787, Emilia in *La Vestale*. When she took her benefit, on 29 March 1787, tickets could be obtained from her at No 39, Suffolk Street, Charing Cross.

During 1786–87 Mme Mara continued to find herself in the midst of controversy. According to John Wolcot (writing as Peter Pindar) in *Ode upon Ode* (1787), one of her scheduled performances in the Drury Lane oratorios had been canceled by order of the King because it threatened a concert of the Society of Ancient Music in Tottenham Court Road. In that same publication Wolcot reported some gossip about the royal family's discourteous treatment of her.

> To Windsor, *several times, and else to Kew,*
> *The R—y–l Mandate* MADAM MARA *drew.*
> *No cheering Drop was* MARA *ask'd to sip—*
> *No Bread was offer'd to her quiv'ring Lip.*
> *Though faint, she was not suffer'd to sit down—*
> *Heav'n help the* Goodness—*Grandeur of the*
> Cr——n!
> . . . .
> *For* MADAM MARA's *Chaise-hire and sweet Note,*
> *Their bounteous M——ies gave—not a Groat.*

She again sang in the Handel Memorial Concerts at the Abbey in May 1787, but not before becoming the object of fresh public criticism. A long and insulting letter signed "Decency" was directed against her in the press on 7 April. The writer charged her with "a wish to be a director and ruler wherever you are," and continued,

from a neglect of what you undertake, the conductors of the first concerts are deterred from engaging you. Your credit is rapidly decreasing—the daily *self-commending puffs* have kept alive, thus far, your drooping name. The period is arriving when your name will scarce ever be mentioned; your rare appearance at the Opera, and at a concert *ill attended*, cannot much contribute to a sickly name. It has been related in the public prints that you have had offers from the directors of the Abbey, at the ensuing meeting, and that you have, with *proper spirit*, refused them: that will not easily be believed. Madame Mara, it is trusted, has more prudence than to decline, at this moment, so important an engagement; nor can it well be credited, that the directors would make any such overture, knowing

what confusion her capricious temper might occasion. . . .

Evidently a paragraph had earlier appeared intimating that Mme Mara had refused to assist in the upcoming Abbey concerts because the Dean and Chapter had insisted on an assessment of £1200 to be paid before any distributions were made to charities. The directors of the Abbey Commemoration, however, denied that any such demand had been made, and on 4 May 1787 Mme Mara also denied ever having expressed her sentiments against the Dean. On 17 May she announced that because the directors "considered her presence as absolutely necessary to promote the charitable purposes of the institution," she had consented to appear; but since she did not wish to deprive Mrs Billington of the situation as first female singer, she would relinquish her part to her. In the end, Mrs Billington did not perform at the Abbey, and Mme Mara was the leading singer. That summer Mme Mara sang at the various music meetings and appeared at Bath and Bristol in December 1787.

A renewal of her quarrels with Gallini prevented her engagement at the King's Theatre in 1787–88. She offered some concerts at the Pantheon and sang in the Drury Lane oratorios. On 7 April 1788 she performed Mandane in *Artaxerxes* at Drury Lane for the benefit of the young Michael Kelly. The announcement that she was appearing for the first time on any English stage obviously was intended to herald her first dramatic performance other than those in opera at the King's Theatre. She sang Mandane for her own benefit at Drury Lane on 28 May 1788. The proceeds totaled £149 17*s.* 6*d.*, free of charges. Her address was then No 64, Pall Mall.

Mme Mara spent the next two years on the Continent. In 1790, she returned to London to engage with Gallini for £850 and a clear benefit. The King's Theatre having burned in 1789, performances of opera in 1790 were given at the Haymarket Theatre, where on 6 April Mme Mara was heartily re-welcomed as Dircea in *L'usurpatore innocente*. She sang Cleofide in *La generosità d'Alessandro* on 29 April, and for her benefit on 28 May 1790 (tickets at her house, No 8, Golden Square), she offered the title role in *Andromaca*. The *Public Advertiser* on 31 May praised her performance:

"Though the superlative talents of this lady are so well known, we make no scruple to affirm, that the extent of her melodious powers never appeared to more advantage." (The author of *The Manager's Notebook* claimed that news of her father's death caused her to solicit the indulgence of the audience "on the 30th of May," but that date fell that year on a Sunday.)

In the summer of 1790 Tate Wilkinson heard Mme Mara sing at Doncaster church, in race week, to an audience of fewer than 100 persons. The fault was not hers, claimed Wilkinson, but the vicar's for having scheduled the concert for noon, when people were occupied with other attractions. In November and early December 1790 she gave a series of subscription concerts in the Assembly Rooms in Bristol.

In 1791 Mme Mara rejoined the opera, now performing at the Pantheon, appearing on 17 February as Armida, with Pacchierotti as Rinaldo. Mount Edgcumbe thought their duettos "the most perfect pieces of execution" he ever heard. Reporting a rehearsal on 10 January the *Morning Post* found Mme Mara "as usual equally beyond praise and competition," and on 23 February the same paper noticed that she sang "with charming impression, though some strange attitudes marked the vacant negligence of each interval." For her benefit on 14 April (her address was No 25, Queen Ann Street, East) she sang the title role in *Idalide*; the trio in the second act, "Di un si crudele istante," by Mara, Pacchierotti, and Lazzarini was mentioned by the *Morning Post* next day "as surpassing anything we have lately heard." On 2 June she sang Emilia in *Quinto Fabio*, revived for Pacchierotti's benefit. In the summer of 1791 she appeared in the Chester Music Festival and also joined Harrison, Kelly, and Mrs Crouch in performances of oratorios at York Minster during the assizes.

Her plans to return to Italy in the autumn of 1791 were delayed, it seems, by the illness of her husband. So she arranged to perform Mandane four nights in November for the Drury Lane company, which was playing that season at the newly built King's Theatre while they awaited construction of their own new theatre. For her appearances on 17, 19, 21, and 22 November she was paid £100 per night, according to Haydn's comments in his second London notebook, and she won "roars of applause." Box office receipts for the four nights exceeded a total of £1777. That month in the press appeared an "Impromptu. To Madam Mara, On her Quitting England. By Peter Pindar":

> *Dear Mara, should'st thou leave our Isle,*
> *No more would heav'nly Music smile;*
> *Thou killest to thy gentle Peter,*
> *And then there dies the Prince of Metre,*
> *No more thy Burgundy he quaffs,*
> *And sings and drinks, and drinks and laughs:*
> *Now to the Muses tunes his chimes,*
> *And happy hear thee sing his rhymes.*
> *If here thou stayest, thou wilt please*
> *A nation that both hears and sees.*
> *On, what a Venice will thou waste thy wind?*
> *Upon a poor old Dog, thats deaf and blind.*

Before their departure to the Continent, Mme Mara's husband signed a contract with John Philip Kemble for his wife to return that spring to sing serious recitative opera at the King's Theatre for 12 nights at a fee of 500 guineas and a benefit, with the usual charges. The agreement also called for Mme Mara to sing 40 nights in the following season with the Drury Lane company, at a salary of 1000 guineas and one benefit, "the profit of which shall be made up to her five hundred guineas by the proprietors."

The soprano returned to England by mid-April 1792 but did not perform until 23 May, when she sang the title role in *Dido Queen of Carthage*, a new opera by Prince Hoare, based on Metastasio, with the music by Storace. The fifth and last performance of the opera was sung for Mme Mara's benefit on 11 June 1792. The total receipts of £233 (less £161 charges) were disappointing, especially when compared against the box office business she had attracted the previous November. In fact, the total receipts for the run of *Dido Queen of Carthage* were only about £1080. Though contracted to receive 500 guineas for singing 12 nights, she sang only five times. *The London Stage* lists her salary for 1791–92 as £600, but that figure presumably includes payments made to her for the November engagement.

The following season Mme Mara made her first appearance for Kemble on 10 November 1792, in *Artaxerxes*. Kemble was referring to her tardiness that season when he wrote in his memorandum book on 12 November: "Mara pretended illness and ruin'd herself with the

Town." She performed for Kemble only six times that season instead of the 40 for which she had been contracted. But Kemble and his patentee R. B. Sheridan shared the King's Theatre that season with the opera, performances of which began in late January under the management of Storace and Kelly. For them, Mme Mara sang Aspasia in *Il giuochi d'Agrigento* on 5 February 1793, the title role in *Teodolinda* on 19 March, and Zenobia in *Odenato and Zenobia* on 11 June. These three operas were performed a total of 17 times. Sheridan was under obligation to the opera managers to pay Mme Mara's salary for those performances. He wrote to his treasurer Thomas Wheatley on 16 January 1793:

Pay Madame Mara the whole sum mentioned in her engagement with Mr Kemble last season, without deduction; and for the present season let her salary of one thousand guineas for forty nights, be paid weekly, on the Drury Lane account, and pay all arrears for the same.

Sheridan wrote again to Wheatley on 4 February 1793: "Mad. Mara must positively be paid [and] have her weekly salary from the beginning of the season immediately or the Opera will be finished up—I will see this money returned from the Opera account. Her engagement is £1000."

For her benefit on 23 May 1793 she sang as Mandane a favorite harp song, "Ah che nel petto io santo," accompanied by the younger Meyer. Receipts were £216 4s. 6d. (less charges of £163 17s. 6d.). Her address was still No 25, Queen Anne Street, East.

In the spring of 1793 she had also sung in the oratorios at Covent Garden under John Ashley's direction, but not without incident. She claimed that illness prevented her from singing the "Mad Bess" song by Purcell in the third part of the oratorio on 6 March 1793, though she had sung in the earlier two parts, and she claimed to have a physician's certificate to prove her condition. On 8 March she was replaced in the oratorio by Mme Dussek. Then followed a curious litigation between Mme Mara and James Harrison, a singer and publisher. In March 1793 Harrison had written a letter signed "Common Sense" to *The World*, in which he complained of the insults to which Mme Mara had subjected the public, especially in respect

to the recent oratorios. Mme Mara obtained the original manuscript of the letter, which proved to be in his handwriting, and sued Harrison. The verdict was in her favor, but the damages awarded amounted to one shilling. Mme Mara refused to sing at the benefit of John Ashley, so he sued Harrison for the losses he claimed to have sustained by her absence provoked by Harrison's publication. Ashley's suit was thrown out of court as groundless in terms of injury done to him. James Harrison, it should be noted, was the brother of the singer Samuel Harrison, who in 1786 had had a short-lived affair with Mme Mara.

After the 1792–93 season Mme Mara received no further long-term engagements in London. During the next ten years she confined herself mostly to concert and oratorio appearances. On 30 April 1796 she sang her old standby, Mandane in *Artaxerxes*, at Covent Garden, and the *Monthly Mirror* reported that she "retains all her sweetness, but has lost much of her power." She made her first London appearance in "a Comic Opera" at Covent Garden on 25 October 1797, when she acted Polly in *The Beggar's Opera*. She was then 49 years old, past her prime in several respects. The *Monthly Mirror* of November 1797 considered her, "to use a vulgar phrase, as upon her last legs. . . . [Her] Polly is downright burlesque; her figure, countenance, and time of life are directly repugnant to our ideas of character; and her foreign accent and gesticulation complete the absurdity." The *Morning Herald* of 26 October 1797 reported:

Mme Mara is merely a singer; her voice is by no means calculated to give effect to the dialogue of the part; and her performance, although she appears to have paid considerable attention to the degree of action necessary for the part, is greatly deficient in point of feeling. . . . Her deficiency in person and performance, however, is amply compensated for in her ability as a singer.

That season she made several other forays into comic opera at Covent Garden, playing Rosetta in *Love in a Village* on 15 November 1797, Lorenza (with additional songs) in *The Castle of Andalusia* on 5 December, Clara in *The Duenna* on 21 April 1798, Clarissa in *Lionel and Clarissa* on 10 May, and Marian in *Marian* on 14 May. For her benefit on 23 April 1798 she acted Polly in *The Beggar's Opera*.

Receipts were £236 3s. 6d., presumably less house charges, so her profits were quite modest. Tickets could be had from her at Mr Monzani's, No 2, Pall Mall. Monzani, the flutist, was no doubt providing a convenience, for in January 1799 her address was again Queen Ann Street, East, as it had been earlier in the decade, through 1794. In May 1796, however, it was No 57, Edgeware Road.

During that period she sang at Ranelagh Gardens in June 1790, at Dublin in July 1796 (for six nights, at 50 guineas per night and a free benefit), again at Dublin in December 1796 (for 12 nights at £50 per night), at Bath in 1798, and at Ranelagh in 1798. She made her first appearance at the new Drury Lane Theatre on 11 March 1800, playing Zemira in the premiere of Franklin's comic opera *The Egyptian Festival*. In his *Dramatic Censor*, Dutton was severe in his judgment, conceding that as a singer Mme Mara's powers were indisputable:

but as a *performer* she exhibits herself in a light which alternately provokes our ridicule and pity. Her delivery is an absolute libel on the profession. To the defects of a foreign pronunciation she joins a natural impediment of speech, which partakes too strongly of a lisp to warrant her bearing part in the prose dialogue of a play. What could possibly induce her to appear before the public under such disadvantages, unless she did it in compliment to the composer, we are at a loss to conjecture; nor less are we puzzled to account for the supineness of an audience which can patiently tolerate such puny efforts.

Her appearance in *The Egyptian Festival* was accounted for by the fact that the music had been written by Charles Haiman Florio, with whom she had been living for six years. It was rumored that she had written some of the music for another of Florio's operas, *The Outlaws*, that had opened at Drury Lane on 16 October 1798 and had run six nights only.

She was back in her element at the Haymarket oratorios in 1801, when she rendered "Angels ever bright and fair," "What tho' I trace," and "Farewell ye limpid streams" with all the taste and skill for which, the *Monthly Mirror* reported kindly, "she is so eminently distinguished." The audience was impressed and "rapturously applauded and encored the songs." On 15 May 1801 she acted Lorenza in *The Castle of Andalusia* at Covent Garden, her only night of playing there that season.

On 3 June 1802 Mme Mara gave a farewell concert at the King's Theatre, at which she benefited by some £1000. Taking her leave of England with Florio, Mme Mara gave some concerts at Paris, at the last of which it was said she received 12,000 francs, made her way through Germany, passing a week in Berlin in February 1803, when she appeared in a farewell concert, and ended finally in Russia, singing in St Petersburg and then in Moscow.

Mme Mara's relationships with her paramours were often as flamboyant as her talents. Her marriage to Giovanni Battista Mara in Berlin about 1772 was destined for conflict and misery. Burney had met Mara in Berlin and thought him a violoncellist "with great ability." But Mara was, nevertheless, a dissolute fellow who wasted his talents and his marriage. He accompanied his wife to London and seems to have involved himself in the negotiations for her various engagements. He also played for a time in the Covent Garden band. Her husband's presence in London hardly inhibited Mme Mara. The fine English singer Samuel Harrison fell under her spell in 1786, when he was 26 and she was 37. That summer they enjoyed the sea at Margate before visiting Paris together. The affair did not long survive (and in 1790 he married the soprano Ann Cantelo).

In the summer of 1794 Mme Mara again left her husband to run off with Charles Florio, this time to Bath. Both had sung in the Covent Garden oratorios that spring. A letter in the Folger Library, dated "Sept 1794," written by Mme Mara to the actress Jane Pope, reveals the singer's feelings about the new scandal:

I hope the disagreeable step I have been forced to take has not injured me in your good opinion. . . . In my present situation I find that I have been wrong in the following particular—*I never sought the friendship of those that write in the public papers* Perhaps I prided myself too much on my talent & private Character to think that I had any thing to fear from them or that their support was requisite they on return finding themselves slighted did not let the least circumstance that happened to me in public slip their notice that would tend to make them Tax me with pride caprice or impertinence—as you will have remark'd—However, this never disturbed my tranquility, for I thought it would not injure me in point of talent nor in point of Character with those persons that knew me. But if I had supposed ever to have been drawn to a step (tho' I have ever so great reason to) could not fail to expose me to spit & malice that had been lurking for an opportunity since so many years, *then* I should have courted the[ir] Friendship and flattered their conceited consequence—then all the compassion, all the praise would have been on *my* side, and all the scandal and calumny on the *other*, and the only thing I should have been blamed for, would have been that I had not taken the resolution ten years ago. It is very cruel that after having maintained my self and family from my Sixth year and afterwards (I am sorry to say it) a husband of an extravagant and Idle disposition the consequence of an excess of inclination to drinking—I am reduced at a time when I should be able to retire and rest myself to begin anew to provide for the future necessaries of life, but I hope those persons who once honoured me with there [*sic*] protection & friendship will not withdraw it now and I dont despair but that in a little while I may do more for my self than I have been able for so many years past—If I may still flatter myself to have a place in your kind remembrance I shall be happy to be convinced of it by a line directed to me at Mr Molini 14 Hanover St Hanover Sq. . . .

Mme Mara and Florio sang together in *Artaxerxes* at Dublin in the summer of 1796 (when Florio was hissed every night). Back in London, Florio and Mme Mara raised more public resentment by living in a house in Brompton and strolling out together. Her estranged husband meanwhile had remained in London, evidently constrained by legal procedures against him. In his *Third London Notebook*, Haydn described an awkward scene at a supper following a concert by Mme Mara at the Hanover Square Room on 24 March 1795:

There was not more than 60 persons in the audience. It is said that she never sang better than at that time. Janiowick conducted.—Mʳ Clementi sat at the pianoforte, and conducted his new grand Symphony, without success. After the concert was over, Madam Mara gave a *Soupé* in the adjoining room. After 12 o'clock Mʳ Mara, very confident, walked in the door, came forward, and asked for a glass of wine. Since Madam Mara saw quite clearly that her husband was raging, and feared the consequences, she turned to her lawyer, who was at the table, and he said to Mʳ Mara: You know our laws; you will have the goodness to leave this room at once, otherwise you will have to pay £200 tomorrow. The poor man left the company. Madam Mara, his wife, went the other day to Bath with

her *Cicisbeo*, but I rather think her obstinacy makes her despicable to the whole nation.

Giovanni Battista Mara left England sometime after that incident. He died in wretched circumstances at Schiedam in the Netherlands in 1808; he is noticed separately on these pages.

Madame Mara left London with Charles Florio in 1801, for a tour which took them to Paris, then to Berlin in 1803, and to Russia in 1807. Florio's extravagance and the burning of Moscow in 1812 both contributed to ruining Mme Mara financially. He speculated disastrously in musical patents and made several trips back to London on that business. He impregnated a Russian servant girl, and when she and the infant were shipped off to England by Mme Mara, the girl contrived to return to lodgings in a Moscow suburb, where Florio resumed the affair. Florio died at Moscow early in 1819, somewhat unbalanced mentally. Additional details of his life with Mme Mara are given in his notice in volume V of this dictionary.

Shortly after Florio's death Mme Mara returned to London, in the autumn of 1819. Some concerts by her were announced for the Argyle Rooms, but those were canceled because of her illnesses. But on 16 March 1820 she made an appearance at the King's Theatre, mysteriously announced as "a most celebrated singer," whom her agents "were not at liberty to name." It was a foolish attempt, for her voice was almost entirely gone. According to *The Manager's Notebook*, however, at the age of 71 "her step was firm, her person erect."

She soon left England for good, and retired to Revel, in Russia, where she died on 20 January 1833.

Mme Mara was regarded by some contemporaries as the most impressive singer from the Continent ever to have come to London, though a bad actress. The "agility and flexibility" of her voice, wrote Mount-Edgcumbe, "rendered her excellent in bravura." Sainsbury wrote of her in his *Dictionary*:

. . . Mara was the child of sensibility: every thing she did was directed to the heart; her tone, in itself pure, sweet, rich, and powerful, took all its various colourings from the passions of the words. . . . Her tone, perhaps, was neither so sweet nor so clear as Billington's, nor so rich and powerful as Catalani's, but it was the most touching language of the soul.

Several years before her death in 1831 she had received from Goethe a birthday poem, "Sangreich war dein Ehrenweg."

Published biographies of Mme Mara include G. C. Grosheim, *Das Leben der Künstlerin* (Cassel, 1823); J. F. Rochlitz in *Für Freunde der Tonkunst* (1868); Rosa Kaulitz-Niedeck, *Die Mara: das Leben einer berühmten Sängerin* (Heilbronn, 1929); and O. Anward, *Die Prima Donna Friedricks des Grossen* (Berlin, 1931).

The singer Mme Mara should not be confused with an actress of that name who performed in Dublin and in other provincial theatres in the 1790s and early 1800s.

Portraits of Mme Mara include:

1. By J. Hutchinson. Pastel drawing, in the Garrick Club (No 311).

2. Engraved portrait by W. S. Leney, after Fouquet. Published by Scatcherd & Whitaker, 1794. A copy was engraved by G. L. Chrétien. These are similar to the engraving by Ridley, after David, below.

3. Engraved portrait by A. Hüssner. A copy by W. Ridley was published by T. Evans, 1792.

4. Engraved portrait by W. Ridley, after J. L. David. Published as a plate to *Monthly Mirror*, 1800.

5. As Armida in *Armida*. Engraving by J. Collyer, after P. Jean. Published by Darling & Thompson, 1794. Copies were engraved by W. Greatbach as frontispiece to Hogarth's *Memoirs of the Musical Drama* (1838), by Rauch, and by J. C. Susemihl.

6. As Mandane in *Artaxerxes*. By unknown engraver. Published as a plate to the *Hibernian Magazine*, August 1792.

7. Caricature of her singing at a "Wapping Concert," 28 February 1786, with text as given above in this notice.

8. In a caricature engraving by Dent entitled "High Committee, or, Operatical Contest," along with other figures representing opera personnel and nobility who were involved in the rivalry between two opera companies in 1791.

9. Caricature, "The Charmers of the Age," engraving by James Sayers, 1786.

10. Caricature, "Ancient Music," engraving by J. Gillray, 1787.

11. In a group portrait consisting of medallion miniatures, with 25 other musicians and singers "of the time of Haydn and Mozart." Engraving by Landseer, from miniature cameos by H. de Janvry, after a plan by De Loutherbourg. Published at London by H. de Janvry, sold by Colnaghi & Co, 1801.

Maranari. *See* MARINARI.

Maranesi, Cosimo   *b. c. 1736, dancer.*
The youthful dancers Cosimo (sometimes Cassimo) Maranesi and Elizabetta Bugiani arrived at London on 9 October 1752, and the next day the press announced that these "two celebrated Italian Comic Dancers from the Opera at Paris" would soon appear at Covent Garden Theatre. They had recently performed with Pietro Sodi at the Opéra Comique of the Foire St Laurent. Probably they had been accompanied to London by Elizabetta's father, Signor Bugiani, who though not a regular member of the company would dance several times at Covent Garden in 1753 and 1754. Maranesi and Signorina Bugiani made their Covent Garden debut on 28 October 1752 in *Les chabonniers* and *Les sabotiers Tyrolese*, two dances which proved popular throughout the season. Their second appearance, on 1 November was reported by the press (in a clipping in the Winston Collection at the Folger Library): "They were just[ly] admired by the whole House for great Execution and amazing Variety of Comic Gestures . . . They are both very young. The Lady, as we are informed, not being above 15, and Signior Maranesi about 16 years old."

After a return visit to Paris in the summer, the couple rejoined the Covent Garden company for the 1753–54 season. Maranesi was scheduled to dance on 20 October 1753 but he broke his arm practicing on the night before, so his first appearance of the season, with Sga Bugiani in *Les savoyards* and *Les taileures*, was delayed until 10 December. On 7 March 1754 they danced *Les jardiniers* and *Les chabonniers*, and for her benefit on 30 March they presented a new dance called *Le matelot*. That dance and several other favorites were offered for Maranesi's benefit on 29 March.

Maranesi and his partner did not return to Covent Garden in 1754–55 but joined the dancers at the King's Theatre, where they made their debut on 9 November 1754 and remained for two seasons. They shared a benefit there on 18 March 1755, dancing a minuet.

Their last benefit at the King's was on 6 April 1756. At that time they were living together in Dean Street, Soho. He was then about 21 and she 20.

Engaged at a combined salary reported as £1000, Maranesi and Sga Bugiani opened at Tom Sheridan's Smock Alley Theatre in Dublin on 3 November 1756 with a comic dance in which he performed in women's clothes and she in men's. Maranesi worked in Dublin for three seasons, but Sga Bugiani seems to have left after 1756–57, perhaps to return to the Continent.

Maranesi evidently interrupted his Irish engagement early in 1758 to make a trip to Italy, whence he returned with a new partner, Signora Provenzali. On their way to Ireland, they stopped in London on 4 April 1758 to perform new dances at the King's Theatre and the following day set off for Dublin, where they danced at both Smock Alley and Crow Street. In 1759–60 they were once again at the King's, dancing under Gallini's direction.

In the autumn of 1760 Maranesi reengaged at Covent Garden, after an absence of six years, at a salary of 16s. 8d. per day, or £150 per season. Also in the company, on the paylist for 13s. 4d. per day or £120 per year, was a Sga Maranesi who made her first appearance at that theatre on 10 October 1760 with him in *The Cossacks*. Since the name of Sga Provenzali disappears from the bills after the 1759–60 season at the King's, we suggest the possibility that she may have married Maranesi and then appeared under her new name at Covent Garden. With his wife, whoever she may have been, Maranesi performed at Covent Garden for three seasons, through 1762–63, appearing in such ballets as *The Pedlar Trick'd*, *The Colliers*, and *The Hungarian Gambols*. She was featured in specialty minuets.

The Maranesis left London, it seems, after 1762–63. *The London Stage* suggests they danced in *La clemenza di Tito* at the King's on 3 December 1765, on the basis of an edition of that opera printed that year, but we believe the cast listed represents the performers from the London production of 15 January 1760. According to M. H. Winter in *The Pre-Romantic Ballet*, Maranesi was engaged at the Naples court during the two decades preceding the French Revolution.

Maranesi, Signora Cosimo, earlier Signora Provenzali? ₁*fl.* 1758–1763₁, *dancer. See* MARANESI, COSIMO.

Marble, Mrs ₁*fl.* 1774–1775?₁, *dancer.*
In the Forster Collection at the Victoria and Albert Museum is a company list that shows the dancer Mrs Marble to have been at Drury Lane in 1774 and probably 1775.

Marcadet, Mons ₁*fl.* 1797₁, *dancer.*
Monsieur Marcadet made his first English appearance on 17 January 1797 at the King's Theatre dancing in *Les délassements militaires* and the role of Tisiphone in *L'Amour et Psiché*. The *Monthly Mirror* was not impressed: "A new dancer, of the name of Marcadet, has been imported from [St Petersburg] Russia, where he was held in high estimation; he may become useful here, but can never eclipse the superior talents of our old favourites." Marcadet danced in the ballet *Pizarre* beginning 7 February and may have been in other dances not named in the bills. It is probable that he was related to Jean-Remy Marcadet, the dancer and dancing master who was at Stockholm from 1778 to 1795.

March. *See* MARSH.

Marchbanks, Mr ₁*fl.* 1799–1813₁, *scene designer and painter.*
The earliest record we have found of Mr Marchbanks is a bill for the Royal Circus dated 25 March 1799; on it Marchbanks (or Marchbank) is credited with helping to paint the scenery for *Almoran and Hamet*. The bill for 23 June 1800 shows that he aided in the execution of the scenery for the pantomime *The Magic Flute*. For the following 13 years Marchbanks busied himself at the Royal Circus. Until 1806 he was usually cited as helping to paint scenery designed by others for such spectacle productions as *The Eclipse*, *The Golden Farmer*, *Gonsalvo de Cordova*, *The Jubilee of 1802*, *The Rival Sisters*, and *Louisa of Lombardy*. The Drury Lane accounts for 1805 show a payment to Marchbanks of £16 16s., so he augmented his income by working at the patent house as well.

From 1806 on, Marchbanks served the Royal Circus as a scene designer as well as painter, one of his first designs being for *Momus and Mercury*, which played on 26 May 1806. Between then and 28 June 1813 (our last record of him) Marchbanks designed scenery for *Juan Fernandez*, *The Cloud King*, *The False Friend*, *Solima*, *Buenos Ayres*, *The Magic Sword*, *The Rival Clowns* (with Greenwood), a ballet based on *Macbeth* (with Greenwood), *The Seven Wonders of the World*, and *The Siberian Exile*. He also helped on the execution of scenes for *Llewelyn, Prince of Wales*, and as a special background for a song sung by Miller he painted a view of Lisbon.

Marchesi, Luigi, called "Marchesini"
1755–1829, singer, composer.

Luigi Marchesi was born in Milan on 8 August 1755, according to the *New Grove*, the son of a horn player who planned a career for his son as an instrumentalist. Young Luigi's voice was of such high quality, however, that his father was persuaded to have the boy operated on at Bergamo to preserve it. Luigi studied singing under Caironi and Albuzzi and music under Fioroni and made his debut at 17 in Rome in a female role in *La serva padrona*.

Harvard Theatre Collection

LUIGI MARCHESI
engraving by Bernardoni

In 1775 he sang another female part, in Florence, in *Castore e Polluce*. That year he sang also in Milan and Munich and was engaged by the Elector of Bavaria for his chapel. That assignment lasted for two years, after which Marchesi returned to Milan to serve as second man to Pacchierotti and then to Venice, where he sang second to Millico. By 1778 he was singing *primo uomo* in Munich, Padua, and Florence.

Perhaps it was in 1778 at Florence that he sang, according to Michael Kelly, "Bianchi's 'Sembianza amabile del mio be sole' with most ravishing taste; in one passage he ran up a voletta of semitone octaves, the last note of which he gave with such exquisite power and strength that it was ever after called 'La bomba del Marchesi.'" Nancy Storace tried to equal that feat, and the jealous Marchesi had her dismissed from the company.

From 1778 to 1780 Marchesi sang at Naples; then he returned to Milan and later toured to Pisa, Genoa, Turin, Rome, Lucca, Vienna, and Berlin. In Turin in 1782 he was appointed court musician to the King of Sardinia at 1500 Piemontese lire and given permission to travel abroad nine months out of the year. In 1785 he was in St Petersburg, but, fearful that the Russian weather might harm his voice, he did not stay the scheduled three years.

He made his first appearance in London on 5 April 1788 at the King's Theatre, singing the title role in *Giulio Sabino*. Mount-Edgcumbe recorded his impressions:

At length in the spring arrived the celebrated Marchesi, whose fame had long reached this country, and who had been extolled to such a degree that impatience and expectation were raised to the highest pitch; and on the first night of his appearance the theatre was not only crowded to the utmost in every part, but on the rising of the curtain, the stage was so full of spectators that it was some time before order and silence could be obtained, and with some difficulty that Marchesi, who was to open the opera, could make his way before the audience. Marchesi was at this time a very well-looking young man, of good figure, and graceful deportment. His acting was spirited and expressive: his vocal powers were very great, his voice of extensive compass, but a little inclined to be thick. His execution was very considerable, and he was rather too fond of displaying it; nor was his cantabile singing equal to his bravura. In recitative, and scenes of energy and passion, he was incomparable, and had he been less lavish of ornaments, which were not always appropriate, and possessed a more pure and simple taste, his performance would have been faultless: it was always striking, animated, and effective. He chose for his début Sarti's beautiful opera of Giulio Sabino, in which all the songs of the principal character, and they are many and various, are of the very finest description. But I was a little disappointed at Marchesi's execution of them, for they were all familiar to me, as I had repeatedly heard Pacchierotti sing them in private, and I missed his tender expression, particularly in the last pathetic scene, and lamented that their simplicity should be injured, as it was, by an overflowery style. But this flowery style was an absolute simplicity to what we have heard in latter days. The comparison made me like Marchesi less than I had done at Mantua, or than I did in other subsequent operas here. He was received with rapturous applause.

At his benefit on 8 May Marchesi sang Megacle in *L'Olimpiade*, making tickets available at No 37, Upper James Street, Golden Square. On 29 May he sang a new song he had composed. His popularity was such that songs he sang in the two operas in which he appeared in 1788 were quickly published.

Marchesi returned for the 1789 opera season in London at a salary of £1500 plus a free benefit and lodgings. He sang Achille in *Ifigenia in Aulide*, Gualtieri in *Il desertore*, and Poro in *La generosità d'Alessandro*. He returned to Milan after the season ended, according to a letter from Dr Burney to Frances Burney D'Arblay in the Hilles Collection at Yale. Marchesi had promised to return to London in 1790, but when he got to Paris on his way to Milan he changed his mind, according to Burney. The opera manager, Gallini, had used him like a dog, Burney wrote, but sent Marchesi carte blanche if he would come back.

The castrato returned for the 1790 season at the Haymarket Theatre; Smith in *The Italian Opera in London* states that his salary was £1150. Marchesi sang Timante in *L'usurpator innocente*, Poro in *La generosità d'Alessandro* again, and Pirro in *Andromaca*. His benefit tickets in 1790 were available from him at No 14, Charles Street, St James's Square. During his visits to London Marchesi also sang at the Oxford Music Room, sometime in 1788 or 1789, and he sang with Pacchierotti at a private concert at Lord Buckingham's—the only time that the two singers appeared together, according to

Heriot. While in London Marchesi published a few ariettes, and he sat for the artist Richard Cosway. Cosway's wife, Maria, like so many other women who saw Marchesi, fell madly in love with the singer. When he left London, she followed him to the Continent, leaving her husband and infant child behind. She followed Marchesi all over Europe for several years, not returning to her husband until 1795.

Heriot quotes a newspaper report dating toward the end of Marchesi's stay in England:

Last night their Majesties and the Princesses honoured the Opera with their presence. The object of attraction was the Marchesi, and the hero, animated by the presence of the Court, exerted himself to the utmost. He has for some time past greatly corrected himself in regard of his flourishes and ornaments. He still demonstrates his wonderful endowments in the science, but not to the injury of the air, by loading it with ornament. Tune, however, is in the ear what vision is in the eye—it may be amended where it is, but cannot be conveyed where it is not. We fear it is not in Marchesi.

Yet Dr Burney held a high opinion of the male soprano:

Marchesi's style of singing is not only elegant and refined to an uncommon degree, but often grand and full of dignity, particularly in his recitatives and occasional low notes. His variety of embellishments and facility of running extempore divisions are truly marvellous. Many of his graces are new, elegant, and of his own invention; and he must have studied with intense application to enable himself to execute the divisions, and running shakes from the bottom of his compass to the top, even in a rapid series of half notes. But besides his vocal powers, his performance on the stage is extremely embellished, by the beauty of his person, and grace and propriety of his gestures. We expected a great singer, but that does not always include a fine actor.

After his London years Marchesi spent most of his time in Venice, carrying on there in 1790 a musical feud with the prima donna Louisa Todi that excited the Venetians. But he also appeared regularly in Milan, and it was there in 1806 that he refused to sing for Napoleon. After the 1805–6 season in Milan he retired from the stage. He died there in mid-December 1829.

By all accounts Luigi Marchesi was one of the finest male sopranos of the eighteenth century, and one of the last. Like so many of the eminent singers, he was greatly fawned upon by his adoring public, and, like many, he had his peculiar vanities. According to Heriot, Marchesi insisted on making his entrances descending a hill on horseback, wearing the usual hero's plumed helmet (in his case, multicolored and a yard high). And he insisted on being announced by a fanfare of trumpets. No matter what character he was singing, he always began with one of his favorite arias, whether it was appropriate to the occasion or not.

The *Enciclopedia dello spettacolo* (which gives Marchesi's death date as 14 rather than 18 December 1829) contains details of the singer's continental career.

Portraits of Marchesi include:

1. By Richard Cosway, present location unknown. Engravings were made by Schiavonetti and published by Colnaghi, 1790, and by "M. F. H.," published in London (n.d.).

2. Engraved portrait by G. Bernardoni, 1829.

3. Lithograph portrait by H. E. Wintter, 1816.

4. Engraved portrait by unknown artist, with caption "Aloys Marchesi Mediolanus."

5. Caricature published by J. Nixon in 1789 called "A Bravura at the Hanover Square Concert," showing Marchesi covered with jewels and playing the conceited coxcomb.

6. An engraving, cited by Heriot, made in the English style in Italy, showing a triumphant Signora Todi and a humiliated Marchesi.

7. Marchesi is shown with a large group of singers in an engraving by Rainaldo, after Fedi, published in Florence between 1801 and 1807.

8. Two benefit tickets for Marchesi were designed by Cosway: one engraved by Condée for Marchesi's benefit at the Haymarket on 29 April 1790, the other engraved by Schiavonetti, undated. Both show cupids playing on a lyre, but neither has a picture of Marchesi.

Marchesini, Signora. *See* ROSSI, SIGNORA PHILIP DE.

Marchesini, Maria Antonia, called "La Lucchesina," later Signora Jacopo Amiconi [*fl.* 1736–1739], *singer.*

"La Lucchesina," as Maria Antonia Marchesini was called, sang in Naples in 1736, for the Opera of the Nobility in 1737, and for Handel beginning in 1738. The *Daily Advertiser* on 26 April 1737 reported that

Signor Rolli's new opera called SABRINA, was rehearsed yesterday in Mr. Heidegger's apartments. The Signora Marchesini, lately arrived from Italy, performed in it with universal approbation; and we hear that their Royal Highnesses the Prince and Princess of Wales, to whom she sung on last Friday night at court, intend to honour the entertainment with their presence this evening at the theatre-royal in the Hay-market. The Signora Marchesini's songs are distributed after such a judicious manner by the ingenious author, so as to rise gradually upon the audience in each act.

La Lucchesina's role in the opera was the title part of Sabrina.

In 1738 at the King's she sang Isifile in *La conquista del vello d'oro*, Rodimonda in *Faramondo*, Arsamene in *Serse*, and Albina in *Alessandro severo*. In 1739 she was heard as Medoro in *Angelica and Medoro*, probably sang in *Jupiter in Argos*, and was possibly the Witch of Endor in *Saul*. Dean in *Handel's Dramatic Oratorios and Masques* calls La Lucchesina a mezzo-soprano, but he also notes that one of David's solos in *Saul* was marked for her, and David was written for a countertenor. The papers differed on the report of the singer of the Witch of Endor in that oratorio; Cecilia Arne was named for it in one paper, and she was a soprano.

In the registers of the Portuguese Embassy Chapel on 17 May 1738 "Mª Antonia Marchesini" married James Amiconi, with Julia Marchesini and George Lewes standing as witnesses. The groom was the scene painter Jacopo Amiconi, who had worked at the King's Theatre since 1729 and did decorative painting as well as scene painting. He left England about 1739, went to Paris and St Petersburg and then to Venice before returning to London in 1741. He returned to Venice and then went to Madrid, in 1747. He died in the latter city in 1752. It is not known whether Maria Antonia was with him from the time of their marriage to his death, but she may have been. We find no further evidence of her having continued her singing career.

Marchetti, Signora [*fl.* 1773–1791?], *singer.*

On 7 December 1773 Signora Marchetti had a principal role in the opera *Il puntiglio amoroso* at the King's Theatre. During the rest of the 1773–74 opera season she took part in *Antig-*

ono, Nitteti, Artaserse, and *L'Olimpiade.* According to Dr Burney, she also sang in *Lucio Vero.* He said she "had a brilliant toned voice, *bel metallo di voce,* with which she might have become a singer of the first class, if want of health had not prevented her from that persevering practice which is so necessary to the vanquishing vocal difficulties." A benefit was granted her at Hickford's Rooms on 9 May 1774, at which she sang a principal character in *Il trionfo della costanza.*

About 1791 was published the recitative and duet *Ah qual orrida scena* as sung by Signora Marchetti and Signor David (i.e. Davide). We do not know when she may have sung with him, but it would have to have been after her appearances in London in 1773–74.

Marcoureau, Guillaume. *See* DE BRÉCOURT, SIEUR.

Marcucci, Felice ₁*fl.* *1764–1771?*₁, *dancer, actor?*

On 21 February 1764 at the King's Theatre a new but unnamed dance was performed by Felice Marcucci and Signor Bernardi. Signora Marcucci (or Marcucis), advertised as just arrived from Italy, had appeared in an untitled dance at the King's the previous 10 January. She may have accompanied her husband to Ireland, but only his name has been found in the bills there. In 1764 Marcucci danced at Smock Alley in Dublin, and in 1765–66 and 1766–67 he danced at the Crow Street Theatre. A "Signora Marcoucci" played Captain Champignon in *The Tars of Old England* at the Theatre Royal in Edinburgh on 20 March 1771; that citation was probably intended for Felice Marcucci.

Marcucci, Signora Felice ₁*fl.* *1764*₁, *dancer. See* MARCUCCI, FELICE.

Mardette. *See* MAUDET.

Mareis, Pasqualino de ₁*fl.* *1736*₁, *violoncellist.*

At a performance of *Alexander's Feast* at Covent Garden by Handel's company on 19 February 1736 Pasqualino de Mareis and Andrea Caporale played violoncellos.

Marella, Giovanni Battista ₁*fl.* *1746– 1777*₁, *violinist, violist.*

Giovanni Battista Marella (or Morella) arrived in Dublin on 29 September 1750 and for four years gave performances on the viola d'amore and violin. In July 1751 he and several others leased the Crow Street Music Hall for six years at an annual rate of £113 15*s.* Though van der Straeten places Marella in London in 1753, the earliest notice we have found of him dates from 29 January 1755, when he played first violin in a performance of *La serva padrona* at the Haymarket Theatre. The following 13 February at the same house he offered a solo on the violin. A year later, on 25 March 1756, he returned to the Haymarket to play a violin solo. Pohl has Marella in London in 1759 playing the viola d'amore, and van der Straeten notes that the musician won a prize at the Catch Club in 1763. He published some violin pieces in 1753 and 1757.

Pue's Occurrences on 1 October 1754 said Marella had married (Eleanor) Oldmixon in Dublin. She was the daughter of the playwright and historian John Oldmixon (1673–1742), and though, according to Faulkner's *History of Brentford,* she sang in 1746 at Hickford's Music Room in London as Mrs Marella, we find her cited as "Miss" Oldmixon on 21 April 1749 at Hickford's and as "Mrs" Oldmixon at a concert in Dublin on 25 January 1752. In 1749 in his *General History* the prompter Chetwood quoted some lines on her:

> *Oldmixon, Syren-voice, improv'd by Art*
> *Steals softly on the Song-enamour'd Heart.*

The Mr "Morella" listed in Mortimer's *London Directory* of 1763 as a teacher of guitar living in Great Pultney Street, Golden Square, was probably Giovanni Battista Marella.

Giovanni Battista and Eleanor (cited as John Baptist and Eleanora) were residuary legatees of George Oldmixon, Eleanor's brother (?). In George's will, dated 27 June 1777, he described the Marellas as of Wandsworth, Surrey, and the parents of a son, John Baptist. The will, abstracted in Crisp's *Somerset Wills,* was proved on 5 June 1779, but there is no certainty that Mr and Mrs Marella were then still alive. Seilhamer stated that the Marellas had a son who changed his name to Oldmixon and was later knighted (supposedly) by the viceroy for his services under the Duke of Portland in

Ireland. That son may have been the John Baptist mentioned in George Oldmixon's will. "Sir" John Oldmixon married the singer and actress Georgina George in 1788.

Marella, Mrs Giovanni Battista, Eleanor, née Oldmixon ₁*fl. 1746–1777*₁, *singer.* See MARELLA, GIOVANNI BATTISTA.

Marenesi. *See* MARANESI.

Mareschi, Signora ₁*fl. 1757*₁, *singer.* On 24 March 1757 at the King's Theatre Signora Mareschi sang in the annual benefit for indigent musicians and their families. *The London Stage* cites a Mareschi singing Ormonte in *Euristeo* at the King's on 31 May, and we take that reference to be to Signora Mareschi.

"Margarina." *See* YOUNG, ISABELLA.

Margherita, Signora. *See* DE L'ÉPINE and GALLIA.

Maria, Signora ₁*fl. 1791*₁, *singer.* Smith in *The Italian Opera* in London lists Signora Maria as one of the singers in the opera company at the King's Theatre from 26 March to 6 June 1791.

Maria, Signora Joanna. *See* "BARONESS, THE."

Mariana, Signora, later Mrs Richards ₁*fl. 1779–1782*₁, *rope dancer.* Signora Mariana performed a rope dance with Lawrence Ferzi at Sadler's Wells on 5 April 1779, and appeared there again in March 1780. By 2 March 1782 she had become Mrs Richards and was performing at Bristol in Andrews's company from London. The bill on that date identified her as "the late Signora MARIANA, from Sadlers' Wells" and claimed that she would "perform on the Tight Rope without touching it with her Feet, never yet attempted by any but herself, she also will Leap over a Garter Six Feet from the Rope, backward and forward,—the *Clown* by Mr. RICHARDS." Later in the evening she performed "Several astonishing Equilibriums on the SLACK WIRE . . ." The performance took place at Coopers' Hall. The troupe continued

performing into April, and on the ninth the show was for the benefit of "the unparalleled Signiora MARIANA."

Marianne, Mlle ₁*fl. 1760–1762*₁, *dancer.* As of 22 September 1760 a female dancer named Marianne was on the Covent Garden paylist at 5s. daily or £50 annually. *The London Stage* lists her as "Mrs Mariane" in 1760–61 and "Mlle Marianne" the following season, but it would appear that there were not two women but one, and she was more frequently cited as Mademoiselle. During 1760–61 she danced in *Comus, The Hungarian Gambols*, and a dance called *The Painter in Love With His Picture*, and from 17 December 1760 to 22 May 1761 she appeared as Air in *The Rape of Proserpine*. In 1761–62 she repeated that part, again participated in *Comus* and *The Hungarian Gambols*, and danced a Follower of Daphne in *Apollo and Daphne.*

Marianne, Miss *b. c. 1784. See* HANDY, MARY ANN.

Maria Theresia, Mme. *See* TERESIA, MME.

Marie, Mrs ₁*fl. 1726*₁, *performer?* On 20 May 1726 a benefit was held at Drury Lane Theatre for Mrs Marie; it is not clear whether that was her Christian name or surname, and the bill did not indicate what her position was in the company—if she held one. Possibly she was a performer.

Mariens, Francis ₁*fl. 1685–1689*₁, *flutist.* Cart de Lafontaine in *The King's Musick* conjectures that references in the Lord Chamberlain's accounts to a Monsieur Mario are to the flutist Francis (or François) Mariens. Mariens was appointed to the King's Musick under James II on 31 August 1685, spent part of the summer of 1687 attending the King at Windsor for 6s. daily above his regular salary of £30 annually (plus livery, one supposes), and was last cited in the accounts on 25 March 1689.

Mariet, Mrs ₁*fl. 1743–1761*₁, *dancer.* At the Pinchbeck and Fawkes booth at Bartholomew Fair on 23 August 1743 Mademoiselle Mariet danced. She seems not to have been mentioned in London bills again until the 1749–50 season, when she appeared with regularity at Drury Lane, sometimes called Mlle, and sometimes Mme, Mariet. That pattern continued for over ten years, and the citations in *The London Stage* to Mlle, Miss, Mme, and Mrs Mariet seem all to be to one dancer, though why there was such inconsistence in styling her for so long a time remains a mystery. In 1749–50 she appeared as a dancer in *The Savoyard Travellers*, *Acis and Galatea*, the *Rural Dance* at the end of *The Chaplet*, the dance of Aerial Spirits in *The Tempest*, and the comic ballet *Venetian Gardeners*. The following season she danced in *The Bird Catchers* and on 18 January 1751 was injured dancing in the pantomime *Queen Mab*. The prompter Cross, who recorded her accident, also noted on 18 February that "Mrs Mariet our Columbine ran away with some Gentleman," but by 24 April she had returned to the cast of *Queen Mab*.

Except for the seasons 1755–56 and 1756–57, when she may have been performing in the provinces, Mrs Mariet danced at Drury Lane, adding to her repertoire unnamed characters in *Harlequin Ranger*, *The Genii*, *Harlequin Enchanted*, *Fortunatus*, and *Mercury Harlequin*. After the 1760–61 season she seems to have left the London stage.

Marigi. *See* MORIGI.

Marinari, Gaetano *1764–1844, scene painter, machinist.*

The Italian painter Gaetano Marinari succeeded Novosielski at the King's Theatre in 1785–86 at a salary of £100, according to the Lord Chamberlain's records. Among his assignments that sason were "a great Variety of magnificent Scenery and Decorations" for the premiere of *Le Premier Navigateur*, a ballet originally created at Paris by Gardel but produced in London by Vestris on 23 March 1786, and scenes for Mortellari's opera *Armida* on 25 May. Marinari served as a painter and machinist at the King's Theatre regularly through 1788–89. His work on operas and ballets (many by Noverre) included: *Alceste*, *Il tutore burlato*, *L'Amore protetto dal cielo*, *Giulio Cesare in Egitto*, *Gli schiava per amore*, and *L'Heureux Evénément* in 1786–87; *Il re Teodoro in Venezia*, *Les Offrandes a l'Amour*, *Giannina e Bernadone*, *Psyché et l'Amour*, *Les Fêtes du tempe*, *Euthyme e Eu-*

chario, *Giulio Sabino*, and *L'Olimpiade* in 1787–88; and *La locandiera*, *La cosa rara*, *Ifigenia in Aulide*, *La villana reconosciuta*, *La Vendemmia*, and *Il barbiere di Siviglia* in 1788–89.

After the King's Theatre burned in June 1789 the opera was conducted in several temporary locales. Marinari did new scenes for *The Generous Slave*, a ballet, at the Haymarket on 13 May 1790, for *La pastorella nobile* at the Pantheon, and for *La Locanda* and *La discordia conjugale* at the Haymarket in 1791–92. Meanwhile he had taken on work at the Royalty Theatre in Goodman's Fields in 1790 for productions of *Paris Federation* and *Arthur, the British Worthy*. For the premiere of Cobb's *Poor Old Drury!*, done by the Drury Lane company at the new King's Theatre on 21 September 1791, Marinari provided, in the words of Michael Kelly, "some beautiful scenery, particularly Mount Parnassus." For the fireworks celebrating the birth of the Duchess of York in May 1792 he designed for Ranelagh Gardens a special building to exhibit the eruption of Mount Etna. The idea for the exhibition had been based on Torré's "Forge of Vulcan" which had attracted great numbers to Marylebone Gardens 20 years earlier. Marinari's scene depicted Mount Etna and the cavern of Vulcan, with the Cyclops forging armor to the accompaniment of music collected from Gluck, Haydn, Giardini, and Handel. As described by the advertisements, "The smoke thickens, the crater on the top of Etna vomits forth flames; and the lava rolls dreadful along the side of the mountain. This continues with increasing violence till there is a prodigious eruption, which finishes with the tremendous explosion."

When the operas and ballets resumed at the King's Theatre in January 1793 Marinari provided scenes for *I giuochi d'Agrigento*, *Venus and Adonis*, *La nozze di Dorina*, *Teodolindo*, and *Iphigenia in Aulide*. He also prepared the scenery for the Margravine of Anspach's new private theatre at Brandenburgh House that opened on 25 February 1793. The following season at the King's found him working on *Il matrimonio segreto*, *I contadini bizzarre*, *Il capriccio drammatico*, *Don Giovanni* and *Ifigenia in Aulide*. For *Don Giovanni* on 1 March 1794 the *Morning Chronicle* (3 March), reported "The decorations were admirable—particularly what M. Noverre calls his *practicable hell*, in which Marinari has displayed very fine talents. It is wonderful what an effect of fire he has produced by the power of transparencies." Blazing torches and reflection from the scene threw flashes of red light into the boxes, "which had most superb effect, in the way of spectacle." For another of Noverre's ballets, *Ifigenia in Aulide*, introduced on 23 April 1793, one of Marinari's machines was the chariot of the sun, "the brilliancy of which is much beyond any former representation of the sort," according to the testimony of the *Morning Herald* (24 April); it passed over the stage, and for some time was suspended over the altar, while the whole corps de ballet offered their "adorations."

In 1794–95 Marinari was replaced at the King's Theatre by Novosielski, but after the latter's death in April 1795, Marinari was reemployed, mainly it seems for altering and redecorating the theatre, at a salary of £300 for 1795–96. He had in the meanwhile taken up a position at Drury Lane Theatre where he continued to be engaged from October 1794 through 1799–1800 at £10 10s. per week. In December 1796 he was paid £50 for painting a new frontispiece for the Drury Lane stage. At that theatre his productions included *The Mountaineers*, *Alexander the Great*, *Jack of Newbury*, and *The Triumph of Hymen* in 1794–95; *Venice Preserv'd*, *The Plain Dealer* (with Capon), and *Mahaud* in 1795–96; *Robinson Crusoe* (with Greenwood) in 1797–98; and *Pizarro* in 1798–99.

During the 1790s he also was engaged occasionally at the Haymarket, executing scenes for the premieres of *Zorinski* (with Rooker) on 20 June 1795, *The Italian Monk* on 15 August 1797, *The Inquisitor* on 23 June 1798 and *Cambro-Britons* on 21 July 1798. He was also employed as a machinist at Covent Garden Theatre in 1796–97.

Evidently Marinari's energies and talents allowed him to make contributions to all the major London theatres in the 1790s. In 1797 he resumed work at the King's Theatre, where he was still painting in 1804 and may have been as late as 1808. There he executed Dragonetti's designs for the premiere of *Ipermestra* on 28 November 1797, for the ballet *Télémaque* on 26 March 1799, the English premiere of *Alessandro e Timoteo* on 15 April 1800, and in 1802–3 he painted for *La Morte de Mitridate*, *Armida*, *Merope e Polifonte*, and *I due baroni*.

The Drury Lane account books record payments to him as house scene painter through at least 1804–5. There in 1802, with Capon and Greenwood, he worked on *The Winter's Tale*. In 1809 he went to Dublin to decorate F. E. Jones's Crow Street Theatre, painting allegorical pictures on the ceiling, the proscenium, and the panels of the several tiers, as well as a new drop scene. He was still there in 1810–11 when he did a setting of clouds and the moon for *Harlequin from the Moon*.

In 1812 Marinari returned to London to resume some of his previous connections, working that season at the new Drury Lane and at the Pantheon. In 1819–20 he was receiving £7 per week for work at the former theatre, where he continued, sporadically, over the next several decades, providing scenes for Kean's *King Lear* and *Coriolanus* in 1820, for Elliston's coronation spectacle in August 1821 (the scene of Westminster Hall, with the King and nobles seated at a banquet, was "the most imposing" part of the spectacle), with Andrews and Stanfield in 1824 and 1828, and for Elliston between 1831 and 1834. In 1836 he was at Covent Garden.

Marinari was still alive about 1844, described by G. Raymond (*Memoirs of Robert Edward Elliston*) as aged 80 and in great poverty. Raymond regarded him as one of the best scene painters in Europe and Gilliland praised his classical mind and fine specimens of architectural scenery. Planché found him inferior to De Loutherbourg. Nothing of his work seems to have survived, save a sketch by J. H. Grieve of Marinari's sun temple design for *Pizarro* in 1798–99, now in the print room of the British Museum.

Marinelli. *See also* MARTINELLI.

Marinelli, Mr [*fl.* 1796–1797], *puppeteer.*

According to the bill for *Harlequin and Oberon* at Covent Garden Theatre on 19 December 1796 "the *Fantoccini* [were] executed by Marinelli." The pantomime had 60 performances during the 1796–97 season.

Marinesi or Marinisi. *See* MARANESI.

Mario, Mons. *See* MARIENS, FRANCIS.

Marionesi. *See* MARANESI.

Mariotti, Mr ₁*fl. 1793–1838*₁, *trombonist.*

On 3 April 1793 Mr Mariotti (or Marriotti) was paid £18 15s. for playing in the Drury Lane band at the King's Theatre at 25 performances of *The Pirates.* According to Doane's *Musical Directory* (1794) Mariotti played trombone at the Oxford Meeting in 1793. The accounts of the King's Theatre indicate that Mariotti was in the band there in 1817 and 1818, and he may well have been performing regularly in earlier years. From February 1834 to February 1838 the trombonist sent letters of thanks to the Royal Society of Musicians for Christmas donations he had received.

Mariottini, Signor ₁*fl. 1773–1774*₁, *dancer.*

The bill for the King's Theatre of 20 November 1773 announced that the dancer Fierville had sprained his ankle at a rehearsal the day before and would be replaced in a *Grand Serious Ballet* and *Grand Chaconne* by "Mariottini who never appeared in England before. . . ." For the rest of the season Mariottini danced regularly in those works plus a Persian pantomime ballet called *Harem of Ispahan*, and in *La Provencal*, *Les Faunes vainques*, and a *New Field Dance*.

Mark, Mrs ₁*fl. 1795*₁, *performer?*

Mrs Mark was a member of the company at the Richmond theatre in the summer of 1795; she was presumably a performer.

Markatchy, Signor ₁*fl. c. 1771?–1785*₁, *equestrian.*

Signor Markatchy (or Markutchy) was an equestrian at Astley's Amphitheatre from perhaps 1771 through 7 April 1785.

Markes. *See* MARKS.

Markham, Mrs ₁*fl. 1721–1722*₁, *actress.*

On 23 May 1721 Mrs Markham shared a benefit with Miss Lindar at Drury Lane, though she was mentioned in no bills previous to that. On 4 August she played Jiltup in *The Fair Quaker*, and the following 27 October she appeared as Dame Pliant in *The Alchemist*. During the rest of the 1721–22 season she acted

Zayda in *Aureng-Zebe* and Beliza in *The Ambitious Stepmother*. On 23 May 1722 she shared a benefit with Boval.

Marklew, ₁**Carolina?**₁ *d. 1778, dancer.*

A Mrs Marklew subscribed 10s. 6d. to the Drury Lane Fund in 1766, and though her name did not appear in the bills there until some years later, she may well have labored obscurely in the dancing chorus from 1766 on. She danced at Norwich in 1772, probably between Drury Lane seasons, and in 1773 and 1774 she was a columbine at Bristol. On 18 May 1774 she danced a hornpipe at Drury Lane and had her benefit tickets accepted. She offered a hornpipe at the China Hall, Rotherhithe, on 3 July and 25 September 1776, and at Drury Lane beginning 31 October 1777 she danced in *Cymbeline*. A notation in the Fund Book indicates that she died in April 1778, but that may have been when the accountant at the theatre received news of her death, for it seems likely that she was the Carolina "Markelev" from St Clement Danes who was buried at St Paul, Covent Garden, on 15 March 1778.

Marks, Mr ₁*fl. 1776–1803*₁, *doorkeeper.*

Nearly every spring, sometime between 21 May 1776 and 30 May 1788, a Mr Marks was cited in the Covent Garden benefit bills. Though he was not mentioned in the 1790s (when he may have had other employment) it is probable that he was the Mr Marks who served Drury Lane as a doorkeeper from 1799–1800 through 1802–3. At Covent Garden his name had regularly been grouped with other house servants.

Marks, Mr ₁*fl. 1780–1792?*₁, *actor.*

Mr Marks had a role in *Fortunatus: Or Harlequin at Stirbitch-Fair* on 5 October 1780 at Stourbridge Fair, Cambridge. He acted Lance in *Wit Without Money* and an unspecified role in *The Taylors* on 25 November 1782 at the Haymarket Theatre in London. Perhaps he was the "Markes" who was acting in 1792 at the theatre at Barking, Essex, under Johnson. Johnson converted the Town Hall into a playhouse, said the *Thespian Magazine* in 1792, and Johnson, his wife, Weston, and the dancer Kirk had some merit. "But for all the rest," stated the journal, "nothing can be said which will by any means prove to their advantage."

Marks, William [*fl.* 1794–1816], *violinist, oboist.*

Doane's *Musical Directory* of 1794 listed William Marks, of Warwick Street, Charing Cross, as a violinist and oboist who was a member of the New Musical Fund and had played in the Handel Memorial Concerts at Westminster Abbey. At some point he became a member of the Royal Society of Musicians, for on 1 August 1813 and 4 February 1816 he sent the Society thanks for benefactions.

Markutchy. See MARKATCHY.

Marlborough, Mr [*fl.* 1781], *actor.*

The part of Brazen in *The Recruiting Officer* at the Crown Inn, Islington, on 15 March 1781 was played by a Mr Marlborough.

Marley, Mr [*fl.* 1759?–1785], *trumpeter.*

The trumpeter Marley who replaced Justice Willis in the King's Musick in 1759 or later was probably the Marley who played trumpet in the Handel Memorial Concerts at Westminster Abbey and the Pantheon in May and June 1784. He performed in the St Paul's Concert on 10 and 12 May 1785. That service indicates that he belonged to the Royal Society of Musicians.

Marlow, Mr [*fl.* 1747], *actor.*

At the Cole Hole in Red Lion Street on 27 January 1747 a Mr Marlow played Mirvan in *Tamerlane.*

Marlton, William [*fl.* 1770–1779], *actor.*

Mr Marlton was in a company of strolling players who performed in Glasgow from January to March 1770. Marlton's roles are not known, but the troupe offered *The Provok'd Wife*, *The Citizen*, and *Jane Shore*. The group returned in February 1771 and performed through April. Marlton was at the Crow Street Theatre in Dublin in 1771–72 and 1772–73 and also acted in Limerick in 1771 and 1772 and at Cork in 1772. On 3 March 1773 a group of Dublin actors signed on to perform with Macklin; among them was William Marlton. On 11 September 1775 Marlton performed in Chester in the Whitlock-Austin troupe. Finally, on 13 October 1779, he tried

London as Colonel Feignwell in *A Bold Stroke for a Wife* at the Haymarket Theatre.

"Marmotte." See GOSNELL, WINIFRED.

Marqui, Signor [*fl.* 1785–1801], *dancer, choreographer.*

Signor Marqui was on the company roster at Astley's Amphitheatre in 1785 as a dancer, though he was not cited in any bills. During the 1786 season he danced in *The Ethiopian Festival*, a new dance "representing the whimsical Actions & attitudes made use of by the Negroes." Marqui was a Dancing Attendant on the Lord Mayor in the musical spectacle *Love from the Heart* on 4 September 1786, and he participated in *The Ethiopian Festival* again in 1788. Marqui composed a dance called *Vindication of Love*, which was performed at Astley's on 8 June 1789, and *La Coquette*, which was presented the following 22 August. On 4 September his *Villagers* was performed.

He was not mentioned in the Astley bills in 1790, but he was frequently cited in 1791 as a dancer in *The Irish Fair*, *The Threshers*, *The Happy Negroes*, *The Animated Statue* (a work of his own composing), and *The Wrestlers*. Signor "Marque" danced in *The Good and Bad*, an opera pantomime, in June 1792, and on 31 January 1793 at the Amphitheatre Royal, Peter Street, Dublin, he danced in the pantomime *La Forêt noire*. He was engaged at the Crow Street Theatre in 1794–95. On 22 August 1795 he was back at Astley's Amphitheatre in London dancing a Gypsy Woman in *Harlequin Invincible*. In 1801 he was performing as a harlequin at Astley's, and on 5 October of that year he appeared at the Royalty Theatre in a ballet called *The Bashaw* and as Lord Ogre in the pantomime *Puss in Boots.*

"Marquis of Hatchet, The." See McGEORGE, HORATIO THOMAS.

Marr, Miss [*fl.* 1756], *house servant?*

Benefit tickets for Miss Marr were accepted at Drury Lane Theatre on 7 May 1756. She was probably one of the house servants.

Marr, Henry d. 1783, *actor, singer, dancer.*

Henry "Dagger" Marr was first noticed in London bills on 23 August 1740, when he played Octavio in *The Harlot's Progress* at the Hippisley-Chapman booth at Bartholomew Fair. He then began an engagement at Goodman's Fields Theatre on 22 November with Pedro in *The Spanish Fryar* and continued during the 1740–41 season with Sir John Gates in *Lady Jane Gray*, the Bookseller in *The Committee*, Mortimer in *1 Henry IV*, a Recruit in *The Recruiting Officer*, Supple in *The Double Gallant*, the Shoemaker in *The Relapse*, Nimblewrist in *Love and a Bottle*, Florio in *The Imprisonment, Release, Adventures, and Marriage of Harlequin*, Hounslow in *The Stratagem*, Wat Dreary in *The Beggar's Opera*, Ludovico in *Othello*, Spitfire in *The Wife's Relief*, Catesby in *Richard III*, the Third Lord in *The Winter's Tale*, an Old Shepherd in *Harlequin Student*, List in *The Miser*, Aelius in *Timon of Athens*, and a Beau in *Lethe* (to which he also spoke the prologue). Marr also danced in *King Arthur*. It seems likely, in view of his extensive repertoire, that he had gained experience in the provinces before his first performances in London.

Marr acted at the Tankard Street Theatre in Ipswich in July and August 1741, one of his roles there being Sir Wittling Rattle in *Lethe*. Then he returned to London to play Vizier Mirza in *Thamas Kouli Kan* at Bartholomew Fair on 22 August. He was again at Goodman's Fields in 1741–42, adding to his list of roles such parts as Simon Pure in *A Bold Stroke for a Wife*, Jack Stanmore in *Oroonoko*, Trapland in *Love for Love*, Manuel in *Love Makes a Man*, Burgundy in *King Lear*, and the Chaplain in *The Orphan*. When David Garrick made his debut as Richard III on 19 October 1741, Marr played Catesby.

He performed at Drury Lane in 1742–43, appearing first on 13 November 1742 as Catesby. His new parts that season included Hotman in *Oroonoko*, Meleager in *The Rival Queens*, Prince John in *1 Henry IV*, Beau Trippet in *The Lying Valet*, Jaques in *As You Like It*, and the Poet in *The Twin Rivals*. During the season he went over the Thames to Southwark on 30 March 1743 to appear as a Recruit in a single performance of *The Recruiting Officer*.

Marr seems then to have left London for a season, returning in June 1744 to play Laertes in *Hamlet* at the Haymarket. Then he disappeared again until 30 March 1745, when he acted Novice in *The Stratagem*. In the fall of 1745, when he rejoined the Drury Lane Com-

pany for the 1745–46 season, Marr began with Noodle in *The Tragedy of Tragedies* on 8 October 1745. He made Drury Lane his winter home through 1776–77, playing such new parts as Guildford in *Henry VIII*, Nimming Ned in *The Beggar's Opera*, Cinna in *Julius Caesar*, Bernardo in *Hamlet*, Gloster in *Henry V*, Abraham in *Romeo and Juliet*, Simon in *The Suspicious Husband*, Philip in *Catherine and Petruchio*, Mirvan in *Tamerlane*, Gadshill in *Henry IV*, Davy in *2 Henry IV*, an Outlaw in *Two Gentlemen of Verona*, an Officer in *Twelfth Night*, an Officer in *Tancred and Sigismunda*, and a large number of other, sometimes unspecified, small parts. After the 1770–71 season his name disappeared from the bills, but since the accounts cited him at a weekly salary of £1 in 1776–77 it is probable that Marr continued performing at least through that season in parts too small to deserve mention in the bills. He was probably the "Narr" listed by *The London Stage* as at Drury Lane in 1775–76.

Over the years at Drury Lane Marr shared benefits, usually with a number of others. His salary as of 1765 was the same as that in 1776–77, and it seems likely that in earlier years he also served at a lowly wage.

Marr's appearances over the years at other houses were probably efforts to augment his modest income. He was at Covent Garden in late June 1746 playing Montano in *Othello* and Lenox in *Macbeth*; on 7 January 1740 he was in Foote's *Auction of Pictures* at the Haymarket; he acted at Bartholomew Fair in August 1740 and at Southwark Fair in September 1753, but that ended his activity at the fairs. In the summer of 1751 he appeared at the Richmond Theatre, playing Tradelove in *A Bold Stroke for a Wife*, and on 27 May 1757 he played the Beggar in *The Beggar's Opera* at Covent Garden.

Marr, despite his long stage career, showed little development as an actor. *The Battle of Players* in 1762 referred to him as "Mar-all," and Tate Wilkinson in *The Wandering Patentee* called Marr "one of the worst actors that ever exhibited in theatre or in barn." Wilkinson told an anecdote about Marr's career as an underling:

Many actors say, that principal characters will make great performers.—I remember *old Mar*, from his inveteracy to Garrick, for not giving him principal characters, always said, the very sound of *Manager* put his frame into a ferment.—If when he fed the ducks in St. James's Park, any one of the feathered race was peculiarly alert, and swallowed more than the others, he would vociferously roar out! "O damn you! you are a Manager."

By 1806, when The Festival of Wit was published, that story had developed so that "Dagger roared out loud enough to be heard by Garrick, who was not far behind him, 'Get out of that you gobbling rascal, I see you are a manager, by G—d!'" Nevertheless, Garrick left Marr an annuity of £10.

The Gentleman's Magazine reported in June 1783 that Harry Marr had died recently, in Duke's Court, Bow Street (Reed said he died abut 23 April). Marr was described as of an ancient family and an actor of humble parts for 50 years. He had been, the Gentleman's Magazine said bluntly, wholly unfit for the stage. Marr had drawn up a short will on 20 April 1782, leaving everything to his wife Martha. He described himself as of the parish of St Martin-in-the-Fields. Mrs Marr proved the will on 2 June.

Marr, Mrs [Henry?, Martha] [fl. 1765–1783?], dresser.

A Drury Lane paylist dated 9 February 1765 listed a Mrs Marr as one of the women's dressers at 1s. 6d. daily or 9s. weekly. On the same list was the actor Henry "Dagger" Marr, and it is likely that Mrs Marr was his wife Martha. Mrs Marr was still working as a dresser at 9s. weekly in 1776–77. Henry Marr died in 1783, leaving his estate to his wife. She proved the will on 2 June of that year.

Marranesi. See MARANESI.

Marrant, Anthony [fl. 1669], musician.

On 17 December 1669 Anthony Marrant and four other men were ordered arrested for performing music without licenses.

Marriot, F. [fl. 1784–1798], actor.

On 22 March 1784, at a specially-licensed benefit for the actress Margaret Cuyler at the Haymarket Theatre, Mr Marriot played the Irishman in the Pit in The Manager in Distress. A Marriot, probably the same, turned up in Everard Sterne's little company at the Red Lion Inn, Lordship Road, Stoke Newington, in March 1787, accompanied by his wife. The

company gave half a dozen performances—all benefits for the company members—and melted away. Marriot was seen as Joseph Surface in The School for Scandal, the Chaplain in The Orphan, one of the Keepers in The Miller of Mansfield, Ottman in Barbarossa, Young Marlow in She Stoops to Conquer, Gibbet in The Beaux' Stratagem, Thomas in The Virgin Unmask'd, Mercutio in Romeo and Juliet, Lord Minikin in Bon Ton, and one of the Scholars in The Padlock. He also wrote and spoke, on the occasion of his and Mrs Marriot's benefit on 29 March "An Occasional Address of Thanks to the Ladies and Gentlemen" and six other pieces of monologue. (A note on a copy of that playbill gives the initial letter of his first name as "F.")

Mrs Marriot, meanwhile, was featured as Mrs Candour in The School for Scandal, Corinna in The Citizen, Peggy in The Miller of Mansfield, Zaphira in Barbarossa, Miss Tittup in Bon Ton, Mrs Sullen in The Beaux' Stratagem, and the Nurse in Romeo and Juliet.

On the opening night of John Palmer's Royalty Theatre, 20 June 1787, Marriot was in the company playing Silvius in As You Like It. He may have continued with Palmer's doomed venture through the troubles of the next few months. But in 1788 Mr and Mrs Marriot can be traced to Mrs Sarah Baker's troupe of itinerants in Kent. Whither the Marriots wandered from there is not known. Our Marriot acted a few parts at Edinburgh's theatre from January to April 1792: Young Clackit in The Guardian, Pierre in Venice Preserv'd, the King in The Surrender of Calais, and Milford in The Road to Ruin. His wife was a Villager in Richard Coeur de Lion on 7 and 9 April. A Marriot was at Windsor Theatre in the summer of 1792 and the same or another ("who last season played with Mr. Fox at Brighton") was at Chelmsford in September 1792, according to the Thespian Magazine of that month. Probably he was the same who acted fleetingly at Derby in March 1793.

Late in 1793 the Marriots (usually now "Marriotts") embarked for America. He apparently made his debut in Charleston with the Thomas Wade West-John Bignall Company on 24 January 1794 as Belcour in The West Indian, his wife playing first on the twenty-ninth as Monimia in The Orphan. They were announced as "from the Theatre Royal in Edinburgh." On 27 January, in the South Carolina Gazette, Mrs

Marriott published a proposal for two volumes of poems by subscription. On 5 February she played Portia in *The Merchant of Venice* while her husband was Bassanio. The fragmentary bills show him also as a Soldier in *The Gamester* on 29 May.

The Marriots then went north to join the Old American Company in the last season that troupe was to play at the Southwark Theatre, or anywhere in Philadelphia. Playbills for the season were seldom specific. We know only that Mrs Marriot played Julia in *The Midnight Hour* on 26 September, that Marriot took some part unspecified in the pantomime *The Danaides* on 8 October, and that for their joint benefit on 17 November they chose her own new afterpiece *The Chimera, or Effusions of Fancy*.

The Marriots accompanied the Old American Company to the John Street Theatre in New York for the 1794–95 season. Marriot opened as Pierre in *Venice Preserv'd* on 18 December. The *New York Magazine* thought his effort failed, though it gained some applause. That journal admired Mrs Marriot's figure as Arabella in *Such Things Are*, a part in which she "appeared much terrified." Yet the Marriots were employed frequently during the season. Her known roles were Statira in *The Rival Queens*, Mrs Euston in *I'll Tell You What*, one of the "Vocal Parts" in *Macbeth*, Lady Louisa in *Love's Frailties*, Charlotte in *Heigho for a Husband*, Regan in *King Lear*, Millwood in *George Barnwell*, Viola in *The School for Greyheads*, Lady Jane in *Know Your Own Mind*, Zelmira in *Zenobia*, Julia in *Which is the Man?*, Clara Sedley in *The Rage*, Belinda in *Modern Antiques*, Perdita in *The Winter's Tale*, and Harriet in *Seduction*. When, on 23 June, Mrs Marriot took her second benefit "having failed in her first," she played Lauretta in her own comedy *Try Again*, written for the occasion.

Her husband took the part of Du Chesne in that piece. During the season Marriot also played Sir Rowland in *The Children in the Wood*, Clytus in *The Rival Queens*, General Fairlove in *Heigho for a Husband*, Seymour in *Love's Frailties*, Tigranes in *Zenobia*, Malvil in *Know Your Own Mind* and Antigonus in *The Winter's Tale*.

In June 1795 the Marriots left the American Company and rejoined the company run by West, now with the widow Bignall (John Bignall having died), in Virginia. Hardly anything is now known of these Virginia comedi-

ans. Seilhamer, however, reported in his *History of the American Theatre* that the Marriots were playing in Dumfries, Virginia, on 16 April 1796 when they took their benefit. Once again, the facile Mrs Marriott furnished the play, *The Death of Major Andre; or, The Land We Live In*. Seilhamer says that she "died soon afterward."

Mr Marriot did not mourn long. When he joined the Boston Haymarket company in the winter of 1796 he brought along a new wife. They made their first appearance on the opening night of the Haymarket, he as Sir George Touchwood in *The Belle's Stratagem*, she as a humble attendant in the musical spectacle *Mirza and Linder*. During the rest of the season she added only Mrs Ledger in *The Road to Ruin* and the Landlady in *The Suspicious Husband*, so far as the record shows. He added Barton in *The Battle of Hexham*, Foigard in *The Beaux' Stratagem*, Norland in *Every One Has His Fault*, Thorowgood in *George Barnwell*, Sir Charles Marlow in *She Stoops to Conquer*, and Rovewell in *The Upholsterer* and was the original Governor Gage in John Burk's bombastic *Battle of Bunker Hill* on 17 February 1797.

Sidney M. Oland has found evidence of Mr Marriot's appearance in Halifax, Nova Scotia, in May 1798. What connections, if any, F. Marriot had with the British provincial actor Arthur H. Marriot or the Miss Marriot who appeared at Covent Garden in the early nineteenth century are not known.

Marriot, Mrs F. *d. 1796, actress.* See MARRIOT, F.

Marriott, E[dward?] *b. 1663?, impresario.*

An advertisement in the Burney Collection at the British Library, dating abut 21 July 1722, announced that at

RICHMOND, This Evening, at E. Marriott's Great Room on the Green, will be an extraordinary Concert of MUSICK, By the Masters from the Opera, in which Mr. KYTCH will perform several pieces on the Hautboy and German Flute, and Mr. JOHN BASTON a Concerto on the Little Flute. N. B. The ROOM is Open every Day, with a very good set of Musick Mornings and Evenings.

E. Marriott is otherwise unknown, but perhaps he was the Edward Marriott, son of Reginald, who was born in Richmond on 2 March

1663 and christened at the Richmond Church the following 12 March. An Edward Marriott was buried at St Paul, Covent Garden, on 23 February 1738, but there is not enough evidence to identify him as the concert hall operator.

Marriotti. *See* MARIOTTI.

Marroni. *See* MAZZONI, SIGNORA.

Marseilles, Mons [*fl.* 1786], *dancer.*
Monsieur Marseilles participated in a *New Divertissement* at the end of the opera at the King's Theatre on 11 March 1786 and subsequent dates, and beginning on 23 March he danced a Lover of Melody, Morpheus, and a priest of Hymen in *Le Premier Navigateur* and participated in a *pas de quatre*.

Marsey, Mrs [*fl.* 1780?], *singer.*
The *Catalogue of Printed Music in the British Museum* cites a Mrs Marsey as singing *There was a Mad Man* in *The Devil to Pay*; the song was separately printed about 1780. Possibly the performer referred to was Mrs Massey, though that woman was primarily an actress of serious roles and not a singer.

Marsh, Mr [*fl.* 1708], *scenekeeper.*
In Vice Chamberlain Coke's papers at Harvard is a list of the staff at the Queen's Theatre as of 8 March 1708; a Mr Marsh is cited as a "Scaene" man at a salary of 7s. 6d. daily.

Marsh, Mrs [*fl.* 1788], *actress.*
Mrs Marsh played Harriet in *The Jealous Wife* in a single performance at the Haymarket Theatre on 9 April 1788.

Marsh, Alphonso 1627–1681, *lutenist, harpsichordist, singer, composer.*
Alphonso Marsh, the son of the court musician Robert Marsh, was christened at St Margaret, Westminster, on 28 January 1627. He served as a musician in ordinary under Charles I, and on 8 February 1648 he contracted his first marriage, with Mary Cheston, at St Margaret's. Marsh shared with John Harding the role of Pirrhus in the historic production at Rutland House in 1656 of Davenant's *The Siege of Rhodes*. At the Restoration, Marsh was reap-

pointed to the King's Musick, replacing Thomas Day as a singer. Alphonso was also a lutenist, like his father. He received an annual salary of £40, and his livery allowance (rarely paid on time) was the standard £16 2s. 6d. Sometimes, as in the summer of 1671 and the late summer of 1678 he attended the King at Windsor and received from 6d. to 8d. additional daily pay. In February 1675 both he and his namesake son (by his first wife) performed in the court masque *Calisto*, the elder Marsh serving as a theorbo (double-necked lute) player, and he also played the "harpsicall." Outside the court Marsh was a warden in the Corporation of Music.

One of the rare personal glimpses we get of Alphonso Marsh comes from Samuel Pepys, who recorded in his diary on 19 August 1661 that he had gone for a walk with Mr and Mrs Marsh, bought them drinks, and heard Marsh sing: "but his voice is quite lost." By the time Marsh died on 9 April 1681 he was married a second time, to a woman whose Christian name was Rebecca. Marsh was buried at St Margaret, Westminster, on 12 April 1681. In his will, dated 12 October 1680, he bequeathed one-third of his arrears in pay from the crown to his son Alphonso; the remainder of his estate he left to his widow. John Abell replaced Alphonso Marsh in the lutes and voices at court on 20 December 1681. A Hester Marsh, doubtless a relative, was buried at St Margaret's on 2 May 1681.

Marsh had a modest career as a composer of songs, some of which were published in *The Treasury of Musick* in 1669 and *Choice Ayres and Dialogues* in 1676. He wrote songs for several plays: *The Law Against Lovers* in 1662, the revival of *The Unfortunate Lovers* and *An Evening's Love* in 1668, *The Conquest of Granada* in 1670, and *The Spanish Rogue* in 1673.

Marsh, Alphonso *d.* 1692, *singer, composer.*
Alphonso Marsh the younger was the son of the court musician Alphonso Marsh (1627–1681) and his first wife Mary, née Cheston, who were married in February 1648. By February 1675 young Marsh had become a performer and sang the role of Africa in the prologue to the court masque *Calisto*. On 25 April 1676 he was sworn a Gentleman of the Chapel Royal, replacing William Howes. The Lord

Chamberlain's accounts mentioned Marsh occasionally after that: he attended the King at Windsor in the late summer of 1678, waited impatiently in 1683 for his annual livery allowances of £16 2s. 6d. for the years 1679 to 1681, marched in the coronation procession of James II as one of the tenors in the Chapel Royal, and was appointed to the private music of William and Mary on 20 July 1689. He apparently went to the Hague with William III in early 1691. Marsh's name is noted in a manuscript of Purcell's music for the King's birthday in 1687.

Marsh died on 5 April 1692 and was buried four days later in the west cloister of Westminster Abbey. A creditor received administration of his estate, Alphonso's cousin Anne Roffey, his next of kin, renouncing. Marsh's wife Cicilia (or "Cilicia" in the Abbey register) had been buried in the west cloisters of Westminster Abbey on 16 January 1691. The couple had had a daughter Mary, who was baptized at St Margaret, Westminster, on 11 September 1685 (those registers cited Mrs Marsh as Cicilia), but the fate of the child is not known and she was not mentioned in connection with Marsh's estate. Of Marsh's cousin Anne Roffey nothing is known, but it is likely she was related to the composer John Roffey, who was active in the 1680s.

Like his father, the younger Alphonso Marsh composed songs, some of which were printed in *The Theater of Music* (1685–1687) and *The Banquet of Musick* (1688–1692).

Marsh, Charles *(fl. 1717–c.1744)*, *trumpeter.*

On 25 November 1717 the Lord Chamberlain issued a warrant to purchase a new trumpet for the court musician Charles Marsh. Marsh continued active until 1744 or shortly thereafter, when he was replaced in the King's Musick by Charles Snow. Marsh and his namesake son had become members of the newly organized Royal Society of Musicians on 28 August 1739.

Marsh, Charles *(fl. 1739)*, *musician. See* MARSH, CHARLES *(fl. 1717–c.1744)*.

Marsh, George *(fl. 1739)*, *musician.*

On 28 August 1739 George Marsh became one of the original subscribers to the Royal Society of Musicians.

Marsh, Richard *d. 1692?, trumpeter.*

On 13 December 1679 Richard Marsh, probably a relative of Alphonso Marsh and his son, was appointed a trumpeter in the King's Musick. He was reappointed under James II on 20 May 1685 and under William and Mary on 12 September 1689. At least some of his duties were in the first troop of guards. It seems very probable that the Richard Marsh, horner, of St Andrew, Holborn, who wrote his will on 8 November 1688 was our subject, since references to Richard Marsh in the Lord Chamberlain's account stop after 1689 (though a Richard Marsh was cited beginning 1698; he, we think, was a second person). The Richard Marsh of St Andrew's left small bequests to his sister Margarett Taylor and his brother John Marsh, designating his kinsman Thomas Milton of Stepney, victualer, his main legatee. The will was proved on 17 March 1692.

Marsh, Richard *(fl. 1698–1700)*, *trumpeter.*

On 19 April 1698, according to the Lord Chamberlain's accounts, a silver trumpet was delivered to Mr Richard Marsh. He was, perhaps, a son of the Richard Marsh who was last mentioned in the records in 1689 and who, we believe, died about 1692. As a trumpeter Marsh received a salary of £91 5s. annually (trumpeters were among the highest paid members of the King's Musick), but on 5 January 1700 he surrendered his post to Joseph Williams.

Marshal, Mr *(fl. 1761)*, *singer.*

Covent Garden Theatre paid a Mr Marshal 5s. on 13 November 1761 for singing in the coronation chorus.

Marshall, Mr *(fl. 1730–1740)*, *actor, singer.*

There were apparently two Marshalls acting in London in the 1730s, one of whom played mostly serious parts but some comedy roles and was perhaps James Marshall, while the other seems to have specialized in roles in farces and pantomimes and was a singer as well as an actor. On only one date, however, 31 December 1736, were both Marshalls named in bills at different theatres on the same night, and the citations for each man dovetail so neatly that one might think that only one man named

Marshall was performing in London. But the roles of James (?) Marshall are enough different from those of our subject that we have assumed that there were two Marshalls active at the same time.

On 29 January 1730 Mr Marshall appeared as Death in *Hurlothrumbo* at the Haymarket Theatre. He then appeared at that house regularly through 3 July, playing a small, unspecified part in *The Cheshire Comicks*, Sharp in *The Half Pay Officers*, a Prisoner and Brainworm in *Love and Revenge*, Scarecrow, Don Tragedio, and Bantomite in *The Author's Farce*, and Noodle and Doodle in *Tom Thumb*. (The following fall the other Marshall made his first appearance.)

Marshall seems not to have performed in London again until 31 December 1736, when he appeared at Drury Lane Theatre as Ben in *The Beggar's Opera*. (That season the other Marshall was at Covent Garden.) During the rest of the 1736–37 season at Drury Lane Marshall played a Forester in *The King and the Miller of Mansfield* and repeated his role in *The Beggar's Opera*. On 4 May 1737 benefit tickets sold by Mr and Mrs Marshall were accepted at Drury Lane. He was again at Drury Lane on 12 January 1738 playing a Constable in *The Harlot's Progress* and then Joe in *John Cockle at Court*, the Forester in *The King and the Miller*, and Philip in *The Rival Queens*.

Marshall remained at Drury Lane through 1739–40, playing his old parts and adding a Keeper in *The Pilgrim*, Poundage in *The Provok'd Husband*, a Man in *An Hospital for Fools*, and Neptune in *The Fall of Phaeton*. His last appearance seems to have been in *The Pilgrim* on 10 March 1740.

Marshall, Mr ₁*fl. 1735–1736*₁, *footmen's gallery keeper.*

Latreille identified a Mr Marshall as the footmen's gallery keeper at Covent Garden Theatre in 1735–36 at a nightly salary of 1s. 6d.

Marshall, Mr ₁*fl. 1765*₁, *actor.*

A Mr Marshall played at the Haymarket Theatre in 1765, appearing in unspecified roles in *The Lyar* on 15 July and *The Orators* on 31 July.

Marshall, Mr ₁*fl. 1771*₁, *bassoonist.*

Mr and Miss Marshall shared a benefit concert at Coopers' Hall in Bristol on 17 January 1771; the bill stated that they were from Nottingham and that Miss Marshall was 11 years old. At Hickford's Music Room in Brewer Street in London on 10 May, Mr and Miss "Marshal" again shared a benefit. He played the bassoon and she sang songs and played the piano and harpsichord. Their lodgings were at Mr La Fountain's in Princes Street, near Leicester Fields.

Marshall, Mr ₁*fl. 1794*₁, *singer.*

Doane's *Musical Directory* of 1794 listed a Mr Marshall, from Lincoln, who sang bass in the Handel performances at Westminster Abbey in London.

Marshall, Mrs ₁*fl. 1736–1739*₁, *actress, singer.*

Mrs Marshall played Monimia in *The Orphan* at the Lincoln's Inn Fields playhouse on 19 October 1736. She was active in Henry Giffard's troupe at that house throughout the 1736–37 season, playing Kate in *1 Henry IV*, an Attendant in *Britannia*, an Attendant in *The Beggar's Pantomime*, an unspecified part in *The Independent Patriot*, Lady Worthy in *A Tutor for the Beaus*, Lady Fancy in *The Maid's the Mistress*, and Cynthia in *The Wife's Relief*. Playing at Drury Lane that season was Mrs (James?) Marshall, who was assigned considerably more important parts.

The Mrs Marshall who was at Lincoln's Inn Fields in 1736–37 appeared at Covent Garden Theatre in the spring of 1738, making her first appearance on that stage on 20 April as Lucy in *The Beggar's Opera*. We take her also to have been the Mrs Marshall at Covent Garden in the summer of 1738 who played Mrs Security in *The Gamester*, Lady Loverule in *The Devil to Pay*, Mrs Prim in *A Bold Stroke for a Wife*, Mrs Goodfellow in *Tunbridge Walks*, Thaisa in *Marina*, and Bullfinch in *Love and a Bottle*. She was engaged at Covent Garden for the 1738–39 season as well, but was named in the bills only for a Country Lass in *The Rape of Proserpine*, a Countrywoman in *The Country Wedding*, Rodriquez in *Don Quixote*, and Mrs Modish in *The Lucky Discovery*. Her last notice in the bills was on 28 May 1739 as Mrs Modish.

Marshall, Miss *b. c. 1760, singer, harpsichordist, pianist.*

The Miss Marshall who sang at Finch's Grotto Gardens about 1765 may have been the little girl of that name who was born about 1760 and had gained a considerable reputation as a singer, harpsichordist, and pianist by 1771. Langdon's song *Ev'ry Bliss that Heav'n can give* was published about 1770 as sung by Miss Marshall at the Grotto Gardens. On 10 January 1771 Miss Marshall performed at Coopers' Hall in Bristol, and on the seventeenth she shared a benefit with her father there. The bill noted that Mr and Miss Marshall were from Nottingham and that she was 11 years old.

On 10 May 1771 Mr and Miss "Marshal" held a benefit concert at Hickford's Music Room in Brewer Street, London, tickets for which were available at their lodgings at Mr La Fountain's in Princes Street, near Leicester Fields. At the concert Mr Marshall played the bassoon and Miss Marshall played the piano and harpsichord and sang. Appended to their advertisement was a testimonial from John Alcock, Doctor of Music, dated 12 December 1770. He declared that Miss Marshall was "of Nottingham," 11 years old, and "the best performer . . . in England" on the piano and harpsichord.

On 17 August 1772 Miss Marshall was again in London, singing the Maid in *The Ephesian Matron* at the Grotto Gardens. According to the entry in *The Dictionary of National Biography* on Anthony Manini, Manini played the violin in 1777 at Miss Marshall's concert in St John's College Hall, Cambridge. Letters now at the British Library from Thomas Twining to Dr Burney referred to Miss Marshall in December 1784 and June 1785. The first letter recommended Miss Marshall to Dr Burney's attention, saying she was from Ipswich and would be going to town (London, presumably) and thirsted for music. She was, Twining said, a decent, sensible, unaffected young lady with considerable merit as a performer. The second letter reported to Burney that Twining had visited Miss Marshall at Ipswich and heard her play the whole evening on the pianoforte.

Marshall, Miss ₍ *fl. 1784*₎, actress.

Miss Marshall played Mrs Tempest in a single performance of *The School for Wives* at the Haymarket Theatre on 16 November 1784.

Marshall, Anne. *See* QUIN, MRS ₍ PETER?₎.

Marshall, Mrs ₍ E.₎ ₍ *fl. 1736–1745?*₎, actress, singer.

The Mrs Marshall who played Mrs Sealand in *The Conscious Lovers* at Drury Lane Theatre on 15 December 1736 was, according to a bill of 1742, Mrs E. Marshall. During the rest of the 1736–37 season at Drury Lane Mrs Marshall appeared as Mrs Peachum in *The Beggar's Opera* and the Nurse in *Love for Love,* and she sang in *Macbeth.* Performing at Lincoln's Inn Fields that season was another Mrs Marshall, possibly a relative, who was assigned less important roles.

Mrs Marshall continued at Drury Lane through the 1739–40 season, playing her old roles and also Mrs Day and Mrs Chat in *The Committee,* Lucy in *The Old Bachelor,* Mistress Overdone in *Measure for Measure,* Lady Bountiful in *The Stratagem,* Mrs Motherly in *The Provok'd Husband,* Lady Pride in *The Amorous Widow,* Mrs Clearaccount and Midnight in *The Twin Rivals,* the Nurse in *The Relapse,* Cloggit in *The Confederacy,* Hob's Mother in *Flora,* Widow Lackit in *Oroonoko,* Mrs Wisely in *The Miser,* Bromia in *Amphitryon,* the Wife in *An Hospital for Fools,* Lady Darling in *The Constant Couple,* the Mother in *The Chances,* the Fourth Wife in *Don John,* Altea in *Rule a Wife and Have a Wife,* and Mrs Stocks in *The Lottery.* After the spring of 1740 her name dropped from the London bills. On 28 July at Canterbury she played the Duchess of York in *Richard III.*

Mrs Marshall's name reappeared in London bills on 22 January 1742, when at Drury Lane she played Mariana in *All's Well that Ends Well.* At Drury Lane on 13 May 1742, according to a bill in the Enthoven Collection, a Mrs E. Marshall had Drury Lane benefit tickets out, and on the following 25 May a Mrs Marshall (the same or a different woman?) had benefit tickets out for the same theatre. Our guess is that the same woman was referred to. The receipts on 13 May came to only £100 so the management may have allowed Mrs Marshall to share in a second benefit.

Mrs Marshall played at the Jacob's Wells Theatre in Bristol from 16 June to 27 August 1742, then returned to London on 14 April 1743 to act Mariana in *The Miser* in a single performance given at the Haymarket Theatre. She was, we believe, the Mrs Marshall who appeared at Norwich from 1743 to 1745; one of her roles there, reported by Sybil Rosenfeld in *Strolling Players*, was Le Beau in *As You Like It* in the summer of 1745.

Marshall, James *b. 1770, instrumentalist.*

On 11 December 1823 the musician James Marshall wrote from Warwick to Sainsbury, supplying the musical biographer with some details of his life. The letter, preserved at the Glasgow University Library, stated that Marshall was born at Olney in Buckinghamshire in 1770. He studied violin, violoncello, pianoforte, and organ under an unnamed "Master" at Oxford, gained the patronage of the Earl of Dartmouth, and was sent to London to study under John Ashley, the assistant conductor "at the Westminster Abbey Meetings." There he added to his list of instruments the viola and double bass, and through Ashley he was engaged to play double bass at the Abbey meeting in 1790. Ashley also helped Marshall get engagements at provincial meetings, including one at Worcester.

Marshall lived in Worcester about a year, he said, then moved to Northampton, where he married. After three and a half years he moved to Rugby, where he was appointed church organist, a post he held until 1801, when he was offered the position of organist at St Mary's in Warwick. There Marshall remained, though he regularly attended the meetings of the three choirs—Gloucester, Hereford, and Worcester. Marshall had two sons and a daughter. The elder son, Frederick, became an organist and pianist, was appointed organist of the Rugby school chapel, and composed a number of hymns and preludes.

Marshall [James?] *d. 1773?, actor.*

James Marshall, who subscribed in 1746 to the works of Henry Ward, may have been the Marshall (sometimes Marshal) who acted in London beginning in 1730. At Drury Lane Theatre on 9 December 1730 the title role in *Oroonoko* was "attempted by a young Actor who never appear'd on this Stage before." Similarly (and perhaps in error) the bill for 22 December at the same house said Oroonoko would be acted by "a young Actor, who never appear'd on this Stage before." The bill for 29 December listed Juba in *Cato* as by "Marshall, who lately perform'd the Part of Oroonoko." Perhaps Marshall was the "new Actor" who had played Sempronius in *Cato* on 1 October 1730 (Juba

was then acted by Wilks). Marshall then acted Bajazet in *Tamerlane* on 19 January 1731, Polydore in *The Orphan* on 17 February, Procles in *Eurydice* on 22 February, Dolabella in *All for Love* on 3 April, Oroonoko for his shared benefit with Rainton on 7 May, Prince John in *2 Henry IV* on 19 May, Charles in *The Busy Body* on 31 May, and Lopez in *Don John* on 11 June.

After that rather spectacular first season Marshall slowed down, for in 1731–32 he played only Oroonoko, Juba, and Polydore again and added Ferdinand in *Injur'd Innocence*. He was not named in London bills in 1732–33, but he returned to Drury Lane in 1733–34 to play Torrismond in *The Spanish Fryar*, Leon in *Rule a Wife and Have a Wife*, Oroonoko, Richmond in *Richard III*, Plume in *The Recruiting Officer*, Bajazet, Essex in *The Unhappy Favorite*, Surrey in *Henry VIII*, Charles in *The Busy Body*, Alcibiades in *Timon of Athens*, Ferdinand in *The Tempest*, Marcian in *Theodosius*, Lovewell in *The Cornish Squire*, Rainford in *The Fatal Falsehood*, and Norfolk in *The Albion Queens*. At Lincoln's Inn Fields Theatre on 9 May 1734 he played Leon in a single performance of *Rule a Wife and Have a Wife*.

Marshall then joined John Rich's troupe at Covent Garden Theatre, appearing there first on 18 September 1734 as Claudius in *Hamlet*. He remained there through 1736–37 playing such new roles as Omar in *Tamerlane*, Norfolk in *Richard III*, Cuproli in *Abra Mule*, Sharper in *The Old Bachelor*, Juan in *Rule a Wife and Have a Wife*, Belford in *The Fatal Marriage*, Hemskirk in *The Royal Merchant*, the Ghost of Laius in *Oedipus*, Pylades in *The Distrest Mother*, Seyward in *Macbeth*, Trebonius in *Julius Caesar*, Vizard in *The Constant Couple*, the Elder Worthy in *Love's Last Shift*, Polyperchon in *The Rival Queens*, Lucius in *Theodosius*, the Governor in *Love Makes a Man*, Dugard in *The Inconstant*, Marcus in *Cato*, Elliot in *Venice Preserv'd*, and Horatio in *Hamlet*. Possibly he was the Marshall who acted Dorilant in *The Country Wife* at a single performance at Lincoln's Inn Fields on 18 October 1736—a night when our subject was not scheduled to perform at Covent Garden. (But we believe the Marshall [fl. 1730–1740] who sang and acted light parts in London in the 1730s must have been a different person.) Marshall in 1735–36 played 172 days at Covent Garden and received 13s. 4d. daily.

Marshall then disappeared from London until 4 November 1740, when he made his first appearance at the Goodman's Fields playhouse as Tamerlane. He stayed there through 1741–42 playing such old parts as Torrismond, Oroonoko, Richmond (on 19 October 1741 when Garrick came on as Richard III), Bajazet, Leon, and Sharper and appearing in such new roles as Osmyn in *The Mourning Bride*, Standard in *The Constant Couple*, Chamont in *The Orphan*, Lothario in *The Fair Penitent*, Southampton in *The Unhappy Favorite*, Laertes in *Hamlet*, Loveworth in *Tunbridge Walks*, Macbeth, Polixenes in *The Winter's Tale*, Volatil in *The Wife's Relief*, Duart in *Love Makes a Man*, the title roles in *King Arthur* and *Timon of Athens*, the King in *All's Well that Ends Well*, and Gloucester in *King Lear*. He was probably the Marshall who acted Alexander in *The Rival Queens* on 4 August 1741 at Tottenham Court Fair.

Then Marshall's name again disappeared from London bills. From March to July 1744 he was in a strolling company that appeared at the Stoke's Croft Theatre in Bristol. There he is known to have played Henry VIII in *Anna Bullen* and Horatio in *The Fair Penitent*. The bill for 2 July noted that the performance was for Marshall's benefit, but he was "in Confinement." The 1744–45 season found Marshall at the Capel Street Theatre in Dublin, appearing on 17 January 1745 as Bassanio in *The Merchant of Venice*, hailed as from England and making his first appearance in Ireland. He also acted Hamlet on 22 January and Standard in *The Constant Couple* on 28 January.

Marshall returned to Drury Lane on 12 October 1745 as Laertes in *Hamlet*. He stayed but one season, playing Omar in *Tamerlane*, Surrey in *Henry VIII*, Frederick in *As You Like It*, Sir Robert Clifford in *Henry VII*, Sebastian in *The Tempest*, and Lieutenant Plunder in *The Humours of the Army*. After that Marshall made only sporadic appearances in London. He was seen at the Haymarket Theatre on 1 September 1755 as Brabantio in *Othello* and on the ninth as Kite in *The Recruiting Officer*. He returned there on 18 January 1758 to play Priuli in *Venice Preserv'd*, and on the following 22 June he received £23 at a benefit held at Drury Lane for some distressed actors who had formerly belonged to the London patent houses.

The Drury Lane accounts for 1773 show a payment of £3 10*s*. "For Mr. Marshall's fu-neral." It is likely that the reference was to the retired actor.

(A performer named Marshall was playing at Norwich from 1726 to 1729 and may have been the subject of this entry, but without further details we cannot be sure. References to a Mr Marshall who sang at Covent Garden in 1761 and was at the Haymarket in 1765 are probably not to the actor we have been following.)

Marshall, Rebecca [*fl.* 1660–1683?], actress.

Rebecca Marshall and her elder sister Anne (who became Mrs Quin) were not, as Pepys thought, the daughters of the Presbyterian divine Stephen Marshall. Yet she was called in 1667 "a presbyter's praying daughter" by Nell Gwynn, according to Pepys, and probably the parents of the girls were Mr Marshall, the chaplain to Lord Gerard, and his wife Elizabeth, née Dutton, of Cheshire, the bastard daughter of John Dutton. Further confusion was caused by the author of *The History of the English Stage* in 1741 when he thought Rebecca was the "Roxalana" who was pursued and duped by the Earl of Oxford. But that was Hester Davenport.

The London Stage lists Rebecca Marshall as a member of the King's Company during their opening 1660–61 season at the Vere Street theatre; in the Lord Chamberlain's accounts she was cited as a company member on a warrant dated 27 March 1661, but a similar warrant canceled her name. That she was active in the King's troupe before the plague is certain, though we have only a sketchy notion of what roles she may have played and when. A Folger copy of *The Royall King*, which may have been performed about 1661–62, has a manuscript cast that includes "Y.M." (the Younger Marshall?) in an unnamed part; a Folger copy of *Love's Sacrifice* has "Beck M." and "B. Marshall" marked for Colona for performances between 1661 and 1664. The editors of volume VIII of the new California Dryden *Works* suggest that Rebecca Marshall may have played Orizia in *The Indian Queen*. The work was acted in January and February 1664. Wiley in *Rare Prologues and Epilogues* has a Mrs Marshall speaking the prologue to *The Parson's Wedding* (it was acted by an all-female cast at Bridges Street in October 1664, but that Mrs Marshall was more likely Rebecca's sister Anne. Rebecca may have spoken that prologue at a revival in later years. She was in the King's Company in 1664–65, and in 1665 complained to the Lord Chamberlain of being molested by Mark Trevor "as well upon the Stage as of[f]." Pepys on 3 April of that year saw her with Nell Gwynn in the audience at the rival Duke's Company playhouse.

Rebecca was molested again in early 1666 and lodged another complaint. On 8 February 1667 (Fitzgerald incorrectly dated it a year earlier, when the theatres were still closed), Rebecca protested that

On Saturday last [2 February] Sir Hugh [Middleton], entering into the tyring house or behind the scenes of the playhouse, Mrs. Marshall taxed him with some ill language he had cast out against the women actors of that house, and wondered he would come amongst them. Sir Hugh, being disgusted, grew into a heat and told her she lied, and concluded the injure with calling her a jade, and threatening he would kick her and that his footmen should kick her. On this, the actress, frightened at his menaces, complained to the King and desired his protection. On the Tuesday evening, having acted in the play and returning to her lodging, in the great entry going out of the playhouse she saw Sir Hugh standing there, which gave her some apprehension that he lay in wait to do her some mischief or affront.

She was walked home by a Mr Quin (probably her sister Anne's husband), but a few doors from the theatre a ruffian pressed hard upon her and then slinked away. Near the entrance to the court where she lived the same bully ran up close to her and clapped a (turd?) upon her face and fled. She believed Middleton had been behind the action.

It is clear that she performed on Tuesday 5 February 1667, when *The Chances* was performed, and J. H. Wilson conjectures in *All the King's Ladies* that perhaps her part was the first Constantia.

On 7 December 1666 Pepys saw Rebecca in *The Maid's Tragedy*: "well acted, especially by the younger Marshall, who is become a pretty good actor . . . " Wilson thinks she may have played Evadne, a role her sister had acted earlier. The two women were cast by Flecknoe in his *Damoiselles à la Mode* as Mlle Mary and Mlle Anne when the play was printed in 1667, but we cannot be certain if the actors followed his

wishes. Before the Bridges Street playhouse burned in 1672 Rebecca was seen as the Lady in *The Scornful Lady*, the Queen of Sicily in *Secret Love*, Edith in *The Bloody Brother*, an unnamed role in *The Cardinal*, Plantagenet in *The Black Prince*, Dorothea in *The Virgin Martyr*, the epilogue speaker in *Hyde Park*, Quisara in *The Island Princess*, Berenice in *Tyrannick Love*, Fulvia in *The Roman Empress*, Calphurnia in *Julius Caesar*, Lyndaraxa in both parts of *The Conquest of Granada*, and Jaccinta in *The Generous Enemies*.

Pepys followed Rebecca's career with interest. When he saw *Secret Love* on 24 May 1667 he told his diary that "though I have often seen [it, yet it] pleases me infinitely, it being impossible, I think, ever to have the Queen's part, which is very good and passionate, and Florimel's part, which is the most comicall that ever was made for woman, ever done better than they are by young Marshall and Nelly." When he saw the play again the following January he felt it was "certainly the best acted of any thing ever the House did, and particularly Becke Marshall, to admiration." In February 1668 he saw *The Virgin Martyr* and found it "finely acted by Becke Marshall." He found her "very handsome near hand" when he sat by her at the Lincoln's Inn Fields playhouse in September 1667, and in May 1668 he "did see Beck Marshall come dressed, off of the stage, and looks mighty fine, and pretty, and noble. . . ."

It was Pepys who reported that Nell Gwynn and Rebecca had had a tiff during which Nell called Beck "a whore to three or four" and said that Beck was "kept by [Henry] Guy an excise man." Pepys also recorded Rebecca's part in bringing Charles Hart and Lady Castlemaine together, as Lady Castlemaine's revenge against the King for his attentions to Moll Davis. Rebecca continued having run-ins with people. One Hannah Johnson went to court against her on 16 January 1668, perhaps for a debt; Beck sued Mary Meggs the theatre concessionaire ("Orange Moll") on 5 November 1669 for abusing her; and on 18 May 1672 one Richard Uttings went to law against the actress for a debt of £7 9s. 6d.

After the Bridges Street Theatre burned on 12 January 1672 the King's Company moved to the Lincoln's Inn Fields playhouse, recently deserted by the rival Duke's players when their new theatre in Dorset Garden opened. There she played Doralice in *Marriage à la Mode* (though she may have acted that as early as December 1671 at Bridges Street), spoke the prologues and epilogues to *Philaster* and *The Parson's Wedding* (the latter in breeches), and played Berinthia in *The Maides Revenge*, Lucretia in *The Assignation*, and Isabinda in *Amboyna*. When the new Drury Lane playhouse opened in 1674 Rebecca was seen as Poppea in *Nero*, Spaconia in *A King and No King*, Francelia in *Brennoralt*, probably Lucina in *Lucina's Rape*, Nourmahal in *Aureng-Zebe*, the title role in *Gloriana*, Olivia in *The Plain Dealer*, Queen Berenice in *The Destruction of Jerusalem*, Lady Lovely in *The Country Innocence*, and Roxana in *The Rival Queens*.

After playing in *The Rival Queens* in March 1677 Rebecca Marshall went over to the rival Dorset Garden playhouse on 31 May (or earlier) to play Maria in *A Fond Husband*, after which she seems to have left the stage. But though gone, she was not forgotten, and satirists for some years made reference to her. An anonymous *Lampoon* (c. 1678) at Harvard amongst some manuscript poems by Rochester and others, said

> *Proud Curtizen Marshall tis time to give o're*
> *Since now your Daughter, shee is turn'd Whore*
> *But be not discourag'd it was in Cambridge shee*
> > *fell*
> *And her London Maiden head, you have still to*
> > *sell.*

How much truth there may have been in that reference to a daughter (and one no longer a child) we have no way of knowing. The *Satyr on both Whigs and Tories* in 1683 suggested that Rebecca Marshall had a liaison with Sir George Hewett. Everything points to her having been a handsome woman (perhaps with the long black hair and dark eyes that Lee describes for her role in *Nero*) and a woman of spirit.

Marshall, [Samuel?] [*fl.* 1711], *musician?*

According to *The London Stage*, a benefit concert for "Sam. Marshall and Geo. Trevor" was held at Clothworkers' Hall on 25 April 1711. In his manuscript index notes to that volume, however, the late Emmett Avery cited Marshall as James, not Samuel.

Marshall, Thomas *d. 1819?, actor, singer.*

Thomas Marshall made his first appearance on any stage at the Haymarket Theatre on 1 June 1781 as Young Meadows in *Love in a Village* (he was described in the bill only as "A Young Gentleman," but the *Morning Herald* the following day identified him as Marshall). The *Morning Chronicle* of 2 June said Marshall's "figure and deportment though not perfect, are far from contemptible. His voice is both pleasing and powerful. . . ." The *Westminster Magazine* in June 1781 identified Marshall as a tailor by trade,

an employment to which we would advise him industriously to apply, as we are told it is extremely profitable; and he seems by action and education to be better suited to it than to that of an Actor. He has a melodious voice, but the powers of it are confined. . . . He would be some years in copying Du Bellamy, who seems to be his model; and in the present state of public taste, success would not reward his pains.

The Secret History of the Green Room in 1792 added that Marshall's father lived in Crown Court, Russell Street.

Bellamy's *Picturesque Magazine* in 1793 provided further information, saying that Marshall was

Harvard Theatre Collection

THOMAS MARSHALL

engraving by Ridley, after Shee

the son of a reputable master taylor, who gave him a liberal education. He early displayed an inclination for the Stage; and in the year 1781, hearing that Mr. Wood, from the York theatre, was prevented by Mr. Wilkinson from fulfilling his engagement at the Haymarket, he applied to Mr. Colman, and was by him (on the sanction of Dr. Arnold's approbation) received into his corps. His first character was Meadows—he was received in a very flattering manner and repeatedly [*recte*: three times total] played the part during the season; he was engaged at two, three, and four pounds a week, but with a restrictive clause, that the article might be dissolved at the end of the first season. This Mr. Colman (we cannot say why) availed himself of, and our hero then directed his march to Edinburgh.

During the remainder of the summer of 1781 Marshall played Young Meadows again and also Harman in *Lionel and Clarissa*, Ensign Williams in *The Silver Tankard*, and Ferdinand in *The Duenna*.

Sybil Rosenfeld in her manuscript on the York Theatre placed a Mr Marshall from Bath at the York Theatre in 1781–82. Our guess is that our Marshall appeared at Bath shortly after his summer performances in London in 1781 and then acted at York, after which, we find from the research of Norma Armstrong, Marshall and his first wife were active at the Theatre Royal, Shakespeare Square, Edinburgh, from January through June 1782. They had married sometime before August 1781.

Tate Wilkinson took credit for introducing Marshall and his wife to York audiences as singers during race week in August 1781. Wilkinson said of Marshall that he had "a very genteel figure, sung very pleasantly, and promised well as an actor. . . ." In Edinburgh Marshall played many roles, including Apollo in *Midas*, Careless in *The School for Scandal*, Ferdinand in *The Duenna*, Filch in *The Beggar's Opera*, Jaques in *As You Like It*, Leander in *The Padlock*, Monsieur in *Love Makes a Man*, Polly Peachum in *The Beggar's Opera Reversed*, Pylades in *The Distrest Mother*, Sir Henry Grovely in *The Maid of the Oaks*, and his London debut role of Young Meadows in *Love in a Village*.

Sybil Rosenfeld's research indicates that a Marshall performed in 1782 in York, advertised as from Edinburgh, and we take it that after his spring engagement in Edinburgh Thomas returned to York. Marshall was in Hull in November 1782, and he was playing

in York in 1783. In 1785–86 Marshall was with the Norwich company. The *Public Advertiser* on 5 December 1785 published a letter from Yarmouth dated 20 November: in the "afterpiece, the Son-in-Law . . . we were also astonished and delighted with a Mr. Marshall's performance of Signior Arionelli. His imitation of the Italian manner, both in acting and singing, were really very capital." We find he was in Brighton for the season that opened on 3 July 1787, was with his wife at the Smock Alley Theatre, Dublin, in 1787–88, and at the Crow Street Theatre there in 1788, described as from the York Theatre. According to the *Newcastle Courant*, the Marshalls had a daughter who was born on 22 July 1789. He and Mrs Marshall played in Manchester at the end of the 1789–90 season, and he appeared in July 1790 at Birmingham. During his provincial career Marshall also performed in Chester.

Marshall then returned to London, making his Covent Garden debut under Harris's management on 17 September 1790, according to John Philip Kemble's notes; he played Bagatelle "(with a song in character)" in *The Poor Soldier*. The *European Magazine* said that Marshall had some merit as a performer but not enough to wipe away the audience's memory of Wewitzer in that character. He was hailed as from Birmingham on that occasion, but the *Newcastle Courant* of 25 September noted that he had played in Newcastle just before his London engagement. Perhaps Marshall and his wife had separated, for he seems to have been busy in London when she died, apparently in December 1790, in North Shields, where she had been a member of Cawdell's company, according to the *North Shields Mercury* of 4 January 1791.

Marshall's three-year engagement at Covent Garden was for £4 weekly in 1790–91; the following season he was raised to £5, and perhaps he went higher during his last season there, 1792–93, but no records have been found. His parts during his three seasons at the patent house included Dr Caius in *The Merry Wives of Windsor*, Colonel Epaulette in *Fontainebleau*, Brazen in *The Recruiting Officer*, Douglas in *1 Henry IV*, Jack Meggot in *The Suspicious Husband*, Osric in *Hamlet*, Antonio in *The Duenna*, Captain Belville in *Rosina*, Captain Sightly in *The Romp*, Cloten in *Cymbeline*, Montano in *Othello*, the Duke of Suffolk in *Henry VIII*, and Picard in *The School for Arrogance*. When his benefit tickets were admitted on 4 June 1791, Marshall's address was given as No 11, York Street, York Buildings.

Bellamy's Picturesque Magazine said Thomas Marshall was received in the character of Bagatelle in *The Poor Soldier*

with distinguished approbation, making it by his style of dress and manner of performing almost a *nouvel* character, and on introducing a song, was given a double encore. Occasionally, in cases of illness, he stepped forward as Macheath, Mr. Belville &c. and though labouring under the disadvantage of the suddenness of the call, and struggling against the impression the audience must feel for superior performers, still he has been favourably received. . . . But on finding himself deprived of that part of Antonio in the Duenna, and from a native diffidence, fearful he had fallen in Mr. Harris's esteem, a modest expostulation took place with that gentleman, in which Mr. Marshall intimated his design of leaving Covent-Garden at the expiration of his article.

Our comedian has engaged himself for the *new* Theatre at Philadelphia, under the management of Mr. Thomas Wignell.

In Arnold Hare's *Theatre Royal Bath*, Thomas Marshall is listed as also at the Orchard Street Theatre in Bath from 1791–92 through 1795–96, but he could have been there only through 1792–93, since he sailed to America at the end of that season. He "married" (Lydia?) Webb about 1793, apparently at Bath.

The Marshalls sailed from England on 15 July 1793 on the *George Barclay*. His American debut may have been at Annapolis, but the first certain notice of him was on 17 February 1794, when he was Don Fernando in *The Castle of Andalusia* at the Chestnut Street Theatre in Philadelphia; Mrs Marshall played Lorenza. On 3 March Marshall acted Bagatelle, a popular role from his London days, which he continued performing for several years. Except for the 1796–97 season, the Marshalls acted in Philadelphia to the end of the century, she attaining popularity in soubrette roles and he appearing in such parts as Carlos in *Isabella*, Belville in *Rosina*, Captain Greville in *The Flitch of Bacon*, Bedamar in *Venice Preserv'd*, Young Meadows in *Love in a Village*, Edwin in *Robin Hood*, Valentine in *The Farmer*, Henry in *The Deserter*, Quaver in *The Virgin Unmask'd*, Sandy

in *The Highland Reel*, Fag in *The Rivals*, Eugene in *The Agreeable Surprize*, Fribble in *Miss in Her Teens*, Tressel in *Richard III*, Horatio and the Ghost in *Hamlet*, Lord Aimworth in *The Maid of the Mill*, O'Carrol in *The Surrender of Calais*, Don Ferdinand in *The Duenna*, Duke Frederick in *As You Like It*, Lionel in *Lionel and Clarissa*, Captain Sightly in *The Romp*, Frederick in *No Song No Supper*, Lorenzo in *The Merchant of Venice*, Christian in *Gustavas Vasa*, Signor Pasticio and Sir Fretful Plagiary in *The Critic*, Azor in *Selima and Azor*, and Pisanio in *Cymbeline*.

Also Amiens in *As You Like It*, Paris in *Romeo and Juliet*, Ennui in *The Dramatist*, Sir Benjamin Backbite in *The School for Scandal*, Inkle in *Inkle and Yarico*, Trueman in *The Volunteers*, Lovewell in *The Clandestine Marriage*, Harcourt in *The Country Girl*, Brownlow in *The East Indian*, Leander in *The Padlock*, Lord William in *The Haunted Tower*, Lord Alford in *The Children in the Wood*, Flutter in *The Belle's Stratagem*, Sir John Loverule in *The Devil to Pay*, Lovel in *High Life below Stairs*, Foigard in *The Beaux' Stratagem*, Lord Grizzle in *Tom Thumb the Great*, Chignon in *The Heiress*, Lubin in *The Quaker*, Friendly in *Hob in the Well*, Marcos in *The Prisoner*, Dr Caius in *The Merry Wives of Windsor*, Macheath in *The Beggar's Opera*, Lord Glenmore in *The Chapter of Accidents*, the Nephew in *The Irish Widow*, Captain Patrick in *Love in a Camp*, Chapeau in *Cross Purposes*, Killeavy in *The Bank Note*, Basset in *The Provok'd Husband*, Frederick in *The Miser*, Lysimachus in *Alexander the Great*, Sicinius Velutus in *Coriolanus*, Charles Dudley in *The West Indian*, Lenox in *Macbeth*, Richard in *Richard Coeur de Lion*, Southampton in *The Earl of Essex*, Patie in *The Gentle Shepherd*, Hotspur in *1 Henry IV*, Hastings in *Jane Shore*, and Beverly in *The Gamester*.

The Marshalls who acted in Boston, New York, and Charleston in the late 1790s were probably the George Marshalls.

Ireland said that Marshall returned to London (without Mrs. Marshall?) in 1801, which is probably correct, for the American bills cease mentioning him after 1800. London bills did not cite him, however, until 24 September 1804, when he reappeared at Covent Garden, again as Bagatelle in *The Poor Soldier*, described as returning after an absence of ten years in

America. The theatre's accounts show his salary to have been £5 weekly in 1804–5. He performed in Brighton in the summer of 1805.

The Drury Lane accounts mentioned him regularly from 1808–9 through 1818–19, his salary remaining at £3 weekly through 1815–16 and dropping to £2 in 1816–17. The report that he died in 1816 would seem to be a mistake. The accounts did not cite him after 1818–19, and Ireland was probably correct in dating Marshall's death in 1819. Ireland and Dunlap both reported that Marshall had become blind and lived on the Drury Lane Fund. His name in the accounts in 1808–9 was cited fully as Thomas Marshall; Charles Beecher Hogan also found Marshall's full name attached to a list of subscribers in 1788.

Thomas Marshall was pictured in an engraving by W. Ridley after M. A. Shee, which served as a plate to *Bellamy's Picturesque Magazine* in 1793.

Marshall, Mrs Thomas the second. *See* WEBB, ₁LYDIA?₁.

Marshall, William ₁*fl. 1724–1729*₁, *actor, officekeeper?*
William Marshall was a member of the Lincoln's Inn Fields troupe under John Rich on 1 August 1724 when, on that anniversary of the Hanoverian succession, he "rode triumphantly in a Turnip-Cart, with a Crown and Pair of Horns on his Head"—until officers committed him to Bridewell. He was soon released, however, for he acted Oswald in *Merlin* at Southwark Fair on 2 September. The account books at Lincoln's Inn Fields cited him occasionally from 1726 through 1729, and one note, on 28 November 1728 ("M.ʳ Chr. Rich by W.ᵐ Marshall 2") suggests that he may have been a worker in the office, arranging for complimentary tickets.

Marson, Mr ₁*fl. 1776*₁, *actor.*
A Mr Marson played Transfer in *The Minor* at China Hall, Rotherhithe, on 9 October 1776.

Marten. *See also* MARTIN.

Marten, Miss ₁*fl. 1747–1748*₁. *See* MARTEN, JOHN.

Marten, Miss ₁*fl. 1761*₁, *actress.*
A Miss Marten was announced in the bills for the part of a Fairy in *Edgar and Emmeline* on 31 January 1761 at Drury Lane Theatre, but Miss Wright acted the part that day. It is probable that Miss Marten played other parts too small to receive notice in the bills.

Marten, John *d. 1764, actor, wardrobe keeper?*
John Marten was probably the Mr "Martin" who acted Tattleaid in *The Funeral* at Covent Garden Theatre on 30 September 1737, though Genest dated Marten's debut at that theatre a year later. On 26 May 1738 Marten made what was advertised as his first appearance on the Drury Lane stage, playing Sir Sampson in *Love for Love*. Then, on 2 October of that year, he played Kite in *The Recruiting Officer* at Covent Garden to begin a full season of performances there. The notices given above were the only ones Marten received up to the fall of 1738.

At Covent Garden in 1738–39 he was also seen as Old Atall in *The Double Gallant*, the Landlord in *The Stage Coach*, Balderdash in *The Twin Rivals*, the Cryer in *Don Quixote*, the title role and Hellebore in *The Mock Doctor*, and Sir Tunbelly and the Surgeon in *The Relapse*. He returned to Drury Lane in 1739–40 to play Bolus in *The Double Gallant*, Mixum in *A Match at Newgate*, the Surgeon in *The Chances*, a Citizen in *Julius Caesar*, Capstern in *Britons Strike Home*, the Poet in *The Mother in Law*, Phaeax in *Timon of Athens*, Charon in *Lethe*, Glumdalca in *The Tragedy of Tragedies*, Kate Matchlock in *The Funeral*, the title role in *The Vintner in the Suds*, Bradshaw in *An Historical Play*, and Mercury in *Amphitryon*. At Drury Lane in 1740–41 he added such new roles as Sands in *Henry VIII*, Sir Roger in *A Fond Husband*, Petulant in *The Plain Dealer*, an Officer in *Twelfth Night*, Truncheon in *The Strollers*, Otter in *The Silent Woman*, and Sly in *Love's Last Shift*. Then he appeared at Bartholomew Fair on 22 August 1741 as Albufazar in *Thamas Kouli Kan*.

Back Marten went to Covent Garden in 1741, and that became his theatrical home until his death in 1764. He was a journeyman player, earning only £1 weekly in 1746–47 and sharing benefits with, usually, two or three others. The accounts show that by 22 September 1760 he was being paid 6s. 8d. daily or £2 weekly. For his modest salary, plus whatever he could make from shared benefits, Marten played a great variety of mostly comic parts, some of them sizeable but many small. (The Miss Marten listed in *The London Stage* as at Covent Garden in 1747–48 must be an error for John.)

Over the years between 1741 and 1764 he added to his repertoire such parts as Scale in *The Recruiting Officer*, Blister in *The Virgin Unmask'd*, Humphrey in *The Conscious Lovers*, the Lord Mayor in *Richard III*, Charles in *As You Like It*, Quack in *The Country Wife*, Goody Gurton in *Orpheus and Eurydice*, the Old Shepherd in *The Winter's Tale*, Bumpkin and Puzzle in *The Funeral*, Cacafogo in *Rule a Wife and Have a Wife*, Lockit in *The Beggar's Opera*, Sampson in *The Fatal Marriage*, Blunder in *The Honest Yorkshireman*, Clodpole in *The Amorous Widow*, Bonniface in *The Stratagem*, Vandunck in *The Royal Merchant*, Bardolph (in *Henry IV*, *Henry V*, and *The Merry Wives of Windsor*), the Soothsayer in *Julius Caesar*, Atticus in *Theodosius*, a Demon in *The Rape of Proserpine*, Bluff in *The Old Bachelor*, Decoy in *The Miser*, Diego in *She Wou'd and She Wou'd Not*, the First Murderer and a Witch in *Macbeth*, the Justice in *The Provok'd Wife*, Captain Hackum in *The Squire of Alsatia*, the Duke in *The Merchant of Venice*, Nicias in *Timon of Athens*, the Town Clerk in *Much Ado about Nothing*, Sackbut in *A Bold Stroke for a Wife*, Poundage in *The Provok'd Husband*, the Miller in *The King and the Miller of Mansfield*, the Surveyor in *Henry VIII*, the First Avocatoro in *Volpone*, Elbow in *Measure for Measure*, Butler in *The Drummer*, the Host in *The Merry Wives of Windsor*, the Duke in *Othello*, Serapion in *All for Love*, Austria in *King John*, Patrico in *The Jovial Crew*, Old Hob in *Flora*, Justice Clement in *Every Man in His Humour*, and the Duke in *Venice Preserv'd*. (On 18 February 1743 he played his old role of Sir Sampson in *Love for Love* at Southwark, his only venture away from Covent Garden.)

The Martin referred to in the *Smithfield Rosciad* of 1763 may have been John Marten:

> And some so pleas'd with Mr. Martin's face,
> Would leave off tea,—to be in CHERRY'S case.
> Can ye dispel the flutter from the breast,

> When he Lord Trincket *enters gaily drest?*
> Can ye conceal the language of the eye,
> And cease to flirt the fan, when he goes by?
> Say, would ye speak, if ther was room to prove
> One little *fault, against that Man of love?*

To augment his income Marten seems to have served Covent Garden as wardrobe keeper; in 1757–58 he received 6s. 2d. daily as an actor and 2s. 7d. daily for his work in the wardrobe. The accounts named him several times in 1760.

William Smith mentioned Marten in a letter to Lord Chedworth (now at the Folger Shakespeare Library, undated, but probably belonging to the 1760s):

We had an Actor of the Name of Martin 6 ft 4 in. in Height, weighing 27 stone who beat Arthur out & out in devouring a fowle in the Busy Body [in the character of Sir Jealous, presumably]. It was always annihilated in 7 mouthfulls. . . . He was a good Fisherman & took a Bett. I won 5 Guineas of him on the Jockey Club Plate, when Forrester, Brilliant &c run. . . .

Marten continued acting to the end. His last appearance seems to have been on 18 May 1764, when he played the title role in *The Miller of Mansfield*. He died at Broxborne on either 24 or 28 July 1764. His widow received a benefit at Covent Garden on 7 May 1765.

Marten, Mrs John   [*fl.* 1760?–1765], *dresser?*

The Mrs "Martin" who was listed on 22 September 1760 as a dresser at Covent Garden Theatre at a daily salary of 1s. 6d. was perhaps the wife of the actor John Marten, who seems to have served the same theatre, at least in 1757–58, as wardrobe keeper. Marten died in 1764 and his widow was given a benefit at Covent Garden (shared with two others) on 7 May 1765.

Martial, Mr   [*fl.* 1769], *actor.*

At the Haymarket Theatre on 28 February 1769 a Mr Martial played Brabantio in *Othello*.

Martiall. *See* MARSHALL *and* QUIN, MRS [PETER?].

Martin. *See also* MARTEN.

Martin, Mr [*fl.* 1710–1715?], *doorkeeper.*

Mr Martin, a doorkeeper at Drury Lane Theatre, shared a benefit with Cartwright on 16 May 1710. Perhaps he was the Martin who shared a benefit at Lincoln's Inn Fields Theatre on 10 August 1715 with the boxkeeper Giles.

Martin, Mr [*fl.* 1756–1760], *wardrobe keeper.*

Mr Martin was cited in benefit bills at Covent Garden Theatre on 19 May 1756, 19 May 1757, and 8 May 1758. The accounts cite Martin (or Marten) as a wardrobe keeper in 1757–58 at 2*s.* 7*d.* daily and on 14 January 1760 show a payment to him of £10 for three months' salary.

Martin, Mr [*fl.* 1762–1767], *dancer.*

The dancer Martin listed as a member of the Covent Garden company in 1762–63 and 1766–67 was probably in the troupe in the intervening years as well. Only twice, so far as we can tell, was he mentioned in the bills: on 26 January 1763 he was a Demon in *The Rape of Proserpine*, and on 27 April 1767 he danced in a turn called *The Wapping Landlady*. Possibly he was related to the fencing master named Martin who, according to *Mortimer's London Directory* of 1763, lived in Clifford's Inn, Fleet Street.

Martin, Mr [*fl.* 1783–1785], *dresser.*

According to the Lord Chamberlain's accounts, a Mr Martin served as a men's dresser at the King's Theatre from 1783 to 1785.

Martin, Mr [*fl.* 1791–1796], *actor.*

On 24 October 1791 Mr Martin made his first appearance on any stage playing Bedamar in *Venice Preserv'd* and Carmine in *Taste* at the Haymarket Theatre. He returned to the Haymarket in 1796 to play Lord Minikin in *Bon Ton* on 22 February and Lord Burleigh in *The Earl of Essex* on 27 April.

Martin, Mr [*fl.* 1793–1794], *watchman.*

The Drury Lane Theatre accounts reveal that a Mr Martin was paid 12*s.* weekly as a watchman in 1793–94. He was still serving the theatre in October 1794.

Martin, Mrs [*fl.* 1695–1708?], *actress.*

Mrs Martin (or Martyn) played Bellasira in *She Ventures and He Wins* at the Lincoln's Inn Fields playhouse in September 1695. The scarce bills of the time reveal that she acted Florella in *The Italian Husband* in November 1697, Marian in *Fatal Friendship* in May 1698, and Esperanza in *Queen Catharine* in June 1698. After that she went to Dublin for a season. In *The Early Irish Stage* W. S. Clark placed Mrs Martin in Dublin from about 1698 to 1702.

Casts for three Etherege plays performed at the Smock Alley Theatre in Dublin in 1698–99 have survived, and Mrs Martin figured in all three: Mrs Grace in *The Comical Revenge*, Mrs Trinket in *She Wou'd If She Cou'd*, and Lady Woodvil in *The Man of Mode*. By mid-April 1699 Mrs Martin was back in London, playing Fidelia in *The Princess of Parma* at Lincoln's Inn Fields. In May she acted Amidea in *The False Friend*, and the following December she played Euphrosine in *Iphigenia*. About December 1700 she was Beliza in *The Ambitious Stepmother*, and between January and August 1701 she was seen as Lady Sobmuch in *The Ladies Visiting Day*, Terresia in *The Czar of Muscovy*, and Sophia in *The Gentleman Cully*. About November 1701 she played Irene in *Antiochus the Great*, after which the sparse records made no mention of her in London until March 1703, when she appeared as Flavia in *The Fickle Shepherdess*. W. S. Clark said Mrs Martin was in Dublin after 1703 and into the 1720s and, indeed, no Mrs Martin was named in London casts until 1725. Mrs Martin was cited for the role of Orada in *The Spanish Wives* in Dublin in 1707–8, after which the Dublin bills did not mention a Mrs Martin until 1714.

Since the Mrs Martin we have been tracing here was playing mature roles—mothers, servants, confidantes—in the late 1690s, and since the Mrs Martin who came from Dublin to London in 1725 had a career that lasted until 1747, our guess is that the later Mrs Martin was, perhaps, the daughter of our subject. Roles for a Mrs Martin in Dublin from 1714 on have been assigned to the younger woman, but some of the parts cited in the 'teens and early 1720s may have belonged to the elder Mrs Martin. The two women played a similar line, and it is tempting to suppose that one Mrs Martin had a career that lasted from 1695 to 1747, but that seems unlikely.

Martin, Mrs ₍*fl.* *1714–1747*₎, *actress, singer.*

The Mrs Martin who acted at the Smock Alley Theatre in the fall of 1714 and in subsequent years may have been the Mrs Martin who appeared in London as early as 1695, but that seems doubtful, for the Dublin actress had a career that stretched to 1747, so we believe there were two women named Martin, playing similar lines—mature women—and they were, perhaps, mother and daughter. William S. Clark in *The Early Irish Stage* listed Mrs Martin as playing Mrs Day in *The Committee* and Teresa Pancha in both parts of *Don Quixote* at Smock Alley in the fall of 1714. Not many of Mrs Martin's roles are known, but in 1716–17 she was seen as Lettice in *The Hasty Wedding*, in 1717–18 as Lucy in *Irish Hospitality*, in the spring of 1719 as Mrs Twist in *The Sham Prince*, and in 1719–20 as the maid Sentry in *The Plotting Lovers*. From 1720 to 1725 at Smock Alley she acted the Nurse in *Love for Love*, Abigail in *The Deceit*, Edging in *The Careless Husband*, Pert in *A Wife and No Wife*, Lady Pride in *The Amorous Widow*, Wishwell in *The Double Gallant*, Mrs Goodfellow in *Tunbridge Walks*, and Viletta in *She Wou'd and She Wou'd Not*.

On 25 October 1725 "Mrs Martin, from the Theatre in Dublin," played Widow Lackit in *Oroonoko* at the Lincoln's Inn Fields Theatre in London, beginning an engagement under the manager John Rich that lasted 22 years. During the rest of her first London season she acted Teresa in *Money the Mistress*, Lucy in *Tunbridge Walks*, Laura in *The Man's the Master*, Mrs Bisket in *Epsom Wells*, Mrs Snare in *The Fond Husband*, Mrs Security in *The Gamester*, and Mrs Queasy in *The Wits*. Perhaps our Mrs Martin spent part of the 1726–27 season in Dublin, for a Mrs Martin was at Smock Alley then, but our subject was on the payroll at Lincoln's Inn Fields (a payment of 15*s*. was made to her on 16 September 1726, and she received 10*s*. on 14 June 1727). The bills show only four parts for her that season: Mrs Snare in *The Fond Husband* on 30 November 1726, Mrs Amlet in *The Confederacy* on 5 April 1727, Necessary in *Woman's a Riddle* on 10 April, and Lucy in *The Country Wife* on 17 May, so she may well have spent part of the winter in Dublin. There was another Mrs Martin active from 1729, however, and since she acted in Dublin in the

1730s and 1740s, perhaps she was the Mrs Martin in Dublin in 1726–27.

Our Mrs Martin continued playing in John Rich's troupe at Lincoln's Inn Fields to the end of 1732 and then at the new Covent Garden Theatre until her retirement in 1747. Typical of her roles over the years were Mrs Peachum and Diana Trapes in the first production of *The Beggar's Opera*, Betty in *Flora*, Jiltup and later Jenny in *The Fair Quaker of Deal*, Mrs Topknot and Mrs Security in *The Gamester*, Lady Darling in *The Constant Couple*, Mrs Quickly in *The Merry Wives of Windsor*, Flareit in *Love's Last Shift*, Mrs Sealand in *The Conscious Lovers*, Mrs Chat in *The Committee*, Dollalolla in *The Tragedy of Tragedies*, the Aunt in *The What D'Ye Call It*, Mrs Cloggit in *The Confederacy*, Mrs Goodfellow in *Tunbridge Walks*, Patch in *The Busy Body*, Viletta in *She Wou'd and She Wou'd Not*, Mrs Motherly in *The Provok'd Husband*, Lady Bountiful in *The Stratagem*, the Hostess in *1 Henry IV*, Widow Blackacre in *The Plain Dealer*, the Nurse in *The Fatal Marriage*, the China Woman in *The Double Gallant*, Lady Wishfort in *The Way of the World*, Mrs Stocks in *The Lottery*, the Nurse in *The Relapse*, Tattleaid in *The Funeral*, Lady Faulconbridge in *King John*, Ruth in *The Squire of Alsatia*, Teresa in *Don Quixote*, Mrs Mannerly in *Orpheus and Eurydice*, Manlove in *The School Boy*, Mrs Fruitful in *Aesop*, and Mistress Overdone in *Measure for Measure*.

She was probably the Mrs Martin who made fairly regular appearances at Richmond and at the late summer fairs. On 25 August 1729, for instance, she acted Hob's Mother in *Dorastus and Faunia* at Bartholomew Fair, and in the summer of 1730 she appeared at Richmond in two of her standard parts: Patch and Mrs Motherly. She was Hob's Mother in *Flora* at Bartholomew Fair in 1731—another part she played at the patent house—and in 1732 she acted again at Richmond and played Lady Sousecrown in *The Perjur'd Prince* at Bartholomew Fair. She was at the fair again in 1733 and 1734, performed at Richmond in September 1734, and on 30 September appeared at Mile End Green as Margery in *The Gardner's Wedding*. After that she seems not to have acted at Richmond or Bartholomew Fair again, but perhaps she was the Mrs Martin who appeared at Bristol in the summers of 1741, 1743, and 1744, but, again, that may as easily have been the Mrs Martin who acted at Dublin during the early 1740s.

Our Mrs Martin may have needed her summer activity to boost her income, for Rich paid her, in 1735–36, only £43 for performing 172 days. Though she was clearly a useful actress in secondary and tertiary roles, she could not command a high salary. In her last season, 1746–47, she was only earning 15s. weekly. The last part she is known to have played at Covent Garden was the Aunt in *Miss in Her Teens*, on 17 January 1747. (The bill called her Mrs Marten.) After that she seems to have left the stage, unless she was the Mrs Martin in Simpson's company from Bath, playing Sulpitia in *Albumazar* on 3 November 1747 at the Jacob's Wells Theatre in Bristol. (*The London Stage* has a Mrs "Marten" down for Butler in *The Drummer* at Covent Garden on 8 December 1752, but that is clearly an error for Mr [John] Marten.)

The Mrs Martin who acted at Norwich in 1731 was probably a different woman, for our subject was occupied in London that year. And we take it that the Mrs Martin who was a puppeteer in 1728 was also a different person.

Martin, Mrs [*fl. c. 1715?*], *impresario*.

The entry on the musician Matthew Dubourg in *The Dictionary of National Biography* states that a Mrs Martin kept a concert room in Sherborn Lane—apparently about 1715, when Dubourg was a boy.

Martin, Mrs [*fl. 1728*], *puppeteer*.

According to George Speaight in his *History of the English Puppet Theatre*, a Mrs Martin exhibited puppets at the Nag's Head in James Street in 1728.

Martin, Mrs [*fl. 1729–1742*], *actress, singer*.

Two women named Martin were active in London from 1729 to 1733, one an actress (fl. 1714–1747) in John Rich's patent company who had come from Ireland in 1725 and performed in London until 1747, and a second Mrs Martin, our subject, who was clearly a younger woman, possibly a relative. This Mrs Martin (or Marten) appeared only at the Haymarket Theatre. Latreille transcribed a bill for that playhouse, dated 6 February 1729, which is not in *The London Stage*: Mrs Martin was to

play Dorinda in *The Stratagem* and the Miller's Wife in *The Humours of Harlequin* for her benefit and advertised that tickets were available "at her shop under Tom's Coffee House, Russell St. Covent Garden."

She had a principal but unspecified role in *The Village Opera* on 8 January 1730, and by the beginning of May had acted the Miller's Wife in *The Humours of Harlequin*, Lucina in *Fatal Love*, Dorinda and later Cherry in *The Stratagem*, an unspecified part in *Love and Revenge*, Seringo in *Hurlothrumbo*, an unspecified part in *The Cheshire Comicks*, Peachum in *The Metamorphosis of the Beggar's Opera*, Mrs Novel in *The Author's Farce*, and Princess Huncamunca in *Tom Thumb*.

Mrs Martin returned to the Haymarket on 10 March 1732 to sing Polly in *The Beggar's Opera* at her shared benefit with Dove. Then she appeared as Mrs Lovely in *A Bold Stroke for a Wife*, Silvia in *The Recruiting Officer*, Nell in *The Devil to Pay*, Dorinda in *The Stratagem*, and, on 27 April, Belinda in *The Recruiting Officer*. A year later, on 21 February 1733, she shared a benefit with Mrs Talbot and played Melinda again. On 19 March she played Dorinda in *The Stratagem* once more. Her last appearances in London were from 5 to 29 April 1734, when she played Mrs Guzzle in several performances of *Don Quixote in England*.

The Mrs Martin who acted in Dublin from 1737–38 through 1741–42 was, we believe, our subject. At the Smock Alley Theatre Mrs Martin played Lucia in *The Squire of Alsatia* on 14 November 1737; Jenny in *The Lottery*, Columbine in *The Hussar*, and Loveit in *The Relapse* in 1739–40; Clodio in *Love Makes a Man* in April 1741; and, at Aungier Street, Columbine in *L'Arlequin Mariner* on 3 September 1741. She must have played many other parts of which we have no record.

Martin, Mrs [*fl. 1758*], *actress*.

Mrs Martin played Rosario in *She Wou'd and She Wou'd Not* and Biddy in *Miss in Her Teens* at the Haymarket Theatre on 12 January 1758. On 16 and 18 January she was seen as the Aunt in *Numps's Courtship*.

Martin, Mrs [*fl. 1760*]. *See* MARTEN, MRS JOHN.

Martin, Master ₁*fl. 1756–1757*₁, *actor.*

On 5 May 1756 at Drury Lane Theatre *Lethe* was performed "By the children," according to the prompter Cross. One of the youngsters was Master Martin, who was also a Lilliputian in *Lilliput* at Drury Lane from 3 December 1756 to 15 February 1757.

Martin, Miss ₁*fl. 1734*₁, *actress.*

Miss Martin played Stormanda in *The Covent Garden Tragedy* at the Haymarket Theatre on 17 April 1734. The work was presented through the end of April.

Martin, Miss ₁*fl. 1740–1741*₁, *performer?*

The Covent Garden Theatre accounts show a Miss Martin at a salary of 5*s.* daily in 1740–41. At that salary she was probably a performer, but her name did not appear in the bills.

Martin, Mrs Christopher. *See* ELRINGTON, MRS RICHARD.

Martin, Edward ₁*fl. 1697*₁, *proprietor.*

Edward Martin was the proprietor of a tavern called the Horns, near Pancras Wells, and advertised in 1697 the virtues of the waters, which had proven a good antidote for vapours, stone, and gravel. For the summer season he advertised dancing every Tuesday and Thursday.

Martin, George *d. 1735, actor.*

The Mr Martin who played Swab in *The Beggar's Wedding* on 6 August 1729 at the Haymarket Theatre was, we believe, George Martin. *The London Stage* lists *The Beggar's Wedding* as being performed again at Drury Lane Theatre (an error for the Haymarket?) on 16 August, with Martin as Scrib. Martin was at the Goodman's Fields playhouse in 1732–33, playing parts too small to gain mention in the bills, and he was there again (or still) in 1734–35. That season he was named for the roles of Spatterdash in *The Fond Husband* on 13 November 1734 and then Longbottom in *The Country Lasses*, a Dropsical Man in *The Chymical Counterfeits*, a Witch in *Jupiter and Io*, Sir Amorous in *Woman's a Riddle*, Cogdie in *The Gamester*, and a Grenadier in *Britannia* (on 3 May 1735, his last appearance in London).

That may well have been his last appearance on any stage. The registers of St James, Bury St Edmund, show that George Martin, a player from London, was buried on 20 July 1735.

Martin, J. ₁*fl. 1763–1767?*₁, *violinist, music copyist?*

J. Martin played violin at Covent Garden Theatre on 13 May 1763. He was probably the Martin who was paid £1 6*s.* by Covent Garden on 27 May 1767 for copying the music for two dances in *Love in the City.*

Martin, Jonathan *1715–1737, organist, composer.*

Jonathan Martin was born in London in 1715, served as a chorister in the Chapel Royal under Croft, and studied organ under Thomas Roseingrave. He sometimes performed at St George, Hanover Square, in Roseingrave's place and at the Chapel Royal in lieu of Weldon. A benefit concert for Martin was held at York Buildings on 15 May 1735, and another was given him on 16 April 1736 at Stationers' Hall. On the latter occasion (and probably on the former as well) he played a solo on the organ. On 21 June 1736 Martin was sworn organist to the Chapel Royal, succeeding Weldon, who had died. On that day Martin and William Boyce signed the following agreement:

whereas the place of Organist has much more duty and attendance belonging to it than the place of Composer (both which were enjoyed by Mr. Weldon lately deceas'd, during whose long indisposition the two places were jointly supply'd by the two persons aforesaid), I the said William Boyce do promise and agree that so long as I shall continue in the place of Composer, I will perform one third part of the duty and attendance belonging to the Organist, provided that I am allow'd one third part of the travelling charges belonging to the place. And I Jonathan Martin promise to compose Anthems or services for the use of his Majesty's Chapel whenever required by the Subdean for the time being.

Grove notes that Martin may not have had to do any composing for the Chapel, for his only known composition was a song for Rowe's *Tamerlane.*

Jonathan Martin did not enjoy his new post for long. According to the funeral book of Westminster Abbey, he died on 4 April 1737 at the age of 22. The newspapers said he died of consumption and that he had been "as much esteemed for his amiable personal qualities as he was admired for his great excellency in his profession." Martin was buried on 9 April in the west cloister of Westminster Abbey.

Martin, Robert [*fl. 1759*], *machinist?*
The accounts at Covent Garden Theatre on 8 October 1759 show a salary payment of £10 to Robert Martin for three months' work. The *Index to the London Stage* calls Martin a machinist, but on what evidence we do not know.

Martin, Signor St. *See* SAN MARTINI.

Martín y Soler, Vicente *1754–1806, composer, conductor.*
The *New Grove* gives Martín y Soler's birthdate in Valencia as 2 May 1754, though the fifth edition of Grove had corrected Martín's tombstone and given 18 June 1754. The *New Grove* also supplies several other names by which the musician was known: Atanasio Martín Ignacio, Tadeo Francisco Pellegrin, Martini,

Civica Raccolta delle Stampe Achille Bertarelli, Castello Sforzesco, Milan

VINCENTE MARTÍN Y SOLER
engraving by Adam, after Kreutzinger

Vincenzo, il Valenziano, Ignaz. He was the son of Francisco Xavier Martín and his wife Magdalena. Vicente studied singing and organ, but by 1776 he had moved to Madrid and turned to composing operas. By 1780 he was in the employ of the Infante. In the early 1780s he had been commissioned to write Italian operas for Naples, Turin, Lucca, and perhaps Florence and Parma. Nancy Storace sang in one of his operas in Venice and was influential in getting Martín to Vienna in 1784 or 1785, where he gained the patronage of Joseph II and began collaborating on operas with the librettist Lorenzo da Ponte. Their first work, *Il burbero di buon cuore*, was presented in Vienna on 4 January 1786. the same year they brought out *Una cosa rara*, which became one of the most popular operas of the period, eclipsing for a time Mozart's *Le nozze di Figaro*. Martín went to St Petersburg in 1788 to serve as court composer to Catherine II; she collaborated with him on librettos. He was given a four-year contract to compose Russian and Italian operas and teach singing.

Da Ponte, who in 1794 was serving as poet to the King's Theatre in London, persuaded Martín to come to London. Their *Una cosa rara* had been performed in London in 1789, so Martín's reputation was well established. On 27 January 1795, with Martín leading from the harpsichord, the first performance of his new opera *La scola de' maritati* (with a libretto by da Ponte) was given at the King's Theatre. It apparently became the practice for Martín to conduct the first three performances of each of his new works. In quick succession his *L'isola del piacere* and *Le nozze de' contadini spagnuoli* came out at the King's, on 26 and 28 May 1795 respectively. For the composer's benefit on the latter date tickets were available from him at No 17, Sherrard Street, Golden Square. Grove (fifth edition) notes that his operas were not very successful in London. Martín also performed at Salomon's opera concerts while in London. Early in 1796 he returned to his duties in St Petersburg.

In 1798 he was made an Imperial Russian Privy Councillor by Paul I, and he served as inspector of the Italian court theatre from 1800 to 1804. Martín composed, in addition to a number of operas, several ballets, some church music, and songs. The *New Grove* lists his works and clarifies the confusion of Martín with Jean Martini. After spending his last years as a singing teacher, Martín y Soler died in St Petersburg on 11 February 1806 (according to the *New Grove*; the fifth edition of *Grove* gave 30 January). He was buried in the Vassily Island Cemetery.

A portrait of Martín engraved by J. Adam, after J. Kreutzinger, was published at Vienna in 1787.

Martindale, Mrs John. *See* WARREN, MRS THOMAS.

Martinelli, Signor [*fl.* 1780–1798], *machinist, puppeteer.*

Signor Martinelli worked as a puppeteer with Micheli in Piccadilly in 1780–81 and alone in Savile Row in 1791–92. He was a machinist at Covent Garden Theatre as early as 1794–95. In *Harlequin's Treasure* in March 1796 audiences saw "The Outside of Pantaloon's House—the Mandarine—the Inside—the Magic Candles—Harlequin from the Tea Urn, &c. invented by Messink and Martinelli." According to the bill for *Harlequin and Oberon* on 19 December 1796 "the Fantoccini [were] executed by Marinelli." That pantomime had 60 performances during the 1796–97 season. He demonstrated his fantoccini again in *Harlequin and Oberon*, beginning 30 October 1797. His puppets were at Ranelagh in 1796–97 and at the Royalty Theatre in 1797–98.

Martinelli was at Birmingham in the summers of 1797 and 1798. The bills there in 1797 spoke of a new dance title *The Contrast; or, Nature and Art*, "in which sig. Martinelli will introduce his celebrated Fantoccini as exhibited at the Theatre Royal in Covent Garden upwards of 100 nights with the most unparalleled applause. . . ." The public was told that "It is universally acknowledged that the Fantoccini . . . are the neatest Collection of Mechanical Figures which have ever been before a Public; the ingenuity, & precision with which they are worked is wonderful, and Dances are evidently the Ne plus ultra of Human Contrivance."

Martini, Signor [*fl.* 1723–1741], *oboist. See* SAN MARTINI.

Martini, Signor [*fl.* 1776], *dancer.*

Signor Martini made his first appearance in England at Drury Lane Theatre on 16 January 1776, dancing a new comic turn called *The Gardners*; the prompter Hopkins noted in his diary: "tolerable." The following day Martini and Signora Paccini offered a dance called *The Jealous Harlequin*. The pair continued appearing into February; Martini received a gratuity of £10 10s. on 5 June.

Martini, Mme [*fl.* 1790?], *singer.*

In an article on Dussek in *Music and Letters* in 1960, S. V. Klima stated that among the singers who performed with Dussek at concerts at the Hanover Square Rooms (which began in March 1790) was a Mme Martini.

Martyr, Margaret, née Thornton, *d.* 1807, *singer, actress, dancer.*

Margaret Thornton was said by several early acounts to be the daughter of a London tailor. The temptation would be strong to dismiss them and assign her as an offspring of the provincial manager Henry F. Thornton, who had several daughters. But he was evidently not born early enough to have been her father. In fact, no connection to those Thorntons is evident. She did, however, have a sister Martha whom she introduced to the stage and who played for some time. It may be that Margaret and Martha were related—perhaps even as daughters—to the Mrs Thornton who was at Dublin in 1780–81.

Margaret's appearance as Rosetta in *Love in a Village* on 13 February 1779 at Covent Garden was advertised, in the coy manner of bills of the day, as by "A Young Lady," being her first appearance on any stage. But she had already been singing at Vauxhall, as she did in summers for many years thereafter. For the remainder of her first Covent Garden season she had to content herself with repetitions of her debut part and such chores as singing Antiope in the masque *Calypso* and joining Mrs Wrighten and Reinhold in the vocal parts of *Gallic Gratitude*.

Margaret Thornton did not return to the Covent Garden company in the 1779–80 season. She sang once at Drury Lane, for Mrs Wrighten's benefit, on 11 april 1780 and rounded out the year at Vauxhall.

Before 13 November 1780 she married a

MARGARET MARTYR
by Condé

man universally reported as "Captain" Martyr and a gentleman. No first name has survived. He died sometime before 1 October 1783, in debt in the King's Bench prison. The *European Magazine* stated that it was well known that he had died of a broken heart, "through the incontinency of a certain lady." The *Thespian Magazine* of July 1792 charged more directly:

Her conjugal virtues were often impeached; and her partiality for Messrs [James] Wild and [Gilbert] Mahon, was very freely talked of in the Green Room. The boasted favours of the latter gentleman having reached the ears of her husband, Captain Martyr reproved him in very severe terms. This produced an open rupture, that proceeded to blows in a coffee-room; but the Captain refused to meet his antagonist in the field, considering a musician beneath him. He was stigmatized as a coward; his wife openly deserted him, and he was soon after imprisoned in the King's Bench, where he died.

Wilde, prompter of Covent Garden, treated her badly. There were separations and reconciliations until 1784, when, he breaking his leg, she deserted him also and took up residence with William Thomas Parke, the celebrated oboist.

The marriage with Martyr, however short and unhappy, had produced a daughter, Margaret (indicated, at least, to be Martyr's child in Mrs Martyr's will). By Parke, whom she never married, Mrs Martyr had at least two children, William Byrne Parke and Henry Parke.

Of middling height, with a figure well-proportioned for breeches parts, Margaret Martyr's black-haired, black-eyed beauty and clear soprano made her an immediate popular success in merry maids and tuneful minxes, the piquant and the pert, for a quarter of a century. She is said to have modeled her singing style (one is tempted to say also her life) upon that of her teacher, the notorious but theatrically effective Ann Catley. "Catley's pupil—Catley's boast," testified Thomas Bellamy in *The London Theatres* (1795): "Sportive, playful, arch, and free, / Lovely MARTYR, hail to thee!"

Except for the single season of 1779–80, Margaret Martyr remained constantly on the roster at Covent Garden Theatre from her debut (as Miss Thornton) early in 1779 through the season of 1803–4. She was at Vauxhall in the summers, with few exceptions: Richmond, Surrey, in 1788 (when she may also have sung in town), 1790, and 1797 ("engaged for a fortnight only"); Birmingham in 1793; Ireland in 1796, when she was at Crow Street Theatre, with excursions to Cork and then to Limerick (*How Do You Do*, on 30 July 1796: "Mrs. Martyr, now we understand Mrs. Parke [!], has been performing with Daly with great success").

Mrs Martyr quickly reaped the rewards of her popularity and she seems to have saved her money. In 1780–81 she earned a respectable £2 a week, excellent for a newcomer. She was raised to £4 in 1781–82 and by 1785–86 she was up to £7. In 1786–87 she was near the top of the list, with £10 per week, and there she stayed for the next dozen years. In 1799–1800 her salary dropped to £7, which is what she made until the end of her career. In addition, she seems to have had generous benefits

MARGARET MARTYR, when Miss Thornton, at Vauxhall

artist unknown

formances of John O'Keeffe's *Lord Mayor's Day*, Ismene in *The Sultan*, the original Phoebe in Frances Brooke's *Rosina*, Euphrosyne in *Comus*, and Juno in *The Golden Pippin*; in 1783–84, Diana in *Lionel and Clarissa*, the original Kathlane in John O'Keeffe's *The Shamrock* (quickly altered to *The Poor Soldier* the same season), Laura in *The Agreeable Surprize*, Cornelia in *The Positive Man*, Urganda in *Cymon*, Florence in *Too Loving by Half*, and William in *Rosina*; in 1784–85, Clorinda in *Robin Hood*, Dollalolla in *Tom Thumb*, the original Nanette in O'Keeffe's comic opera *Fontainebleau*, the original Page in Thomas Holcroft's and William Shield's *The Follies of a Day; or, The Marriage of Figaro* (the first presentation in England of Beaumarchais's fable), Lorenza in *The Castle of Andalusia*, Terisa in William Pearce's comic opera *The Nun-*

(the *Monthly Mirror* reported £480 in 1799) and she supplemented her patent-house income at the pleasure gardens and summer theatres.

Margaret Thornton Martyr's known roles, in the approximate order in which she learned them, were: in 1799–80, Antiope in *Calypso*, Sylvia in *Cymon*; in 1780–81, Pastoral Nymph in *Comus*, Camilla in the first performances of Charles Dibdin's *The Islanders*, Meriel in *The Jovial Crew*, Maudlin in *Poor Vulcan*, and Mandane in *Artaxerxes*; in 1781–82, Camilla in *The Marriage Act*, Jenny Diver in *The Beggar's Opera*, Venus in *The Golden Pippin*, Rosetta in *Love in a Village*, Virtue in James Messink's *The Choice of Harlequin; or, The Indian Chief*, Citronella in *Vertumnus and Pomona*, Mauxalinda in *The Dragon of Wantley*, Cornelia in *The Positive Man*, and Louisa in *The Duenna*; in 1782–83, Polly in *The Beggar's Opera*, Theodosia in *The Maid of the Mill*, Aerial Spirit in the first per-

MARGARET MARTYR, as Rose

by De Wilde

nery, and the original Clara in Leonard Macnally's comedy *Fashionable Levities*; and in 1785–
86, Captain Macheath in *The Beggar's Opera*,
the first Jaqueline in Thomas Holcroft's comic
opera *The Choleric Fathers*, Cherry in *The Beaux'
Stratagem*, Oberea in *Omar*, Flora in *She Wou'd
and She Wou'd Not*, the original Flora in John
O'Keeffe's musical farce *Love in a Camp; or,
Patrick in Prussia*, the first Glib in Macnally's
musical farce *April Fool*, Harriet in *The Two
Misers*, Donella in *The Bird in a Cage*, the title
role in *The Deserter*, Lucy in *The Country Mad
Cap*, Lubin in *Annette and Lubin*, Arethusa in
The Contrivances, Polly in *Piety in Pattens*, and
Miss Jenny in *The Provok'd Husband*.

In 1786–87 Mrs Martyr added to her rep-
ertoire Arabella in *The Girl in Style*, the title
role in *Nina*, Miss Linnet in *The Maid of Bath*,
and Colin in *Rose and Colin*; in 1787–88, Molly
Maybush in *The Farmer*, Mrs Townly in *The
Lady of the Manor*, Lucy in *The Beggar's Opera*,
Florizel in *The Winter's Tale*, Diana in *The Royal
Chace*, and Patty in *Marian*; in 1788–89,
Wowski in *Inkle and Yarico*; in 1789–90, Moggy
in *The Highland Reel*, Dorcas in *Thomas and
Sally*, Fanny in *The Maid of the Mill*, a Shepherdess in *Harlequin's Chaplet*, Ellen in *The
Czar*, a new comic opera by John O'Keeffe,
Miss Dolly Bull in *Fontainebleau*, Mungo ("with
a new Negro song, composed by Reeve") in
The Padlock, Sylvia in Frederick Reynolds's new
melodrama *The Crusade*, Mrs Vermilion in *The
Wives Revenged*, and Laura in *The Female Adventure*; in 1790–91, Ismene in *The Sultan*, the
original Peggy in the musical interlude *A Divertissement* by J. C. Cross, Dolly in Henry Bate's
new comic opera *The Woodman*, Gillian in *The
Quaker*, the first Peggy in *The Union*, a musical
interlude by Richard Wilson; in 1791–92,
Fatima in Hannah Cowley's comic opera *A Day
in Turkey*, and Patty in *Marian*; in 1792–93,
the original Judith in the anonymous opera
Just in Time; in 1793–94, Jane in *Wild Oats*,
Susan in *Hartford Bridge*, George Streamer in
Sprigs of Laurel, Maresa in *The Midnight Wanderers*, the original Jaquenetta in *The Ward of
the Castle*, Mrs Burke's new comic opera, the
first Nerinda in Henry Bate's comic opera *The
Travellers in Switzerland*, and Clara in *The Sicilian Romance*.

In 1794–95, she was the original Seraphil
in *Mago and Dago*, an elaborate pantomime
prepared by Mark Lonsdale, Nelti in *Columbus*,

Harvard Theatre Collection

MARGARET MARTYR, as Phoebe
by De Wilde

the original Thisbe in Thomas Hurlstone's
Crotchet Lodge, Hymen in the enormous spectacle *Windsor Castle*, Sally in *The Sailor's Prize*,
Mora in *The Death of Captain Faulkner*, and
Minetta in *A Bold Stroke for a Husband*; in
1795–96, Pleasure in *Harlequin's Treasure*, the
original Phelim in O'Keeffe's *The Lad of the
Hills*, and Mat Midships in J. C. Cross's new
musical *The Point at Herqui*; in 1796–97, the

original Kitty in *Abroad and at Home*, a comic opera by J. G. Holman, Catherine in *Netley Abbey*, the original Annetta in the comic opera *Italian Villagers* by Prince Hoare, Cymbalo, "a Negro Boy" in *The Surrender of Trinidad*, J. C. Cross's interlude, Maud in *Peeping Tom*, and Lady Marygold in *The Village Fete*; in 1797–98, Sylph in *Harlequin's Return*; in 1798–99, a Huntress in *The Norwood Gypsies*; and in 1799–1800, Rhodope in *A Peep behind the Curtain*.

A glance at those roles demonstrates how constantly she sang in comic opera and pantomime, how often she was used to introduce new pieces, and how eagerly she went into breeches to exploit her figure—Macheath, Mungo, William, Lubin, Colin, Hymen, Phelim, Mat Midships. It does not suggest how incessantly she was called upon for entr'-acte songs, to bolster choruses, and to participate in musical dialogues. Some two dozen songs "as sung by" her are listed in the *Catalogue of Printed Music in the British Museum*.

For some years, her address changed frequently, judging from her benefit bills: in 1784, No 32, St Martin's Street, Leicester Fields; in 1785, Mr Robley's, Bow Street, Covent Garden; in 1786, No 31, Tavistock Street; in 1788, No 28, Great Pultney Street (her parents were that year in Southampton Buildings, Holborn, where her mother died on 9 December); and in 1789, No 13, King Street. But by 22 April 1790 she was at No 16, Martlet Court, Bow Street, where she remained through at least 1801. When she made her will on 19 May 1807 she was "of Long Acre in the County of Middlesex, widow."

Upon the usually acerbic (and often cruel) critic John Williams ("Anthony Pasquin") she had an intoxicating effect, as his comment in *The Children of Thespis* (1792) shows:

See Harmony joyant burst wild on the stage,
To give a young sorceress up to the age;
'Tis all-alive Martyr who claims Beauty's throne,
And marks indirectly each gazer her own.—
Feel the aggregate raptures that live in her sigh,
See the love-darting blaze of her black rolling eye;
Which eloquent speaks all the wish can desire,
And silently whispers—the pulse is on fire!
Mark that killing air-riant exalting her strains,
See Dignity bowing, and Passion in chains;
Not the regal Persephone look'd more divine,
Whom Dis bore triumphant to hell's aweful shrine:
Those rich sable locks, which o'ershadow her brow,

Frigidity warms and provokes the fierce vow;
In irregular ringlets they happily wave,
To hook the blithe hearts of the wise, young, and brave;
In delicious disorder they artlessly break
On those soft snowy mountains which hallow her neck.
Could Ptolemy's relict such witcheries have wore,
Who rul'd the Egyptian on Nile's fruitful shore,
To have call'd such all-potent enchantments her own,
She'd have given a province, perhaps too—her throne;
For sure gallant Caesar could never have fled,
Had tresses so lovely but play'd round her head.
*   While simplicity charms, shall her* PHOEBE *be priz'd;*
When she sings, that calm stillness is praise un-disguis'd;
Her arch replication's her fame's surest guard,
And her CHERRY *demands every critic's regard:*
But should sentiment fail in conveying its zest,
Her beauty obtrudes, and performs all the rest.—

Mrs Martyr died on the afternoon of 7 June 1807 having been (according to a contemporary news account) "in a rapid state of decline, which the most skilful medical treatment was found incapable to resist." Her will appointed William Thomas Parke executor:

Whereas I have lately agreed with my Dear Daughter Margaret Martyr to sell and dispose of a ffarm lands and hereditaments at Yalding in the County of Kent charged with an Annuity to me of seventy six pounds eighteen shillings and six pence during two lives and that the money therefrom shall be equally divided between us now I do hereby give my moiety . . . unto my Dear Sons William Byrne Parke and Henry Parke in equal shares. . . .

The will makes plain that both boys were minors. A notation in the *Thespian Magazine* implies that she had given birth, probably to one of the sons mentioned, in October 1793, and Thomas Dutton, in *The Dramatic Censor* (1800) remarked that "In consequence of Mrs. Martyr's *accouchement*, on the very night of her own Benefit [7 May 1800] the part of Dolly [in *The Woodman*] was sustained by Mrs. Sims."

The rest of her property was to be divided, half to her daughter, one quarter each to her sons. The daughter Margaret sang in the Covent Garden oratorios in the spring of 1801, advertised as a pupil of Madame Mara. She played her first role at Covent Garden in May 1803 on the occasion of her mother's benefit. She performed at Edinburgh in the spring of

1809. She was evidently still acting in London, as Mrs Hudson, as late as 1825–26.

Portraits of Mrs Martyr include:

1. Engraved portrait by J. Condé. Published as a plate to the *Thespian Magazine*, 1792.

2. Engraved portrait by W. Ridley, "From an original picture." Published as a plate to Parsons' *Minor Theatre*, 1794.

3. Engraved portrait by Mackenzie, a reversed copy of the Ridley engraving (No 2 above). Published as a plate to the *Thespian Dictionary*, 1805, and marked "Deighton del." The same plate was also printed in *The Myrtle and the Vine*, 1800 (vol I). A copy by an unknown engraver had been published in *The Busy Bee* by J. S. Burr, 1790.

4. When Miss Thornton; singing at Vauxhall. By unknown engraver. Published as a plate to *Vocal Magazine*, 1778.

5. As Aura in *The Country Lasses*. Engraving by W. Leney, after S. De Wilde. Published as a plate to *Bell's British Theatre*, 1792.

6. As Cherry in *The Beaux' Stratagem*. Engraving by Murray, after Cruikshank. Published by Roach, 1799.

7. As Dolly Fairlop in *The Woodman*. Engraving by Springsguth.

8. As the Enchantress in *Omai*. Engraving by J. Dean, after M. Brown, 1786.

9. As Euphrosyne in *Comus*. Painting by Gainsborough Dupont. In the Garrick Club (No 38).

10. As Euphrosyne. Engraving by N. C. Goodnight. A copy was also issued in lithograph.

11. As the Page in *The Follies of the Day*. By Mather Brown. According to William Dunlap, *History of the Arts of Design* (I, 269) this portrait was exhibited in the outer room, Somerset House, in 1785.

12. As Phebe in *Rosina*. Water color by De Wilde, 1805. In the Harvard Theatre Collection. Engraving by Cooke, published as a plate to Cawthorn's *Minor British Theatre*, 1806.

13. As Rose in *The Recruiting Officer*. Painting by De Wilde. In the Garrick Club (No 211). Similar to No 14, below. Engraving by P. Audinet as a plate to *Bell's British Theatre*, 1792. A copy was printed for C. Cooke, 1806.

14. As Rose. Watercolor by De Wilde. In the Garrick Club (No 66C). Similar to No 13, above.

15. Portraits of "Lord Toper and Clorinda [Mrs Martyr]" appear together in the tête-à-tête column of *Town and Country Magazine* in 1787.

Marviller, Mr [*fl.* 1776–1777], *dancer?*

Mr Marviller (or Mavillier), possibly a dancer, was twice cited in the accounts at Drury Lane Theatre. On 5 October 1776 he, Helme, and Younger were paid £4 18*s.*, and sometime between 9 June and 19 July 1777 he received £70—or perhaps that was an accounting of his season's salary.

Mary, Lady. *See* FINDLEY, MR.

Mary Ann, Miss. *See* HANDY, MARY ANN.

Marylook, Mrs [*fl.* 1722], *actress?*

Fitzgerald in his *New History* listed the rosters of the two London patent houses as of 12 April 1722, drawing upon British Museum manuscript Add 2201. Included as a member of the Lincoln's Inn Fields troupe was Mrs Marylook, possibly an actress and otherwise unknown. She is not listed in *The London Stage*.

Marzi, Pasqualino di [*fl.* 1763], *violoncellist.*

Mortimer's London Directory of 1763 listed Signor Pasqualino di Marzi as a violoncellist living in Russell Street, Covent Garden—which suggests that he may have played at one of the theatres.

Masena, Mr [*fl.* 1790], *puppeteer.*

According to the Pie Powder Court Book at the Guildhall, Mr Masena paid 8*s.* for a license to exhibit his puppets at Bartholomew Fair in 1790.

Masi, Girolamo *b. 1768, pianist, composer.*

Born in Rome in 1768, Girolamo Masi was first instructed in music by his father, a harpsichordist and a pupil of Durante. In 1786, at the age of 18, Masi was appointed pianoforte teacher to the duchessa Braschi, niece of the incumbent pope. In 1789 he replaced his father, who had become blind, as director and composer of the Royal Spanish Church in Rome. After holding that position for four years, during which he wrote sacred music and two operas, Masi settled in Naples. When the French invaded Italy, he left for England in the company of Sir John Legard, with whom he subsequently resided for many years.

On 7 April 1798 Masi played the pianoforte in a concert given at Willis's Rooms, King Street, for the benefit of Mrs Franklin. He performed his own concerto on the pianoforte in a concert led by Raimondi at Willis's Rooms on 27 March 1800, again for Mrs Franklin's benefit.

In 1823 when Sainsbury was gathering information for his *Dictionary of Music*, Masi was teaching in London. Among his published compositions were his arrangements for *Twelve original German waltzes for the piano-forte or harp*; *Six canzonetts with an accompaniment for the piano-forte, selected from Pope's Elisa*; *Auld Robin Gray. A favorite Scotch song, adapted with variations for the harpsichord, or the piano-forte*; *A Set of Preludes*, published by Monzani; and *Tocatta*, published by the Harmonic Institution. He reduced symphonies by Beethoven, Mozart, Woelfi, and others to septets and quintets, and he also published a number of rondos, airs, and variations.

Maskell, Edward [*fl. 1739*], *musician.*
Edward Maskell was one of the original subscribers to the Royal Society of Musicians when it was established on 28 August 1739.

Mason, Mr [*fl. 1746–1747*], *house servant?*
Mr Mason, possibly a house servant, had benefit tickets out at Drury Lane Theatre on 19 May 1746 and 11 May 1747. He was evidently not M. Mason, a boxkeeper at Covent Garden Theatre, who had a benefit there on 6 May 1746.

Mason, Mr [*fl. 1780*], *actor.*
Advertised as making his first appearance, a Mr Mason played Sprightly in *The Detection* at a single performance at the Haymarket Theatre on 13 November 1780.

Mason, Mr [*fl. 1786*], *house servant?*
Benefit tickets for a Mr Mason were admitted on 2 June 1786 at Covent Garden Theatre. He was probably one of the house servants.

Mason, Miss [*fl. 1793–1794*], *singer.*

The Miss Mason who appeared at the Theatre Royal, Norwich, in 1793 was probably the Miss Mason who was advertised as making her first appearance in public (in London) singing in the oratorios at Drury Lane Theatre on 9 April 1794.

Mason, Alice. *See* HEAPHY, MRS TOTTENHAM.

Mason, George [*fl. 1749–1759*], *musician.*
The establishments lists for 1749 and 1759 named George Mason as one of the musicians in the King's Musick earning an annual salary of £40.

Mason, John d. 1677?, *violinist, wind instrumentalist.*
John Mason was probably related to the court wind instrumentalist Thomas Mason of Jacobean times. By 15 July 1628 John was a member of the King's Musick and listed with performers on the oboe and sackbut—but which was his instrument, the Lord Chamberlain's warrant did not say, nor did later warrants in the 1630s clarify the matter. When Mason was reinstated in the King's Musick in 1660 he was given a post among the violins as well as one in the wind instruments, at least for a time, though he was chiefly a wind player. On 13 September 1662 he and three other court musicians were each granted £60 annually for life to teach (again, each) two boys music, particularly flute and cornet. A special livery allowance of £29 16s. 8d. was also granted each of the four teachers for clothing their students for half a year; that sum was then subdivided among the students.

Mason attended the King at Windsor in the summer of 1663, but he seems otherwise to have stayed in London devoting the bulk of his time to the training of, presumably, a sequence of young boys in the Chapel Royal.

Mason continued active in the King's Musick as a teacher until 1674, after which references to him in the accounts cease until 24 December 1677, when Francis Garrard was appointed to replace John Mason, deceased, at wages of 1s. 8d. daily plus a livery allowance of £16 2s. 6d. annually—presumably what Mason had been earning as a teacher.

On 6 March 1672 John Mason, of Woking,

Surrey, made his will, leaving £20 to his cousin Magdalen Blagrave; £10 each to his sister Ann Blagrave, and his cousins Anthony Blagrave, Allan Blagrave, Bridgett Johnson, and John Burton; and £5 each to his godson John Goodwin, his cousins Ann Searle, Ann Ealmes, cousin Cheney Blagrave's son Thomas, and his goddaughter Mary Blagrave, the daughter of his cousin Allan Blagrave. He made his kinsman Thomas Blagrave his executor. The Blagraves, Searles, and Goodwins were all musical families.

Mason, John ₍fl. 1703?–1708₎, singer.
A Mr Mason, who had never appeared on a stage before, sang between the acts at Drury Lane on 25 November 1703. *The London Stage* roster for 1703–4 has him as Mason Shaw. He was cited in the bills regularly during the winter of 1703–4, and in 1704 the song "Cease, cease, Gentle, gentle Swain" by Daniel Purcell was published in *Monthly Masks*. According to a separately published copy of the song (titled just *Cease gentle Swain*) the same year, the song was sung by Mason in *Macbeth*. The singer was very likely the John Mason who was sworn a Gentleman of the Chapel Royal on 12 June 1708 upon the death of Edward Braddock.

Mason, John ₍fl. 1706–1734₎, musician, singer, actor, composer.
The John Mason who, according to the Lord Chamberlain's accounts, attended the King at Windsor and Hampton Court in 1706 was probably the Mason who was active until 1734. Mason was at Windsor again in 1708 and subsequent years through 1725 as one of the Gentlemen of the Chapel Royal. As a member of the Chapel we take it that Mason was a singer, and he was probably the John Mason whose song *The Admiring Lover* was published about 1730. Our guess is that he was also the Mason who played the Poor Poet Radian and the English Taylor in *The Mad Lovers* at the Haymarket Theatre on 2 March 1732. That Mason also sang Damon in *Acis and Galatea* at the Haymarket on 17 and 19 May 1732 and played Axalla in *Tamerlane* on 4 November 1734 at the Great Room in the Ship Tavern. The John Mason who was one of the Children of the Chapel Royal who was granted an allowance on 29 May 1725, after his voice had changed, was perhaps our subject's son.

Mason, John ₍fl. 1725₎, singer.
On 29 May 1725 the Lord Chamberlain ordered an allowance for John Mason, a former Chapel Royal boy whose voice had changed. He was perhaps the son of John Mason (fl. 1706–1734).

Mason, Joseph ₍fl. 1793₎, musician.
The establishment list for 1793 named Joseph Mason as a musician in the royal band, but his salary apparently did not come from the Crown.

Mason, M. ₍fl. 1734–1759?₎, boxkeeper.
M. Mason and his fellow Haymarket boxkeepers Skinner and Cossins had to advise the public on 18 March 1735 that the report of a benefit for them the following night was false. Mason and three others shared a benefit the following 25 April. We take it that our subject was the Mr "Masons" who shared a benefit at Covent Garden Theatre on 14 May 1742 and was listed in that theatre's bills as a boxkeeper through May 1750. He was probably also the house servant Mason who was paid 10s. 6d. each year for working at the *Messiah* performances at the Foundling Hospital in May 1758 and May 1759.

Mason, Michael ₍fl. 1743–1758₎, actor.
Michael Mason appeared at the Smock Alley Theatre in Dublin in 1743–44, sharing a benefit with three others on 2 February 1744. The research of the late William S. Clark revealed that Mason was at the Capel Street playhouse in 1746–47 and at Smock Alley again in 1747–48. On 1 April 1748 he and Miss Mason—his daughter, one supposes—shared a benefit.
At Southwark Fair in London on 7 September 1748 and at Blackheath on 1 October a Mr Mason played Butler in *The Fair Maid of the West*, and we believe that actor to have been Michael. Mason was at Capel Street in Dublin in 1749–50. On 31 March 1755 at the Jacob's Wells Theatre in Bristol, at the desire of the brotherhood of Masons, Simpson's company from Bath performed *The Gamester*, with Mr Mason as Bates. The last notice we have of Mason is again Irish: he and Mrs Mason were at the Smock Alley Theatre in Dublin in 1757–58.

Mason, Mrs Michael [*fl. 1746–1765*], actress.

Mrs Michael Mason performed, as did her husband, at the Capel Street Theatre in Dublin in 1746–47. She was, it seems likely, the Mrs Mason who played Maria in *The London Merchant* on 29 December 1748 at the New Wells, Clerkenwell, in London, for Mr Mason was in London that fall. Mrs Mason appeared at the Smock Alley playhouse in Dublin in 1752–53, was there with Mr Mason in 1757–58, performed at the Crow Street Theatre in 1759–60, and appeared in 1765 at Cork. A Miss Mason, presumably the daughter of Mr and Mrs Michael Mason, acted at Smock Alley in the spring of 1748 but seems not to have appeared in London.

Mason, Robert *b. 1755, violoncellist, violinist, violist, composer.*

Robert Mason was born in 1755. At St Andrew, Holborn, on 1 June 1775 he married Ellen Fisher, and by July 1781, when Mason was recommended for membership in the Royal Society of Musicians, they had three children, the eldest being then five years of age. Mason's recommendation statement by the musician Joseph Gehot said Mason was first violoncellist at Drury Lane Theatre and played also the violin and viola. Mason seems not to have been admitted to the Royal Society of Musicians until 1784.

In May and June 1784 he played violoncello in the Handel Memorial Concerts at Westminster Abbey and the Pantheon, and a year later he was one of the 'cellists at the St Paul's Concert sponsored by the Royal Society of Musicians in May. He continued working at Drury Lane, and some years during the oratorio season he was called upon to offer a 'cello solo, as on 29 March 1786, 25 March 1789, and 13 April 1791. He also served as an accompanist to singers, as on 11 March 1791, when he accompanied Cecilia Davies in "O Liberty" from *Judas Maccabaeus*. In February 1793 he was at the King's Theatre, accompanying Miss Poole, and the following month he accompanied Harrison at the Haymarket Theatre.

Despite his appearances at other theatres, Mason seems to have been regularly employed in the band at Drury Lane. Though he had worked there since 1781, accounts for that

house did not begin citing him until 18 February 1791, when his salary was raised 1s. 8d. (from what base we do not know). The accounts in 1803–4 listed him at a weekly salary of £3, a sum he was still receiving in 1816–17, the last mention of him in the accounts. During the 1790s he played fairly regularly at the St Paul's Concert each May, and from 1804 to 1810 he played during the summers in the band at the Haymarket. Doane's *Musical Directory* in 1794 gave Mason's address as in Upper Marylebone Street.

After 1817 Mason seems to have retired. The Royal Society of Musicians granted him a monthly allowance of five guineas on 2 November 1828 and may have been giving him a pension in earlier years. A note in the Society's books on 3 November 1828 stated that Robert Mason was "a married man and 73 years of age." The last mention of him in the accounts was on 7 February 1830, when his allowance was withheld because his financial status was not certain.

Robert Mason composed some violin solos and violin and 'cello duets; the *Catalogue of Printed Music in the British Museum* dates their publication about 1795 and 1800.

Mason, Susanna [*fl. 1732–1734*], singer, actress.

References in playbills from 1732 to 1734 to Mrs and Miss Mason all seem to refer to the same performer, and we believe she was the singer Susanna Mason, who took the role of Publick Virtue in the opera *Britannia* at the Haymarket Theatre on 16 November 1732. The previous 13 March "Mrs" Mason had made what was apparently her first public appearance as Augusta in *Amelia* at the same house. On 4 June 1733 Mrs Mason played Huncamunca in *The Opera of Operas* at the Haymarket.

The London Stage lists a Mrs and a Miss at Drury Lane Theatre in the spring of 1734, but, as before, we believe that there was only one woman named Mason there. On 3 January she appeared as a Shepherdess in *The Cornish Squire*, and on 4 February she was seen as Venus in *Cupid and Psyche*, a role she played many times through 24 May. She also tried Juno in *Cupid and Psyche*, a Grace in *Love and Glory*, and a Grace in *Britannia*. On 31 May 1734 Mrs Mason sang at the James Street Theatre.

Massey, Mr ₍*fl. 1708*₎, *flutist.*

In his manuscript index to his volumes of *The London Stage* the late Emmett Avery noted that a Mr Massey played flute at a concert at Epsom on 26 July 1708; it was Massey's second appearance in public.

Massey, Mr ₍*fl. 1748–1749*₎, *actor, singer.*

On 4 April 1748, Mr Massey acted Worthy in *The Recruiting Officer* at the New Wells, Goodman's Fields (not Clerkenwell as stated in *The London Stage*). A month later, on 4 May, at the New Wells, Shepherd's Market, he sang "By Jove, I'll be free," and he probably acted in *Miss in Her Teens* and *Harlequin Fortune Teller*, but no casts were given in the advertisements. The play and pantomime also had been performed on 3 May, but Massey's song had not been announced then. It was advertised again when the bill was repeated on 5, 6, and 9 May.

At Phillips's Bartholomew Fair booth in August 1748 Massey played Constant in *The Rival Lovers* and Stephano in *The Tempest*. At the same place in August 1749 he again acted Stephano, and was seen as Mordecai the Jew in *The Harlot's Progress*. With Phillips's company at Southwark Fair that September he played Constant in *The Industrious Lovers; or, The Yorkshireman Bit*, a role which suggests he was the Massey who had acted at Norwich in 1748.

Massey, Mr ₍*fl. 1758–1760*₎, *actor.*

On 28 December 1758 Mr Massey and Matthew Skeggs performed an additional scene in the burletta *Galigantus* at the Haymarket Theatre. At the same theatre on 30 April 1760, Massey and Skeggs appeared in *Britannia's Triumph*. They were members of Christopher Smart's company.

Massey, Mr ₍*fl. 1776–1778*₎, *actor.*

A playbill in the London Guildhall Library, hand dated 3 July 1776, indicates that a Mr Massey acted in *The Rivals* at China Hall, Rotherhithe. (This performance is not noted in *The London Stage*.) He was there again with the same company in the early fall of that year, when he played General Savage in *The School for Wives*, Pan in *Midas*, Gardiner in *Henry VIII*, Jobson in *The Devil to Pay*, Obadiah Prim

in *A Bold Stroke for a Wife* (on 30 September 1776, when tickets could be had from Massey at the Bell and Dragon, near Prince's Stairs), Griskin in *A Trip to Scotland*, Blunder in *The Honest Yorkshireman*, the Lord Mayor in *Richard III*, and Lord Grizzle in *The Life and Death of Tom Thumb*.

In May and June 1778 a Mr Massey performed at China Hall on the same nights that another Massey (who was, we believe, the Norwich actor) played at the Haymarket. The Massey at China Hall acted the Servant in *Douglas*, the Music Master in *Catherine and Petruchio*, Crispin Heeltap in *The Mayor of Garratt*, Diggory in *She Stoops to Conquer*, Ratcliffe in *Jane Shore*, Beaufort in *The Citizen*, the Footman in *The Devil to Pay*, the Butler in *The Busy Body*, Sir Jeffrey Constant in *The Ghost*, an Officer in *The Earl of Essex*, and Catesby in *Richard III*.

The Mrs Massey who acted Zaphira in *Barbarossa* on 27 September 1776 and the Queen in *Richard III* on 4 October 1776, at China Hall, was no doubt his wife.

Massey, Mr *d. 1784, actor, singer.*

Mr Massey acted at the Crow Street Theatre, Dublin, in 1766–67. He made his first appearance at Covent Garden Theatre on 14 September 1767, as Jasper in *The Mock Doctor*. Sylas Neville wrote in his diary that night: "Young Jasper pretty well by one Massey." His salary for that season was 3*s*. 4*d*. per night, but his name appeared infrequently in bills. Among his roles were Cob in *Every Man in His Humour* and Gargle in *The Apprentice*. In September and October 1768 he joined some other Covent Garden actors in an engagement at Richmond, Surrey, where on 10 October he played Peachum in *The Beggar's Opera*.

Perhaps he was the Massey who was with Austin and Heatton's provincial company in 1770; they were at Chester in June and at Whitehaven in October. In 1772–73 Massey was with a strolling company playing at Cooper's Hall, Bristol.

On 1 February 1775 Massey played Hawthorne in *Love in a Village* and Jobson in *The Devil to Pay* at the Haymarket, for Miss Woodman, the Covent Garden singer. Announced as making his first appearance there in eight years, Massey returned to Covent Garden on 9

May 1775 to act Trapland in *Love for Love*, for Quick's benefit. Massey then was engaged at Norwich, making his debut there as Jobson in *The Devil to Pay* on 26 December 1775. On 8 April 1776 the Norwich proprietors "Ordered That Mr and mrs Massey have Notice to leave the Company at the End of the Season." On 30 May 1776 they "Ordered, That Mr Massey's Note of £3.3.0 be given up to him as a Compensation for Mrs Massey's Performing before the Commencement of her Salary." Mrs E. Massey had made her Norwich debut on 13 January 1776. Mr and Mrs Massey were not with the company when, at the end of the Norwich season, it went to play for a while at Dereham, about 16 miles west.

In the summer of 1777 Massey and his wife joined Colman's company at the Haymarket, where he appeared on 15 May in an unspecified part in *The English Merchant*. He played many roles that summer, including Tubal in *The Merchant of Venice*, Vanderbluff in *Polly*, a Gravedigger in *Hamlet*, Bardolph in *1 Henry IV*, Sir Jasper Wilding in *The Citizen*, and (his most substantial) Sir Jacob Jollup in *The Mayor of Garratt* on 30 July 1777, the night when Foote, playing Major Sturgeon, made his last appearance on the stage.

In the first half of 1778 Massey made occasional appearances at the Haymarket: as Thomas in *The Irish Widow* on 9 February (for a benefit shared with his wife, when tickets were available from him at No 17, Portugal Street, Lincoln's Inn Fields), Norfolk in *Richard III* on 24 March, Sir Philip Modelove in *A Bold Stroke for a Wife* on 31 March, Thomas in *The Irish Widow* and Acasto in *The Orphan* on 9 April (when benefit tickets were available from him at Marshall's, Bedford Court), Vulture in *The Country Lasses* on 29 April, and Sterling in *The Clandestine Marriage* on 30 April. That summer he was again with Colman at the Haymarket, where he was engaged regularly through 1783, and acted dozens of roles, in a supporting line, in comedies and comic operas. When he played Lockit in *The Beggar's Opera* in June 1778, he was criticized by the *Morning Chronicle* for not being fully familiar with his part and for applying too much burnt cork upon his eyebrows—"Lockit is drawn as the character of a man, not of a monster." For his benefit at the Haymarket on 13 October 1779 he played Obadiah Prim in *A Bold Stroke for a*

Wife and a principal character in the London premiere of O'Keeffe's *The She Gallant*. Tickets were available from Massey at No 4, St Martin's Street. Among his roles in his last Haymarket season, 1783, were Kilderkin in *The Flitch of Bacon*, Basil in *The Spanish Barber*, Pantaloon in *The Genius of Nonsense*, Hodge in *Love in a Village*, Kitchen in *Man and Wife*, and Bundle in *The Waterman*.

In 1778–79 Massey had played at Crow Street, Dublin. Early in 1781 he had acted with his wife at Edinburgh; among his roles there was Stanley in *Richard III* on 8 January. Later that year he was again a member of the Norwich company.

Massey died in the summer of 1784, according to Reed's "Notitia Dramatica" in the British Library. In George Frederick Cooke's obituary in the *Gentleman's Magazine* for November 1812, it was stated that Massey had been a member of the "Choice Spirits Club," which included Cooke, G. A. Stevens, Ned Shuter, and Michael Rooker.

Massey, Mr ₁*fl. 1786*₁, *dancer.*
At Astley's Amphitheatre, Westminster Bridge, on 4 September 1786, Mr "Massi" performed a Dancing Attendant on the Lord Mayor in the musical spectacle *Love from the Heart, a Trial of Skill for a Wife*. On 17 September, now advertised as Massey, he danced in the review *A Sale of English Beauties at Grand Cairo*.

Massey, Mrs ₁*fl. 1776*₁, *actress. See* MASSEY, MR ₁*fl. 1776–1778*₁.

Massey, Mrs E. ₁*fl. 1776–1783*₁, *actress.*
Mrs E. Massey may have acted elsewhere in the provinces before her Norwich debut on 13 January 1776 as Zara in *The Mourning Bride*. Her husband, a veteran provincial stroller, was also a member of the Norwich company that season. On 8 April 1776 the Norwich proprietors "Ordered That Mr and Mrs Massey have Notice to leave the Company at the End of the Season." On 30 May 1776 they "Ordered That Mr Massey's Note of £3.3.0 be given up to him as a Compensation for Mrs Massey's Performing before the Commencement of her Salary."

In the summer of 1777 the Masseys joined

Harvard Theatre Collection

MRS MASSEY, as Christina

engraving after Roberts

April 1778, when her husband shared benefit tickets with Freeman.

By 18 May 1778 Mrs Massey was in York, where she played Widow Brady on that date. She had made the journey from London at some expense in expectation of a benefit, which she received on 22 May, when she acted Jane Shore and Zara. The account books show that the receipts totaled a disappointing £16 os. 6d. Massey had a "wonderful opinion" of his wife's abilities, according to Tate Wilkinson, the York manager, and "the lady was not behind hand in the same." Wilkinson thought her "very *so, so*, though not destitute of some degree of merit."

Returning to the Haymarket for the summer, on 10 June 1778 Mrs Massey played Al-

Harvard Theatre Collection

MRS MASSEY as Albina and WILLIAM DI-MOND as Edward

artist unknown

Colman's Company at the Haymarket Theatre, where she first appeared on 7 August as Queen Elizabeth in *Richard III*. She was seen as Marcia in *Cato* on 14 and 18 August and Queen Catherine in *Henry VIII* on 29 August and 5 September. A correspondent to the *Morning Chronicle* of 5 September was "amazed so little notice should be taken" of this young actress, for he judged her "by far the best in Mr. Colman's troop." In a letter to that paper on 9 September 1777 she signed "Mrs E. Massey."

She and her husband seem to have remained in the London area for the early months of 1778, though neither had an engagement in either of the winter patent houses. They made several appearances, however, in specially-licensed performances at the Haymarket. On 9 February 1778 for their benefit she acted the title role in *Jane Shore* and Widow Brady in *The Irish Widow* (with Massey as Thomas); tickets were available from them at No 17, Portugal Street, Lincoln's Inn Fields. She acted Monimia in *The Orphan* and Widow Brady on 9 madine in the premiere of Walpole's interlude *Nature Will Prevail*. The critic for the *Public Advertiser* on 12 June 1778 thought that she had "a fine voice" for singing but she "rather tragedizes too much in her tone." Her other roles that summer included Queen Catherine in *Henry VIII*, a Daughter in Colman's adaptation of *Bonduca* on 30 July, Lady Macbeth, and Cordelia in *King Lear*. She then traveled to Dublin, where she made her debut at the Crow Street Theatre on 22 December 1778.

Mrs Massey continued to be engaged at the Haymarket every summer through 1781. On 31 July 1779 she acted the title role in the premiere of Mrs Cowley's *Albina, Countess Raimond*. *The Gazetteer* of 4 August 1779 described her as one "who from a natural timidity, which too frequently depresses real merit, retains the errors of a young and inexperienced actress much beyond the usual period." At the Haymarket on 13 October 1779, for a specially-licensed benefit for her husband, she acted Anne Lovely in *A Bold Stroke for a Wife*.

On 3 January 1781 Mrs Massey made her first appearance at Manchester, as Belvidera in *Venice Preserv'd*. On 8 January she acted Queen Elizabeth in *Richard III* and her husband played Stanley. In 1782 she was in Dublin again, acting at the Capel Street Theatre until the last day of the year. In December of 1783 she acted with Pero's company at Derby.

The Mrs Massey who acted at China Hall, Rotherhithe, in 1776 we believe was a different actress. A Mrs Eleanor Massey Fitzgerald acted in productions given by British troops quartered in New York in 1781 and 1782 and in Ryan's company there in 1783. In October 1783 she defrauded Ryan of £46 16s. by absconding from her indenture to him and the manager offered a reward of £20 for information concerning her whereabouts. We are unable, however, to link that actress to our subject.

A portrait by an unknown engraver, after J. Roberts, of Mrs Massey as Christina in *Gustavus Vasa* was published as a plate to *Bell's British Theatre* in 1778. There is no record of her having played that role in London. An anonymous engraving of her as Albina, with William Dimond as Lord Edward, in *Albina, Countess Raimond* was published in the *Lady's Magazine* in November 1779.

Massey, Hugh [*fl. 1688?*], *fiddler*.

A portrait of Hugh Massey by Marcellus Laroon, engraved by J. Savage, was published as a plate to Tempest's *Cryes of London* (1688) with the title "The Merry Fidler."

Massey, James [*fl. 1740–1748*], *constable*.

In 1740–41 James Massey earned 2s. per day as a constable at Covent Garden Theatre. On 29 September 1740 he was paid 10s. for five nights. His name was still on the theatre's paylist in 1747–48. On 6 May 1748 he shared benefit tickets with other house servants.

Massey, John *d. 1775, ballad singer*.

An entry in Sir William Musgrave's *Obituary Prior to 1800* (1899–1901) gives the death

HUGH MASSEY

engraving by Savage, after Laroon

JOHN MASSEY

engraving by Smith, after Carter

date of "Massey, Jno., ballad-singer" as 1775. An engraved portrait by J. R. Smith, after G. Carter, shows Massey standing by a wall, holding broadside ballads, with a young woman and a boy as his audience. The portrait was published in 1775.

Massey, Robert [*fl.* 1789–1797], *violinist, horn player, music seller.*

Robert Massey, a music seller in Manchester, was listed in Doane's *Musical Directory* in 1794 as a violinist, horn player, and a subscriber to the New Musical Fund. In 1789 his name had appeared as "R. Massey, Music seller, Manchester" on the imprint of *A New Sett of Hymns and Psalm Tunes . . . Composed by J. Leach, Rochdale.* About 1797 *A Second Sett of Hymns and Psalm Tunes* was issued with Massey's name similarly inscribed.

Massi. *See* MASSEY.

Massimino, Signor [*fl.* 1777], *singer.*

Signor Massimino replaced the singer Trebbi as Nardone in *La Frascatana* for one performance at the King's Theatre on 15 May 1777.

Massingham, Mr [*fl. c.* 1790–1830], *doorkeeper, office keeper.*

In the *Monthly Magazine* in November 1830 appeared an article describing Mr Massingham sitting in the "privilege-office" at Drury Lane Theatre: "a quite broad, shrewd-looking, elderly gentleman; who sitting in a nook that fits him like a great-coat, with his hat drawn a little over his eyes, to shade them from the glare of the lamp beside him, has received your credentials. . . ." Massingham told the reporter that he had been sitting there for 40 years, through the reigns of Mrs Siddons, Kean, and others; "I have not seen a play or a farce for these forty years," he boasted. He did not even go to his own benefits.

From that we can guess that Massingham began working at Drury Lane about 1790; the earliest mention of him in the accounts was in 1791–92, and the earliest benefit bill that cited him was that for 15 June 1792 when the Drury Lane company was acting at the King's Theatre. The accounts made frequent mention of Massingham (and at least once of a Massingham Junior, probably his son) during the 1790s and throughout the first two decades of the nineteenth century. Mrs Massingham was also named in the books once—in June 1802— but seems not to have been employed at the theatre during the eighteenth century. Massingham was cited in the accounts in various ways: cheque taker, pit doorkeeper, boxkeeper, box bookkeeper, and renter's office keeper. Possibly some of those designations concern the younger Massingham. Figuring out Massingham's salary is difficult, for the accounts seem to show him at both 9s. and at 12s. weekly in 1803–4 (the lower salary may have been for the younger man), £1 10s. weekly in 1812–13, 12s. weekly in 1815–16, and 18s. weekly in 1818–19.

Massingham's address in his benefit bill on 5 June 1795 was given as No 85, King Street, Golden Square. He was still living there in 1810, but a Haymarket bill on 14 October 1824 noted that tickets and places for the boxes could be had of Massingham at No 58 (late No 83), King Street, Golden Square, opposite Cross Street.

Massingham, Mr [*fl. 1795–1804?*], house servant.

The benefit tickets of Massingham junior were accepted at Drury Lane Theatre on 5 June 1795 and the accounts cited him in 1795–96 among the house servants. He was, presumably, the son of the doorkeeper and office keeper Massingham, who worked at Drury Lane for 40 years. How long the younger man was employed at the theatre is difficult to determine, but the accounts in 1803–4 cited Massinghams at 9s. weekly and at 12s. weekly, and perhaps the lower figure was for the younger Massingham. His duty is also hard to determine, for the accounts attach a number of different tasks to the name Massingham (they are discussed in the elder Massingham's entry), but the 9s. salary was for work as a cheque taker, and perhaps that was one of the younger man's duties.

Massinghi. *See* MAZZINGHI.

Massink. *See* MESSINK.

Masson. *See* MASON.

Masters, Mr [*fl. 1794*], violinist.

Doane's *Musical Directory* of 1794 listed Mr Masters as a violinist who played for the Handelian Society and in the Handel performances at Westminster Abbey. Masters was from Greenwich, Kent, and was very likely a relative of Joseph Masters, who was bound apprentice to John Hindmarsh on 26 September 1792 to study violin, viola, and clarinet. Joseph's father was William Masters, a wine merchant from Greenwich. Joseph is not known to have performed professionally before the end of the eighteenth century.

Masters, Mr [*fl. 1794–1803*], singer.

Mr Masters was named in *Mirth's Museum* in 1794 as the singer of four songs by Reeves: "The Antiquity of Bulls," "Ben Block," "Knowing Joe and the Shew Folk," and "The Vestry Dinner." The periodical did not say where Masters sang those pieces.

As early as 17 April 1795 Masters was working at the Royal Circus, singing a principal character in *Veluti in Speculum*. On 1 October he had a major role in *The Jew and the Gentile*, a burletta. The bills for the Circus reveal that on 6 October 1800 Masters was a principal character in the burletta *The False Friend* and sang "The Merry Merry Bells." He was given benefits on 11 November 1802 and 15 November 1803. The last notice we have found for Masters is the Royal Circus bill of 28 November 1803, when he sang "The Merry Bells." He may have been the husband of the Mrs Masters who performed in London from 1788 to the end of the century.

Masters, Mrs [*fl. 1675*], singer, actress.

Mrs Masters, apparently not one of the ladies of the court but a regular performer, sang and acted one of the Shepherdesses in the court masque *Calisto* on 15 February 1675.

Masters, Mrs [*fl. 1713–1715*], dressmaker.

The Drury Lane accounts at the Folger Shakespeare Library name Mrs Masters, a dressmaker, on 29 January 1713 and again in March 1715. She appears to have been on the theatre staff.

Masters, Mrs, née Lalauze b. 1753, dancer.

Charles Laulauze's daughter was born in 1753 and on 25 April 1759 made her stage debut at Covent Garden Theatre dancing a minuet with her father and Miss Toogood. The bill stated that Miss Lalauze was between five and six years old. A year later, making what was advertised as her second appearance, she danced *La Petite Bergere*, and on 23 April 1760 at her father's benefit she repeated that dance and with Lalauze performed a serious dance and a louvre. Her next stage appearance came a year later, when she again did her *Petite Bergere* dance and performed a minuet with an eight-year-old boy, a scholar of Lalauze. When she danced at her father's benefit on 29 April 1763 with one of her father's young pupils, the children were advertised as making their last appearance on any stage. That would clearly not prove true of Miss Lalauze.

On 29 March 1764 she danced at the King's Theatre; in April 1769 she danced a louvre and minuet with her father at his Covent Garden benefit; on 14 February 1770 at the Haymarket Theatre father and daughter again danced a louvre and minuet; and on 11 March 1771 at his Haymarket benefit they danced a louvre, minuet, and allemande. At Covent Garden on 4 May 1776 the benefit bill listed a Mrs Masters as one of many beneficiaries, and she was identified as formerly Miss Lalauze.

Mrs Masters's first advertised performance at Covent Garden came on 13 October 1775, when she was a Nymph in *Orpheus and Eurydice*. During the rest of that season she was seen in that part many times and played Trippet in *The Lying Valet*, Lucia in *The Cheats of Scapin*, Arante in *King Lear*, an unnamed role in *The Weathercock* (but she was dropped after the first performance). Mrs Masters also sang in *Prometheus*, and on the day her benefit tickets were accepted she danced a minuet with D'Egville. It is probable that the Mrs Masters who played soubrettes and was a columbine at Bristol in 1778–79 was the same performer.

Masters, Mrs [*fl.* 1788–1809], *actress, singer.*
The benefit tickets of Mrs Masters were accepted at Covent Garden Theatre on 31 May 1788. *The London Stage* lists a male Masters as selling benefit tickets for 6 June 1789 at Covent Garden, but that citation is probably an error for Mrs Masters, who was named regularly in benefit bills during that period but was not named in *The London Stage* company rosters in 1788–89. She sang in the chorus in *Romeo and Juliet* on 14 September 1789 and in *Macbeth* on 12 October. Beginning on 21 December she was a Fishwoman in *Harlequin's Chaplet*, and on 1 March 1790 she began doubling as a Milliner in that piece. She sang in *All for Love* on 24 May and had her benefit tickets out for 27 May.

Her career at Covent Garden continued in a similar vein through 1803–4, and for her labors as a player of bit parts and a member of the singing chorus Mrs Masters received £1 weekly. Some of her assignments were a Prisoner in *The Crusade*, an Aerial Spirit in *Blue-Beard*, a Shepherdess in *Orpheus and Eurydice*, a Lady in *Harlequin's Museum*, a Housemaid in *The Invasion*, a Biscayan Girl in *The Midnight Wanderers*, a Country Girl in *The Mysteries of the Castle*, an Irish Peasant in *Bantry Bay*, Cloe in *High Life below Stairs*, a Nun in *Raymond and*

Agnes, an Attendant in *The Volcano*, and a chorus member in a number of other musical pieces.

On 18 June 1792 Mrs Masters began spending her summers at the Haymarket Theatre, where her assignments were again minor ones. On that date she was a Villager in *The Battle of Hexham*, after which she appeared in *The Surrender of Calais* and as Parthenope in *The Rehearsal*. In subsequent summers she was seen as a Lady in *The Pad*, a Peasant in *The Mountaineers*, a Bacchante in *Comus*, and a chorus member in *The Iron Chest*, *The Italian Monk*, *Cambro-Britons*, *The Red-Cross Knights*, *Obi*, and *What a Blunder*. Mrs Masters continued at the Haymarket at least through the 1801 summer season and at Covent Garden through 1808–9. She was probably the wife of the singer Masters who performed for several seasons at the Royal Circus.

The Mr Masters cited in *The London Stage* as having benefit tickets out on 6 June 1789, 4 June 1794, 18 May 1798, and 17 May 1799 was surely Mrs Masters. In all cases the name comes from the accounts and not the bills, and the citations dovetail neatly with the rest of Mrs Master's citations.

Masterson, Mrs [*fl.* 1775], *singer.*
Mrs Masterson sang in the "Solemn Dirge" at the end of performances of *Romeo and Juliet* at Covent Garden Theatre from 25 September to 27 December 1775.

Masying. *See* MAZZINGHI.

"Match Matilda." *See* EDWARDS, MRS [*fl.* 1786–1794].

Mates, Mr [*fl. c.* 1715], *barber.*
According to the Drury Lane Theatre accounts at the Folger Shakespeare Library Mr Mates was a company barber about 1715.

Matheis, Mr [*fl.* 1734], *singer.*
The Earl of Egmont noted in his diary that Mr Matheis was one of the professional singers at his private concerts on 15 February and 8 March 1734. On 27 November of the same year Matheis participated in a concert at the Crown and Anchor.

Mather, Mr ₁*fl. 1772–1790*₁, *carpenter.*
A Mr Mather was on the account book of Drury Lane Theatre at a salary of 9*s.* per week in the season of 1789–90. His function was not indicated, but he may have been the carpenter who received a benefit at Sadler's Wells in October 1772.

Mather, Mrs ₁*fl. 1743*₁, *house servant?*
A Mrs Mather shared benefit tickets with the Widow Dupre at Covent Garden on 7 April 1744. She may have been a servant of the theatre.

Mather, Mrs ₁*fl. 1800*₁, *singer, actress.*
A Mrs Mather was in the company at Sadler's Wells in the spring and summer of 1800. She made her first appearance at the Haymarket on 16 September, the night after the close of the season there, in a performance for the benefit of the prompter F. G. Waldron.

Mather, Richard, *See* MATHER, ROBERT.

Mather, Robert ₁*fl. 1681*₁, *boxkeeper.*
The London Stage lists a Richard Mather as a member of the King's Company at Drury Lane in 1680–81, but that would appear to be an error for Robert Mather. A Lord Chamberlain's warrant dated 28 April 1681 directed that Robert should replace the boxkeeper Henry Hailes. On 26 October of that year Anthony Collins petitioned against Robert Mather for a debt, and on 8 November he was allowed to sue.

Mathew, Mr ₁*fl. 1784–1786*₁, *tumbler.*
Mr Mathew, also identified in the advertisements as "The English Mercury," was a tumbler at Sadler's Wells in the summers of 1784 and 1785. "The English Mercury" also performed acrobatics at Bristol in 1785–86. His son, Master Mathew (fl. 1784–1786), performed with him at both places.

Mathew, Master ₁*fl. 1784–1786*₁, *tumbler.*
Master Mathew performed tumbling feats with his father, Mr Mathew (fl. 1784–1786), also known as "The English Mercury," at Sad-

ler's Wells in the summers of 1784 and 1785 and at Bristol in 1785–86.

Mathewes, Thomas ₁*fl. 1671–1672?*₁, *musician.*
Thomas Mathewes was one of several musicians apprehended by the Corporation of Music on 4 August 1671 for teaching music or performing in public without a license. Possibly he was the Thomas Mathewes whose daughter Susanna was christened at St Paul, Covent Garden, on 11 August 1672. That man's wife was named Mary.

Mathews. *See also* MATTHEWS.

Mathews, Mr ₁*fl. 1663*₁, *swordsman.*
Samuel Pepys went on 1 June 1663 to the Vere Street Theatre, recently vacated by the King's Company when their new house in Bridges Street opened, and saw some swordsmanship:

And here I came and saw the first prize I ever saw in my life: and it was between one Mathews, who did beat at all weapons, and one Westwicke, who was soundly cut several times both in the head and legs, that he was all over blood: and other deadly blows they did give and take in very good earnest, till Estwicke [*sic*] was in a most sad pickle. They fought at eight weapons, three boutes at each weapon. It was very well worth seeing, because I did till this day think that it had only been a cheat; but this being upon a private quarrell, they did it in good earnest; and I felt one of their swords, and found it be very little, if at all, blunter on the edge, than the common swords are. Strange to see what a deal of money is flung to them both upon the stage between every bout. But a woeful rude rabble there was, and such noises, made my head ake all this evening.

Mathews, Mr ₁*fl. 1708*₁, *house servant?*
Among Vice Chamberlain Coke's papers at Harvard is a paylist for the Queen's Theatre dated 8 March 1708; a Mr Mathews is down for a salary of 2*s.* 1*d.* daily, but his duties were not specified. At that salary he was probably one of the house servants.

Mathews, Mr ₁*fl. 1739?–1771*₁, *dancer, tumbler, manager.*
The dancer Mr Mathews who had an adult career on the London stage for over 25 years

probably was the child Master Mathews, a scholar of Davenport, whose first notice in the bills was on 21 May 1739 at Covent Garden Theatre when he performed a harlequin dance. In 1739–40, Master Mathews and Miss Wright, another of Davenport's pupils, appeared many times at Drury Lane Theatre in a *Scots Dance*, which they performed for the first time on 16 October 1739. At Goodman's Fields Theatre in 1740–41, still under Davenport's instruction, Master Mathews was seen regularly in an untitled comic dance and several times in a pierrot dance. He performed again at Covent Garden on 30 November and 9 December 1741. At Drury Lane on 25 May 1742 Master Mathews and Miss Wright danced in *Celadon and Phyllis* and *The Medley of Jokes*. That summer he was a member of the Sadler's Wells Company. Again with Miss Wright he performed *The Swedish Gardeners* ("after the Manner of the Fausans") and *The Medley of Jokes* at the Haymarket on 23 March 1743 and returned to Drury Lane to offer the *Scots Dance* and *Tambourine* on 26 May 1743, when Miss Wright shared a benefit with Morgan and Walker.

In the summer of 1745 an English pantomime director named Mathews (whom we believe to have been Master Mathews, grown up) brought a troupe to play at the Opéra Comique in Paris, under the auspices of Favart, that theatre's producer. The English company performed during the Saint Laurent Fair, giving *Le Désespoir favorable* on 16 July 1745, *L'Oeil du Maître* on 24 July, *L'Expédition militaire* on 7 August, and *Les Vendanges de Tempé* on 28 August. The manager of that company was no doubt the Mr Mathews who danced the next season at Covent Garden Theatre, appearing in a peasant dance on 22 March 1746, when the bills announced he was making his first appearance on that stage in four years. On 7 April 1746 he was one of the Aerial Spirits in *The Royal Chace*, with Miss Vandersluys. In 1746–47 Mathews was on the Covent Garden paylist for 30s. per week.

The bills in the spring of 1747 present some confusion, for sometimes, as on 23 April 1747, they indicate that a Master Mathews performed a comic dance with Miss Vandersluys, and at other times, as on 4 May 1747, that Mr Mathews performed a peasant dance with her. There seems to be no doubt, however, that

an adult Mathews was dancing regularly at Drury Lane Theatre in 1747–48, and that he remained there at least through 1766–67, appearing in numerous ballets, masquerades, and specialty dances. His salary in 1766–67 was 5s. per night, or £1 10s. per week. He had also appeared at Sadler's Wells in April 1746, at the New Wells, Clerkenwell, on 20 October 1746, at the Haymarket Theatre on 5 September 1748, and at the James Street Theatre on 26 December 1748 (on the same night that he danced *The Sailors Revels* at Drury Lane). In April 1748 he lived at the Golden Ball in Duke's Court, Drury Lane, in April 1751 in Fountain Court in Aldermanbury, and in April 1752 in Longacre Street, near St Martin's Lane. The *Daily Advertiser* of 6 February 1752 reported that he was recovering from an accident.

In March and April 1750 Mathews, along with Dancer and Yeates, managed theatrical performances at the New Wells, London Spa, Clerkenwell, in the afternoons (while Mathews continued to dance evenings at Drury Lane). On 16 April 1750 at the New Wells they gave *The Sacrifice of Iphigenia* and *Harlequin Mountebank*.

By 1757 Mathews had also turned to rope- and wire-dancing and tumbling, exhibiting such feats along with his dancing at Sadler's Wells in 1760, 1762, 1768, and 1769. On 3 July 1762 Joseph Reed noted in his *Diary* seeing Mathews perform at Sadler's Wells before the Cherokee Kings. In the summer of 1763 Mathews and Hardy took a troupe to play at Bristol and Bath. At the Coopers' Hall, Bristol, in May and June Mathews (described as from Covent Garden Theatre) performed equilibres on the wire. One night in early June the seats collapsed and Mathews apologized in the press for the accident, assuring the public "he has taken proper Methods to prevent any thing of the Kind happening for the future." The advertisements for his appearance at the Orchard Street Theatre in Bath on Tuesday, 21 June 1763, described his act:

He puts the Wire in full Swing, and turns himself round; sits on a Chair on the Wire in full Swing, and carries a balance on his Nose at the same Time. He walks upon a Deal Board on the Wire, turns himself round on the Wire as swift as the fly of a Jack, and carries a Balance while in full Swing. He stands upon his Head in full Swing, and quits his hold at the same time; and performs a Variety of other curious Equilibres, all without a Pole. He will balance a half-pound weight on The top of a Straw, and stand on his Head on the Foot of a Drinking Glass. . . .

From 1769 to 1771 Mathews was a regular performer at Sadler's Wells. Also dancing with him at the Wells in 1770–71 was a Master Mathews, no doubt a son, as may have been the Master Mathews who danced at Drury Lane in June 1759.

The Mrs "Matthews" who performed at Drury Lane for 16 years between 1749 and 1765 was perhaps Mr Mathews's wife. In addition to the two dancing sons, the actress Elizabeth Mathews, who later became Mrs Josiah Millidge, was probably their child.

Mathews, Mrs ₁*fl. 1749–1753*₁, *actress, singer.*

A Mrs Mathews appeared with a company at Richmond and Twickenham regularly each summer between 1749 and 1753. Among her roles were Penelope in *Tunbridge Walks* in 1749; Hortensia in *Philaster*, Rodriguez in *Don Quixote*, and Mrs Tattoo in *Lethe* in 1750; Gipsy in *The Beaux' Stratagem*, Isabella in *The Conscious Lovers*, Scentwell in *The Busy Body*, Teraminta in *The Wife's Relief*, Lucy in *The Beggar's Opera*, Foible in *The Way of the World*, Jenny in *Two Nights from Land's End*, Lady Humpkin Bus in *The Diversions of a Morning*, a Laughing Lady in *The Inconstant*, Myrtilla in *The Provok'd Husband*, and Charlotte in *The Mock Doctor* in 1751; Mrs Motherly in *The Provok'd Husband*, Mavis in *The Silent Woman*, and Mrs Topknot in *The Gamester* in 1752; and Madge in *The King and the Miller of Mansfield* and a vocal part in *Macbeth* in 1753.

Mathews, Master ₁*fl. 1747–1749*₁, *dancer.*

On 23 April 1747 a Master Mathews performed a comic dance with Miss Vandersluys at Covent Garden Theatre. In August 1749 Master Mathews danced with Mrs Annesley in *The Medley of Jokes* and *French Peasants* at Cross and Bridges's booth during Bartholomew Fair. He was probably related to the dancer and tumbler Mr Mathews (fl. 1739?–1771).

Mathews, Master ₁*fl. 1759*₁, *dancer.*

A Master Mathews, a child five years of age, danced a hornpipe at Drury Lane on 28 June 1759. Also performing that evening, as Tag in a performance by children of *The Lying Valet*, was Elizabeth Mathews, no doubt his sister, who became Mrs Millidge. Probably Master and Miss Mathews were the children of the Drury Lane dancer Mr Mathews (fl. 1739?–1771).

Mathews, Master ₁*fl. 1770–1771*₁, *dancer.*

A Master Mathews danced at Sadler's Wells in the summers of 1770 and 1771. Sometime in September 1770, according to undated advertisements, he danced a minuet with Miss Hitchcock and appeared in *Cupid's Frolick*. On 24 September 1771 he performed with Mr Mathews (probably his father), the Hamoirs, and Miss Wilkinson.

Mathews, Master ₁*fl. 1784*₁, *singer.*

A Master Mathews was one of the boy sopranos who sang in the Handel Memorial Concerts at Westminster Abbey and the Pantheon in May and June 1784. Perhaps he was the son of William Mathews, of Oxford and London, who also sang in those performances.

Mathews, Elizabeth. *See* MILLIDGE, MRS JOSIAH.

Mathews, James ₁*fl. 1783–1800*₁, *singer, actor, music seller and publisher.*

James Mathews, who was described by the *Bonner & Middleton's Bristol Journal* in January 1783 as "a respectable butcher of Bath," made his debut as a singer on the Bath stage on 22 January 1783. After appearing at Bath and Bristol concerts in 1783–84 and 1784–85, he ventured to London, where he obtained a principal role in a piece called *Burletta*, which was performed at the Royal Circus, St George's Fields, in 1785. Mathews continued to perform at the Royal Circus in 1786. On 9 June 1786 he made his first appearance at the Haymarket Theatre as Giles in *The Maid of the Mill*. (The *Town and Country Magazine* of July alluded to his former occupation as a butcher.) Mathews's other roles at the Haymarket in the summer of 1786 included Steady in *The Quaker* on 17 June and Hawthorn in *Love in a Village* on 19 June.

Mathews returned to the Haymarket for the next three summers, adding to his repertoire Muzzy in *Harvest Home*, Jupiter in *The Golden Pippin*, a Bacchanal in *Comus*, and Jupiter in *Midas* in 1787; Father Frank in *The Prisoner at Large*, a character in *The Gnome*, the President in *The Catch Club*, and the female role of Venus in *Chrononhotonthologos* in 1788 (he also sang "The High-minded Soldier" on 28 August and several other songs on 2 September); a principal character in *Ut Pictura Poesis!*, a Lawyer in *The Miser*, Lockit in *The Beggar's Opera*, and a Robber in *The Battle of Hexham* in 1789.

When the younger Colman assumed the Haymarket management after the summer of 1789, he discharged a number of performers, according to the *Oracle* of 15 October 1789, and Mathews was among them.

Perhaps he was the Mathews who had sung in the oratorio *Judas Maccabaeus* in the Great Room, Prince's Street, Bristol on 17 September 1787, but that performer may have been William Mathews of Oxford. In 1790 our subject was in the company at the Royalty Theatre, Goodman's Fields; on 5 April of that year he sang with others in *Arthur*. Also in 1790 was published Thomas Costellow's song *You lov'd and I was blest* as sung by Mr Mathews at the Royalty in *A Pill for the Doctor; or, The Triple Wedding*. Doane's *Musical Directory* of 1794 listed Mathews as a tenor in the Bath Theatre and in the Handelian concerts at Westminster Abbey.

While carrying on his modest stage career, Mathews also established a music and book shop in the High Street, Bath. James Mathews, "Stationer and Bookseller, Bath, and of T. R. London," was listed as a subscriber to George Parker's *Life's Painter of Variegated Characters*, published 1789. About 1794 Mathews moved his shop to Milson Street, and then about 1795 to No 3, George Street, where he remained until 1800. Among the pieces he published were some of his own compositions, including *Howe and the Glorious First of June. A new Song, written by Earl Mulgrave. The Air composed . . . by J. Mathews* [1794]; *Nelson & the Tars of Old England, a New Song* [1798]; *Marriage has its Pleasures various* [1795?]; *The Western Volunteer. A New Song, adapted for the Piano Forte, Guitar, German Flute, One, or Two*

Voices [1800?] and *The Pleasures of Spring. A Favorite Duett Original* (1800).

Mathews, William [*fl.* 1767–1794], *singer, music seller.*

William Mathews was a music seller in Cat Street, Oxford, in 1767; about 1775 he moved to the High Street, opposite All Saints Church. At the Theatre Royal, York, in March 1770 he and Tenducci were featured in the oratorios. One of the most prominent bass singers in the Oxford Music Room during the last quarter of the century, Mathews also performed in the Handel Memorial Concerts at Westminster Abbey and the Pantheon in May and June 1784. The Master Mathews who was a boy soprano in those concerts was probably his son. Advertised as from Oxford, the elder Mathews sang in the oratorios performed in the Great Room, Prince's Street, Bristol, in April 1788, among which were *Alexander's Feast* on the sixteenth and the *Messiah* on the eighteenth. In 1794 Mathews was listed in Doane's *Musical Directory* as a principal bass in the Westminster Abbey Concerts. He was one of the Esquires Bedel of Oxford University and probably sang in some college choirs.

"Matt Medley." *See* ASTON, ANTHONY.

Matteaux. *See* MOTTEAUX.

Mattei, Colomba [Signora Trombetta], [*fl.* 1754–1763], *singer, manager.*

Colomba Mattei was first noticed in London on 9 November 1754, singing Elpinice in *L'Ipermestra* in the first of 15 performances of that opera at the King's Theatre that season. She probably sang in several or all of the following pieces in the season's repertoire, *Penelope*, *Siroe*, *Ricimero*, and *Ezio*. All were several times repeated, but no casts were given. On 17 March 1755 she sang "Sorge nell'alma mia" at a concert of music "For the Benefit and Increase of a Fund to Support Decay'd Musicians, or their Families," at the King's Theatre.

For the next seven seasons (with the exception of 1756–57) Colomba Mattei's name appears on bills at the King's, and, as in her first season, because of a paucity of information she was probably more active than the surviving evidence suggests. In order, her roles were:

Lucius in *Tito Manlio* in 1755–56; Narsea in *Solimano*, and the title role in *Zenobia* in 1757–58; Semiramide in *Attalo* and Mandane in *Il Ciro riconosciuto* in 1758–59; Berenice in *Vologeso*, Tusnelda in *Arminio*, the title role in *Antigona*, Vitellia in *La clemenza di Tito*, and Astrea in the cantata *La Gran Brettagna emula della antica Roma* in 1759–60; Servilla in *Tito Manlio* and Arianna in *Arianna e Teseo* in 1760–61; and Cleofida in *Alessandro nell' Indie* in 1761–62. She was also heard in special concerts, as on 16 March 1756, when she sang in *Alexander's Feast* in the Great Room in Dean Street, Soho.

If Charles Burney was correct, she was also managing during most of that period: "After the resignation of [Felice] Giardini and [Regina] Mingotti, . . . the state remained without a chief, till Mattei and her husband Trombetta made interest for the chance of speedy ruin, and obtained the management." He also specified that it was Mattei who engaged Gioacchino Cocchi as "composer to the opera."

The opera bill for the performance of *Zanaida* on 31 May 1763 noted:

As Signora Mattei will leave England soon after the Operas are over; and as Mr. Crawford will have no further concern with the Management of Operas, all the Cloaths used in the Burlettas and Dances, with many other articles, being his own Property and that of Signora Mattei's, will be sold. The particulars of which may be had of Mr. Crawford at the finishing of the season.

(Those statements would seem to negate assertions by Wilkinson and Michael Kelly, made long after the event—and the first evidently derived from the second—that Francesco Vaneschi was the manager.) *The London Stage* is in error in assigning her a part in a performance at the King's Theatre on 3 December 1765. The cast is taken from the 1765 edition of *La clemenza di Tito*, which lists her for Vitellia, a part she had sung in 1760.

Burney called Mattei "a charming singer and a spirited and intelligent actress." Oliver Goldsmith in his essay in *The Bee*, "The Opera in England," agreed: "Signora Mattei is at once both a perfect actress and a very fine singer: she is possessed of a fine sensibility in her manner, and seldom indulges . . . [in] extravagant and unmusical flights of voice. . . ."

Mattei, Filippo. *See* AMADEI, FILIPPO.

Matteis, Nicola [*fl.* 1671–1714], *violinist, guitarist, composer.*

Nicola Matteis called himself a "Napolitano" in some of his publications, but of his birth and early life nothing is known. Roger North is the source of much of the information we have on Matteis, and North said that before coming to England Matteis traveled across Germany on foot with his violin on his back. Upon his arrival in London he made friends with a merchant who helped support him, but the violinist was what North called "inexpungably proud, and hardly prevailed with to play to anybody." Wilson, the editor of North, guesses that Matteis was in England no later than 1671; Michael Tilmouth in his admirable article in *Musical Quarterly* in 1960 is mute on that point.

Matteis soon learned that his annoyance at people who insisted on whispering while he was playing lost him patronage. He performed before members of the nobility, including the Duke of Richmond, but failed to win a patron and was not granted a position in the King's Musick. "At length," North said,

great persons, and hopes of presents, had some influence upon him. Sr Wm Waldegrave and Sr Roger Lestrange, (pair of vertuosos and our cheif conoiseurs, at that time) found him out and perceiving his value courted him very much, and [did it] by discoursing how much it would be for his interest to complye with the genius of the English nation, who declined those that stood upon high termes, and were most obligding to such as were complaisant and familiar. This good councell and starving brought the man over, and he became the most debonaire and easy person living; he came to litle meetings and did just what they would have him. He soon found his account by scollars, of which sort he had plenty, and began to feel himself grow rich, and then of course luxurious.

Even if some Englishmen were offended by the violinist's manner at first, they did not question his ability. On 19 November 1674 John Evelyn reported:

I heard that stupendious Violin Signor *Nicholao* (with other rare Musitians) whom certainly never mortal man Exceeded on that Instrument: he had a strock so sweete, & made it speake like the Voice of a

Man; & when he pleased, like a Consort of severall Instruments: he did wonders upon a Note: was an excellent Composer also: here was also that rare *Lutinist* Dr Wallgrave: but nothing approch'd the *Violin* in *Nicholao's* hand: he seem'd to be *spiritato'd* & plaied such ravishing things on a ground as astonish'd us all.

Evelyn heard him again at Mr Slingsby's on 2 December, when the playing of Matteis "struck all mute. . . ." Evelyn was so carried away that he went again to concerts at Slingsby's in which Matteis participated in January 1675 and November 1679.

North was equally impressed. "I have knowne him hold a room full of Gentlemen and ladyes by the Ears for hours, and Not a whisper scarce to be perceived among them, which I never observed of any Musicall Enterteinment before or since." North attributed much of the change in English musical taste from the French to the Italian style to Matteis. North compared him to Corelli and commended his compositions as "full of the most artfull harmony, and his fire exquisite."

In addition to reshaping musical taste, Matteis was largely responsible for introducing to English violinists a new and better way of handling their instruments. Said North:

His manner of using his violin was much out of the comon road of handling, but out of it he made the utmost of sound, double, single, swift, and all manners of touch, which made such impressions that his audience was not onely pleased but full of wonder at him, and his way of performing. He was a very tall and large bodyed man, used a very long bow, rested his instrument against his short ribbs. . . . In short the caracter of that man, to those who never saw or heard him, is incredible; but out of that awkwardness he taught the English to hold the bow by the wood onely and not to touch the hair, which was no small reformation. . . . His devision was wonderfull swift; but whether upon a comon or triple ground, the plain song was distinctly perceivable under it, and (so far from loosing his time and emphases that) one might imagine an harmony in each note. And when the raptures came, which his attendant bases were aware of, and conformed to, one would have thought the man beside himself. And then came his superior powers, an *arcata* as from the clouds, and after that a querolous expostulary style, as just not speaking, all which and other signall excellencys might then be perceived but now may not be described, so vio-

lent was his conference of extreams, whereof the like I never heard before or since. And that which was most remarkable of him was that he bore up to the quickest touches of his part with all his bases that were very loud, and if he touched *forte* and *piano* the latter was always heard as distinct as the other.

North said also that Matteis "had an absolute power of his trill, and used it always in time; and so slow, as permitted the ingredients in his shakes to be distinctly heard sounding. . . ."

Though he was best known as a violinist, Matteis was expert on the guitar as well and performed so powerfully "as to be able to contend with the harpsichord in concert." One of his many publications, *The False Consonances of Musick* (1680), contained "Instructions for the playing a true Base upon the Guitarre, with Choice Examples and Cleare Directions to enable any man in a short time to play all Musicall Ayres."

Much of his performing was of a private nature, but toward the end of the century he evidently performed in public. The London *Gazette* of 26–30 May 1698 noted that "This present Monday being the 30th of May, Mr Nichola's Consort of Vocal and Instrumental Musick will be performed in York Buildings." Matteis also served as one of the stewards at a St Cecilia Day celebration in Oxford in 1696.

Most of the musician's energies were devoted to teaching, composition, and publication. The first, in 1676, was typical of many of his publications; the *Gazette* on 11 December announced that "The famous and long expected Musicks of Two Parts, by Nicola Matteis are now published; consisting of Ayres of all sorts, fitted for all hands, and capacities, and 190 Copper-plates. . . ." Matteis in many of his publications was careful to help students locate within a book of his pieces those selections best suited to their abilities. He was also careful to present copies of his books to persons of quality in order to "obtain plenty of Ginnys." He went to France late in 1678 and attempted a similar but unsuccessful publishing venture. He returned soon to England and continued turning out books of his compositions. The musician John Jenkins much admired the works of Matteis; of one of the violinist's airs Jenkins said "he had never heard so good a peice of musick, in all his life."

Matteis brought out most of his works in Italian and English versions, and the translation of some sections of *False Consonances* may have been his own. Here is his delightful advice to young musicians:

Good advice to play well.

You must not play allwayes alike, but sometimes Lowd and sometimes softly, according to your fancy, and if you meet with any Melancholy notes, you must touch them sweet and delicately.

Secondly it is very necessary to make a Clever shake sweet and quick which is the Chief method for those that play of these sort of instruments.

Thirdly that you don't play your tune to fast, because your quick playing is apt to Confuse you, so that you ought too play clearly and easily.

To set your tune off the better, you must make severall sorts of Graces of your one Genius, it being very troublesome for the Conposer to mark them.

Advice about Composing in few Words.

When you will Compose any Tune as an Almand Saraband & *cet*: upon ye Harpsecord, Theorb, Lute, Kittar, or any other Instruments, you must besure to intermix a Base now and then because your naked playing has little Harmony, and [is] not Gratfull at all.

Secondly it is very necessary to give a discord now and then which is as much as to say a false Strock ending pleasantly which will set your Composition Extremely of.

Thirdly that your Tune be not to long and tedious, nor yet to Short but of a Medium.

And so on.

By the end of the seventeenth century Matteis had a namesake who was gaining a reputation as a fine violinist. Nicholas Matteis (d. c. 1749) was probably born soon after the elder Matteis arrived in England. North said that the lad was taught violin "from his cradle." Of the elder Matteis's (first?) wife we know little, but the following entries in the registers of St Martin-in-the-Fields, if they do in fact pertain to Matteis the violinist, give us her Christian name: the daughter of Nicola and Frances, Bridget Matteis, was born on 10 January 1691, baptized six days later, died in the summer of 1693, and was buried at St Martin's on 31 July. The registers of St Paul, Covent Garden, first showed "Nichola" and Frances (sometimes "Francis") Matteis in 1694. Their child John-Nichola was christened on 27 December 1694, Elizabeth on 27 February 1696, Sarah on 4 June 1697 (but she died and was buried four

days later), and Katharin on 8 September 1699. Frances, the wife of "Nichola" Matteis, was buried on 22 September, possibly from complications following the birth of her daughter Katharin.

Upon becoming a man of means Matteis, according to North, "took a large hous and had a thing called a wife, and pretended to entertein, which by the Nicety of his Wine shewed he was no detter to his Genius." Tilmouth quotes the London *Post* of 29 January 1700 on a (second) marriage Matteis contracted which may have been to the "thing called a wife" North referred to: "Signior Nicolao, the famous Italian Musician, is married to one Madam Timperley, a Widow of 300 pounds Joynture, with one Child of about 12 Years of Age, who has 1600 pounds *per annum*, the management of which, she has till he comes of Age." Tilmouth discovered that Susanna Timperley was the daughter of Sir John Sparrow; she had married Henry Timperley, who died in France in 1690. She came back to England in 1694 and settled in Hintlesham, the family manor in Suffolk. She was joined there by her son Henry in 1699. Susanna lost the management of Henry's income when she was superseded as his guardian, so Matteis did not get to enjoy her wealth. Young Henry Timperley squandered his estate by 1721 in any case. In 1714 he sold his manor of Colkirk in Norfolk to Nicholas Matteis, and Tilmouth believes that perhaps Colkirk was the "large hous" North mentioned as having been acquired by Matteis.

But in his *Letters from the Dead to the Living* in 1702 Tom Brown wrote of Matteis as dead, and it could be that some of the references to Matteis after 1700 concern his son. North did not date the death of "Nichola" Matteis, but he said that "Excess of pleasure threw him into a dropsie, and he became very poor; he made his condition knowne to his friends, but would take no bounty, but upon his obligation, such was his pride, to repay it. He came at last to loos both his Invention, and hand and in a miserable state of body purs and mind, dyed."

Though the younger Nicholas Matteis had a distinguished career as a violinist and composer, he seems not to have performed publicly in London. He was invited to the Hapsburg court in Vienna, where he was from 1700 to

1737. When he returned to England he settled in Shrewsbury as a teacher of languages and violin. He died there about 1749.

A portrait of Nicola Matteis by Kneller, owned by William Barrow of Llandudno in the 1960s, was offered for sale by Miss D. Weir, Barrow's heir, at Sotheby's on 16 May 1973 but did not attract the reserve price of £200, although £190 was offered. It was offered again at Sotheby's on 25 September 1974 (lot 135) without a reserve price and was purchased by a bidder unknown to us. The painting was reproduced in *Musical Quarterly* in 1960, when it was still owned by Barrow.

Matteis, Nicola   *d. c. 1749, violinist, composer.*

The younger Nicola Matteis (or Nicholas Matheis) was probably born in the 1670s, since, as the *New Grove* points out, a "Balleto for Young Nicola," in manuscript, dates about 1682. The younger Matteis studied violin under his father, but Roger North found his playing effeminate compared with his father's. The *New Grove* has it that the younger Matteis performed successfully in London near the end of the seventeenth century; we have found no concrete evidence of such performance. He was invited to the Hapsburg court in Vienna, where he lived from 1700 to 1737, working as a director of instrumental music and as a violinist until his retirement in 1730. He returned to England and settled in Shrewsbury, where he died about 1749.

Matthews. *See also* MATHEWS.

Matthews, Mr   [*fl. 1735–1746*], *actor, singer.*

A Mr Matthews acted Scale in *The Recruiting Officer* at the Haymarket Theatre on 13 December 1735. Eight years later a Mr Matthews, perhaps the same person, played Morelove in *The Careless Husband* at the James Street Theatre on 10 December 1744. Probably he was the Matthews who acted Sharp in *The Lying Valet* and sang a "Welsh Song" and 'Monmouth's Glory" for his own benefit, "By Desire of the United Body of Gentlemen Salesmen," at the old Southwark Theatre on 6 November 1746.

Matthews, Mr   [*fl. 1759?–1766*], *actor.*

A Mr Matthews was a member of Spranger Barry's company from Ireland which acted at the King's Theatre in August and September 1766. His known roles were the First Ruffian in *King Lear* and Ernesto in *The Orphan*. Perhaps he was the Mr Matthews who had performed at the Smock Alley Theatre, Dublin, in 1759–60.

Matthews, Mr   [*fl. 1794–1804*], *scene painter, machinist.*

A Mr Matthews was listed in the bills as a scene painter with Spitzer and Seward for *Harlequin in His Element* at Astley's Amphitheatre, Westminster Bridge, on 8 September 1794. There he also designed the machines for *Harlequin Invincible* on 22 August 1795 and *The Magician of the Rocks* on 16 May 1796. In 1804 Matthews was painting scenery with Coyle at Manchester; one of their productions was *Harlequin's Progress to the Temple of Mars* in January.

Matthews, Mrs   [*fl. 1749–1765*], *singer, dancer, actress.*

A Mrs Matthews appeared as a Shepherdess in *The Triumph of Peace* at Drury Lane Theatre on 23 February 1749. Over the next 16 years Mrs Matthews (sometimes Mathews) sang, danced, and evidently acted at that theatre. She had a vocal part in *Romeo and Juliet* in 1750–51 and danced in *The Genii* in 1752–53 and *The Chinese Festival* in 1755–56.

Mrs Matthews appeared as Venus in *Chrononhotonthologos* on 29 April 1756 and as Wheedle in *The Miser* on 29 July 1760, the latter performance being a benefit for "a Gentleman who has written for the Stage." In 1760–61 she again sang in *Romeo and Juliet* and danced in many performances of *The Genii*.

According to a Drury Lane paylist, supposedly in Garrick's hand, which H. H. Furness printed in *Notes and Queries* on 13 June 1885, a Mrs Matthews was being paid 2s. 6d. per day, or 15s. per week, as an actress in 1764–65. We have not found her name in the bills that season, so she must have been performing very minor roles.

Perhaps this performer was the wife of the dancer Mr "Mathews" (fl. 1739?–1771), who was at Drury Lane during the same period.

Matthews, Catherine Mary *1772–1787, dancer.*

Catherine Mary Matthews made her first appearance at Covent Garden Theatre dancing a hornpipe on 1 May 1772. Probably she was a young girl at that time. Announced as making her second appearance on that stage, Miss Matthews (sometimes Mathews) danced with Master Harris at Covent Garden on 22 May. In the next season there she danced with Master Blurton in *The Cumberland Corn Thrashers* on 24 April 1773, in a new comic dance with master Harris on 26 April, and in *Minuets* and *Cotillons* on 26 May. At the end of the following season she appeared again to perform a triple hornpipe with Miller and Eves on 15 April 1774, a new dance called *The Pilgrim* on 16 April, and in various dances on 18 and 20 May. She appeared in similar dances in 1774–75. In the summer of 1775 she danced at Richmond and Sadler's Wells.

On 13 October 1775 she appeared as Colombine in a revival of the pantomime *Orpheus and Eurydice* and then played that part many times during that season. On 23 January 1776 she replaced Sga Vidini in *Prometheus*.

Miss Matthews continued to dance in ballets and pantomimes at Covent Garden through 1784–85. She was also at Richmond again in the summer of 1776 and at Sadler's Wells in the summers of 1783 and 1784. In addition to many appearances at Covent Garden in specialty numbers, she danced such roles as Colombine in *The Royal Chace* and *The Choice of Harlequin*, Pierrot's Wife in *The Norwood Gypsies*, and a principal character in *The Medley*.

After the 1784–85 season Miss Matthews evidently retired from the stage. In his will, dated 2 April 1787 and proved 31 August 1787, the Covent Garden housekeeper Charles Sarjant, the younger, left in trust £3333 6s. 8d. in three per cent bank annuities for the benefit of "Catherine Mary Matthews Spinster who now resides in my House in King Street Covent Garden . . . during the term of her natural life." Miss Matthews also was bequeathed £100 immediately and all of Sarjant's furniture, linen, china, and other household effects. Sarjant specified, however, that should Miss Matthews's mother, Harman Matthews, be still alive at the time of his death, she was to have for life the proceeds of £1000. Since Sarjant named no wife or children in his will,

it is possible that Harman Matthews was his common-law wife and that Catherine Mary Matthews, upon whom he was settling the bulk of his estate, was his child.

Matthews, Mary Ann. *See* WRIGHTEN, MRS JAMES.

Mattock. *See* MATTOCKS.

Mattocks. *See also* MADDOCKS and MADDOX.

Mattocks, Miss [*fl. 1746–1748*], actress.

Miss Mattocks was first recorded at the New Theatre on the Bowling Green in the time of Southwark Fair, 6 October 1746, playing Lappet in *The Miser*. On 16 October she was Dorinda in *The Stratagem*.

When she moved to Goodman's Fields Theatre on 27 October as Kitty in *The Lying Valet* the bill printer spelled her name "Maddocks." Next evening he changed her to "Maddox" when she played Rose in *The Recruiting Officer*. On 31 October she was seen as Cherry in *The Stratagem* and on 6 November as Miss Prue in *Love for Love*. She was "Maddocks" again and Lucy in *The London Merchant* on 13 November.

In January and May of 1748 Miss Mattocks played Biddy at least five times in *Miss in Her Teens*. After that she dropped from the record.

Mattocks, George *1735–1804, singer, dancer, actor, manager.*

George Mattocks sang, as "Master Maddox," when he was 12 years old, at Hussey and Phillips's booth on the Bowling Green during the time of Southwark Fair, in September 1747. In August 1748 he was at Bartholomew Fair, singing and dancing between the acts of the drolls at "Hussey's Great Theatrical Booth facing the Hospital Gate."

Still called "Master Maddox," he was a Shepherd in *The Triumphs of Peace* at Drury Lane Theatre on 23 and 24 February 1749. But when he returned to Drury Lane to present a song in the first act of *The London Merchant* in September of that year, the spelling of his name in the bills had been corrected to "Mattocks." His service at Drury Lane in 1749–50 was almost invariably tuneful. In the next sea-

Harvard Theatre Collection

GEORGE MATTOCKS

engraving by Laurie, after Dighton

son, 1750–51, he was utilized infrequently; perhaps at that time—between his fifteenth and sixteenth year—his voice was changing.

Mattocks had sung in chorus and had contributed entr'acte songs, but his named roles had been few and small: the Second Spirit in *Comus*, Palaemon in *The Chaplet*, Mercury in *Lethe*, Janus in *The Secular Masque*, some principal part unspecified in *Robin Hood*, and (his only nonmusical dramatic part that year) Donalbain in *Macbeth*. But Mattocks would never be a clever actor. He was willing enough, but diligence could not substitute for talent. The comment of the prompter Cross in his diary, when Mattocks attempted in the middle of his third season his first big straight role in London, Golding in *Eastward Hoe*, on 29 December 1751, is instructive: "Mr Ross being ill Mr Mattocks did his part at a Day's Notice, wch at the end of the 4 Act Mr Woodward told the Audience, & tho Mr Mattocks was hiss'd before, when he next appear'd they gave him great Applause. Mattocks never play'd a principal part before in London."

The qualifier "in London" was necessary because of Mattocks's summer service in 1750 and 1751 with the Richmond-Twickenham company, where a few surviving bills show him playing not only the minor roles of Contabali in *Diversions of the Morning*, Poins and Sir Richard Vernon in *1 Henry IV*, Quaver in *The Virgin Unmask'd*, Slur in *The Wife's Relief*, Leander in *The Mock Doctor*, Charles in *The Busy Body*, Simon Pure in *A Bold Stroke for a Wife*, Benvolio in *Romeo and Juliet*, Fantom in *The Drummer*, and Damon in *Damon and Phillida* but also Aimwell in *The Beaux' Stratagem*, Mirabel in *The Way of the World*, and Macheath in *The Beggar's Opera*. He returned to Richmond in the summer of 1752. He seems to have suffered only a one-season eclipse because of the voice-change, for in 1751–52 he sang dozens of solos at Drury Lane. He also appeared from time to time in the 1748-to-1750 period in concerts at Cuper's Gardens.

Our understanding of the career of George Mattocks for the following few years is dim. In 1754 he was on the roster of the summer company at Jacob's Wells Theatre in Bristol, and then disappeared from the records until, on 1 November 1757, he returned to London to sing Macheath in *The Beggar's Opera* at Covent Garden. He was that night advertised as "Mattocks, who never appeared on that stage or any other these 6 years." On 1 February 1758 he sang in the sizeable chorus to the opera *The Prophetess*, which was repeated many times through April. He had one named part that season, Damon in *The Chaplet*, on 24 April.

Mattocks remained at Covent Garden during 25 successive winter seasons, at first singing principally in supporting choruses of masques, spectacles, musical farces, and tragedies—the "Solemn Dirge" which had become customary in *Romeo and Juliet*, or as one of the Recruits in *The Fair*—or providing entr'acte songs. Gradually he moved into the leads of ballad opera, pastoral opera, and comic opera. Sometimes he was thrust on in straight comic roles, but they were not his forte. He rarely had straight parts in tragedy.

Mattocks's named characters over the years (in addition to ones already listed) included, in the order he assumed them, the following: in 1758–59, Mercury in *The Judgement of Paris*; in 1759–60, Vincent in *The Jovial Crew* and

Jupiter in *The Rape of Proserpine*; in 1760–61, Friendly in *Flora*, Lovemore in *The Lottery*, the Second Spirit in *Comus*, Rovewell in *The Contrivances*, Lorenzo in *The Merchant of Venice*, and Harry Hunter in *Phebe*; in 1761–62, the original Sir James Elliot in Foote's comedy *The Lyar*, and Silence in *Apollo and Daphne*; in 1762–63, Wellbred in *Every Man in His Humour*, Amiens in *As You Like It*, and the original Young Meadows in Bickerstaff's immensely popular dramatic opera *Love in a Village*; in 1763–64, Rimenes in *Artaxerxes*, Perseus in *Perseus and Andromeda*, and Joe in *The Miller of Mansfield*; in 1764–65, Lord Planwell in *The Guardian Outwitted*, Lord Aimworth in *The Maid of the Mill*, and Worthy in *The Spanish Lady*; in 1765–66, Frederick in *The Summer's Tale*, Apollo in *Midas*, Lorenzo in *The Mistake*, and Chasseur Royal in *The Royal Chace*; and in 1767–68, the original Harrol in *The Royal Merchant*, Thomas Linley's operatic alteration from Beaumont and Fletcher, Lionel in *Lionel and Clarissa*, Clerimont in *The Old Maid*, and Frederick in *Amelia*.

Mattocks in 1768–69 was the original Tom in Joseph Reed's comic opera *Tom Jones*. He also added Orpheus in *Orpheus and Eurydice* that season. In subsequent years he continued to expand his repertoire as follows: in 1769–70, Agenor in *Amintas*; in 1770–71, Theano in *Medea*, Artabanes in *Artaxerxes*, Sir Amintor in *Daphne and Amintor*, and Ballad in *The Country Madcap*; in 1772–73, Paris in *The Golden Pippin* and a Witch in *Harlequin Sorcerer*; in 1775–76, Lively in *The Two Misers*, the original Ferdinand in Richard Brinsley Sheridan's successful comic opera *The Duenna*, and Captain Grenade in *The Sirens*; in 1776–77, the first Abdallah in Charles Dibdin and Edward Thompson's comic opera *The Seraglio*, Ferdinand in *The Tempest*, and Sir John Loverule in *The Devil to Pay*.

In 1777–78 Mattocks was Colonel Bully in *The Provok'd Wife*, the original Young Brumpton in Thomas Hull's comic opera *Love Finds the Way*, and the first Jupiter and Stud in Charles Dibdin's burletta *Poor Vulcan!*; in 1778–79, the original Mr Vermillion in Dibdin's comic opera *The Wives Revenged*, the original Sir John Manly in William Kenrick's comic opera *The Lady of the Manor*, and the first Lively in Dibdin's comic opera *The Chelsea Pensioner*; in 1779–80, Lieutenant Beauclerc in *Plymouth in an*

Harvard Theatre Collection

GEORGE MATTOCKS, as Apollo

artist unknown

Uproar, the original Apollo in *The Widow of Delphi*, Richard Cumberland's comic opera, and the first Beauclerc in Frederick Pilon's musical farce *The Siege of Gibraltar*; in 1780–81, the original Garcia in Dibdin's comic opera *The Islanders*; and in 1781–82, Jupiter in *Jupiter and Alcmena* and the first Fernando in John O'Keeffe's comic opera *The Banditti*, which failed.

On 2 November 1782 O'Keeffe brought out his wildly successful comic opera *The Castle of Andalusia*, an alteration of *The Banditti*. Mattocks took the leading role of Don Fernando. It was his last original part at Covent garden, and after the 1782–83 season he departed from its company, though his wife continued to act there. He was then earning £8 per week, his wife £10.

The comparatively few critical notices of Mattocks's talents which survive are in agreement that his singing was excellent and his acting lamentable. *The Rational Rosciad* (1767) went directly to the point:

> *Mattocks, for gentle trip and shuffle famed,*
> *Ought as an Actor scarcely to be named,*
> *But as a singer merits much applause,*
> *There truth with candour justifys his cause.*

That judgment agreed with Hugh Kelly's admiration, in his *Thespis* (1767), of Mattocks's "delicately clear" and "sweet-toned softness." The critic of the *Macaroni, Savoir Vivre, and Theatrical Magazine* (1773) wrote:

> As an actor, Mr. Mattocks has very little title to public favour,—as a singer, he claims very respectful notice: his voice is clear, soft, melodious and expressive. The next his figure, which is well proportioned; yet he wants that manly grace his sex demands, and animation to inspirit the several characters he performs; as for instance, in Sir George Airy, in the Busy Body, in which he is destitute of that manliness and politeness the character requires, or, to speak in Mr. Dryden's phrase, that self breeding which is necessary to adorn that character.—As a vocal performer, I look upon Mr. Mattocks to be the best on either Theatre in point of voice; and, did he possess more compass in this last-mentioned, he, probably, would be the best on any stage.

William Hawkins, in *Miscellanies in Prose and Verse* (1775) echoed the opinion. A dozen songs "as sung by" Mattocks are listed in the *Catalogue of Printed Music in the British Museum.*

Mattocks never acted in London in summers, except for a few performances at the Haymarket in 1778, and perhaps casual singing engagements in concerts. Around 1759 he had begun to look to the provinces again for some supplemental income. Gilliland asserts that "At the conclusion of the [1760] season, [John] Arthur sold the concern [at Plymouth] to Madame Capte Deville [Mlle Capdeville], an eminent dancer engaged in the company, for five hundred guineas, who appointed Mr. Mattocks to officiate for her [as manager]. In 1761 Mattocks bought half the property, which two years afterward he sold to Anthony Kerby

. . . who purchased the other half." He was also acting and singing at Bristol in July 1761. In the company was his current mistress, Harriet Pitt, by whom he either had already had, or was to have, two illegitimate children. Also present were his future wife, Isabella Hallam, then only 15, her guardian-aunt Ann Hallam Barrington, and one of her Hallam uncles. He married Isabella four years later, in 1765.

Mattocks and his wife were becoming summer favorites at Liverpool by 1767. On 24 July that year Thomas King wrote to David Garrick that they were in great repute in that city. The *London Chronicle* for 13–16 April 1771 reported that "Mr. Mattocks, of Covent Garden Theatre, has purchased the Playhouse at Portsmouth, which is now decorating for the ensuing season." But we have no information about his management there except Tate Wilkinson's report that Mattocks's deputy was Wright and that "it was during the American War." In 1773 and 1774 the burghers of Manchester began to petition Parliament for a patent for a new theatre erected there, according to Gilliland's account, and Mattocks and Joseph Younger, the veteran prompter at Covent Gar-

Harvard Theatre Collection

GEORGE MATTOCKS, as Achilles
engraving by Terry

den, assumed its management, opening in Whitsun week, 1774.

In 1775, according to James Winston's *The Theatric Tourist* (1805), Younger and Mattocks teamed with the Covent Garden actor Thomas Kniveton to take over the Liverpool Theatre. (Winston also asserts that Mattocks was at some period again in the management at Manchester, Sheffield, and Birmingham with Younger, one of the Robertsons, and Nathaniel Herbert.) Kniveton died in mid-August 1775 and evidently Younger dropped out, leaving Mattocks to direct affairs at Liverpool alone. A playbill for the Birmingham Theatre dated 18 September 1775 states that the Mattockses would play that evening for the only time that season. They were briefly at Birmingham again in the summer of 1776. Tate Wilkinson reported them at York for race-week in August 1776, and then at Leeds for "three or four nights," and then at Wakefield. Wilkinson also remembered Mattocks in management at Birmingham in the summer of 1779, in opposition to Miller, who had the New Theatre in the city, and named the members of Mattocks's company: Lewis, Wilkinson himself, the younger Bannister, Aickin, Davis, West, Doyle, Mrs Kennedy, Mrs Lewis, Mrs Charlton, and Mrs Melmoth—Mrs Mattocks was not mentioned.

Several accounts suggest that Mattocks's provincial theatrical speculations ruined him. But he evidently continued to find a livelihood in the provinces. The *Monthly Mirror*, both in 1799 and in 1801, described him as "treasurer" of the Liverpool company and in 1802 reported his benefit gross there as £164. Yet James Dibdin in *The Annals of the Edinburgh Stage*, placed Mattocks at the Edinburgh Theatre in 1801–2. He was certainly in Edinburgh in 1802–3, and in 1804–5 the bills asserted that he was the stage director there.

Mattocks died on 14 August 1804. The "Recorder's Book of the Calton Burying Ground" in the General Register Office for Scotland, in Edinburgh, contains the following entry, dated 18 August 1804: "George Mattox Treasurer to the Theatre Royal Ed^r from John Graham's No 5 Sheakspear Square died of a Decline of Nature Buryed 2 y^{ds} N of Mr Jackson's Ground. Aged 69."

Mattocks had made his will on 1 January

1768, nearly 37 years before his death, and had never altered it.

This is the last will of George Mattocks of the parish of Saint Paul Covent Garden in the county of Middlesex Comedian as follows I give and bequeath all my ready Money Jewels plate Household ffurniture Securities for Money and all other my personal Estate of whatsoever nature kind or quality after payment of my legal Debts to my dear Wife Isabella Mattocks late Isabella Hallam and one of the Performers at the Theatre Royal Covent Garden. . . .

Isabella was named executrix. The witnesses were one Michael Downs and the actors Ellis Ackman and Thomas Baker. Isabella proved the will on 2 October 1804.

Because of George Mattocks's liaison with Harriet Pitt, which had produced two children before the couple parted, the Hallam family had been decidedly opposed to Isabella's union with Mattocks. But she and George had defied them, eloping to France and marrying on or about Easter Sunday (7 April) 1765. The marriage endured for nearly 40 years, until Mattocks's death, but it was not free of dissension. The 1795 edition of *The Secret History of the Green Room* charged that Isabella had received the actor Robert Bensley as a lover and that Mattocks had separated from her until he discovered that doing so meant the loss of her salary. The account states, further, that Mattocks had retaliated in kind with the widow of the actor William Powell shortly after that lady had married her second husband, the musician John Abraham Fisher: "Mrs Mattocks, who was on the most friendly terms with her rival, remonstrated calmly, and obtained her promise to desist; but a second discovery excited her greatest indignation, and she openly, and even triumphantly, exposed her dear spouse and the chaste wife of the Musician, in the Green-Room."

The Mattockses had one child, Isabella Anne, who was briefly on the stage before her marriage, on 8 January 1801, to "Nathaniel Huson of the Inner Temple, London, Esquire, a Bachelor." The Husons gave Mrs Mattocks (by that time George was dead) a granddaughter, also named Isabella Ann.

The two children of Harriet Pitt by George Mattocks retained their mother's name. Cecil

Pitt was in the band at Sadler's Wells in 1803 during the management of the younger Charles Dibdin, his half-brother. Mattocks's daughter Harriet Pitt was for a time a dancer. She is said by Pinks, in his *History of Clerkenwell*, to have died in the Clerkenwell Poor House. The mother of those children had attached herself to the elder Charles Dibdin and had produced for him two illegitimate sons, Charles Isaac Mungo Dibdin and Thomas John Dibdin. She went for some years under the Dibdin name but later acted as Mrs Davenett.

Portraits of George Mattocks include:

1. Engraved portrait by R. Laurie, after Dighton. Published by W. Richardson, 1799.

2. As Achilles in *Achilles*. Engraving by Thornthwaite, after Roberts. Published as a plate to *Bell's British Theatre*, 1777.

3. As Achilles. Engraving by Terry. Published as a plate to an edition of the play, 1779.

4. As Apollo in *Midas*. By unknown engraver. Published as a plate to *Vocal Magazine*, 1778.

5. As Don Ferdinand, with John Quick as Mendoza, in *The Duenna*. By unknown engraver. Published by C. Bowles, 1777.

6. As Ferdinand, with Ann Cargill as Miranda, in *The Tempest*. Engraving by C. Grignion, after Dighton. Published for T. Wright, 1777. Reproduced in volume 3 (p. 66) of this dictionary.

7. As Lord Aimworth, with Elizabeth Bannister as Patty, in *The Maid of the Mill*. Engraving by Collier, after Dodd. Published as a plate to Lowndes's *New England Theatre*, 1782.

8. As Macheath, with Ann Cargill as Polly, in *The Beggar's Opera*. Engraving by Walker, after Dighton. Published as a plate to Lowndes's *New England Theatre*, 1782.

Mattocks, Mrs George, Isabella, née Hallam 1746–1826, actress, singer, dancer, instrumentalist.

Isabella Hallam, born in 1746, was the youngest of four children of the elder Lewis Hallam (1714?–1756?), the actor and manager, and his wife, an actress whose first name is not known but who was connected in some way with the Rich family of Covent Garden Theatre. Isabella was allied through blood or marriage with performers of many kinds and several degrees of distinction. Her grandfather,

the minor actor Thomas Hallam, had died as a result of a notorious green-room scuffle with Charles Macklin a decade before Isabella was born. But she was surrounded from birth with her uncles and aunts who (with the exception of one who was a distinguished naval officer) all became performers and married performers. Her Aunt Ann and Ann's second husband the actor John Barrington, assumed the guardianship of the young Isabella when Isabella's father and mother left for America in 1752. She certainly saw performances by her uncles—Adam, George, and William—some of them at William's theatre, the New Wells, Lemon Street, and others at one or another of the fair booths her family sometimes ran.

She herself acted at a very early age, as she testified in a letter to "J. Hill Esq. [of] Henrietta St. Covent Garden" on 19 June 1800. The letter contains, however, some misstatements, whether inadvertent or deliberate is not certain. "I was born," she wrote, "in the year—46." But at another point: "I was only 4 years old" when the Hallam theatrical group left for America; and that was in 1752. She remembered that "at 4 years & a half only I perform'd for my Uncle's benefit at Cov: Garden the part of the 'Parish Girl,' in the 'What d'ye call it.' I was so little that a gentleman whimsically said 'he could hear me very well, but he cou'd not see me without a glass.'" The performance she alludes to was probably that of 2 October 1752, her first recorded appearance in that part—not, however, on the night of anyone's benefit. She had first been seen in the bills only 10 days before, in the traditional debut role for youngsters, the Duke of York in *Richard III*, when her aunt, Mrs Barrington had played Lady Anne. She was also allowed to walk on as the Page in *The Orphan* on 27 October 1752 and to play the Duke of York again on 18 May 1753. In the 1753–54 season she repeated that part twice and the Page once. In September 1754 she repeated each part once.

That was the pattern that Mrs Barrington chose for the careful seasoning of her niece for the next few years—one or two performances in each of the familiar parts and much coaching by and observation of her elders. (Isabella must have been a juvenile success, though. A surviving list of payments notes: "Paid Charlotte Lane for making a Callimanco Coat & Breeches loop'd and bound with silver for Miss Hallam [in *The Orphan*]," followed by itemized sums for "silk garters, . . . 2 coat, 9 breast silver'd buttons," and so on.) In 1754 also, she accompanied her elders to act at Bristol, and Tate Wilkinson remembered her and the Barringtons at Maidstone in Kent in June 1754, acting at a booth in the Star Yard. At Covent Garden in 1755–56 she was eight times in the playbills; however, she failed to add any new roles to her slender repertoire. In 1756–57 she was in a dozen performances, but added only the Page in *The Rover*. James Winston, in *The Theatric Tourist* (1805), remembered that: "In 1757 Wignall, an under actor at Covent-Garden, collected a sharing company for the summer season; among whom were the late Tate Wilkinson, Jefferson, Miss Hallam (now Mrs. Mattocks), [and] Miss Morrison. . . ." In 1757–58 she repeated her former parts and added the Page in *Love Makes a Man* and Robin in *The Merry Wives of Windsor*. Then she left the London boards for two years. Evidently she spent much of that time in Bristol, with her aunt, Mrs Barrington, for whose benefit at Jacob's Wells Theatre on 8 August 1760 there was, among other delights, "Singing & Playing on Guitar by Miss Hallam." The surviving bill of Jacob's Wells for 24 July 1762, for *The Funeral*, in which Barrington played Counsellor Puzzle and Mrs Barrington Lady Brumpton, carries Miss Hallam as "Lady Harriot . . . introducing airs from *Artaxerxes*."

At Covent Garden on 10 April 1761, at age 15, Isabella, under the conventional designation "A Young Gentlewoman," made her first "adult" appearance, playing Juliet to Ross's Romeo, with her Aunt Ann Barrington as Lady Capulet. It was her Aunt's benefit evening, and to add an extra fillip to the occasion Isabella danced a minuet with young Poitier. In her letter to Hill in 1800 Isabella proclaimed that "from that time to this (with the exception of one winter pass'd in Liverpool When Mr Mattocks was Manager there) I have invariably continued at Cov: Garden [in the winter season]." It was loosely true, although she does not seem to have acted at Covent Garden again after her Juliet debut until 12 April 1762 when she (so identified by Stone in *The London Stage*) disguised again as "A Young Lady" played Catharine in *Henry V*.

Her other roles, first as Miss Hallam, and then, after 7 April 1765, as Mrs Mattocks, were as follows, roughly in order of assumption: in 1761–62, Laura in *The Chaplet*, and Dorinda in *The Stratagem*; in 1762–63, Isabella in *The Wonder*, Parisatis in *The Rival Queens*, Catharine in *Henry V*, Serina in *The Orphan*, Selima in *Tamerlane*, Diana in *All's Well that Ends Well*, the original Lucinda in Isaac Bickerstaffe's new dramatic opera *Love in a Village*, Angelina in *Love Makes a Man*, Belinda in *The Provok'd Wife*, Rosara in *She Wou'd and She Wou'd Not*, Narcissa in *Love's Last Shift*, Angelica in *The Constant Couple*, the Lady in *Comus*, and Miss Hoyden in *The Relapse*; in 1763–64, Teresa in *The Squire of Alsatia*, Phillis in the masque to *Perseus and Andromeda*, Nysa in *Midas*, and Ann Lovely in *A Bold Stroke for a Wife*; in 1764–65, Cordelia in *King Lear*, Lady Harriet in *The Funeral*, Lady Julia in *The Guardian Outwitted*, Nancy in *What We Must All Come To*, Flora in *The Country Lasses*, Patty in *The Maid of the Mill*, and Sally in *Thomas and Sally* (her last new role as Miss Hallam); in 1765–66, Maria in *The Citizen*, Amelia in *The Summer's Tale*, Lucia in *Cato*, and Rachel in *The Jovial Crew*; and in 1767–68, Molly in *The English Merchant*, Jessica in *The Merchant of Venice*, Lucy in George Colman's new comedy *The Oxonian in Town*, Valeria in *The Roman Father*, Sophy in *The Musical Lady*, Gertrude in *The Royal Merchant*, Fanny in *The Clandestine Marriage*, Clerimont in *The Old Maid*, the original Jenny in Bickerstaffe's new comic opera *Lionel and Clarissa*, Harriet in *The Jealous Wife*, and Maria in *George Barnwell*.

In 1768–69, Isabella Mattocks added Dame Kitely in *Every Man in His Humour*, Aspasia in *Cyrus*, Ophelia in *Hamlet*, and the original Honour in Joseph Reed's new comic opera *Tom Jones*; in 1769–70, the original Lettice in Colman's comedy *Man and Wife*, Eliza in *Amintas*, Parisatis in *The Court of Alexander*, the title role in *The Spanish Lady*, and Aurelia in *The Twin Rivals*; in 1770–71, Arbaces in *Artaxerxes*, some "Principal Part" in *True Blue*, Polly in *The Beggar's Opera*, and Millwood in *George Barnwell*; in 1771–72, Miss Melville in *An Hour Before Marriage*, Roxana in *The Rival Queens*, the original Mrs Frankly in Mrs Elizabeth Griffith's comedy *A Wife in the Right*, Belzara in *Ximena*, Mrs Strickland in *The Suspicious Husband*, Olivia in *Twelfth Night*, Hermione in *The Winter's Tale*, and Mrs Sullen in *The Stratagem*; and in 1772–

73, the title role in *The Country Madcap*, Mariana in *The Miser*, Emily in *The Deuce is in Him*, the original Albina in William Mason's "dramatic poem" *Elfrida*, Venus in *The Golden Pippin*, Phaedra in *Amphitryon*, and Lady Brumpton in *The Funeral*.

In the summer of 1773, at Liverpool with her husband and Mrs Barrington, Mrs Mattocks expanded her tragedy repertoire by adding Statira in *The Rival Queens*, Monimia in *The Orphan*, Queen Mary in *The Albion Queens*, Octavia in *All for Love*, and four Shakespearean serious roles: Portia in *The Merchant of Venice*, Constance in *King John*, Juliet in *Romeo and Juliet*, and Lady Macbeth. She also played, apparently for the first time, the Second Constantia in *The Chances*, Mariana in *The Miser*, Estifania in *Rule a Wife and Have a Wife*, Angelica in *Love for Love*, Bisarre in *The Inconstant*, and Rosetta in *The Foundling*. She was eventually to bring all these characters to London.

Back at Covent Garden in the winter season of 1773–74, Mrs Mattocks went on adding parts to her list: Mordyma in *Don Sebastian*, Alicia in *Jane Shore*, and the Queen in *Richard III*. In 1774–75 she added Phillis in *The Conscious Lovers*, Charlotte in *The West Indian*, Arethusa in *Philaster*, Caelia in *As You Like It*, Athenais in *Theodosius*, Emilia in *Othello*, Lavinia in *The Fair Penitent*, Daraxa in *Edward and Eleonora*, Isabinda in *The Busy Body*, and Miss Prue in *Love for Love*; and in 1775–76, Lydia in *The Rivals*, Jenny in *The Two Misers*, Bettris in *The Man's the Master*, the original Louisa in R. B. Sheridan's comic opera *The Duenna*, Queen Eleanor in *Henry II*, Parthenope in *The Sirens*, and Lady Plyant in *The Double Dealer*.

Mrs Mattocks added to her repertoire in 1776–77 Lady Restless in *All in the Wrong*, Mrs Marwood in *The Way of the World*, Lady Froth in *The Double Dealer* and Miss Dormer in *A Word to the Wise*; in 1777–78, Lady Bell in *Know Your Own Mind*, and Eriphile in *Iphigenia*; in 1778–79, Lady Teazle in *The School for Scandal*; in 1779–80, the original Adelaide in Charles Dibdin's comic opera *The Shepherdess of the Alps*; in 1780–81, Miss Hardcastle in *She Stoops to Conquer*, Lady Easy in *The Careless Husband*, the original Mrs Sparwell in Hannah Cowley's short-lived comedy *The World as it Goes*, Mrs Brittle in the anonymous new farce *Barnaby Brittle*, and Catherine in *Catherine and*

Petruchio; in 1781–82, Phaedra in *Jupiter and Alcmena*, Victoria in *The Banditti*, Miss Hardy in *The Belle's Stratagem*, Arabella in *The Wife's Relief*, Mrs Ford in *The Merry Wives of Windsor*, the original Amelia in Leonard Macnally's farce *Retaliation*, and Clara in *Duplicity*; and in 1782–83, Colombine in *The Wishes*, Miss Pendragon in *Which is the Man?*, Mrs Richly in *The Discovery*, and the original Olivia in Hannah Cowley's comedy *A Bold Stroke for a Husband*. She played often but added no new roles in 1783–84.

What Isabella Mattocks remembered, in her 1800 letter to Hill, as a hiatus in her Covent Garden career of only one winter seems actually to have been two— the seasons of 1784–85 and 1785–86. Before the entry for 16 September 1784, the opening date of the Covent Garden season, Reed's "Notitia Dramatica" bears the notation "Mr. & Mrs. Mattocks dismissed." The couple went to Liverpool, where he was manager, and remained there through the summer of 1786. A Folger manuscript shows that they netted £109 19*s*. at their joint benefit in September.

When she regained her place on the Covent Garden roster in the fall of 1786 at £10 per week, Mrs Mattocks left her husband in Liverpool. She threw herself into her broadening comic line with renewed vigor, adding, in 1786–87, Violante in *The Wonder*, Lady Tremor in *Such Things Are*, Edging in *The Careless Husband*, Bridget in *The Chapter of Accidents*, and Miss Walsingham in *The School for Wives*; in 1787–88, Kitty Pry in *The Lying Valet*, Mademoiselle in *The Provok'd Wife*, Lettice in *The Intriguing Chambermaid*, Betty Blackberry in *The Farmer*, Flora in *The Midnight Hour*, Lady Carrol in *All on a Summer's Day*, Lady Grace in *The Provok'd Husband*, Miss Walsingham in *The School for Wives*, Miss Dolly Bull in *Fontainebleau*, Lissette in *Animal Magnetism*, Lady Bonton in *The Ton*, and Letty in *Tit for Tat*; in 1788–89, Lappet in *The Miser*, Mrs Clerimont in *The Tender Husband*, Susan in *The Follies of a Day*, Margaret in *Hide and Seek*, and Mrs Worldly in *A School for Widows*; in 1789–90, Miss Tittup in *Bon Ton*, Miss Sterling in *The Clandestine Marriage*, and Marchioness Merida in *The Child of Nature*; in 1790–91, the original Lady Peckham in Thomas Holcroft's comedy *The School for Arrogance*, Mrs Racket in *The Belle's Stratagem*, Lady Racket in *Three Weeks*

Courtesy of the Garrick Club

ISABELLA MATTOCKS, as Lady Restless
by De Wilde

after Marriage, the original Mrs Cockletop in John O'Keeffe's farce *Modern Antiques*, and Florizet in *National Prejudice*; 1791–92, Mrs Sneak in *The Mayor of Garratt*, Jacintha in *Lovers' Quarrels*, the original Lauretta in *A Day in Turkey*, a comic opera by Hannah Cowley, the original Mrs Warren in Thomas Holcroft's greatly successful comedy *The Road to Ruin*, and Nerina in *The Intrigues of a Morning*; in 1792–93, Adriana in *The Comedy of Errors*, Lady Flippant in *Fashionable Levities*, Lady Amaranth in *Wild Oats*; in 1793–94, Lady Placid in *Every One Has His Fault*, Muslin in *The Way to Keep Him*, Mary the Buxom in *Barataria*, the original Mrs Albert in O'Keeffe's comic opera *The World is a Village*, the original Nannette in Holcroft's comedy *Love's Frailties*, the original Lady Philippa Sidney in Henry Bate's comic opera *The Travellers in Switzerland*, Lady Freelove in *The Jealous Wife*, Susannah in *Tristram Shandy*; 1794–95, the original Lady Sarah Savage in Frederick Reynolds's comedy *The Rage!*, Patch in *The Busy Body*, the original Mrs Fancourt in Hannah Cowley's comedy *The*

Town Before You, the original Annette in the melodrama *The Mysteries of the Castle*, by Miles Peter Andrews and Frederick Reynolds, the original Mrs Bloomfield in William Macready's *The Bank Note*, and the original Mrs Sarsnet in Holcroft's comedy *The Deserted Daughter* (the last two on contiguous nights!).

Mrs Mattocks was now in her fiftieth year, with no sign of diminution of vigor or talent. In 1795–96 she added to her string of roles Mrs Grub in *Cross Purposes*, the original Mrs Auburne in O'Keeffe's farce *The Doldrum*, and the original Clementina Allspice in Thomas Morton's comedy *The Way to Get Married*; in 1796–97, the original Miss Union in Reynolds's comedy *Fortune's Fool*, the original Miss Vortex in Morton's comedy *A Cure for the Heart-Ache*, the original Lady Mary Raffle in Elizabeth Inchbald's comedy *Wives As They Were and Maids As They Are*, Wishwell in *The Double Gallant*, the original Lady Nettleton in Benjamin Hoadley's comedy *The Tatlers*, Lady Rodolpha Lumbercourt in *The Man of the World*, Mrs Frail in *Love for Love*; in 1797–98, the original Sally Downright in Morton's comedy *He's Much to Blame*, Mrs Candour in *The School for Scandal*; in 1798–99, Mrs Changeable in *The Jew and the Doctor*, the original Lady Maxim in T. J. Dibdin's comedy *Five Thousand a Year*, Mrs Oakley in *The Jealous Wife* (at the Haymarket in the summer of 1799); and in 1799–1800, the original Rachel Starch in Mrs Inchbald's drama *The Wise Man of the East*, Mrs Croaker in *The Good-Natured Man*, and Tilburina in *The Critic*.

Mrs Mattocks continued—though at a diminished rate—to add principal parts to her repertoire through her final years on the stage: in 1800–1801, the original Miss Lucretia McTab in Colman's comedy *The Poor Gentleman*, the original Norah O'Blarney in W. W. Dibdin's farce *The Cabinet*, and Betty Hint in *The Man of the World*; in 1802–3, the original Mrs Sapling in Frederick Reynolds's *Delays and Blunders*, and the original Fiametta in Holcroft's *A Tale of Mystery*; in 1803–4, Fish in *Appearance is Against Them*; in 1804–5, the original Mrs Glastonburg in *Who Wants a Guinea?*, a comedy by Colman; in 1805–6, the original Camilla in "Monk" Lewis's melodrama *Rugantino* and Viletta in *She Wou'd and She Wou'd Not*; in 1806–7, the original Githa in Dimond's melodrama *Adrian and Orsila* and the original Lady Trot in *Town and Country*, a comedy by Morton; and in 1807–8, Lady Wrangle in *Too Friendly by Half* and Flippanta in *The Confederacy*.

In those last few years she also played less often. Her final performance was as Flora in *The Wonder* on 7 June 1808, when she took a benefit and spoke a farewell address. Mrs Mattocks acted at Liverpool in some summers until late in the 1790s. She was also seen at Edinburgh in the summer of 1798 playing 10 of her favorite parts, and she did one-night stands in provincial towns throughout her career. Those engagements supplemented a salary at Covent Garden which was constant at £10 per week during most of her final years there. She had prosperous benefits at both London and Liverpool.

Isabella Mattocks had a fine singing voice which was heard frequently in oratorios and sometimes in concerts, as well as often in comic operas, especially in her earlier years. She was an excellent speaker of prologues and epilogues. She very quickly won favor with the public, but critical approval was slower and was sometimes captious. The critical ambiguity persisted until late in her career. "Sir Nicholas Nipclose" (Francis Gentleman) in *The Theatres* (1772) generally commended her in both comedy and tragedy and summed her up:

A figure happily dispos'd, tho' small,
Striking in nought, agreeable in all:
Sometimes too earnest in desire to please,
She steps beyond the boundaries of ease,
Forces her features into painful state,
And rather sinks, attempting to be great:

But he admitted that "few, for general use, can rivals stand."

The *Macaroni and Savoir Vivre Magazine* in 1773 considered her a "universal and judicious actress." "She has an exceeding good natural voice that stamps her a very good second singer; which, on the whole, from a pleasing person, together with a good share of judgement, renders her one of the most useful performers in the theatre she is engaged in." Two years later William Hawkins treated her art respectfully in *Miscellanies in Prose and Verse*, calling her "useful and pleasing . . . in the lively, spirited parts of comedy" and placing her "foremost among the favourite daughters of Thalia." Even

in tragedy, she has had "all the success the diminutive size of her figure will permit."

By 1792 she had advanced to near the head of the list of London comediennes, but her mannerisms, several critics thought, had become too pronounced. The harsh "Anthony Pasquin" (John Williams) pilloried her in the thirteenth edition of *The Children of Thespis* (1792):

With a sort of a cobweb-like half-tatter'd pride,
That is gay but not good, like a lustring thrice
dy'd;
With the jerk of a Thais, an eye mark'd by cunning,
And a small mincing step that's nor walking or
running
All confident Mattocks befeather'd descry,
Who, ere her tongue speaks, her front says—Here
am I!
In high life or low, in the palace or cot,
Her mind s leading feature is never forgot:
Be the part old or young, witty, flippant, or dull,
A rustic, a countess, a romp, or a fool;
The jig indecorous steps in to confound it,
And like dogs when distracted, runs rapidly round
it—
Unappropriate grins, like a fool at confession,
Or the shrugs of a Gaul at the void of expression;
With impertinent titterings, make up that measure,
Which Wit meant an offering for rational Pleasure.—
She was once prais'd by Truth, happy, artless and
gay,
But a wish to be more makes her efforts outré*;*
Thus old belles patch their wrinkles when vanities
mad 'em,
To regenerate charms they mis-us'd when they had
'em
When she aped Lady Racket (as Phrenzy once tried
her)
Her address near effected what Nature denied her;
The bold minx turn'd a thief, in the Muses' abode,
And stole all she could, from bright Abington's
code;
She would hide the rich theft, when the credulous
praise her,
But Truth draws the curtain, and, angry, betrays
her;
Now 'tis seen thro' and thro' by a curious eye,
Like the transparent wing of a summer-dry'd fly;
Or the unnapp'd remains of—an honest man's coat,
Or the old water-mark of a hacknied bank note.
Yet her Peckhams, her Flirts, and her Adelaides
charm me,
And her epilogue speaking *can gladden and warm*
me,

*In that Envy's minions must own when they mind
     her,
She leaves Competition—a furlong behind her.*

But the critic of the *Thespian Magazine* the same year, contemplating her mature achievement, praised "the delicacy of her person [and] the vivacity of her temper":

It is the peculiar distinction of this actress, that she possesses so lively a sensibility about her, as to *realize* her parts; nor is she deficient in judgment to prevent that sensibility from verging to the unnatural: to these advantages, she unites a pleasing person, and agreeable voice. . . .

As time went on, the voice faded, and Thomas Bellamy in *The London Theatres* (1795) mourned that

*The rising race will now small credence give,
When, from their elders, they are gravely told,
That* Billington *by* MATTOCKS *was outdone.*

Harvard Theatre Collection

ISABELLA MATTOCKS, as Lettice
engraving by Williamson, after De Wilde

Still, Bellamy marked the survival of the "aspect penetrating, strong and bold" of "Ma'am Maddocks, still alert and gay" at half a century.

*In vulgar epilogues the lady shines;
In snip-snap chat, to her the palm resign,
Ye chambermaids, and all ye lowly herd . . .*

Also in 1795, the actor Francis G. Waldron wrote of her in *Candid and Impartial Strictures on the Performers*:

In our opinion, an unrivalled performer in a certain line of acting, and the best of all good speakers of an epilogue. Her deportment is considerably injured by a buckram mechanism in her walk that is extremely disgusting. Her face, likewise, is sometimes made disagreeable by an unmeaning stare, and an exhibition of teeth and gums, that approaches to the frightful. These abominable practices ought to be corrected, if for no other reason than for fear of terrifying the children in the boxes, or occasioning an accident to some female auditor labouring under certain delicate sensations.

The author of *The Secret History of the Green Room* in 1795 gave her the following

Poetical Character
Though MATTOCKS *never was decreed to shine
A first-rate Actress of the tragic line,
In scenes of humour she might always please,
If she cou'd conquer her dislike of ease:
But (as if studious of restraint) she tries
Nature with affection to disguise;
Thro' all her form it constantly presides,
In drawling accents from her tongue it slides,
Glares in her eyes, and ev'ry gesture guides.
A false ambition to appear well bred,
To this strange stiffness in her acting led;
For, to this darling foible ever true,
She strives the Lady still to keep in view,
E'en if she's playing Hoyden or Miss Prue
But though she thus can ludicrously toil
Her native talents for the Stage to spoil,
Yet in some characters her scenic worth
Spite of the wild attempt will struggle forth
With sprightly freedom Lady Bell she shews,
Designs with judgment, and with nature glows;
And in Maria's gaily-varied mien,
A perfect proof of comic skill is seen.*

In February 1798 she annoyed the critic of the *Times*: "Mrs Mattocks has of late habituated herself to a constant titter, which destroys the effect of her best scenes." And in 1800 Thomas Dutton in *The Dramatic Censor* wrote tartly:

"Mrs. Mattocks's flippancy may please some persons, but we, for our part, would never wish to see her in any other characters, than pert chambermaids, and vulgar house-wives." But the *Monthly Mirror* reviewer that year praised her devotion to the comic muse, "whose cause she supports with admirable spirit, and with a peculiarity of humour, which, though it may sometimes exceed the precise limitations of critical propriety, is richly comic, and . . . perfectly original."

Leigh Hunt, in *Critical Essays of the Performers* (1807) was particular:

In her performance of the intriguing Betty Hint in *The Man of the World* she personifies with the happiest effect the breathless anxiety and hushed communication of the mischief-maker; her expressive stare at the beginning of her speeches, prophetic of her interlocutor's amazement, her very preparatory swallow (excuse me this vulgarism) as if she were unable to commence her direful tales, and the pretended gaiety of hurry with which she slurs over her real want of information as though it were a confirmed knowledge of facts, form a picture of great variety and truth.

Mrs Mattocks's steady admirer James Boaden wrote, in his *Memoirs of the Life of John Philip Kemble, Esq* (1825):

In her private manners she was rather refined, and had some of the graceful ease of the old school. On the stage she had a taste for the greatest *breadth* of effect, and excited probably as much laughter as Lewis himself. She was the *patent* representative of all WIDOWS of distinction, whether they were discriminated by valuable or mischievous properties. Nor were her chambermaids without the usual dexterity of the class, and probably with something beyond their usual assurance.

Boaden added, in his *Memoirs of Mrs Inchbald* (1833):

Mrs Mattocks has had no successor on the English stage. . . . She was the paragon representative of the radically *vulgar* woman, of any or no fashion, of whatever condition or age. The country *Malkin*, too, was taken to "Lunnun" by her, with her "stumping gait," and "idiot giggle," so as to banish from her spectators the remotest suspicion that she herself could be the refined and sensible lady she was in private life. Her favourite partners on the stage were [John] Quick and [William Thomas] Lewis; and exquisite merriment proceeded from their union.

The American manager William Burke Wood, who saw her when she was "far advanced in life," nevertheless remembered a half century later his "delight in her excellence, and surprise that while resembling her brother [Lewis Hallam the younger] in many respects, she should be so unlike him in her style of acting." Her talents struck him as "of the first class," as he recalled comparable actresses in his *Personal Recollections of the Stage* (1855).

Isabella Hallam had eluded the vigilance of her guardians to elope to France and marry George Mattocks in April 1765. Her relations had opposed the match with Mattocks, who was eleven years her elder and who had already fathered two illegitimate children. The family's misgivings proved correct. The marriage endured but was not happy. There was unfaithfulness on both sides. She took the actor Robert Bensley as lover and Mattocks made the actress Mrs J. A. Fisher his mistress. Those affairs were brief, but there were perhaps others. The relationship was further exacerbated by a disparity in professional standing. Mattocks had a pleasant singing voice but was not a good actor. Mrs Mattocks possessed both talents and developed them.

George Mattocks died in 1804 in Edinburgh. Isabella Mattocks inherited very little because of her husband's losses, sustained in several provincial theatrical adventures. But she had lived frugally and had saved a large sum. She settled part of her fortune on her daughter Isabella Anne, the only child of her marriage, and turned £6000 over to the management of her son-in-law Nathaniel Huson, a barrister. Huson quickly spent it all and then died.

On 24 May 1813 her old colleagues Mrs Jordan, Quick, Palmer, Fawcett, and others gave her a benefit at the King's Theatre. It realised £1092, which was invested in an annuity for her.

Isabella Mattocks died at her house in the High Street, Kensington on 25 June 1826. She left plate, books, jewels, household effects, and cash for her daughter, with residuary legatees her "dear granddaughter Isabella Anne Huson" and John and Jane Merriman. Merriman was named executor and proved the will on 11 July 1826.

Portraits of Isabella Mattocks include:

1. By Richard Crosse. Location unknown.

The ledgers of this deaf and mute miniaturist record the painting of Mrs Mattocks's portrait on 29 November 1776.

2. By George Dance, Jr. Pencil drawing, owned by Iolo Williams in 1949.

3. Engraved portrait by R. Laurie, after W. Dighton. Published by W. Richardson, 1780.

4. Engraved portrait by W. Ridley, after Miller. Published as a plate to the *Monthly Mirror*, 1800.

5. Engraved portrait by Ridley & Co, after S. Drummond. Published as a plate to *European Magazine*, 1807.

6. Speaking the epilogue to *Know Your Own Mind*. Engraving by Cook, after Dodd. Published by Fielding & Walker, 1780.

7. As one of the chorus, with Hull as Edwin and Elizabeth Hartley as Elfrida, in *Elfrida*. Engraving without artist or engraver named, undated, in the Harvard Theatre Collection (but not in the catalogue of portraits).

8. As Elvira in *The Spanish Fryar*. Engraving by J. Corner, after S. De Wilde. Published as a plate to *Bell's British Theatre*, 1791.

9. As Elvira. Engraving by Thornthwaite, after J. Roberts. Published as a plate to *Bell's British Theatre*, 1777. A copy by an anonymous engraver was published in the same work.

10. As Elvira, with Henderson as Edwin. Pencil and wash drawing by unknown artist. In the Folger Shakespeare Library.

11. As Isabella in *The Wonder*. By unknown engraver. Published by Harrison & Co, 1781.

12. As Jacinta in *Lovers' Quarrels*. Engraving by Alais. Published by J. Roach, 1806.

13. As Lady Restless in *All in the Wrong*. Painting by S. De Wilde. In the Garrick Club (No 250). Engraving by Audinet published as a plate to *Bell's British Library*, 1792.

14. As Lady Wishfort in *The Way of the World*. Engraving by Chapman, after Moses. Published as a plate to *British Drama*, 1807.

15. As Lettice in *The Intriguing Chambermaid*. Pen and red chalk drawing by S. De Wilde. In the British Museum. Engraving by Williamson published as a plate to Cawthorn's *Minor British Theatre*, 1807.

16. As Louisa in *The Duenna*. Engraving by Dunkarton, after J. Russell. Published by J. Walker, 1777.

17. As Louisa. Painting by Gainsborough Dupont. In the Garrick Club (No 410).

18. As Louisa, with Leoni as Carlos. By unknown engraver.

19. As Louisa. Watercolor drawing by unknown artist. In the Widener Collection, Harvard University.

20. As Louisa, with John Quick as Sir Isaac, in *The Duenna*. Engraving by W. P. Carey, after J. Rowlandson. Published by J. R. Smith, 1784.

21. As Nysa in *Midas*. By unknown engraver. Published as a plate to *Vocal Magazine*, 1779 (song 1250).

22. As Princess Catherine in *Henry V*. Colored drawing by J. Roberts. In the British Museum. Engraving by Grignion published as a plate to Bell's *Shakespeare*, 1775.

23. As Miss Prue, with Wilson as Ben, in *Love for Love*. Engraving by B. Reading, after E. Edwards. Published as a plate to Lowndes's *New England Theatre*, 1776.

24. As Mrs Warren in *The Road to Ruin*. By unknown engraver. Published as a plate to *Attic Miscellany*, No XXX, February 1792.

Mattox. *See* MATTOCKS.

Maudet, Mrs? [*fl. 1740–1743*], *dancer, actress.*

A female dancer cited in *The London Stage* from 1740 to 1743 as Mardette, Maudet, Modett, Moudette, etc., and sometimes designated Mrs and sometimes Miss was very likely just one person, and since she was most frequently called Mrs we have tentatively listed her as married. During the 1740–41 season she danced at Drury Lane as a Pilgrim in *The Fortune Tellers* from 4 December 1740 and was seen also during the season in *Comus* and as a Villager in *Orpheus and Eurydice* and the fourth Sylvan in *The Rape of Proserpine*. On 22 August 1741 she played Mrs Goodshot in *The Matrimonial Squabble* at Bartholomew Fair. In 1741–42 and 1742–43 she was at Covent Garden dancing an Amazon in *Perseus and Andromeda*, a Shepherdess in *Rural Assembly* within *The Winter's Tale*, and a Country Lass in *The Rape of Proserpine*. She was also seen in the ballets *La Provençale* and *Mars and Venus*. At Bartholomew Fair on 25 August 1742 she danced *English Maggot* with Monsieur Blondel at Hippisley and Chapman's booth. Though *The London Stage* does not show her active at Drury Lane in 1743, she was in the corps de ballet there, probably in the fall, according to Egerton manuscript 2320.

Maugridge. *See* MAWGRIDGE.

Mauly, Mons ₍*fl. 1749*₎, *actor.*
Monsieur Mauly was one of the French players who engaged with the manager Monnet for a season in London, opening on 14 November 1749 at the Haymarket Theatre with *Les Amans réunis.* Anti-gallic sentiment ran strong and the rioting at the theatre brought the engagement to an end in mid-December. On 22 May 1750 Monnet was given a benefit at Drury Lane in order to make up some of his losses. He published an account showing that Mauly and another player, Hamond, contracted for £301 8s. 9d. but settled for £238. Perhaps Mauly was related to the dancer Mademoiselle Mauly who was at Toulouse in 1756.

Maund, Mr ₍*fl. 1708*₎, *pitkeeper.*
Among Vice Chamberlain Coke's papers at Harvard is a paylist for the Queen's Theatre dated 8 March 1708; Mr Maund is listed as one of four pitkeepers at a daily salary of 2s. 8d.

Maunsel. *See* MANSEL.

Maunsell, Miss. *See* FARREN, MRS WILLIAM and MANSEL, ELIZABETH.

Maunsell, Dorothea. *See* TENDUCCI, MME GIUSTO FERDINANDO.

"Mauxalinda." *See* YOUNG, ISABELLA.

Mavillier. *See* MARVILLER.

Mawby, Edward ₍*fl. 1784–1815*₎, *violoncellist.*
Edward Mawby played violoncello in the Handel Memorial Concerts in May and June 1784. Doane's *Musical Directory* of 1794 noted that Mawby was then playing at Sadler's Wells Theatre and resided in Ratcliffe Row, Ratcliffe Highway. Mawby was a subscriber to the New Musical Fund in 1794, 1805, and 1815, and on 15 January 1798 played in the *Messiah* at the Haymarket Theatre.

Mawgridge, John *d. 1688, drummer.*
On 20 June 1660 the elder John Mawgridge (or Maugridge) was appointed drum major in the King's Musick. Another drummer in the royal musical establishment was John's brother Richard. The John Mawgridge who was appointed a drummer in ordinary without fee on 30 August 1671 was probably the drum major's nephew John, Richard's son. The Lord Chamberlain's accounts cited the elder Mawgridge from time to time over the years: submitting a bill for red baize, receiving livery payments of £52 17s. 8d. annually (often not on time), receiving livery payments for the four drummers and fife player who were his responsibility, being petitioned against by his nephew Robert when he withheld Robert's livery in January 1684, and receiving a bounty of £20 from James II on 3 April 1688.

The post of drum-major general had come into existence by 1676, and as Grove points out, John Mawgridge assumed the duties of that office as well as those connected with the post of drum major of the royal household. In October 1676 Mawgridge recruited drummers for service in Virginia, and on 10 April 1679 he was paid £5 12s. for "impressing and furnishing 16 drummers for the eight companies added to the Coldstream Guards in 1678."

John Mawgridge died in early 1688 and was succeeded by his nephew (we think) John. He had written his will on 21 November 1687, leaving bequests of 1s. each to his nephews Robert and John Mawgridge, sons of his brother Richard. Everything else he left to his wife Sara, who proved the will on 19 April 1688. Mawgridge described himself in his will as of the parish of St Paul, Covent Garden, but the parish registers there contain no mention of him. As late as 1692 Sara Mawgridge was owed her late husband's arrears in livery payments.

On the other hand, the registers of St Margaret, Westminster, which contain references to many court musicians, mention a John and Sarah Mawgridge who were doubtless the drum major and his wife: their daughter Mary was christened on 8 December 1662, their son Henry on 4 February 1664, and their son John on 28 May 1665 (and assuming that that John was, in fact, the drum major's son, he would have been far too young to have joined the King's Musick in 1671).

Mawgridge, John [fl. 1671–1705], drummer.

The John Mawgridge who was appointed a drummer in ordinary without fee in the King's Musick on 30 August 1671 was probably the elder John Mawgridge's nephew, the son of Richard Mawgridge, who was also a drummer in the royal musical establishment. Authorities have taken the younger John to have been the son of the elder, but the only parish register information we have found concerning the elder Mawgridge shows that his son John was born in 1665. Upon the death of the elder John Mawgridge, the younger John was appointed to his post as drum major of the royal household and drum-major general, the two posts having been combined at least as early as 1676. The appointment came on 10 April 1688, according to a warrant in the Lord Chamberlain's accounts, and chiefly involved recruitment of drummers for the service. With the coming of William and Mary in 1689 John Mawgridge was reappointed drum major, and in January 1691 he accompanied William III on a trip to the Hague.

From a warrant dated 1696 we learn that Mawgridge's livery allowance was £40 annually, some £12 less than the allowance granted under Charles II. Charles had usually been delinquent in his livery payments to court musicians, and so was William: John's 1696 warrant was a request for livery due him in 1692. A warrant dated 1699 shows that Mawgridge received a yearly salary of £30 (the drummers under him were paid £24). He may have been the John Mawgridge of St Margaret, Westminster, who married Barbara Mason, also of that parish, at St Paul, Covent Garden on 17 July 1702—though that could as easily have been John the son of the elder John Mawgridge. The drum major's post passed from John Mawgridge to Robert Mawgridge on 1 February 1705, according to Dalton's *English Army Lists*. Robert was, we think, the brother of the younger John Mawgridge.

Mawgridge, Richard [fl. 1661–1687?], drummer.

Richard Mawgridge was appointed a drummer in the King's Musick on 19 February 1661;

he served under his brother John, who was the drum major. On 19 March 1677 Edward Wharton replaced Richard, but the reason was not specified in the Lord Chamberlain's warrant. However, since the warrant did not specify that Richard had died (such warrants usually did if a post was vacated because of death), we can assume he either decided to retire or took a position outside the court. Richard's brother John's will, dated 21 November 1687, included one-shilling bequests to Richard's sons John and Robert, and the wording would suggest that Richard was then still alive.

Mawgridge, Robert d. 1708, drummer.

Robert Mawgridge was appointed a drummer in the King's Musick on 7 April 1662, serving under the drum major John Mawgridge, who was probably his uncle; his father was Richard Mawgridge. Robert's appointment was renewed on 24 August 1665 when he took over the post left vacant by Jeremiah Crewes (Robert may until then have served without fee). Robert's wages were 1s. daily and a livery fee of £16 2s. 6d. When the 1665 warrant was repeated on 15 December 1669 the daily salary was given as 12d.

It is possible that the following entry in the parish register of St Martin-in-the-Fields refers to the drummer: Hugh "Moggride" the son of Robert and Elizabeth was born and baptized on 25 February 1680. But the name Mawgridge, variously spelled, was remarkably common in the Restoration period and can be found in several registers.

A warrant in the Lord Chamberlain's accounts dated 15 October 1680 stated that Robert Mawgridge could continue as a kettledrummer (in which capacity he must have been serving) providing he could find a man capable of replacing him as a drummer; he evidently found someone, for on 8 June 1682 Robert took over permanently the post of kettledrummer left vacant by the death of Walter Vanbright. A warrant dated 12 January 1684 shows that Robert petitioned his uncle John for his livery allowance, which the drum major had for some reason withheld.

In the coronation procession of James II, as described by Sandford, the kettledrums "with their banners of crimson damask richly fringed and embroidered with His Majesty's arms and supporters" were followed by Robert Mawgridge in his elegant livery.

Upon the death of the drum major John Mawgridge in early 1688 the younger John Mawgridge—his nephew and Robert's brother, we believe—became drum major. Robert was reappointed a drummer in ordinary on 10 April 1688, when John moved up to drum major; warrants thereafter cited Robert regularly as the kettledrummer in the group of drummers under John. In the mid-1690s Robert had two scrapes with the law. William Bull petitioned against him on 23 April 1694 for using "scandalous words," and William Holland went against him on 14 February 1696 for a debt of £4. Robert's salary, as of 1699, was £24 annually.

Dalton in his *English Army Lists* stated that Robert Mawgridge succeeded (his brother) John to the post of drum major on 1 February 1705. According to Luttrell, Robert killed Captain Cope, son of Sir John Cope, on 17 June 1706 in the guard room at the Tower, fled to the Continent, and was brought back and executed at Tyburn on 28 April 1708. The Robert Mawgridge who was granted administration of his mother Dorothy's estate on 3 December 1716 was perhaps a son of the kettledrummer; she was described as a widow from the parish of St Margaret, Westminster.

Mawgridge, Robert [*fl.* 1702–1720], *kettledrummer.*
Robert Mawgridge Junior, probably but not necessarily the son of the elder Robert Mawgridge, was listed as a kettledrummer in the royal musical establishment as early as 1702. His salary then and as late as 1714 was £24 annually. At some point he was made drum major, and on 18 February 1720 John Clothier apparently replaced "Maugridge" in the King's Musick. By that time the post was worth £40 yearly.

Mawley, Mr [*fl.* 1733–1734], *actor.*
Mr Mawley played Shadow in *2 Henry IV* at the Haymarket Theatre with Theophilus Cibber's seceders on 12 October 1733 and subsequent performances through 19 January 1734.

Mawley, Mr [*fl.* 1784], *treasurer.*
According to *The Case of the Opera-House Disputes* (1784) a Mr Mawley replaced Crawford

as treasurer at the King's Theatre; he had advanced money to the trustees on the condition that he would receive the appointment with an increase in salary. He apparently did not last long, for Crawford was back as treasurer and manager before the year was out.

Maxene. *See* MAXFIELD, GEORGE.

Maxfield, Mr [*fl.* 1744–1756?], *actor.*
At Goodman's Fields Theatre Mr Maxfield played the Welsh Collier in *The Recruiting Officer* on 26 December 1744, Mustacho in *The Tempest* beginning 14 February 1745, and James in *The Miser* on 7 March. He had a solo benefit on 2 April. Perhaps he was the Maxfield who played Foigard in *The Beaux' Stratagem* at Canterbury on 27 July 1756.

Maxfield, George [*fl.* 1662–1675], *singer.*
The George "Maxene" mentioned in the Lord Chamberlain's accounts as a Chapel Royal boy in 1662 was very likely the George Maxfield who was a member of the King's Company in 1673–74 and the Mr "Maxsine" who was paid in May 1675 for singing in the court masque *Calisto* the previous 15 February.

Maximilian, Christopher. *See* MILLER, MAXIMILIAN JOHN CHRISTOPHER.

Maxsine. *See* MAXFIELD, GEORGE.

Maxwell, Mrs [*fl.* 1798], *house servant?*
The Drury Lane Theatre accounts show a payment of 7s. to a Mrs Maxwell on 24 February 1798 for two days of work. She was cited again exactly a month later. Her benefit tickets were accepted on 11 June. She was probably a house servant.

May, Mr [*fl.* 1721–1727], *house servant?*
Mr May shared benefits at Drury Lane Theatre, usually with one other employee, from the spring of 1721 to the spring of 1727, excepting only 1723—and that may merely be a gap in the discovered records. He was probably a house servant and related to (if not the same as) the Mr May of 1747.

May, Mr ₍fl. 1747₎, *house servant?*
A Mr May shared a benefit at Drury Lane
Theatre with five others on 14 May 1747. He
may have been (or been related to) the Mr May
who was at Drury Lane from 1721 to 1727.

May, Mr ₍fl. 1755₎, *actor.*
Mr May was a member of Theophilus Cibber's troupe at the Haymarket Theatre in the
late summer of 1755, and perhaps he was one
of the players who, it was said, had never
appeared on any stage before. On 9 September
he acted Fidler in *The Devil to Pay* and two days
later he was a Servant in *Lethe.* He repeated
the latter role on 15 September.

May, Mr ₍fl. 1794–95₎, *carpenter.*
Mr May was listed in the Covent Garden
accounts for 1794–95 as one of the theatre's
carpenters earning 19s. weekly.

May, Benjamin d. 1759, *manager.*
A notation in the Winston transcriptions in
the Folger Shakespeare Library calling Benjamin May "for many years principal Director of
Entertainments at [the] King's Theatre" gives
his death date as 9 January 1759. The *Grand
Magazine of Magazines* for January 1759 called
him "manager" of the theatre and stated that
he died on 1 January. Nalbach's study of the
King's Theatre contains no mention of May.
May had written his will on 28 June 1753,
describing himself as of the parish of St James,
Westminster. He asked that his wife Theresia
give to her son Peter Crawford, jeweller (and
treasurer of the King's Theatre), and Henry
Kipling of St George, Bloomsbury, £1000 for
the purchase of securities in behalf of Mrs May.
Peter Crawford was left £500, and £200 was
to go to young William Bright of St Anne,
Westminster, silversmith, when he should reach
the age of 21; until that time he was to receive
£6 annually as maintenance. Philip Crown of
St Marylebone was given an annuity of £6, and
May's friends Lewis Petitt and John Murod
were bequeathed 20 guineas each. May left
five guineas to each servant in his employ at
the time of his death. The rest of his estate he
left to his wife. The will was proved on 18
January 1759.

May, Elizabeth. *See* JEFFERSON, MRS
THOMAS *the first.*

May, ₍Richard₎ ₍fl. c. 1715₎, *house servant.*
In the Drury Lane Theatre accounts at the
Folger Shakespeare Library "Rᵈ May" is named
about 1715. He appears to have been a house
servant.

**Mayers, Elianor, later Mrs John-Philip
du Ruel** ₍fl. 1703–1706₎, *dancer, choreographer.*
In volume 4 of this dictionary we noticed
"Mme Du Ruel." We have since discovered in
the registers of St Paul, Covent Garden, the
entry concerning her marriage and can now
identify her more precisely as the dancer Mrs
Mayers. A document in the Public Record
Office headed "Establishmᵗ of yᵉ Company,"
previously dated by scholars 1707 but now
shown by Judith Milhous to date about 1703,
listed a Mrs Mayers as a dancer at an annual
salary of £40 (about the middle of the scale).
Monsieur "De Ruell" was listed at the same
salary. Mrs Mayers's first notice in the bills
came on 12 January 1704 when she, du Ruel,
and others danced at Drury Lane. Thereafter
she was regularly at both Drury Lane and Lincoln's Inn Fields (once at both theatres on the
same day) through 17 April.
On 17 April 1704 at St Paul, Covent Garden, John-Philip du Ruel and Elianor Mayers
were married, and beginning 20 April 1704
she began dancing at Drury Lane under her
married name. She appeared regularly with du
Ruel through July, dancing the *Country Frenchman and his Wife*, the *Dutch Skipper*, and other
turns which were left undescribed in the bills.
On 1 July she danced a solo chaconne. The
pair danced again at Drury Lane in the 1704–
5 season. On 24 February 1705 Madame du
Ruel composed and danced a piece called *The
Heroine*, and on 1 March she received a benefit.
She and her husband returned to France for
the summer and upon their return were engaged to dance at the Queen's Theatre in the
Haymarket. The Drury Lane manager, Christopher Rich, seems to have prevented that,
however, and on 24 November 1705 the du
Ruels were at Drury Lane, making their first
appearance since their return. They danced
there for the rest of the season, but not as
frequently as before. After the spring of 1706
Madame du Ruel disappeared from the London
stage.

Her seasons in England brought her enough fame to warrant a poem by Samuel Phillips, published in the *Diverting Post* on 17 March 1705:

> *Gods, how she steps! see how the blushing Fair,*
> *With nimble Feet, divides the yielding Air,*
> *As tho' she'd throw the common Method by,*
> *And teach us not to Walk, but how to Fly!*
> *Look with what Art the Nymph displays her*
>   *Charms;*
> *Observe the curling Motions of her Arms!*
> *See in what Folds her flowing Garments stream;*
> *At once they cool and kindle up a Flame*
> *In e'ery Breast, but her's!—she's still the same.*
> *She, like chast Cynthia, does on all Men shine,*
> *But to Endymion she is only kind:*
> *Ill-sorted Fate! that only One must be*
> *Repriev'd from Death, enjoy Felicity,*
> *While Thousands daily do dispair, and die.*

Maylan, Evan ₍*fl. 1696*₎, *harper.*

On 3 February 1696 the Lord Chamberlain ordered the harper Evan Maylan to be appointed to the King's Musick without fee; he was to receive a salary when a post became vacant, but since the accounts make no further mention of him, he must have given up and left the royal musical establishment.

Mayle, Mr ₍*fl. 1741–1744*₎, *office keeper.*

Mr Mayle, an office keeper at Drury Lane Theatre, was cited in the benefit bills each spring from 14 May 1741 to 15 May 1744.

Maynard, Mr ₍*fl. 1733*₎, *actor.*

The role of Old Laron in *The Old Debauchees* at the Haymarket Theatre on 27 March 1733 was played by a Mr Maynard; the work was not repeated.

Mayo, Mrs ₍*fl. 1756–1757*₎, *actress.*

Mrs Mayo made her first appearance on any stage playing Lady Townly in *The Provok'd Husband* at Covent Garden Theatre on 8 May 1756. Her second appearance, and apparently her last in London, was on 21 October 1757 at the same theatre as Zara in *The Mourning Bride*.

Mazzinghi, Joseph *1765–1844, instrumentalist, composer, director of music.*

Joseph Mazzinghi was born in London on 25 December 1765, the son of Thomas Mazzinghi (d. 1775), wine merchant, composer, violinist, and descendant of an ancient Corsican family. Joseph's mother was the sister of Cassandra Frederick, a musician who married the wealthy landowner Thomas Wynne. Early memoirs credit his aunt Cassandra with encouraging Joseph's musical talents and placing him under J. C. Bach. In 1775, at the age of ten, he served as organist at the Portuguese Chapel. He received further instruction from Bertolini, Sacchini, and Anfossi.

According to Sainsbury's *Dictionary of Music* (1827) at the age of 19 Mazzinghi became composer and director of music at the King's Theatre. But serving in those capacities until the summer of 1786 was Mazzinghi's teacher, Pasquale Anfossi, whom he may have assisted. Mazzinghi's first notice in connection with the King's Theatre was in 1786 when the music for *Le Premiere Navigateur; or, The Force of Love* (a ballet by Gardel which had been produced on 23 March 1786) was published as "Selected and adapted for the Piano Forte or Harpsichord by Sig^r Mazzinghi." The same year also was published *The favorite Opera Dances performed at the King's Theatre*, also selected and adapted for the same instruments by Mazzinghi. Similar editions of Mazzinghi's music for the opera dances came out in 1787, 1788, 1789, and 1792. In 1789 some of his overtures for the opera were published.

On 9 January 1787 Cimarosa's *Giannina e Bernardone* was presented under Mazzinghi's direction. He provided music for the ballet *Zemira and Azor* on 13 February 1787, and on 8 December 1787 he played at the harpsichord when *Il rè Teodoro in Venezia* was performed. He wrote ballet music for *L'Amour et Psiché* on 29 January 1788. He directed the London premiere of Marchesi's *Giulio Sabino* on 5 April 1788, Marchesi's *L'Olimpiade* on 8 May 1788 (in which his song "Grandi e ver son le tue pene" was sung by Signor Giuliani), Martini's *La cosa rara* on 10 January 1789 (in which his song "Dolce mi parve un di," was sung by Sga Delicati). Mazzinghi provided a grand march for a performance of Cherubini's *Ifigenia in Aulide* on 24 January 1789.

When the King's Theatre burned to the ground on 17 June 1789, Mazzinghi seems not to have joined the make-shift opera productions at the Haymarket Theatre the next season. He busied himself with composing a series of sonatas for pianoforte, violin, and violoncello that were published between 1789 and 1792. (He also published sonatas in 1795, 1799, and 1800.) In 1791 he became composer to the opera at the Pantheon, until it was destroyed by fire on 14 January 1792. There he altered Zini's *La bella pescatrice* and directed it on 1 March 1791 and produced Paisiello's *La locanda* on 16 June 1791. The following year, on 28 February 1792 he directed *La locanda* at the Haymarket; the *Morning Herald* of 5 March reported that "the original score of this beautiful opera was destroyed in the conflagration at the Pantheon. Mazzinghi and Cramer have been able, from recollection, to bring it again before the public." Mazzinghi wrote the music for the premieres of Cowley's comic opera *A Day in Turkey* on 3 December 1791 and Merry's comic opera *The Magician No Conjurer* on 2 February 1792, both produced at Covent Garden Theatre.

When opera was resumed at the new King's Theatre in January 1793, the house composers were Storace and Federici and the leader of the band was Cramer. Mazzinghi, however, continued to supply music for productions there and at other places. Those at the King's included *Paul et Virginie* in 1794–95; *La bella Arsene, The Bouquet, Il Tesoro,* and *Les Trois Sultanes* in 1795–96; *Les Délassements Militaires, Pizarre* (on 7 February 1797, when the ballet was described as "Magnificent, perhaps beyond parallel on the British stage," but much too long), *Sapho et Phaon,* and *L'Albero di Diana* in 1796–97; and *Eliza* in 1797–98. In 1794 Doane's *Musical Directory* gave his address as Newman Street, Oxford Street.

When the Margravine of Anspach produced her own comedy *The Smyrna Twins* as a birthday gift for her husband at Brandenburgh House, Hammersmith, on 25 February 1796, Mazzinghi was in charge of the music. He composed several airs for the Margravine, played the harpsichord, and conducted the band, which included Dragonetti on the double bass, Harrington on the oboe, Pieltain on the horn, and Holmes on the bassoon.

Mazzinghi's compositions for Cobb's comic opera *Ramah Droog* at Covent Garden on 12 November 1798 were called by the *Morning Herald* "some of the best music the English stage has for some time been able to boast."

Also at Covent Garden he and Reeve provided music for Thomas Knight's *The Turnpike Gate* on 14 November 1799 and Cobb's musical farce *Paul and Virginia* on 1 May 1800. Mazzinghi wrote the overture for the latter piece. On 5 July 1800 he and Reeve were paid £50 for the music in *Paul and Virginia*, probably a payment on account. Again with Reeve at Covent Garden he composed for Morton's *The Blind Girl* and Hoare's *Chains of the Heart* in 1801. He was paid £100 by Drury Lane in 1803–4 for the music to *The Wife of Two Husbands.* Again at Covent Garden, he collaborated with Bishop on the music for Reynolds's *The Exile* in 1808 and wrote music for *Free Knights* in 1810.

About 1790 Mazzinghi had become a partner in Goulding, D'Almaine, & Co, the music printers who published most of his music after that time. He organized the concerts at Carlton House and the Concerts of the Nobility which were established in 1791 and were held in private houses on Sunday evenings. Many of Mazzinghi's miscellaneous compositions were popular at the various professional concerts, in which he also performed on the harpsichord. He enjoyed an extensive practice as a teacher for many years, counting among his many pupils from the nobility the Princess of Wales, later Queen Caroline.

For almost 57 years Mazzinghi was a member of the Royal Society of Musicians, to which he had been admitted on 3 June 1787. In the 1790s he played in the Society's annual concerts at St Paul's and in 1800 he served on the court of Assistants.

While on a visit to his son, Mazzinghi died at Downside College, Bath, on 15 January 1844, in his seventy-ninth year, and was buried, as he requested in his will, in the vault of the Catholic Chapel in Chelsea on 25 January.

Biographers have been confused about the identity of the musician named Mazzinghi who was reported to have been made a count somewhere in Italy in 1834. Some accounts state that the ennobled one was Joseph's brother Thomas, a violinist who did not perform in London in the eighteenth century and about whom little is known. It seems to have been Joseph, however, who went to Corsica in 1834 to claim his title. Our subject's will, drawn on 16 January 1841, begins "This is the last Will and Testament of me Count Joseph Mazzinghi now residing at No 22 in Duncan Terrace City Road." Several places thereafter in the will he is referred to as a count.

In his will Mazzinghi made bequests to many relatives, including a daughter, Catherine Amelia Josephine French, who was married to Anthony French, and a minor son, George Dominick Mazzinghi. The latter must have been the issue of a second marriage, since the death of Mazzinghi's wife was announced in the *Monthly Mirror* of January 1800. The second wife, not mentioned in his will, presumably was also dead by 1841. Two brothers, Thomas and Dominick, were also dead by that date. The widow of Dominick Mazzinghi received £50. Joseph left bequests to his nephew Thomas Mazzinghi of the Inner Temple and his nieces Cassandra Mazzinghi and Juliet Mazzinghi Worthington, all presumably the children of his brother Dominick. Generous residual provisions were made by Joseph for his sister Cassandra Edwards, wife of George Edwards, and her children: Mary, wife of George Nicholson, Margaret Edwards, Cassandra Edwards, Frederick Edwards, and Maria Valareale ("lately" Maria Edwards, wife of Signor Valareale living in Palermo, Sicily). Mazzinghi left an annuity of £20 to a sister-in-law, Maria Nicholl, wife of John Nicholl; presumably she was the sister of Joseph's second wife.

Mazzinghi gave his nieces and nephews £500 each. His sister Cassandra Edwards received £100 and the right to continue to reside in the house in Duncan Terrace. His freehold houses in Cleveland Row and Cleveland Square, St James's, and all other real and personal estate, including a bond of £1000 from his son-in-law Anthony French, Mazzinghi left to his daughter Catherine Amelia Josephine French. Curiously, his son George Dominick received only an annuity of £100, to be provided for by his sister's investments in bank stocks. Mazzinghi gave £100 to the Royal Society of Musicians, £100 to the Charity Schools, Whitehead's Grove, Chelsea, and £120 to Downside College. The will was proved at London on 7 February 1844 by his executors and solicitors Thomas Farthing, John Squire, and Frederick Squire, all of Pall Mall East.

In the *New Grove*, Roger Fiske notes a John Mazzinghi who translated several Italian operas and who in his *New and Universal Guide through London* (1785) claimed to be foreign born; he had an eldest son, also named Joseph, born in London. John Mazzinghi was likely the brother of Thomas Mazzinghi, our subject's father.

Long lists of Mazzinghi's sonatas, glees, songs, ballet and opera music, and incidental compositions are published in Sainsbury's *Dictionary of Music* and the *Catalogue of Printed Music in the British Museum*.

Although he was prominent and wealthy, no portraits of Joseph Mazzinghi are known.

Mazzinghi, Thomas   *d. 1775, violinist, composer.*

Thomas Mazzinghi was a descendant of an ancient Corsican family, one of whom was the chevalier Tedici Mazzinghi, a diplomat posted to the court of Naples in 1697. Other members of the family lived in Pisa, Florence, and Leghorn. When Thomas (or Tommaso) Mazzinghi came to London is unknown, but in 1763 his *Six Solos for the Violin with a Thorough-Bass for the Harpsichord* was published there by Welcker. Mazzinghi also established himself as a wine merchant and married the sister of the musician Cassandra Frederick (later the wife of Thomas Wynne, a wealthy landowner in South Wales).

According to Daniel Lysons's *Environs of London* and Cansick's *St Pancras Epitaphs*, Mazzinghi was a violinist and leader of the band at Marylebone Gardens when the establishment was under Dr Arnold's direction.

Mazzinghi died in London on 20 May 1775 (not in November 1771 as stated in the *New Grove*) and was buried in St Pancras churchyard. His son Joseph Mazzinghi (1765–1844), who had a successful career as a composer and musician for the opera, is noticed separately on these pages. Another son, Thomas Mazzinghi the younger, about whom little is known except that he was a violinist, seems not to have performed in London in the eighteenth century. One John Mazzinghi, a translator of some Italian operas in the 1790s and author of a *New and Universal Guide through London* (1785), was perhaps our subject's brother. No doubt also related was Felice Mazzinghi, who published a keyboard sonata about 1771; five manuscript sonatas by him are in the British Library.

Mazziotti, Antonio *[fl. 1763–1764]*, singer.

The singer Antonio Mazziotti is mentioned as one of a group of opera performers contracted for by Felice Giardini for the opera in London in 1763–64 by the writer "R. P." of the satirical pamphlet *A Defense of F. Giardini, from the Calumnies, Falsehoods, and Misrepresentations, of Cacophon, published by Him in the Name of Gabriel Leon . . . 1765.* Leone, a continental broker, is asserted to have cheated both the impresario and the performers. Among other sums mentioned are "fifteen hundred sequins," which was supposed to be Mazziotti's salary ("the most spirited Actor, and most brilliant singer, that ever trod the stage," says the author sardonically) and "three hundred of the fifteen hundred," supposedly Leone's commission. The pamphlet is at least the second of an unknown number in a dispute about opera finances and procurement of foreign singers which is impossible now to disentangle.

Mazzoni, Signora *[fl. 1773–1774]*, dancer.

The London Stage lists a male dancer at the King's Theatre in 1773–74 named Marroni; that is an error: the dancer's name was Signora Mazzoni. On 20 November 1773 at the King's she and others entertained with "A *Pastoral Dance* with a *Pas de Trois*, de Deux, &c." After that she appeared frequently during the season in entr'acte dances, among them the "New Grand Heroic-Comic-Pantomimical Ballet" *Orfeo e Euridice*, a *Grand Chaconne*, *La Provençal*, a *Pastoral Ballet*, the *Harem of Ispahan*, *La Bagatelle*, the heroic ballet *The Tempest; or, The Happy Shipwreck*, the comic ballet *La Bauquetiera*, *Les Faunes vainques*, and a *New Field Dance*.

Mc. *See* MAC.

Meachen. *See* MACHEN.

Mead, Mr *[fl. 1799–1817]*, singer.

Mr Mead was first noticed in the bills at Drury Lane on 4 February 1799, when he sang in the chorus of Villagers in *Feudal Times*. Thereafter he sang in the chorus of Soldiers in the same work, was one of the Janizaries in *Blue-Beard* and Camazin in *Lodoiska*, and sang in *The Tempest*, *Pizarro*, and *De Montfort* before

the end of the century. "Meade" was on the Drury Lane paylist at £1 0s. 10d. in 1810–11 and sang in the chorus at the Lyceum from 1811–12 through 1816–17 for £1 5s. weekly.

Meadows, William *[fl. 1779–1809]*, singer, actor.

When James Whitely gathered a company to act at Stourbridge Fair, near Cambridge, in the summer of 1779, Meadows, "from Richmond [Surrey]," was among them. He was, we believe, the wandering singer and actor William Meadows.

Meadows was said to have been from the Manchester Theatre when he turned up at the Crow Street Theatre, Dublin, with his wife in the summer of 1783. He acted also at Cork and at Smock Alley that summer, joining Crow Street's company in the autumn for the 1783–84 season. No roles are available for those engagements.

He made his first London appearance on 12 February 1785 in a specially-licensed performance at the Haymarket Theatre, in *The Quaker*—"In which Meadows (from the Theatre Royal, Dublin) will make his first appearance in the Kingdom," probably in the role of Lubin. (The prevarication by which the bill ignored his Richmond and Manchester performances was not unusual.) He played Young Meadows in *Love in a Village*, to open his summer activities in 1785, when he alternated performances at the Haymarket with appearances among Francis Godolphin Waldron's small group of players at the Windsor Castle Inn, King Street, Hammersmith. At the Haymarket he added to his known repertoire Ralph in *The Maid of the Mill*, William in *Rosina*, Mungo in *The Padlock*, Snip in *William and Susan*, a vocal part in *The Sons of Anacreon*, and Filch in *The Beggar's Opera*; and at Hammersmith, Trippit in *The Lying Valet*, Derby in *Jane Shore*, Truman in *The Clandestine Marriage*, a Soldier in *The Spanish Fryar*, a Courier in *The Follies of a Day*, Jeremy in *She Stoops to Conquer*, and a Savage in *Robinson Crusoe*.

Meadows joined the Covent Garden company in the 1785–86 season, singing in choruses and adding a few small named parts to his repertoire: Carlos in *The Duenna*, a Bacchanal in *Comus*, Damaetas in *Midas*, Apollo in *Poor Vulcan*, a Constable in *Omai*, and a Sailor in *The Peruvian*. The address on his benefit bill was simply John Street, Golden Square. Once again, in the summer of 1786, he divided his time between Haymarket and Hammersmith, adding at the Haymarket Captain Wilson in *The Flitch of Bacon*, Sprightly in *The Devil in the Wine-Cellar*, Loader in *The Minor*, Watty Cockney in *The Romp*, Junk in *The Siege of Carzola*, and the Bird Catcher in *Harlequin Teague* and at Hammersmith Guildenstern in *Hamlet*, a servant in *The Country Girl*, Cudden in *The Agreeable Surprise*, a Servant in *The Heiress*, and an Officer in *Venice Preserv'd*.

He was not rehired at Covent Garden in 1786–87, but in the summer of 1787 he was again at the Haymarket, where he added Glanville in *Harvest Home*, Osric in *Hamlet*, Eugene in *The Agreeable Surprise*, Balthasar in *Much Ado about Nothing*, Mercury in *The Golden Pippin*, and the Mate in *Inkle and Yarico*.

On 12 May 1788 Meadows made his first appearance at Sadler's Wells, singing unspecified characters in the musical sketches *The Clown Turned Beau* and *Saint Monday*. He sang again in a part unknown and a piece unknown on 7 June. Doubtless he was more fully employed but the surviving notices for Sadler's Wells are few. He was called "Meadows, late of the Haymarket" when he lent his efforts as Lubin to a compassionate benefit for James Fearon's widow and her eight children at Covent Garden on 16 June 1790.

We lose track of him until 16 January 1792 when he played Sir Christopher Curry in *Inkle and Yarico* and Puff in *Miss in Her Teens* in a pickup company at the Crown Inn, Islington. At some time in 1792 he acted also at the little Parson's Green Theatre, Fulham. But by March he was in Edinburgh at the Theatre Royal, Shakespeare Square, where he stayed for a year and acted, in addition to some of his old parts, Selim in *A Day in Turkey*, the Governor in *Richard Coeur de Lion*, Haulyard in *The Reprisal*, Azor in *Selima and Azor*, Captain Gorget in *Gretna Green*, Eugene in *The Agreeable Surprise*, the Fisherman in *The Triumph of Harlequin*, Leander in *The Padlock*, Linco in *Cymon*, Lord William in *The Haunted Tower*, Lorenzo in *The Merchant of Venice*, and Moscoso in *Columbus*. He cannot have been the Meadows in Franklin's troupe at the Amphitheatre in Bristol on 20 April 1793, for he was still in Edinburgh on 27 April. And it is unlikely he was the miserable Meadows acting under Duckworth's

management at Farnham, Surrey, in June 1793 who was stigmatized by the *Thespian Magazine* as "the most disgusting brute we ever beheld." He was, in any event, on his way to Dublin.

In the summer season of 1793, advertised as from Edinburgh, Meadows was once more in Ireland, active at Crow Street, where he and two of his daughters were hired for the winter season 1793–94. The trio returned to Crow Street in 1796–97 (when Meadows evidently did bird imitations).

A benefit bill for the Royal Circus, St George's Fields, London, dated 6 October 1800 features "Mr Meadows (from the Theatres Royal of Dublin and Liverpool), being his first Appearance on this Stage." In the same performance were the "Misses A. and G. Meadows."

That is the last we hear of Meadows. A Mrs Meadows was at Covent Garden from 1806–7 to 1808–9. One at least of his daughters was again or still at the Royal Circus in 1806 and 1807. One died at London on 29 June 1809, according to the *Gentleman's Magazine* of July.

Meads, Mrs ₍fl. 1740₎, *dancer?*
Mrs Meads was a Sea Nymph in *Neptune's Palace* at Hallam's booth at Bartholomew Fair on 23 August 1740.

Meares. *See also* MORRIS *and* MYERS.

Meares, Mr ₍fl. 1749–1760₎, *tailor, dresser?*
The Mr Meares who was paid £2 11s. on 29 September 1749 for work done as a tailor at Covent Garden was probably the "Mearns" on that theatre's paylist on 22 September 1760 listed as a dresser at a daily wage of 2s. 6d. Meares was mentioned frequently in accounts in 1759 and 1760.

Meares, Milbert. *See* MORRICE, MILBERT.

Mears. *See also* MEYERS *and* MORRICE.

Mears, Miss ₍fl. 1730–1733₎, *dancer, actress.*
Miss Mears played a Shepherdess in *The Fairy Queen* at Drury Lane Theatre on 15 May 1730. She was a Follower of the Deities of Pleasure and a Syren in *Cephalus and Procris* beginning 28 October 1730. She remained at Drury Lane

until the end of November 1733, frequently offering entr'acte dances and appearing as a Beggarwoman in *The Jovial Crew*, one of John's wives in *Don John*, Juno in *Bayes's Opera*, an Hour of Sleep, an Attendant on Andromeda, and a Mezzetin Woman in *Perseus and Andromeda*, a Servant in *The Devil to Pay*, Nonparel in *The Covent Garden Tragedy*, Lucy in *The Mock Doctor*, Mrs Vixen in *The Beggar's Opera*, Isabella in *The Devil of a Duke*, a Milkmaid, the second Yeoman's Wife, and a Peasant in *The Country Revels*, a Country Lass in *Betty*, Teazer in *Caelia*, a French Woman in *Harlequin Restor'd*, a Gardener's Wife (and her role of a Syren) in *Cephalus and Procris*, Pallas in *The Judgment of Paris*, a Fingalian and Palla in *The Harlot's Progress*, and Iris in *Harlequin Doctor Faustus*. At the Fielding-Hippisley booth at Bartholomew Fair on 22 August 1732 Miss Mears danced an unspecified role in *The Envious Statesman*.

"Mechanical Artist From London, The." *See* KENYON, MR.

Mechel. *See* MICHEL.

Mechin. *See* MACHEN.

Mechlin or **Mecklin.** *See* MACKLIN.

Medbourne, Matthew *d. 1680, actor, playwright.*

Matthew Medbourne was a member of the Duke's Company at the Lincoln's Inn Fields Theatre in 1661–62 and one of the players who assaulted Edward Thomas, a messenger from the Revels office, on 4 July 1662. All the actors involved in that incident were identified as from the parish of St Clement Danes, but Medbourne was a Roman Catholic and not a member of that church. He and his fellows confessed to beating up poor Thomas and on 18 July were fined 3s. 4d. each.

Medbourne's earliest role is not known. A manuscript cast in a copy of *The Witty Combat* at Ohio State University has him down for the King; the Duke's Company production of that play may date 1662–63. He certainly played Delio in *The Duchess of Malfi* on 30 September

1662, and his part (or sides) for the character of Trico in *Ignoramus*, performed at court on 1 November 1662, is now at Harvard. On 23 February 1663 he was Filomarini in *The Slighted Maid*. In 1663–64 he appeared as Capito in *The Step-Mother*, Cardinal Campeius and Cranmer in *Henry VIII*, and the Count of Blamount in Boyle's *Henry V* (though the prompter Downes remembered Medbourne as playing Clermont). In 1664–65 he was Lennox in *Macbeth* and Thuricus in *Mustapha*.

During the plague that closed the theatres Medbourne may have turned his hand to playwriting. *Saint Cecily or the Convert Twins*, a tragedy, was published in 1666 with a dedication signed by Medbourne. The title page lists E. M. as the author; *The London Stage* indexes the play as by an anonymous author, but Nicoll assigns it to Medbourne. In any case, it seems not to have been acted.

After theatrical activity resumed, Medbourne was again a member of the Duke's players, but *The London Stage* does not list him as active until 1668–69, and for that season no roles are known for him. The following season he ran into difficulties. A Lord Chamberlain's warrant dated 9 December 1669 directed that Medbourne should be arrested for disorderly behavior, and he was suspended from the Duke's Company. He petitioned against the actor-managers Betterton and Harris, asking to be promoted or discharged; a hearing was called on 8 January 1670, the outcome of which is unclear. His version of *Tartuffe*, was published in 1670 and performed either about May of that year, as *The London Stage* lists it, or the fall or winter of 1669–70, as Robert Hume argues. In any case, Medbourne spoke the epilogue, and the performance took place at the King's Company playhouse in Bridges Street.

By 10 January 1671 Medbourne was again in the Duke's Company, acting Smerdis in *Cambyses* at Lincoln's Inn Fields Theatre. During the remainder of that season he appeared as Sir Grave Solymour in *The Six Days' Adventure*, Friendly in *The Town Shifts*, and Theodore in *Juliana*. *The London Stage* lists him as playing Herod in *Herod and Mariamne* in September 1671, but Hume has made a case for that work not having been performed until about August 1673. At the new Dorset Garden Theatre in late November 1671 Medbourne played Alphonso in *Charles VIII*, and during the rest of the season he was Delio in *The Duchess of Malfi* and Don Gerardo in *Fatal Jealousy*.

Except for the 1673–74 season, during which we have no record of him, Medbourne performed at Dorset Garden from 1672–73 to his imprisonment in 1679 in connection with the Popish Plot. His parts included Muchland in *The Morning Ramble*, Lenox in *Macbeth*, Lysander in *The Reformation*, Hametalhaz in *The Empress of Morocco*, Clarmount in *Love and Revenge*, the King of China in *The Conquest of China*, the Ghost in *Hamlet*, Agis in *Alcibiades*, Lord Drybone in *The Country Wit*, Morat in *Ibrahim*, Rui-Gomez in *Don Carlos*, Mendozo in *Abdelazer*, Don Ruis de Moncado in *The Wrangling Lovers*, Captain Tilbury in *Madam Fickle*, Paulinus in *Titus and Berenice*, Montano in *Pastor Fido*, Canidius in Sedley's *Antony and Cleopatra*, Don Pedro in *The Rover*, Traumatius in *The Constant Nymph*, Lysimachus in *The Siege of Babylon*, Demetrius in Shadwell's *Timon of Athens*, Carlos in *The Counterfeits*, and Agamemnon in *The Destruction of Troy* (in November 1678, his last known new role).

Medbourne was accused of high treason on 23 October and sent to Newgate on 26 November 1678. In the *Calendar of State Papers Domestic* under the date 3 February 1679 is a note by Sir J. Williamson: "Mr. Oates. Phillips in Black Friars at the Wonder Tavern.—Swears that Medbourne's wife, in presence of another woman, offered in her husband's name to make him a man for ever, if he could invalidate Oates' testimony. Mrs. Medbourne at Thavies' Inn in Plough Yard &c." On 7 February he wrote, "Phillips swears a certain woman brought to him by Mrs. Medbourne offered him money to swear that Oates offered him money to bring witnesses against Medburne." The actor was still languishing in prison on 8 February 1679, though others had been released.

About mid-May 1679 Medbourne declared his will: he wished everything he owned to be given to his wife Catherine. He was at that time still in Newgate and sick. He gave his address as the parish of St Andrew, Holborn. Matthew Medbourne died on 19 March 1680. Langbaine said that Medbourne was "One, whose good parts deserv'd a better fate than to die in prison, as he did in the time of the late Popish-Plot; thro' a too forward and indiscreet Zeal for a mistaken Religion." Davies, writing over a century later, called Medbourne a man

of learning and accomplishments who had been favored by the Earl of Dorset. Summers, citing Smith's *Intrigues of the Popish Plot* and Dates's *True Narrative*, says that the actor had belonged to a club that met at the Pheasant Inn in Fuller's Rents which did not allow religious discussions and was made up of both Protestants and Catholics. Medbourne may have been unjustly accused.

Medicine, Joseph [*fl.* 1787], *equilibrist.*

A Chester playbill of 29 October 1787 advertised a troupe from Sadler's Wells in London. The bill provided that

The CLOWN, JOSEPH MEDICINE, Will perform many NEW and CURIOUS EQUILIBRIUMS, Particularly He will go through a HOOP with a PYRAMID of THIRTEEN GLASSES on his HEAD—Stand on his HEAD on TWO TABLES and TWO CHAIRS, and drink a GLASS of WINE backward from the Floor, beating a DRUM at the same Time.

No descriptions have been found of Medicine's London performances.

Medina, Miss [*fl.* 1740–1749], *actress, singer.*

On 31 December 1740 at the Goodman's Fields playhouse, Polly in *The Beggar's Opera* was performed by "a Gentlewoman who never appeared on any stage before." She was Miss Medina, and in addition to Polly, she appeared during the 1740–41 season in the title role in *Flora*, Angelica in *The Anatomist*, and Thalia in *Harlequin Student*. She also sang in *King Arthur* and offered entr'acte songs. Even before her first appearance an anonymous poet was moved to send some anticipatory verses in her praise to the *Daily Post*, on 12 December 1740:

Still Polly's tender notes our ears invite,
New charms we find & taste again delight.

The poet was convinced that "Gay modell'd every line for you alone." Miss Medina used Polly for her solo benefit on 8 April 1741.

She continued at Goodman's Fields in 1741–42, singing between the acts and playing an unnamed part in *Trick for Trick*, Cicely in *Pamela*, Mrs Trippit in *The Lying Valet*, and Betty in *The Way of the World*. Tickets for her shared benefit with Mrs Yates on 19 April 1742 were made available at her lodgings at Mr Fearnley's in Somerset Street, Goodman's Fields, according to a clipping in the Enthoven Collection. Then Miss Medina was not mentioned in London bills until 18 February 1746, when she returned to Goodman's Fields to sing Arne's "Behold the sweet Flowers," "Come Rosalind," and "Blow ye Bleak Winds around." She sang again on the twenty-seventh.

Miss Medina was absent from the London stage, again for three years, and when she returned it was as a Shepherdess in *The Triumph of Peace* at Drury Lane on 21 February 1749; she was replaced after that one performance and not heard from again.

Medina, Maria. *See* VIGANÒ, SIGNORA SALVATORE.

Medley, George ₍*fl.* 1794–1796?₎, *singer.*
Doane's *Musical Directory* of 1794 listed George Medley, of No 13, Grosvenor Place, Pimlico, as a tenor who sang in the choirs of the Chapel Royal and St Peter's (presumably Westminster Abbey). He may have been the Mr Medley who played Skirmish in the musical farce *The Deserter* at Drury Lane Theatre on 11 May 1796. The *European Magazine* in June reported the performance:

A riot took place this evening, occasioned by the performance of Skirmish by a new actor. This person, wanting every quality requisite for the stage, performed so very much to the dissatisfaction of the audience, that the piece was mutilated in such a manner that for some time it was insisted on that the whole should be repeated more perfectly and by another actor. This being impossible, some mischief was threatened, but after a short time the disturbance ceased.

"Medley, Matt." *See* ASTON, ANTHONY.

Medlicott, Mr ₍*fl. c.*1786–1787₎, *dancer.*
The bills for the Royal Circus show that Mr Medlicott danced in a piece called *Nobody; or Two Faces are Better than One*, probably in the spring of 1786. He danced again at the Circus in 1787. He was probably related to Miss Harriet Medlicott, but in what way we do not know.

Medlicott, Harriet ₍*fl.* 1769–1786₎, *dancer, actress.*
On 19 October 1769 Thomas King, the manager of Sadler's Wells, signed an agreement with Peter D'Egville, the Drury Lane dancer, agreeing that Harriet Medlicott and other pupils of D'Egville would not dance anywhere but at the "Theatres Royal in London" unless King gave his permission. At that time Miss Medlicott probably danced at Sadler's Wells and Drury Lane. She was certainly performing at Drury Lane in the fall of 1777, for on 15 November she was paid £2 18s. for 29 days.

On 30 June 1778 she played a principal but unspecified role in *Dissipation* at the Richmond Theatre, and she also danced that night. She performed there throughout the summer season. The Mrs Medlicott who was listed as a figure dancer at the King's Theatre in 1783 (in a document in the Lord Chamberlain's accounts) was probably Harriet. About the spring of 1786 Miss Medlicott danced at the Royal Circus in *Nobody; or Two Faces are Better than One.* Also in that piece was a Mr Medlicott, doubtless a relative. The following October Harriet danced in *The Industrious Mechanick* at the Circus, after which references to her ceased.

Megalli, Domenico ₍*fl.* 1760₎, *singer.*
Domenico Megalli sang Alceste in *Antigona* at the King's Theatre on 17 April 1760—and presumably at other performances through 15 May, though casts were not named in the bills.

Meggs, George ₍*fl.* 1761₎, *pugilist.*
According to Pierce Egan's *Boxiana* George Meggs fought Bill Stevens at the tennis court in James Street (a sometime theatre) in 1761.

Meggs, Mary *d.* 1691, *concessionaire.*
Mary Meggs, better known as "Orange Moll," was considered a regular member of the King's Company in early 1663. Upon payment of £100 on 10 February 1663 the widow Meggs of St Paul, Covent Garden, was granted by the theatre sharers "full, free, & sole liberty, licence, power, & authority to vend, utter, & sell oranges, Lemons, fruit, sweetmeats, & all manner of fruiterers & Confectioners wares & commodities" in all parts of the theatre except the upper gallery of the new Bridges Street playhouse. Her license ran for 39 years, and cost her a daily fee of 6s. 8d. The rules governing her sales activity were that she should employ no more than three people in one day, two in the pit and one in the boxes "& lower rooms."

The Lord Chamberlain's accounts contain

numerous references to Mrs Meggs over the years. On 21 November 1664 she was sworn a "Comoedian" in the King's troupe (the term applied to any member of the company, regardless of duties); on 1 April 1668 she went to law against the court musician John Singleton (probably for a debt); in September 1669 one John Bathurst sued her; and on 5 November of that year the actress Rebecca Marshall had Mrs Meggs apprehended for abusing her and "Comitting other Misdemeanours." William Grant, Vicar of Isleworth sued Mary on 13 June 1670 for money she owed him for the previous three years for eight acres of fruit trees. In November Henry Poole was given permission to sue Mrs Meggs and the musician Singleton. The fire that consumed the Bridges Street Theatre in January 1672 began under the stairs where Mrs Meggs kept her supplies. On 10 November 1682 Mrs Meggs went to law against Charles Killigrew over the lease to sell fruit at Drury Lane under the new union of the King's and Duke's troupes. That squabble was a serious one, for the United Company evidently planned to oust Mrs Meggs and put someone of their own choosing in charge of the concession. Mary claimed in court in 1684 that the managers kept her out of Drury Lane until October 1683.

The managers allowed her to return, but by 1690 they complained that she had fallen behind in her rent (for a few years she had apparently been allowed to operate without payment). Mary claimed that after 10 February 1690 the managers had prohibited her from selling her fruit, so she had retaliated by refusing to pay her rent. The court case brought out the fact that she kept no business records but operated on a day-to-day basis.

Orange Moll was more than a concessionaire, as we learn from the diary of Samuel Pepys. In August 1667 he spoke of Moll being the carrier of messages to him from his actress friend Mrs Knepp and the purveyor generally of theatre gossip, especially concerning the intrigues of former orange girl Nell Gwynn. She performed emergency operations, too. The following November, wrote Pepys, "a gentleman of good habit, sitting just before us, eating some fruit in the midst of the play, did drop down as dead, being choked; but with much ado Orange Moll did thrust her finger down his throat, and brought him to life again."

It is probable that the Mrs Meggs who owned two pieces of property shown on Lacy's 1673 map of the parish of St Paul, Covent Garden was Mary. The plots measured approximately 125' by 40' and 50' by 25' and were adjacent to one another in the center of the block bounded by Russell Street, Bridges Street, Drury Lane, and the back side of White Hart Yard. The property was apparently accessible by means of a narrow lane from Bridges Street. That Mrs Meggs was fairly prosperous is indicated by the will she caused to be written for her on 24 April 1682. The lease on her concession was by that time worth from £150 to £200; she bequeathed it to her friend Philip Griffin, the actor. To her brother, a mariner, she left three houses, one of which was in 1682 rented for £50 annually to a minister. Mary left to her niece Mary Thomas a diamond ring, a "Turky stone" ring, and all of her wearing apparel. When she made her will she was of the parish of St Martin-in-the-Fields and described herself as still a widow and "weake in body." If she had been ill, she recovered, for she continued operating her concession at the theatre for nine more years. She signed the will by her mark, and it is probable that she was illiterate.

Though Mrs Meggs had once sued the musician John Singleton, they must have become close friends. Not only did she join him in suing Henry Poole in November 1670, but when Singleton wrote his will on 21 January 1685 he appointed Mrs Meggs his co-executor and left her £100. The other executor, Alexander Hicks, did not participate in the proving of Singleton's will on 23 November 1686.

Mary Meggs died on 21 January 1691. Philip Griffin proved her will on 2 December of that year.

Mehun. *See* MOHUN.

Meire. *See* MAER.

Malachlin *See* MACKLIN.

Melini. *See* MELLINI.

Mell, Daniel. *See* MELL, DAVIS.

Mell, Davis   *1604–1662, violinist, composer.*

Davis Mell was born on 15 November 1604 at Wilton, near Salisbury, the son of a servant of William Herbert. He was apprenticed to a clockmaker, but by 1625 he had become a violinist in the King's Musick. At that time Leonard Mell, violinist, and Thomas Mell, wind instrumentalist, were also in the King's Musick. The Lord Chamberlain's accounts mentioned Davis Mell (sometimes Davies or David) occasionally in the 1630s, twice in connection with payments to him for music books and a violin. During the Commonwealth, he supported himself by teaching, and in 1657 was one of the signers of a petition to establish a college of music. He was apparently a court musician for Cromwell.

Anthony à Wood wrote in March 1658 of Mell visiting Oxford and being entertained by local music lovers. "The Company did look upon Mr. Mell to have a prodigious hand on the violin, and they thought that no person, as all London did, could goe beyond him. . . . [He] played farr sweeter than Baltzar, yet Baltzar's hand was more quick." Wood liked Mell, even though he came to be overshadowed as a violinist by Baltzar; Mell "was a well-bred gentleman, and not given to excessive drinking as Baltzar was."

At the Restoration Mell's post in the King's Musick was restored to him, and he was also granted Woodington's place "for the broken consort also" (the band of violins?). The latter post brought him a high salary of £110 annually, to which was added £16 2s. 6d. yearly as a livery allowance (but it was seldom paid on schedule). Pulver states that on 31 May 1661 Mell and George Hudson were given joint direction of the King's band of violins, and Grove says that Mell succeeded Lanier as Master of the King's band at the Restoration. Nicholas Lanier was regularly listed as master of the King's Musick from 28 August 1660 until his death in 1666, when he was replaced by Louis Grabu. The accounts do not name Mell as leader of the band of 24 violins. The warrant of 31 May 1661 concerning Mell and Hudson stated that they were empowered to report negligence on the part of any members of the band of violins.

The *New Grove* says Davis Mell died on 4 April 1662. Pulver notes that a warrant dated 30 August 1662 stated that William Yowckney was to replace Davies Mell, deceased, at wages of 1s. 8d., but then Pulver cited a warrant of 20 March 1663 showing John Banister as a replacement in the private music for Mell at £110 annually; Pulver took that to mean that Mell probably died in early 1663. But that assumption is incorrect, for Mell's will was proved on 16 May 1662. Mell obviously held two positions at court, as many of the musicians did, a general one as musician in ordinary and a special one as a member (leader?) of the band of violins.

"David" Mell of Poplar in the parish of Stepney had his will drawn up on 3 April 1662, at which time he described himself as sick and weak of body. To his wife Ann he left the income from a house in which Edward Cabell was then living, plus a £10 annuity during her lifetime and £50 in arrears from the King (in 1667 Ann Mell was still owed her late husband's livery allowance from 1661). The remainder of the estate, after all bills were paid, was to go to Mell's daughters Elizabeth and "Abigall," and they were to serve as executrices. Mell's brother-in-law John Allen and Thomas Furner received £5 each for helping his daughters execute his will. "Abigail" Mell alone proved the will on 16 May 1662.

The "Daniel" Mell once mentioned in the Lord Chamberlain's accounts in March 1663 was clearly an error for Davis Mell. Some of Davis Mell's compositions appeared in collections such as *Court Ayres* in 1655, *Courtly Masquing Ayres* in 1662, and the *Division Violin* in 1685. But more significant was Mell's part in the production of Shirley's *The Triumph of Peace* in 1633–34; he received £20 for composing music for the antemasques and accompanying the Grandmasquers' dances. Aubrey in his *Miscellanies* told of a child of Davis Mell who was cured of a crooked back by the touch of a dead hand.

Mell, Thomas   *d. 1666, flutist, sackbut player.*

In his *History of the Violin* van der Straeten states that Thomas Mell was appointed a flutist in the King's Musick in 1612, but there was no mention in the Lord Chamberlain's warrants of Mell until 1625, when he was listed as one of the wind instrumentalists who had been in the service of the late James I. He and the violinists Leonard and Davis Mell were doubtless related in some way; all three were members of the King's Musick under Charles I. An odd warrant dated November 1631 assigned Mell to the place in the wind instruments vacated by the death of William Nokes, yet on 13 December 1632 Mell petitioned for a post in the winds and was told that he would succeed William Nokes. There may have been some reshuffling of positions at that time.

What happened to Thomas Mell during the interregnum is not known; he was again in the King's Musick after the Restoration and performed at the coronation of Charles II. Mell and three others were granted £60 each for life. Each musician was to teach two boys to play instruments, particularly flutes and cornets. Mell also received a livery allowance for his students; warrants for those payments were repeated over the years until Thomas Mell's death in 1666. Administration of his estate was granted on 18 May 1666 to his widow Elizabeth; Mell was described as late of Deptford, Kent. His post at court was filled on 7 December 1666 by Edward Hooton. He still had arrears in salary of £46 10s. 10d. as of 9 January 1669 which, one supposes, his widow kept trying to collect.

Mellini, Eugenia ₁fl. 1748–1755₁, *singer.*
Eugenia Mellini was the first woman (serious roles) in the burletta company, managed by Croza, which performed at the King's Theatre beginning 8 November 1748. The casts were not listed for any of the productions. On 21 March 1749 Signora Mellini sang at the King's Theatre annual benefit for indigent musicians and their families. In 1749–50 the troupe performed at the Haymarket Theatre until 13 January 1750, on which date they returned to the King's. Signora Mellini sang Lavinia in *Il trionfo de Camilla* on 31 March and in the annual benefit for poor musicians on 10 April. Latreille's transcriptions of bills indicates that she probably sang in *Madame Ciano* at the Haymarket on 18 and 21 April. She had a benefit at that house on 28 April, when *Don Calascione* was presented. She was again in London on 29 January 1755, singing in *La serva padrona* at the Haymarket.

Mellish, Mr ₁fl. 1736₁, *actor.*
Mr Mellish played Butler in *The Devil to Pay* at York Buildings on 26 April 1736.

Mellon ₁ or **Malone?or Kinnear?**₁, **Harriot, later Mrs Thomas Coutts the second, then Duchess of St Albans** 1778?–1837, *actress, singer, dancer.*
Seekers after the circumstances of the birth and early life of Harriot Mellon are offered contradictory accounts which seem equally unsatisfactory. Mrs Cornwell Barron-Wilson's account, in *Memoirs of Miss Mellon afterwards Duchess of St Albans* (1887), drawn long after the actress's death, from materials the source of which the author coyly conceals, is fiercely and sentimentally partisan. The memoir by Richard Malloy Westmacott, in *The Age* in 1837, is by an editor who had energetically persecuted his subject in print during the last 20 years of her life. He claimed to have had his facts from a provincial manager who knew Harriot's father.

Harvard Theatre Collection

HARRIOT MELLON

engraving by Ridley, after Allingham

Mrs Barron-Wilson tells a tale of one Sarah (last name unknown), an Irish cotter's handsome daughter, who was a milliner at Cork and who joined Kena's strolling company as wardrobe mistress and ticket seller. She is said to have met and married, on 6 January 1777, a mysterious "Lieutenant Mathew Mellon of the Madras Native Infantry," home on convalescent leave, who shortly departed again for India and died on the voyage. Sarah and her infant, fruit of the brief union, resumed strolling with the Kenas.

Westmacott's version varies greatly:

Harriett [*sic*] Mellon or Malone (the latter being her real name) was born at Kendal in the county of Westmoreland about the year 1770 [*sic*]. Her mother was a servant of all work who travelled with the family of the Bibbys, an itinerant company, who for many years exhibited in the towns on the verge of Lancashire, and Yorkshire, and Westmoreland. Her father and mother were both Irish; the [father] is said to have been a person at one time of some consequence as a commercial man in Dublin, who, becoming charged with treasonable and seditious offences, fled from Ireland and being a man of lively talent and attractive person, sought a refuge from poverty in the profession of a strolling actor—his real name was John Kinnear [*sic*], and if old Mr. Bibby's information was correct, in whose company he acted, his death took place during the infancy of his illegitimate daughter.

Whatever the degree of truth or fiction of that version, Harriot's mother apparently not only always insisted on the father's name having been Mellon, but also hinted broadly that the name was assumed in order to disguise his noble birth. Because of the "nobility" of the father, Sarah's expectations for Harriot and her demands on her, both professional and social, were extravagant. The mother was, in fact, psychotic, veering between extremes of sentimental indulgence of the child back to sudden cruelty to her. Those difficulties were added to the usual hardships of the itinerant performer. In addition, bizarre things happened in Harriot's picaresque youth: Harriot was once so frightened of her mother's violence that she ran away, slept exhausted in a charcoal pit, dreamed that its fires were hell, and reappeared to frighten the company, black from head to foot. Their lodgings were once in a cellar next to a graveyard; a weak wall gave way and a coffin burst through it. Harriot acquired a varied experience of life on the road.

At Wigan, Lancashire, sometime around 1782, Sarah Mellon at 29 married her second husband, a meek 18-year-old violinist named Thomas Entwisle. An early history of Wigan compiled in 1829 says that Harriot played "boys' and girls' characters" there. Kena's company falling on hard times, the Entwisles deserted and went to Preston, and it was only then, insists Mrs Barron-Wilson, that they met Thomas Bibby and joined his company. During a long pause of the company at Ulverstone, Harriot was given her first regular schooling. At age 10 she looked at least 13, and Bibby chose as her first advertised part Little Pickle in *The Spoiled Child*, which, the surviving bill shows, she played on 16 October 1787. It was a resounding success, prompting a gift to Harriot of 10*s*. from the manager, which her mother promptly appropriated. Harriot's second part was Priscilla Tomboy in *The Romp*. Thus she had already fallen into her most admired line of roles, farce. But she also sang. On 11 February 1789, according to a bill of the Leigh Theatre, she played the First Speaking Witch in *Macbeth* and Lucinda in *Love in a Village* and sang "The Sooner the Better, a favourite Scotch song."

By the end of 1789 she was playing older parts, like Phoebe in *As You Like It*, Narcissa in *Inkle and Yarico*, and Gillian in *The Quaker*. Harriot was on her way. But the Entwisles had a joint salary of only 17*s*. 6*d*. per week, which Entwisle tried to supplement by teaching. They began to see Harriot as an economic mainstay; so when Bibby refused to pay her more than 4*s*. 6*d*. per week, the family deserted him for the management of Stanton, who headed a sharing company based on Stafford, but which made the rounds of Newcastle-under-Lyne, Barton, Ashbourne, Walsall, Bridgewater, Nantwich, Newport, Drayton, Leek, and Lichfield. Harriot was patronised by a prominent Stafford banker named Wright, whose daughters took delight in giving her clothes and lending her jewelry for important roles. She added to her repertoire Sophia in *The Road to Ruin*, Betty Blackberry in *The Farmer*, Jenny Wronghead in *The Provok'd Husband*, Kathleen in *The Poor Soldier*, Cowslip in *The Agreeable Surprise*, Beatrice in *Much Ado about Nothing*, Celia and Audrey in *As You Like It*, Lydia

Languish in *The Rivals*, and Moggy in *The Highland Reel*, in which she excited the young bloods with her dancing.

In October 1794 Richard Brinsley Sheridan happened to come from London to Stafford for the races and saw her as Letitia Hardy in *The Belle's Stratagem* and Priscilla Tomboy in *The Romp*. Sheridan expressed polite approval and also politely (but insincerely) promised, when pressed, to consider her for his Drury Lane company. He was not allowed to forget, for the determined Mrs Entwisle and her daughter showed up in London in June 1795 and took lodgings in the Strand. When Sheridan shunned them they moved to a cottage in New Street, Southwark, and wrote to the banker Wright, who successfully exerted pressure on Sheridan to engage Harriot.

Her London debut has generally been said to have been as Lydia Languish, which, indeed, she played on 30 October 1795, advertised only as a "Young Lady" from the Stafford Theatre. But she had first stepped onto the Drury Lane stage on 1 October, as one of the innumerable Captives in the spectacle *Lodoiska*. Of her Lydia Languish, a newspaper critic said: "Her appearance was strikingly handsome, her voice musical, her action powerful when not checked by fear, and there were some tones of archness at times which practice may increase; so it would be unfair to call last night a failure, though she did not succeed." Sheridan established her salary at 30s. a week.

Harriot had ample opportunity that first season to study her idol, the incomparable Dorothy Jordan, in the effervescent line of girlish characters which Harriot most coveted. But for the time being she had to be content to understudy her betters and fill any vacancy of which she was capable. The bills show many additions to her repertoire during the 1795–96 season: both Nell and Clara in *The Adopted Child*, Lady Godiva in *Peeping Tom*, one of the "General Chorus" of *The Pirates*, Lucy in *The Recruiting Officer*, Maria in *The Spoiled Child*, Lucy in *The Country Girl*, Miss La Blonde in *The Romp*, one of the chorus of *The Surrender of Calais*, Blanche in *King John*, Peggy in *The Suicide*, a Villager in *The Mountaineers*, the original Minerva in William Linley's pantomime *Harlequin Captive*, the original Mary in James Cobb's musical farce *The Shepherdess of Cheapside*, Lettice in *The Plain Dealer*, Berinthia in *The Trip to Scarborough*, one of the chorus of George Colman's new, ill-received melodrama *The Iron Chest*, the original Margery in Samuel Birch's melodrama *The Smugglers*, one of the Nieces in *The Critic*, one of the chorus of Prince Hoare's new melodrama *Mahmoud; or, The Prince of Persia*, Jenny in *The Gentle Shepherd*, and Miss Grantham in *The Liar*.

On 14 March 1796 "The Publick" were "most respectfully informed that, on account of the sudden Indisposition of Mrs Jordan, Miss Mellon will undertake the character of Amanthis [in *The Child of Nature*] and humbly solicits their indulgence." On 6 May Harriot replaced Maria Theresa De Camp as Penelope in *The Romp*. On 23 May, as a mark of favor, she was given the original Philotes in J. P. Kemble's alteration of Dryden's and Cibber's *Comical Lovers*, for Mrs Kemble's farewell benefit. On 17 March 1796, having found the three-mile distance from Southwark too exhausting, Mrs Entwisle and Harriot moved to No 17, Little Russell Street, directly opposite the theatre.

Michael Kelly testified that in her first Drury Lane season Harriot "proved herself a valuable acquisition to our dramatic corps. She was a handsome girl and much esteemed" by all. Mrs Barron-Wilson quoted an actor who, she says, came to Drury Lane about the time of Harriot's debut: "Miss Mellon was a remarkably handsome brunette, but did not look a bit like an actress. She was much more like one of the genuine beauties of a quiet village two hundred miles from town." He declared that she was at first very little noticed among the reigning fascinators then at Drury Lane—Mrs Jordan, Mrs Goodall, Miss de Camp, the majestic Mrs Siddons, "the Cleopatra looking Mrs Powell, and that most graceful and lovely of all syrens, Mrs Crouch. These ladies had a style, you could classify them as divinities; but Miss Mellon was merely a countrified girl, blooming in complexion, with a tall, fine figure, raven locks, ivory teeth, a cheek like a peach, and coral lips. All she put you in mind of was, a country road and a pillion." Prominent actors

spoke very highly of her indeed . . . and she was often praised for her good-natured readiness to play for anyone in cases of illness, &c. On these occasions (if very sudden) the higher performers would say, "Miss Mellon can do it; I saw her play it very well at such a place [in the provinces]." These things made her very popular with management, for she

HARRIOT MELLON, as the Comic Muse

by Stump

was indefatigable; and, after flaunting as the fine lady in the absence of some greater actress, she returned to the secondary business she was accustomed to play with a good grace and good humour. Old Wewitzer was her friend and adviser. . . . I fancy he was a friend of the family; he knew her mother very well.

Harriot was also much befriended by Elizabeth Farren, soon to be Countess of Derby, and by the veteran comedian Dicky Suett. Suett chided her for piling on makeup and advised her that her own natural, dramatic, high coloring— the astonishing complexion and jet black hair— was more effective.

In the summer of 1796 Harriot went to the Liverpool Theatre Royal. Mrs Siddons came there for a fortnight's engagement and kindly and pointedly spoke of her before the as-

sembled company as her "young friend," a person of strict principles and good manners, giving Harriot great cachet at that theatre, then and later. She blossomed at Liverpool that summer, taking more than 50 roles, many of them leading ones which she would seldom or never play in London. The ones that we have not yet found her playing included: Julia Faulkner in *The Way to Get Married*, Sophia in *The Road to Ruin*, Ophelia in *Hamlet*, Maria in *The School for Scandal*, Phoebe in *Rosina*, Fatima in *The Revenge*, Nancy Lovell in *The Suicide*, Hero in *Much Ado about Nothing*, Tilburina in *The Critic*, Rosina in *The Spanish Barber*, Estifania in *Rule a Wife and Have a Wife*, Roxalana in *The Sultan*, Cecilia in *Speculation*, Mariana in *The Dramatist*, Thisbe in *Crotchet Lodge*, Joanna in *The Deserted Daughter*, Nancy in *Three Weeks after Marriage*, Cherry in *The Beaux' Stratagem*, Miss Woburn in *Every One Has His Own Fault*, Angelina in *Love Makes a Man*, Madge in *Love in a Village*, Rosalind in *As You Like It*, Miss Tittup in *Bon Ton*, Miss Leeson in *The School for Wives*, Emmeline in *The Doldrums*, Maud in *Peeping Tom*, Louisa Dudley in *The West Indian*, Miss Lucy in *The Virgin Unmask'd*, Flora in *The Wonder*, Sabina Rosni in *First Love*, the title role in *Polly Honeycomb*, the Page in *The Follies of a Day*, Fanny in *Lock and Key*, Clara in *The Masked Friend*, Lady Touchwood in *The Belle's Stratagem*, Joanna in *The Page*, Agnes in *The Mountaineers*, Lady Flippant in *Fashionable Levities*, Dorothy in *Heigho for a Husband*, Nell in *The Devil to Pay*, Annette in *Robin Hood*, Emily Tempest in *The Wheel of Fortune*, Annabel in *The Man in Ten Thousand*, Barbara in *Love and Money*, Mrs Kitty in *High Life below Stairs*, and Miranda in *The Tempest*. Her benefit night netted her the goodly sum of £130.

The critic for the London journal *How Do You Do* assured its readers on 24 September 1796 that "Miss Mellon improves amazingly, and will with practice become a valuable addition. . . . She seems in a fair way to have [that practice]." Indeed, with two dozen roles in her first London season and an extensive provincial repertoire, Harriot was already an experienced trouper before she was 20. In her second London season, 1796–97, she played many of her former roles and learned several new ones: Charlotte in *Who's the Dupe?*, Phillis in *The Conscious Lovers*, Cleone in *The Distrest Mother* (on an evening when at short notice she also replaced Maria Theresa De Camp in the second performance of S. J. Arnold's comic opera *The Shipwreck*), Inis in *The Wonder*, Clarissa in *All in the Wrong*, Lucetta in *The Suspicious Husband*, Nancy in *A Bold Stroke for a Wife*, and the original Cicely Copsley in Frederick Reynolds's comedy *The Will*.

Harriot was winsome and hard-working and lucky but she would for many years labor in the shadow of Dorothy Jordan, whose talents in the same lines of acting were far larger and who would not leave Drury Lane until 1809. Their chief types—singing and dancing flirts, charming soubrettes, hoydenish country girls, and mischievous serving wenches—being vir-

Harvard Theatre Collection

HARRIOT MELLON, as Anne Lovely

engraving by Alais

tually the same, Miss Mellon was of course accused of imitation. "Could prettiness do all she wishes alone / She might sit as incumbent on Fame's glassy throne," but, alas, " 'tis Jordan in all," decided John Williams in *A Pin Basket to the Children of Thespis* (1797).

But neither the looks nor the personalities of Mrs Jordan and Miss Mellon were at all alike, and as time went on Harriot developed a style of her own. She also gained a considerable following in London, not to speak of the devotees she had accumulated at Liverpool, where she returned on 21 June 1797 for a long engagement. The *Monthly Mirror* reported in July that she "is the regular heroine and is in considerable esteem with the Liverpool people." That year Harriot displayed her characteristic generosity when she invited the widow of the actor Robert Benson, who had committed suicide in 1796, to share her house.

In Liverpool she went on building her repertoire: Maria in *George Barnwell*, Jessy Oatland in *A Cure for the Heartache*, Flora in *The Midnight Hour*, Miss Dorellon in *Wives as They Were*, Agnes in *Raymond and Agnes*, Ruth in *The Honest Thieves*, Dolly in *The Woodman*, Annette in *Robin Hood*, Lady Danvers in *Fortune's Fools*, Harriet in *He Would Be a Soldier*, Josephine in *The Children of the Wood*, Chloe in *The Lottery*, and Rosalba in *The Italian Monk*.

At Drury Lane in 1797–98, she acquired Betty in *The Clandestine Marriage*, a part in Birch's new farce *Fast Asleep*, Kitty Sprightly in *All the World's a Stage*, Susan in *The Follies of a Day*, the original Grace in John O'Keeffe's comedy *She's Eloped*, and Alithea in *The Country Girl*. At Liverpool in the summer of 1798 she added Rose Sydney in *Secrets Worth Knowing*, Charlotte in *The Apprentice*, Fanny in *The Shipwreck*, Eva in *Curiosity*, Jacinta in *Lovers' Quarrels*, Angela in *The Castle Spectre*, Fadladinida in *Chrononhotonthologos*, Jane in *Wild Oats*, Donna Olivia in *A Bold Stroke for a Husband*, and Miss Price in *Ben the Sailor*. She cleared £240 at her benefit. She had been scheduled to act in the afterpiece *The Deserter* on 2 August, but that was prevented by the death onstage that night of John Palmer, who was acting a leading role in the mainpiece.

In 1799 J. C. Cross offered Harriot twice her Drury Lane salary (of £4 a week) to perform at the Royal Circus, and old Philip Astley tried to inveigle her to Dublin to star in the minor theatre he planned to erect there. She refused them both. She did, however, allow herself to be persuaded to two performances at the George Inn in Epsom that year. Perhaps her reluctance to cut ties to Drury Lane is understandable, when the hard road which led her there is considered. Still, she was dissatisfied with the number and quality of her roles, being hemmed in on the low-comedy side by Mrs Jordan and the high-comedy side by Miss De Camp.

The critics gave her full credit for professionalism within her limitations. When the *Dramatic Oracle* reviewed her Patty in *Inkle and Yarico* in the 1800–1801 season, the reviewer thought that "The archness and cunning, the pertness and loquacity, of the chambermaid, she admirably exhibited; and such an exhibition must be acknowledged to evince no inferior powers of comic delineation." Her Wishwell, in *The Double Gallant*, elicted from the *Morning Chronicle* the opinion: "Where playfulness rather than sensibility is to be portrayed, she certainly stands unrivalled."

In 1801–2, her salary was £5, but her only notable acquisition was Lady Contest in *The Wedding Day*. That season, she served as stage-manager of the amateur theatricals at Strawberry Hill, with the Earl of Mount Edgecumbe, Lady Elizabeth Cole, the Misses Berry, and other fashionables. In 1801–2 her new part was Sophia in *The Brothers*. Her salary that season was still £5 per week, compared to Mrs Jordan's £30 and Miss De Camp's £12. In 1802–3, though she added the well-received characters Alexa in *The Hero of the North*, Mary Woodland in *The Marriage Promise*, and Rosaria in *She Wou'd and She Wou'd Not*, critics were still offering her the oblique compliment. For her Lydia Languish—her London debut-character and still one of her favorites—the *Post* said she was "entitled to no common praise. She has much of the *naïveté* and giddy cunning of Mrs. Jordan, with grace and simplicity spontaneously imparted by her own nature and judgment." And again, when she played Alithea along with Mrs Jordan's Miss Peggy on 3 January 1804, the *Post* found that "Her manner [was] full of sweetness, simplicity and refinement." Yet, she "in many respects most happily imitate[d] Mrs. Jordan" and "drew, next after" that lady, "the greatest share of attention and applause."

During those first nine years of their London

residence the fiery and uncertain temper of Mrs Entwisle, however uncomfortable it was for Harriot, had proved in other ways useful. She stood between Harriot and the managers. She insisted on strict application to theatrical duty on Harriot's part. Most important from her point of view—and, as it turned out, from her daughter's as well—she fended off the attentions of impecunious actors and others who did not meet the exalted social and financial qualifications she had drawn up for any permanent connection with her daughter. But by 1804 Harriot, at about 26, was ready for a show of independence and she had temper nearly equal, when aroused, to her mother's. When her stepfather, who had been engaged for years in the Drury Lane band, was dismissed in March 1804, the Entwisles, pushed by Harriot, removed themselves to Cheltenham and opened a music shop in the High Street. Harriot and a friend, Sarah Stevenson, went on living in Little Russell Street.

But fate was preparing a scenario which would be very agreeable to everybody in the Entwisle family. Harriot twice visited her mother at Cheltenham during the summer of 1804, each time playing a few nights before and after going to reap her golden harvest at Liverpool. Greatly admired at Cheltenham, she was given a benefit under the patronage of Viscountess Templeton. She also obtained, through the influence of a Colonel MacMahon, an intimate of the Prince of Wales, the appointment of her stepfather as postmaster of the town. Finally, whether by accident or the deliberate contrivance of her mother, she met Thomas Coutts.

Coutts, a son of the Lord Provost of Edinburgh, had founded, with his brother James, the banking company of Coutts and Company in the Strand and had become in 1778 its sole proprietor. Supposed to be one of the richest men in England, he was certainly, as money manager for George III and numbers of the Court, one of the most influential. When Harriot met him he was a lonely, diffident, shabbily dressed man of 69, shrewd in business and very charitable, but with few other interests except occasional theatre-going. His wife, the former Susan Starkie, had been a servant of his brother's. She was in 1804 a housebound invalid with no memory, completely oblivious to her surroundings, but Coutts cared for her devotedly in his own house in Stratton Street.

National Portrait Gallery

HARRIOT MELLON, when Duchess of St Albans
by Beechey

Their three daughters had been married for years—Sophia in 1793 to Sir Francis Burdett, Bart., Susan in 1796 to the Earl of Guilford, and Frances in 1800 to the Marquis of Bute. Coutts, like everyone else, was charmed with Harriot, and she found him kind and fatherly. Mrs Entwisle found him in every way satisfactory.

It is difficult to believe, as some of Harriot's earlier defenders affected to believe, that the relationship was, for ten years or even for very long, platonic. But it is easy to see—from letters left by both principals and from the sympathetic accounts of friends—that there was great and loyal affection on both sides, and a considerable degree of understanding from Coutts's daughters. Many of the public paragraphers and caricaturists were not so understanding. They needed someone besides Dora Jordan and her Duke of Clarence to pillory, and it was from this period that the notoriety of Harriot Mellon began. There were attempts, at first, to conceal the relationship. When a decided difference in the style of Harriot's living at the Little Russell Street house became apparent, her old friend the actor Ralph Wewitzer invented a tale that she had won £5000 in a lottery and declared that he had bought the ticket for her.

Meanwhile, Harriot continued with her career. In 1804–5, she added two parts of particular interest, Polly in *The Land We Live In* and Volante in John Tobin's *The Honeymoon*, the latter a role in which she would be warmly approved season after season. With the career of Mrs Jordan gradually winding down, Harriot was finally achieving something like stardom. She added few new roles in her later years but was sustained by audiences delighted to see her in her long-accumulated repertoire of standard parts. Her professional satisfactions were interrupted by some annoyances. She had to endure the child acting sensation Master Betty, the "Young Roscius," as Captain Flash to her Miss Biddy in *Miss in Her Teens*. When Charles Lamb's farce *Mr. H.* was produced, he insisted on casting it with her as heroine and R. W. Elliston as hero; Elliston was drunk as usual, and it failed. Some of her "younger" roles she was finally forced in 1812, because of her increasing size, to abandon to the eager hands of Mrs Glover, Miss Kelly, or Mrs Orger. By 1814–15 she was earning £12 per week,

but that sum was now, of course, only symbolically important.

With Coutts's money, Harriot had already expanded to some extent the scale of her impulsive generosity. A woman who recalled being taken, as a child, to the site, on the evening after the terrible fire which destroyed Covent Garden Theatre on 20 September 1809, described Miss Mellon standing at the window of her house opposite, watching the exhumation of bodies from the ruins: "She was dressed in a blue satin pelisse, looking lovely in her anxiety; and each time she appeared at the window she was received with animated cheers by the crowd, who seemed ready to worship her." She had provided a large barrel of ale for the laborers and paid them £5 for each person found alive and £2 for the recovery of each corpse.

By the beginning of the 1814–15 season, rumors of her imminent departure from the stage had increased to the point that certain new parts which she desired—like Ellen in Poole's farce *Intrigue*—were denied her because it was thought a waste of time to rehearse her in them. On 4 January 1815 Mrs Thomas Coutts died, three weeks after scalding herself terribly in an accident, and she was buried on 14 January. A curious train of occurrences followed. On 17 January, as the record in the Vicar General's Office shows, Harriot went in person to that Office and obtained a marriage license. On 18 January she and Coutts were secretly married at St Pancras Church by the curate, the Reverend W. R. Champneys. The ceremony was witnessed, according to the parish register, by the actor James Grant Raymond and one William H. Houghton. But when the surprised vicar of the church read in the *Times* of 2 March a reference to the recent marriage in his church of the richest man in London and a comedienne of note, he investigated. He found that only one of the required two witnesses, Raymond, had actually been present. The Bishop disciplined Champneys the curate for the illegal rite, and another curate presided over a second marriage for Thomas and Harriot, on 12 April 1815. Raymond, despite the bungled first ceremony, is supposed to have received £1000, handed him in a silver snuff-box, for his part in arranging the proceedings.

Thomas Coutts had acquired a rustic estate

in Highgate called Holly Lodge, and there, soon after her marriage, Mrs Coutts embarked on her formidable career as London hostess, on one occasion giving a dinner attended by the Dukes of York, Clarence, Kent, and Sussex. She also embarked on a career of lavish and almost indiscriminate alms-giving. The news spread to the poor of London, whose ranks were swelled in 1817 by thousands of recently discharged soldiers and sailors. As one of her pamphleteering critics wrote: "The construction of a tent at the entrance to her pleasure grounds, the assemblage of an immense crowd of supplicants of every description to whom in her own presence her donations of clothing, food, and money were . . . distributed, was bitterly ridiculed by her enemies and imputed to ostentation. . . ."

Thomas Coutts died on 24 February 1822 at the age of 87 at their house in Stratton Street. Mrs Coutts was chief mourner in the long procession of noblemen's carriages which followed the hearse on its five-days' journey to interment at Wroxton, Oxfordshire. The *Morning Post* reported excitedly:

> Some time previous to his death [Coutts] settled upon Mrs. C. the sum of £600,000 with the house in Stratton Street, all the plate, linen, etc.—the service of plate is said to be the most valuable of any in the country . . . together with the house at Highgate. . . . Mrs. C. is likewise left half-proprietress of his immense banking establishment. . . . [I]t is said there is a balance of £67,000 due to Mrs. C. which will be proved under the will. The whole amount of property (with the annual profits of half the banking business) makes her the richest widow in the United Kingdom.

It was all true.

After 18 months of decorous widowhood Mrs Coutts gave an enormous fête at Holly Lodge, attended by above 700 people of fashion, including the Duke of York, three European princes, three other dukes, six marquises, and 12 earls, with their ladies. Some 2000 coachmen and footmen were also entertained "in the house of the victuallers in the neighborhood," according to the *Post*. The affair drew down on Harriot's head a series of attacks by Theodore Hook in the "Ramsbottom Letters" in *John Bull* and by several others, in which she was aspersed for social climbing, insuffi-

cient distribution of her fortune to Coutts's daughters, and ingratitude to old friends (especially to old Wewitzer, who was seen as one of the authors of her good fortune, left to die neglected). The tone of the attacks may be judged from the title of one of the worst: *Mr. Percy Wyndham's Strictures on an Imposter and Old Actress, formerly Bet the Pot Girl, Alias the Banker's Sham Widow, with Particulars of her Appearance at the Bar of Bow Street, of the Child Manufactory at Highgate, and Madam's Sleeping at the Horns of Kensington.*

Many a mother of a titled but needy son peered covetously at the new widow's wealth. But Harriot's requirements were strict. She wanted not only a peer, but a duke. She wanted not only a kind heart with his coronet—someone like Thomas Coutts, but much younger; she wanted someone she could manage. By 1823 the 46-year-old actress had met and captivated the gentle, rather simple-minded 23-year-old Lord Burford, heir to the land-rich and money-poor old Duke of St Albans. (Perhaps there was a sort of genetic affinity. Burford was descended from the first Duke of St Albans, the illegitimate son of Charles II and the actress Nell Gwynn.) In the autumn of 1824 she toured north to Scotland with Burford, chaperoned by Lady Caroline, one of his sisters. Harriot had known Sir Walter Scott for some years and they liked and respected each other. Scott's biographer Lockhart lightly satirizes her visit to Abbotsford:

> [A]lthough she was considerate enough not to come on him with all her retinue, leaving four of the seven carriages with which she travelled at Edinburgh, the appearance of only three coaches, each drawn by four horses, was rather trying to poor Lady Scott. They contained Mrs. Coutts, her future lord, the Duke of St. Albans, one of his Grace's sisters, a *dame de compagnie*, a brace of physicians, for it had been considered that one doctor might himself be disabled . . . and besides other menials of every grade, two bedchamber women for Mrs. Coutts's own person . . . because in her widowed condition she was fearful of ghosts, and there must be one Abigail for the service of the toilet and a second to keep watch by night. With a little puzzling and cramming all their train found accommodation; but it so happened that there were already in the house several ladies, Scotch and English, of high birth and rank who felt by no means disposed to assist their host and hostess in making Mrs. Coutts's visit agreeable to her.

Harvard Theatre Collection

HARRIOT MELLON, as Louisa Dudley
engraving by Alais

Lockhart's persiflage aside, we know from other testimony that the coldness and rudeness of the ladies was severe enough to penetrate even Harriot's well-tried social armor. Though Scott scolded them, and they behaved better, Harriot and Burford left next day.

But Harriot's generosity and social ingenuity—and the gradual realization by the nobility that she was not only rich but now wielded great influence at Coutts's Bank—made her for some months acceptable to all but a few of society's grand dames. She was invited to the Duke of Devonshire's weekends and was re-

ceived kindly at Court and she gave a *déjeuner* for the Duke of Gordon on his ninetieth birthday. But then rumors of her forthcoming marriage with Burford, who succeeded to the dukedom of St Albans in July 1825, excited another series of printed vilifications. A man named Mitford first tried to blackmail her, then published *The Secret Memoirs of Harriot Pumpkin*, full of dull scurrility. Society began to draw away from her again. She made another visit to Scott and denied to him her intention to marry. He shrewdly surmised otherwise. On 25 November 1825 he wrote in his diary:

If the Duke marries her, he ensures an immense fortune; if she marries him she has the first rank. If he marries a woman older than himself by twenty years, she marries a man younger in wit by twenty degrees. I do not think he will dilapidate her fortune; he seems good and gentle. I do not think she will abuse his softness of *disposition*—shall I say or of—*head*? The disparity of ages concerns no one but themselves; so they have my consent to marry if they can get each other's.

In the months just following, the Duke was constantly with her in her travels, to her house in Brighton, and to her estate near Chelmsford in Essex. On 16 June 1827 their marriage was celebrated privately in the house in Stratton Street by the Duke's clerical uncle, the Reverend Lord Frederick Beauclerk. The Duchess gave her husband £30,000 as a wedding present. Then she, whom Sir Walter had called the "burly, brisk, and jolly" Harriot, "a kind, friendly woman, without either affectation or insolence in the display of her wealth," sat down to write him, who had offered his congratulations. The letter was typically without pretense:

I am a Duchess at last, that is certain, but whether I am the better for it remains to be proved. The Duke is very amiable, gentle, and well disposed, and I am sure he has taken pains enough to accomplish what he says has been the first wish of his heart for the last three years. All this is very flattering to an old lady, and we lived so long in friendship with each other that I was afraid I should be unhappy if I did not say I *will* (whisper it, dear Sir Walter). The name of Coutts—and a right good one it is—is, and ever will be, dear to my heart. What a strange, eventful life has mine been, from a poor little player child, with just food and clothes to cover me, dependent on a very precarious profession, without talent or a friend in the world, "to have seen what I have seen, see what I see." Is it not wonderful? Is it true? Can I believe it?—first the wife of the best, the most perfect being that ever breathed, his love and unbounded confidence in me, his immense fortune honourably acquired by his own industry, all at my command . . . and now the wife of a Duke. You must write my life; the *History of Tom Thumb*, Jack the Giant Killer, and Goody Two Shoes will sink compared with my true history written by the Author of *Waverley*; and that you may do it well I have sent you an inkstand. Pray give it a place on your table in kind remembrance of your affectionate friend, HARRIOT ST. ALBANS.

The Duchess of St Albans resumed and augmented her lavish entertainments. The hostile press, led by Westmacott, editor of *The Age*, resumed and intensified their virulent attacks. On the first anniversary of their marriage the Duke and Duchess gave "A Grand Fête Champêtre" at Holly Lodge, which surpassed everything before and set the pattern for future entertainments: while singers from among her old friends at the theatres sang boat-songs, she presented the Duke with a six-oared cutter, while the crew, attired in his silks, stood by. There were Russian, Spanish, and German ballets and young women vying for archery prizes. The predictable deluge of ridicule followed, *The Age* leading the pack with a poem titled "The Loves of Queen Dollalolla and Lord Noodle." (St Albans and his lady spent some weeks in France in 1828. A short biography in the newspaper *Le Mentor* referred to Harriot's debut as Lydia Languish with unintentional drollery: "Ella debuta à Londres . . . dans le role de Lydie des Longueurs.")

To the end of her life, the Duchess never failed to attend Court in the Season. Though she was still denied entrance to the circles of the most fastidious of the fashionables—the Duchesses of Rutland and Leinster and the Countess of Jersey did not receive her, and she was barred from Almack's Club—she continued to give her fêtes to appreciative crowds of aristocrats. At one, according to the approving description of *The Court Journal*, "A pretty little pastoral incident was arranged on the lawn, where two Alderney cows were introduced dressed in flowers *à la Suisse*, and when Madam Stockhausen had sung the *Ranz des Vaches* which

their appearance suggested, a syllabub . . . was prepared on the spot, which the Duchess distributed with her own hands to several of the most distinguished visitors, his Highness of Gloucester in particular, who seemed to approve it mightily." The cow and the syllabub became permanent features of the fêtes.

The lives of the childish Duke and his shrewd but childlike Duchess wore away in alternation between the delights of Holly Lodge and Stratton Street, varied by Brighton in the winter and summer visits to inspect the tenantry on the Duke's estates. The cholera and influenza epidemics of 1832 sent them flying to Cheltenham, Tunbridge Wells, and Brighton. During the years 1833 through 1836 the Duchess accelerated the rate of her hospitality, sometimes giving three or four elaborate dinners in a week.

In the spring of 1837 she fell ill of a fever which confined her to Holly Lodge for weeks. Then, according to one newspaper account, she "requested to be removed to Piccadilly [Stratton Street]. There on the ground floor, in the great dining-room she lay for two months, quite tranquil and without pain, and then desired to be carried into the room where Mr. Coutts died. There her Grace also expired," on the morning of 6 August 1837. She was buried several days later on the Duke's estate at Redbourne, Lincolnshire, where the Duke erected a monument to her memory.

The Duchess signed her will on 14 March 1837. The sum of £20,000 was to be invested for the benefit of Dame Sophia Burdett, wife of Sir Francis Burdett, Bart. (a daughter of Thomas Coutts), "above the sums I have already given to her," which amounted to £118,602 15s., "and all other sums I may hereafter give her," all such gifts to be free of control of any husband.

To Sophia Burdett's youngest daughter, Harriot's favorite, Angela Georgina Burdett, the bulk of the fortune was bequeathed. To her went "all my watches, jewels, trinkets, and ornaments of the person" and the Duchess's share of the banking house of Coutts. Residuary legatees were to be, in order, the first son (if there should be one) of Angela Georgina; Johanna Frances Burdett (another daughter of Sophia); her male heir; Clara Maria Burdett (another daughter of Sophia); her heir;

Dudley Coutts Marjoribanks, one of Thomas Coutts's godsons; his heir; and Coutts Lindsay, a grandson of Coutts Trotter. Each of those persons, if and when the inheritance should fall to them, were required to change their surnames to Coutts, and the males were to be known as Thomas Coutts.

The Duke of St Albans was left an annuity of £10,000, and life tenure of Holly Lodge and the residence in Stratton Street. He could have an additional £10,000 immediately, to "furnish" the Stratton Street house and could select "so much of the plate purchased by me as shall be of the value of two thousand pounds sterling." Dudley Coutts Marjoribanks and Harriot Marjoribanks, children of Edward Marjoribanks, were each bequeathed £5,000, as was Margaret Trotter, daughter of Sir Coutts Trotter, Bart. A long list of persons in England and Scotland, including the Duchess's servants, were left annuities ranging in size from £50 to £500. The size of the Duchess of St Alban's personal fortune at her death was estimated to be £600,000.

Mrs Barron-Wilson's biography of Harriot Mellon we have had to correct and supplement with contemporary sources, particularly as regards the acting record. But despite its inaccuracies and sentimentalities, it is useful in providing a fund of revealing anecdote. Charles E. Pearce's *The Jolly Duchess, Harriot Mellon, afterwards Mrs. Coutts and the Duchess of St. Albans, A Sixty Years' Gossiping Record of Stage and Society (1777 to 1837)* (1915), is less about the Duchess than about her times. But it sets the record straight on the illegal Coutts marriage and records many rare caricatures.

Portraits of Harriot Mellon include:

1. By W. Beechey. Full-length, when Mrs Coutts. Exhibited at the Royal Academy in 1818. In the National Portrait Gallery, the bequest of W. L. A. Burdett Coutts, 1921.

2. By J. Stump. Miniature. Location unknown. Engraving by J. Hopwood, published by J. Bell, 1813; copies were engraved by T. Blood, as a plate to *European Magazine*, 1815, and by Cooke, as a plate to Oxberry's *New English Drama*, 1822.

3. By John Nixon. Drawing of her at the Bowmen's Theatre, 1799. In the Garrick Club.

4. Engraving by W. Clerk. "The late Duchess of St. Albans, when Miss Mellon." Published 26 August 1837 with *Novelty* No. 2.

5. Engraving by S. J. Stump. As the Comic Muse, when Miss Mellon. Published by Stump, 1803.

6. Engraving by W. Ridley, after C. Allingham. Published as a plate to the *Monthly Mirror*, 1803.

7. Engraving by Sears & Co. Published by Knight & Lacey, 1828, No 41.

8. By unknown engraver. Published by Dean & Munday as a plate to *Lady's Monthly Magazine*, 1816.

9. As Ann Lovely. Engraving by Alais. Published by J. Roach, 1816.

10. As Louisa Dudley in *The West Indian*. Engraving by Alais. Published by J. Roach, 1805.

11. As Mrs Page in *The Merry Wives of Windsor*. Engraving by W. Say, after J. Masquerier. Published by Say, 1804. A copy engraved by H. R. Cook was published by T. & I. Elvey as a plate to *The Drama*, October 1822.

12. As Volante in *The Honeymoon*. By W. Beechey. Payments were made to the artist by Miss Mellon: £60 on 4 June 1807 and £60 on 29 March 1809. Engraving published by J. P. Thompson, 1806. A copy engraved by T. Woolnoth was published by Dean & Munday as a plate to *Ladies' Monthly Museum*, 1822; another copy, by an anonymous engraver, was published by H. Colburn, 1839; and a copy engraved by J. Rogers was published as a plate to Oxberry's *Dramatic Biography*, 1825.

13. Engraving by G. Cruikshank, published 1 December 1822 by W. N. Jones. A caricature entitled "Management-Or-Butts & Hogsheads," depicting various theatrical persons in a satire on the management of the new Drury Lane Theatre. Miss Mellon, "with much-exposed breasts," appears with Coutts, from whose pocket hangs a paper, "Mellon, payable at Coutts." A detailed commentary is given in *Political and Personal Satires in the British Museum* No 11940.

Charles E. Pearce records in *The Jolly Duchess* (1915) a number of engraved caricatures, some of which he reproduces. They are:

14. "Paul Pry at Widow Cout's," by Cruikshank, 1822.

15. "A Frolic at the Melon Shop in Piccadilly," by an anonymous engraver, 1826.

16. "A Visit to Court," by an anonymous engraver.

17. "A Sketch at St Albans or *Shav*ing the

new *Maid* Dutchess!!!," by an anonymous engraver, 1827?

18. "The Honey Moon and the MAN in the MOON, or a Peep through a *Holly Bush*," by an anonymous engraver, July 1827.

19. "The Presentation of Dollallola accompanied by the Mighty Thumb," by an anonymous engraver, 1828?

20. "Run Neighbors Run St AL——NS is Quadrilling It," an anonymous engraver, May 1829.

21. "The Duchess of St Albans in 1835," by an anonymous engraver, 1835? Pearce records, in addition (with no attributions to engravers):

22. "The New Banking Company's Scales of Equity," 1825.

23. "The Morning after Marriage," June 1827.

24. "A New Farce in High Life," June 1827.

25. "One of the Graces," July 1827.

26. "Feasting During Pleasure," July 1827.

27. "A Scene in the Honeymoon," 1828?

28. "A Dream of Retrospection," 1828.

29. "A View of the Grand Barge," 1828.

30. "Making Decent," 1828.

31. "Lady Day at Court," 1829.

Harvard Theatre Collection

COURTNEY MELMOTH

engraving by Ridley, after Beach

Mellor, Mr [*fl.* 1794], *singer.*

Mr Mellor, a tenor from Lancashire, sang in the Handel concerts at Westminster Abbey, according to Doane's *Musical Directory* of 1794.

Melmoth, Courtney, stage name of Samuel Jackson Pratt 1749–1814, *actor, manager, author.*

The sometime actor and prolific miscellaneous writer Courtney Melmoth, whose real name was Samuel Jackson Pratt, was born at St Ives, Huntingdonshire, on 25 December 1749. His father, a brewer of St Ives, twice served as high sheriff of the county and died at St Ives in 1775. Young Pratt received some of his education at Felstad school in Essex and also may have received private tuition from Hawkesworth. After he was ordained, his poem "Partridges, an Elegy," was published in the *Annual Register* for 1771 as by the "Rev. Mr. Pratt of Peterborough . . . an esteemed and popular preacher." About 1772 Pratt cut short his clerical career by eloping to Dublin with a pretty boarding school miss, whose Christian name was Charlotte and whose family name perhaps was Melmoth, the pseudonym that Pratt was to adopt for his stage ventures and under which she also acted. Pratt's alliance with Charlotte was much disapproved of by his parents, causing in later years dissension and litigation concerning family property.

Announced as "A Young Gentleman," Pratt made his debut at the Smock Alley Theatre on 22 February 1773 as Antony in *All for Love*. He cut a tall genteel figure but lacked conviction in his acting. On 25 March his name was given in the bills as Courtney Melmoth, "the Gentleman who performed . . . Antony." On 8 May 1773 "Mrs Melmoth" made her debut as Monimia in *The Orphan*, for his benefit. At the end of the Smock Alley season Melmoth turned country manager, building a little theatre in Drogheda capable of holding about £40, which he opened by playing Shylock to Mrs Melmoth's Portia.

When the Drogheda project failed after three months, the Melmoths turned toward London, where she made her debut at Covent Garden

Theatre on 26 February 1774 as Calista in *The Fair Penitent*. Early the following season, on 20 October 1774, Melmoth made his first appearance at Covent Garden as Philaster, again announced as a gentleman, but identified in the prompter Hopkins's notes. That month the *Westminster Magazine* described his debut optimistically;

Although his stile of playing convinced us that he is no new adventurer, we are happy to subscribe our testimony to that merit which he discovered, and which is confessedly his due. His voice in the tender scenes has a pleasing compass; but in the more nervous and impassioned, it wants that swell and fullness which Tragedy requires. He discovered a critical knowledge of his author, and frequently availed him-self of it, so as to produce some pleasing situations. His person is rather *petite*, but not ungraceful, except when he gives a full, horizontal extension to his arms, and then he is disgusting. Upon the whole, this gentleman is certainly a credit to the Theatre.

His name was in the bills as Melmoth when he acted Leontes in *The Winter's Tale* on 19 November, with Mrs Melmoth as Hermione. After repeating Leontes two nights later, his next role was Hamlet on 20 February 1775. In his poem *The Drama* (1775), Frederick Pilon wrote that Melmoth's person wanted weight but his heart sprung in his words and animated each part. In his "remarks on the inferior performers" in *Miscellanies in Prose and Verse* (1775), William Hawkins listed Melmoth's name but confused him with John Brunton, whom Hawkins's text describes.

Though Melmoth would depend on his pen for a livelihood over the remaining years of his life, he did persist as an itinerant actor and reciter for another decade. Sometime late in 1775 he solicited a loan from Mrs Montague:

This instance of your delicacy encourages me to impart a Circumstance of particular, and pathetic Import—I have engaged this Season to give a Course of Oratorical and Classical Lectures in Scotland at Edinburgh, whither my Wife is gone to perform as a first figure at the Theatre. A most heavy Chancery Suit, by the late result of which, I have lost *many* thousand Pounds, and the costly contingencies resulting from such a Misfortune, have exhausted my little finances; and *anticipated* many of the resources I derive from my trifling literary Efforts. To depend too much on the Emoluments of Science is, alas, a desperate dependence—In a word

Madam, I have to settle a few small Matters here, and to prepare for my Journey, and if you could have sufficient confidence in my Integrity, and indeed my Sense of Honour, as to accomodate me with about £15 more—Indeed Madam, I feel myself blush—I would most gratefully return it in the Course of Two Months. Allow, I beseech you Madam for my visible embarrassment, and believe me to be incapable of abusing the benevolence, which cannot but flow from the purest, and most Christian Principle.

When in Edinburgh he acted Jaffeir to his wife's Belvidera in *Venice Preserv'd* at the Theatre Royal, Shakespeare Square, on 20 March 1776. He performed at Bath in 1778–79 and returned to Edinburgh in 1779 to act Don Carlos in *The Duenna* on 15 February and 29 March. Probably he played occasionally in Dublin, where Mrs Melmoth was engaged regularly from 1780–81 to 1788–89.

According to *The Grove*, a satire by Thomas James Mathias, Melmoth lived off his wife's talents. They traveled together through England and Wales telling fortunes and giving public readings and lectures. At Swansea they took £20 by performing a tragedy, "without any other actor, stage-sweeper, scene-shifter, or candle-sniffer but themselves; PRATT being at all of these, except the first, an amazing adept." Melmoth's failure as an actor, according to John Taylor in *Records of My Life*, was due to his peculiar mannerism, including a walk which was "a kind of airy swing that rendered his acting at times rather ludicrous." Sometime after 1781, when they were playing at Dublin, the Melmoths, who no doubt had never been married by ceremony, separated. Eventually, in 1793, she went to America to assume some importance as a stage queen, and he went to the Continent to glean ideas for future literary efforts. On 5 July of that year the press contradicted reports of his death in Switzerland, stating he was in good health. Upon his return to England Melmoth applied himself with great industry to the publication of voluminous works ranging over a wide variety of subjects and interests, including seven plays, some of which appeared under his real name and some under his pseudonym.

He had begun his professional writing career before his Covent Garden debut in the autumn of 1774 by publishing his verses *The Tears of Genius, Occasioned by the Death of Dr. Goldsmith*,

Harvard Theatre Collection

COURTNEY MELMOTH

engraving by Chapman, after Peat

composed a few hours after Goldsmith died on 4 April 1774; it was reissued in 1775 as *The Tears of Genius, an Elegy on the most favourite English Poets lately deceased, imitative of the Stile of Each.* Other early efforts included *The Progress of Painting*, a poem (1775); *Liberal Opinions, or the History of Benignus* (six volumes, 1775–77, four volumes 1783); *Observations on the Night Thoughts of Dr Young* (1776); "Garrick's Looking Glass or the Art of Rising on the Stage," a poem (1776), and *An Apology for the Life and Writings of David Hume* (published anonymously in 1777 with supplement, also new edition 1789, and issued as *Curious Particulars and Genuine Anecdotes respecting Lord Chesterfield and David Hume*, 1788).

About 1776 Pratt entered partnership with Clinch, a bookseller at Bath on Milsom Street, a location subsequently known as Godwin's Library. After Clinch's death, the acquisition of a new partner changed the firm's designation to Pratt and Marshall, but Pratt abandoned that enterprise after a few years and returned to London. His extensive travels, foreign and domestic, provided the materials for some of his publications: *Gleanings through Wales, Holland, and Westphalia* (three volumes, a sequential fourth volume being *Gleanings in England*, 1795–99); *Harvest Home, consisting of supplementary Gleanings* (three volumes, 1805); *The Contrast, a Poem, with Comparative Views of Britain, Spain, and France* (1808); and *A Brief Account of Leamington Spa Charity with the Rides, Walks, &c.* (published anonymously in 1812 and subsequently enlarged as *Local and Literary Account of Leamington, Warrick, &c. By Mr. Pratt*, 1814)

His first effort for the stage was *Joseph Andrews*, a two-act farce acted at Drury Lane for Bensley's benefit on 20 April 1778 (not published and not in the Larpent Collection of manuscripts at the Huntington Library). More successful was *The Fair Circassian*, a five-act tragedy first played at Drury Lane on 27 November 1781 and acted a total of 21 times that season; its popularity is further attested by three editions before the end of the year. His next piece, *The School for Vanity*, a five-act comedy, was given one performance at Drury Lane on 29 January 1783, with prologue and epilogue probably by the author; it was published in 1785 and the manuscript is in the Larpent Collection. His comedy *The New Cosmetic; or, The Triumph of Beauty* was published in 1790 but was not acted in London. Three plays, *Fire and Frost*, *Hail Fellow Well Met*, and *Love's Trials; or, The Triumphs of Constancy*, were not acted but were published in 1805 in the second volume of his *Harvest Home*. *The Fatal Interview*, a tragedy produced at Drury Lane on 16 November 1782, is usually credited to Thomas Hull but has also been ascribed to Pratt, who provided the epilogue. The play was not published but the manuscript survives in the Larpent Collection.

In 1779 was published *The Shadows of Shakespeare. A Monody occasioned by the Death of Mr. Garrick. Being a Prize Poem written for the Vase at Bath-Easton. By Courtney Melmoth.* The monody was spoken by Matthew Browne at his benefit on 19 July 1787 at the Haymarket and no doubt was used as a specialty recitation by other actors throughout the provinces. An epitaph by Pratt was engraved on the monument to Garrick raised in Westminster Abbey in 1797; the lines were characterized by Lamb as "a farrago of false thoughts and nonsense."

Pratt died at Colmore Row, Birmingham,

on 4 October 1814 after a long illness aggravated by a fall from a horse. Mrs Melmoth, having been separated from him since 1793, died in New York in 1823.

Extensive lists of his publications, in addition to those named above, are in *The Dictionary of National Biography* and the *Cambridge Bibliography of English Literature*.

According to Taylor in *Records of My Life*, Pratt had shown him a manuscript of a two-volume autobiography, but it was never published. Taylor thought well of him, writing that "if Pratt had been born to a fortune, a great part of it would have been devoted to benevolence." But Pratt often injured his relationships by displays of rancor and viciousness, especially in his correspondence. In 1784 he wrote an offensive letter to Mrs Siddons, a sometime friend, because she had requested the return of a small loan, denouncing her for unfeelingly asking him for "the trifling sum" when she was making so much money. That year Mrs Siddons' husband had extended a loan of £500 to Pratt. "Poor man! I respect his talents and pity his imprudence," Mrs Siddons wrote to the Whalleys on 21 June 1784. They were still quarreling in October 1787, evidently because Pratt believed that Mrs Siddons was not doing her best to promote his plays with the managers. In what seems to be an extraordinary presumption, Pratt accused her of "ingratitude," as she wrote to Mrs Thrale, "calling himself the ladder upon which I have mounted to fame, and which I am kicking down." Some years earlier, in 1769, Pratt had written a curious and begging letter to Samuel Johnson. In Isaac Reed's commonplace book at the Folger Shakespeare Library is a copy of a letter that Pratt wrote to the bookseller Evans on 25 January 1784 complaining about his treatment in a new edition of *Biographia Dramatica*:

I was shocked by the Anecdotes which your Editor has given of myself. Anecdotes which sink upon the reader all the lights and discover all the shades and which in a few vague poisnous Sentences are every way calculated—perhaps the only ones in the book that are *glaringly* so—to tear down my fame as a Writer, my prosperity as a Tradesman, and my bosom peace as a Man. The deed being done . . . it is in vain to appeal from the Severity to the Candour of your Editor, who hath dealt my damnation

thro the land in this most wanton and unnecessary manner—wanton because he seems aware that I deriv'd much emolument from publick employ, and unnecessary because he has not been liberal enough to connect it with the least favourable account of those performances which made me his publick mark, nor with any mention at all of those productions which have lately earn'd me those honest Wreaths which it has been his pride and pleasure to rend from my temples. . . .

A portrait of Pratt was painted by Thomas Lawrence in 1807. It was sold from the collection of Sir Richard Phillips at Christie's on 9 July 1886; it was with Leggatt in 1925 and with Colnaghi in 1926. The present location of Lawrence's painting is unknown but it was engraved by C. Watson and published by Phillips in 1805. A portrait by Peat, also untraced, was engraved by Chapman (from the original) and published by Longman & Rees on 12 August 1800. Other portraits of Pratt include engravings by Ridley, after Beach, published as a plate to the *Monthly Mirror*, 1803; by Turner, after Masquerier, published by Turner, 1802; and by an unknown engraver, published (on a plate with a portrait of J. Ward, R.A.) by Cundee, 1807.

Melmoth, Mrs Courtney, Charlotte, stage name of Mrs Samuel Jackson Pratt *1749–1823, actress, singer.*

Charlotte Melmoth presumably was the young woman who in the early 1770s ran away from a boarding school with the clergyman and miscellaneous writer Samuel Jackson Pratt. Her maiden name is unknown, but perhaps it was Melmoth, for that was the stage name adopted by Pratt when he went on the boards for the first time at the Smock Alley Theatre, Dublin, in February 1773. Several months later, "Mrs Melmoth" made her debut there on 8 May 1773 as Monimia in *The Orphan*, for his benefit. At the end of the 1772–73 season at Smock Alley, "Courtney Melmoth" turned country manager and built a little theatre at Drogheda capable of holding £40, which he opened as Shylock to Mrs Melmoth's Portia.

The Drogheda venture failed within three months. Soon after, the couple made their way to London, where she made her debut at Covent Garden on 26 February 1774 as Calista in *The Fair Penitent*. The bills announced her only

Harvard Theatre Collection

CHARLOTTE MELMOTH, as Elizabeth

engraving by Collyer, after Dodd

as a gentlewoman but the prompter Hopkins identified her by name in his diary. The *Westminster Magazine* for March 1774 reported that

she was lately a boarder with the celebrated Charlotte Hayes; a circumstance which will inform our readers that her figure is pleasing and also that she is young and handsome. It is but justice, however, to add that she possesses the internal as well as external requisites of a good actress; for she discovers great feeling and sensibility; and indeed promises to be an ornament to the theatre.

The Fair Penitent was repeated on 5 and 10 March 1774; on 11 April Mrs Melmoth acted Mandane in *Cyrus*, her only other role that season.

Early in her second season at Covent Garden, Mrs Melmoth appeared as Roxana in *Alexander the Great* on 4 October 1774 (re-

peated on 10 October), and then on 20 October she played Bellario when Mr Melmoth made his London debut as Philaster. Her other roles included the Queen in *Richard III*, Queen Eleanor in *King Henry II*, Hermione in *The Winter's Tale* (with Melmoth as Leontes), and Queen Elizabeth in *The Earl of Essex*. In his *Miscellanies in Prose and Verse* (1775), William Hawkins, remarking on the "inferior performers," judged her to have been "very respectable" in the several tragic parts she had so far offered.

In the first half of 1776, the Melmoths played in Edinburgh, where she acted a number of capital parts which included Alicia in *Jane Shore*, Belvidera in *Venice Preserv'd*, Desdemona, Euphrasia in *The Grecian Daughter*, Lady Macbeth, Lady Randolph in *Douglas*, Marcia in *Cato*, Mrs Belville in *The School for Wives*, Queen Catherine in *Henry VIII*, Viola in *Twelfth Night*, and Zara in *The Mourning Bride*.

She returned to London in the autumn of 1776 to make her debut at Drury Lane Theatre as Lady Macbeth on 25 November. Hopkins recorded in his prompter's diary that she "was very wild in the Part, met with some Applause." After repeating Lady Macbeth on 26 and 30 December and playing Roxana on 17 February 1777 (for which efforts she was advanced £10 on 9 December 1776 and paid £50 in full on 11 April 1777), Mrs Melmoth once more retreated to the provinces, never again to act in London.

Engaged with her husband at Edinburgh in 1778 and 1779, she added several comic roles to her repertoire: Lady Sneerwell in *The School for Scandal*, Lady Townly in *The Provok'd Wife*, Mrs Lovemore in *The Way to Keep Him*, Mrs Oakly in *The Jealous Wife*, and Mrs Sullen in *The Beaux' Stratagem*. In the summer of 1779 they acted at Birmingham and then wandered from engagement to engagement. According to *The Grove*, a satire by Thomas James Mathias, Melmoth lived off her talents:

But their extravagance rendered it necessary for the lady to quit a regular company, and they travelled together in various characters through England and Wales. Sometimes she told fortunes and MELMOTH took the money; at others they had public lectures; and at Swanzea [*sic*] they performed a tragedy, and actually got twenty pounds, without any other actor, stage-sweeper, scene-shifter, or candle-snuffer but themselves; PRATT being at all of these, except the first, an amazing adept.

Between 1782 and 1792 Mrs Melmoth often appeared in various Irish towns: Cork in 1782 and 1786; Limerick in 1785 and 1786; Waterford in 1786 and 1792; Belfast in 1790 and 1791; and Derry in 1791. In Dublin she played at Smock Alley between 1780 and 1783, and from 1785 to 1788; at Crow Street in 1781–82 and 1788–89; and at Fishamble Street in 1784–85. The song *Tell me, my lute*, as sung by Mrs Melmoth in the character of Octavia in *The Duenna*, was published in the *Hibernian Magazine* in December 1780. The *Thespian Dictionary* claimed that previous to her Dublin benefit in 1786, she made known her intention of becoming a Roman Catholic and began to attend chapel every morning; "but the receipts of the house not corresponding with her expectations, she found it was likely to be of no benefit to her in *this* world, and therefore did not think proper to change her road to the next." Dunlap, on the other hand, in his history of the American theatre, wrote that she was a Roman Catholic; and, indeed, she was buried in a Catholic cemetery.

The Melmoths, who probably never had married, separated sometime after they performed together at Smock Alley in 1781. He turned to the voluminous production of writings, including several plays that found their way upon the London stage. She turned to the New World.

Announced as "from the Theatres Royal of London and Dublin," Mrs Melmoth advertised in the New York *Daily Advertiser* on 30 March 1793 that she would offer recitations in the City Assembly Rooms at Corre's Hotel on the evening of 9 April. Her program, which she repeated several times in April, included selections from *Julius Caesar*, *Macbeth*, *Paradise Lost* and Collins's *Ode to the Passions*. On 10 April *Loudon's Register* reported that the entertainment "must have afforded infinite delight to every rational mind."

That fall Mrs Melmoth became a member of Hodgkinson's company at the John Street Theatre, where she made her debut on 20 November 1793 as Euphrasia in *The Grecian Daughter*. On 9 December she acted Belvidera in *Venice Preserv'd* and subsequently that season was seen as Arabella in *Such Things Are*, Widow

Racket in *The Belle's Stratagem*, Lady Randolph in *Douglas*, Calista in *The Fair Penitent*, Zara in *The Mourning Bride*, Lady Macbeth, Marcia in *Cato*, Portia in *Julius Caesar*, Arpasia in *Tamerlane*, Alicia in *Jane Shore*, Mrs Beverley in *The Gamester*, Roxalana in *The Sultan*, and other roles. She was the original Matilda in Dunlap's *The Fatal Deception* on 24 April 1794. On 16 May she recited "Shelah's Voyage to America." She had refused to speak the epilogue to *Tammany*, a new opera written by Mrs Siddons's eccentric sister Ann Hatton, which was premiered on 3 March 1794. The *New York Journal* of 12 March reported that Mrs Melmoth disapproved of "the patriotic sentiments" contained in the opera and the paper called for a boycott of her:

She is to appear on the stage *this night*. I hope she will be *convinced*, by the *absence* of republicans when she appears that *the people* resent her impertinence. I think she ought not to be suffered to go on the New York stage again.

Dunlap claimed that in 1793 Mrs Melmoth "was the best tragic actress the inhabitants of New York, then living, had ever seen." Though past her prime, she still possessed a handsome face and a commanding figure. "To a fine face and powerful voice," wrote William Wood in his *Personal Recollections*, "she added an exquisite feeling of the pathetic, which in Lady Randolph, Lady St Valori, and other parts of tenderness, left an impression which years fail to efface." She ranked with Mrs Wignell and Mrs Whitlock as "an actress of matrons," though her "poetical *enthusiasm*" sometimes caused her to overact. According to the New York *Spectator* of 4 January 1800 her manner of speech tended to be "artificial and declamatory." In her later years, Mrs Melmoth expanded to dimensions described by Dunlap as "far beyond the sphere of *embonpoint*." When she played Euphrasia one night, after having achieved such great bulk, at her crying out to save her father, "Strike here, here you will find blood enough!" the audience laughed heartily.

Mrs Melmoth was engaged at the John Street Theatre until 1798, when she went with Hallam and Hodgkinson to the new Park Theatre. Her salary at the latter house in 1798–99 was $20 per week. She also had acted in Philadelphia in the fall of 1794 and in Hartford in the summer of 1795.

In 1802 Mrs Melmoth quarreled with Dunlap and left the Park Theatre, only to return next season and remain until Dunlap went bankrupt in 1804–5. Then she acted at the Chestnut Street Theatre in Philadelphia in 1805–6. On the road to take up an engagement for 1811–12 at the Olympic Theatre in New York, she suffered an accident in which she "met with a severe fracture of her arm." Rumors of her death circulated, and her engagement was prevented. On 12 August 1812 she solicited the patronage of the public for her last benefit, "having been deprived by accident of all pecuniary resources from an inability to appear in her profession." That night at the Olympic she gave her last performance, as Fiammetta in *The Tale of Mystery*.

The *Thespian Dictionary* stated that during the time she was still acting she kept a "respectable tavern" in New York. After her retirement from the stage she kept a school for elocution on Washington Street, near the Albany Basin. She also bought a house on Long Island between Brooklyn and Fort Swift, with land enough to carry on some dairy farming.

Mrs Melmoth died in New York on 28 September 1823 (not in 1805 as stated in *The Dictionary of National Biography*), at the age of 74, and was buried in the cemetery adjoining the first St Patrick's Cathedral, a burial ground which was in use until 1833.

A portrait of Mrs Melmoth as Queen Elizabeth in *The Earl of Essex* engraved by Collyer, after Dodd, was published in Lowndes's *New English Theatre*, 1777. An engraving by Walker, after Dodd, of her as Roxana, with Lawrence Clinch as Alexander in *The Rival Queens*, was published by Lowndes in 1776 and is reproduced in volume 3, page 335, of this dictionary.

Melville. *See also* MELVIN, JOHN.

Melville, Miss [*fl.* 1795–1797], *actress, singer.*
The Sadler's Wells bills at the Folger Shakespeare Library show that Miss Melville played a Fairy in *Chevy Chase* on 4 August 1795 and a Lass in *England's Glory* on 31 August. Also in 1795 she played Pandora in *Pandora's Box* and Spinner ("with a song") in *Momus's Gift*. *The Morning Herald* on 8 July 1796 reported that Miss Melville, from Sadler's Wells, was at

Brighton, and a Tunbridge Wells bill dated 24 August 1797 stated that she was making her first appearance there—again having come from Sadler's Wells.

Melvin, John *1771–1817, dancer, actor, monologuist.*
The first recorded appearance of a Mr Melvin was among nearly thirty others dancing in the pantomime *Harlequin's Invasion* at Drury Lane on 27 December 1792. But he was probably the Melvin who had performed in Duckworth's company at the New Theatre, Parson's Green Fulham, earlier that year. He probably danced obscurely in the Drury Lane ballet corps the rest of the 1792–93 season. Whether or not he was there in following seasons is unknown.

In the summer of 1796 Melvin was at Sadler's Wells, where from 16 to 25 June he gave "his imitations of the following London performers: Mr. Kemble, Mr. Bensley, Mr. Macklin, Mr. Wroughton, and Mr. Quick." He was said to be from the Margate Theatre when he turned up at the Edinburgh theatre in January

Harvard Theatre Collection
JOHN MELVIN
engraving by Ridley and Holl, after Bates

1797. He seems to have remained in the Scottish capital until May, to have spent the summer at York, and then to have returned to Edinburgh. His known roles at Edinburgh were, in order: Sheva in *The Jew*, Mr Bronzely in *Wives As They Were and Maids As They Are*, Young Flourish in *Abroad and at Home*, Lord Miniken in *Bon Ton*, Tanjore in *The Way to Get Married*, Young Mirabel in *The Inconstant*, Dick Dowlas in *The Heir-at-Law*, Brush in *The Clandestine Marriage*, Sir Robert Ramble in *Every One Has His Fault*, Hassan in *The Castle Spectre*, Heartwell in *The Farmhouse*, and Lord Trinket in *The Jealous Wife*. His Lord Trinket was scolded by "Timothy Plain" the Edinburgh critic as "execrable." Plain found his Dick Dowlas "below criticism."

By 6 April 1799 Melvin was again in the York Company, at Hull, and apparently he remained on that circuit until at least 1802, becoming a leading player. The *Monthly Mirror* in December 1800 had decided that he needed more study. Evidently he took the hint and improved. W. Burton, in *A Pasquinade Upon the Performers at York* (1801) praised him as "That comedian of spunk."

In 1806–7 Melvin was on the Covent Garden roster. His benefit that year grossed £408 6s. He took a benefit at Crow Street, Dublin, on 19 May 1808. In 1809–10, 1810–11, and 1811–12 he played in the Drury Lane Company at the Lyceum. (In 1810 he was living at No 9, Surrey Street, the Strand, according to a note by James Winston.) By 1811–12 his salary was £11 per week.

According to both the "Dramatic Register" manuscript in the Harvard Theatre Collection and O. Smith's manuscript stage history in the British Library, Melville died on 19 November 1817, aged 46. The "Register" furnishes his first name. Smith adds that he was buried in St Pancras churchyard, London.

A portrait of Melvin engraved by Ridley and Holl, after Bates, was published in the *Monthly Mirror*, 1806.

Memi, Mrs. *See* FORCADE, MME LÉONARD.

Menage, Mons *d. c. 1818?, dancer.*
Monsieur Menage, progenitor of a dancing family, was an obscure chorus dancer at Drury Lane Theatre by 1775–76; though his name seems not to have appeared on the bills in that and several subsequent seasons, he was on company lists on 9 May 1776 and 5 October 1776. On 3 May 1794 his salary was raised 1s. 8d. per day. In 1795–96 his salary was £1 per week, by 1800–1801 it was £3, and by 1803–4 it was £5. His name was still on the Drury Lane list in 1807–8.

Among the assignments for which his name appeared in the Drury Lane bills were the pantomime dance *The Sportsmen Deceiv'd* on 10 December 1779 (repeated 17 December), dancing in *Cymbeline* on 18 April 1780, Don Henriques in *Don Juan* on 10 May 1782, dancing in *Robinson Crusoe* on 15 May 1782, a minuet with Miss Collet on 28 September 1782, a minuet with Miss Stageldoir on 22 May 1784, dancing in *Daphne and Amintor* on 24 April 1786, and dancing in *Cymbeline* on 29 January 1787.

At the Haymarket Theatre in the summer of 1785, Menage appeared in *Don Juan* on 15 and 18 April. At Palmer's Royalty Theatre he danced as one of the Countrymen in *Hobson's Choice* on 3 July 1787 and in *Harlequin Mungo* in November of that year. Again at the Haymarket in 1789 his performances included a new dance called *The Graces* with Miss Bury and the two Misses Simonet on 22 May, a hornpipe on 10 June, and a new dance called *The Happy Sisters* with Miss De Camp and the Simonet girls on 8 July. He danced in the chorus of the King's Company (playing at the Pantheon) in 1791.

His son Frederick Menage, and his daughters Mary Menage, Arabella Menage (later wife of the painter Michael William Sharp), and possibly a third girl Miss E. Menage, all danced on the London stage in the 1790s and beyond. We have assumed that the elder Menage was the dancer who was at Drury Lane and his son Frederick the one who was at Covent Garden in the first decade of the nineteenth century.

The elder Menage also performed at Sadler's Wells at the same time his son was there, appearing as Justice Minikin in *Goody Two Shoes* and a Sailor in *British Amazons*, both in 1803.

According to a manuscript notation in the British Library (Add 18586), Menage died about 1818; in this notation he is mistakenly confused, however, as the original player of Tuckey in *Obi* at the Haymarket in 1800, a role actually played by his son Frederick, who died in 1822, so this death year must be suspect. The Arabella Menage, of Brighton, who was buried at St Paul, Covent Garden, on 22 May 1827 at the age of 65 was no doubt his wife, for his daughter Arabella had died ten years before in 1817 as Mrs Michael William Sharp.

Menage, Arabella, later Mrs Michael William Sharp *d. 1817, dancer, actress.*

Arabella Menage was the younger daughter of the Drury Lane chorus dancer Mons Menage and his wife Arabella. Her birth date is unknown to us, but her elder sister Mary was born in 1778 and her elder brother Frederick in 1788. She was very young indeed when, advertised as Miss Menage Junior to differentiate her from her sister Mary, she appeared on the stage of Drury Lane on 27 December 1792 as a dancer in *Harlequin's Invasion*, a piece in which her father, brother, and sister also appeared. But Arabella seems to have performed even earlier. According to *The London Stage* a Miss E. Menage danced in *The Enchanted Wood* at the Haymarket Theatre on 25 July 1792

Harvard Theatre Collection

ARABELLA MENAGE

engraving by Cheeseman, after Sharp

and five other times that summer. Since her sister Mary also was in that production, and we have no other record of an "E." Menage, we assume that this listing was an error for "B," as Arabella was later billed.

According to Gilliland's *Dramatic Mirror* (1808), Bella was "brought upon the stage in infancy," and was instructed by Didelot and D'Egville, the latter making her "accomplished" in the hornpipe. By 1798–99 she was performing quite regularly at Drury Lane, dancing that season in the choruses of *Blue-Beard*, *The Captive of Spilburg*, and *Feudal Times*. On 1 January 1799 she replaced Mrs Bland as Zingarella in *Aurelio and Miranda*, for that night, and on 7 January she appeared as Irene in *Blue-Beard*. On 17 May 1799 she took over Nelly in *No Song No Supper*.

On 19 October 1799 Bella's salary was 13*s.* 4*d.* per week, but on the following 9 November it was raised to £2. In 1799–1800 her roles included Beda in *Blue-Beard*, Cicely Copsley in *The Will*, Cicely in *The Haunted Tower*, a Captive in *Lodoiska*, Sophia in *Of Age To-Morrow*, and Viola in *The Strangers at Home*.

At the Haymarket Theatre in 1801 she appeared as Rosina in *The Castle of Sorrento* and Patty in *Inkle and Yarico*; the ballet *The Corsair* that summer, according to Gilliland, owed its success entirely to her dancing. She was also at the Haymarket in 1804.

At Drury Lane, where she continued her regular engagement into the nineteenth century, her salary was £2 10*s.* in 1802–3. In August 1804 the *Monthly Mirror* announced that Bella Menage had "lately" been married to Michael William Sharp (d. 1840), late pupil of Sir William Beechey and successful portrait painter. He was the son of the oboist Michael Sharp (d. 1800) and Elizabeth Sharp. Michael William Sharp's mother Elizabeth was one of the daughters of the Drury Lane prompter William Hopkins (d. 1780) and the actress Elizabeth Hopkins (d. 1801) and the sister of Priscilla Hopkins, who eventually became Mrs John Philip Kemble. Thus Bella Menage's husband was the nephew, by marriage, of the great Kemble. On 29 September 1804, Sarah Siddons, Kemble's sister, wrote to Mrs Thrale:

I know of no deaths, births, or Marriages, except one of the latter Sort which I am very Sorry for because I know it will afflict his poor Mother and

Courtesy of the Garrick Club

ARABELLA MENAGE
by Wood

Sister . . . It is the Marriage of Michael Sharpe to (I'm afraid) a naughty little dancing Girl at Drury Lane called Miss Menage.

As Mrs Sharp, Bella continued to perform with the Drury Lane Company from 1804–5 through 1811–12. Between 1805–6 and 1808–9 her salary was £5 per week. Though her husband was a musician as well as an established painter there is no evidence he played professionally in the theatre. He did, however, sometimes sign for his wife's salary at Drury Lane.

Gilliland decribed Bella Sharp in 1808 as an "excellent dancer, and pretty little woman," possessed of a small but elegant figure and regular and pretty features.

Mrs Sharp died at her home in Duke Street, Portland Place, on 9 January 1817 (by report of the *Gentleman's Magazine* of that month). Her husband, who later did some paintings of theatrical scenes, is noticed in *The Dictionary*

of National Biography. He died in 1840 at Boulogne. Bella's father, Mons Menage, died about 1818; and her mother Arabella Menage was buried at St Paul, Covent Garden, on 22 May 1827. She was 65 years old when she died. Bella's brother Frederick died in 1822 and her sister Mary in 1830.

A pencil and watercolor drawing of Bella Menage by W. Wood is in the Garrick Club. Her husband's portrait of her was engraved by T. Cheesman for Gilliland's *Dramatic Mirror* in 1807 and by S. Freeman for the *Monthly Mirror* in 1808. An engraving by Barlow, after Cruikshank, of Frederick Menage as the Boy and Miss Menage as the Girl in *The Children in the Wood* was published by J. Roach in 1793; the Miss Menage pictured is Mary, not Bella as in the Harvard Theatre Collection catalogue of engraved portraits.

Menage, Miss E. *See* MENAGE, ARABELLA.

Menage, Frederick *1788–1822, dancer.*
Frederick Menage, born in 1788, was the son of the Drury Lane chorus dancer Mons Menage and his wife Arabella Menage (1762–1827). He was first noticed in London bills when he danced under D'Egville's direction in *The Enchanted Wood* at the Haymarket Theatre on 25 July 1792. Among the many children also performing that night were his sisters Mary Menage and Miss E. (*recte* B.?) Menage. At Covent Garden, on 11 March 1793 Master Menage was the Grandchild in *The Governor*, a pantomime ballet that had seven performances that season. On 31 May 1793 he danced *Le Pas Russe* with his sister Mary at the King's Theatre, where the Drury Lane company was temporarily housed. At the King's on 3 June 1793 he was added to the dancers in *Le Jaloux puni*.

During the 1790s Master Menage was employed at the three major patent houses, but most regularly at the Haymarket winter seasons until Colman's management between 1793 and 1800. There in 1793–94 he appeared as a Boy in numerous performances of *The Children in the Wood* and *Harlequin Peasant*, roles he was also seen in later, at Drury Lane. On 2 July 1800 he performed Tuckey in the premiere of Fawcett's very popular pantomine *Obi*. At Drury Lane he played the Son of Darius in *Alexander the Great* in 1794–95 and Fleance in *Macbeth*,

Harvard Theatre Collection

FREDERICK MENAGE, as Chimpanzee

engraving after Nixon

beginning in 1796–97. He was also in the dancing chorus at the King's Theatre from 1794 through 1800.

The *Monthly Mirror* of October 1796 reported that "Young Menage (the boy) may now be called, emphatically, *the child of promise.*" According to the Drury Lane account books he received about 10s. per night in 1796–97.

Still billed as Master Menage, he worked at the Haymarket in the summer of 1801, appearing in the ballet *The Corsair*. In 1800–1801 he became engaged at Covent Garden, where he enjoyed popularity as the Chimpanzee in *Perouse, or The Desolate Island*, a successful pantomime that premiered on 28 February 1801. He also was in Dibdin's company at Sadler's Wells in 1803, when he performed the title role in *Jack the Giant Killer*, Master Bull in *New Brooms*, Young Perkins in *Red Riding Hood*, and Beaufidelle, a monkey, in *Philip Quarll*. By 1803–4, he was old enough to be

billed as Mr Menage at Covent Garden, where he remained through 1814–15, earning £2 per week in 1804–5 and a constant £3 per week thereafter. A Covent Garden pay receipt of 1808 (British Library Add MS 29,631) bears his full signature. Between 1815 and 1817 he also made £3 per week as a member of the Haymarket Company.

Frederick Menage was buried at St Paul, Covent Garden, on 15 January 1822, at the age of 34. His will consisted of one sentence: "I bequeath the whole of my property to my mother Mrs. Arabella Menage in case of my decease ffeby 17–1820—F. Menage." There were no witnesses. On 4 February 1822 James Vincent Menage (a son or brother?), occupation turner, of No 29, Frith Street, Soho Square, and Robert Howard Fish of No 34, Greek Street, Soho Square, a watchmaker, testified to

Harvard Theatre Collection

FREDERICK and MARY MENAGE in *The Children of the Wood*

engraving by Barlow, after Cruikshank

their knowledge of the deceased, who had lived at No 28, Frith Street. Administration of the will was granted on 6 February 1822 to Arabella Menage, mother and next of kin. Frederick's father had died about 1818. His sister Mary Menage died in 1830 and his sister Arabella Menage Sharp had died in 1817, after successful stage careers.

An anonymous engraving, after J. Nixon, of Master Menage as the Chimpanzee in *Perouse* was published by W. Holland in 1801. An engraving by Barlow, after Cruikshank, of Master Menage and his sister Mary in *The Children in the Wood* was published by J. Roach in 1793. The catalogue of engraved portraits in the Harvard Theatre Collection incorrectly identifies the girl as Bella Menage, the younger sister.

Frederick Menage was also depicted, with John Bannister as Walter and Thomas Caulfield as Oliver, in a scene from *The Children in the Wood* painted by R. Westall. The location of the painting is unknown to us, but an engraving by Lundan (under the direction of James Heath) was published 1 May 1797. If the picture was intended to represent the cast of the original production at the Haymarket in October 1793, then the little girl is Mary Menage; if the cast of the production at Drury Lane in 1796–97 was pictured then the "little girl" is Master W. S. Chatterley.

Menage, Mary *1778–1830, dancer, singer, actress.*

Mary Menage was born in 1778, the eldest known child of the Drury Lane chorus dancer Menage and his wife Arabella. She was the sister of the performers Frederick Menage and Arabella Menage (later Mrs Michael William Sharp). At the Pantheon in 1791 she appeared as a Nymph in D'Auberval's ballet *Amphion et Thalie* on 17 February, Cupid in *Telemachus in the Island of Calypso* on 22 and 24 March, and a Niece in *The Deserter* also on the 24th. Again at the Pantheon on 17 December 1791 she performed Cupidon in *L'Amant déguisé*. Her first notice at the Haymarket Theatre was for dancing in *Le Volage fixé* on 10 March 1792, followed by Zorzi in *Le Foire de Smirne; ou, Les Amans réunis* on 14 April, the Prince of Wales in *The Battle of Hexham* on 19 and 21 June, and in the chorus of *The Enchanted Wood* on 25 July 1792 (and five other times that summer).

In the last piece the bills also listed a Miss E. Menage as a dancer, but we take that as an error for Bella Menage, Mary's younger sister.

During the 1790s, Mary danced, sang, and acted at Drury Lane, the Haymarket, and the King's Theatre, in a number of youthful roles. In the bills she was advertised as Miss or Mlle Menage, as differentiated from her younger sister who was listed as Miss Menage Junior or Miss B. Menage. Mary's roles in the Drury Lane Company at the King's Theatre in 1792–93 included the Page in *Love Makes a Man*, a Spirit in *The Cave of Trophonius*, the Duke of York in *Richard III*, and Fleance in *Macbeth*. At the Haymarket in 1793–94 she was a character in *The Mountaineers*, the Girl in many performances of *The Children in the Wood* (in which her brother Frederick played the Boy), Julia in *The Mariners*, a Peasant in *Harlequin Peasant*, and a Page in *The Purse*. She was at Drury Lane and the Haymarket regularly each season through 1799–1800. Among her other assignments at Drury Lane was singing in the choruses of various peasants, goatherds, and assorted characters in such pieces as *Lodoiska*, *The Cherokee*, *Alexander the Great*, *The Mountaineers*, *Feudal Times*, *Blue-Beard*, and *The Captive of Spilburg*. At the Haymarket she appeared as Aminadab in *A Bold Stroke for a Wife* in 1795, in the chorus of *The Iron Chest* in 1796, as Louisa in *No Song No Supper* in 1797, as an Attendant in *Obi* (in which brother Frederick was Tuckey), Carolina in *'Tis All a Farce*, and Viletta in *What a Blunder* in 1800, among other roles. She was also at the King's Theatre in 1796–97.

In 1799 the *Authentic Memoirs of the Green Room* stated that having served her apprenticeship to the stage Miss Menage had outgrown "the characters in which she lately shined," particularly the Girl in *The Children in the Wood*, and "At present she assists the chorus singers." She remained at Drury Lane in her modest service through 1811–12, and at the Haymarket until 1810. In the early 1800s her Drury Lane salary was 16s. 8d. per week and at the end of her career in 1811–12 it was only £1. Her sister, who became a somewhat more successful performer, was earning £2 by the end of the eighteenth century. Mary Menage also performed at Birmingham in the summer of 1802. Her first name was given in the Drury Lane account books on 18 October 1800 (at the Folger Shakespeare Library). The *Thespian Dictionary* (1805) identified her as Bella's elder sister.

Mary Menage, described in the registers as of St Giles in the Fields, was buried at St Paul, Covent Garden, on 12 November 1830, at the age of 52.

An engraving by Barlow, after Cruikshank, of Mary Menage and her brother Frederick in *The Children in the Wood* was published by J. Roach in 1793. The catalogue of engraved portraits in the Harvard Theatre Collection incorrectly identifies the girl as Bella, the younger sister. Mary Menage is probably the little girl pictured in a painting by R. Westall of a scene from *The Children in the Wood*, with her brother Frederick as the boy, John Bannister as Walter, and Thomas Caulfield as Oliver. The painting seems lost, but an engraving by Lundan (under the direction of James Heath) was published on 1 May 1797. If the picture was intended to show the cast at Drury Lane in 1796–97, then the "little girl" is Master W. S. Chatterley.

Menaste, John ₁*fl. 1694*₁, *house servant?*
In the Lord Chamberlain's accounts is a warrant for payment to the United Company for plays performed before royalty; the bill was signed by Thomas Davenant, Christopher Rich, and John Menaste. Menaste was probably a house servant, perhaps an accountant working in the theatre office.

Mence, Benjamin ₁*fl. 1744–1775*₁, *singer.*
Benjamin Mence was sworn a Gentleman of the Chapel Royal in place of Francis Hughes, deceased, on 14 April 1744. Evidently he was still a professional singer in 1775. A letter dated 11 June 1775, from Anself Bayly to Garrick concerning Bayly's pupil, the young singer Harriet Abrams, mentions Mence's singing to her in his "enforcing" manner and approving her professional abilities.

Mence, Samuel *d. 1786, singer.*
Samuel Mence was described as one of the lay vicars of Lichfield Cathedral in his obituary in the *Gentleman's Magazine*, following his death on 20 February 1786. When his brother, the Reverend William Mence, was granted administration of his property the following June,

Samuel Mence, "late of the close of the Cathedral Church of Litchfield" was said also to have been "one of the Gentlemen of the Chapel Royal at St James a Batchelor."

"Mendenia, Signora" ₁*fl. 1754*₁, *singer?*
The "Signora Mendenia" who had a vocal part in *Mrs Midnight's Concert* at the Haymarket Theatre on 22 April 1754 was paired off in the bill with "Signora Gapatoona." Both names were pseudonyms made up by Christopher Smart (Mrs Midnight).

Mendez, Mr ₁*fl. 1763–1767?*₁, *treasurer, actor?*
A benefit was held at the Haymarket Theatre on 11 August 1763 for Samuel Foote's treasurer, Mr Mendez. Tickets were available from Mendez in Bow Street, Covent Garden. A Mr Mendez, very possibly the same person, acted with Foote's troupe at the same house in the summer of 1767. He was Sampson in *Romeo and Juliet* on 22 June and had a part in *The Patron* on 12 August.

Mendez, Mr ₁*fl. 1781*₁, *actor.*
A Mr Mendez had an unnamed principal part in *The Spendthrift* at the Haymarket Theatre on 12 November 1781.

Mendoza, Daniel *1764–1836, pugilist, manager.*
Daniel Mendoza was born of Jewish parents on 5 July 1764 in Aldgate, London. Most of his youth was spent in the East End, where he received a Jewish education and worked at various times for a glazier, then in a fruit and vegetable shop, and in a tea shop. He was working as a tobacco salesman when, at the age of 16, he turned to pugilism, an art at which he had become skillful in the streets of the East End. In his *Memoirs* Mendoza characterized himself as a gentle man, but clearly he had an instinct for brawling. His professional bouts with Tyne, Matthews, and Nelson brought him to the attention of the Prince of Wales, who was intrigued by the young boxer and took him up as a protégé. Through the Prince's influence a bout was arranged with Samuel Martin, "the Bath Butcher," at Barnet racecourse on 17 April 1787. Mendoza won an easy victory in 20 minutes, whereas it had

DANIEL MENDOZA

engraving by Gardiner, after Robineau

taken two hours for Richard Humphreys, a prizefighter of repute, to subdue Martin. The victory, when all wagers were settled, is said to have brought Mendoza about £1000 and a reputation for incomparable boxing skill.

About 1786 Mendoza opened a boxing academy in Capel Court, where he gave lessons and sold portraits of himself to those who came to witness his sparring exhibitions. About this time he married a Jewess, to whom he made a promise to abandon the prize ring, but he was lured back by the challenge of Richard Humphreys.

When he was a young East End scrapper, Mendoza had been befriended by Humphreys, "the gentleman boxer," from whom it is said he derived his scientific knowledge of fighting. But that friendship was eroded by jealousies, and by the time they met at Odiham, Hampshire, on 9 January 1788, the combat had assumed the aspect of a grudge fight. The bout, fought on a stage before a large crowd, engendered suspicions of "foul play" in the umpiring against Mendoza, and when he

sprained his foot in a fall the match had to be ended after 20 minutes.

A contest of words carried out in the *World*, consisting of a barrage of letters between the two fighters, provoked a great anticipation for the second bout. After training at a camp set up at the Essex home of Sir Thomas Price, Mendoza met Humphreys again on 6 May 1789, at Henry Thornton's park in Stilton, Huntingdonshire. A specially erected building housed a ring 48 feet in circumference and rows of gallery seats reported to have accommodated nearly 3000 spectators. Mendoza prevailed after a long battle and became champion and a national hero. The third and final encounter with Humphreys occurred on 29 September 1790 at an inn yard at Doncaster, before 500 people who paid a half-guinea each for admission. Again Mendoza prevailed, somewhat easily.

After that third bout with Humphreys, Mendoza became even more immensely popular throughout England. Songs were written about him and his feats were mentioned in at least three theatrical productions, *The Duenna*, *The Farmer*, and *The Road to Ruin*. A sparring match had been introduced in the Irish fair scene of O'Keeffe's *Aladin* at Covent Garden on 30 December 1788 which originally featured Humphreys and another pugilist named Death. On 5 January 1789, however, Humphreys was replaced by Mendoza, who appeared again on 7 January and was paid £21 on 9 January. During July 1790 exhibitions of boxing were given at the Royal Circus by Mendoza, Jackson, Ryan, and Ward. In a tour of the British Isles Mendoza attracted large crowds wherever he went, and he gave exhibitions in packed theatres.

In 1791 Mendoza opened a small theatre at the Lyceum in the Strand for sparring exhibitions. "In his managerial capacity," explained Pierce Egan in *Boxiana* (1812), Mendoza "assured the public, by a very neat and appropriate address, that the manly art of boxing would be displayed, divested of all ferocity, rendered equally as neat and elegant as fencing." Imitations of "celebrated ancient and modern pugilists" were displayed, and everything was to be conducted "with the utmost propriety and decorum, that the female part of the creation might attend, without their feelings being infringed upon, or experiencing any unpleasant sensations." At Dublin in February

By permission of the Trustees of the British Museum

DANIEL MENDOZA

by Gillray

1792 Mendoza appeared in an entertainment called *A Peep at London's Amusements* produced at Astley's Amphitheatre in Peter Street and he gave boxing exhibitions there at a salary of £60 per week.

In the flush of his success, Mendoza, who was ill-versed socially and financially unsophisticated, began to play the role of bon vivant too enthusiastically. For a Jew from the East End to be conveyed in the royal coach to meet and engage in a long conversation with the King of England was heady stuff, indeed. But Mendoza was a bad manager of money, and in 1793 he found himself confined for a while as a prisoner within the rules of the King's Bench.

Mendoza had boxed with William Warr, of Bristol, at Smitham Bottom near Croydon on 14 May 1792, and though he was knocked down by a punch to the jaw in the fourteenth round he rallied to win in the twenty-third.

He defeated Warr again, this time in 15 minutes, on Bexley Common on 12 November 1794. Mendoza lost his championship, however, when he met the powerful John Jackson at Hornchurch, Essex, on 15 April 1795 before 3000 people. In the fifth round of that bout, which was fought for 200 guineas, Jackson held him by the hair as he pummeled him, until the exhausted Mendoza surrendered.

After his defeat by Jackson, Mendoza toured theatres throughout England and Wales for several years. In his *Memoirs* the fighter printed a copy of the bill for his appearance in Stretton's company at Stafford which was typical of performances:

Theatre Stafford. For One Night Only.

Messers. Stretton and Mendoza, who have had the honour of performing before their Majesties, under the sanction of the Reverend the Vice-Chancellors of Oxford and Cambridge, and most of the Nobility in this kingdom, present most dutiful respects to the Ladies and Gentlemen of Stafford, its Vicinity, and publick in general, and having procured copies from the original manuscripts of Mr Dibdin's celebrated Entertainments, thus humbly invite them to a performance entirely nouvelle, which they offer for their amusement, and which they hope will prove a source of entertainment to that publick, whose patronage and support it will ever their highest ambition to merit.

On Monday evening, January 28, 1799, will be presented a Selection of the most admired Songs and Recitations, written, composed, and performed by Mr Dibdin, at San Souci, Leicester Place, London; taken from the Christmas Gambols, Castles in the Air, and the General Election.

Between the parts, Mr Mendoza, the celebrated pugilist, will display his scientific knowledge of Self-Defence against a practiced pupil, by which he has foiled many an opponent.

End of Part 1st Mr Mendoza will exhibit and lecture upon the scientific skill and method of fighting of those celebrated pugilists, Big Ben, Johnson, Broughton, and Perrins.

End of Part 2d. will be displayed others equally skilful in the science; Humphreys, Ward, Wood, and George the Brewer.

The ladies are respectfully informed, there is neither violence or indecency in this spectacle, that can offend the most delicate of their sex; as an affirmation of which, Mr Mendoza has, by repeated desire, performed before their Majesties and the Royal Family.

The whole to conclude with Mr Mendoza's own Original Attitude

Mendoza retired from boxing to become publican of the Admiral House in Whitechapel. He also served as a Middlesex sheriff's officer and, it is said, was at some time a baker. In 1802, according to the *Memoirs* of the younger Charles Dibdin, Mendoza sparred with Jem Belcher one night on the stage of Sadler's Wells before a crowded house. He came out of retirement to fight a grudge match on 21 March 1806 on Grimstead Green, near Bromley, Kent, with Henry Lee, who had forfeited bail Mendoza had posted for him. Mendoza emerged the victor in 52 rounds, and won 50 guineas.

At the time Egan wrote *Boxiana* in 1812, Mendoza was a publican in Kennington. Subsequently he gave exhibitions of boxing in tours throughout the three kingdoms. His last appearance was in July 1820, when he was defeated by Tom Owen. He had a public benefit in 1820.

When he died in Horseshoe Alley, Petticoat Lane, on 3 September 1836, at the age of 73, Mendoza left a widow and 11 children, but little money. One of his cousins, Aaron Mendoza, was also a pugilist.

Daniel Mendoza was about five feet seven inches tall, and possessed strong arms, long stamina, and great courage. He had introduced into boxing a style which relied on quickness and finesse rather than brute strength.

His East End heritage permeated much of Mendoza's life, and his achievements and social influence for a while buoyed the spirits of London's Jews. He was often billed pugnaciously as "Mendoza the Jew," and to his neighbors he was the "Light of Israel."

The Odiad, or Battle of Humphries and Mendoza, was published in 1788. In 1789 Mendoza published *The Art of Boxing. The Memoirs of the Life of Daniel Mendoza,* written by himself, appeared in 1816; it was reissued in 1975 with an introduction by Paul Magriel.

Portraits of Daniel Mendoza include:

1. By S. Einsle. "The Match between Richard Humphreys and Daniel Mendoza at Odiham, Hants., 9th January 1788." Engraving by J. Grozer.
2. By T. Robineau. Depicts Mendoza standing in a field, in fighting posture. Present location unknown; the painting was in the possession of T. Hotchkin in 1789 when an engraving by H. Kingsbury was published by Fores. An engraving of the head only, done by

W. N. Gardiner, was published by Tagge in 1789.

3. By unknown artist. "Jackson-Mendoza Fight." Painting at Brodick Castle. Reproduced in this dictionary with the notice of John Jackson, pugilist.
4. Engraving by J. Gillray. Depicts Mendoza standing in the ring, in fighting posture. Published by Lewis.
5. By unknown engraver. View of the Humphreys-Mendoza bout in 1790. Published as a plate to Egan's *Boxiana* (1812).
6. By unknown engraver. Depicts Mendoza standing on a platform, in fighting posture.
7. Mendoza is shown with Humphreys on a mug commemorating their match at Odiham in 1788.

Menel, Mr ₍*fl. 1789–1792*₎, *violoncellist.*

Haydn in his *First London Notebook* cited Mr Menel as a violoncellist active in London in 1789. According to van der Straeten's *History of the Violoncello,* Menel made his London debut that year and in 1791 was a soloist in Salomon's concerts. Menel played at Haydn's benefit concert at the Hanover Square Rooms on 9 February 1792 and appeared there again on 3 May.

Menene, Signora. *See* FLETCHER, MARIA.

Menessier. *See* MANESSIER.

Mengotti. *See* MINGOTTI.

Mengozzi, Bernardo *1758–1800, singer, composer.*

Born at Florence in 1758, Bernardo Mengozzi there studied voice with Guarducci. Later he was taught by Pasquale Potenza, cantor of St Mark's, in Venice. From 1784 to 1786 he sang in oratorios at Venice. With the singer Anna Benini, whom he had married about 1785, he came to London, where on 17 February 1787 he made his debut at the King's Theatre, singing Don Leandro in Paisiello's *Il tutore burlato,* in which his wife performed Rosina. On 27 February he performed Bernardone in *Giannine e Bernardone,* in place of Morigi, with whom Burney confused him in his *General History of Music.* He also sang Tolomeo in *Giulio Cesare in Egitto* on 1 March, Don Berlico in

Gli schiava per amore on 24 April, and Domiziano in *La Vestale* on 1 May. On 15 March he played a principal role in *Virginia* and sang two new songs.

Mengozzi's voice suffered from the English climate, so he left London to settle at Paris. Before the Revolution he sang at concerts sponsored by Marie Antoinette and performed with the Italian company at the Théâtre de Monsieur. During the Revolution he was nominated for the directorship of the company, to be shared with Puppo. Upon the establishment of the Conservatoire in 1795 Mengozzi became professor of singing. He also wrote 14 comic operas for the Montansier and Feydeau theatres, and he gave private lessons.

He worked for many years on a *Méthode de Chant du Conservatoire*, but died in Paris in 1800 before he finished it. The work was edited by Langlé and published by Cherubini in 1804. A list of Mengozzi's productions in the Paris theatres is given in the *Enciclopedia dello spettacolo*, where he is characterized not as an innovator, but as an important link between the "scuola belcantista" and the "nuovi ideali vocali" of the eighteenth century.

Mengozzi's wife, who is noticed in this dictionary as Anna Bernini, seems to have been active professionally at least until 1791.

Mengozzi, Signora Bernardo. *See* BENINI, ANNA.

Meniucci, Mr (*fl.* 1776–1777), puppeteer.
Messrs Meniucci and Braville displayed their Chinese shadow puppets in St Alban's Street in 1776–77.

Menivale. *See* MERRIVALE.

Mennage. *See* MENAGE.

Mennie. *See* MEUNIER.

Mensell, Mr (*fl.* 1739), musician.
Mr Mensell was one of the original subscribers to the Royal Society of Musicians when it was established on 28 August 1739.

Menton, Mr (*fl.* 1735–1736), house servant.
The accounts of Covent Garden Theatre show that a Mr Menton was a house attendant at a salary of 2s. daily in 1735–36. He worked 179 days that season.

Mentorini, Signora (*fl.* 1754), dancer, actress.
In Christopher Smart's entertainment called *The Old Woman's Oratory* at the Haymarket Theatre on 11 March 1754 an *English Ballet* was performed by "Timbertoe, Signora Mentorini." Smart often used pseudonyms, and Timbertoe certainly sounds like one, but Signora Mentorini (or Mentoreni) may have been a dancer's real name. The pair danced again on 30 March, and on 1 April she had a principal part in *The Adventures of Fribble*.

Mercerot, Mons (*fl.* 1791–1806), dancer, choreographer, actor.
Astley's Amphitheatre at Westminster Bridge advertised on 26 and 27 August 1791 an "Operatical Dance" composed by Monsieur Mercerot, "just arrived from one of the principal theatres in Paris." The rare and scattered bills of Astley's demonstrate that he was employed at the amphitheatre as choreographer, dancing master, and a principal performer for at least the following 15 seasons. For example, on 30 August 1791 there was a "Dramatic Dance composed by the celebrated Mons. Mercerot called *Love and Valour; or, Astley's New West Indian.*" From 17 to 19 September 1791 he danced in the ballet *The Animated Statue*. On 17 July he was the Demon in a pantomime *Good and Bad; or, Jupiter's Vengeance*. From 5 to 14 August 1792 his "Pastoral Dance" *The Florists* held sway at Astley's.

In the winter of 1792–93 Mercerot and the rest of the company were at Astley's Amphitheatre Royal in Peter Street, Dublin, and on 31 January he danced in the pantomime *La Forêt noire; or, The Natural Son*. Evidently that pantomime was the same as *Maternal Affection; or, The Dark Forest*, which he appeared in when the company returned to London in the spring.

The first appearance of Madame Mercerot in England was advertised at Astley's for 3 April 1793 when she and Mercerot danced in a fête *Champêtre* of his composition. His *Florists' Festival* was danced in May 1794. She danced with "Tassells" (Lascelles Williamson) on 27 July 1795 in Williamson's *Rustic Sports; or, Win Her and Wear Her.*

On 16 May 1796 at Astley's (at that time called the Amphitheatre of Arts) Mercerot danced Hymen in *The Magician of the Rocks* and his wife danced in the corps and stepped out for a hornpipe with West. The evidence is missing after 1796 until 5 October 1801, when Madame Mercerot danced with Banks, Whitmore, and Laurent in *The Spaniard and the American* "got up by Mr. Mercerot," and the Mercerots teamed as featured dancers in the ballet *The Bashaw.*

The *Monthly Mirror* occasionally and briefly mentioned Mercerot's presence in the company at Astley's until 1804. The Drury Lane accounts in the Folger Library show Mercerot receiving a weekly salary of £1 5s. in the 1807–8 season. (A Miss Mercerot, doubtless his daughter, earned the same salary as a dancer at Drury Lane during the previous season.)

In April 1807 the *Monthly Mirror,* reviewing an unnamed Amazonian extravaganza at Astley's in which Mme Mercerot then had a part, remarked that she was "too big with child to take the sword and mingle in the fight. Though she conquers her man . . . her feats are more alarming than agreeable."

Mercerot, Mme ₁*fl.* 1793–1807₁, *dancer. See* MERCEROT, MONS.

Merchant, Mrs ₁*fl.* 1677₁, *actress.*
At Drury Lane Theatre, Mrs Merchant played Petulant Easy in *The Rambling Justice* in late February 1678 and Lucilla in *Trick for Trick* in March.

Merchant, S. *See* DIBDIN, THOMAS JOHN.

Merchant, Mrs S. *See* DIBDIN, MRS THOMAS JOHN.

Merchants, Mr ₁*fl.* 1688₁, *musician.*
Mr Merchants, a member of the King's Musick, attended the King at Windsor from 24 July to 20 September 1688 and for his services received 6s. plus a daily fee of 1s. 6d.

Mercier. *See also* LEMERCIER.

Mercier, Mons ₁*fl.* 1773₁, *exhibitor.*
The Philadelphia *Journal* on 12 May 1773 and following, carried advertisements for a "New PROSPECTIVE THEATRE which the Sieur MERCIER has brought over" from London, and which could be seen at the Southwark Theatre in Philadelphia on Mondays, Wednesdays, Fridays, and Saturdays. Thomas Clark Pollock, in his *The Philadelphia Theatre in the Eighteenth Century* (1933), conjectures "this was apparently a combination of 'magic lanthorn'; marionettes, and panorama."

Mercucius, Signora ₁*fl.* 1764₁, *dancer.*
Signora Mercucius danced at Sadler's Wells in 1764. Her name is found on surviving advertisements for entertainments on 28 April and 22 September of that year.

"Mercury, The English." *See* MATHEW, MR ₁*fl.* 1784–1786₁.

Mercy, Louis *c.* 1695–*c.* 1750, *recorder player, flutist, composer.*
Louis Mercy (or Merci), born about 1695, was an Englishman of French extraction who excelled on the recorder and wrote several solos for it. At the Lincoln's Inn Fields Theatre on 9 April 1716 he played two entertainments on the flute, and he performed on 13 February 1719 at Hickford's Music Room. Mercy was at Cannons about 1720 as a flutist at £10 per quarter. Since the recorder was going out of fashion and being replaced in public favor by the German, or transverse, flute, Mercy joined with the instrument-maker Thomas Stainsby, the younger, to promote a modified recorder which he called an English flute. That was in 1735, so it is likely that when Mercy performed compositions of his own for his benefit at York Buildings on 1 April 1735 he used the new instrument. The *New Grove* says Mercy died about 1750.

Meredith, Mr ₁*fl.* 1773–1782?₁, *singer.*
Mr Meredith, "who never performed in public," sang with Sga Galli, Vernon, Miss Harper, and others in the *Messiah* at the Haymarket Theatre on 26 February 1773. The same singers presented *The Prodigal Son* on 6 March and five other times until 2 April, *The Resurrection* on 24 March, the *Messiah* again on 26

March, and *Goliath* on 23 April and 5 May. About 1775 the song *Hark the hills and dales resounding* was published as sung by Meredith. During the mid-seventies Meredith began singing at Ranelagh Gardens. He was announced as from there in the newspaper bills advertising the opening of the new Vauxhall Gardens at Bristol in July 1776. He was a principal singer in *Acis and Galatea* at Covent Garden during the oratorio season in March 1778. Perhaps he was the Meredith who sang a duet with Gaudry at a concert of the Edinburgh Musical Society on 8 March 1782.

A collection of *The Favourite Songs sung at Ranelagh Gardens by Mr. Meredith and Miss Sharpe* was published in 1777. Other songs published as performed by Meredith at Ranelagh included *Arise, arise, thou blushing Rose, As t'other day o'er the green meadows I pass'd*, and *When the snow descends*, all in 1778.

Meredith, Mr   *d. 1777, housekeeper.*

A Mr Meredith was a house servant at the Haymarket Theatre by 4 March 1745 when it was advertised that tickets could be had of him at the theatre. On 20 December 1751 the Haymarket bills identified him as housekeeper. The *Morning Chronicle* of 7 May 1777 announced that he had died the previous day.

Meredith, Mr   [*fl. 1789–1804?*],   *actor.*

Announced as a gentleman making his first appearance on any stage, Mr Meredith acted the title role in *Alexander the Great* at Covent Garden Theatre on 28 April 1789, for Aickin's benefit. An occasional address written by Vardill was spoken by Middleton to introduce Meredith, who was identified in the *European Magazine* that month.

Perhaps he was the Meredith who acted at the Theatre Royal, Norwich, in 1791. A Meredith played Buckingham in a specially-licensed performance of *Richard III* at the Haymarket Theatre on 16 April 1792 for the benefit of the Literary Fund, but probably he was an amateur. On 23 January 1797 a Meredith was a member of Wilkinson's Company at the Haymarket, playing a role in *The Battle of Eddington* and Tiptoe in *Ways and Means*. On 10 May of that year, at the Haymarket, *The Battle of Eddington* was again offered with the afterpiece *The Romance of an Hour*, in which Meredith acted Orson. On 26 March 1798 Meredith

returned with Wilkinson to the Haymarket to act Shiva in *The Jew*, Sam Stern in *A Naval Interlude*, Sir Jacob Jollup in *The Mayor of Garratt*, and Trusty in *The Ghost*—a busy evening. Announced as making his first appearance at Covent Garden, Meredith played Duke Murcia in *The Child of Nature*, for the benefit of the General Lying-in Hospital on 11 June 1798. In 1804 a Meredith was acting with the company at Richmond, Surrey.

Meredith, Mr   [*fl. 1793*],   *equestrian. See* **MEREDITH, MASTER.**

Meredith, Mr   *d. 1810, singer.*

Among the performers in the grand concert of Handelian music by which the new Drury Lane Theatre was opened on 12 March 1794 was Meredith, a bass singer from Liverpool, making his first appearance in London. Similar concerts were given several times in March and April. On 12 April the Drury Lane treasurer paid Meredith £73 10s. "in full."

Harvard Theatre Collection

MR MEREDITH

engraving by Haughton, after Turmeau

The *Examiner* of 24 January 1810 reported that "Meredith the Bass Singer," having survived the amputation of his leg but a short time, had died at Wrexham on 6 January.

The Musical Chace, a hunting song by Charles Wilton, was published at Liverpool about 1790 and at London in 1795 as sung by Mr Meredith. A portrait of him engraved by M. Haughton, after J. Turmeau, was published by the artist in 1803.

Meredith, Master, called "The Child of Promise" *b. 1786, equestrian.*

In April 1793 Thomas Franklin's equestrian show was performed at the amphitheatre in Limekiln Lane, Bristol, and the advertisements reported that "His Troop now consists of Thirteen of the best performers in the Universe, among whom is Master Meredith, a native of this city." In October 1793 Franklin brought young Meredith to the Royal Circus in London, where he was advertised as seven years old and called "The Child of Promise." (The original "Child of Promise" was Mary Ann Handy.) Thomas Frost in *Circus Life and Circus Celebrities* (1875) placed a "Mr" Meredith, an equestrian, at the Royal Circus in 1793; if that person was not actually Master Meredith, perhaps he was his father.

Merefield. *See* MERRIFIELD.

Merighi, Antonia Margherita [Signora Carlo Carlani] [*fl.* 1717–1740], *singer.*

Antonia Margherita Merighi was a Bolognese and served the Dowager Grand Duchess Violante Beatrice of Tuscany. She sang in Venice from 1717 to 1733, making appearances also in Bologna, Naples, Parma, Florence, Turin, and London. A contralto, she often sang male roles.

The *Daily Journal* reported on 2 July 1729 that Handel had recruited Signora Antonia Merighi, "a Woman of a very fine Presence, an excellent Actress, and a very good singer—A Counter Tenor" for the opera season at the King's Theatre (Burney called her a "contralto profondo"). Her salary for the season was £800 (Rolli reported £900 or £1000). According to the 1729 edition of *Lotario*, she sang Matilde in that work when it was given on 2 December 1729, then she was heard as Rosmira in *Partenope*, Erissena in *Poro*, Palmira in *Ormisda*, and

Elisa in *Tolomeo*, in which she sang soprano music transposed for her. During the 1730–31 season she again sang Erissena and also appeared as Armira in *Scipione*, Armida in *Rinaldo*, and, according to Deutsch's reconstruction, Unulfo in *Rodelinda*. She was not in London again until the 1736–37 season. She returned to sing at Kensington, according to the *Daily Post* of 18 November 1736, then at the King's Theatre she portrayed Amira in *Siroe*, the title role in *Merope*, and Cleonice in *Demetrio*. The following season, 1737–38, she sang Statira in *Arsaces*, Gernando in *Faramondo*, Alessandro in *Alessandro Severo*, Peleo in *La conquista del vello d'oro*, and Amastre in *Serse* (her last role in England, according to Grove).

Mrs Pendarves wrote to her sister Ann Granville in late November 1729 that Signora Merighi's voice was "not extraordinarily good or bad, she is tall and has a very graceful person, with a tolerable face; she seems to be a woman about forty, she sings easily and agreeable." By 27 November 1736 after Signora Merighi's return, Mrs Pendarves wrote that the singer had "*no sound*" in her voice, but thundering action—a beauty with *no other merit . . .* " Rolli, on the other hand, wrote to Riva that "Merighi is really a perfect actress and that is the general opinion." Handel certainly thought well of her talent, giving her important roles.

Signora Merighi sang in Florence in 1732 and Modena in 1735; in Munich in 1740 she sang in two operas and then retired. Her husband, Carlo Carlani (1716–1776), was a tenor, but he seems not to have appeared in England.

A caricature of Antonia Margherita Merighi by Anton Maria Zanetti is in the Fondazione Giorgio Cini in Venice.

Merimée. *See* MEUNIER.

"Merit, Miss" [*fl.* 1753], *performer.*

In Christopher Smart's *Old Woman's Concert* at the Haymarket Theatre on 13 March 1753 one of the principal parts was taken by "Miss Merit, an English Lady of an ancient Family, almost extinct." The pseudonym was a typical Smart concoction, and there is no telling whether Miss Merit was a human being or a trained animal. With her in the cast were such other Smart creations as "Mynheer Puffupandyke; Mlle Rompereau; Mme Hophye."

Merlin, John Joseph *1735–1803, mechanical instrument maker, exhibitor.*

According to notations to "Lyson's Collectanea" in the British Library, the Belgian John Joseph Merlin was born at Huys on 17 September 1735 and came to England on 24 May 1760 in the entourage of the Spanish Ambassador Extraordinary, the Count de Fuentes. He worked with Gabriel Cox, proprietor of Cox's Museum, Spring Garden, until 1773, and then went on his own, setting up a shop at No 11, Princes Street, Hanover Square. By 1783 his establishment was styled "Merlin's Mechanical Museum," where he offered afternoon tea and coffee and private evening parties to persons desiring to view his ingenious mechanical gadgets.

Among Merlin's inventions, some of them of practical use, were a bell-communication system to summon servants, a mechanical chariot, a mechanical garden, a self-propelling wheel chair, a "Hygeian Air-Pump" to expel foul air, a mechanical carousel, and a prosthetic device for "a Person born with Stumps only."

Merlin also constructed musical instruments. A pianoforte with a compass of six octaves that he made for Dr Burney preceded by some fifteen years Broadwood's five-and-a-half-octave span in 1790. Other inventions included a barrel organ-harpsichord that played 19 tunes and a one-man orchestra that consisted of:

Five instruments always in tune,
It's a sight you can't always survey;
Composed in one instrument's use,
All of which one Musician can play.

In Dr Burney's article on the harpsichord in *Rees's Cyclopaedia*, the musicologist wrote: "A *double* harpsichord used to have two sets of keys and three strings, two unisons and an octave to each note. Merlin, we believe, was the first

The Iveagh Bequest, Kenwood (GLC)

JOHN JOSEPH MERLIN
by Gainsborough

who changed the octave stop into a third unison, about the year 1770, which rendered the instrument equally powerful, and less subject to go out of tune."

Fanny Burney filled her diary with comments about Merlin, who was "a great favourite" in the Burney household:

He is very diverting also in conversation. There is a singular simplicity in his manners. He speaks his opinion upon all subjects and about all persons with the most undisguised freedom. He does not, though a foreigner, want *words*; but he *arranges* and *pronounces* them very comically. He is humbly grateful for all civilities that are shown him; but is warmly and honestly resentful of the least slight.

At a fashionable masquerade at Bath on 10 April 1780 she saw Merlin disguised as "A Sick Man in his Morfus Chair, as he calls it."

In a revival of *The Tempest* at Drury Lane Theatre on 4 January 1777, with new settings by De Loutherbourg, according to the *Morning Chronicle* "The Musical Instrument (played behind the Scenes)" was Merlin's invention.

In his *Concert Room and Orchestra Anecdotes* (1805), Thomas Busby related a serio-comic incident:

One of his ingenious novelties was a *pair of skaites*, contrived to run on wheels. Supplied with these and a violin, he mixed in the motley group of one of Mrs Cornelys' masquerades at Carlisle House; when, not having provided the means of retarding his velocity, or commanding its direction, he impelled himself against a mirror of more than five hundred pounds value, dashed it to atoms, broke his instrument to pieces and wounded himself most severely.

Merlin died at Paddington in May 1803, at the age of 68. In his will he directed that his thirty-year-old horse be shot. Having died unmarried, he left his property to two brothers and a sister, living abroad. Details of his inventions are given by Richard Altick, *The Shows of London* (1978). An engraving showing Merlin and his mechanical chariot was published in Kirby's *Wonderful and Scientific Museum* (1803). An engraving of his mechanical wheel chair appeared in *Ackermann's Repository of Arts* (1811). Merlin's portrait in oils by Thomas Gainsborough is at Kenwood House, Hampstead; on loan from an anonymous owner since 1973, it was purchased by Kenwood in 1983.

Merrick, Mr ₁*fl. 1745–1747*₁, *gallery keeper.*

One Merrick, gallery keeper, is the subject of two entries in a surviving Covent Garden paylist in the British Library. On 8 December 1746: "gal. keeper—arrears £6.9.0 for last season"; on 1 June 1747: "for his attend. this season 7.2.4."

Merrick, James ₁*fl. 1794–1803*₁, *scene painter.*

James Merrick was an assistant scene painter at Covent Garden Theatre from August through October 1794, at a salary of 8*s.* per day, according to British Library MS Egerton 2293. He was probably the Merrick (sometimes "Meyrick") who was paid as a painter at Drury Lane Theatre from October 1802 through the season of 1807–8 and again, at the Lyceum, in 1811–12. He assisted Thomas Greenwood, Jr, at the Royal Circus with the scenery for *Louisa of Lombardy* and *Number Nip* in 1803 and was one of six executants working to designs by Latilla and Whitmore for *Aballino; or, The Bravo's Bride* in 1805.

Merrifield. *See also* MERRYFIELD.

Merrifield, John ₁*fl. 1762–1776*₁, *dancer.*

John Merrifield (Merefield, Merifield, Merryfield, at the whim of the bill printer) was in the corps of dancers at Covent Garden Theatre from 1762–63 through 1775–76. He was never a soloist and usually danced in company with two or more of the usual crew with whom he shared his annual benefits: Dumay, Hussy, Miss Daw, Davis, Holtom, and the like. On 22 May 1764 he did share the comparative distinction: "A Double Hornpipe by Merefield, first time & Miss Daw." His shared benefits were often failures, with deficits incurred because of house charges, and at the end of several seasons the account book bore notations such as : "Rec'd . . . in payment of deficiencies for last season's bt. . . . " Merrifield's last recorded performance was on 15 May 1776 when he danced "Minuets and Cotillions" with seven others.

John Merrifield's first name and the spelling he apparently approved of for his family name were furnished by his signature to a letter in the *Theatrical Monitor* of 5 November 1768.

Merrivale, Thomas *b. c. 1703, actor, author.*

The poet Thomas Merrivale was born about 1703 and was the author in 1724 of a poem entitled *The Necromancer; or, Harlequin Doctor Faustus*, a tribute to John Rich's successful pantomime, *The Necromancer*. Chester Burgess has suggested to us that Thomas Merrivale was the Mr "Merrival" who was hired by Rich at the Lincoln's Inn Fields Theatre on 20 May 1723. His daily salary, according to a note in the theatre's accounts dated 24 September 1724, was 3*s*. Merrivale is known to have acted Mortimer in *1 Henry IV* on 20 May 1724 at a benefit he shared with two others (gross income £114 7*s*.) and Phorbas in *Oedipus* at the Bullock-Spiller booth at Southwark on 24 September.

Merry, Mrs Anne. *See* WIGNELL, MRS THOMAS.

"Merry Trumpeter, The." *See* "CHARLES THE MERRY TRUMPETER."

Merryfield, Robert *1732–1789, actor.*

When in February 1775 a special benefit was arranged at the Haymarket Theatre for Mrs Woodham the singer and her five orphaned children, Robert Merryfield essayed Justice Woodcock in *Love in a Village* ("Merryfield, first Appearance on any Stage"). But, pitifully, the expenses exceeded the receipts of the performance and a collection had to be taken up for the widow.

There was another benefit at which the dubious talents of Merryfield were called upon, this time for the actor Jacobs on 3 October 1776. It was "By Particular Desire of the Masons," and both Jacobs and Merrifield were called "Brothers" of the lodge. Merryfield repeated his Justice Woodcock. That was his last performance, so far as we know, though he may have acted outside London. He seems to have been more than an amateur, for according to *A Collection of Epitaphs* (1806), which furnishes his full name, he was buried at the "actors' church," St Paul, Covent Garden, after his death on 28 August 1789, aged 57.

Merryman, Mr [*fl.* 1782?–1785], *equestrian.*

Mr Merryman was an equestrian with Philip Astley's troupe in Brussels (probably the tour Astley made in 1782), according to references to him in John Williams's *A Pin Basket to the Children of Thespis*. He was still with Astley, in London, in July 1785, when he was "much admired" for his horsemanship.

Messing. *See also* MESSINK.

Messing, Junior. *See* MESSINK, JAMES.

Messing, Frederick [*fl.* 1733–1763?], *horn player.*

The first notice of Frederick Messing (if indeed it was he; no first name was given) was in the bill for Hickford's Room on 5 April 1734, when Messing and Charke the singer and violinist took a benefit. During the concert that night was "introduc'd Adonis Chace, consisting of two Aubaden for four French Horns," in which Messing perhaps bore a part. "Frederick Messing" is listed as one of the original subscribers to the Royal Society of Musicians in the Declaration of Trust establishing the Society on 28 August 1739.

Among the surviving scattered bills of the musical taverns is one for another benefit for Messing, at the Devil Tavern on 19 February 1741, a concert "in which will be introduced several Pieces on a new-invented Instrument, called the Corno Cromatico." (This "chromatic horn," a stage of development of the "French" horn from a hunting to a widely-used orchestral instrument, employed a series of "crooks," rings of tubing of several sizes which could be inserted into the parent unit to alter the key. R. Morley Pegge, writing in *Grove's Dictionary* (5th edition) credits Frederick Messing as "probably being the first" to use crooks in public in England.) Lysons in his *Environs* cites a bill of the Devil Tavern:

Mr. MESSING

Goes to the Devil this present Thursday, to prepare a polite serenade, both vocal and instrumental, for the entertainment of his well-wishers and benefactors.

A Frederick Messing is cited in Mortimer's *London Directory* (1763): "Performer on the French horn and violin. Compton-street, Soho."

He may, however, have been a son of the subject of this entry.

Messing, Frederick ₍*fl. 1763?*₎, *French-horn player, violinist.*

When Frederick James Messing (1754–1798), "the Mad Fidler," made his deposition to the Royal Society of Musicians in 1782 he testified that "My Grandfather and Father belonged to [the Society for] many years." Inasmuch as the 1739 list of charter subscribers to the Society carried the name of only one Messing—Frederick Messing the well-known horn player—he must have had a son, Frederick James Messing's father, who joined the Society later. But there is no record of that Messing in the Minute Books of the Society, which are by no means complete.

Charles Burney, writing in Rees's *Encyclopedia*, said that "The Messings were the first [horn players] who pretended to perform in all keys in England, about the year 1740," making it certain that there was a second Messing active at about that date, which was too soon for Frederick James Messing. He may have been the Frederick Messing listed in *Mortimer's London Directory* in 1763: "Performer on the French horn and violin. Compton-street, Soho."

Messing, Frederick James *1754–1798, violinist, violist, violoncellist, guitarist, copyist.*

Frederick James Messing was 27 years old on 17 December 1781. So he declared on the occasion of his admittance to the Royal Society of Musicians in 1782. His other statements on a curious document with 17 numbered lines, a statement to a line ("1st, . . . 16th, 17th") provide an outline of his life and condition to that date, and perhaps also a hint of the eccentricity which would grow to madness: "My Grandfather and Father belonged to [the Society] many years." "I profess the Violin, Viola, Violoncello, Guittar with copying of musick." "I am married ye 10th of March 1781 and have had no children nor is there the least likelyhood of my having any at present." "My wife will be 22 years of age next March [1783]."

In his sixth to sixteenth allegations Messing deposed:

I have played at ye Antient Concert at ye Crown and Anchor 10 years. I have played at his Majesty's [Birthday] Odes 7 years. I have played at most of

By permission of the British Library Board

FREDERICK JAMES MESSING

artist unknown

the Publick Places [pleasure gardens and musical taverns]. I play at Annual Concerts [of various musical Societies like the Academy of Ancient Music]. . . . I have got my Bread by the said Profession above these 12 years. Bless God I and my Wife are in perfect Health. I have always Employ more or less [*sic*]. Furniture and everything in my Lodgings is my own property which cost me above £150. and don't owe a Farthing. My principal gain is by Teaching and Copying.

His "gain" had not been to that point large, though it was growing. He says he "got by ye above professions" in 1779 £65 13*s*. 6*d*., in 1780 £79 14*s*., and in 1781 £123 16*s*. 7*d*.

Burney listed Messing among the "tenors" (violas) when the Handel Memorial Concerts of May and June 1784 were performed at Westminster Abbey and the Pantheon. He was on the list in the Minute Books of the Royal

Society of Musicians to play tenor at the annual charity concerts at St Paul's on 10 and 12 May 1785, and to play violoncello on 12 and 14 May 1789. His name is on a surviving list of instrumentalists and singers employed for the 1787–88 season of concerts by the Academy of Ancient Music. (He earned £6 6s. playing violin.)

Little more is known about Messing's career. Sainsbury in the *Biographical Dictionary of Musicians* (1824) tells us that he was called "the Mad Fiddler." "He called himself Handel's son, whose monument he visited daily, went with his head shaved, and dressed in black, with a star. He died in London in 1797, at the age of forty-three. His children were educated at the expense of the Musical Fund."

The onset of Messing's madness, its tragic consequences for his family, and the charitable operation of the Fund are preserved in memoranda in the manuscript Minute Books of the Royal Society of Musicians. On 7 February 1790 he personally applied for relief, informing the Governors that he and his family were in the utmost distress. A committee was deputed to look into the facts and authorize a sum not to exceed six guineas. But on 7 March the committee reported that Messing's need was not caused by age, infirmity or unavoidable misfortune. On 4 April his petition was denied, but the governors ordered two guineas to be applied to relief of his children. He was rebuffed again in May, but in August evidence was offered "that his mind was deranged."

Two guineas a month were authorized to the Messing family on a temporary basis; he was ordered to appear and produce an accounting of his earnings in October. Upon his admission that he had "refused a regular engagement" of one guinea a week, he was told that future applications would be disregarded. On 7 August 1791 "Mr. Denman informed that Mr. Messing had been committed to Bridewell for an assault, that his wife had thrown herself from a two-story window & lay in the hospital not only very much bruised but deranged in her senses, that application had been made to him as a governor to prevent the society being disgraced by the children being sent to the Parish and that he had placed them with temporary nurses. . . ."

From then until 1810 the Governors of the Society sponsored the education and training of Messing's children, putting the son Frederick James apprentice to a blacksmith, a daughter Henrietta to a shoemaker, and Phebe to a mantua-maker. Apparently there was yet another, younger, daughter. All were provided with apparel.

Frederick James Messing did not die in 1797 as Sainsbury thought. A portrait of Messing by an unknown engraver is in the British Museum, its inscription reading: "Fred.ᵏ James Messing, well known by the name of the Mad Fidler, he was a member of the Royal Society of Musicians, and was by them interred in Sᵗ. Pancras Churchyard, died Augˢ 4ᵗʰ 1798 Aged 44." A bit too late, on 5 August 1798, more money was alloted for medicine for him by the Society. On 2 September Penelope Messing, his widow, prayed for relief and was granted £1 15s. per month and £5 1s. to pay for his funeral. Her allowance was raised to £2 per month on 6 February 1820. On 3 March she, "being above 70 years old," got a gratuity of £6. On 1 August 1830, £8 was granted for her funeral.

Messinck. *See* MESSINK.

Messink, Mr ₁*fl. 1726*₁, *painter.*
A Mr "Missing" (we think that may have been a scribal error for "Messink") was recorded in accounts of Lincoln's Inn Fields Theatre preserved in the British Library (Ms Egerton 2266) as receiving £11 on 18 February 1726 "for painting 8 habits [*sic*] in the Rape of Proserpine." The painter, of whom there is no further trace in London, may have been related to the later performer-painter James Messink or even to the musicians Messing.

Messink, Barnard ₁*fl. 1774–1775*₁, *machinist. See* MESSINK, JAMES.

Messink, James *1721–1789, singer, dancer, wire-dancer, actor, machinist, scene-painter, pantomime deviser.*
It seems likely that citations to the singer "Messing" in Covent Garden and Haymarket playbills occasionally from 1742 through 1748 refer to James Messink. A Messing was allowed benefit tickets at Covent Garden on 27 March 1742. On 2 February 1743 and for several nights following, Messing played the Dragon

in *The Dragon of Wantley* at the Haymarket
Theatre and on 24 March was Osmyn in *Amelia*
at the Haymarket. Both were specially-licensed
benefits at that house, normally dark in the
winters. Similarly, on 19 January 1744, Messing sang the role of the Marquis in *The Queen
of Spain; or, Farinelli in Madrid* at such a benefit.

At Covent Garden in March 1744 and in
January, February, and March 1745, Messing
was one of the Attendant Spirits in *Comus*. Very
likely he was obscurely employed in the choruses during that season and during the next,
when he earned a share of the benefit night of
29 April 1746. On 26 April 1748 at Covent
Garden he shared a benefit with Plummer the
boxkeeper. On 9 December 1748 a Messing,
"Jun[ior]" (perhaps our subject, perhaps his
son) sang for the benefit of the bass singer
Gustavus Waltz.

On 13 December 1750 at Drury Lane the
afterpiece was the new musical entertainment
Robin Hood in which "Messink" sang Robin
Hood. He (like the earlier "Messing") is undoubtedly to be identified as James Messink,
who began his Irish career later that same season as a harlequin at Smock Alley Theatre in
Dublin.

James Messink remained at Smock Alley
through 1758–59. In his second season there
for his own shared benefit on 21 May 1751 he
added another specialty to his growing list, for
the bill announced: "Messink [dancing] on the
wire (after the manner of the celebrated Mahomet Caratta), being his first attempt of that
kind in Publick." On 3 April 1752, for his
benefit, he offered equilibres on the wire:

1st, He will balance a Straw on the Edge of a Glass.
Next, he will balance a Feather on his Nose, and
afterwards blow it from his Nose on his Forehead.
Next, He will wheel a Lapland Dog in a Wheel-
Barrow. Next, He will play on the Pipe and dou[b]le
Taber standing on the Wire. Next, He will toss
the Balls. And lastly, He will balance a Horizontal
Wheel of Fire works.

In the 1758–59 season Messink alternated between Smock Alley and the Crow Street Theatre. In 1761–62 and continuously through
1766–67 he was with Barry at Crow Street.

Over the years in Ireland he began to apply
his great dexterity and ingenuity to devising
pantomimes and creating elaborate machinery.

He composed his first pantomime, *Mercury
Harlequin*, for production at Crow Street on 16
April 1763 and his second *The Enchanted Lady*
for that theatre in February 1766. Robert
Hitchcock in *An Historical View of the Irish Stage*
(1788) called him "the first machinist ever
known in this kingdom." During his time in
Ireland he also often walked on in a variety of
inconsiderable characters—servants, porters,
pirates, plebeians—and a few named roles like
Longbottom in *The Country Lasses*, Vasquez in
The Wonder, and Hounslow in *The Stratagem*.
In the summers or autumns of 1757, 1758,
1760, 1762, 1763, 1764, and 1766 he also
acted or perhaps devised pantomimes at Cork.

Messink's versatility had come to Garrick's
attention, and in 1767 he was brought to Drury
Lane at £4 per week to supervise machinery
and help devise pantomimes. But he continued
to act, sing, and dance in them, too, playing
a Beggar here and a Recruit there, sometimes
an Irishman, sometimes a Shepherd or a Lover,
Clinch in *The Ghost*, Roger in *The Mayor of
Garratt*, but also sometimes acting a minor
role in Shakespeare like William in *As You Like
It* or Tubal in *The Merchant of Venice*. He remained at Drury Lane for a decade, contriving
or assisting in such pieces as *The Elopement*
(1767), and *Pigmy Revels*.

When Garrick sought to recoup some of his
losses from his disastrous Shakespeare Jubilee,
held at Stratford in 1769, by transferring some
of its features to the stage, Messink was invaluable. He devised a procession, employing
elaborate arrangements of machinery and lavish use of costumes and scenery in 11 "pag-
eants," or floats, drawn across the stage, bearing
Shakespearean characters in famous scenes—
Romeo and Juliet in the tomb, Cleopatra on
her barge, Richard III in the tent scene, and
so on—as an adjunct to Garrick's successful
farce, *The Jubilee*. Messink also walked in the
procession of Shakespearean characters. (The
Folger Library holds a manuscript scenario entitled "Pageant of *Shakespeare's Jubilee* in the
year 1770" with Messink's own notes to Garrick in his own rather original spelling, e.g.,
for *Coriolanus*: "The pageant to represent a kind
of trone comeposed of Tropheys of arms and
Speers—Tullius Afegius siting on the right
hand of Coriolanus. . . ." A complete description of the manuscript is given by G. W. Stone,
Jr. in *The London Stage 1660–1800*. Another

manuscript, with some variations, is at the Huntington Library and has been published by Elizabeth P. Stein in *Three Plays by David Garrick*.)

In 1777 Messink went over to Covent Garden where his *Harlequin Freemason* (1780) and *Choice of Harlequin* (1781) were popular. In 1783 he returned to Ireland this time to a third Dublin Theatre, Capel Street. There he designed the models for scenery by William Jolly, working under Giordani and Leoni. He thus helped create the scenery for *The Enchantress* (1783) and *The Maid of the Mill*, *The Genius of Ireland*, and *Orpheus and Eurydice* (1784). At Smock Alley in 1785 he was composer, machinist, and painter for the elaborate *Island of Saints, or Institution of the Shamrock*.

James Messink died at his house in Charlotte Street, Rathbone Place, London, on 19 November 1789. He left his wife, Jane, née Cartwright, whom he had married in Dublin in 1756 (probably his second wife, for a "Mrs Messink" was on the roster at Smock Alley in 1751–52), and several children. His will, made 19 February 1787 and proved by his wife on 9 December 1789, provided handsomely for his family out of what was apparently an ample fortune, partly made and partly inherited from his son, Barnard Messink.

The reasons for Messink's inheriting from his son are involved in a curious episode in theatrical history: David Garrick had been applied to by some gentlemen of the East India Company's forces at Calcutta for assistance and advice in setting up an English-language theatre. "In consequence of which," noted the *London Chronicle* of 10–13 December 1774, "he sent them over the best dramatic works in the language, together with complete setts of scenery, under the care of an ingenious young Mechanist from Drury-lane, whom he recommended to superintend that department." In June 1775 the gentlemen of Calcutta sent Mrs Garrick some Indian chintz and Garrick some Madeira. On 21 August 1775 Gilbert Ironside, evidently a Colonel in the East India Company's forces, wrote to Garrick from Patna, India, praising Mr Messink for help in setting up a theatre at Fort William and assuring Garrick that he would do everything he could to advance the young man's fortune. "I have some thoughts," wrote Ironside, "of setting at work his happy invention for Machinery, & the skill he has in the artificial slights or deceptions of the Stage, in the manufacturing a Pantomime by way of Vehicle for the introduction of the fashions habits dances & music of this Country." Many years later Charles Lee Lewes, in a vignette of "my once loved Messink" in his memoirs, declared that "after a very short stay" in India young Messink had amassed a fortune of £27,000, and died suddenly at Bencoolen on his way back to England.

Evidently Lewes considerably exaggerated Barnard Messink's wealth. James deposes: ". . . by the last will and Testament of my late son Barnard Messink I am appointed one of his . . . Executors . . . by which will a Sum of two thousand pounds is given to myself . . . upon Trust to invest . . . for the use and benefit of his Natural Daughter Sarah now under my care." James passed on the trusteeship and guardianship to his wife Jane.

James Messink left his wife Jane £1,000 and the household effects. A ring of "50 guineas' value" went to Messink's daughter Gertrude Talfrey, with an explanation for not leaving her "a full and equal share with the rest of her sisters": that Gertrude's husband was sufficiently wealthy. The "rest and residue" of James's property and money was invested for the benefit of "three younger daughters," Elizabeth, Frances, and Henrietta.

Messis, Mrs [*fl.* 1733], *dancer.*
At Goodman's Fields Theatre on 7 May 1733 the part of Venus in *The Contending Deities* was danced by "Mrs Messis, from the Opera House."

Mestayer, Henry [*fl.* 1773], *prompter.*
In the *Morning Chronicle* on 4 May 1773 was a card signed by Henry Mestayer, prompter at the Haymarket Theatre, regarding the opening of the season at that house.

Mettalcourt, C. [*fl.* 1780–1795], *dancer.*
Mr Mettalcourt, for his first appearance at Covent Garden Theatre, danced a new Polish dance on 5 December 1780 (for that night only). In the *Morning Chronicle* on 9 September 1795 he advertised that he was planning to give dancing lessons. He signed his name C. Mettalcourt.

Metteer, Mr [*fl. 1755*], *actor.*

Many of the members of Theophilus Cibber's troupe at the Haymarket Theatre in August and September 1755 had not appeared on the public stage before, and perhaps Mr Metteer was one of them. During the first two weeks of September he was advertised as playing Lodovico in *Othello*, Guttle in *The Lying Valet*, Slango in *The Honest Yorkshireman*, the Conjurer in *The Devil to Pay*, Balance in *The Recruiting Officer*, and Smith in *The Rehearsal*, after which his name disappeared from London playbills.

Meunier, Mons [*fl. 1782–1787*], *acrobat, dancer, clown.*

Monsieur Meunier (or Mennie, Munie, Meunis, Merimée) made his first appearance in England in a tumbling act at Sadler's Wells on 1 April 1782. He and his partner Dubois lived at No 7, Tayler's Buildings, Islington Road. They had a benefit in April 1783. Meunier performed acrobatics in the wake in *Hob in the Well* at Bristol on 20 October 1783 and subsequent dates, appeared again at Sadler's Wells in London in the summer of 1784, and returned to Bristol by 11 December 1784, when he served as a clown and tumbler at Coopers' Hall with the Sadler's Wells troupe. He remained in Bristol until January 1785, making guest appearances at Bath. Then he performed at Astley's Amphitheatre in London in August, September, and October 1785. He was at Bath in December. Meunier was last mentioned in April 1787, when he was a member of a "CAPITAL GROUP" of performers on the trampoline at the Royal Circus.

Meurs, Milbert. *See* MORRICE, MILBERT.

Mew, Mr [*fl. 1723*], *actor.*

At the Haymarket Theatre Mr Mew played Bonniface in *The Stratagem* on 14 March 1723, Brazen in *The Recruiting Officer* on 15 April, and the Doctor in *The Anatomist* on 22 April.

Meyer, Frederic Charles *1780?–1840,* *harpist, composer.*

In a letter to the editor Sainsbury in 1823, Philip James Meyer, the younger, stated that his brother Frederic Charles Meyer had been born at Strasbourg in 1780 (though *The Dictionary of National Biography* gives 1773 as his birth-year). Frederic Charles Meyer—usually called Charles Meyer—was the younger son of Philip James Meyer, the Strasbourg harpist who settled in London in 1784.

Doane's *Musical Directory* in 1794 listed "Meyers, Charles Junr," of Queen Ann Street, East, as a harpist in the Drury Lane oratorios, and *The London Stage* places him at Covent Garden Theatre and the Pantheon in 1791–92. The *Morning Herald* of 17 April 1792 identified the young Meyer who played the harp in the ballet *La Foire de Smirne* at the Haymarket Theatre on 14 April as Charles Meyer. But most of the other notices of performances by a "Meyer Junior" in the 1790s, we believe, refer to Charles's elder brother Philip James.

Charles Meyer spent most of his career teaching the harp and composing. At the King's Theatre on 25 April 1816 he and five other musicians played "a New Bardic Overture" for six harps, as it had been performed at the Drury Lane oratorios.

The Dictionary of National Biography dates his death in 1840. He published sonatas dedicated to Miss Leader, Miss Weeks, and Miss Beauclerk. Other compositions included *Divertimento Delia*, *Il Pensieroso*, *Introduction and Solo*, and *Fantasia and Solo*.

A portrait of Charles Meyer by Sir William Beechey, signed and dated 1820, was illustrated in Christie's catalogue for a sale on 22 November 1974. The painting was offered again at Sotheby's on 26 November 1975 and was purchased by someone unknown to us.

Meyer, Philip James *1737?–1820?,* *harpist, composer.*

According to the manuscript biography of his father which the younger Philip James Meyer provided to Sainsbury in 1823, the elder Philip James (or Philipp Jacob) Meyer was born at Strasbourg in 1737 (and not in 1732 as stated by *The Dictionary of National Biography*). He was sent to the college in his native city to prepare for the Protestant ministry. There he sang in the church choir, learned the organ, and cultivated a knowledge of German music. Having become interested in the German harp, he left college at about the age of 20 to pursue music. At Paris, with the help of an instrument maker, he set out to improve the harp, which at that time, Sainsbury tells us, was "very incomplete; the occasional semitones were then produced by means of hooks turned with the left hand, which operation, during the continuance of performance, rendered the resources of modulation extremely confined." Meyer added several pedals, and in 1767 he published *Methode sur la vraie manière de jouer la Harpe, avec les règles pour l'accorder.* He also studied German music with Müthel (a student of Johann Sebastian Bach) and wrote some sonatas. On a return visit to Strasbourg in 1768 he married.

Meyer visited London in 1772 and is reputed to have been the first person to play the pedal harp in England, at a concert in the Hanover Square Rooms. During the period of the American Revolution he returned to Paris and busied himself with composing. Among his compositions was a setting of Pitra's dramatic poem *Damète et Zulmis.* He was invited by Voltaire to compose music for a serious opera about Samson, but the author died before it was finished.

In 1784 Meyer settled in London with his family. He performed little, if at all, but devoted himself to composing and teaching. Sainsbury wrote that "as he had neglected a talent, which, at the best of times, through his insurmountable timidity, proved ungrateful to him, he gave up all pretension as a performer." His son's memoir stated that Meyer died in 1819, aged 82, though *The Dictionary of National Biography* provides the death-date of 17 January 1820. Nothing is known to us about his wife. His two sons, Philip James Meyer (1770–1849) and Frederic Charles Meyer (1780?–1840), both harpists in London, are noticed separately.

In the words of his son Philip James, Meyer "was a staunch enthusiast of the German school, and in his compositions . . . he obstinately avoided the florid changes of the modern style and taste." His compositions included: *Two Collections of French Songs for the Harp* (1800); *Two Sonatas for the Harp, with an Accompaniment for the Pianoforte or two Violins, Viola, and Cello* (1800); *Irish Melodies arranged as Duets for the Harp and Piano* (1800); and *A Collection of Hymns and Psalms arranged for the Harp* (1815). He also wrote sonatas, several fugues, and duets, which he dedicated to various noble ladies.

Meyer, Philip James *1779–1849, harpist, composer.*

In a letter to Sainsbury in 1823 Philip James Meyer stated that he had been born at Paris in 1770, when his father Philip James Meyer (1737?–1820) was among the first performers on the harp in that city. Philip James and his younger brother Frederic Charles were brought to London by their father in 1784.

In 1794 Doane's *Musical Directory* identified "P. J. Meyers" of Queen Ann Street, East, as a harpist with the opera. The reference seems to have been to the younger Philip James since by that year the father had ceased to perform. Usually advertised in the bills as "Meyer Junior," Philip James in the 1790s played in a number of concerts and as accompanist to ballets. His first notice was on 15 June 1789, when he accompanied the dances at the King's Theatre in *Les Follies d'Espagne.* He played for the Covent Garden oratorios in 1791 and the Drury Lane oratorios in 1791–92, and he also gave occasional concerts at those theatres.

Meyer was among the musicians who played in a concert at the new Drury Lane Theatre on 9 April 1794, accompanying Miss Mason's singing of "Hope told a flattering tale." At the same theatre on 4 May 1795 he accompanied Miss Leake in a favorite song. In 1798–99 he was an instrumentalist with the opera at the King's Theatre. He also joined his colleagues in private concerts: Charles Burney wrote his daughter Fanny on 25 May 1799 about supping at Mrs Walker's, where he heard Meyer play the harp.

Meyer was among the professional subscribers to the New Musical Fund programs in 1815 and served on the Court of Assistants. Some letters and his manuscript biography of his father, which he sent to Sainsbury in October 1823 from No 13, Delancy Place, Camden Town, are in the Glasgow University Library. Meyer, a highly respected teacher, was also harpist to Queen Adelaide. He died in 1849, according to his notice in *The Dictionary of National Biography*, to which information was contributed by his grandson Sebastian W. Meyer.

Meyers. *See also* **MEYER.**

Meyers, George ₁*fl. 1794–1799*₁, *singer.*

George "Meyer," of No 24, St James Street, Westminster, was listed in Doane's *Musical Directory* in 1794 as a singer in the Concert of Ancient Music, the Academy of Music, and the Chapel Royal. Probably he was the chorus singer at Drury Lane Theatre whose name appeared regularly in the playbills as Mr Meyers between 1796–97 and 1798–99. Among the productions in which he sang were *A Friend in Need* in 1796–97, *Richard Coeur de Lion* and *Blue-Beard* in 1797–98, and *Feudal Times* in 1798–99. He seems not to have been related to the Meyer family of harpists.

Meyrick. *See* MERRICK.

Meziere, Mlle [*fl.* 1785–1788], *dancer.*
A Mlle Meziere was in the corps of dancers at Astley's Amphitheatre in 1785 and 1788. At the King's Theatre in 8 December 1787 a "Mezierres," presumably a man and related to (but possibly the same as) the subject of this entry, was among a number of dancers in *Les Offrandes à l'amour* at the end of the opera.

Mezierres, Mons [*fl.* 1787], *dancer. See* MEZIERE, MLLE.

Michael, Mr [*fl.* 1744], *actor.*
As a member of Theophilus Cibber's troupe at the Haymarket Theatre, Mr Michael played Friar John in *Romeo and Juliet* on 29 September 1744 and subsequent performances through 17 December.

Michal. *See* MICHEL.

Michan. *See* MACHIN.

Michel. *See also* COREY, MRS JOHN, MICHELL, MITCHELL.

Michel, Mons [*fl.* 1734–35], *wardrobe keeper.*
Monsieur Michel was the wardrobe keeper in Francisque Moylin's troupe, which performed at the Haymarket Theatre from 26 October 1734 to 3 June 1735 and at Goodman's Fields on 23 May and 4 June 1735.

[**Michel, Master?**] [*fl.* 1741], *dancer.*
A "little French boy" shared a benefit at Covent Garden Theatre on 20 April 1741 with

François Michel and his son and daughter. The boy joined them in *Les Sabotiers de Piemont* and played a Drawer in *Harlequin Barber*. It is probable that the lad was another of Mons Michel's children.

A Smock Alley, Dublin, bill of 29 June 1747 announced "Les Savoyards by Monsieur and Mademoiselle Mechel [the son and daughter cited above], Monsieur Mechel sen. [François] his Son and others." We take "his Son" to have been yet another boy, the "Boy of 6" who made his second appearance the following 13 July. He could hardly have been the little French boy who performed in London in 1741. The youngster who danced in Dublin seems not to have appeared in London.

Michel, Master [*fl.* 1776–1790], *dancer.*
Master Michel, who was probably the son of Pierre Bernard Michel, made his dance debut at the Crow Street Theatre in Dublin in 1776–77. He and Miss Michel (his sister Lucy, later Mrs Philip De Rossi and then Mrs James Byrn) danced at Fishamble Street in 1784. They were seen for the first time in England at the Haymarket Theatre in London on 1 July 1785 in *La Giardinier Italiene.* They then joined the company at the Orchard Street Theatre in Bath, where they danced from 1786–87 through 1788–89. They were also named in the bills at Bristol from 1787 to the summer of 1790. Though Miss Michel continued her career after that (as her entry under Signora Rossi shows), Master Michel seems to have left the stage.

Michel, Mlle [*fl.* 1739–1750?], *dancer, actress, singer.*
With the Opéra Comique at the St Laurent Fair in 1739 Mlle Michel danced with her brother Pierre and her father François. At Covent Garden Theatre in London on 22 December 1739 a French boy and girl made their first appearance at that house dancing *French Peasants.* The lad also presented a wooden shoe dance and the girl a musette and a tambourin. They repeated those turns many times during the 1739–40 season and also appeared in a popular *Miller and His Wife* and a *Swiss Dance.* On 13 May 1740 they shared a benefit with Bencraft and Gibson and danced *La Pantomime de suisse & d'Alemande.* During that season Mlle Michel repeated her tambourin and was an Arcadian Shepherdess in *Orpheus and Eurydice.*

The two youngsters were called Michel and Mlle Michel (or Mechel) most of the time during the 1740–41 season. Mlle Michel's Christian name is not known, but the evidence points to the brother and sister being the dancers at the St Laurent Fair in 1739. In 1740–41 they again offered their *Miller and His Wife* and *Swiss* turns and appeared in such new pieces as a *Harlequin Dance*, a *Peasant Dance*, *The Matelots*, *Les Niaise*, and a musette. At their shared benefit on 20 April 1741 they were seen with their father, François Michel, and, it seems, a younger brother. Mlle Michel danced with her father that night in a minuet and a French rigadoon and was Colombine in *Harlequin Barber*. The Mons and Mlle Michel who danced at the Jacob's Wells Theatre in Bristol in the summer of 1741 and received a benefit on 7 August were probably François and his daughter.

In 1741–42 Mlle Michel and her brother Pierre were at Drury Lane Theatre, where they made their first appearance on 26 September 1741 in *The Swiss*, a number they repeated many times during the season. The pair also danced their *Miller and His Wife* and tried out such new pieces as a *Pierrot Dance*, *The Italian Peasants*, *Les Perelins voyageur*, and *Le Boufon*, and they danced in a group piece called *Le Genereux Corsair*. As before, Mlle Michel made occasional appearances in her tambourin and in a dance called a *Concerto*. At the benefit she shared with her brother on 8 April 1742 she, her brother, and her father presented *A Grand Ball Dance*, *The Cuckow Dance*, and *The German Hussar*. During the season Mlle Michel also danced in *Comus*.

After an absence of a few years the Michels returned (from France) to Drury Lane for the 1745–46 and 1746–47 seasons. The brother and sister team appeared frequently, but the bills often said only that there would be dancing by the Michels. Among their new dances were a *Ball Country Dance*, a *Sailor's Dance*, louvres, and minuets, and they danced in *Comus*. At their benefit on 16 April 1746 they were in *Harlequin Incendiary* and she danced *Les Characteres de la Dance*.

The family moved to Dublin after the 1746–47 season. Mlle Michel danced at the Smock Alley Theatre in June 1747 and remained for the 1747–48 season to try her hand at Polly in *The Beggar's Opera* on 21 April 1748. The Dub-

lin prompter Chetwood quoted in his *General History* in 1749 some lines (from a poem by George Anne Bellamy) that referred to Mlle Michel:

> *Or should* Mechel, *all languishing, advance,*
> *Her Limbs dissolv'd in well-conducted Dance*

Perhaps Mlle Michel was still performing about 1750, when some dance tunes by Hesse were published, with "Mons and Mme [*recte*: Mlle?] Michal" named among the performers.

Michel, François [*fl.* 1739–1748], *dancer.*

Marian Hannah Winter in *The Pre-Romantic Ballet* identifies the Michel (or Mechel) who danced in London with his children in the 1740s as François Michel. One of his sons seems certainly to have been Pierre Bernard Michel; François apparently had at least one other son and a daughter. All of the children danced. François was ballet master and dancer with the Opéra Comique at the St Laurent Fair in 1739, where his daughter and one of his sons also danced.

The Covent Garden Theatre accounts show a payment £4 4s. to Monsieur "Michell" on 10 October 1740, and he received several payments of £5 5s. (weekly, evidently) through March 1741. The payments to Michel seem to have been for the performances of his children, who had been appearing since 1739–40. At a benefit held on 20 April 1741 for himself, his son and daughter (usually called "the French Boy and Girl"), and another "Little French Boy" (another son, we believe), Mons Michel "the Father" was advertised as making his first appearance in any theatre in England. The elder Michel danced a minuet and a French rigadoon with his daughter. Tickets for the benefit had been available at the family lodgings in Newport Street "next door to the Printseller."

Mons and Mlle Michel danced at the Jacob's Wells Theatre in Bristol in the summer of 1741 and were given a benefit on 7 August. We suppose that pair was the father and daughter.

In 1741–42 Michel and his family—Master, Mademoiselle, and perhaps another boy— danced at Drury Lane Theatre. "M and Mlle Mechell (the French Boy and Girl)" appeared for the first time on 26 September 1741. The

Drury Lane bill of 8 April 1742 advertised "A Grand Ball Dance by Mechel Sen, Mechel Jr, and Mlle Mechel." On 8 April the Michels (presumably all three) also danced *Les Jardiniers Suedois*, *The Cuckow Dance*, and *The German Hussar*. The evening was a benefit for Mechel and Mlle Mechel—probably the youngsters, since they had been dancing all season. The receipts came to £110.

The Michels returned to Drury Lane on 26 September 1745, advertised as lately arrived from Paris. Most of the appearances in 1745–46 were made by the young brother and sister, while the father, François, occupied his time teaching them and guiding their careers. On 16 April 1746 a benefit was held for "M. and Mlle Mechel" and *The Peasant and Sabotiere* was danced by "Mechel and Young Mechel." The Mechels—presumably all three—performed a *Swiss Dance*, a minuet, and a louvre. Similarly, "the Mechels" had a benefit on 2 April 1747.

The Michels went to Dublin in the summer of 1747. The bill at the Smock Alley Theatre on 29 June 1747 announced "A new Comick Dance called Les Savoyards by Monsieur and Mademoiselle Mechel, Monsieur Mechel sen, his Son and others." Four Michels were cited in that statement: father, daughter, and two sons. In 1747–48 "M. Mechel," identified as the father of "M. and Mlle Mechel," advertised in Dublin that he was setting up as a dancing master and would teach pupils at their homes or at his own lodgings at the Black Boy in Fishamble Street.

Michel, Lucy. *See* ROSSI, SIGNORA PHILIP.

Michel, Pierre Bernard [*fl.* 1739–1790], *dancer, choreographer.*

Pierre Bernard Michel was probably the son of the dancer François Michel who danced with his father and sister at the Opéra Comique at the St Laurent Fair in 1739. The French boy and girl who danced for the first time at Covent Garden Theatre in London on 22 December of that year were Master and Miss Michel (or Mechel), referred to in later bills as "M. and Mlle Mechel." The boy was, we believe Pierre Bernard. In 1739–40 Pierre offered a *Wooden Shoe Dance* and paired off with his sister (Christian name unknown) in *French Peasants*. The youngsters proved very popular and were named regularly in the bills, often cited as dancing a

Miller and His Wife and a *Swiss Dance*. At their shared benefit with Bencraft and Gibson on 13 May 1741 they performed *La Pantomime de Suisse & d'Alemande*. Master Michel did not often do solo turns. Beginning on 12 February 1740 he had a part in a pantomime: a Woman Dwarf in *Orpheus and Eurydice*.

On 19 September 1740 at Covent Garden "M and Mlle Michel (the French Boy and Girl)" danced the *Miller and Wife* number and *The Swiss*. During 1740–41 young Michel appeared many times with his sister, some of their new pieces being a *Harlequin Dance*, a *Peasant Dance*, *The Matelots*, *Les Niaise*, and a musette. At their shared benefit on 20 April 1741 *Harlequin Barber* was performed with "Mechel Jr" (Pierre, we assume) as Pierot, Mlle Mechel as Colombine, and a "Little French Boy" (another son of François) as a Drawer. At that performance François made his first appearance in England dancing a minuet and French rigadoon with his daughter, and "Mechel the son" (Pierre?) danced a minuet with Miss Polly Woffington. Michel (Pierre?), Mlle Michel, and Miss Woffington danced *The Metamorphoses of the Windmills*, and the evening concluded with a wooden shoe dance called *Les Sabotiers de Piemont* with Michel Sr, Michel Jr, Mlle Michel, and the little French boy. The bill said the benefit was for Michel and Mlle Michel "(the French Boy and Girl)"—that is, Pierre and his sister—and noted that tickets were available from Michel in Newport Street. During that season Pierre continued playing his role in *Orpheus and Eurydice* and occasionally appeared in a solo *Wooden Shoe*.

The 1741–42 season found the Michels at Drury Lane, where the brother and sister made their first appearance on 26 September 1741 in a pantomime ballet called *The Swiss*, and Pierre danced *The Peasant*. The pair revived their *Miller and His Wife*, joined several other dancers in *Le Genereux corsair*, and appeared in such pieces as a *Pierrot Dance*, *The Italian Peasants*, *Les Perelins voyageur*, and *Le Boufon*. They also danced in *Comus*, and Michel alone danced *Matelote Polonnes*. At their shared benefit on 8 April 1742 they danced *Les Jardiniers Suédois* and were joined by Michel Sr in *A Grand Ball Dance*, *The Cuckow Dance*, and *The German Hussars*.

The Michels left England after that season, but they returned, from Paris, to appear again at Drury Lane on 26 September 1745. Our subject was now referred to occasionally in the bills as Young Michel (as opposed to Master or just M) to distinguish him from his father, but since Pierre and his sister did most of the performing, the bills usually cited them simply as Michel and Mlle Michel. The pair offered a new piece called a *Ball Country Dance*, but most of the bills gave no dance titles. The pair danced in *Harlequin Incendiary*, and at their benefit on 16 April 1746 they were joined by their father. François Michel and "Young Mechel" danced *The Peasant* and *Sabotiers* and "the Mechels" (all three? all four?) danced a minuet, louvre, and a *Swiss Dance*. The Michels were again at Drury Lane in 1746–47, offering their usual entr'acte dances.

They went to Dublin for the summer season of 1747. With them was yet another younger brother, for a young Michel danced on 29 June and was probably the "Boy of 6" who made his second appearance on 13 July. The Michels remained in Dublin for the 1747–48 season and brought the manager, Sheridan, under criticism because the Michels were Catholic and subjects of the French King. After that the family probably left Ireland. Some dance music by Hasse, published about 1750, named "Mons and Mme Michal" among several who had danced to his tunes at the theatres in London—but that may have been a reference to earlier days. The Mme was probably an error for Mlle.

If we are correct in identifying the young Michel of the 1740s as Pierre Bernard Michel, he went on to a considerable career on the Continent. Citing Gennaro Magri's *Trattato Teorico-Prattico di Ballo* of 1779, Marian Hannah Winter in *The Pre-Romantic Ballet* notes that Michel was in Lisbon with choreographers Andrea Alberti and Giuseppe Salamoni in 1754, at the Vienna Burgtheater with Magri and Giovanni Guidetti in 1759, in Venice with the Magri and Giovanni Battista Galantini troupes in 1760 and 1761, in Venice with Clarice Bini as his partner in 1762, and at the court of Modena from 1761 to 1765. Magri credited Michel with the invention of at least 23 capriols and called him "the greatest grotesque dancer that France has produced."

W. S. Clark's culling of Dublin theatre notices shows that Pierre Michel performed at Smock Alley in 1766–67, advertised as hav-ing come from the Haymarket in London—but *The London Stage* lists no Haymarket bills naming Michel during the 1760s. In 1767–68 and 1768–69 Michel performed at the Crow Street Theatre, Dublin; in 1770 he moved to the Capel Street Theatre; and in 1771–72 he was again at Smock Alley. Years later, on 26 July 1793, the *Hibernian Journal* described the dancer Signora Rossi as the daughter of the former Crow Street Theatre ballet master. We take it, then, that Pierre Bernard Michel was the father of Lucy Michel (born in 1771), who became Signora Philip De Rossi and later Mrs James Byrn.

After his years in Dublin Michel moved to Bath, where he set up as a dancing master. He was apparently the Michel who danced in *L'Amour jardinier* at the King's Theatre in London on 1 April 1786 and subsequent dates through 11 July. His daughter Lucy and a son whose name we do not know danced at the Orchard Street Theatre at Bath from 1786–87 through 1788–89. On 5 December 1790 at Bath Abbey Lucy Michel of Walcot, Bath, spinster, married, with the consent of her parent (not named in the registers), Philip De Rossi, bachelor. He was a teacher of French and Italian (*The London Stage* is incorrect in calling him Joseph; there was another man, Joseph Rossi, who was a dancer). Witnessing the marriage of Lucy Michel and Philip De Rossi was Pierre Michel, according to the register at Bath Abbey. Curiously, he was not identified as Lucy's father, but it seems certain that he was.

Michell. *See also* MICHEL *and* MITCHELL.

Michell, Mr [*fl. 1800*], *dancer.*

Mr and Master Michell made a single appearance on the London stage, on 29 April 1800, dancing at Covent Garden Theatre. They were advertised as from the Theatre Royal Edinburgh. That leads us to beleive that Master Michell may have been Master T. Michell, whose name was in the bills at the York theatre in 1798. Perhaps they were related to the actors Mr and Mrs W. B. Michell, who performed in the 1790s at Hull, Edinburgh, and York but did not appear in London.

Michell, Master [T.?] [*fl. 1798?–1800*], *dancer. See* MICHELL, MR.

Michell, Thomas ₁*fl. early eighteenth century?*₁, *proprietor.*
Davis and Waters in *Tickets and Passes* state that Restoration Gardens was established in the reign of Charles II and closed in 1755; at some point Thomas Michell was proprietor of the music house there, according to a token that has survived.

Michelle. *See* DE MICHELI.

Michelli. *See* DE MICHELI.

Michim. *See* MACHIN.

Middlehurst, Mrs. *See* LOUCH, MRS.

Middlemist, ₁**Robert?**₁ *1741–1791?, dancer.*
Throughout most of the latter half of the eighteenth century groups of Scottish actors, some of them professionals, hired the Haymarket Theatre one of several times each year to act Allan Ramsay's *Patie and Roger; or, The Gentle Shepherd* and to sing traditional Scots tunes and dance traditional dances.
From 1761 through 1764 a dancer named Middlemist was regularly featured on those occasions. He did not appear again until 1769 when he danced twice, in February and December. He reappeared in 1772, 1775, 1776, 1779, 1780, 1782, 1784, and 1785. Probably between appearances he sustained himself by teaching, perhaps in Scotland. For he may have been the subject of an entry in the Burial Records of the Calton Ground, Edinburgh (now in the Scottish Record Office): 18 April 1791, buried "Robert Middlemost [*sic*] a Dancing Master from Mr Havison's Land Lith Wynd Died of a Consumption Buried 6 yards 1 foot SW from the SW c[orner] of James Stewarts Grave and close to the sid[e] of the Walk Aged 50 years."

Middlemore, Richard ₁*fl. c.1671–1709*₁, *concessionaire.*
About 1671, according to the investigations of Leslie Hotson, set forth in *The Commonwealth and Restoration Stage*, Richard Middlemore was occupying one of the two apartments over the porch of the Dorset Garden Theatre and was a

sharer in the Duke's Company patent. His rent was £16 yearly, and his neighbor in the other apartment was the company actor-manager Thomas Betterton. Possibly Middlemore took up occupancy when the new playhouse opened on 9 November 1671. On 30 May 1687 Middlemore and Andrew Card purchased Dame Mary Davenant's rights of income from the fruit-selling concession at the theatre. Middlemore was still a sharer in the patent in March 1709.
The Brownlowe family also held a share in the patent, and Richard Middlemore figured in two Brownlowe wills. The elder Sir John Brownlowe, whose will was proved on 28 June 1680, left his cousin Richard Middlemore two bequests: £100 for his own use and another sum for the use of his sister Elizabeth Middlemore (who had become Elizabeth Lambe by the time Sir John died). Richard Middlemore was also mentioned in the will of the younger Sir John Brownlowe, which was proved on 2 September 1697. It is impossible to tell how deeply involved Middlemore may have been in the affairs of the Duke's Company, then the United Company, and then Christopher Rich's troupe, or how much he had to do with the concession at Dorset Garden. But the fact that he lived in the theatre suggests something more than a financial connection.

Middlemost. *See* MIDDLEMIST.

Middlesex, Lord. *See* SACKVILLE, CHARLES.

Middleton, Mr ₁*fl. 1734–1750*₁, *actor, booth proprietor.*
Mr Middleton acted Leatherside in *The Covent Garden Tragedy* on 17 April 1734 at the Haymarket Theatre. The notice in the bills that he had "never appeared on this stage before" suggests that he probably was a provincial player. He performed the same role there the next two nights and on 29 April 1734. No doubt he was the same Middleton who was a member of the company performing in the booth operated by Lee and Phillips at Bartholomew Fair in the summer of 1740; on 23 August he played Squire Shallow in *Harlequin Restor'd*, a pantomime in which Mrs Middleton was a Milkmaid.
On 4 August 1741 Middleton opened his

own booth at the Tottenham Court Fair, playing Teague in *A Wife Well Manag'd*. At the
May Fair in 1744 Middleton and Cushing operated a booth, and there the following year
Middleton managed his own "Great Theatrical
Booth." At Bartholomew Fair in August 1749
he was a member of Cushing's company playing in a booth facing the King's Head, Smithfield; among Middleton's roles was Jeffery
Holdfast in *The Adventures of Sir Lubberly Lackbrains and his Man Blunderbuss*. In September
1750, Middleton was once more seen in a fair
booth, this time with Phillips at Southwark
Fair, where he played Stocks in *The Constant
Couple* and Columbine's Father in *The Imprisonment of Harlequin*.

Sometimes appearing in these performances
at the fairs was Mrs Middleton, presumably
his wife.

Middleton, Mrs ₍fl. 1722–1741₎, ac-
tress, dancer.
Mrs Middleton was a performer in Pinkethman's Bartholomew Fair booth in August and
September 1722; probably she played Zara or
Selima in *The Distress'd Beauty* and she also
danced. She returned to that fair in August
1723, when her roles included the Widow in
The Blind Beggar of Bednal Green. That September probably she was with Pinkethman's company in Richmond. For that manager at Southwark Fair toward the end of September she
again played the Widow in *The Blind Beggar*
and Mrs Blake in a droll based on *Jane Shore*.

Perhaps she was the same Mrs Middleton,
the wife of the actor Middleton, who occasionally performed in London in the 1740s. In Lee
and Phillips's booth at Bartholomew Fair on
23 August 1740 she was a Milkmaid in *Harlequin Restor'd*. That autumn she joined Giffard's company at the Goodman's Fields Theatre, where she acted Belinda in *The Old Bachelor*
on 21 October 1740 and subsequently was
seen as Sylvia in *The Recruiting Officer*, Emilia
in *Othello*, Doris in *Aesop*, Millwood in *George
Barnwell*, and Trueman in *The Drummer*. Her
last performances at Goodman's Fields seems
to have been as Mrs Page in *The Merry Wives of
Windsor* on 15 November and Angelina in *Love
Makes a Man* on 18 November 1740. In Middleton's booth at the Tottenham Court Fair in

August 1741 she acted Diligence in *The Rival
Queens*.

Middleton, Miss ₍fl. 1784₎, *singer.*
Miss Middleton was listed by Dr Burney as
a treble singer in the Handel Memorial Concerts at Westminster Abbey and the Pantheon
in May and June 1784.

Middleton, David ₍fl. 1670–1676₎,
scenekeeper, guard.
The London Stage lists David Middleton and
William Middleton (brothers, perhaps?) as
scenekeepers at the King's Company Theatre
in Bridges Street. The Lord Chamberlain's accounts cite William on 2 August 1671 and
David on the twenty-sixth. No further trace
has been found of William, but David was a
guard at the new Drury Lane playhouse in
1675–76; in the new King's Company rules,
dated 9 December 1675 in the accounts, David
Middleton was assigned to guard the tiring
house door.

**Middleton, James, stage name of James
Magan** *c. 1769–1799, actor.*
James Middleton, whose family name was
Magan, was born about 1769 at Dublin, where
his father was, according to early stage memoirs, "an eminent surgeon." James received his
education at the academy in Dublin run by
Samuel Whyte, who was teacher to a large
number of nobility, and then he was placed
with Robert Bowes, head of the Royal College
of Surgeons, according to some sources, or
with a Dr Kerr, according to others. While
engaged in some private theatricals—his first
role reputedly was Sciolto in *The Fair Penitent*—he attracted the attention and encouragement of the actor Joseph Holman. Magan
determined to abandon the dissecting room for
the dressing room. Realizing he could not keep
his ambition a secret if he tried to launch his
career in Dublin, because the manager Daly
was "a near relative," Magan set out for London.

Through the influence of the dramatist W. C.
Oulton, Magan was given an audition by Harris at Covent Garden, probably sometime late
in 1787. That manager evidently promised
him an engagement for the next season and
recommended him to the Bath management

Harvard Theatre Collection

JAMES MIDDLETON
by J. C.

for the interval. Gilliland claimed that the mental problems which Middleton suffered throughout the remainder of his short life began just before his Bath debut. It seems that the young man found himself unable to get to Bath "through a deficiency of pecuniary means" and at the same time received a letter from Daly which outlined the extraordinary difficulties of theatrical life and urged him to return to his friends and profession. Middleton became "suddenly disordered" in his mind, and only the efforts of a friend with whom he lodged prevented him from committing suicide.

Presumably it was at that time that Magan adopted the pseudonym Middleton, either to spare his father's feelings or to unburden himself of a name he felt was too dull and ordinary for an actor. Nevertheless, for his debut at Bath on 31 January 1788, when he acted Othello,

he was advertised anonymously as "A Gentleman." The local press praised the performance, describing him as scarce 20, tall, well-formed, with a soft voice like Barry's. His second Bath role was Romeo, "in which he gained the good opinion of the Bath critics," reported the *Monthly Mirror*. He also acted Othello and Romeo at Bristol several times in February and March.

Middleton made his first appearance at Covent Garden on 22 September 1788, as Romeo. After four more performances of Romeo, he acted Chamont in *The Orphan* on 27 October, and during the season was also seen as O'Donovan in the premiere of O'Keeffe's *The Toy* on 3 February 1789, Harry Neville in the premiere of Reynolds's *The Dramatist* on 15 May, and Florizel in *The Winter's Tale* on 22 May. During that first year in London, though his salary was only £1 10s. per week, Middleton lived in expensive lodgings, attended by a footman. "Thus commenced his career of folly," lamented the *Monthly Mirror* in October 1799, and "he never could disentangle himself from the perplexities into which this first extravagance precipitated the thoughtless youth."

After his debut season Middleton suffered two blows: he was not re-engaged at Covent Garden, and his wife Sophia died at Mile End on 6 August 1789, at the age of 31. Middleton returned to Dublin, where, beginning in the late summer of 1789, he acted at the Crow Street Theatre through the season of 1791–92. He seems to have enjoyed success in his native city, though the press described him in 1790 as a novice, who ranted too much most of the time but when he spoke with judgment recalled the tone of Barry. Appearances in the Irish provincial towns included Waterford in October 1789 and Cork in August and September 1789 and August 1791. At the Crow Street Theatre on 29 March 1792 Middleton appeared in Michael Fitzgerald's new tragedy *Elwina*, the prologue and epilogue to which were written by Whyte, Middleton's old schoolmaster and the father of his second wife. On 28 June 1791 the *Dublin Chronicle* had reported Middleton's marriage at Dublin to Martha Ann Whyte.

Middleton appeared at the Theatre Royal in Shakespeare Square, Edinburgh, on 16 January 1793 as Othello. He then acted there Hamlet, Jaffeir, Romeo, and Irwin in *Every One*

JAMES MIDDLETON, as Salisbury
by De Wilde

JAMES MIDDLETON, as Eumenes
engraving by Chapman, after De Wilde

Has His Fault. On 1 April 1793 he made his debut, as Romeo, in Belfast, where he remained until the middle of May.

After an absence of five years Middleton was re-engaged at Covent Garden in 1793–94 at a salary of £6 per week. He appeared as Othello on 23 September 1793 and that season acted Romeo, Laertes, Neville in *The Dramatist*, Marquis in *The Midnight Hour*, William in *The World in a Village*, Charles in *The West Indian*, Edmund in *King Lear*, Altamont in *The Fair Penitent*, Crevelt in *He Wou'd be a Soldier*, Louis in the premiere of Boaden's *Fontainville Forest* (for which he also gave the prologue) on 25 March 1794, the Duke in *The Chances*, Colloony in *The Irishman in London*, Captal de Buche (and the prologue) in the premiere of Pye's *The Siege of Meaux* on 19 May, Muley Zeydan in *Don Sebastian*, and Ferrand (and the

prologue) in the premiere of Henry Siddons's melodrama *The Sicilian Romance* on 28 May. That last night, which was for his benefit, he also acted Alexander in *Alexander the Great*. Gross receipts were £203 13*s*. 6*d*. and tickets were available from Middleton at Vint's perfumer, No 3, Tavistock Row, Covent Garden. When he acted an unspecified character in *The Death of Captain Cook* on 19 May 1794 the *Thespian Magazine* advised him "not to *drivelize* his character, but to be less lavish of his tremulous tears in future."

Middleton remained at Covent Garden for three more years, through 1796–97, at a constant salary of £6 per week. In the summers he played out of town—at Derry in 1794 and at Birmingham in 1795 and 1796. Among his roles at Covent Garden during that period were Arviragus in *Cymbeline*, Sir George Gauntlet in *The Rage*, Macduff in *Macbeth*, Junius in

Bonduca, Clement in *The Deserted Daughter*, and Ulric in *The Secret Tribunal* in 1794–95; Heartwell in *The Farm House*, Captain Arable in the premiere of Reynolds's *Speculation* on 7 November 1795, Sir Richard Vernon in *1 Henry IV*, Sir Harry Groveby in *The Maid of the Oaks*, Allworth in *A New Way to Pay Old Debts*, Radsano in *Zorinski* and M'Scrape in *Netley Abbey* in 1795–96; and Frederic Bertram in *The Jew*, Leeson in *The School for Wives*, Virolet in *The Mountaineers*, Lord Randolph in *Douglas*, Pharamond in *Philaster*, Woodville in *The Tatlers*, Lewson in *The Gamester*, Captain Manley in *The Honest Thieves*, Portius in *Cato*, and Doricourt in *The Belle's Stratagem* in 1796–97. He lived at No 53, Great Marlborough Street, Oxford Street, in June 1795, at No 20, Great Russell Street in May 1796, and at No 16, Buckingham Street, York Buildings, in June 1797.

Critics continued to note the similarity of his voice to Barry's, but generally they found him a mediocre talent. F. G. Waldron wrote in *Candid and Impartial Stricture on the Performers* . . . (1795) that Middleton's voice had a harmony and sweetness which resembled

more the strains which used to flow from the lips of the all persuasive *Barry*, than any we have heard since his time. Like his also we are satiated with too much sweetness. . . . His Person good in other respects, is considerably injured by his knees turning inward. . . . His face . . . inexpressive . . . eyes that are deficient of every power but that of *squinting*. His action is nerveless and effeminate, and his deportment possesses that studied mechanism we would expect to meet in the hero of a country theatre.

George Frederick Cooke, who acted with Middleton in Dublin, thought he possessed "a pleasing, harmonious voice," and a "genteel person & address" but that by the mid-1790s Middleton's abilities were much on the decline, particularly his memory. In a (for him) somewhat sober thought Cooke wrote in his diary when reflecting on Middleton's death that "He seemed good natured & facetious, a pleasant (perhaps for his own good too pleasant) companion." Middleton, indeed, had become another alcoholic actor who kept late hours and bad company. His dissipation led to a disorderly mind and a disintegration of his professional behavior. While acting Nerestan

in *Zara* at Covent Garden on 19 December 1796, Middleton after the first scene "retired abruptly into the wardrobe," reported the *Monthly Mirror* in January 1797, "pulled off his coat, and telling the dresser he should be back in ten minutes, left the theatre; he did not return, however, according to his appointment, and Davenport read the remainder of the character: a fit of insanity is supposed to have seized him." He had gone to a neighboring tavern and had written a note to the stage manager that he did not intend to perform any more that evening. "In the consequent apology in the Journals," wrote John Williams in *A Pin Basket to the Children of Thespis*, "the public were informed that Mr. MIDDLETON was deranged!" After that incident Middleton did not reappear on stage until 27 February 1797, when he acted Septimus in *The Doldrum*.

Middleton lost his engagement at Covent Garden at the end of 1796–97. He went to play at Crow Street in Dublin for a year, but "through frequent repetitions of ill-conduct," he lost that position also. During the summer of 1798 he performed with various provincial companies. In the Sterling Library, Yale University, is a letter from Middleton to an unidentified recipient (but evidently the editor of the *Monthly Mirror*), written from Cheltenham on 3 September 1798, in which he requests as many copies of the number containing his portrait as the enclosed shilling would buy. "I have performed here 6 nights," he reported, "to full Houses Romeo, Young Sadboy [?], young Marlow, Dick in the apprentice, Doricourt, & on Saturday Charles Surface in the School for Scandal by desire of the Dowager Countess of Salisbury. I have concluded a second engagement here & performed Romeo at Gloucester with much applause. . . ."

Nevertheless, in the autumn of 1798 Middleton found himself back at London in desperate straits. He told a writer for the *Monthly Mirror* that "he would accept with gratitude and joy any situation on the London boards, however menial or disgraceful, if it would but yield him a bare subsistence." Drury Lane took him on at wages reported by *The London Stage* to have been £6 per week, a salary in the middle range. (Packer, for example, earned £5 and Robert Palmer £7.) A manuscript in the Folger Library, however, indicates Middleton was put on the Drury Lane list on 10 November 1798 for 6s. 8d. per day. He first appeared there on 13 October 1798 as Aimwell in *The Beaux' Stratagem*. On 19 December he acted Don Duart in *Love Makes a Man*, and on 19 January 1799 he was Henry in the premiere of the younger Colman's melodrama *Feudal Times*, which was acted a total of 39 times that season. His last Drury Lane performance was in that role on 17 April 1799.

Old habits overpowered Middleton. Brandy was his constant companion, for which he borrowed heavily from the backstage personnel. He lost his memory, because "filthy in person, depraved in principle," and soon was thrown into Newgate. There he received supplies from his fellow actors. Just before the beginning of the 1799–1800 season he was released through the generosity of Charles Kemble, but he was in no condition to act. On 14 September 1799 he tried to raise some money by reciting speeches from *Romeo and Juliet*, *The Orphan*, and other pieces, at a small private theatre in Pimlico.

On Sunday morning, 13 October, a shoemaker found Middleton lying in the street, drenched with rain. The shoemaker took him to his own home, cared for him several days, and then transferred him to lodgings in King Street, Westminster. As the *Monthly Mirror* for October reported:

By this time, the comedians had become apprised of his situation, and hastened to his relief. They found him lying upon a rug, *upon the floor*, his lower half without sense or motion. . . . His face was bloated, and almost of a *crimson-red*, with the effects of the liquor which his attentive host, from a mistaken principle of kindness, had given to his entreaties. In one day he had demanded, and drank, between four and five quarts of shrub and brandy.

He died in inebriated senselessness on Friday, 18 October 1799, at about the age of 30. His funeral expenses were paid for by a subscription raised by the actors of both patent houses. Attended by Holman, Kelly, H. Johnston, and C. Kemble, he was buried in the Broadway Chapel, Westminster, in a coffin upon which his real name Magan was inscribed. An entry in the Drury Lane account books for 7 January 1800 reads: "The Proprietors' Gift to Bury Mr. Middleton 5/5/–."

For some time Middleton had been separated from his second wife, who took up teaching at Bath to support their two children. The baptism of one of the children, Samuel Eusta Magan, son of James and Martha, born on 16 December 1795, occurred at St Paul, Covent Garden, on 17 January 1796.

Portraits of James Middleton include:

1. Engraved portrait by "J. C." Published as a plate to *Thespian Magazine*, March 1793.

2. As Artaxerxes in *The Ambitious Stepmother*. Engraving by W. Leney, after J. Roberts. Published by Cawthorn as a plate to *Bell's British Theatre*, 1795.

3. As Douglas in *Douglas*. Canvas by Gainsborough Dupont. In the Garrick Club (No 461).

4. As Eumenes in *Merope*. Engraving by J. Chapman, after S. De Wilde. Published as a plate to *Bell's British Theatre*, 1795.

5. As Romeo in *Romeo and Juliet*. Engraving by W. Ridley, "from an Original Painting." Published as a plate to *Monthly Mirror*, May 1796.

6. As Salisbury in *The Countess of Salisbury*. Canvas by S. De Wilde. In the Garrick Club (No 254). Engraving by P. Audinet published as a plate to *Bell's British Theatre*, 1793.

Middleton, Robert [*fl.* 1778–1788], *actor, dancer.*

Robert Middleton, who probably had a modest acting career in the provinces, performed occasionally in London between 1778 and 1785. His first known appearance was on 22 June 1778 at China Hall, Rotherhithe, when at the end of the mainpiece he delivered the monologue "Bucks have at ye All." He was no doubt the Middleton who, announced as making his first appearance on any stage (presumably in a speaking character), played with other novices in *The Macaroni Adventurer* at the Haymarket Theatre on 28 December 1778.

All Middleton's subsequent London appearances were at the Haymarket in specially-licensed productions during the winter season. His performances included Timothy in *The Humours of Oxford* on 15 March 1779; Aminadab in *A Bold Stroke for a Wife* and a character in *The She Gallant* on 13 October 1779; a character in *Love at a Venture* and Headlong in *The Tobacconist* on 21 March 1782; a hornpipe and "Bucks have at ye All" on 6 May 1782; Taylor in *The Temple Beau*, Quildrive in *The Citizen*, and a hornpipe on 21 September 1782; Roger in *Wit Without Money*, a character in *The*

Taylors, and a hornpipe (over 12 eggs, blind-folded) on 25 November 1782; a character in the premiere of Oulton's farce *A New Way to Keep a Wife Home* on 17 September 1783; and hornpipes on 9 February 1784 and 31 January 1785.

The *Gazetteer* of 9 November 1780 reported that Middleton had married a Miss King at St Katharine Cree, Leadenhall Street, on 7 November. The last notice of him was on 30 May 1788, when the *Gazetteer* denied a report of his death, provided his full name, and identified him as a dancer.

Middleton, William [*fl.* 1670–1671], *scenekeeper. See* MIDDLETON, DAVID.

Midford, Mr. [*fl.* 1726–1728], *house servant?*

The accounts at the Lincoln's Inn Fields playhouse contain notices of a Mr Midford from 1726 to 1727. Typically the citations said "Mr Midford for M^r Ch. Rich." That would suggest that Midford may have been a house servant who helped with the accounts. A note on 8 April 1728, however, reads: "Mr Midford Rent"—which suggests he may have been a box renter.

"Midnight." *See* SMART, CHRISTOPHER.

Midoleta, Mr [*fl.* 1799], *house servant?*

The Drury Lane Theatre accounts show a payment of £1 13*s.* 4*d.* to a Mr Midoleta for five days of work. His duties were not specified; perhaps he was a house servant.

Miell, William 1753–1795, *actor, manager.*

William Miell was probably an itinerant actor before he was engaged by Foote for the Haymarket summer company of 1768. He acted the Servant in *The School Boy* on 25 and 29 July and Drawer in *The Beggar's Opera* on 27 July and several times thereafter. Those modest roles seem to have been his only assignments in London, after which he labored in the provinces for some 27 years.

Miell was a member of the Norwich Company by 24 August 1772, on which date the committee in charge of that theatre ordered his salary continued at £1 5*s.* per week. Evi-dently he refused the terms, for less than a week later, on 29 August, the committee approved the advance of his salary to £1 11*s.* 6*d.* per week, provided "he will article for two years or more." By 26 May 1773 he was living with Mrs Margaret Forbes, a former London singer; on that date it was recorded in the Norwich Committee Books that Mr and Mrs Miell's application for an advance of £20 would be rejected unless they signed articles for 1773–74. In that season they also acted at the Smock Alley Theatre, Dublin. Subsequently they played at Norwich in 1774–75 at King's Lynn in 1776, and at York in 1776, 1777, and 1779. In 1779 he was acting-manager of Giordani and Leoni's opera company at the Capel Street Theatre in Dublin, where he remained a while. He performed at the Stourbridge Fair, near Cambridge, with Glassington's company in 1780 and with John Palmer's in 1780 and 1786, and in the following year, according to the *Thespian Dictionary*, he gave up a chance to play at Drury Lane (upon Mrs Siddons's recommendation) in order to join Palmer at the Royalty Theatre. But that venture was repressed after one performance on 20 June 1787, for which Miell's name was not found in the bills. Colman rejected his application for an engagement at the Haymarket, thus relegating him to the provinces. Miell was at Derby from 1787–88 through 1789–90 and at Shrewsbury in 1792. He played at Leominster in June 1794, and soon became manager of the theatres at Worcester, Wolverhampton, and Shrewsbury.

Miell was buried at St Chad's, Shrewsbury, on 16 December 1795, at the age of 42. His death was reported in the *European Magazine* of January 1796. In his will drawn on 26 April 1787, when he was living at Furnivall's Inn Court, London, he left an unspecified estate in trust "to maintain educate and apprentice . . . the two infants William Benjamin Miell Who is now at the Reverend Mr Bowmans Academy and Amelia Miell Who is now with *my truly* loving and *unnatural wife* in Jermyn Street Saint James." Amelia Miell was no doubt the daughter of William and Margaret Miell who was baptized at St Michael le Belfrey, York, on 22 May 1777. Administration of the will was granted on 1 February 1797 (when the deceased was described as "late of Shrewsbury") to his son, who had by then reached his majority. Since Mrs Miell was not mentioned in the probate, we assume she was not alive at the time of its registration. Mentioned in the will, however, were his sister Ann Watkins, to whom he bequeathed £20, and his late sister Martha Clayton, to each of whose two daughters he left £10.

Miell, Mrs William, Margaret. *See* FORBES, MRS MARGARET.

Milan. *See* MELLON.

Milbank. *See* MILBOURNE.

Milbourn, James [*fl.* 1794], *singer.*
Doane's *Musical Directory* (1794) lists a James Milbourn, a bass singer who lived in the Strand, sang in oratorios at Drury Lane, and belonged to the Choral Fund. Nothing further or more specific is known about him.

Milbourne, M. Charles [*fl.* 1777?–1809], *scene painter, actor, dancer, singer.*
A Mr "Milborn" was listed among house personnel under Joseph Fox at the Brighton Theatre in 1777 by Porter in his *History of the Theatres of Brighton.* Conceivably he was Charles Milbourne, who was working at Portsmouth in 1791–92, where, for the performance on 17 January of the pantomime *Harlequin Revels at Portsdown Fair*, he designed and painted a Temple of Hymen. Rosenfeld and Croft-Murray, in *Theatre Notebook* 19, cite payments to him of two guineas per week at Covent Garden Theatre, where he was an assistant scene painter from October 1785 until, at earliest, October 1789.

But Milbourne had other abilities and on 13 July 1785 he was noticed in the Haymarket Theatre's bill ("Milbourn") as Teague Harlequin, the companion of Robert Palmer's Harlequin Teague, in *Harlequin Teague; or, the Giant's Causeway.* He also appeared in that pantomime's subordinate sketch "Characters Out of Character," as a Harlequin with One Leg. On 19 August following he was featured as Harlequin Mum in *The Genius of Nonsense* and on 31 August was the original Harlequin Skip in Carlo Delpini's pantomime *Here and There and Everywhere*, which ran through 16 September 1785.

Scattered bills of the Smock Alley Theatre show Milbourne, announced as "from the Haymarket" at the Dublin house in the 1785–86 winter season. On 6 February 1786 he produced at Smock Alley his own pantomime, *The Wizard of the Rocks; or, Harlequin Conqueror*, in which he played Harlequin.

Milbourne continued to act occasionally at the Haymarket and, after November 1788, at Covent Garden, until May 1791. His other recoverable London roles were: at the Haymarket in 1787, Crack in *Gretna Green*; in 1788, the original Harlequin for Ralph Wewitzer's pantomime *The Gnome; or, Harlequin Underground*; at Covent Garden (usually as "Milburne") in 1788–89, Puritan in *Duke and No Duke*, the Taylor in *Catherine and Petruchio*, Barnaby in *The Old Bachelor*, and Sneak in *The Lady of the Manor*; at the Haymarket in 1789, a Soldier in *The Battle of Hexham*; at Covent Garden in 1789–90, the Jew's Man in *The Little Hunchback*, Harlequin in *The Touchstone* (the *Public Advertiser* commended "Milbank" in the part), and a Grave Digger in *Hamlet*; at Covent Garden in 1790–91, some character unspecified in the ballet pantomime *Provocation!*, the Gardener in *The Picture of Paris*, the Second to Hephestion in *Alexander the Little*, and one of the original Sailors in John O'Keeffe's *Wild Oats*; and at Covent Garden in 1791–92, a "Principal Character" in *Blue-Beard*, a Shepherd in *A Peep behind the Curtain*, and some role unspecified in Thomas Hurlstone's new comic opera *Just in Time*, which perished after one performance on 10 May 1792. That performance was Milbourne's last appearance in London. He had lived for some time at No 5, Broad Court, Bow Street, the address he gave when he exhibited a watercolor at the show of the Society of Artists of Great Britain in 1790.

In 1792 Thomas Wignell came to England, hunting for performers to fill the stage of the splendid new theatre then rising in Chestnut Street in Philadelphia. But first he needed an artist to decorate its interior and help devise scenes for its opening productions. Scene painters and decorators were at a premium in London, with the huge new theatres being built and the increasing demand for spectacle in the patent houses, at the opera, and at the gardens and circuses. As small a fish as Charles Milbourne was, he must have seemed a desirable catch to Wignell, who sent him on to

Philadelphia late in 1792. That was nearly a year ahead of the arrival of the performing company on 15 July 1793. (He was accompanied by his young daughter, but no Mrs Milbourne was mentioned by William Dunlap, Seilhamer, Pollock, or any other chronicler of the early American theatrical scene.)

Evidently Milbourne was responsible for finishing the painting, gilding, and other interior decoration of the Chestnut Street Theatre designed by John Inigo Richards, who had redesigned Covent Garden Theatre. Early accounts exclaim in satisfaction over his work. Evidently, also, Milbourne painted a great deal of scenery for the theatre during the following few seasons, though John Durang remembered in 1818 that, at the opening of the house on 17 February 1794, John Joseph Holland was "Principle [*sic*] scene painter." Milbourne he called "Painter and actor; ground Harlequin." But Dunlap thought Milbourne's scenery as far surpassed "any stage decorations heretofore seen in the country as the building surpassed former American theatres."

Few indeed are Milbourne's performances as "ground Harlequin" or in any other specialty that Pollock preserves in *The Philadelphia Theatre in the Eighteenth Century*: Harlequin Skip and Clown in *The Birth of Harlequin* on 14 July 1795, repeated on 18 July and, in the new season, 8 and 10 December 1794; Clown in *The Elopement; or, Harlequin's Tour* on 29 June 1795; and Tubal in *The Merchant of Venice* on 27 March 1797. One may guess that Milbourne painted "A Grand Display of the Great Falls of Niagara" for *Harlequin's Tour*, which was first presented on his benefit night.

J. R. Wolcott in *Theatre Survey* 18 called attention to surviving prints of scenery painted by "M. C. Milbourne" for *The Triumph of Virtue; or, Harlequin in New York* at Rickett's Circus in New York in the summer of 1796. Wolcott there asserted that Milbourne remained at Philadelphia only to the end of 1795–96; but Pollock found both him and his daughter active there through the season of 1799–1800. (The daughter played a variety of parts of growing importance after a slow start in colombines and other pantomime parts. She later acted as Mrs Darby.)

In the season of 1807–8 at the Park Street Theatre, New York, according to G. C. D. Odell's *Annals*, Milbourne painted scenery with Holland and Hugh Reinagle for *Adrian and Orilla* and *Cinderella* and in 1808–9 he was still bouncing across stages as Harlequin.

Miles. *See also* MOYLE.

Miles, Mr [*fl. c.* 1769], *exhibitor.*
Henry Morley in *Memoirs of Bartholomew Fair* (1859) mentions a Miles who "was another chief of menagerie" at Bartholomew Fair about 1769. His booth, "Miles's Menagerie," is shown in an engraving of Bartholomew Fair of a much later period than 1769, for it was engraved by John Nixon after Thomas Rowlandson.

Miles, Mr [*fl.* 1784–1785], *constable.*
On the "List of Persons" at the King's Theatre in the 1784–85 opera season (Lord Chamberlain's Records in the Public Record Office) is a Mr Miles, the theatre's constable. Paid by the management, not by the City of Westminster or the Crown, he was considered part of the house establishment.

Miles, Mrs [*fl.* 1689–1692], *actress.*
A manuscript cast in a Claremont College copy of *Valentinian* shows that Mrs Miles played Celinda during the 1689–90 season, probably at Drury Lane, one of the United Company's two playhouses. She acted the Niece in *The Successful Strangers* in January 1690 and was still a member of the United Company in 1691–92.

Miles, Mrs Abram Allen. *See* GUEST, JANE MARY.

Miles, Francis 1716–1771, *dancer, actor.*
According to an epitaph published in the Dublin *Public Journal* of 1 May 1771, shortly after the death of Francis Miles, he was born in 1716. The place of his birth is not known.

Miles played one of four Tritons in *Neptune's Palace* at Hallam's booth on 23 August 1740 during the time of Bartholomew Fair. That was his first known appearance before a London public which he was to entertain, as dancer and minor actor, at booths and patent theatres for 40 years.

Miles returned to Hallam's booth during the Fair of 1741, dancing Africa in *The Triumph of Britain Over the Four Parts of the World*, according to a bill of 22 August 1741. On 2 October 1744 he turned up at Drury Lane Theatre in a "Grand Turkish Dance," with a number of dancers who included also Mrs Miles. On 19 October Miles was added to the cast of the pantomime *The Amorous Goddess; or, Harlequin Marry'd*. On 14 January 1745 and following he was one of the dancers in *Comus*.

Miles was either submerged anonymously in the corps or not at the theatre until the spring of 1746 when he was named with many others on the Drury Lane bill for the odd new pantomime commenting on the recent Jacobite rebellion, *Harlequin Incendiary; or, Colombine Cameron*. The next season, 1746–47, saw him and his wife at Goodman's Fields, Lemon Street, with his old booth friends the Hallams. During the season he performed often—both with Mrs Miles (a Scotch dance particularly) and alone—his *Drunken Peasant* and a hornpipe. But he also suddenly discovered a talent for acting, not only that required by ballet, as in his portrayal of Setebos in the masque of the Dryden-Davenant *Tempest*, but also in minor "straight" parts: Bardolph in *1 Henry IV*, a Boor in *The Royal Merchant*, Jack in *The Twin Rivals*, the Doctor in *Macbeth*, Simple in *The Merry Wives of Windsor*, Theodore in *Venice Preserv'd*, and Burgundy in *King Lear*.

After spring, 1747, there is a gap of a year in the record. We next see Miles on 4 April 1748, when he and his wife performed a dance titled *The Country Wake* in the theatre called New Wells, Lemon Street, where Lewis Hallam's company performed that night only.

Where was Francis Miles earning his bread between the spring of 1747 and the fall of 1750, when we pick up his trail again? Perhaps he danced or acted in the pleasure gardens, theatrical taverns, and fair booths of London and the suburbs, records of which are at this date skimpy. More likely he was in Ireland or the provinces of England. But when he returned to London he settled down at Covent Garden Theatre until virtually the day of his death. There he stepped into the rich pantomime tradition of John Rich and was the successful athletic Harlequin in many performances of those lavish and ingenious spectacles: in 1750–51, *Perseus and Andromeda* and *Merlin's Cave*; in 1751–52, *The Miller Outwitted*; in 1752–53, *Harlequin Statue*; in 1753–54, *Harlequin Skeleton*; in 1754–55, *The Jealous Farmer*

Deceived; in 1759–60, *The Fair* and *The Rape of Proserpine*; 1761–62, *Apollo and Daphne*; in 1762–63, *Harlequin Sorcerer*; in 1765–66, *The Royal Chace*; in 1767–68, *Orpheus and Eurydice* and *Harlequin Doctor Faustus*; and in 1769–70, *Harlequin's Jubilee*.

In his final season, 1770–71 Francis Miles added only some role unspecified in George Colman and Samuel Arnold's new pantomime *Mother Shipton*. It was likely, also, to have been the last part he played. The *Public Advertiser* lists him as the Landlady in *Mother Shipton* for 12 April. But that is highly dubious, for a benefit had been given for him on the eighth, and he died on 15 April 1771. On 26 April a benefit was given for his widow, Mary Miles.

Francis Miles was earning £3 per week in 1761, a decent but not munificent salary which was probably not much more at the time of his death. His will, signed on 1 April 1771, shows that he had been frugal. The sum of £700, three per cent "consolidated Bank Annuities my Property now standing in my name" on the books of the Bank of England was given in trust to his executors, the well-known actors Thomas Hull and Charles Clementine Dubellamy, to be invested for the benefit of his wife Mary. His daughter Ann, wife of John King, was residuary legatee of that amount.

The will minutely inventoried dozens of household items of value in his house in Wild Court, St Giles, which he left to his wife— ". . . my light day Clerk and Escritoire and Book Case, and also the use of my pint Silver Mug which was the property of my said Wife Mary before our Marriage and also my Six Silver Tea Spoons Two Tongs and Strainer two Silver Table Spoons and Silver Milk Pott . . ." and so on, down to pans, warming pans, and a "Copper Coal Scuttle." Joseph Besford, long-time property man at Covent Garden Theatre, was one of the witnesses to the will, proved by Miles's widow on 30 April 1771.

Miles, Mrs Francis, Mary ₁*fl.* 1744– 1780?₁, *dancer, actress.*

Mrs Miles joined her husband Francis and numerous others in a *Grand Turkish Dance* after the play at Drury Lane on 2 October 1744. That was her first recorded performance. Her second was on 17 October following, when she was one of three Shepherdesses in a pantomime, *The Amorous Goddess; or, Harlequin Mar-*

ry'd. She was in the dance corps when *Comus* was performed on 14 January 1745. She followed her husband to Goodman's Fields Theatre for the 1746–47 season and was featured in the bills several times with him in "Scotch" and "comic" dances. She was once, on 18 November 1746, thrust into service as an actress, playing Mrs Trusty in *The Provok'd Husband*. When the Hallam company gave its lone performance at the New Wells, Lemon Street, on 4 April 1748, Mary Miles danced with her husband a figure called *The Country Wake*. It was her last known appearance. After Francis Miles's death on 15 April 1771, Mrs Miles was given a benefit at Covent Garden on 26 April. She was the chief beneficiary of his will (see his entry). She was perhaps "the widow of the late Miles" who on 23 May 1780 was allowed benefit tickets at Covent Garden.

Miles, James *d. 1724, proprietor*
About 1697 Sadler's Wells was operated by the musician Francis Forcer the elder and his partner James Miles, a glover, but by 1699 Forcer seems to have dropped out of the management. Possibly Forcer had married a relative of Miles: at St James, Clerkenwell, on 9 March 1671 "Frances Forster" married a Mary "Milles." Early records of entertainments at the Wells are scarce, but the *Postman* No 465 advertised that on 23 May 1698 there would be "a concert of vocal and Instrumental music . . . and will continue every Monday and Thursday during the season of drinking the waters." The *Protestant Mercury* on 24 May 1699 said that one of the entertainments was a man who, after a full meal, ate a live chicken, feathers and all. Ned Ward in the same year spoke of the Wells as having entertainments of singing and dancing, fiddlers, and juvenile sword dancers, as well as drinking the waters, ale, and cider, and eating custards.

Morley in his *Memoirs of Bartholomew Fair* notes that in 1699 James Miles kept the "Gun Musick Booth" at that fair, where some of the dances exhibited were

a Dance between Three Bullies and Three Quakers; the Wonder of her Sex, a Young Woman who dances with the Swords and upon the Ladder with that Variety, that she challenges all her Sex to do the like; A Cripples' Dance by Six Persons with Wooden Legs and Crutches in Imitation of a Jovial Crew; and a New Entertainment between a Scaramouch,

a Harlequin, and a Punchinello, in imitation of Bilking a Reckoning.

"Jacobos" Miles kept a music booth at Stourbridge Fair, Cambridge, from 1717.

In June 1711 the *Inquisitor* called Sadler's Wells "a nursery of debauchery," and on 14 August 1712 a murder was committed at "The famous Place called Sadler's Wells, otherwise Miles's Musick-House. . . ." Lillywhite in *London Coffee Houses* reports *Parker's London News* of 15 April 1724 as saying that "Mr. Miles, who diverted the town, and was the favourite of Beaux, Butchers, Bawds, &c., by his entertainments at Sadler's Wells, is lately dead." The registers of St James, Clerkenwell, show that James Miles of Sadler's Wells was buried on 17 April.

The son and namesake of Francis Forcer may have been in some way connected with the management of the Wells after his father died in 1705 and before Miles died in 1724, for he married Miles's daughter, Frances. She was the widow of a Mr Tompkins, by whom she had two sons, Henry and John. When James Miles died, he left most of his possessions, according to Arundell's *Story of Sadler's Wells*, to his daughter and her sons.

Miles, John [*fl. 1697–1712*], *treasurer.*
The *London Stage* lists John Miles as treasurer of Betterton's company at the Lincoln's Inn Fields playhouse in 1697–98 and either treasurer or subtreasurer in 1699–1700. On 1 November 1704 the troupe acted *The Committee* at the Inner Temple, and apparently Miles was the one who received the payment. A document in Vice Chamberlain Coke's papers at Harvard concerning the actor George Bright mentions Miles as an agent for the troupe at the new Queen's Theatre about 1707 or 1708, and another document lists him at a salary of 2s. 8d. daily. Notes left by the late Emmett Avery show that on 2 November 1712 (a Sunday, so possibly an incorrect date) John Miles received payment from the Inner Temple for a performance given there, presumably on 1 November, the traditional date, by players from the Drury Lane company.

"Military Horse, Little." *See* **Learned Horse, The Little Military."**

Mill, David. *See* MELL, DAVIS.

Millar, Mr [*fl.* 1776], *singer? actor?*
On 22 April 1776 one Millar was teamed
with another unknown, Miss Barret, in speaking (or singing) "an Epithalamium" in Act II
of *Isabella*, in a benefit given at the Haymarket
Theatre for Mrs Fisher.

Millard, Mr [*fl.* 1785–1788], *performer.*
Mr Millard's name is found on lists of the
company at Astley's Amphitheatre, Westminster Bridge, in 1785 and 1788. Surviving bills,
however, do not reveal his performing specialties.

**Millard, Marie Elizabeth Anne, née
Boubert, later Mme Pierre Gabriel Gar-
del the second** *1770–1833, dancer.*
Born at Auxonne on 8 April 1770, Marie
Elizabeth Anne Millard was the daughter of
Monsieur Boubert, a musician at the Théâtre
des Grands-Danseurs du Roi. (*Grove's Diction-
ary* gives his name as Francois Xavier Houbert
and identifies him as a musician in a French
artillery regiment.) Her mother, Elisabeth
Boubert, née Chemitre, remarried, to the Pol-
ish musician and composer Ernest Ludwig
Mueller, sometimes called Krazinski Miller.
As Mlle Miller, Marie made her debut at the
Paris Opéra on 13 January 1786, dancing in
Dardanus. In his *Etat des Personnes* in 1788, the
Opéra manager Antoine Dauvergne described
her as "an excellent dancer, a bit cold. Works
without let-up to become a *premier sujet*." Mlle
Miller danced at the Opéra until 1792, and
was called in reviews "Terpsichore incarnate."
Noverre wrote "she was to the dance what
Venus de Milo was to sculpture."
Announced as from the Paris Opéra, and
advertised as "Mlle Millerd," she made her
debut at the King's Theatre on 26 January
1793, dancing in a new *Divertissement* and *Les
Caractères de la Dance* (in Noverre's *Les Époux du
Tempe*), with Mlle Hilligsberg, Nivelon, and
Favre Gardel (Guiardele). On 29 January the
Public Advertiser reported:

The charming Miss Millard, who was the most
accomplished dancer at the Opéra of Paris, made
her debut in England; she was received with the
warmest applause, and never was applause so cor-
dially requited. The great talent of Miss Millard is

the unparalleled neatness of her motion. "The many
twinkling feet" are peculiarly adapted to her dancing—for never perhaps did the English spectator
see such graceful rapidity as she possesses in the
demi-caractère.

She danced in the same pieces on 5 February,
and on 26 February appeared as Venus in
Noverre's heroic pantomime ballet *Venus and
Adonis*, set to new music by Storace. Her ballets were repeated on 6 April. On 23 April she
danced Clytemnestra in *Iphigenia in Aulide*, a
ballet by Noverre and set to music by "Millerd," meaning her step-father Krazinski Miller,
who worked at the Opéra but seems not to
have been in London at this time. On 1 June
Mlle Millard danced in *La Jaloux puni*, a piece
that was repeated on 4, 8, and 11 June. On
that last night she also appeared in *Iphigenia in
Aulide* and in a *Court Minuet* with Guiardele.
Her last performance at the King's Theatre was
on 29 June 1793.
After that one season in London, Mlle Millard returned to Paris, where on 24 December
1795 she became the second wife of the choreographer Pierre Gabriel Gardel (who is noticed in volume 5 of this dictionary). His first
wife had been the dancer Anne Jacqueline Cou-
lon. Mme Gardel retired from the Opéra in
1816, after 30 years on the stage. Her pension
was 4000 francs. She died on 18 May 1833
(according to Campardon's *L'Académie Royale
de musique*, and not in 1823 as given by Grove).

Millau. *See* MILLARD.

Milledge. *See* MILLIDGE.

Miller. *See also* MILLAR and MILLARD.

Miller, Mr [*fl.* 1708], *bill carrier.*
In Vice Chamberlain Coke's papers at Harvard is a paylist for the Queen's Theatre dated
8 March 1708; a Mr Miller was named as a bill
carrier at a daily salary of 4s.

Miller, Mr [*fl.* 1745], *actor.*
When Townly was given his benefit at
Goodman's Fields Theatre on 21 March 1745,
one Miller played the Doctor in *The Mock Doctor*—"By Desire," the playbill said. He may
have been some popular amateur.

Miller, Mr [*fl.* 1754–1758]. *See* MILLER, JOHN WEITZEN.

Miller, Mr [*fl.* 1761], *actor.*

An anonymous "Gentleman" made his debut in some part unspecified in *All in the Wrong* in the Foot-Murphy Company at Drury Lane on 15 June 1761. He was identified in Isaac Reed's "Notitia Dramatica" in the British Library and in a notation by James Winston at the Folger Library as "Miller." When the play was repeated for the third time on 18 June the bill carried the information: "Mr. Miller, 3rd appearance." "Millar" got some role in *The Citizen* when it was acted on 2 July, and another in Richard Bentley's new pantomime *The Wishes; or, Harlequin's Mouth Opened.* Presumably he was in both mainpiece and afterpiece when the little company of irregulars closed their season on 8 August with *All in the Wrong* and *The Citizen*.

Miller, Mr [*fl.* 1770–1776], *house servant.*

A British Library manuscript, Egerton 2272, lists a Mr Miller as "first gallery office-keeper" at Covent Garden in 1766. He was very likely the male house servant named Miller who shared in benefits with numerous others in May 1770, and nearly every year through 1776.

Miller, Mr [*fl.* 1773–1790], *dancer.*

On 24 April 1773 a hornpipe was danced at Covent Garden Theatre by "Miller (Scholar to Fisher [James Fishar])." On 30 April Miller danced again, and again on 25 May. Those were the brief solo appearances used to introduce every young dancer to the audiences. But it is noteworthy that they were fewer than usual and that Miller (unlike the usual "pupil" of the dancing masters) was never called "Master." He must have been verging on manhood when he came to the stage.

He was almost certainly in the regular corps of dancers at Covent Garden in the 1773–74 season, his presence concealed under the ampersand which usually ended the incomplete list of dancers on the playbill. For the manuscript account book carries the notation as of 15 January 1774 "Paid Mr Miller [£2] for performing 8 nights in *The Sylph*," a new pantomime which was to net Miller, in two additional payments, £4 15s.. for 20 more nights of dancing.

But Miller was assuredly not a headliner. At Covent Garden on 22 May 1776 he shared a benefit with many others. On 9 October 1777 he danced a hornpipe at the Haymarket. On 3 January 1780 he was singled out in the Haymarket bill for dancing at the end of Act II of the mainpiece. Perhaps by then he had lost his small place at Covent Garden, for he took up teaching. At Drury Lane on 5 May 1780 "Master Butler, scholar to Miller" made his appearance dancing a hornpipe for the benefit of his father, the theatre's carpenter. The youth danced for similar May benefits at Drury Lane in 1781, 1782, 1784, and 1785—and those were the only occasions in which we find Miller the dancer's name in the playbills.

Perhaps Miller was dancing anonymously again at Covent Garden after 1785–86. He could have had engagements at Sadler's Wells or one of the Circuses. On 5 May 1787 he was allowed benefit tickets at Covent Garden, with other underlings of the company, and danced, with Mr and Mrs Ratchford, "a new dance, The Sailor Caught Napping." He had therefore been a regular at least some part of the 1786–87 season. On 30 May 1788 he and the Ratchfords again were allowed tickets and danced *The Cobler of Castle Dormot.* The last knowledge we have of Miller the dancer is of 27 May 1790, when he, the Ratchfords, Blurton, and Jackson presented *A Dance of Jockies* at Covent Garden.

Miller, Mr [*fl.* 1777–78], *constable.*

Mr Miller, a constable employed by Covent Garden Theatre, was allowed to distribute benefit tickets, which were accepted at Covent Garden Theatre on 24 May 1777. He was accorded the same privilege on 22 May 1778.

Miller, Mr [*fl.* 1784], *horn player.*

Charles Burney listed a Miller as a horn player in the Handel Memorial Concerts at Westminster Abbey and the Pantheon in May and June 1784.

Miller, Mr [*fl.* 1784], *singer.*

Charles Burney listed a Miller as a bass singer in the Handel Memorial Concerts at Westminster Abbey and the Pantheon in May and June 1784.

Miller, Mr ₍fl. 1784₎, violinist.

Charles Burney listed a Miller among the second violins at the Handel Memorial Concerts in Westminster Abbey and the Pantheon in May and June 1784.

Miller, Mr ₍fl. 1784₎, violist.

Charles Burney listed a Miller, "tenor" (i.e., viola) among the instrumental musicians in the Handel Memorial Concerts at Westminster Abbey and the Pantheon in May and June 1784.

Miller, Mrs ₍fl. 1758₎, actress? house servant?

A Mrs Miller was allowed benefit tickets, along with four known actors, at Drury Lane Theatre on 29 May 1758. Her function at the theatre is not known.

Miller, Miss ₍fl. 1769–1779₎, actress.

Miss Miller made her debut on 18 October 1769 at Covent Garden, billed only as "A Young Gentlewoman, never on any Stage before," playing Monimia the female lead in *The Orphan* on a night when the well-known William "Gentleman" Smith was playing Castalio the male lead for the first time. The young woman survived that difficult challenge to repeat the part on 14 November, when her name first appeared in the bills. In fact, she remained at the theatre in good tragedy roles until the end of the 1773–74 season, despite the objections of some among her fellow actors and some critics.

Charles Macklin, in his resentful deposition in the 1770 lawsuit between the Covent Garden managers Thomas Harris and George Colman, scolded Colman for engaging Miss Miller at 50s. per week to portray leading tragedy characters which, he said, had been capably shared among several other actresses, including Macklin's daughter Maria.

The *Theatrical Review* (1771) reported that "Miss Miller dandles through the Part of Irene [in *Barbarossa*] with her usual constitutional insipidity." Francis Gentleman in *The Theatres* (1771) thought that she should be deprived of "foremost characters." With her, "grief or declamation drooping flags, / And screech-owl screams tear passion into rags." The *Macaroni and Savoir Vivre Magazine* for October 1773 both gave and took away:

Miss Miller has merit in many parts of Tragedy, such as, Roxana, Alicia, Cordelia, &c. and in comedy she is useful in several parts; but her talent is mostly inclined to the former: her fault lies in a want of expression, and next in her voice, which is not exactly tunable, and wants compass; yet the above characters in tragedy, and several others, she performs with judgment and great spirit.

William Hawkins, in *Miscellanies in Prose and Verse* (1775) also found her voice not "tunable" and added that she should rid herself of a certain "stiffness in her gait" in the less haughty roles.

But other critical pens were employed in her praise, like that of the writer in the *St James Chronicle* quoted by Noyes in *Ben Jonson on the English Stage*: "*Miss Miller* is the very Caelia of the Play [*Volpone*]; her Look, Manner, Voice Deportment, and Execution creates [sic] every Emotion in the Spectator which that Character should raise!"

Miss Miller also excited strange behavior. Fanny Burney in her *Early Diary* (1775) speaks of a certain gloomy clergyman, the Reverend Mr Penneck, who conceived such a violent passion for Miss Miller "that upon suspecting Mr. [George] Colman was his rival, this pious clergyman, who is twice the heightt [sic] at least of Mr. Colman, one night, in the streets, knocked him down, when he was quite unprepared for any attack." Mr Penneck's suspicions were probably well founded. They were shared by Macklin, who in one of his manuscript jottings published in the *Monthly Mirror* as "Mackliniana," twins her with Mrs Lessingham as a "Manager's mistress."

These, then, are the roles awarded Miss Miller, however she earned them: in 1769–70, Monimia in *The Orphan*, the female lead in *Tancred and Sigismunda*, Marcia in *Cato*, Imoinda in *Oroonoko*, and Athenais in *Theodosius*; in 1770–71, Rutland in *The Earl of Essex*, Cordelia in *King Lear*, Irene in *Barbarossa*, Alicia in *Jane Shore*, Desdemona in *Othello*, Roxana in *The Rival Queens*, and Juliet in *Romeo and Juliet*; in 1771–72, the Queen [Elizabeth] in *Richard III*, Caelia in *The Fox*, Amanda in *Love's Last Shift*, Lady Seaton in *A Wife in the Right*; in 1772–73, Jenny in *The Gentle Shepherd*, Queen Elizabeth in *The Albion Queens*, and Octavia in *All for Love*; in 1773–74, Fanny in *The Clandestine Marriage*, the Lady in *Comus*, Arpasia in *Tamerlane*, Albina in *Elfrida*, Mrs

Boothby in *The Duellist*, and Leonora in *The Revenge*.

William Hawkins declared in 1775: "Miss Miller at present is disengaged from Covent-Garden, occasioned by the late alteration at that theatre." The alteration was the departure from the managerial partnership of Miss Miller's friend George Colman, who had sold his share to Thomas Hull. After 4 May 1774 Miss Miller never appeared at Covent Garden. But our subject may have been the Miss Miller who helped a miscellaneous group of actors put on a revival (after 49 years) of James Miller's *The Humours of Oxford* at the Haymarket on 15 March 1779.

Miller, Alexander *d. 1796, actor, manager.*

When Alexander Miller was buried at St Mary's, Nottingham, in 1796 the register identified him as "Son of James Miller," presumably the sometime Worcester and Shrewsbury manager, who had died in July 1791. Alexander was probably the Miller who acted and managed on the Derby circuit in February 1769.

Billed only as "A Young Gentleman," Miller played Antony in *Julius Caesar* at the Haymarket on 11 September 1769. He was identified by the *Whitehall Evening Post* of 12 May 1770, which predicted that he would resume at the Haymarket in the summer of 1770. There is no evidence in the playbills that he did; yet he was one of the 28 players whom Samuel Foote took with him to Edinburgh's Theatre Royal, Shakespeare Square, for a winter campaign opening on 17 November 1770. Norma Armstrong's manuscript calendar yields the following roles for Miller: the Duke in *The Merchant of Venice* on 3 December, Alonzo in *Rule a Wife and Have a Wife* on 10 December, the Duke in *As You Like It* on 7 January 1771, Duncan in *Macbeth* on 13 March, and Lieutenant Lyon in *The Tars of Old England* on 20 March.

Miller was back at the Haymarket when it opened on 15 May, playing an unspecified part in *The Devil upon Two Sticks*. Thereafter that season he played Old Knowell in *Every Man in His Humour*, Richard Wealthy in *The Minor*, one of the Mob in *The Mayor of Garratt*, Hortensio in *Catherine and Petruchio*, some role in *The Orators*, Robert in *The Mock Doctor*, and a Member of the Mob in *The Contrivances*. Griffiths had replaced him in his parts by 5 Au-

gust, and he seems not to have returned to London to act.

From 29 November 1771 through February 1772, Miller was acting and managing at the theatre at St Mary's Gate, Derby. Tate Wilkinson weaves one of his circumlocutory anecdotes around Miller's issuing a writ for £10 due him from Mrs Bridgemore, one of his former actresses.

Alexander Miller was for some years in partnership in provincial theatrical managership with the better-known Thomas Shaftoe Robertson. Miller died in May 1796. He was buried at St Mary's, Nottingham, on 22 May 1796.

Miller, Anne *d. 1805, actress, singer.*

The actress Miss Miller who performed at Drury Lane Theatre between 1794 and 1799 is called a "Daughter of Miller of St. James's Coffee House" in a manuscript (Add 8586) in the British Library, and her first name, Anne, is furnished by another (Add MS 38,607).

Her first appearances at Drury Lane were as one of a large number of female Captives in J. P. Kemble's new melodrama *Lodoiska* after its premiere on 9 June 1794. She continued that duty the following fall, but on 28 October, when she was given the title role in Joseph Berington's new tragedy *Emilia Galotti*, her name was concealed on the bill under the designation then conventional for debutantes in named parts: "A Young Lady (who has never appeared on any stage)." *The Authentic Memoirs of the Green Room* (1798) declared, however, that she had already played in "the country." *Emilia Galotti* died quietly after the third performance but Anne Miller continued for five seasons at Drury Lane, playing important secondary roles, with occasional leads. An unidentified clipping dated only 1795, in the Folger Library, informs us that "Miss Miller who made so interesting a Figure on the D.L. Boards last Season, was a Kind of Pupil to Mrs. Kemble the Mother of Mrs. Siddons."

Her roles as she added them season by season were, after Emilia, as follows: in 1795–96, Diana in *All's Well that Ends Well*, Zorayda in *The Mountaineers*, Parisatis in *Alexander the Great*, Lady Douglas in *Mary Queen of Scots*, the original Zobeide in Prince Hoare's melodrama *Mahmoud*, Galeria in *The Roman Actor*, and Lady Touchwood in *The Belle's Stratagem*; in

Harvard Theatre Collection

ANNE MILLER, as Zaphira

engraving by Leney, after De Wilde

Giles, Cripplegate, the previous 26 February. The registers described Edward Miller as a player and noted that his son had died of convulsions. Miller acted again at the Haymarket in February and March 1723, playing Renault in *Venice Preserv'd* and Gibbet in *The Stratagem*, after which he seems to have given up London for the provinces. Tate Wilkinson in *The Wandering Patentee* placed Edward Miller at York in 1727, playing Heli in *The Mourning Bride* for Orfeur's benefit (Miller's first appearance in London had been for Mrs Orfeur's shared benefit). Miller is known to have acted the title role in *The Pilgrim* at the Smock Alley Theatre in Dublin on 4 May 1737, and when he played there again on 4 May 1738 he was advertised as from the Edinburgh theatre.

Miller, Mrs [**Edward?**] [*fl. 1723–1735*], actress.

Dorinda in *The Stratagem* at the Haymarket Theatre on 14 March 1723 was played by Mrs Miller, presumably the wife of the actor Edward Miller, who acted Gibbet. She was probably the Mrs Miller who was seen as Mrs Sullen in *The Stratagem* at Southwark Fair on 24 September 1730, Hillaria in *Tunbridge Walks* on 8 March 1732 at the Haymarket, Lady Trueman in *The Drummer* on 28 May 1735 at Tottenham Court and then, at the Haymarket in July and August of that year, Mrs Motherly in *The Provok'd Husband*, the Maid in *The Mock Doctor*, and Florella in *The Orphan*.

1796–97, Maria in *The School for Scandal*, Maria in *The London Merchant*, Miss Neville in *Know Your Own Mind*, Juliet in *Romeo and Juliet*, and Miranda in *The Tempest*; in 1797–98, Dorinda in *The Tempest*; and in 1798–99, Angelina in *Love Makes a Man*.

Anne Miller died at Wandsworth on 20 August 1805, according to the *Gentleman's Magazine* for August 1805. A portrait of her as Zaphira in *Barbarossa*, engraved by W. Leney, after De Wilde, was published as a plate to *Bell's British Theatre*, 1795.

Miller, Edward [*fl. 1722–1738?*], actor.

The Mr Miller who played Horatio in *The Wife's Relief* on 17 December 1722 at the Haymarket Theatre was very likely the Edward Miller whose son William was buried at St

Miller, Edward *1735–1807*, organist, impresario, composer.

Edward Miller was born at Norwich on 12 September 1735, according to the account of his life in the *New Grove*. He was apprenticed to his father, a paviour, but deserted his apprenticeship for music and studied under Charles Burney. He is said to have played flute "in Handel's oratorio orchestra during the 1750s" though we can find no confirmation of this claim. He was elected organist of Doncaster, Yorkshire, on 15 July 1756 at the recommendation of James Nares, succeeding John Camidge.

Miller proceeded Doctor of Music at Cambridge in 1786. The rejection of George Smart by the Royal Society of Musicians gave rise to the New Musical Fund, in which Miller took an early and prominent part. A letter from

John Wall Callcott to Dr Charles Burney dated 25 September 1802 recollects: "Dr. Miller's letter also in behalf of [allowing] Country Musicians [to participate in the Fund] was the inducement to appoint him with Dr [Philip] Hayes conductor of their annual performance the first (I believe) of which was held April 12, 1787." (British Library Add MS 27667).

Miller directed the Sheffield Festival of 1788. Tate Wilkinson, in his *Wandering Patentee* describes an occasion in 1790 when "he heard [Madame Gertrud] Mara sing at Doncaster church in the race week [in oratorios conducted by Miller] and not one hundred persons there." Miller was a teacher, for the prominent violinist and pianist Charles Cummins testified in a letter to John H. Sainsbury that he had received his first musical instruction from Miller. He was usually called Miller "of Doncaster" but he seems to have spent much time in London. He was married in 1763, according to *New Grove*; his wife died 10 years later and he remarried in 1796.

Miller was best known as a composer. His *Elements of Thorough Bass and Composition* contains patterns for performance. His *Psalms of David for the Use of Parish Churches, the Words Selected . . . by the Rev⁴ G. H. Drummond* contains the famous hymn tunes "Rockingham" and "Galway." *David's Harp*, in which Miller collaborated with his son, a Methodist clergyman, offers about 300 tunes for Wesleyan hymns. He also wrote a respectable *History of Doncaster*.

Edward Miller died at Doncaster on 12 September 1807.

Miller, Elizabeth. *See* BAKER, MRS THOMAS.

Miller, George [*fl.* 1763], *double-bass player.*
Mortimer's London Directory (1763) carried the cryptic entry for George Miller: "Double Bass. Bedfordbury. Covent-garden."

Miller, James William [*fl.* 1779–1792?], *actor.*
At the Haymarket Theatre on 18 October 1779 a Mr Miller played Charles in *The Busy Body* in a special performance for the benefit of Thomas Dibble Davis. It was called his "first appearance." In another such performance, on 23 February 1784, a Mr Miller, perhaps the same, was given a part in *The Patriot*, a play by an anonymous author. On 6 February 1792, when Mrs Churton took a benefit at the Haymarket, a Miller played the Duke in *Othello*. The Lord Chamberlain's records for February 1796 show the application of James William Miller for a license to stage a performance at the Haymarket for his benefit. The performance occurred on 22 February, when "Previous to [the] mainpiece an *Occasional Address*" was given by Miller. The mainpiece was *The Mourning Bride*, in which Miller assumed the lead male role of Osmyn.

There are no proofs that the Miller of 1779 and that of 1784 were the James William Miller of 1792. But far less likely was J. W. Miller to have been the dancer (fl. 1773–1790) or the singer (fl. 1794). The *London Stage* indexes conflate the three records incorrectly.

Miller, Jo [*fl.* 1743–1754?], *actor.*
On 7 April 1743 at the James Street Theatre a benefit was held for "Jo. Miller," nephew of the late Josias ("Joe") Miller (1684–1738); the younger Miller's Christian name may also have been Josias, though the elder comedian was often called Joseph, so that may have been his nephew's name. At James Street Miller acted Teague in *The Committee* and Muckworm in *The Honest Yorkshireman*, the former being one of his uncle's favorite roles. On 21 March 1745 he tried the title role in *The Mock Doctor* at Goodman's Fields, and from 2 June 1746 he acted at the Jacob's Wells Theatre in Bristol for 4*s.* per performance. On 24 August 1748 he was seen as Ben Board'em in *The Consequences of Industry and Idleness* at Bartholomew Fair, and it is probable that the Mrs Miller who acted at the fair in 1749 was his wife. Perhaps he was the Mr Miller who acted at the theatre in Water Street, Philadelphia, from 15 April to 24 June 1754 playing Puff in *Miss in Her Teens*, Old Hob in *Flora*, and Stratocles in *Tamerlane*.

Miller, Mrs [Jo?] [*fl.* 1749], *actress.*
The Mrs Miller who played Sycorax in *The Tempest* at Bartholomew Fair from 23 to 28 August 1749 may have been the wife of Jo Miller, though we have found no record of his appearance at the Fair that particular year.

Miller, John *d. 1770, bassoonist.*

When the Royal Society of Musicians was established on 28 August 1739, one of the original subscribers was the musician John Miller. At the Haymarket Theatre on 3 February 1741, a concert of instrumental music was presented with a Mr Miller, probably John, participating; he played the bassoon at concerts at Hickford's Music Room the following 5 and 6 March, at the King's Theatre on 14 March, and at Hickford's on 10 April. In March 1743 he performed at the annual benefit for indigent musicians held at the King's Theatre, as he did in March 1744 and for many years following.

On 14 February 1745 Miller played a bassoon solo at the Haymarket, and the following April he participated in the oratorios at Covent Garden Theatre. For Waltz's benefit he played at the Haymarket in December 1748; in May 1758 he participated in the performance of the *Messiah* at the Foundling Hospital for a fee of 10s. 6d. (another Miller was among the trumpets and drums); on 22 November 1766 Miller played bassoon at the Oxford Music Room; and on 22 September 1760 his name was on the Covent Garden paylist at 5s. daily. The last piece of information suggests that Miller may have been performing in the theatre band for many years and making side appearances at the annual King's Theatre benefits and elsewhere. He was cited on the paylist at Covent Garden again on 14 September 1767, when he was still earning 10s. 6d. daily. The *Whitehall Evening Post* for 26 March 1770 carried notice of the recent death of John Miller, said to be a musician belonging to Covent Garden Theatre. Dr Burney described Miller as "the best bassoon I can remember."

It is quite possible that John Miller was related to the music publishers and musical instrument sellers of the seventeenth and early eighteenth century, noticed in the entry of Mrs John Miller.

Miller, Mrs John, Elizabeth ₁*fl. 1707–1727*₁, *impresario, publisher.*

According to Humphries and Smith's *Music Publishing in the British Isles*, Elizabeth Miller, the widow of the music and musical instrument seller and publisher John Miller, ran her late husband's shop at the sign of the Violin and Hautboy on London Bridge from 1707 to

about 1727. Dudley Ryder in his *Diary* wrote that on 21 November 1715 he "went to Mrs. Miller's concert upon London Bridge. There was no great matter of a concert." How much of a career she made of putting on concerts we do not know. Her husband had had his shop on London Bridge from 1695, but no information has been found concerning her activity until her husband's death, which must have been in 1707.

It is probable that John and Elizabeth Miller were related to other Millers in the music publishing and instrument selling business in the seventeenth century, virtually all of whom operated not far from London Bridge. George Miller ran a shop in the Blackfriars from 1601 to 1646; his son Abraham succeeded him there and ran the operation until 1653. Another George Miller, doubtless a relative, had a business near the Royal Exchange in 1676, and in 1707 J. Miller (not John, apparently) sold music at premises in Birchin Lane, which ran south from Cornhill. It also seems probable that the bassoonist John Miller active in the middle of the eighteenth century was also related.

Miller, John ₁*fl. 1775*₁, *musician.*

A manuscript in the Forster Collection in the Victoria and Albert Museum, endorsed by David Garrick, "List of our Band [at Drury Lane Theatre] for the present year 1775," contains the name of John Miller. Perhaps he was the son of the bassoonist John Miller who died in 1770.

Miller, John Weitzen ₁*fl. 1749–1759*₁, *trumpeter, horn player.*

John Weitzen Miller was cited several times in the Lord Chamberlain's accounts as a trumpeter in the King's Musick. He evidently replaced Charles (?) Snow in 1749 and was replaced by John Richards sometime after 1759. His salary was £40 annually. Since his full name was regularly given, we take it that he was not the bassoonist John Miller (d. 1770); the use of the middle name would suggest that the record keepers were trying to distinguish between the two musicians. John Weitzen Miller was probably the Miller who played horn in the performance of the *Messiah* at the Foundling Hospital in May 1745 for a fee of 10s.

6d.. He was there again in May 1758, listed among the trumpets and kettledrums.

Miller, Josias [or Joseph] *1684–1738, actor, singer, dancer.*

Born in 1684 and possibly related to (Patrick?) Miller, who operated fair booths at the turn of the century, Josias Miller may have made his first appearance on 25 March 1704 as the Watchman in *Love at First Sight* at the Lincoln's Inn Fields playhouse. Among the manuscripts at the British Library is a note that the Miller acting that part was "one who never appeared before." A Miller was again cited in London bills on 1 August 1705, when he acted Julio in *The Cares of Love* at Lincoln's Inn Fields.

The same manuscript notes that Miller's first appearance at Drury Lane was on 28 November 1709, when "one who never Acted on that Stage before" played Teague in *The Committee*; Teague became one of "Joe" Miller's favorite roles. The following 3 December Miller was named in the bill for Jeremy in *Love for Love*. On 10 December he acted a Senator in *Timon of Athens*, seven days later he played Clip in

Harvard Theatre Collection

JOSIAS MILLER, as Teague
engraving by A. Miller, after C. Stoppelaer

The Confederacy, and on 31 January 1710 he was Guzman in *The Successful Strangers*. He was the singing Pedlar in *The Maid of the Mill* on 14 March, shared a benefit with Knapp on 21 March, and was the second Sailor in *Bickerstaff's Burial* on 27 March.

After that promising beginning Miller seems to have left London for five years, returning (probably from playing in the provinces) on 4 February 1715 to act Sneak in *The Country Lasses* at Drury Lane. He performed there through 1729–30, building up a large repertoire of mostly comic parts that included Kate Matchlock and later Trim in *The Funeral*, Sir Roger in *The What D'Ye Call It*, Clincher Junior and later Beau Clincher in *The Constant Couple*, Old Wilful in *The Double Gallant*, Tallboy in *The Jovial Crew*, Cokes in *Bartholomew Fair*, Sir Thomas Reveller in *Greenwich Park*, Robin in *The Contrivances*, the Lord Mayor in *Richard III*, Sir Jolly Jumble in *The Soldier's Fortune*, Sir Amorous LaFool in *The Silent Woman*, a Carrier in *1 Henry IV*, a Coachman in *The Drummer*, Sir Mannerly Shallow in *The Country Wit*, Roderigo and the Mad Englishman in *The Pilgrim*, Nicodemus Somebody in *The Stage Coach*, Clodpole in *The Amorous Widow*, Sly in *Love's Last Shift*, Lance in *Wit Without Money*, Sir Harry Gubbin and Humphrey in *The Tender Husband*, Ptisan in *Three Hours after Marriage*, Hothead in *Sir Courtly Nice*, Sir Joseph in *The Old Bachelor*, Don Lewis in *Love Makes a Man*, Widgin in *The Northern Lass*, Sir Martin in *The Feign'd Innocence (Sir Martin Marall)*, Bumpkin in *The Old Troop*, Whackum in *The Scowrers*, Sampson in *The Little French Lawyer*, Bullock in *The Recruiting Officer*, Ben in *Love for Love*, Le Prate in *Love for Money*, Trinculo in *The Tempest*, Foigard in *The Stratagem*, Smart in *The Masquerade*, Lurcher in *Chit Chat*, Roderigo in *Othello*, Jaqueline in *The Fatal Marriage*, Asotus in *The Bondman*, Marplot in *The Busy Body*, Osric in *Hamlet*, and Isander in *Timon of Athens*.

He also added Belfond Senior in *The Squire of Alsatia*, Silence in *2 Henry IV*, the Shoemaker in *The Relapse*, Sir Wilfull in *The Way of the World*, Franvil in *The Sea Voyage*, Mizen in *The Fair Quaker*, Squire Hartford in *The Lancashire Witches*, a Citizen in *Julius Caesar*, Kastril and Abel Drugger in *The Alchemist*, Sir Gregory in *The Rival Fools*, Sir Philip Money Love in *The Artifice*, Thisbe in *Love in a Forest*, Petulant in *The Plain Dealer*, Duratête in *The*

Inconstant, Macahone in *The Strollers*, Crack in *Sir Courtly Nice*, Pierrot in *Apollo and Daphne*, the title role in *Hob*, Cholerick in *Love Makes a Man*, Teague in *The Twin Rivals*, Razor in *The Provok'd Wife*, Pantaloon in *Apollo and Daphne*, Trappanti in *She Wou'd and She Wou'd Not*, a Countryman in *Harlequin Doctor Faustus*, the title role in *The Humorous Lieutenant*, the first Ruffian in *Caius Marius*, Ernesto in *The Adventures of Five Hours*, the Shoemaker in *The Man of Mode*, John Moody in *The Provok'd Husband*, Sir Apish Simple in *Love in Several Masques*, Timothy Peascod in *The What D'Ye Call It*, Antonio in *The Chances*, Cimon in *Love in a Riddle*, Brush in *The Village Opera*, Sands

Harvard Theatre Collection

JOSIAS Miller, as Sir Joseph Wittol
engraving by Cornac

in *Henry VIII*, Varole in *The Lovers Opera*, and the Squire in *The Comical Distresses of Pierot*.

From time to time Miller offered entr'acte songs and dances, and, as can be seen from his roles, he occasionally participated in pantomimes and ballad operas that would have displayed his singing and dancing talents. He enjoyed solo benefits for most seasons during his stay at Drury Lane.

At first Joe's allegiance was to Drury Lane alone, and if he performed during the summers it was there, but in July and August of 1718 he acted at Pinketham's playhouse in Richmond, playing an unnamed part in *The Spanish Fryar*, the title role in *The Busy Body*, and Teague in *The Committee*. After that his name was often found in the bills for the late summer fairs and elsewhere, though he performed regularly during the normal theatrical season at Drury Lane. Sybil Rosenfeld in *Strolling Players* places Miller at Richmond again in August 1719, but he performed that month at Drury Lane as well, and he shared the management of a booth at Bartholomew Fair on 24 August and played Sir Anthony Noodle in the droll *Jane Shore*. At the Pinkethman-Norris booth at tht fair in August 1720 he acted Roger in *Maudlin*; in 1721 he joined with those two at both Bartholomew and Southwark fairs and played Sousecrown in *The Injur'd General*. Miller was at Richmond again in July and August 1722, acting Tony Souscrown in *Richmond Wells* and Wantbrains in *Distress'd Beauty*; the latter roles he repeated at Bartholomew Fair at the booth he operated with Pinkethman and Boheme. At Southwark Fair that September he managed by himself at the Angel Tavern, producing and acting in *The Faithful Couple*. On 3 August 1724 he played Somebody at Richmond, then in September at the booth run by Bullock and Spiller at Southwark Miller acted Adrastus in *Oedipus*.

Then he took a few summers off, returning on 21 August 1727 to run a booth at Bartholomew Fair with Hall and Milward, at which they produced *The Humours of Anthony Noodle* with Miller in the title part. With Hall in 1728 at the Fair he presented *Bateman* and played Sparrow in it. He did not engage in activity at any fair in 1729, but *Fog's* on 19 July of that year ran a note that may have referred to Joe: "We hear that Mr Miller having left performing as usual, at Windmill Hill, Mr

Spencer intends to Entertain the Town with an antient Catalogue of Plays. . . ." It could be that in previous summers Miller had been producing plays at Windmill Hill, but no bills for such activity have been found.

Miller was not at Drury Lane in 1730–31, and perhaps he acted in the provinces. He was at Bartholomew Fair in August 1731, however, operating a booth with Mills and Oates (not with Oates and another Miller, as Nicoll has it in his *History of English Drama*, II, 366). They put on *The Banish'd General*, with Miller playing Hobble Wallop; the work was repeated by them at Southwark Fair the following month.

Joe was referred to as Joseph in the *Daily Post* on 31 December 1731, and called that regularly, though Josias seems to have been his Christian name. He played Teague in *The Committee* at the Goodman's Fields Theatre on 3 January 1732 and was advertised as making his first appearance on any stage in two years. He acted there through May, reviving many of his favorite roles: Ben, Roderigo, Sir Joseph, Beau Clincher, Bullock, Don Lewis, Hob, Foigard, Trappanti, the Mad Englishman, Marplot, Somebody, and Old Wilful, among others. But he tried some new roles: Father Burn in *Father Girard*, Daniel in *Oroonoko*, the first Gravedigger in *Hamlet*, Noddy in *The Footman*, Numps in *The Tender Husband*, and Jobson in *The Devil to Pay*. In August he rejoined his old friends Mills and Oates to present the droll

Benefit ticket for JOSEPH MILLER
by Hogarth

Henry VIII at Bartholomew Fair, in which he acted Numpskull.

Miller returned to Drury Lane on 22 November 1732, using Teague in *The Committee* to celebrate his return; then he played a run of his favorite parts, as he had done at Goodman's Fields, and introduced such new ones as Jack Straw in *Wat Tyler*, James in *The Miser*, and Alexander Whittle in *Deborah*. With Mills and Oates he produced the droll *Jane Shore* at Bartholomew Fair in August 1733, playing Sir Anthony. That summer Miller and other players from Drury Lane joined with Theophilus Cibber in a stage mutiny, pictured by Jack Laguerre in his print of that name, complaining against the patentees of theatre and especially John Highmore and threatening to desert the troupe. In a letter to the *Daily Post* on 4 June the patentees stated their case, noting by the way that Miller's salary had been £5 weekly and that they had paid him a total of £40 before he began acting for them again (for the period from September through December 1732). In Theophilus Cibber's response the rebel leader noted that Miller's absence from the stage had been caused by the Drury Lane patentees; Miller "was kept out of any Business upwards of Two Years, and was a Sufferer above 300 l." The £40 which the patentees paid Miller upon his return to Drury Lane in January 1733 had been in recompense of his losses during the seasons preceding, an arrangement apparently urged by Cibber.

Miller played Galindo in *The False Friends* on 10 September 1733 at Richmond (for Chapman's benefit and Miller's own diversion), then he joined Cibber at the Haymarket with a number of the other Drury Lane rebels. On 26 September he acted Ben in *Love for Love* for his first appearance at that playhouse. At the Haymarket he provided his standard repertoire of comic roles and attempted only one new one: Dr Diascordium in *The Mother-in-Law* on 12 February 1734, just before the troupe won their case against Drury Lane and returned to their old house in triumph. Exactly a month later Miller repeated the same role for his reappearance at Drury Lane.

At Drury Lane from March through May 1734 Miller repeated some of his old parts but added no new ones, and on 2 September he appeared again at Richmond, playing in *The*

Stage Coach. In 1734–35 at Drury Lane Miller's new roles were the Host in *The Merry Wives of Windsor* and Reynard in *The Man of Taste*. At the end of the season a new management arrangement was considered but not carried out: a committee of actors, including Miller, were to rent Drury Lane from the new patentee Fleetwood for 15 years at £900 annually; perhaps the reason their plan was not implemented was the bill before Parliament to govern the playhouses more tightly; it might have ruined any players who did not actually hold a patent. Miller was one of many actors who signed a petition against the bill in 1735.

Miller remained at Drury Lane until his death in 1738, playing his usual run of comic parts and expanding his repertoire very little: a Witch in *Macbeth* (one is surprised that he had not taken such a part before; the witches were usually played by a company's low comedians), Sir William in *The Squire of Alsatia*, Caius in *The Merry Wives of Windsor*, the Miller in *The King and the Miller of Mansfield*, the Clown in *Measure for Measure*, Cockade in *The Man of Taste*, Fruitful in *Aesop*, Jeffrey in *Art and Nature*, and the title role in *Sir John Cockle at Court*. His last appearance seems to have been as Clodpole in *The Amorous Widow* and the Miller in *The King and the Miller of Mansfield* on 30 May 1738. (He had gone over to Lincoln's Inn Field's to play a Carrier in *1 Henry IV* on 14 April 1736.)

As of March 1737 Miller had been living in Clare Street, Clare Market, but he must have moved shortly after that. The *Daily Advertiser* on 17 August reported that "Yesterday Morning died at his House at Strand on the Green [Chiswick] after three Days Illness, Mr Joseph Miller, a celebrated Comedian." The *Daily Post* that day said he died the morning of the sixteenth of a pleurisy. He was buried in the burial grounds of St Clement Danes, in Portugal Street, near Clare Market.

Miller was given a sentimental epitaph, by Stephen Duck:

> Here lie the Remains of
> Honest JOE MILLER,
> who was
> A tender Husband,
> A sincere Friend,
> A facetious Companion,
> And an excellant Comedian.

> He departed this Life, the 15th Day of August,
> 1738,
> Aged 54 Years.

> If Humour, Wit, and Honesty could save
> The Hum'rous, Witty, Honest, from the Grave
> The Grave had not so soon this Tenant found,
> Whom Honesty and Wit and Humour crown'd.

> Or could Esteem and Love preserve our Breath,
> And guard us longer from the Stroke of death;
> The Stroke of Death on him had later fell,
> Whom all mankind esteem'd and lov'd so well.

Victor called Miller "a natural, spirited Comedian; he was the famous *Teague* in the *Committee*, and all the Comedies where that Character is introduced; and though the Gentlemen of *Ireland* would never admit that he had the true Brogue; yet he substituted something in the room of it, that made *Teague* very diverting to an *English* audience. . . ."

Victor said that Miller never learned to read, and got married expressly to have "a Wife learned enough to read his Parts to him"— which may or may not have been true. His wife was named Henrietta Maria, and on 14 December 1738 Drury Lane granted her a benefit which was so crowded that spectators were given seats on the stage, and there was hardly room left for the actors. Mrs Miller died in 1766 at the age of 83; she was buried in the same grave with her husband on 10 July. Another Joe Miller, who advertised himself as a nephew of our subject, acted from 1743 on.

Miller was a convivial fellow and is said by

Harvard Theatre Collection

"JOE MILLER'S WHIM"

artist unknown

some to have kept a tavern somewhere near his lodgings in Clare Market, but there appears to be no proof of that, and the story may have developed from the one that has Miller an habitué of the Bull's Head in Spring Gardens, Charing Cross, or the Black Jack in Portsmouth Street, Clare Market. In any case, he seems to have been remembered as a hearty drinker. He was also remembered as a jester, and in 1739 John Motley compiled *Joe Miller's Jests*, a collection of 247 so-called witticisms drawn from earlier sources, and, perhaps, from Joe Miller himself. A few of the jokes name Miller, but Esar in *The Legend of Joe Miller* has demonstrated that many of the items can be found in other joke books, such as *Polly Peachum's Jests* (1728) with no reference to Joe. Among the better jests in the collection is this one:

4. *Joe Miller* sitting one Day in the Window at the *Sun-Tavern* in *Clare-Street*, a Fish Woman and her Maid passing by, the Woman cry'd, *Buy my Soals; buy my Maids*: Ah, you wicked old Creature, cry'd honest *Joe*, *What are you not content to sell your own Soul, but you must sell your Maid's too?*

By which one may judge the general level of the work.

A Joe Miller benefit ticket, for a performance at Drury Lane of *The Old Bachelor*, possibly on 25 April 1717, inscribed "W. Hogarth F^t" but listed by Paulson in *Hogarth's Graphic Works* among the "Joseph Sympson, Jr." etchings, shows a scene from Act III of the play but cannot be said to provide a clear portrait of Miller. Paulson stated that he could not find a benefit for Miller at which *The Old Bachelor* was performed, and since the benefit ticket was taken to belong to 1738, Paulson supposed that for his last benefit, on 13 April of that year, the play had been changed from *Love for Love*. That is certainly possible, and 1717 would have been very early for a Hogarth or a Sympson engraving.

Miller was represented as Sir Joseph in *The Old Bachelor* in the frontispiece to *Joe Miller's Jests* in an engraving by Charles Mosley. An engraving by C. Stoppelaer in 1738 shows Joe as Teague. The Stoppelaer portrait was engraved by A. Miller, W. Greatbach, N.G., H. Burgh, and an anonymous engraver. An engraving by Brocas Jr was made from a painting in the possession of the Rt Hon J. P. Curran.

Miller is shown in John Laguerre's satirical print, "The Stage Mutiny" (1733) carrying a stick.

Miller, Maximilian John Christopher
1674–1734, giant.

Born in Leipzig in 1674 and remarkable from infancy for his size and strength Maximilian John Christopher Miller (probably Müller originally) was exhibited in his native city, toured the Continent, and visited England shortly before his death. Caulfield in his *Remarkable Persons* wrote that

He attracted considerable notice in London, where Boistard [*recte*: Boitard] drew his portrait from the life, in April 1733. At this time Miller was fifty-nine years of age, and measured nearly eight feet in height, his hand measured a foot, and his finger was nine inches long.

By permission of the British Library Board

MAXIMILIAN JOHN CHRISTOPHER MILLER
engraving after Boitard

Hogarth, in his inimitable print of Southwark fair, has introduced the figure of Miller on a *showcloth*, which evidently proves he was in the habit of exhibiting himself at public places, as well as receiving company in private for money. His face and head were of an enormous size . . . He wore a sort of Hungarian jacket, a fancy-wrought cap, with an immense plume of feathers; and, upon the introduction of visitors, he assumed an air of the utmost importance, with a gilt sceptre in his right hand, and his left placed on the handle of a tremendous falchion, richly mounted, parading the apartment with great state and dignity.

The *Grub Street Journal* on 23 May 1734 stated that "Yesterday morning the wife of the tall Saxon, who performs in Goodman's-fields Play-house, being disordered in her senses, hang'd herself, which is thought to be owing to the misfortune of having lately lost 2 India bonds." The statement is somewhat ambiguous, but it would seem that Miller, not his wife, was a performer at Goodman's Fields. The *Daily Courant* reported that Miller was taken into custody "on suspicion of murdering his wife, she having been found hanged in an odd posture in her apartment belonging to the Playhouse," but the *Daily Post Boy* said that report was false. In any case, Miller died in 1734, aged 60 years. He left a minor son, Alexander. In 1735 a power was granted Elizabeth Sayer, the wife of Thomas Sayer and aunt of young Alexander, to administer Miller's estate for the benefit of his son. Miller's parish was given as St Clement Danes.

As Caulfield noted, Hogarth pictured Miller in "Southwark Fair" in 1733, and L. Boitard drew a portrait of him the same year. R. Grave engraved the Boitard portrait for Caulfield's *Remarkable Persons* in 1820. An earlier engraving of the Boitard portrait by an unknown engraver (n.d.) was sold by S. Lyne, print seller, at the Globe in Newgate Street.

Miller, Patrick [*fl. 1696?–1704*], *actor, manager.*

At May Fair in 1696 entertainments were provided "At Miller's Loyal Association Booth at the upper end of the market near Hyde Park Corner." The same Miller, we think, had a booth at Bartholomew Fair on 23 August 1699 next to that operated by Barnes and Appleby, produced *Crispian and Crispianus* at May Fair on 5 May 1702, and offered the droll, *The Tempest*, at Bartholomew Fair the following August.

Our guess is that the Miller in question was Patrick, who, with a number of other "Stage-players; Mountebanks, Rope-dancer, Prize-players, Poppit-showers, and such as make the shew of motions and strange sights," had to pay local constables 2s. daily for licenses about 1702. That information, contained in a clipping (hand-dated 1702) at the Huntington Library, was set forth by the Master of the Revels, Charles Killigrew.

Miller, Robert [*fl. 1689*], *performer.*

A Lord Chamberlain's warrant dated 9 September 1689 called for the arrest of Robert Miller for playing drolls without a license.

Miller, Sarah. *See* ELKINS, SARAH.

Miller, William [*fl. 1794*], *violinist, singer, dancing master.*

A William Miller of No 19, Brayn's Row, Spa Fields, appears in Doane's *Musical Directory* (1794) as a violinist, a dancing master, and a member of the Choral Fund.

Miller, William *d. 1819, equestrian, clown, actor, singer.*

William Miller the equestrian and actor appeared regularly with Philip Astley's troupe at the Amphitheatre at Westminster Bridge from 1778 or earlier until 1793 or later doing trick riding (including, on 21 March 1782, riding "the curious Dromedary"). At some time before 29 May 1792 he assumed also the duties of "Clown to the Horsemanship."

He had during this period sometimes appeared in other arenas, as for instance on 25 April 1786, when the bill for the Equestrian Amphitheatre, Union Street, Whitechapel—Jones's troupe—promised "Horsemanship burlesqued by Miller," and when he joined Handy's troupe for "Horsemanship Incomparable" at Bristol in April 1788.

There are large gaps in the record. We know nothing of his activities between 1793 and 1802, except for one Royal Circus appearance (on a newsbill dated only 1798). Charles Dibdin recalled in his *Memoirs* that Miller—"celebrated for playing vulgar Sailors in a superior slang style (and an apprentice of Mr. Hughes)"—

was with Dibdin when the reorganized Royal Circus opened in 1800. (But Speaight, Dibdin's modern editor, believes he did not join full-time until the season of 1802.) When next we meet him, at the Royal Circus on 4 August 1806, he has acquired an ability to act in pantomimes and is playing Hassan Alhabal ("an old Gardner") in *Cloud King; or Magic Rose*. Later that summer-fall season of 1806 he was Will Surge in *False Friend; or, Assassin of the Rocks*, Grigsby Concave, the Theatrical Barber in *A Stage Letter*, and Heavy Ralph, Harlequin's Man in *The Parcae; or, Harlequin and Time*.

In the 1807 season he acted, sang, and danced, Jack Oddfish in *Solima; or, The Maid of the East*, Captain Cockswain, "with (by particular desire) the favourite song of Bound 'Prentice to a Waterman" in *Buenos Aires; or, Love and Perfidy*, and Old Christuphe Centuple in *Rodolph and Rosa*.

Much of this time he was still performing the arduous duties of Clown to the Ring, in connection with which he may have been injured. For in 1808 he appeared first on 4 July, singing comic songs with Mr Hall and playing Poor Old Jemmy ("with a song in character") in *The Witch and the Wizard*. On 19 September the Royal Circus bill read: "Mr. Miller will make his fifth appearance (since his accident) in an entire New Song called 'Junot's Defeat, or Wellesley for Ever!' Which he will sing in the character of a Wounded Seaman. . . ."

Where he went then or when he died is not known to us. His first name was furnished in James De Castro's *Memoirs* (1824), and by the *Gentleman's Magazine* for May 1819, which spoke of his service at "the Summer Theatres, under the name of *Miller the Seaman*," and dated his death 16 May 1819.

De Castro called him "the most original actor a minor theatre ever produced, he was a pupil of old [Jean Baptiste] 'Dubois.'"

Miller was pictured standing, full length, in an anonymous engraving published by Laurie & Whittle, 1806. Beneath the picture four stanzas of the song "Bound 'Prentice to a Waterman" are printed.

Miller, William Edward ₍*fl.* 1791?– 1805?₎, *singer, violinist, harpist, composer, music publisher?*

William Edward Miller was perhaps the son, certainly some relative, of the well-known musician of Doncaster, Yorkshire, and of London, Dr Edward Miller, for he was said to be a resident of Doncaster by Doane in the *Musical Directory* (1794). Miller was proficient on the violin and harp and had performed in one or several of the Handel commemorations in Westminster Abbey (the latest of which had been in 1791).

C. B. Hogan in *The London Stage* identifies a singer in the oratorios at Drury Lane from 12 March 1794 as William Edward Miller. The *Theatrical Journal* cites a Mr "Millar" singing at the Town Hall, Windsor, in 1794.

Longman and Broderip published about 1793 a song *The Queen of France*, "words and music by W. E. Miller." British Library Add MS 29710 shows payments of £4 per week at Drury Lane in the spring of 1794 to a musician named Miller. A payment on 28 February 1795 of £30 to Miller for "Music in Alex," i.e., arranging and copying music for, perhaps also performing in, the elaborate serious new pantomime by J. H. D'Egville, *Alexander the Great*, the music and dances for which had required 54 rehearsals. It ran for over 30 successive nights. A William Miller, possibly the same, "Bookseller to His Royal Highness," of No 5, Old Bond Street, published music, some of it by Dr Edward Miller, including his well-known *Psalm Tunes* (1805).

"Miller the Seaman." *See* MILLER, WILLIAM *d.* 1819.

Millett, Mr ₍*fl.* 1798–1802₎, *dancer.*
The Drury Lane Theatre accounts listed Mr and Miss Millett as supernumerary dancers during the 1798–99 season. Millett seems to have continued serving the theatre an an extra dancer, apparently at 15*s.* weekly, until the end of the 1801–2 season. Miss Millett was mentioned as one of the lasses in the ballet *Our Dancing Days* on 11 February 1801 but may not have been employed beyond the 1800–1801 season. Mrs Millett, also a dancer, was named on the company list at the end of the 1801–2 season and noted as receiving a weekly salary of £1 0*s.* 10*d.* in October 1802, but she seems not to have performed in the eighteenth century.

Millett, Miss [*fl.* 1798–1801], *dancer. See*
MILLETT, MR.

Millico, Giuseppe 1739–1802, *singer,
composer.*

The soprano castrato Giuseppe Millico, who
was born at Terlizzi, near Bari, in 1739, sang
in various opera houses on the Continent, and
was at the Russian court from 1758 to 1765.
In the latter year he returned to Italy, and in
1769 he sang with great success at Parma in
Gluck's *Le feste d'Apollo*, attracting the admiration of the composer, who brought him to
Vienna that year to sing the role of Paris in
Paride ed Elena. Millico also became singing-
master to Gluck's niece.

In the spring of 1772 Millico arrived in
London, where his debut at the King's Theatre
was scheduled for 21 April as Arbaces in *Artaserse*. But that opera was canceled that night
because Millico was suddenly taken ill with a
cold and hoarseness, and *La pazzie di Orlando*
was substituted. He was recovered sufficiently
to sing Arbaces on 25 April. *Artaserse* was
heard nine other times before the end of the
season. Millico possibly sang in *La buona figliuola* on 19 May and *Demetrio* on 3 June 1772.

The following season at the King's Theatre
witnessed the arrival of the composer Sacchini,
in whose *Il Cid* Millico sang on 19 January
1773 and 25 other times that spring. He also
appeared in Sacchini's *Tamerlano* on 6 May. He
was heard in *Artaserse* 17 other times, in *Sofon-
isba* on 14 November 1772, and in a performance of the original Vienna version of Gluck's
Orfeo on 9 March 1773. In a concert at the
King's Theatre for the benefit of the musicians'
fund on 5 February he sang with Sga Carara
and Sga Girelli. For his benefit on 25 February
Millico offered two cantatas in English of his
own composition, in which he sang "several
songs accompanied by Fishar on the *Hautboy*,
and some by himself on the *Harp*."

Young Fanny Burney recorded in her diary
a *soirée* with Millico, Sacchini, and Celestini on
25 February 1773; the evening was "heav-
enly"—Millico "is of a large or rather an immense figure, and not handsome *at all*, at all;
but his countenance is strongly expressive of
sweetness of disposition, and his conversation
is exceedingly sensible." At this early point in
her listening career Fanny was enraptured when
Millico obliged the company with his new air
in the opera: "I have no words to express the
delight which his singing gave me." Dr Burney
described Millico as a "judicious performer,
and worthy man, who was not an Adonis in
person, and whose voice had received its greatest beauties from art." But Millico and Sacchini
were victimized by cabals against them. Millico, who was of a dark complexion, and perhaps was of Negro blood, aroused a hostility
which his artistic excellence eventually molli-
fied. As Dr Burney reported:

None of the friends of their predecessors would allow that Millico could sing or the new master
compose. Violent and virulent means were used to
poison, or at least to shut the ears of the unpreju-
diced public; but not with much success. Indeed,
at first both the Music and performances were frequently hissed; but, at length, Sacchini's compositions were generally allowed to be admirable, and
Millico's importance was manifested by a crouded
house at his benefit, composed of the first persons
for taste and rank in the kingdom; and at the end
of the next season, several who had boldly pronounced that neither Sacchini could compose nor
Millico sing, would have given a hundred pounds
if they could have recalled their words. . . .

Millico returned to the King's for the opera
season of 1774, performing in *Nitteti* and *Lucio
Vero*, among others. On 9 May 1774 at Hickford's Room, for the benefit of Sga Marchetti,
he appeared in *Il trionfo della costazza* with
Fochetti and Sga Galli.

In the autumn of 1774 Millico joined Gluck
at Paris, and they traveled together to Zwei-
brücken and Mannheim. Subsequently Millico
was engaged at Berlin, until in 1780 he took
up the post of *maestro da capella* to the Royal
Chapel at Naples (in which service he taught
Lady Hamilton). He died at Naples on 2 October 1802.

Busby found that Millico's excellences consisted "in power and sweetness of his voice, the
sensibility of his expression, and simplicity,
yet nobleness of his manner." He was, however,
"ambitious and perfidious" in his Neapolitan
position, persecuting "every foreign singer who
neglected to court his protection."

His compositions include three cantatas and
several collections of cazonets published in

London. A list of his works is in the *Repertoire International des Sources Musicales*; included are *Le cinesi* and *L'isola disabitata*, operas written at Naples for the Bourbon princesses Teresa and Luisa, and *La pietà d'amore*, an opera published at Naples in 1782.

Millico's portrait as Orpheus was published in the libretto of *Le feste d'Apollo* at Parma in 1769. He also appears in Antonio Fedi's "Parnaso," an engraving by Rainaldi of a large group of Italian singers that was issued at Florence between 1801 and 1807.

Millidge, Mrs Josiah, Elizabeth, née Mathews *d. 1800, actress, dancer.*

When a young child, Elizabeth Mathews, who may have been the daughter of the dancer Mathews (fl. 1739?–1771), appeared as Toadel in the premiere of Garrick's farce *Lilliput* at Drury Lane Theatre on 3 December 1756. After several more performances in that role, she appeared as Colombine in *Harlequin's Frolic*, a pantomime played by children at the Haymarket Theatre on 15 June 1757 and many other times that summer as part of Theophilus Cibber's series of medley concerts. At Drury Lane again she was the Queen in *The Oracle* on 7 December 1758 (repeated on 2 February 1759) and Tag in *Miss in Her Teens* on 5 April 1759; both pieces were played by children.

During the next six years Elizabeth Mathews seems to have been absent from the stage. She was probably the Miss Mathews who was paid 2*s*. 6*d*. per day, or 15*s*. per week, as a Drury Lane dancer in 1764–65. In the summer of 1766 a Miss Mathews acted at Richmond and also played Miss Biddy in *Miss in Her Teens* with Spranger Barry's Company at the Haymarket on 1 September.

In 1766–67 Miss Mathews's salary at Drury Lane was 3*s*. 4*d*. per day, or £1 5*s*. per week. After acting again at Richmond in the summer of 1767, she returned to Drury Lane, where for several seasons she appeared mainly in such pantomimes as *Harlequin's Invasion*. In 1767–68 she also acted Kitty in *The Lyar* and Betty in *Flora*. In a special performance at Drury Lane before the King of Denmark on 18 August 1768 she played the Milliner in *The Suspicious Husband*.

When the 1768–69 season at Drury Lane began, Miss Mathews's name was in the bills

as Sukey Chitterlin in *Harlequin's Invasion* on 23 September. Within a day or two, she married Josiah Millidge at St Martin-in-the-Fields (the *Public Advertiser* of 27 September 1768 stated "a few days since") and on 26 September she was billed in the pantomime as Mrs Millidge. She remained at Drury Lane through 1775–76, earning her regular salary of £1 5*s*. per week. On 4 October 1774 she signed her name as a witness to the actor John Hartry's will. Among the roles she added to her repertoire as Mrs Millidge were Tippet in *All in the Wrong*, Sally in *False Delicacy*, Toilet in *The Jealous Wife*, and Jenny in *The Lottery* in 1768–69; Betty in *The Clandestine Marriage* and Betty in *Hob in the Well* in 1769–70; Ursula in *Much Ado about Nothing* and Miss Fuz in *A Peep behind the Curtain* in 1770–71; Kate in *The Miller of Mansfield* and Muslin in *The Way to Keep Him* in 1771–72; a character in *The Pigmy Revels* in 1772–73; the Advocate in *The Fair Quaker* and the Maid in *The School for Wives* in 1773–74; a character in *Harlequin's Jacket* and Kitty in *The Brothers* in 1774–75; and Betty in *Old City Manners* and Trusty in *Epicoene* in 1775–76.

When Drury Lane changed hands at the end of 1775–76 Mrs Millidge either was not reengaged by the new management or she decided to give up the stage. The *Morning Chronicle* of 13 May 1777 reported that her husband Josiah Millidge, printer of the *Westminster Gazette*, had been tried for libel on 13 May and sentenced to six months in prison. In his Fund Book, now at the Folger Shakespeare Library, James Winston recorded that Mrs Millidge, whose first name he provided, had subscribed 10*s*. 6*d*. to the Drury Lane Theatrical Fund in 1766, claimed on that fund in 1786, and died in January 1800.

Millon, Mr $_{[fl.\ 1728]}$, *actor.*

Mr Millon played a Countryman in *The Rivals* at the Haymarket Theatre on 21 February 1728 as a member of Mrs Violante's company.

Mills, Mrs $_{[fl.\ early\ eighteenth\ century]}$, *exhibitor.*

In his *Shows of London* Richard Altick reproduces an undated bill for Mrs Mills's waxworks. It probably dates from the early years of the eighteenth century:

Mills, Mr [*fl. 1774–1784?*], *actor.*

A Mr Mills took the part of the Butler in a pickup performance of *The Busy Body* at the Haymarket Theatre on 24 January 1774. There is no way of knowing whether or not he was the younger brother of John Mills or if he was the Mills who was at Norwich at some time in 1774. A Mills, possibly the same, was with Austin and Whitlock's company at Chester's New Theatre in September 1775 and in the early 1780s.

But on 24 March 1778, in another specially-licensed performance at the Haymarket, a Mills played Tressel in *Richard III*. A Mills was Young Ape-all in *The Humours of Oxford* at the Haymarket on 15 March 1779; and on 18 October 1779 at the same theatre a Mills was Marplot in *The Busy Body*. This Mills or another returned to the Haymarket on 23 February 1784, in another casual company, to assume an unspecified part in *The Patriot*. In a special benefit for Watts, on 8 March 1784, Mills acted Num in *The Man's Bewitch'd*.

Mills, Mr [*fl. 1774?–1788*], *dancer.*

A little Master Mills, advertised as a pupil of Grimaldi's, danced at Bristol occasionally in 1774. He was probably that Master Mills who danced a hornpipe after the second act of *The Gentle Shepherd* in a special performance by a mixed company of Scottish amateurs and London professionals "By Desire of the Masons," at the Haymarket Theatre on 21 November 1775. T. J. Dibdin in his *Reminiscences* recalled that, when Garrick's *Jubilee* was revived at Drury Lane in 1775–1776, he was chosen to represent Cupid but fell ill and was replaced by Master Mills. "I could have killed that boy," he wrote. This was certainly the Master Mills who, with little Miss Grimaldi, danced the comic turn called *The Cow-keeper* at Drury Lane Theatre on 26 September 1778. He and Miss Grimaldi were in the Drury Lane bills again, two of a number of performers of a "Grand Dance" on 5 May 1779.

Likely he was the adult dancer who appeared on the Drury Lane bill for 31 May 1783 dancing a hornpipe at the end of *The Maid of the Mill*. He figured in a *Dance of Sailors* with Miss Stageldoir, Williamson, and others on 27 September and a *Treble Hornpipe* with Miss Stageldoir and Wilkinson on 4 November. He was similarly and frequently employed at Drury Lane in the seasons of 1784–85, 1785–86, 1786–87, and 1787–88. He was very likely the Mills who appeared from time to time dancing at the Royal Circus in 1785 and 1786.

Mills, Mr [*fl. 1785–1791?*], *singer? violist?*

A Mr Mills, "tenor" (presumably a singer, but conceivably a violist), a resident of Birmingham, assisted in the "grand performances" in Westminster Abbey, according to Doane's *Musical Directory* of 1794. Those were commemorations of Handel begun in 1784 and continued in 1785, 1786, 1787, and revived in 1791. Mills participated in some or all of the latter four, inasmuch as his name does not appear on Charles Burney's comprehensive list for 1784.

Mills, Mr [*fl. 1793*], *house servant.*

An obscure transaction is recorded on the Drury Lane account book on 3 July 1793: "Mills return'd 4*d*. night 36 nights he not attend[g] the Opera [i.e. the Drury Lane Company at the King's Theatre]." Mills was evidently a minor house servant.

Mills, Mrs ₁*fl. 1728*₁, *concessionaire?*
Among the Lincoln's Inn Fields papers at Harvard is a note on the free list for 9 October 1728: "M.͞ J. Rich by M.ͬ͛ Mills the Fruit Woman 1 [*s*.?]." Perhaps she was the theatre concessionaire.

Mills, Mrs ₁*fl. 1736*₁, *actress.*
A Mrs Mills played Celia in *The Female Rake* at the Haymarket Theatre on 26 April 1736. She was apparently not Mrs William Mills.

Mills, Mrs ₁*fl. 1785–1788*₁, *dresser, washer.*
A Mrs Mills was a dresser in Drury Lane Theatre during (at least) the seasons of 1785–1786 through 1787–88. Scattered payments were made to her also in that period for washing clothes.

Mills, Mrs ₁*fl. 1795–1804*₁, *singer, actress.*
A Mrs Mills, otherwise unidentified—but who probably could not have been Mrs Henry Mills—was in a large chorus of singers when *The Cherokee* was revived at Drury Lane Theatre on 30 October 1795. She was one of several Gipsies in *Harlequin Captive* on 18 January 1796, returning the following season to sustain the same trifling role. It is probable that she was in other Drury Lane productions during the 1795–96 and 1796–97 seasons, but she was not named in the bills.

Her next London performance, so far as playbills show, was at Drury Lane on 29 November 1798, as Betty Doxey in *The Beggar's Opera*, which she repeated several times. On 17 December following, she (if it was the same performer) played Cloe in *High Life below Stairs* in a special benefit at the Haymarket. She repeated Betty Doxey for Bannister's benefit at the Haymarket on 10 August 1799, and five times during the ensuing season at Drury Lane.

It is not known whether or not a payment of 16*s*. 8*d*. on 3 February 1798 to "Mrs Mills (late Miss Davis)" refers to her or not. She was, possibly, the Mrs Mills at Weymouth in the summer of 1799. A Mrs Mills, proclaimed as "from the Theatre Royal, Drury Lane" donned breeches to play Patrick in *My Poor Soldier* at the Haymarket on 20 June 1801. Even though she was said to be making her first appearance on that stage, she seems to have been our Mrs

Mills. She went on to singing parts in comedy that summer. Conceivably she was the Mrs Mills playing Ophelia and singing the mad song, who provoked the *Townsman* in Manchester in January 1804 to call her effort "a convincing proof that we are in want of a female-singer of the first talents."

Mills, Miss. *See also* BROWN, MRS J.

Mills, Miss ₁*fl. c. 1795–1801*₁, *actress.*
Miss Mills, first name now unknown, was the daughter of John Mills the actor (d. 1787) probably by his first wife, née Stamper, and the stepdaughter of the actor John Fawcett, Jr. She was the sister of the Miss Mills who married the musician John Loder, and of the actor Henry Mills.

Miss Mills acted in the provinces before coming from the Southampton theatre to Covent Garden, where her brother Henry and sister-in-law, Louisa Henrietta Hannah Keys Mills were performing. She made her debut there as Cherry in *The Beaux' Stratagem* on 7 January 1800. Her salary was £1 10*s*. per week.

Her roles for the rest of that season were Anna in *Douglas*, Ruth in *The Honest Thieves*, Jenny in *Liberal Opinions*, Helen in *Cymbeline*, Cecilia in *Speculation*, Norah in *Love in a Camp*, Donna Anna in *Don Juan*, and Constance in *Fashionable Levities*. Thomas Dutton, in his *Dramatic Censor* that year, observed that "The elegance of this . . . lady's person, in male attire, attracted general observation." The Covent Garden accounts in the British Library note, at the end of the 1800–1801 season "Miss Mills gone."

Mills, Edward ₁*fl. 1672*₁, *musician.*
Edward Mills was ordered apprehended by a Lord Chamberlain's warrant dated 2 October 1672 for playing music without a license.

Mills, Eleanor. *See* CHALMERS, MRS JAMES.

Mills, G. ₁*fl. 1791–1792*₁, *porter.*
The Folger Drury Lane accounts list a G. Mills who on 25 February 1792 was paid £1 "120 Nights bring.ᵍ Trunks." Presumably it was a partial payment.

Mills, Henry *b. 1776, actor, singer.*
Henry Mills, born in 1776, was one of several children of John Mills the actor by his first

wife, née Stamper. Not only Henry's father but his mother, his sisters, and four of his aunts and uncles and their several spouses and grandparents were performers. He was connected by blood and marriage to one of the most widespread and well-known theatrical families in Great Britain.

It is therefore no surprise to find that he was on the stage by the time he was eight years old. His father John was connected both to the Edinburgh Theatre Royal, Shakespeare Square, and to Tate Wilkinson's York circuit from time to time after leaving Covent Garden Theatre in 1783. On 17 April 1784 Master Mills was first noticed at the Edinburgh Theatre playing the little Prince in *Edward and Eleanora*. He was on the York and Hull bills in parts unspecified in 1785–86, and is traceable to Edinburgh again, on 11 April 1785 as Medea's Child in *Medea*; on 11 March 1786 as the Child in *Isabella* (repeated on 24 June 1788 and 12 July 1791); on 16 February, 10 March, and 3 April 1788 as Fleance in *Macbeth*; on 31 October 1789 and 3 and 13 January 1790 as the Prince of Wales in *The Battle of Hexham*, and on 3 January 1790 as Tom Thumb in *Tom Thumb the Great*.

Henry's father had died in 1787 and the boy was afterwards probably under the direction of the second (and common-law) Mrs John Mills (née Susan Moore) and of John Fawcett the younger, whom Miss Moore apparently married in May 1788. Fawcett is several times mentioned in accounts as "stepfather" to the Mills brood. Nothing is known of Henry's adolescent struggles. But apparently he endured financial rigor. He was probably the Mills who was at Edinburgh in May and June 1794 playing a Waiter in *The Farmer*, Doctor Shopman in *The World in a Village*, a Waiter in *My Granddaughter*, and a Waiter in *The Jew*.

Tate Wilkinson was just finishing the writing, in the summer of 1794, of his *Wandering Patentee* (1795) when, he said, Henry was "strongly recommended to my notice." Wilkinson made the matter an occasion for one of his lengthy homilies on thrift and sobriety:

Mr. H. Mills has barely attained his 18th year, and is at present very servicable to the theatre. At this early time of life there is certainly (with study and strict attention) time to allow for improvement; and I think, with perseverance, he may in a few years attain to an honest and creditable competence. . . . But young Mills should never forget that he has been left as the Child of Sorrow and Adversity; and that should (now he is on the road to credit) be the stimulus to pursue what is good and creditable. . . .

—with several pages more to the same effect.

Wilkinson in his rambling account mentioned "Harry Mills" only once more, in connection with a stage accident while he was rehearsing the Green Man in a pantomime, *Valentine and Orson*. In "furious conflict" with Edwin and Mitchell, playing the mock-heroic champions, "he nearly lost his thumb in the practice." He was probably the Mills who was briefly at Edinburgh in March and April 1796 acting Benin in *The Highland Reel*, the Postilion in *The Way to Get Married*, and the Printer's Devil in *The Manager's Last Stake*.

On 17 April 1797 Henry Mills married the young actress Louisa Henrietta Hannah Keys at St Michael le Belfry, York. He followed her to Covent Garden in 1799, apparently under the embarrassing conditions expressed by the *Authentic Memoirs of the Green Room* (1799), which remarked that he would never have been known in London except for the fact that Thomas Harris had to accept him in order to hire his wife. He was extremely young, possessed few abilities, but would "undertake anything to serve the manager, from an humble messenger to a walking gentleman." His younger sister, Miss Mills from the Southampton theatre, joined the Covent Garden company on 7 January 1800.

Henry Mills evidently lasted at Covent Garden only until some time early in the 1800–1801 season, though his wife was employed there with modest success until her final illness in 1804. His parts, so far as recorded, were only Jemmy Twitcher in *The Beggar's Opera*, at his debut on 18 September 1799, and then Donalbain in *Macbeth*, a Midshipman in *The Death of Captain Cook*, Burgundy in *King Lear*, and a walk-on among two dozen other pantomime characters in *The Volcano*. His last London appearance seems to have been on 10 January 1800. A Mills, doubtless Henry, was at Edinburgh on 27 January 1800 as Philip in *The Brothers* and a Taylor in *The Miser*.

Mills, Mrs Henry, Louisa Henrietta Hannah, née Keys *d. 1804, actress, singer, dancer.*

Louisa Henrietta Hannah Mills was the daughter of the country actors Mr and Mrs Simon Keys. Her sister Sarah Jane Keys, who married the actor-manager Henry Lee, was also on the London stage, and her brother (whose first name is not known) was a theatrical musician. An obituary account of 1804 asserted that she had made her debut at Weymouth.

Both Louisa and her sister Sarah were on the stage as children and young women. Hence there is some uncertainty as to which Miss Keys is meant in bills of various provincial performances, at least up to July 1793, when Sarah became Mrs Lee. But, proceeding on hints from later accounts of Louisa's career, we assume it was she who made a "first appearance" at Sadler's Wells on 9 April 1792, singing some unspecified part in a musical spectacle, *Queen Dido*. She was listed in two other performances in the surviving Sadler's Wells bills in 1792, as Industry in *The Fourth of June* and in some "vocal part" in *The Savages*, date unknown. After that she moved on, evidently by

Courtesy of the Garrick Club

MRS HENRY MILLS, as Little Pickle
by De Wilde

way of Portsmouth and Plymouth, to Dublin, where she signed on with Richard Daly's company for the 1792–93 season.

The obituary clipping cited above informs us that she sang Rimines to Gertrud Mara's Mandane in *Artaxerxes*, but that her performance displeased Daly. In the "ensuing" (1793?) summer she joined some strollers under the management of Moss. (W. S. Clark found that she played at Kilkenny in August 1793.) Her excellent acting and "genteel" private conduct procured the patronage of two powerful Irish families, the Leighs and the Leslies, who found her a position in the private Dublin theatricals of Frederick Edward Jones and his group of young aristocrats at the theatre in Fishamble Street. There she danced, sang, and acted. She is said to have gone to the Galway theatre and thence to England after a disagreement with Jones. No more is known of her activities in the period 1793 through 1796.

Early in 1797 Louisa turned up in Tate Wilkinson's company on the York circuit as "from Dublin." There she acted, but was featured as a solo singer. On 6 March her sister Sarah Jane Lee died. On 17 April 1797, at St Michael le Belfry, York, Louisa married the provincial actor Henry Mills. In the season of 1798–99 Thomas Harris, the Covent Garden proprietor, brought her to London, where on 3 October 1798, she made her first appearances as Sophia in *The Road to Ruin* and Little Pickle in *The Spoiled Child*. She earned £4 per week.

The *Monthly Review*'s critic, who had seen "her perform several years back at *Sadler's Wells*, [where] even in that situation she indicated talents of no mean promise," now approved her highly in farcical Little Pickle, less so in the more serious role of Louisa.

She played the part [of Little Pickle] with astonishing point and spirit, and, without any coarse imitation of the original, made it often more playful and entertaining, if that be possible, than Mrs Jordan herself. The first song is too *plaintive* for the nature of her voice, which has none of the sweet tones nor exquisite cadence with which Mrs. Jordan embellishes the "sadly-pleasing strain," but seems better suited to the brisk "enlivening air," of which the effect depends more upon the art of the actress than the musical taste of the singer. Mrs. Mills has some skill also in *dancing*, which was displayed to particular advantage in the song she introduced from the works of Dibdin.

Harvard Theatre Collection

MRS HENRY MILLS, as Dorinda

artist unknown

Her forte is evidently the *Hoyden*; her manner is bold and effective; and her spirits appear to be inexhaustible. Her figure, like [her sister] Mrs. Lee's, is slight, but by no means so well proportioned. She will add materially to the strength of the female part of the Covent Garden company. . . .

And so she did, during the few years she spent at the theatre.

In 1798–99 she gave Covent Garden audiences Priscilla Tomboy in *The Romp*, Julia in *The Irish Mimic*, Maugrette in *Raymond and Agnes*, Little Pickle in *Tagg and Tribulation*, Fanny Dickens in *Life's Vagaries*, and Columbine in *The Norwood Gypsies* and popularized the sea song "A Sailor's Life's a Life of Woe" by a rousing rendition in the evening's entertainment called *A Divertissement*. In the 1799–80 season she added Betty Doxey in *The Beggar's*

Opera, the original Margaret in James Cobb's comic opera *Ramah Droog*, Jacintha in *The Suspicious Husband*, Miss Fuz in *A Peep behind the Curtain*, Nancy in *The Camp*, Garnet in *The Good-Natured Man*, Jenny in *The Deserter of Naples*, the original Alambra in Cobb's musical farce *Paul and Virginia*, Fanny Liberal in *Liberal Opinions*, the Page in *Follies of a Day*, and Grace in *Fashionable Levities*. During the 1799–80 season she had been joined at Covent Garden by Henry Mills, her husband, who was evidently much her inferior as a performer, and his younger sister, who had been acting at Southampton.

On 20 June 1801 Louisa began a series of performances at the Haymarket Theatre, advertised as her first appearances there: Patrick in *The Poor Soldier*, Gavretta in *False and True*, Lucy in *The Beggar's Opera*, and Judith in *The Iron Chest*.

Louisa was carried on the Covent Garden roster through the 1803–4 season at increasing salaries of £6, £7, and £8. But she had evidently been battling consumption for some years and in May 1804 she seems to have left the stage. Her manager, Harris, is said to have contributed £2 per week to her support. Her other friends were generous. Her brother, the musician, then residing at Canterbury, brought her down to his house and attempted to revive her health. But she died on 7 July 1804, soon after her arrival there.

Mrs Mills, according to her obituary notice, was good-natured, playful, honorable, and just. "She was [,moreover,] studious and attentive to her profession; not only correct herself, but could prompt any person that was at a loss."

A watercolor portrait by S. De Wilde of Louisa Mills as Dorinda in *The Beaux' Stratagem* is in the Harvard Theatre Collection. De Wilde's painting of her as Little Pickle in *The Spoiled Child* is in the Garrick Club (No 222). A similar portrait of her as Little Pickle, in watercolor by De Wilde, signed and dated 1802, is owned by Ian Mayes.

Mills, Mrs James [or John]. *See* VINCENT, MRS RICHARD, ISABELLA, NÉE BURCHELL.

Mills, John *d. 1736, actor, manager.*
John Mills was a member of Christopher Rich's troupe at the Drury Lane and (occasion-

JOHN MILLS

engraving by Clamp, after Harding

ally) Dorset Garden theatres from mid-April 1695, when he is known to have played the "Ynca of Peru" in *The Indian Queen* at Dorset Garden. His other recorded parts in 1695–96 suggest that he was already an important, though not leading, player: Nennius in *Bonduca* in September 1695, Jack Stanmore in *Oroonoko* in November, Pedro in *Agnes de Castro* in December, the Lawyer in *Love's Last Shift* in January 1696, Castillo in *Neglected Virtue* in mid-February, Mustapha in Pix's *Ibrahim* in late May, Peregrine in *The Cornish Comedy* in June, and Pisano in *The Unhappy Kindness* in July. With the exception of *The Cornish Comedy*, all performances were at Drury Lane.

With Rich's company before the end of the century Mills added to his repertoire such parts as Mr Awdell in *The Female Wits*, Sir John Friendly in *The Relapse*, Rinaldo in *The Triumph of Virtue*, Ned Stanmore in *The World in the Moon*, Leontius in *The Humorous Lieutenant*, Winlove in *Sauny the Scot*, Artan in *Imposture Defeated*, Vitellius in *Caligula*, Merops in *Phae-*

ton, Dorange in *The Campaigners*, Ruidias in *The Island Princess*, Lovewell in *Love and a Bottle*, Trulove in *Love Without Interest*, Vizard in *The Constant Couple*, Arcas in *Achilles*, and Lord Stanley in *Richard III*. He was sufficiently involved in company affairs to be named among six actors when a contract was drawn up with the scene painter Robert Robinson.

According to Fitzgerald's *New History*, John Mills was married to a woman named Margaret, and since we know that the family was of the parish of St Martin-in-the-Fields (Mills was cited as of that parish in Coram Rege Roll, Michaelmas 1701), it is very likely that the following item in the registers pertains to our man: William Mills, the son of John and Margaret, was born on 14 June 1701 and christened at St Martin's on the twenty-ninth. We do not know when John and Margaret Mills were married, but she was acting as Mrs Mills from as early as mid-February 1696.

John Mills continued at Drury Lane through the 1705–6 season, after which the management shifted and the players went to the new Queen's Theatre. By about 1703 Mills could count on an annual salary of £60, according to a document relating to the establishment of a new acting company about that time. Mrs Mills was listed as a singer at £20 yearly. Some of the new parts Mills played during those early years of the new century were Arcadius in *The Grove*, Cleremont in *The Reform'd Wife*, Freelove in *Courtship a la Mode*, Don Duart in *Love Makes a Man*, Charles VIII in *The Unhappy Penitent*, Wilson in *The Humours of the Age*, Colonel Standard in *Sir Henry Wildair*, Menelaus in *The Virgin Prophetess*, Colonel Philip in *The Bath*, Roderigo in *The Pilgrim*, Trusty in *The Funeral*, Don Guzman in *The False Friend*, Octavio in *She Wou'd and She Wou'd Not*, Trueman in *The Twin Rivals*, Loveworth in *Tunbridge Walks*, Sir Charles in *The Fair Example*, Octavio in *Love's Contrivance*, King Lear (on 27 October 1703, for his benefit), Clerimont in *The Tender Husband*, Archas in *The Loyal Subject*, Lord Worthy in *The Basset Table*, and Willmore in *The Fashionable Lover*. He made what may have been his first appearance at Bartholomew Fair on 27 August 1706, as Colonel Lovewell in *The Siege of Barcelona*.

Owen Swiney lured Mills and others from Drury Lane to the Queen's Theatre in the fall of 1706, Mills's first role there being Douglas

in *1 Henry IV* on 26 October. During the rest
of the 1706–7 season he was one of the busiest
and most important of Swiney's actors, play-
ing, among other parts, the King in *The Maid's
Tragedy*, Morelove in *The Careless Husband*,
Bertran in *The Spanish Fryar*, Worthy in *The
Recruiting Officer*, Don Leon in *Rule a Wife and
Have a Wife*, Lord Belguard in *Sir Courtly Nice*,
Southampton in *The Unhappy Favorite*, Blunt
in *The Committee*, Volpone, Freeman in *She Wou'd
If She Cou'd*, Clerimont in *The Silent Woman*,
Francisco in *Wit Without Money*, Octavius Cae-
sar in *Julius Caesar*, Medley in *The Man of
Mode*, Cortez in *The Indian Emperor*, Don Hen-
rique in *The Adventures of Five Hours*, Hubert
in *The Royal Merchant*, the Duke of Norfolk in
Henry VIII, Aimwell in *The Stratagem*, Amphi-
tryon, the Ghost in *Hamlet*; Rashly in *The Fond
Husband*, Villeroy in *The Fatal Marriage*, Timon
of Athens, Petruchio in *The Taming of the Shrew
(Sauny the Scot)*, Tom Wilding in *The City Heiress*, and Quarlous in *Bartholomew Fair*.

The venture at the Queen's under Swiney
continued to January 1708, with Mills continuing in his many solid secondary roles and
adding, as might be expected, Horatio in *Hamlet*
on 22 November and Banquo in *Macbeth* on
27 December 1707. By 31 January 1708 he
was back at Drury Lane, the Queen's having
been turned over to the opera singers; on that
date Mills played Cassander in *The Rival Queens*.
The remainder of the season saw him in some
of his old roles and as Merry in *The Country
Wit*, Aratus in *Irene*, Pharnaces in *Mithridates*,
and Bellfort in *The Lancashire Witches*. He continued at Drury Lane through 1708–09, es-
saying such new parts as Sharper in *The Old
Bachelor*, Oronces in *Aesop*, Trusty in *The Funeral*, Young Loveless in *The Scornful Lady*,
Corvino in *Volpone*, Ramble in *The London
Cuckolds*, Muly Hamet in *The Empress of Mo-
rocco*, Prospero in *The Tempest*, Edmund in *King
Lear*, Creon in *Oedipus*, Surly in *The Alchemist*,
Abdelmelech in *The Conquest of Granada*, Harcourt in *The Country Wife*, and Agamemnon in
Troilus and Cressida.

Mills had become a good friend of Steele and
of the leading actor in the Drury Lane Company, Robert Wilks. Colley Cibber wrote later
in his *Apology* that Mills "was an honest, quiet,
careful Man, of as few Faults as Excellencies,
and *Wilks* rather chose him for his second in
many Plays, than an Actor of perhaps greater

Harvard Theatre Collection

JOHN MILLS, MARY PORTER, and SUSANNA
CIBBER, in *Tartuffe*

artist unknown

Skill that was not so laboriously diligent."
Zachary Baggs, the troupe's treasurer, published a report of actors' salaries in July 1709
that showed Mills at £4 weekly and his wife at
£1 weekly. Mills could count on benefit receipts of over £50, which brought his annual
income to more than £170. That was a very
substantial income for a secondary player.

On 30 March 1709 Mills contracted with
Owen Swiney to perform at the Queen's Theatre for five years at an annual salary of £100
plus a benefit in March (that is, early, and very
desirable) with £40 house charges and a vaca-
tion from mid-June to mid-September. The
new Queen's venture lasted only from Septem-

ber 1709 to November 1710, after which the musical chairs that had been played for several years by the actors and managers ceased. Under his new contract at the Queen's Mills acted such roles as Rhodophil in *Marriage à la Mode*, Charles in *The Busy Body*, Smith in *The Rehearsal*, Mortimer in *Edward III*, and Warner in *Feign'd Innocence*.

The *Tatler* included a few notes on Mills on 21 July 1710, five days before his benefit:

When I called to know if any would speak with me, I was informed that Mr. Mills, the player, desired to be admitted. He was so; and with much modesty acquainted me, as he did other people of note, "that Hamlet, was to be acted on Wednesday next for his benefit." I had long wanted to speak with this person; because I thought I could admonish him of many things, which would tend to his improvement. In the general I observed to him, that though action was his business, the way to that action was not to study gesture, for the behaviour would follow the sentiments of the mind.

Action to the player is what speech is to an orator. If the matter be well conceived, words will flow with ease; and if the actor is well possessed of the nature of his part, a proper action will necessarily follow.

Presumably Mills was faulty in that respect.

He returned to Drury Lane on 20 November 1710 to play Southampton in *The Unhappy Favorite*, and at Drury Lane he remained for virtually the rest of his life. Between 1710 and 1736 he continued in many of his old parts (for instance, in the fall of 1736 he was still acting the Ghost in *Hamlet*, Corvino in *Volpone*, and Bertran in *The Spanish Fryar*) and played also such roles as Melantius in *The Maid's Tragedy*, Pierre in *Venice Preserv'd*, Antonio in *The Jew of Venice*, the title role in *The Gamester*, Macbeth (on 20 October 1711), Mithridates, Pylades and Orestes in *The Distrest Mother*, Sempronius in *Cato*, Bellmour in *Jane Shore*, Julius Caesar, Chamont in *The Orphan*, Buckingham in *Richard III*, Aboan in *Oroonoko*, Falstaff in *1 Henry IV* (on 3 March 1716), Bajazet in *Tamerlane* (Dudley told his diary that Mills "did it mighty well and expressed that furiousness and rage and malice and ambition admirably well in his gesture at the end, but, which is his distinguishing character, very well kept up throughout"), Frederick in *The Chances*, Titus Andronicus, Apemantus in *Timon of Athens*, the King and Osmyn in *The Mourning*

Bride, Cassius in *Julius Caesar*, Cribbidge in *The Fair Quaker*, Cleomenes, Face in *The Alchemist*, Cranmer in *Henry VIII*, Memnon in *The Ambitious Stepmother*, Ventidius in *All for Love*, Sir John Bevil in *The Conscious Lovers*, Torrismond in *The Spanish Fryar*, Manly in *The Provok'd Husband* (Cibber said he excelled himself), Balance in *The Recruiting Officer*, Timoleon, Syphax in *Sophonisba*, Horatio in *The Fair Penitent*, the Emperor in *Aureng-Zebe*, Othello (on 1 December 1730), the King in both parts of *Henry IV*, Cato, Jupiter in *Amphitryon*, Hamlet (on 11 November 1732, with his son as Claudius!), the title role in *Junius Brutus*, Gloucester in *King Lear*, and Wolsey in *Henry VIII*. The *Daily Post* on 4 June 1733 reported that Mills was paid £1 daily for 200 days certain and a benefit free of house charges.

Mills played briefly at the Haymarket Theatre in the winter of 1733–34 with Theophilus Cibber's rebel group. His first part there was Valentine in *Love for Love* on 26 September 1733; then he acted several of his standard parts as well as Othello and Hamlet, both of which he seems to have played only on occasion in the 1730s.

About 1714 Mills had petitioned the Lord Chamberlain's office to be taken into the management of Drury Lane, since Thomas Doggett had been inactive as a co-manager. Mills claimed he had been with the company for 18 years and had often "assisted in the Management." Mills certainly did not join the triumvirate of Cibber, Wilks, and Booth, who ran Drury Lane, but Barker in his *Mr. Cibber of Drury Lane* notes that in 1727 Theophilus Cibber supplanted Mills as manager of the Drury Lane summer company. It is not clear how long he had held that post.

Mills was also involved in the late summer fairs. On 19 September 1715 Dudley Ryder visited Southwark Fair, fell into a conversation about actors, and observed that Mills was the "most virtuous of all the players. . . ." He was "a man of good reputation in the neighbourhood, goes often to prayers and the sacrament and avoids ill and loose company and enjoys himself with his wife alone. Most of the rest are very debauched and loose." Perhaps Mills was associated with Southwark Fair that early, but his name did not begin appearing in the fair bills until 26 August 1731, when he was named with Miller and Oates as a manager of a booth at Bartholomew Fair where *The Ban-ish'd General* was produced. The same trio operated at Southwark Fair on 8 September with the same play. They were at Bartholomew Fair again in 1732 with *Henry VIII*, but Mills seems not to have performed. In August 1733 at that fair they presented *Jane Shore* and *The Gardens of Venus*. Mills forsook the fair on 2 September 1734 to perform in *The Fair Penitent* and *The Stage Coach* at Richmond.

It is clear from the list of just some of the roles Mills played over the years that he was a good utility actor, capable of playing a great variety of roles, small and large, in comedy and tragedy. *The London Stage*, using the 1721–22 season as an example, notes that there were 70 plays acted at Drury Lane, and Mills played at least 50 different parts. Near the beginning of that season he appeared in 12 different roles in 12 nights, and he probably acted 160 out of the 192 nights the theatre was open. Even when he was older, in 1734, he played 170 out of 180 nights. For his labors he received, as of 1729, £200 annually, and his benefit assured him of another £60.

The prosperous years which Drury Lane had enjoyed for so long ended in 1733. Fleetwood became the patentee, and at the end of the 1734–35 season a new arrangement was considered but, apparently, not carried out: a committee of actors, Mills included, were to rent Drury Lane from Fleetwood for 15 years at £920 per year. The players used that as an argument against the bill before Parliament for the governing of the playhouses, claiming that the bill would ruin them financially. As things turned out, Fleetwood remained the Drury Lane patentee.

The last role John Mills played was the King in *2 Henry IV* on 4 December 1736. Thomas Davies in his *Dramatic Miscellanies* said Mills "was taken ill a few days after he had acted it, and died, I believe in November 1736. His name was announced in the bills for Macbeth, but Quin was obliged to supply his place. I saw him hurrying to the playhouse between five and six in the evening." Davies was incorrect in his dates, Mills died, according to the *Evening Post*, about six in the morning of 17 December 1736; Quin replaced him as Macbeth on the twenty-third. The paper said Mills had been ill for 10 or 12 days. On 20 December he was carried from his house in Martlet Court, Bow Street, to St Martin-in-the-Fields, where he was buried. His pall was supported by a group of theatre folk: Fleetwood, Quin, Colley and Theophilus Cibber, Ben Johnson, and Griffin.

The papers were in agreement about the character of John Mills. The *Evening Post* said "He liv'd so generally and deservedly belov'd that his Loss is not only a great Misfortune to the Stage and his brethren, but to the Publick in general, he being in all Respects a very worthy and good Man." Mills was remembered by his fellows on 26 April 1737, when a charity benefit was given for his daughter (unnamed). Mills's wife Margaret had died in 1717, and Mills apparently never remarried. His son William had a considerable career as an actor, often performing with his father; our subject's grandson may have been the actor John Mills who died at Hull in 1787.

Davies described Mills as "inclined to the athletic size; his features large, though not expressive; his voice was manly and powerful, but not flexible; his action and deportment decent. . . ." Pickering in *Reflections Upon The-atrical Expression* in 1755 said:

Whoever remembers old Mr. Mills, will recollect that he had a *Stamp* with his Foot, which, in *some* of his Parts, appeared to be directed by his Judgment; but as he introduced it also in others which in no ways allow of it, it appeared to be rather a *Habit*. It had a very fine Effect in the Part of Leon, in *Rule a Wife*, &c: . . . As also in others of the rough, haughty, and *stern* Kind.

That lukewarm response to Mills as an actor was fairly typical. Victor called him "the most useful actor that ever served a theatre" and said his person was "nearly approaching to the graceful; and his voice a full deep melodious tenor, which suited the characters of rage." Aaron Hill in a letter to Booth dated 31 October 1733, was most unflattering in speaking of Mills as Bajazet in *Tamerlane*: instead of raging in real agony, Mills was full of nods, flings, and jerks. Hill said, "much of what he rants, would be better suited to the character, if it were to be strained through the teeth, with an indignant, suppressed anger, or the galling maliciousness of scorn."

But the prevailing style in the 1730s was far from natural. After seeing Mills play Bajazet (and well, too) Dudley Ryder noted that "the manner of speaking in our theatres in tragedy is not natural. There is something that would be very shocking and disagreeable and very unnatural in real life. Persons would call it theatrical, meaning by that something stiff and affected." Davies thought that Pierre in *Venice Preserv'd* was Mills's best part. He played it "so much to the taste of the public, that the applause bestowed on him in this part, exceeded all that was given to his best efforts in everything else. . . . I confess, I never saw Mills in Pierre without a great degree of approbation."

A portrait of Mills by Van Bleeck, about 1730, shows him as Pierre in *Venice Preserv'd*. Once owned by the actress Jane Pope, it is in the Garrick Club (No 395). A copy by S. Harding, engraved by R. Clamp, was published in Harding's *Biographical Mirror*, 1796. In the Harvard Theatre Collection is an anonymous engraving of a scene from *Tartuffe* showing Mills, Mrs Cibber, and Miss Porter.

Mills, Mrs John, Margaret d. 1717, actress, singer.

By mid-February 1696, when she played Emilia in *Neglected Virtue* with Christopher Rich's company at Drury Lane Theatre, Margaret Mills was the wife of the actor John Mills, who was also in the troupe. When they married is not known. They had a son William, who was born on 14 June 1701 and christened at St Martin-in-the-Fields on 29 June, and a daughter, who received a benefit at Drury Lane in 1737 and about whom nothing else is known.

Margaret Mills is known to have played Phoebe in *The Lost Lover* in March 1696, Zada in Pix's *Ibrahim* in late May, Margaret in *The Cornish Comedy* in June, and Trudge in *Love and a Bottle* in December 1698. The records for the end of the seventeenth and the beginning of the eighteenth century are very incomplete, and she may have been far more active than those few roles would suggest. Leveridge's song *On Sunday after Mass* was published about 1700, with Mrs Mills listed as the singer, but when and where she sang it we do not know. Her name does not otherwise appear in theatrical documents between 1698 and 1703, and it is certain that during part of that period she was pregnant and perhaps not performing.

On 10 April 1703 Mrs Mills played Lettice in *The Fair Example* at Drury Lane, and she shared a benefit with Mrs Shaw when *Secret Love* was acted on 11 July 1704. By that time she was probably earning £20 annually as a singer, and it may be that her chief employment was singing in choruses and between the acts. In 1706–7 she was at the Queen's Theatre, playing Betty in *The Platonick Lady* on 25 November 1706 and then Lucy in *Wit Without Money*, Cordelia in *The Fond Husband*, Julia in *The Fatal Marriage*, Chloe in *Timon of Athens*, and Biancha in *The Taming of a Shrew* (*Sauny the Scot*). Mrs Mills was at Drury Lane again in June and July 1708, her known new roles being Jane in *The London Cuckolds*, Theodosia in *The Lancashire Witches*, Hippolita in *The Sea Voyage*, and Mrs Overdo in *Bartholomew Fair*. In the early months of 1709 at Drury Lane she acted Lady Centaure in *The Silent Woman*, Favourite in *The Gamester*, Scentwell in *The Busy Body*, and Betty in *The Comical Revenge*. She was on the roster at the Queen's as of 24 December 1709 and shared a benefit on 10 April 1710, but no parts are known for her, and perhaps she confined her activity to singing.

At £20 annually she acted again at Drury Lane in 1710–11, appearing on 29 May 1711 at her benefit and playing a Witch in *The Lancashire Witches* on 3 August. The rest of her career followed the same pattern: each spring from 1712 through 1714 she received summer shared benefits, but the bills showed little indication of her performing. She was Peg in *Epsom Wells* on 23 February 1712. In July and August 1715 Mrs Mills sang in *The Indian Queen* and *Bonduca*, and on 7 August 1716 she played Amphitrite in *The Tempest*. Her last known appearance was as Lady Centaure in *The Silent Woman* on 25 May 1717 at her shared benefit. The following 27 November she died. She was, according to the diarist Dudley Ryder, a very respectable woman, just as her husband was a man of unimpeachable character.

Mills, John d. 1787, actor, singer, manager.

If John Mills the London and provincial actor of the late eighteenth century was the brother of the actresses Mrs James Chalmers, Mrs Brown, and Mrs Hugh Sparks, as the *London Chronicle* of 28–31 January 1786 and other contemporary sources attest, then he was the son of Joseph and Mary Mills, for the register of St Michael le Belfry, York, records the baptism on 3 April 1782 of "Sarah, second child of James Chalmers, Comedian, son of James and Sarah Chalmers, and Eleanor, daughter of Joseph and Mary Mills." Joseph and Mary were evidently performers.

William Hazlitt, working from the notes of the actor-author Thomas Holcroft, describes a rural company to which Holcroft had belonged, whose "original founder . . . was Mills, Scotchman. He and his family had formerly travelled the country [of Scotland] playing nothing but Allan Ramsay's Gentle Shepherd. This they continued to do for several years without scenery or music."

Holcroft remembered—perhaps embroidered—much more about the little family company, in which John Mills may have learned his art:

As the younger branches of the family grew up, one of them became a scene-painter, and some of the others learned to fiddle. They now, therefore, added scenes and music to the representation of their circuit, and made excursions into the North of England: and though the loves of Patie and Peggy were a never-failing source of delight on the otherside of the Tweed, their English auditors grew tired of this constant sameness.

Thus gradually, the company added other fare.

Still, however, during the life-time of [Joseph] Mills, the whole business of the theatre, even to the shifting of the scenes, or making up of the dresses was carried on in the circle of his own family. At his death, the property of the theatre was purchased by a Mr. Buck (formerly of Covent Garden theatre), who kept an inn at Penrith . . . [apparently William Buck, d. 1777, who managed a circuit covering Carlisle, Kendal, Durham, and Berwick].

Mrs. Sparks, of Drury Lane Theatre, was an actress in this company at the time Mr. Holcroft belonged to it, and the youngest daughter of Mills, the late manager.

In the early stages of his career the John Mills of this entry is difficult to disentangle from others of his last name. He was certainly the Mills at Edinburgh's Theatre Royal, Shakespeare Square, in the winter of 1773–74, playing the following: the Boatswain in *The Tempest*, the Fisherman in *The Rehearsal*, Gayless in *The Lying Valet*, Harlequin in *The Invasion of Harlequin*, Jack Rugby [*sic*] in *The Merry Wives of Windsor*, a King of Brentford in

The Rehearsal, Leander in *The Padlock*, Lint in *The Mayor of Garratt*, Octavius in *Julius Caesar*, Razor in *The Provok'd Wife*, Rosencrantz in *Hamlet*, Sir Charles Freeman in *The Beaux' Stratagem*, Trapland in *Love for Love*, Whittle in *The Irish Widow*, Lord Aberville in *The Fashionable Lover*, and parts unspecified in *Alonzo*, *The Bankrupt*, *The Nabob*, and *Eldred*.

John Mills returned to Edinburgh in each winter season from 1775–76 through 1778–79. The *Edinburgh Rosciad* (1775) had some critical advice for him:

MILLS *is just rising in theatric field;*
In Little Skirmish *he to few will yeild:*
Yet take a friend's advice, for all your art,
Don't Skirmish *be in ev'ry Comic part:*
If you desire to follow Nature chaste,
Have some more ease, and study some more taste.
In SCOTTISH *characters, we all agree*
You're not the most nat'ral that we ere did see.
But ne'er again in Harlequin appear
His tartan suit will put you in the rear
Of ranks theatric;—look at WOODWARD's *Mien,*
Few parts he plays, but Harlequin is seen.

At Edinburgh he added, in these seasons and in approximately the following order Belcour in *The West Indian*, Dick in *The Apprentice*, Eustace in *Love in a Village*, Harlequin in *Harlequin Highlander* (cause of the critical admonition), Lennox in *Macbeth*, Ranger in *The Suspicious Husband*, Skirmish in *The Deserter*, Little Skirmish in *Little Skirmish*, Tester in *The Suspicious Husband*, Valerius in *The Roman Father*, Young Beverly in *All in the Wrong*, Captain Ironsides in *The Brothers*, Cassio in *Othello*, Colin Macleod in *The Fashionable Lover*, Colonel Tivy in *Bon Ton*, the Copper Captain in *Rule a Wife and Have a Wife*, Donald M'Gregor in *The Lecturer*, Donald M'Intosh in *The Register Office*, the First Recruit in *The Recruiting Officer*, Lovegold in *The Miser*, Maclaymore in *The Conscious Lovers*, and the Prince of Wales in *Henry II*.

He also played Scotch Spouter in *The Apprentice*, Archy Macsarcasm in *Love à-la-Mode*, Tony Lumpkin in *She Stoops to Conquer*, Captain O'Cutter in *The Jealous Wife*, Crispin in *The Anatomist*, Diggery in *All the World's a Stage*, Don Jerome in *The Duenna*, Evander in *The Grecian Daughter*, Horatio in *Hamlet*, Macduff in *Macbeth*, Renault in *Venice Preserv'd*, Romeo in *Romeo and Juliet*, Sciolto in *The Fair Penitent*, Sir Anthony Absolute in *The Rivals*, Southampton in *The Earl of Essex*, Dogberry in *Much*

Ado about Nothing, Gloucester in *Jane Shore*, Hawthorn in *Love in a Village*, Jobson in *The Devil to Pay*, M'Pherson in *The Devil upon Two Sticks*, Ralph in *The Maid of the Mill*, Peachum in *The Beggar's Opera*, Nerestan in *Zara*, Morton in *The Countess of Salisbury*, Orlando in *As You Like It*, the Prince of Wales in *The Institution of the Order of the Garter*, Sir Harry Muff in *The Rival Candidates*, Sir John Restless in *All in the Wrong*, Villeroy in *Isabella*, Sir Peter Teazle in *The School for Scandal*, Lord Grizzle in *Tom Thumb the Great*, Lusignan in *Zara*, Lord Ogleby in *The Clandestine Marriage*, Midships in *The Liverpool Prize*, Pisanio in *Cymbeline*, Sir Bashful Constant in *The Way to Keep Him*, Scrub in *The Beaux' Stratagem*, Seyfert in The *Heroine of the Cave*, and Sir William Wildman in *The Lady of the Manor*.

As the list shows, Mills mastered the ability to play Caledonian characters. Tate Wilkinson wrote that "he had been a country manager in various parts of Scotland, by which means he was become a perfect master of the language, and spoke it more easy, natural, and fluent, than any performer within the ken of my observation."

On 30 April 1782 John Mills suddenly turned up at Covent Garden Theatre, advertised as "from the Theatre Royal, Edinburgh" to play Jerome in *The Duenna*. He was thereafter that season McDougal on the opening night and first run of Leonard Macnally's *A New Occasional Prelude*, the Barber in John O'Keeffe's new afterpiece *Lord Mayor's Day*, Sir William Belmont in *All in the Wrong*, and Verges in *Much Ado about Nothing*. He shared benefit tickets with Wewitzer and Ledger on 15 May. After that he disappeared from Covent Garden's records.

He went in the summer of 1783 to the Bath-Bristol company and in November to the York circuit. Tate Wilkinson, his manager at York, thought him "a truly good actor, 'take him for all in all,'" when he was cool; but he often let an enemy into his mouth to steal away his brains." Wilkinson asserted that Mills had failed the test of London because, "at the time of onset and the day of trial, he was assailed from the climate with a bad cold, and to make it better, he armed himself with weapons mete for defence," that is, that he drank heavily and was thus ineffective.

But he served the York circuit faithfully, and

Wilkinson called him "the Edwin, the Shuter of my company, the darling Darby, &c. of the public" before he went into "a rapid decline" and died of a "dropsy" at Hull in the fall of 1787.

John Mill's domestic relationships are not in every circumstance clear. News accounts reported his marriage to the daughter of the "late" F. Stamper (i.e. Francis Stamper, d. 1766, and his wife née Sarah Kirk, both actors) in March 1775. Miss Stamper acted but briefly and only in the provinces. John's children (all actors), Henry Mills, the Miss Mills who became Mrs John Loder, and the Miss Mills who made her Covent Garden debut on 7 January 1800, were probably the fruits of his marriage to Miss Stamper. At some point, however, Mills and his wife separated and he began living with the actress Susan Moore, who proceeded for awhile under his name. She is recorded in only two London performances, but according to Wilkinson was a fine and conscientious actress. John Fawcett the younger seems to have assumed responsibility for Mills's minor children.

Mills, Mrs John. *See* Fawcett, the first Mrs John the younger, Susan, née Moore.

Mills, Sarah. *See* Sparks, Mrs Hugh.

Mills, Peter [*fl.* 1661–1662], *designer.*

Ogilby's *Relation* stated that Peter Mills, Surveyor of the City, and another person who preferred to remain nameless, designed "The Architectural Part" of the coronation pageant for Charles II on 22 April, 1661. On 23 August 1662 Peter Mills managed *Aqua Triumphalis* on the Thames to celebrate the King's arrival at Whitehall from Hampton Court.

Mills, Theodosia [*fl.* 1748–1794?], *actress.*

The Miss Mills who appeared at the James Street Theatre on 31 October 1748 as Lucy in *The London Merchant* was probably Theodosia Mills, and it seems certain that she was a daughter of William and Theodosia Mills. During the 1752–53 season Miss Mills acted at Drury Lane Theatre, appearing first on 8 December 1752 in *The Rehearsal*. She doubtless acted regularly during the season, but her roles were too small to be named in the play-bills. In the summer of 1753 she performed at Richmond as the Chinawoman in *The Fine Lady's Airs* on 30 June, Milliner in *The Suspicious Husband* on 7 July, Myrtillo in *The Provok'd Husband* on 14 July, Gipsey in *The Beaux' Stratagem* on 24 July, a Witch in *Macbeth* on 28 July, Lamorce in *The Inconstant* on 20 August, and Scentwell in *The Busy Body* on 8 September. Miss Mills returned to Drury Lane for the 1753–54 season to appear in *Harlequin Ranger* and *The Knights*.

Either Miss Mills was away from the London stage in 1754–55, or she acted parts too inconsiderable to receive mention in the bills. She was back at Drury Lane in 1755–56, however, and there she remained through 1765–66. Her roles over the years continued to be small: Tatlanthe in *Chrononhotonthologos*, a Lady in *Richard III*, Iras in *Antony and Cleopatra*, Pompey in *The Way to Keep Her*, Lady Restless and Marmalet in *All in the Wrong*, Honoria in *Love Makes a Man*, Wheedle in *The Miser*, Galatea in *Philaster*, Maria in *The Register Office*, and Trusty in *The Clandestine Marriage*.

During her stay at Drury Lane Miss Mills had, in 1763, sung for Lowe at Marylebone Gardens. Her Drury Lane salary as of 9 February 1765 was 2s. 6d. daily—at the bottom of the scale for actresses; she was up to 3s. 4d. by 24 January 1767—in the middle of her last season, during which she received no attention in the bills. On 4 June 1767 she was advanced a loan of £5 5s. by the Drury Lane management, but the following September found her, along with the elder George Colman, at Covent Garden. Her salary there was 3s. 4d. daily.

She acted in *The Rehearsal* on 14 September 1767, after which she appeared as Trusty in *The Provok'd Husband*, Galatea in *Philaster*, Helen in *Cymbeline*, Toilette in *The Jealous Wife*, Furnish in *The Way to Keep Him*, Iras in *All for Love*, Honoria in *Love Makes a Man*, Clara in *Rule a Wife and Have a Wife*, and Francisca in *Measure for Measure*. After appearing in *The Way to Keep Him* on 24 September 1770, Miss Mills temporarily left Covent Garden.

On 29 October and 14 December 1770 Miss Mills went over to the Haymarket Theatre to appear as Ursula in *The Padlock*. She returned to Covent Garden to play in *Measure for Measure* on 12 January 1771, after which she seems to

have left the stage. At some point Miss Theodosia Mills became the mistress of George Colman, probably after his wife Sarah died in 1771. (We erred in our Colman entry in calling her *Mrs* Theodosia Mills.)

There was a Miss Mills acting major roles and serving as a Columbine in Edinburgh from 1776 to 1780, but that actress could hardly have been Theodosia.

Theodosia Mills was named in two wills, most importantly in that of George Colman, who described her as late of Bristol and now (in April 1789, when the will was made) of Tavistock Street, Covent Garden, spinster. He left her £20. To a later mistress, Mrs Sophia Croker, he was far more generous. The will was proved on 8 December 1794, but we do not know whether or not Theodosia Mills was then still alive. She was also named in the will of the actress Elizabeth Bennet for a bequest of ten guineas. The will was drawn on 24 August 1791 and proved on the following 20 September.

Mills, Thomas ₍*fl.* 1672₎, *musician*.

The Lord Chamberlain issued a warrant for the arrest of Thomas Mills on 2 October 1672 for playing music without a license.

Mills, William ₍*fl.* 1701–1750₎, *actor*.

William Mills, the son of the actors John and Margaret Mills, was born on 14 June 1701 and christened on 29 June at St Martin-in-the-Fields. With other youngsters he performed in 1712 at the playhouse in St Martin's Lane, acting Southampton in *The Unhappy Favorite* on 21 May and Charles in *The Busy Body* on 18 June. Both roles were in his father's repertoire, and surely John Mills coached his son. William played the title role in *Don Carlos* at Drury Lane Theatre on 17 June 1715, acting with other offspring of company players. "Mills' son" shared a benefit with Miss Lindar on 27 May 1718, and, according to the 1719 edition of *Love in a Vail*, he acted Diego, probably on 17 June 1718. On 28 January 1719 he played Messala in *Julius Caesar*, and beginning on 7 March he was Auletes in *Busiris*. He shared a benefit with Chetwood on 2 May and appeared as Timagoras in *The Bondman* on 9 June.

For the following five seasons Mills continued as a minor actor, playing a few named parts each season but probably spending most of his time bearing spears and playing roles too small to be mentioned in advertisements or cast lists. Characters he is known to have acted include Mandrocles in *The Spartan Dame*, Artamon in *The Siege of Damascus*, Norfolk in *2 Henry IV*, a Suitor in *Wit Without Money*, Cleanthes in *The Ambitious Stepmother*, Idwall in *The Briton*, Petruchio in *The Chances*, Charles in *Love in a Forest*, Humphrey Stafford in *Humphrey, Duke of Gloucester* (which, according to the *Weekly Journal or Saturday's Post* of 23 February 1723, was "wretchedly perform'd," except for two of the actresses), Granius in *Caius Marius*, the Earl of Cambridge in *Henry V*, Hilliard in *The Jovial Crew*, and Story in *The Committee*. He shared benefits yearly with one other employee, usually the prompter Chetwood.

Beginning with the 1724–25 season William Mills seems to have come into his own. He was much more frequently cited in the bills, and his parts grew in importance: Bellmour in *Jane Shore*, Lelius in *Sophonisba*, Alexas in *All for Love*, Young Loveless in *The Scornful Lady*, Selim in *The Mourning Bride*, Stanmore in *Oroonoko* (one of several parts William acted during his career that had been played by the elder Mills), Malcolm in *Macbeth*, Freeman in *The Plain Dealer*, Farewell in *Sir Courtly Nice*, Vizard in *The Constant Couple*, Richmore in *The Twin Rivals*, Scandal in *Love for Love*, Surly in *The Alchemist*, Heartfree in *The Provok'd Wife*, Beaufort in *The Comical Revenge*, Fainall in *The Way of the World*, Edmund in *King Lear*, Prince John of Lancaster in *2 Henry IV*, Pylades in *The Distrest Mother*, Antonio in *The Rover*, Lodovico in *Othello*, Claudius in *Hamlet* (his father played Horatio; later William played Claudius to his father's Hamlet), Juan in *Rule a Wife and Have a Wife*, Haly in *Tamerlane*, Cabinet in *The Funeral*, the King in *The Maid's Tragedy*, Antonio and Ferdinand in *The Tempest*, Manuel in *Love Makes a Man*, Sir Walter in *1 Henry IV*, Norfolk in *Henry VIII*, Apemantus in *Timon of Athens*, Sir Charles in *The Stratagem*, and Sempronius in *Cato* were all in his repertoire by the end of the 1720s.

In 1727, sometime between 19 and 28 September to judge by the bills, William Mills married the dancer and actress Theodosia Tenoe, and the two performed for several years at Drury Lane. She died in 1733, and on 10 September 1737 Mills married the actress Elizabeth Holliday at St Anne, Soho. She continued performing after William's death in 1750 but retired in 1755.

In the 1730s Mills added to his list of parts at Drury Lane such characters as Bonario in *Volpone*, Cribbidge in *The Fair Quaker*, Prince Hal in *2 Henry IV*, Aboan in *Oroonoko*, Sir George in *The Busy Body*, Trueman in *The London Merchant*, Quarlous in *Bartholomew Fair*, Douglas and Prince Hal in *1 Henry IV*, Johnson in *The Rehearsal*, Pyrrhus in *The Distrest Mother*, the Beggar in *The Beggar's Opera*, Iago in *Othello*, Hastings in *Jane Shore*, Blunt in *The Committee*, Lorenzo in *The Spanish Fryar*, Amphitryon, Dorimant in *The Man of Mode*, Chamont and Polydore in *The Orphan*, Sir Charles in *The Careless Husband*, Pinchwife and Horner in *The Country Wife*, Townly in *The Provok'd Husband*, Jaffeir in *Venice Preserv'd*, Juba in *Cato*, Blandford in *Oroonoko*, Buckingham in *Henry VIII*, the title role in *Julius Caesar*, Plume in *The Recruiting Officer*, Dolabella in *All for Love*, Myrtle in *The Conscious Lovers*, Subtle in *The Alchemist*, Laertes in *Hamlet*, Truewit in *The Silent Woman*, Mosca in *Volpone*, Osman in *Zara*, Lysimachus in *The Rival Queens*, Banquo in *Macbeth*, Archer in *The Stratagem*, the Copper Captain in *Rule a Wife and Have a Wife*, Cholerick in *Love Makes a Man*, Vernish in *The Plain Dealer*, Axalla in *Tamerlane*, Young Raleigh in *Sir Walter Raleigh*, and Altamont in *The Fair Penitent*.

During the 1730s he was at the late summer fairs, appearing first at Bartholomew Fair as Montfort in *The Banish'd General* on 26 August 1731. On 23 August 1732 he played the title role in a version of *Henry VIII*, and the following year he was Shore in *Jane Shore*. That seems to have been the extent of his activity at Bartholomew Fair. Mills also appeared at Richmond, on 10 September 1733 as John in *The False Friend*, for Chapman's benefit and for his own diversion. Mills was a participant in Theophilus Cibber's revolt from Drury Lane in 1733–34 and appeared for a few months at the Haymarket Theatre playing in several of his standard parts, such as Scandal in *Love for Love*, Prince Hal in both parts of *Henry IV*, Blunt in *The Committee*, Jaffeir in *Venice Preserv'd*, Amphitryon, Subtle in *The Alchemist*, and Plume in *The Recruiting Officer*. His only other venture away from Drury Lane seems to have been on 14 April 1736, when he played Prince Hal in

1 Henry IV at Lincoln's Inn Fields. According to a letter in the *Daily Post* of 4 June 1733, Mills was at that time earning £3 weekly at Drury Lane; together with his wife he received £5 10*s.* weekly, but she rarely acted.

It is clear that Mills, like his father, played a great variety of parts and was doubtless very useful to the company, but there is little to indicate that he had more than a routine talent. One of the earliest notices of him came when he acted Buckingham in *Richard III* on 1 October 1737. Egerton MS 2320 states that the receipts came to £83 and that Mills was "hiss'd." The *Apology for the Life of T......C........* in 1740 (probably written by Fielding) said William Mills was "not excellent in Tragedy, the Inanity of his Voice being unequal to the Swellings and Throws of the Sublime. . . ." But he was usually perfect in his lines and "always very busy on the Stage"—which could be taken two ways. He succeeded to some of Robert Wilks's parts and "caught something of his Catch in the voice."

The London Stage shows two different men named Mills in the cast of *Cato* on 12 September 1738 at Drury Lane, one playing Juba and the other acting Marcus. John Mills died in 1736, and no other Mills than William is known to have been performing at Drury Lane in the late 1730s. We assume that the listing of a Mills as Marcus is an error; William Mills usually played Juba in that decade. Since Hill acted Marcus in September 1737, he was probably the actor intended for Marcus in 1738.

William Mills continued at Drury Lane throughout the 1740s, playing many of his earlier parts and also appearing in such roles as Duke Senior and later Orlando in *As You Like It*, Orsino in *Twelfth Night*, Antipholus of Ephesus in *The Comedy of Errors*, Bertram in *All's Well that Ends Well*, Duncan in *Macbeth*, Gratiano in *The Merchant of Venice*, Salisbury in *King John*, and Cassio in *Othello*—to mention only his Shakespearean parts, which he tended to play more and more as time went on. Toward the end of the decade his name appeared less frequently in the bills, however. He seems to have confined his acting to Drury Lane with one exception: in September and October 1744 he joined Theophilus Cibber at the Haymarket Theatre.

The reason Mills bolted Drury Lane was the tyranny of the manager Fleetwood. In 1743 *Queries To Be Answered* claimed that Mills was in a desperate financial situation, because Fleetwood had not been paying him, and he had been "arrested for Five Hundred Pounds." Fleetwood responded in *Queries Upon Queries*, saying that he had immediately put up bail for Mills, and that Mills's debt was being paid. But *An Impartial Examen* in 1744 stated that Mills and his wife had been turned out of Drury Lane because Mills dared to complain about Fleetwood's conduct. Mills made his first appearance at the Haymarket in 12 years on 25 September in *The Careless Husband*. On 11 December the bill called the performance of that work a concert for Mills's benefit:

A Concert both Serious and Comic; Consisting of the most favourite Airs taken from the most favourite Operas and Oratorios, by the best Masters. Boxes 5*s.* Pit 3*s.* Gallery 2*s.* 6 P.M. To the Publick. Gentlemen and Ladies: I humbly beg Pardon for troubling you in this Manner, but being Unfortunately excluded (I don't know for what Reason) from both the Theatres, and consequently deprived of getting my Living by my Profession, the Favour of your Company at a Concert which I take for my Benefit on Tuesday the 11th instant, at the Little House in the Haymarket, will be a very great Obligation to Your most faithful and devoted humble Servant, William Mills. Tickets to be had of Mr Mills at his House in Nassau St., near Soho. Note: After the Concert will be perform'd (gratis) a Comedy call'd *The Careless Husband.*

Other roles acted by Mills at the Haymarket were Plume in *The Recruiting Officer*, Myrtle in *The Conscious Lovers*, Sir Anthony Wildwit in *The Prodigal*, and Pyrrhus in *The Distrest Mother*.

Fleetwood's reign at Drury Lane ended after a riot on 19 November 1744; the patent was sold, and Lacy took over as manager. Mills and his wife returned to their home theatre, and there they remained until his death. He was still in debt, and Drury Lane gave him a benefit to allow him to pay his creditors, on 1 March 1746, for which tickets could be purchased from Mills at his lodgings in Bow Street, whence he seems to have moved sometime during 1745. Perhaps his brother Masons gave him some help, too; he and his wife spoke the prologue and epilogue respectively to the assembled Masons at Mills's benefit on 16 May 1747.

In addition to his financial problems in the 1740s Mills was plagued toward the end of the decade by illness. His last appearance was as Gratiano in *The Merchant of Venice* on 22 February 1750. He was reported to be at the point of death on 22 March, but on 31 March Mills advertised an appeal for his benefit, scheduled for 21 April, "finding himself every day rather worse than better." Garrick volunteered to play Archer in *The Stratagem* for him, but Mills did not live to enjoy his benefit. The prompter Cross recorded in his diary on 16 April 1750 that Mills died that day (most other reports stated that Mills died on 17 April). The *General Advertiser* of 18 April said the cause of death was dropsy. Mills was, the paper said, an honest man and indulgent husband. According to Cross, Mills was buried at St Martin-in-the-Fields on 20 April. (*The London Stage* editor misread the entry in the Cross-Hopkins diary and said the church was St Mark's.)

In his account of Garrick's life Thomas Davies admitted that William Mills was "frequently seen, though not so much admired as any of his most celebrated contemporaries." He was tall, large, awkwardly made, and not well suited to the comedy parts he usually played. But, like his father, William Mills had great industry and an inoffensive character that gained him many friends and no enemies. Paul Whitehead, said Davies, dubbed Mills "Sir Friendly Huff." Davies quoted an unpublished recommendation by Fielding for Mills's benefit:

Mr Mills, who, from his peculiar facetious and good-humoured disposition, retains still the name of Billy Mills amongst his familiars, is a strong example of the fickleness and inconstancy of fortune. He hath by slow degrees risen to the top of theatrical greatness, and by as slow degrees tumbled down again. He succeeded to the graver parts in comedy of Booth, and to the gayer characters in which Wilkes [*sic*] had shone; and maintained both with equal ability.

In tragedy he hath likewise been very considerable; where, not to dwell on every particular excellence, he is thought of all others to have made the best appearance through a trap-doore. For this reason, those characters which are in some part of the play to enter upon the stage head-foremost generally fell to his lot.

He was at all times a very safe actor; and, as he never shocked you with any absurdity, so he never raised horror, terror, admiration, or any of those turbulant sensations, to that dangerous height to which Mr. Garrick (however good a man he may otherwise be) hath been guilty of carrying them.

From the pinnacle of theatrical greatness, where he was once seated, he hath by degrees fallen, not through his own demerit, for he is now as good as ever he was, but the greatest misfortune in the world, namely, successful rivals. This reverse of fortune he hath borne with heroic constancy and christian resignation; he hath indeed continued honest Billy Mills; nor have envy, malice, or any other species of malignity, been able to hurt his natural good disposition.

Indeed his character in private life is so amiable, that, if the ladies will patronize one of the best and kindest husbands, and the world in general will encourage an honest, good-natured, and inoffensive man, he and his little family will owe many a future happy hour to the public on Monday next; and his benefit, though one of the last, will not be one of the least.

That may have been written for the benefit on Monday 10 April 1749, which Mills shared with his wife.

In *The Actor* in 1750 Hill was not very kind to the memory of Mills:

It is recorded of Mr. Mills, that he long valued himself among his friends for speaking a soliloquy in one of our comedies, which, as he express'd it, poor Mr. Wilks never could remember when he acted that part; but he was at length thoroughly mortify'd by being told by a very great judge of dramatic writing, that there was more merit in Mr. Wilks's forgetting that speech than in all that ever he had remembered in his life.

Mills, Mrs William the first, Theodosia, née Tenoe *d. 1733, dancer, singer, actress.*

The first theatrical notice of Miss Theodosia Tenoe came on 10 October 1717, when she made her first stage appearance dancing at Drury Lane Theatre, advertised as a scholar of Fairbanks. She was presumably the daughter of the singer Tenoe. The bills of the time would make it appear that there was a Mrs Tenoe also dancing at Drury Lane in 1717–18, but even though some bills, such as the one on 30 May 1718, name both Mrs Tenoe and Miss Tenoe, it seems clear from the kind of performances assigned that all the references are to Theodosia. The indifferent use of Miss or Mrs suggests that she was probably about 21. She was called Miss or Mrs through May 1723, after which references to Mrs Tenoe ceased.

During her initial season Miss Tenoe was often named in the bills and seems to have been an immediate success. On 12 October

1717 she was a Grace in *The Loves of Mars and Venus*; on 29 May 1718 she made her first attempt as an actress, playing Rose in *The Recruiting Officer*; at her benefit on 30 May she sang a "Widow's Dialogue" with Rainton; and throughout the season she was named as an entr'acte dancer, often in partnership with Topham. She remained active at Drury Lane during the summer of 1718, playing Jenny in *Love for Money* on 11 July, Miranda in *The Tempest* on 1 August, and Martha in *Love in a Wood* on 15 August.

She worked steadily at Drury Lane in the years that followed. From 1718–19 to her marriage to William Mills in September 1727 she added to her repertoire such roles as a Harlequin Woman in *The Dumb Farce*, Holdup in *The Northern Lass*, Violante in *Greenwich Park*, Parly in *The Constant Couple*, Sylvia in *The Old Bachelor*, Jenny in *The Fair Quaker*, Lady Gentry in *The Rival Fools*, a Punch Woman in *The Escapes of Harlequin*, Wishwell in *The Double Gallant*, Viletta in *She Wou'd and She Wou'd Not*, Lucy in *The Old Bachelor*, Pert in *The Man of Mode*, Cherry in *The Stratagem*, Lucy and Charlotte in *Oroonoko*, Colombine in *Harlequin Turn'd Judge*, Galatea in *Acis and Galatea*, Celemena in *A Wife to be Let*, Cymaena in *The Impertinent Lovers*, Fainlove in *The Tender Husband*, Iris in *Harlequin Doctor Faustus*, Damaris in *The Amorous Widow*, Theodosia in *The Lancashire Witches*, Flareit in *Love's Last Shift*, Hoyden in *The Relapse*, Daphne's Follower and a Shepherdess in *Apollo and Daphne*, Kitty in *The What D'Ye Call it*, Sentry in *She Wou'd If She Cou'd*, Phaedra in *Amphitryon*, Edging in *The Careless Husband*, Mrs Clearaccount in *The Twin Rivals*, Mrs Hartshorn in *The Lady's Last Stake*, the Miller's Daughter in *Harlequin's Triumph*, and Moretta in *The Rover*.

Though she acted many roles, a large number of them hoydenish, her specialty remained dancing, and every season she was used again and again as an entr'acte entertainer. Usually the dances had no names, at least in the bills, but sometimes they did: *Maggot* (a dance created by her master Fairbanks), a *Pastoral Dance of Myrtillo*, *Shepherd and Shepherdess* (which she danced with Lally), *Two Dutch Lasses* (with Miss Smith), *Country Maid*, a "Passacaille," *Two Farmers and Their Wives*, and *The Cobler's Jealous Wife*. Only rarely did she sing, one occasion being on 9 August 1723, when she and Miss

Lindar offered "A Dialogue between a Rake and a Country Maid."

Performing regularly with her at Drury Lane was William Mills, and sometime between 19 and 28 September 1727 they were married. The bill of 14 November still referred to Theodosia by her maiden name, but that was certainly a mistake. As Mrs Mills she continued performing at Drury Lane until her death in 1733. Among her new parts were Lady Wishfort in *The Way of the World*, Rose in *Sir Martin Marall*, Mrs Trusty in *The Provok'd Husband*, Columbine in *Harlequin Happy and Poor Pierrot Married*, Joan in *Acis and Galatea*, Dolly in *The Village Opera*, Mrs Tattleaid in *The Funeral*, Sylvia in *The Recruiting Officer*, Patch in *The Busy Body*, and Tippet in *Phebe*. She continued in many of her old parts as well, danced between the acts less frequently, and did little singing.

Theodosia Tenoe Mills died on 19 May 1733. The patentees of Drury Lane, trying to fight against growing complaints, sent a letter to the *Daily Post* on 4 June 1733 claiming that Mills and his wife together had been receiving £5 10s. weekly (£3 of which was his salary) even though Mrs Mills had not been able to perform during much of the winter; the bills would indicate that that was not quite true. She performed to the middle of January 1733. Latreille quoted a newspaper notice dated 26 May 1733 saying that Mrs Mills "died of a consumptive illness at her lodgings at Paddington. . . ." *The London Stage* incorrectly lists her as a member of the Drury Lane company in the spring of 1734.

Mills, Mrs William the second, Elizabeth, née Holliday   *[fl. 1723–1755],* actress, dancer.

The Miss Holliday who shared a £112 benefit with three others at Lincoln's Inn Fields Theatre on 3 June 1723 was probably Elizabeth Holliday—or Hollyday, Holladay—and occasionally cited in bills as Mrs, which might suggest she was about 21 in the early 1720s. The theatre accounts for 25 September 1724 show "Mrs Hollyday" at a daily salary of 3s. 4d., and "Mrs" Holliday shared a benefit with three others on 14 May 1725, splitting gross receipts of over £170. She was probably playing walk-ons or parts too small to be mentioned in cast lists.

Her name was not cited in theatrical documents in 1725–26 or 1726–27, but on 29 January 1728 she was named as Mrs Coaxer in *The Beggar's Opera*. She followed that with the First Country Girl in 2 *Don Quixote* on 24 April and, at her shared benefit with Miss Warren on 8 May, Rose in *The Recruiting Officer*; they shared over £120.

Beginning with the 1728–29 season at Lincoln's Inn Fields Miss Holliday, as she was then usually called, was more frequently mentioned in the bills. Between 1728–29 and her transfer to Drury Lane Theatre in 1733 she was seen in such parts as Anne Page in *The Merry Wives of Windsor*, Peggy in *The London Cuckolds*, Belinda in *Tunbridge Walks*, Ophelia in *Hamlet* (on 23 April 1729 for Milward's benefit), Mariana in *Measure for Measure*, Miranda in *The Busy Body*, Mrs Squeamish in *The Country Wife*, Cherry in *The Stratagem*, Corinna in *The Confederacy*, Angelina in *Love Makes a Man*, Lucinda in *The Conscious Lovers*, Philadelphia in *The Amorous Widow*, Teresia in *The Squire of Alsatia*, Jessica in *The Jew of Venice*, Silvia in *The Old Bachelor*, and (at Covent Garden in January 1733) Eliza in *The Plain Dealer*.

She received regular benefits in the spring and was evidently a great attraction. For example, at her solo benefit on 6 May 1731 at Lincoln's Inn Fields, the income, apparently before house charges, was over £170, and, according to the *Gentleman's Magazine*, she "received from the Royal Family, over and above the usual Present, a large Gold Medal, weighing about 50 Guineas, with the Bust of her Majesty as Electress of Hanover in each Side." At that performance, which was presented by command of his Royal Highness, she played Angelina in *Love Makes a Man* and the Nymph of Ida in *The Judgment of Paris*.

Miss Holliday's last performance under John Rich's management at Covent Garden was on 31 January 1733; on 8 February she made her first appearance at Drury Lane, playing Cherry in *The Stratagem* (the Prince of Wales was present, and one wonders if he was in any way responsible for her changing theatres). At Drury Lane until her marriage to the actor William Mills in 1737 she played such new characters as Sylvia in *The Double Gallant*, Angelica in *Love for Love*, Isabinda in *The Busy Body*, Harriet in *The Miser*, Hyppolito in *The Tempest*, Arbella in *The Committee*, Lady Harriet in *The Funeral*, Mrs Clerimont in *The Tender Husband*, Kate in *1 Henry IV*, Anna Bullen in *Henry VIII*, Lady Anne in *Richard III*, Hellena in *The Rover*, Cordelia in *King Lear*, Aspasia in *The Maid's Tragedy*, Lady Betty in *The Careless Husband*, Hillaria in *Love's Last Shift*, Lucia in *Cato*, Parisatis in *The Rival Queens*, Mrs Foresight in *Love for Love*, Dorinda in *The Stratagem*, and Lady Macduff in *Macbeth*. She chose for her first benefit at Drury Lane, on 19 April 1733, Margery Pinchwife in *The Country Wife*; the performance was commanded by the Prince of Wales, who was present.

Aaron Hill devoted a great deal of attention to Miss Holliday just after she moved to Drury Lane. He wrote to her saying her "action and voice, in Lady Ann" so charmed everyone "that, now I am positive, it is in your power, to reach everything upon the stage, that is either natural, or amiable." In *The Miser* she tended to hurry her speeches instead of "swelling the significant words" and "distinguishing the periods." He had high hopes for her as Imoinda in *Oroonoko* (which she acted on 7 December 1733 and had probably acted on the previous 8 October) but was disappointed:

I can't say, she answered the hopes, I had conceiv'd of her; she spoke with too low, and faint a voice; and look'd and mov'd, with too little force: But of this I am sure, that, if her voice is not, *naturally*, too weak (which I find, is every body's opinion) it will be easy enough, to inspirit her motion and gesture: But it must be done, not by *written* but personal instruction.

I would have given a good deal, to have known, but a fortnight before, that she was to appear, in that character: It is a terrible misfortune to the house, that nothing is so little thought of, as improving the natural capacities of the actors; whereas, you know very well, that the greatest, and most accomplish'd orators of antiquity, both thought it necessary, and submitted, with pleasure, to seek the advice, and opinion of their friends, before they became able to shine in their profession.

Hill praised Miss Holliday's figure and clearly thought she could rise to the top of her profession. But he complained of her modesty and diffidence, which kept her from expressing the "shining passions" of Zara (in *The Mourning Bride*, presumably) or the misery of Selima (in *Tamerlane*). She was, thought Hill, too sweet.

During the 1730s Miss Holliday ventured to Lincoln's Inn Fields thrice—26 March 1733 to act Bellinda in *Tunbridge Walks*, on 15 April 1734 to play Harriet in *The Miser* for Stoppelaer's benefit, and again three days later to act Serina in *The Orphan* for the benefit of some "Young Author."

Elizabeth Holliday married William Mills at St Anne, Soho, on 10 September 1737. The bills still mentioned her occasionally as Miss Holliday during the rest of the 1737–38 season—an indication, perhaps, of her popularity over the years. But gradually everyone became used to her married name, and as Mrs Mills she appeared regularly and almost exclusively at Drury Lane for the rest of her long career. Some of her new parts were Euphronia in *Aesop*, Fidelia in *The Plain Dealer*, Andromache in *The Distrest Mother*, Alinda in *The Pilgrim*, Millamant and Mrs Fainall in *The Way of the World*, the Lady in *Comus*, Eurydice in *Oedipus*, Desdemona in *Othello*, Luciana in *The Comedy of Errors*, Monimia in *The Orphan*, Statira in *The Rival Queens*, Lavinia in *The Fair Penitent*, Lady Grace in *The Provok'd Husband*, Lady Fidget in *The Country Wife*, Portia in *Julius Caesar*, Melinda in *The Recruiting Officer*, Araminta in *The Confederacy*, Mrs Frail in *Love for Love*, Queen Elinor in *King John*, and Mrs Page in *The Merry Wives of Windsor*.

In the 1740s the tyranny of the manager Fleetwood forced William Mills and his wife into debt, and, briefly, out of Drury Lane Theatre. They appeared a few times at the Haymarket Theatre in late September and early October 1744, with Mrs Mills playing Lady Betty in *The Careless Husband*, Silvia in *The Recruiting Officer*, and Mrs Scrape in *The Prodigal*. On 13 November 1746 she acted Angelica in *The Anatomist* at Goodman's Fields, according to *The London Stage*, but we think that may be an error for Mrs Miles, who was a dancer at Goodman's Fields at the time and who did, indeed, dance that evening. She occasionally acted. In the mid-1740s Mr and Mrs Mills lived in Nassau Street near Soho.

After her husband's death in April 1750 Mrs Mills appears to have reduced her performing schedule, and by her last season at Drury Lane, 1754–55, she was appearing rarely. Her final performance was as Lamorce in *The Inconstant* on 24 April 1755. That was for her benefit, for which she made tickets available at Mr Gardner's, the printer, in Russell Street, Covent Garden. Receipts came to £130. Mrs Mills

retired and, according to the prompter Cross on 13 September 1755, "is gone to end her days in Wales, with an allowance of £20 per An: from the managers."

Milne, Mrs [*fl.* 1794], *singer. See* MILNE, MRS S.

Milne, Miss [*fl.* 1791–1795], *singer.*
Miss Milne was a popular singer at Vauxhall Gardens from 1791 to 1795, as evidenced by a number of published songs which named her as vocalist. Among them were collections of songs by James Hook in 1791, 1792, 1793, 1794, and 1795; *The Eccho Song*, which she sang with Master Shepherd (1792?); *The Silver Moon* (1793); *Poor Annette the Savoyard* (1793?); and *The Happy Milk Maid* (1795?). Doane's *Musical Directory* of 1794 noted that Miss Milne was a soprano and lived in Lambeth Walk.

Milne, Mrs S. [*fl.* 1794], *singer.*
Doane's *Musical Directory* of 1794 listed Mrs Milne and Mrs S. Milne as singers in the Handel performances at Westminster Abbey. They were from Lancashire.

Milton, Mr [*fl.* 1784], *singer.*
Mr Milton sang bass in the Handel Memorial Concerts at Westminster Abbey and the Pantheon in May and June 1784.

Milward, Mr [*fl.* 1792], *singer.*
According to Wroth's *The London Pleasure Gardens*, a Mr Milward sang at Bermondsey Spa Gardens in 1792.

Milward, William [*fl.* 1663], *trumpeter.*
The Lord Chamberlain issued a warrant on 23 May 1663 appointing William Milward a trumpeter extraordinary (without fee) in the King's Musick. Since the accounts did not mention Milward again, a salaried post for him must not have materialized, and he probably left the court.

Milward, William 1702–1742, *actor.*
In his *General History of the Stage* W. R. Chetwood provided some fairly detailed information on William Milward:

From the Collection of Edward A. Langhans

Benefit ticket for WILLIAM MILWARD

by Hogarth

THIS Gentleman was born at *Lichfield* in *Stafford-shire* on 29th of September in the Year 1702. His Great Grandfather Sir *Thomas Milward* was Chief Justice of *West-Chester*, and raised a Troop of Horse in Defence of that unhappy Monarch King *Charles* the First, and was then a County Palatine, which occasioned the *Rump Parliament* in the Year 1659, to vote their Charter void; and I do not find it ever restor'd. The Family were originally from *Derby-shire*. The Father of our Actor, a few Years after the Birth of his Son, removed to *Uttoxeter* (commonly called *Tociter*) in the County of *Stafford*, distant from *London* 126 measured Miles, formerly a Colony of the *Romans*.

He had his Education in a School of that Town, accounted one of the best in that Part of the Country.

(Coincidentally, a William "Milword," son of Robert and Patience Milword, was christened at St Clement Danes, London [where the actor William Milward was buried in 1742], on 29 March 1702. He may have been a relative.)

By 1717 the Milwards were in London, and William's father apprenticed him to an apothecary in Norfolk Street. *The History of the Stage* (1741) claimed that Milward worked there for eight years, but Chetwood's version of the story has William giving up his apprenticeship (which would have lasted only seven years) because *"there were so many Dangers in the Employment, that he could never like it."* The circumstances causing Milward to give up his work were also described by Chetwood:

He was ordered by his Master to carry his Pre-scriptions to a Gentleman and Lady ill of different Maladies at the same time; the Labels were wrong directed, but he did not discover this Mistake till the next Day, when he carried other Medicines to the same Persons, and by his Judgement in the Operation soon found out the Mistake. He was greatly terrified, but for fear of more, he let fall the Phial he had in his Hand, as by Accident, ran back to his Master, and told him what had been done. The Master ordered more proper Doses, the Patients recovered and all was well.

"Mr. Milward's first Essay in Acting was among young Gentlemen, privately, for their own diversion . . . " according to Chetwood. They performed at the Hoop Tavern in St Alban's Street, the *History* said. Soon afterward he joined a provincial company, and the manager of the Lincoln's Inn Fields Theatre in London (John Rich, presumably) saw him and brought him to London to act. That could be a fiction, since *The London Stage* shows Milward making his first professional stage appearance at the Haymarket Theatre on 12 December 1723; he spoke the prologue and acted True-man in *The Female Fop*. At the same house on 5 February 1724 he played Belguard in *Sir Courtly Nice*, and on the thirteenth, when he acted the title part in *Oedipus*, he was given a solo benefit. On 9 March he shared a second benefit with three others.

After an absence from the London stage of a season and a half, Milward reappeared on 19 February 1726, playing Wingrave in *Money the Mistress* at the Lincoln's Inn Fields Theatre. Could it have been just before this that Rich had found him touring the provinces? At Lincoln's Inn Fields during the remainder of the 1725–26 season and the summer Milward was seen as Cornwall in *King Lear*, Antonio in *The Rover*, Octavio in *Love's Contrivance*, Rashly in *The Fond Husband*, Reynard in *Tunbridge Walks*, John in *The Man's the Master*, Bevil in *Epsom Wells*, Lovewell in *The Gamester*, Camillus in *The Spanish Wives*, and Young Palatine in *The*

Wits. On 13 May he shared a benefit with two others that brought in over £100.

Milward was again at Lincoln's Inn Fields in 1726–27, his salary at the opening of the season being 15*s.* nightly. He remained there (and, from 1732, at Covent Garden) in Rich's troupe through the spring of 1733, playing such new characters as Phorbas and Haemon in *Oedipus*, Sparkish and Dorilant in *The Country Wife*, Raymond and Bertran in *The Spanish Fryar*, the Chaplain and Acasto in *The Orphan*, Gibbett, Aimwell, and Sir Charles in *The Stratagem*, Horatio, Claudius, and the Ghost in *Hamlet*, Blandford in *Oroonoko*, Cunningham in *The Amorous Widow*, Hemskirk and Woolfort in *The Royal Merchant*, Albany and Glouceser in *King Lear*, Bonario and Voltore in *Volpone*, Malcolm and Banquo in *Macbeth*, Balance and Worthy in *The Recruiting Officer*, Bedamar, Jaffeir, and Priuli in *Venice Preserv'd*, Trueman in *The Squire of Alsatia*, Manuel in *Love Makes a Man*, Maskwell and Touchwell in *The Double Dealer*, Colonel Feignwell in *A Bold Stroke for a Wife*, Sharper in *The Old Bachelor*, Marcus in *Cato*, Manly in *The Provok'd Husband*, Gratiano in *The Jew of Venice*, Massinissa in *Sophonisba*, Lodovico and Brabantio in *Othello*, Octavius in *Julius Caesar*, Angelo in *Measure for Measure*, the Mad Scholar in *The Pilgrim*, Dervise and the title role in *Tamerlane*, Strato in *The Maid's Tragedy*, Hephestion in *The Rival Queens*, Rovewell in *The Fair Quaker of Deal*, Sir John in *The Conscious Lovers*, Vizard in *The Constant Couple*, the title role in *1 Henry IV*, the Duke in *Rule a Wife and Have a Wife*, Arcas in *Damon and Phillida*, George Barnwell in *The London Merchant*, Charles in *The Busy Body*, Herod in *Mariamne*, Altamont in *The Fair Penitent*, and the title role in *Timon of Athens*. By 24 April 1731 the energetic and versatile Milward had risen to solo benefits at Lincoln's Inn Fields; on that date the receipts came to over £135.

During his years under John Rich, Milward is known to have made some appearances elsewhere: as Shore in *Jane Shore* on 21 August 1727 at a Bartholomew Fair booth which he operated with Miller and Hall; as Charles in *The Busy Body*, Torrismond in *The Spanish Fryar*, and Manly in *The Provok'd Husband* at Richmond in June and July 1730; and Dorilant in *The Country Wife*, Standard in *The Constant Couple*, Ford in *The Merry Wives of Windsor*,

Loveless in *Love's Last Shift*, and Young Bevil in *The Conscious Lovers* at Richmond in July 1731.

On 10 October 1733 Milward played Hotspur in *1 Henry IV* at the Haymarket Theatre with Theophilus Cibber's group of Drury Lane seceders. Before the players returned to Drury Lane in March 1734 Milward added to his already extensive repertoire such parts as York in *2 Henry IV*, Clerimont in *The Double Gallant*, the title role in *Oroonoko*, Frederick in *The Miser*, Portius in *Cato*, Welford in *The Scornful Lady*, Thorowgood in *The London Merchant*, and Careless in *The Committee*. Milward must have taken a risk when he gave up his engagement at Covent Garden (not long after the new theatre opened) to join Cibber's malcontents at the Haymarket. In *Theatrical Correspondence in Death* (1743) is an epistle from Anne Oldfield in which the ghost of Milward explained why he left:

I was but One—had Reasons, and those very cogent ones for my Proceedings—I desired not Others to follow me—If they were not paid enough, or so quick as they could have wished, I always left it to their own Judgments, to move as they thought proper—I apprehend that every Man, when his Articles are expired, has an Option to continue, or to go to the other House—This was always my Way of thinking—without endeavouring to draw after me Others, thereby harassing, oppressing, perhaps ruining the Managers.

On 12 March 1734 Milward made his initial appearance at Drury Lane Theatre playing Heartly in *The Mother-in-Law*. Before the end of the season he also acted Marc Antony in *All for Love*, Brumpton in *The Funeral*, Hotspur, York, and Cranmer in *Henry VIII*, and Sealand in *The Conscious Lovers*. He returned to Richmond in the summer.

In 1735 Milward and other players petitioned against Barnard's bill before Parliament for the governing of the playhouses; Milward was listed as one of several who had joined a group to lease Drury Lane for 15 years. The players claimed they would be ruined should the bill be enacted. Nothing seems to have come of the leasing project, nor did Barnard's bill pass.

The rest of Milward's London career, which lasted until the spring of 1742, was spent at Drury Lane, save for a single appearance on 14

April 1736 at Lincoln's Inn Fields Theatre as Hotspur at a benefit in which Macklin shared. As of 25 March 1738 Milward was living in Brownlow Street, Drury Lane; by the spring of 1740 he was at No 15, Craven Buildings, at the lower end of Drury Lane. (There was a Milward acting at Norwich from 1727 to 1729, 1732 to 1735, in 1738, and in 1740–41, but he was probably another person; William Milward was active in London during those years, at least during the winter seasons.) On the other hand, William Milward did act in Dublin, arriving there on 10 June 1739 for a summer season at the Smock Alley Theatre. He is known to have acted Hamlet, Oroonoko, Bajazet, Castalio, Cassius, Voltore, Edgar, Macduff, Orestes, Sealand, Loveless, Hotspur, Essex, Antony, Ventidius in *All for Love*, and Charles in *Love Makes a Man*.

At Drury Lane over the years his new parts included Osmyn in *The Mourning Bride*, Carlos in *Love Makes a Man*, Mirabel in *The Way of the World*, Dauphine in *The Silent Woman*, Davison in *The Albion Queens*, Valentine in *Love for Love*, Amintor in *The Maid's Tragedy*, Wolsey in *Henry VIII*, Freeman in *The Plain Dealer*, Medley in *The Man of Mode*, Dudley in *Lady Jane Gray*, Pedro in *The Pilgrim*, Jupiter in *Amphitryon*, Hastings in *Jane Shore*, the Elder Brother in *Comus*, Orlando in *As You Like It*, Sebastian in *Twelfth Night*, and Bassanio in *The Merchant of Venice*. His last known appearance was on 22 January 1742, when he played the King in *All's Well that Ends Well*.

According to Davies, William Milward caught a distemper while playing in *All's Well* in October 1741; if that date is correct, his illness came when the play was in rehearsal, for it was not performed until the following January. Davies claimed that Milward wore for his role a "too light and airy suit of clothes. . . ." On 1 February 1742 the bill had to be changed because of Milward's indisposition, and on 6 February David Garrick, fresh from his London debut, wrote to his brother Peter that "Poor Milward is taken very dangerously ill of a Spotted Fever & given o'er (they say) by ye Physicians." Milward died that day. He was buried at St Clement Danes on 10 February, and his widow Mary (then pregnant) and her four children were granted a benefit at Drury Lane on 9 March which brought in £230. They received a second benefit, at Covent Garden, on 25 March, and another, at Lincoln's Inn Fields, on 11 April 1743.

In his day Milward, who patterned his acting after the style of Barton Booth in the role of Lusignan in Hill's *Zara*, was considered one of London's foremost players. Davies found his Lusignan

> not much inferior to Mr. Garrick's representation of that part. —Milward chose Booth for his model; and, notwithstanding his inferiority to that accomplished tragedian, he was the only performer in tragedy, who, if he had survived, could have approached to your great Roscius; who, though he would always have been the first, yet, in that case, would not have been the only actor in tragedy.

"Gentleman" Smith wrote to Coutts in April 1818: "Ryan, Delane, & Milward were Actors of Eminence: You don't remember *Milward*. He was very early in my recollection in Elegance & Expression very like our great Master Roscius."

To have been compared with Garrick by those who saw both was high praise indeed, and the parts assigned to Milward testify to his ability. Chetwood said Milward rose at Lincoln's Inn Fields and Covent Garden (even before he began receiving his best parts) to the "foremost Rank of Perfection." Davies said that "All the surviving spectators of Milward's Prince of Denmark will be pleased to have him recalled to memory; for . . . he was not only an agreeable, but a skilful actor; his voice was full and musical; and, in this character, he seemed to forget that love of ranting, which was his singular fault." The ranting was doubtless a trait picked up from Booth and belonged to the more stylized period preceding Garrick's debut.

James Eyre Weeks in *A Rhapsody on the Stage* in 1746 wrote:

> Milward *had all the Sweetness that cou'd move*
> *The fair one's pity to lament his Love,*
> *The tuneful Voice, the lively open grace*
> *Mellow'd his tongue, and mounted to his Face.*

In *Reflections on Theatrical Expression* (1755) Pickering felt that Milward, "though not of the *first* Rank, was very far from being an *indifferent* Actor." Milward, he said, claimed that by listening closely to the speeches of other actors on stage (which some other players must not have done) he could rouse his own feelings and sometimes bring up real tears. That sounds more like the natural style of Garrick than the artificial one of Booth.

The author of *An Apology for the Life of T......C......* (1740) praised Milward's fine voice and said he was "very well turn'd for the Lover or the Heroe." Milward was sometimes indolently negligent, the author said, though not wanting in judgment. Best suited for the passions of grief, love, pity, or despair, the author thought, Milward excelled in low comedy as well. Indeed, the range of parts he is known to have played would suggest that he was one of the most versatile, if not the finest, actor of the decade preceding the arrival of Garrick.

Milward belonged to the distinguished Freemasons' lodge that met at the Bear and Harrow in Butcher Row, east of the Tower. Other members included Theophilus Cibber, Richard Leveridge, James Quin, and William Hogarth.

A benefit ticket for Milward, ascribed to Hogarth, for *A Bold Stroke for a Wife* at Lincoln's Inn Fields on 23 April 1728, shows, oddly, a scene from *The Beggar's Opera*, in which work Milward acted the Player. Hayman evidently drew a portrait of Milward, for in the Enthoven Collection is a verse titled "On Mr. Milward's Picture As Drawn by Mr. Hayman."

Mimes, Mr *d. 1765, actor.*

In two documents at the British Library (Burney 939 b 1 and Add 18586) a Mr Mimes is noted as having died in 1765. In the first document he is described as an actor, or we might guess that the person in question was the house servant Mines of earlier years.

Mimi, Mme. *See* FORCADE, MME LEONARD.

"Mimicotti, Signora" [*fl. 1757–1760*], *singer?*

In *A Medley Concert* given by "Mother Midnight" (Christopher Smart) and fellow burlesquers at the Haymarket Theatre 28 June 1757, "Sga Mimicotti" sang an Italian air accompanied by "Myn Heer Van-Poop Broomsticato." The identity of Sga Mimicotti is unknown, but the name is intended as a parody of Sga Regina Mingotti, a celebrated singer and manager of the opera at the King's Theatre the previous season. The burlesque program, sometimes joined with Theophilus Cibber's "Auction of many choice Curiosities," was offered a number of times during the summer of 1757 and as late as 3 October. Several years later, on 8 September 1760, Sga Mimicotti returned with Mrs Midnight for another concert at the Haymarket.

Minchine, Mr [*fl. 1784*], *singer.*

Mr Minchine sang tenor in the Handel Memorial Concerts at Westminster Abbey and the Pantheon in May and June 1784.

Mines, Mr [*fl. 1717–1744*], *gallery office keeper, boxkeeper.*

Mr Mines worked for John Rich at Lincoln's Inn Fields from as early as 3 June 1717, when he shared a benefit with four others that brought in £118 8s. 6d. His position at that time was not specified, but by 12 May 1726, when he shared £137 5s. with two others, he was called the gallery office keeper. His salary as of 25 September 1724 was 5s. daily (possibly an error in the accounts, for twice in 1726 he received payments of 7s. 6d. for three days, which indicates a weekly salary of 15s.). His shared benefits continued through the years at Lincoln's Inn Fields and then Covent Garden. Once, on 19 May 1740 he was called a boxkeeper, but at his last recorded benefit, on 11 May 1744, he was listed as the gallery office keeper. His salary in 1735–36 was 2s. 6d. daily. Possibly he was the Mr Mimes who was recorded as dying in 1765, but that person was said to have been an actor.

Though our subject's name seems pretty consistently to have been spelled Mines, there is a possibility that he was related to the Mrs Mynns who was a booth operator at the late summer fairs in London until her death in December 1717. But the date of her death and the date of the first mention of Mines in theatrical records may be only a coincidence. One wonders, though, if Mines was her son.

Minet or **Mynet.** *See* MYNITT.

Mingotti, Signora Pietro, Regina, née Valentini *1722–1808, singer, manager.*

Regina Mingotti was born at Naples on 16 February 1722, the daughter of an Austrian

"The Idol"—REGINA MINGOTTI

artist unknown

army officer named Valentini. Despite the Italian name, her father and mother were reported to have been of German origin. When she was about a year old she was taken to Gratz in Silesia, where her father had been posted and where a few years later he died. An uncle placed her in an Ursuline convent. There she learned music and sang in the choir, but her uncle's death terminated the pension which had supported Regina's education, and at the age of 14 Regina was returned to her mother and two sisters, evidently at Dresden. Principally to rescue herself from the great unhappiness of her youth, in 1746 she married the impresario Pietro Mingotti, about 20 years her senior. With his elder brother Angelo Mingotti, Pietro ran an opera company of some distinction that usually headquartered in Dresden but frequently toured northern European cities.

Mingotti placed his young wife under Porpora's tuition, and her quick development won her an engagement in the Dresden court opera, where on 25 May 1747 she made her debut in Scalabrini's *Merope*. Her success in that theatre supposedly drew the envy and ire of the celebrated Faustina, who with her composer-

husband Hasse left the city for Italy. Soon after, Sga Mingotti also left Dresden to sing at Naples. According to Sainsbury, she had so closely studied Italian that when she made her Neapolitan debut as Aristea in Galuppi's *L'Olimpiade* "she surprised the Italians as much by the purity of her pronunciation, as by her melodious voice, and expressive and natural manner of acting." That performance drew many lucrative offers from Italian companies, all of which she refused in order to return to the Dresden court at a salary "considerably raised." Her performance of *L'Olimpiade* at Dresden was enormously successful. Burney reported a story about Sga Mingotti and Hasse, who had returned to Dresden as Kapellmeister. She accepted his offer to compose expressly for her the adagio, "Se tutti i mali miei," to be sung with only a pizzicato violin accompaniment. Hasse, it is said, deliberately arranged the composition so that any faults committed in singing it would be all the more clearly heard. But Sga Mingotti realized that a snare had been laid for her and was stimulated to a performance of the adagio so exquisitely correct as to win even the silent respect of the composer and his jealous spouse.

In 1751 Sga Mingotti left Dresden for Spain, where for two years she sang with Gizziello in operas produced under the direction of Farinelli, who was so strict in his demands for discipline and application that it is said he would not permit her to sing anywhere but at the opera theatre and forbade her practice in a room which looked toward the street. Among the many favors bestowed upon her while she was in Spain was a diamond necklace from the Queen.

From Spain she went for a time to Paris, and thence to London in 1754. On 24 September of that year *The Entertainer* announced her engagement for the opera and reported "The Lady has been admired at Naples and other parts of Italy, by all the *Connoisseurs*, as much for the elegance of her voice as that of her features." At the King's Theatre on 9 November 1754 she made her debut as Ipermestra in *L'Ipermestra*, an opera by Hasse and Lampugnani that proved to be very popular that season. She sang in *Penelope* on 21 December 1754 (some of Galuppi's airs in that opera were published that year as sung by her), and probably in *Siroe* on 14 January 1755. She appeared in Galuppi's *Ricimero* on 18 February 1755 and several times thereafter, though on 15 March Sga Frasi took Sga Mingotti's place because she had not yet recovered from her "Indisposition." But two days later, on 17 March, evidently Sga Mingotti had recovered well enough to sing in a concert for the benefit premiere of Hasse's *Ezio*. Another performance of that opera scheduled for 31 May was deferred on account of her illness, to 7 June. Nevertheless, Sga Mingotti's appearances that season had saved Vaneschi's management, for, as Burney wrote, the sum total of all his pieces and singers could not "keep the manager out of debt, or hardly out of jail, till the arrival of Mingotti."

The following season at the King's Theatre she appeared 11 November 1755 in Jomelli's *Andromaca*, in which her singing of the air "Eccoti il figlio" was, by Burney's testimony, "truly dramatic and affecting." But the success of *Andromaca* was dampened, as Burney wrote, by her frequent illnesses, which required Sga Frasi to step in for her. Indeed, suspicions arose "that Mingotti's was a mere dramatic and political cold," which put the public out of humor. But her singing in the London premiere of Jomelli's *Demofoonte* on 9 December 1755 gained her more applause, and "augmented her theatrical consequence beyond any period of her performance in England." By her rendition of "Se tutti i mali miei" the audience seemed "to feel her powers of expression, for the first time." Her style was always grand, continued Burney:

and she was a most judicious and complete actress, extending her intelligence to the poetry, and every part of the drama; yet her greatest admirers allowed that her voice and manner would have been still more irresistible, if she had had a little more female grace and softness. The performance in men's parts, however, obviated every objection that her greatest enemy could make to her abilities, either as an actress, or singer.

In a *Concerto Spiritual* given at Drury Lane Theatre on 2 April 1756 for the benefit of the Lock Hospital, Sga Mingotti and Ricciarelli sang the *Stabat Mater* of Pergolesi, the first performance of that work in London. In a letter Thomas Gray stated that Sga Mingotti had "just lain in," but we find no baptismal record.

Perhaps the child died before it could be christened. Gary later heard her sing at Cambridge in May 1759 and thought "her voice (wch always had a roughness) is considerably harsher, than it was, but yet she is a noble Singer."

During the 1755–56 season the Mingotti—as she was often called—had differences with the manager Vaneschi that brought on numerous private and public quarrels. Their contentions, Burney said prejudiced the public against both. One of Sga Mingotti's supporters, Mrs Fox Lane, espoused her cause "with great zeal, entering into the spirit of all her theatrical quarrels as ardently as if they had been her own." A story circulated that when Mrs Lane told a certain general the minute details of the singer's case against Vaneschi, the general asked with seeming ignorance and indifference "And pray, ma'am, who is Madam Mingotti?"—thus provoking the lady to exclaim "Get out of my house! . . . you shall never hear her sing another note at my concerts, as long as you live." On the other hand, Horace Walpole wrote to Bentley of the impertinence of the singer:

The Mingotti, a noble figure, a great mistress of music, and a most incomparable actress, surpassed anything I ever saw for the extravagance of her humour. She never sang above one night in three, from a fever upon her temper; and would never act at all when Ricciarelli, the first man, was to be in dialogue with her. Her fevers grew so high, that the audience caught them, and hissed her more than once; she herself once turned and hissed again. . . . Well, among the treaties which a secretary of state has negociated this summer he has contracted for a *succedaneum* to the Mingotti. In short, there is a woman hired to sing when the other shall be out of humour!

Vaneschi went bankrupt, spent time in the Fleet, and then ran from England in the summer of 1756. Sga Mingotti, the *Connoisseur* for 8 July 1756 reported, also went abroad for the summer, "till her affairs in England can be settled." She returned in the fall to become co-manager of the opera with Giardini, and, as Burney wrote, they assumed "for awhile the sovereignty of the opera kingdom, by which gratification of ambition they were soon brought to the brink of ruin." The company of singers went through the 1756–57 season "with great eclat" under the direction of Giardini and Mingotti. Probably she sang in *Alessandro nell'Indie* on 11 December 1756. On 18 January 1757 she appeared as Eliza in *Il re pastore*. She sang in a concert for the benefit of the Musicians' Fund on 24 March at the King's Theatre, and the next night she performed in Hasse's oratorio *I pellegrini*. She sang the title role in *Rosmira* on 30 April, Eliza, with the addition of some favorite airs, for her benefit on 10 May, and Antigona in *Euristeo* on 31 May. In the *Public Advertiser* on 13 June 1757 Sga Mingotti thanked her public for their subscriptions that past season, in which, she acknowledged, "the Entertainments have been greatly inferior to my intention, which was entirely owing to My not having the Theatre till almost the usual time for the Operas to convene." (That summer at the Haymarket a singer named "Sga Mimicotti" burlesqued her by singing Italian airs in performances of *A Medley Concert* in which "Myn Heer Van-Poop Broomsticato" and "Madam Midnight" also appeared.)

Though Sga Mingotti advertised in June 1757 for subscriptions for the next season, on 31 May Vaneschi had announced in the *Public Advertiser* that he had secured the license from the Lord Chamberlain and would be the director of the operas. It seems, however, that Sga Colomba Mattei actually was the manager of the operas in 1757–58, and Sga Mingotti faded into the background. The latter's name did not appear in any opera bills that season. The most successful operas were *Demetrio* and *Zenobia*, in which Sga Mattei was the first woman. At Drury Lane on 10 March 1758, however, Sga Mingotti sang an air and a duet with Ricciarelli for the benefit of the Musicians' Fund. A similar situation prevailed in 1758–59, though on 14 May 1759 Sga Mingotti received a benefit at the King's Theatre when a concert of instrumental and vocal music was presented. Ten days earlier, on 4 May, she had sung at Covent Garden, again for the Musicians' Fund.

Perhaps for the next several years Sga Mingotti was back on the Continent. Her husband Pietro Mingotti died at Copenhagen on 28 April 1759. Her name was not again associated with London until, Sga Mattei having left England, the Mingotti and Giardini assumed the management of the King's Theatre in 1763–64 and with a small company produced 52 performances of ten operas. She sang in *Cleonice* on 26 November 1763, *Siroe* on 13 December, *Senocrita* on 21 February 1764, *Leucippo* for her

benefit on 29 March, and *I pellegrini* on 5 April. Probably she also performed that season in *Alessandro nell' Indie* and *Enea e Lavinia*, and perhaps it was in the latter that she made her last London appearance on 12 June 1764.

Afterwards Sga Mingotti sang in Italy and Germany. She settled in Munich in 1772 to enjoy a comfortable and amiable society. In 1787 she retired to Neuburg on the Danube, where she began teaching. She may have accompanied one of her pupils, Mme Lops, when the latter made her London debut in 1791. Sga Mingotti died at Neuburg on 1 October 1808.

She was, in Burney's phrase, "a complete mistress of her art," a celebrated singer and an admired actress. She had told Burney in 1772 "that she was frequently hissed by the English for having a toothache, a cold, or a fever, to which the good people of England will readily allow every human being is liable except an actor or a singer." She was a sophisticated student of music and an animated conversationalist. She knew Latin, Spanish, and English; and was so perfect in French, Italian, and German that it was difficult to distinguish her native tongue.

Grove reports her portrait in crayons by Mengs to be (or to have been) in the Dresden Gallery. It is said that the dog painted in Hogarth's "The Lady's Last Stake" was hers. A satirical print by an unknown engraver, published in 1756, depicts her addressing a party of English admirers, among whom is Lord Holderness, the Secretary of State. The print satirizes her £2000 per annum: one of the gentlemen remarks, "We shall have but 12 songs for all this Money."

"Miniature Woman." *See* "WOMAN IN MINIATURE."

Minns. *See* MYNNS.

Minors, Sybilla, later Mrs John Walker *1723–1802, actress, singer.*

The place of birth of Sybilla Minors (often Myners) is not known, nor is her parentage. Her age at death in 1802 having been given as 79, her birth-year is calculated as 1723.

Sybilla was, then, about 18 when, on 11 November 1741, she made her first appearance, as one of the Gypsy Women in *The Fortune Tellers*, at Drury Lane Theatre. Her apprenticeship was short, and after it her success was immediate in the lines she was principally to sustain—hoydenish country girls, frisky ingenues, pert servants, occasional singing parts or minor roles in tragedy—she was, said Francis Gentleman in *The Dramatic Censor* (1770) "happy in the whole girlish cast." She returned to Drury Lane from 1741–42 through 1758 except for the seasons 1743–44 and 1748–49, for which there is no record of her activity in the winters. (She acted at the Haymarket in the summer of 1744 and did not return to Drury Lane until January 1745. On 7 September 1748 she played Madge in *Harlequin Imprison'd* in Phillips's booth at Southwark Fair.)

In May 1758 Sybilla Minors married the Drury Lane actor John Walker and in the fall the newlyweds were lured by Spranger Barry and Henry Woodward to the new theatre in Crow Street, Dublin. There they remained for the next four winter seasons, though they apparently acted at Bristol in the summers of 1760 and 1761. In June 1762 they returned to England and made their way to London by means of acting engagements at Birmingham and Bristol.

In the 1762–63 season the Walkers joined the company at Covent Garden Theatre, where they remained through the 1766–67 season. After one more summer season at Bristol, Walker retired from theatrical activity, and evidently his wife did also.

The playbills show the development of Sybilla Minors Walker's repertoire season by season, as follows: at Drury Lane in 1741–42, a Gypsy Woman in *The Fortune Tellers*, a Lady of Honor in *Chrononhotonthologos*, Gipsy in *The Stratagem*, and some character in *The Rehearsal*; in 1742–43, Hoyden in *The Relapse*, Harriet in *The Miser*, and Cherry in *The Stratagem*; in the spring of 1745, Miss Price in *Love for Love*, Florella in *The Orphan*, Jessica in *The Merchant of Venice*, Lucilla in *The Fair Penitent*, and Blanche in *King John*; in 1745–46, Isabella in *The Stage Coach*, Jessica in *The Merchant of Vennice*, Betty in *The Contrivances*, Betty in *The Lying Lover*, Beliza in *The Comical Lovers*, Mrs Slammekin in *The Beggar's Opera*, Diana in *The She Gallant*, Hippolita in *The Sea Voyage*, and Jenny Firelock in *The Humours of the Army*; and in 1746–47, Edging in *The Careless Husband*, a Lady in *Macbeth*, Charmion in *All for Love*, Mariana in *The Wild Goose Chase*, Busy in *The Man of Mode*,

Night in *Amphytrion*, Milliner in *The Suspicious Husband*, Molly Brazen in *The Beggar's Opera*, Regan in *King Lear*, and Cephisa in *The Distrest Mother*. At Covent Garden in the 1749–50 season she added Lucetta in *The Suspicious Husband* and Biddy in *Miss in Her Teens*.

Again at Drury Lane, Miss Minors added to her repertoire in 1750–51, Anne Page in *The Merry Wives of Windsor*, Ursula in *Much Ado about Nothing*, Mincing in *The Way of the World*, Jenny in *The Tender Husband*, Wishwell in *The Double Gallant*, Laura in *Gil Blas*, Rose in *The Recruiting Officer*, the usually juvenile part of King Edward V in *Richard III*, a role unspecified in Woodward's new farce *A Lick at the Town*; and in 1751–52, Charlotte in *The Intruiging Chambermaid*, Mrs Tattoo in *Lethe*, Flametta in *A Duke and No Duke*, Serina in *The Orphan*, Foible in *The Way of the World*, Mildred in *Eastward Hoe*, Kitty Pry in *The Lying Valet*, Jenny in *The Tender Husband*, an Attendant in *Phaedra and Hippolitus*, Bridget in *Every Man in His Humour*, Cephisa in *The Distrest Mother*, Lucy in *The London Merchant*, Maria in *Twelfth Night*, Laura in *Tancred and Sigismunda*, Flavia in *The Comical Lovers*, Maria in *The Man of Taste*, Parly in *The Constant Couple*, Jezebel in *Don Quixote in England*, Rose in *The Recruiting Officer*.

In 1752–53 she added Lucy in *Oroonoko*, a character in *The Genii*, Corinna in *The Confederacy*, Ismene in *Merope*, Miss Giggle in *Bayes in Petticoats*, and Alithea in *The Country Wife*; in 1753–54, Busy in *The Man of Mode*, Betty in *The Refusal*, Jenny in *The Knights*, Manage in *The Grumbler*, and Peggy in *The King and the Miller of Mansfield*; in 1754–55, Cleone in *The Distrest Mother*; in 1755–56, Jenny in *The Fair Quaker*, a Slave in *Barbarossa*, the original Charlotte in Arthur Murphy's farce *The Apprentice*, Dorcas in *The Winter's Tale*, Serina in *The Orphan*, and Heartshow in *The Lady's Last Stake*; in 1756–57, Arante in Tate's adaptation of *King Lear*, Inis in *The Wonder*, Arabella in *The Modern Fine Gentleman*, Betty in *A Bold Stroke for a Wife*, and a Lady in *Richard III*; and in 1757–58, parts unspecified in *Harlequin Ranger* and *The Male Coquette*, Philotis in *The Frenchified Lady*, and Lucia in *The Squire in Alsatia*.

After her marriage and sojourn in Ireland, Mrs Walker returned to London to round out her career with five years at Covent Garden. Some of the parts she added to her now-large list she had doubtless played in Dublin, Bristol, and elsewhere. As they now occurred, they were, in 1762–63, Miss Harlow in *The Old Maid*, the original Deborah Woodcock in Isaac Bickerstaffe's "New Dramatic Opera" *Love in a Village*, Altea in *Rule a Wife and Have a Wife*, Lucy in *Wit Without Money*; and in 1765–66, the original Lady Bridget in Elizabeth Griffith's comedy *The Double Mistake* and Jiltup in *The Fair Quaker of Deal*. In her final season, 1766–67, she added no new roles.

After his retirement, her husband John Walker became a notable lexicographer and teacher of elocution. Nothing is known of Sybilla Walker after she left the stage, except that she died on 29 April 1802, according to George Clinch in *Marylebone and St Pancras* (1890), who took the information from her tombstone, now disintegrated. F. T. Cansick in *Epitaphs of Middlesex* (1890) confirms that she was buried at St Pancras Church. Cansick supplies her first name from the church register.

Minton, Mr [*fl.* 1797–1819?], *actor, singer?*

Mr Minton played Syphax in *Cato* at the Haymarket Theatre on 4 December 1797. He was apparently not the Minton who acted at the Haymarket in the summers of 1805 and 1806, for that performer was said to be making his first appearance on that stage on 14 June 1805. A Mr "Mintern" was earning £1 5s. weekly at Drury Lane in 1807–8 and by 1815 had risen to £2 10s. He was active at Drury Lane into the 1818–19 season. Another (?) Minton performed at the Theatre Royal, Edinburgh in 1817–18 and 1818–19, playing such roles as Damon in *Cymon*, Jemmy Twitcher in *The Beggar's Opera*, a Robber in *The Castle of Andalusia*, Sancho in *The Duenna*, and William in *The Cobler of Preston*. There is not enough information to determine whether or not one of the Mintons active in the nineteenth century was the Minton who acted in London in 1797.

A Mrs Minton was a dancer at Drury Lane in 1808–9; a Miss Minton performed at the Royal Circus as early as September 1802 and was active at Drury Lane as late as 1816–17; and Anne Minton, later Mrs Charles Justin Macartney was at Sadler's Wells in 1795 and performed at least as late as 1808. All of the Mintons were probably related.

Minton, Anne, later Mrs Charles Justin Macartney *b. 1785, actress, singer.*

Anne Minton was born in 1785, and possibly she was the daughter of the Mr Minton who acted in London in 1797. On 4 August 1795 she played a Fairy in *Chevy Chase* at Sadler's Wells. In 1800 the younger Charles Dibdin engaged Anne. She was, he said, about 13 or 14 years old and had been a pupil of the late Mrs Crouch. He called her "a pretty interesting figure." Dibdin opened on Easter Monday with *Boadicea*, in which Miss Minton appeared. She spent the summer at the Birmingham theatre, and perhaps it was there she met Charles Justin Macartney.

Aris's Birmingham Gazette on 1 September 1800 reported that the couple had been married at Aston on 27 August. The *Gentleman's Magazine* in October reported the marriage and noted that Miss Minton was 15 years old. On 18 June 1804 Mrs Macartney played Lissette in *The Wild Girl* at the Royal Circus; then Dibdin, he said, engaged her again at Sadler's Wells for the 1804–5 season (but George Speaight, who edited Dibdin's *Memoirs*, did not find her mentioned in Sadler's Wells bills until 1807). She was a singing Lady in *The Knights of the Garter* at the Royal Circus on 29 April 1805 and appeared there again in the summer of 1806. The last notice of Mrs Macartney was on 18 April 1808, when she was the Witch of the Well in the pantomime *The Farmer's Boy* at the Royal Circus.

Mirail. *See* DUMIRAIL.

Miranda, Mrs. *See* WAINWRIGHT, SARAH.

Mire. *See* MYER.

Misdale, Mr [*fl.* 1760–1766], *actor.*

Mr Misdale played Canker in *The Minor* on 28 June 1760 at the Haymarket Theatre. At the New Concert Hall in Edinburgh Misdale was in *The Clandestine Marriage* in April 1766 and played Aladdin in *Barbarossa* there the following August.

Mislebrook, [Stephen?] [*fl.* 1752?–1763], *lobby doorkeeper, billsticker.*

Perhaps the Mislebrook (or Mislebroke) who was a house servant at Covent Garden Theatre in the 1750s and early 1760s was Stephen "Misslebrooke," whose son Stephen was christened at St Paul, Covent Garden, on 6 February 1752. The mother's name was Mary. But the name Mislebrook can also be found in the registers of St George, Hanover Square: in December 1754 William Mislebrook married Ann Ward, and in September 1756 Joseph Mislebrook married Mary Hacker.

Our subject was a lobby doorkeeper at Covent Garden when he was first mentioned in the playbills on 20 May 1757 as one of several whose benefit tickets would be accepted. He was similarly cited each spring in the years that followed, but the account books on 22 September 1760 showed that he had changed his post to that of billsticker, at a daily salary of 2s.; after that, others were named in the bills as lobby doorkeepers. Mislebrook's last notice was on the benefit bill of 26 May 1763.

Missing. *See* MESSINK.

"Miss Romp." *See* JORDAN, DOROTHY.

"Mistress of Fashion, The." *See* ABINGTON, MRS JAMES.

Mitchell. *See also* MICHEL *and* MICHELL.

Mitchell, Mr [*fl. 1672*], *musician.*
The Lord Chamberlain issued a warrant on 2 October 1672 for the apprehension of one Mitchell for playing music without a license.

Mitchell, Miss [*fl. 1776–1779*], *actress.*
A Miss Mitchell played Scentwell in *The Busy Body* at a specially-licensed performance, at the Haymarket Theatre, by a group of unengaged performers on 18 October 1779. No other London appearance by Miss Mitchell is known. She may have been the Miss Mitchell listed in the Bath company in 1776–77 by Arnold Hare in *The Orchard Street Calendar*.

Mitchell, Miss *d. 1799, actress, singer.*
When Miss Mitchell played Yarico in *Inkle and Yarico* for her first appearance at Covent Garden Theatre, on 26 September 1798, she was advertised as "from the Theatre Royal, Bath," and, indeed, a Miss Mitchell had been with the Bath-Bristol Company in 1797–98,

according to Arnold Hare in *The Orchard Street Calendar*.

Though the critic of the *Monthly Mirror* for October 1798 thought that "At present Miss Mitchell is no very promising actress, though as a singer she is entitled to some respect, and will be found useful in parts of a secondary nature," but the *Authentic Memoirs of the Green Room* (1799) judged that, in her debut she had "proved that with care and attention, she will be an actress as well as a singer." She had a chance to prove herself as Angelina in *Robin Hood* on 8 October 1798 and in the long run of James Cobb's popular new comic opera *Ramah Droog* on and after its premiere on 10 November 1798, when she sang Eliza. But after being reduced to one of three Principal Witches in the pantomime *Harlequin's Chaplet* on 13 May, she was allowed only Laura in *Lock and Key* ("for that night only") for her benefit, shared with Mrs Litchfield, on 31 May 1799. (She gave her address to ticket seekers as No 38, Bedford Street.) After that night, when she divided £304 15s. 6d. with Mrs. Litchfield, she was seen no more on London's boards.

Miss Mitchell died at Wimbledon on 28 July 1799, according to the *Morning Post* of 31 July.

Mitchell, Colin *d. 1789, actor.*
The Mitchell who acted at the Crow Street Theatre, Dublin, in season, from 1770–71 through 1773–74, appears to have been Colin Mitchell rather than George Mitchell, with whom Colin is liable to be confused. An affidavit tipped into a Huntington Library copy of Kirkman's *Macklin* and dated 3 March 1773 contains among the signatures of eight Crow Street actors that of "C. Mitchell."

Edward Cape Everard, in his *Memoirs of an Unfortunate Son of Thespis* (1818), calling Mitchell, a "good, sound actor, from Dublin," asserts that he acted with him at the little China Hall Theatre, Rotherhithe, in 1778. Certainly he was the Mitchell who played Gloster in *King Lear* in a special benefit mounted at the Haymarket Theatre on 17 September 1778 for the veteran West Digges. Mitchell's name did not show up in any London bills until 22 February 1779, when he picked up another of the special jobs sometimes available to actors at liberty. This time the Haymarket benefit was "for a Family under Misfortune."

He played Sir Charles Raymond in *The Found-ling*, and Colonel Ancient in *The Prejudice of Fashion* and spoke an "Occasional Prologue." Those services evidently gained him enough sympathy amongst his fellows for them to assist at his own Haymarket benefit, shared with another actor from the provinces, Sinclair. Mitchell played Old Norval in *Douglas*. Tickets could be had of him at the Old Castle Tavern, near Gray's Inn Gate, Holborn.

Evidently discouraged, Colin Mitchell returned to Dublin, where he signed on with Richard Daly at the Smock Alley Theatre from 1780 through 1783. He tried one more assault on London in 1785. On 10 February he joined a group of some 20 other casuals in putting on a new anonymous comedy, *The Fair Refugee; or, The Rival Jews*, and two afterpieces at the Haymarket. The evening was by special permission of the Lord Chamberlain and presumably for the sole emolument of the actors. No roles were given in the playbill. After that, Mitchell was seen no more in London, so far as the record shows.

In 1787 he joined Robert Owenson's company at the Fishamble Street Theatre, Dublin, according to *The Thespian Dictionary* (1805). The *Dublin Chronicle* reported that he died in Galway in December 1789.

Mitchell, Katherine. *See* COREY, MRS JOHN.

Mitchell, Richard [*fl.* 1741], *house servant?*
The Covent Garden performance of *The Conscious Lovers* and *The School Boy* on 11 December 1741 was given for the benefit of one Richard Mitchell. What entitled him to the benefit was not stated. He was perhaps a servant of the house.

Mitermayer, Mr [*fl.* 1757], *scene painter.*
Mr Mitermayer (or Mittermayer) painted a new scene for *Antigono* at the King's Theatre for the production that opened on 8 March 1757.

Mitteer, Mrs [*fl.* 1774], *actress.*
Mrs Mitteer acted at the Haymarket Theatre in September 1774, appearing in an unnamed role in *The Fair Orphan* and the Governess in

The Rival Fools on the seventeenth and the Duchess of York in *Richard III* on the thirtieth. She may have been related to the "Mittier" who acted at the Smock Alley Theatre in Dublin in 1759–60 or to the Mr and Mrs Mitteer who acted in the provinces in the first decade of the nineteenth century.

Moase, Y. [*fl.* 1724–1726], *performer.*
The Lincoln's Inn Fields Theatre accounts contain several references to a Y. Moase (or Moisr); the "Y" could stand for "young" or be an initial. Moase—if that was his name—was a performer of some sort, possibly a singer or musician. One entry called for the payment to him of £1 5s. "by Dr. Pepush" the musician, for participation for five nights in "the Sorcerer" (probably *The Necromancer; or, Harlequin Doctor Faustus*). Whatever he did, Moase seems to have been paid daily most of the time and was probably not a regular member of the company. The first reference to him in the accounts was on 29 January 1724, when he was paid 10s. for two nights, and the last was on 29 October 1726, when he was still earning 5s. nightly.

"Modern Hercules, The" [*fl.* 1798], *acrobat.*
At the Royal Circus on 23 April 1798 the "*Infant Pierrot* and *Modern Hercules*" made their first appearance in a tumbling act which included a display of "ANIMATED ARCHITECTURE."

Modett. *See* MAUDET.

Moeller, Mr [*fl.* 1784], *horn player. See* MOELLER, MR, *trombonist or sackbut player.*

Moeller, Mr [*fl.* 1784], *trombonist or sackbut player.*
Two men named Moeller played in the Handel Memorial Concerts at Westminster Abbey and the Pantheon in May and June 1784. One was listed among the trombones and sackbuts and the other was a horn player.

Moench, Simon Frédéric 1746–1837, *scene painter, designer.*
Born in Stuttgart in 1746, Simon Frédéric Moench (or Mönch) began working at the King's Theatre as a scene painter in 1773, succeeding

Biggari. That season he designed the scenery for *Le Cid*, *Tamterlano*, and Gluck's *Orfeo*, and for the latter he also created the costumes. In 1783 he was working in Paris, and in 1791 he designed for the Pantheon Theatre in London the ballets *La Fille mal gardée* and *Le Siège de Cythére* and the opera *La Locanda* and *La Bella pescatrice*. Moench died in 1837.

Moffat, Mr ₍*fl.* 1776–1777₎, *dresser.*

The Drury Lane Theatre accounts named Mr Moffat as a dresser in 1776–77 at 9*s.* weekly. A Mrs Moffat, probably his wife, worked as a dresser at the same house in June 1775.

Moffat, Mrs ₍*fl.* 1775₎, *dresser. See* MOFFAT, MR

Moffett, ₍Grace?₎ ₍*fl.* 1724–1749?₎, *actress.*

Mrs Moffett made her first appearance on any stage playing Lucinda in *Love and a Bottle* at the Lincoln's Inn Fields playhouse on 23 June 1724. During the remainder of the summer she was seen there as Sophonisba, Almeria in *The Indian Emperor*, Belleraza in *Massaniello*, and an unnamed character in *The Roman Maid*. The account books reveal that Mrs Moffett acted 18 times between 23 June and 20 August. Her daily salary during the following season was 10*s.*, but the books show that in 1726 she received some subsistence payments, apparently over and above her regular salary.

During 1724–25 and 1725–26 Mrs Moffett played such new roles as Isabella in *The False Friend*, Mrs Ford in *The Merry Wives of Windsor*, Clara in *Every Man in His Humour*, Teresia in *The Squire of Alsatia*, Cordelia in *King Lear*, Araminta in *The Old Bachelor*, Diana in *Money the Mistress*, Parisatis in *The Rival Queens*, Lucia in *The Cheats of Scapin*, Araminta in *The Confederacy*, Lady Macduff in *Macbeth*, Clarinda in *The Female Fortune Teller*, Arsinoe in *Mariamne*, Rosalinda in *Sophonisba*, and Leonara in *The Walking Statue*. On 13 May 1726 she shared with two others receipts of £105 12*s.* 6*d.*

She seems then to have been absent from the London stage until 21 August 1727, when she played the lead in *Jane Shore* at the Miller-Hall-Milward booth at Bartholomew Fair. She returned briefly to Lincoln's Inn Fields in the fall to appear as Valeria in *The Rover* and Alithea in *The Country Wife*, after which she again left the stage, perhaps for the provinces, though there is a possibility that she was the Grace Moffett who, according to Chetwood's *General History* in 1749, kept the Bell and Dragon in Portugal Street (which must have been very close to the Lincoln's Inn Fields playhouse). Grace Moffett (or Moffet) was the daughter of the second wife of the actor John Hall, Chetwood said. The last theatrical mention of Mrs Moffett was on 23 August 1743, when she was in *The Cruel Uncle* at Bartholomew Fair.

Mohun, Mr ₍*fl.* 1663–1677₎, *actor, boxkeeper.*

At the Folger Shakespeare Library is a copy of the 1633 edition of *Love's Sacrifice* which has a manuscript cast with "Moons Brother" written in as a replacement for Loveday in the role of Petruchio. "Moon" was the actor Michael Mohun, one of the leading members of the troupe. The play was presented by the King's Company at the Bridges Street Theatre sometime during the 1663–64 season, judging by the cast. Since that is the only reference to Mohun's brother as an actor, perhaps he gave up acting to serve the company as a house servant. The *Theatrical Inquisitor and Monthly Mirror* of July 1816 printed a document which was reported to be accounts for performances at the King's Company Theatre in December 1677 for *All for Love* on the twelfth and *The Rival Queens* on the twenty-sixth. Mr Mohun was listed as a boxkeeper.

Mohun, Michael 1616?–1684, *actor.*

Wright's *Historia Histrionica* stated in 1699 that Michael Mohun had been trained as a boy actor under (Christopher) Beeston at the Cockpit. G. E. Bentley in *The Jacobean and Caroline Stage* conjectures that Mohun must therefore have been in Queen Henrietta's company before the formation of Beeston's Boys in 1636. When an order was issued on 12 May 1637 suppressing acting at the Cockpit, the performers named were Christopher and William Beeston, Theophilus Bird, Ezekiel Fenn, and "Michael Moone." That would indicate, Bentley notes, that by then Mohun was one of the more important members of the Beeston company and was probably an adult. If so Mohun's birthdate may have been around 1616, rather than 1620, as *The Dictionary of National Biography* and other sources suggest.

Harvard Theatre Collection

MICHAEL MOHUN

engraving by Harding, after unknown artist

Bentley also reports that Mohun was fifth on the list of Cockpit players granted tickets of privilege on 10 August 1639, and the following 3 May 1640 he was one of three performers ordered arrested for acting an unlicensed play at the Cockpit and for not closing the theatre on the order of the Master of the Revels. About 1642 or earlier Mohun played Bellamente in *Love's Cruelty*, the only part we know of for him before the theatres were closed. Wright said that, like many players, Mohun joined the royalist forces during the wars. Mohun was a captain in the army and served in Flanders at the pay of a major; he was referred to as Major Mohun after the Restoration.

In the *Calendar of State Papers Domestic* is a report of an entertainment presented by Newcastle at Antwerp for Prince Charles, soon to return to England in triumph as Charles II:

The King was brought in with music, and all being placed, Major Mohun, the player, in a black satin robe and garland of bays, made a speech in verse of his lordship's own poetry, complimenting the King in his highest hyperbole. . . . Then they danced again 2 hours more, and Major Mohun ended all

with another speech, prophesying his Majesty's re-establishment.

In 1659–60 Mohun was back in London, performing in the company at the old Red Bull Theatre and then at the Cockpit in Drury Lane. Possibly he was active at the Red Bull as early as 12 May 1659, as we know Anthony Turner and Edward Shatterell were. Mohun seems certainly to have been performing by 24 March 1660, with other old actors at the Red Bull, in a company that contained players who shortly settled into either the Duke's Company under Sir William Davenant or the King's Company under Thomas Killigrew. The troupe at the Red Bull was partly or fully under Mohun's management, at least by the end of May, and in August 1660 his group came to terms with Sir Henry Herbert, the Master of the Revels, concerning payment of fees for the privilege of performing. They agreed to give Herbert £10 at once, £2 each for any new plays and £1 for any revived plays which they performed, and £4 weekly when they acted. That agreement, according to Hotson's invaluable *Commonwealth and Restoration Stage*, lasted only a month; the players stopped paying Herbert after 10 September, aware that his authority was not complete.

About 1 October 1660 Thomas Killigrew, in his attempt to gain control of the company, had the players silenced and briefly imprisoned. From 8 October to 3 November Mohun was with a group at the Cockpit in Drury Lane that was, in essence, the King's Company, as John Freehafer demonstrated in *Theatre Notebook* 20. Sir Henry Herbert sent a letter, addressed on 13 October "To Mr. Michael Mohun, and the rest of the actors of the Cockpitt playhouse in Drury Lane," stating that Killigrew and Davenant had complained of the high prices being charged at the Cockpit. Herbert stated that prices should be no more than those charged years before at the Blackfriars Theatre. He also insisted that Mohun and his fellow players bring to him all the old plays they intended to act, so he could censor them. All of that was a matter of Herbert, Davenant, and Killigrew jockeying for control over theatrical activity in London. In their response the players pointed out to the King that what Herbert really wanted was his weekly fee, and that they would not be molested. They refused to pay, because Herbert had obviously not been able to prevent Killigrew and Davenant from trying to exercise control over the players.

After some shuffling, two companies emerged, and the King's troupe went into business officially on 5 November 1660 at the Red Bull. Within days their converted tennis court playhouse in Vere Street was ready, and the troupe moved into it. With Mohun in the King's Company was his brother (Christian name not known), who played bit parts and was later a house servant.

Michael Mohun is known to have played his pre-war role of Bellamente in *Love's Cruelty* on 15 November 1660 at Vere Street, and on 17 November he acted Melantius in *The Maid's Tragedy*. Pepys saw him in *The Beggar's Bush* on 20 November but did not name the role Mohun played. The diarist said "it was well acted: and here I saw the first time one Moone, who is said to be the best actor in the World, lately come over with the King. . . ." Two days later Mohun played the title role in *The Traitor*; in December he acted Face in *The Alchemist*, Mardonius in *A King and No King*, and Aubrey in *The Bloody Brother*. The casts for many other plays presented in the 1660–61 initial season at Vere Street are not known or did not include Mohun.

On 20 December 1661 Mohun was one of the signers of an agreement to lease a plot of ground for a new playhouse in Bridges Street. Like most of the actors who purchased shares in the building, he could afford—or perhaps was allowed to purchase—only two; only one player, Lacy, bought more (4) out of the total of 36 shares. What the shares cost is not known, but the building sharers were to get £3 10s. from the acting company (of which all except Sir Robert Howard were members) for each acting day once the new theatre opened. That sum had to be split into 36 parts, of course, but in time the sharers could expect to gain back their original investments and realize a profit. The theatre was to have opened in December 1662 but was not ready until 7 May 1663, so the sharers had to wait a long time before they began getting anything back on their investments. Mohun also purchased shares in the acting company for an unknown figure; he held one and a quarter shares out of the total of 12 ¾, and Hotson estimated that the theoretical maximum annual income from one share was perhaps £280, though the actual income was probably less.

At Vere Street Mohun regularly acted major and leading roles, among which were Ziriff in *Aglaura*, Don Leon in *Rule a Wife and Have a Wife*, Caraffa in *Love's Sacrifice*, and Mopus in *The Cheats*. When the Bridges Street Theatre opened on 7 May 1663 Mohun was Leontius in *The Humorous Lieutenant*, and before that playhouse burned in 1672 he played Fernando in *Love's Sacrifice*, Fernando (Lorenzo) in *The Siege of Urbin*, the title roles in *Volpone* and *The Indian Emperor*, probably Mascarillo in *Damoiselles à la Mode* (that was the author's intention), Truewit in *The Silent Woman*, Alberto in *Flora's Vagaries*, Philocles in *Secret Love*, King Edward in *The Black Prince*, Bellamy in *An Evening's Love*, Rudyas in *The Island Princess*, Cethegus in *Catiline*, Iago in *Othello*, Maximin in *Tyrannick Love*, Valentius in *The Roman Express*, Cassius in *Julius Caesar*, Abdelmelech in both parts of *The Conquest of Granada*, Dapperwit in *Love in a Wood*, and Don Alvarez in *The Generous Enemies*. In his edition of Sedley's *Works* Pinto conjectured that Mohun may have acted Everyoung in *The Mulberry Garden*, and the editors of the new California *Dryden* suggest that Mohun may have played Rhodorigo in *The Rival Ladies* and Ynca in *The Indian Queen*. Mohun was also one of the company's regular speakers of prologues and epilogues.

For a time in 1663–64 Mohun, Charles Hart, and John Lacy—the three leading actors in the King's Company—were managing the company for the proprietor Thomas Killigrew. To pay themselves for their services they split three-fourths of one share in the acting company; where they got the share is not certain, but they may have taken it from a sharing actor and turned him into a hireling at £100 annual wages. Their action caused the delegated powers to be withdrawn, and the share was returned to the company. Just what Mohun's duties may have been during that period we do not know.

Nor is there much information about Mohun's life outside the theatre. He is known to have been one of six actors in the troupe who built three houses in the parish of St Martin-in-the-Fields about 1663. Hotson reports that one of their houses was leased on 10 June 1663 for 24 years at £24 annually to Margaret Nephway, widow. About that time Pepys noted in his diary how some of the players had grown rich and proud, and the actor Clun was said to have made a tremendous profit selling his two building shares in the Bridges Street playhouse.

Michael Mohun was a member of the church of St Giles in the Fields, and the registers there contain several references that may concern him. The earliest was dated 17 February 1664, when an "abortive" female child of "Maior Michaell Mohun" was buried. Elizabeth, daughter of "Michaell" Mohun was buried on 2 October 1672, and Jane, the daughter of Michael "Moone" was buried on 26 August 1675. "Michaell Moone," perhaps a grown son, was buried on 2 December 1679. Mohun's wife was the former Ann Bird, daughter of the actor Theophilus Bird, who had performed with Mohun before the wars. As will be seen later, the actor and his wife were both buried at St Giles in later years. The *Survey of London* states that "Major Moone" lived in Russell Street, Covent Garden, in 1665 and in Bow Street in the same parish from 1671 to 1676.

In late 1667 something caused Mohun to cease acting. On 7 December Pepys noted that the King's Company had been silenced due to some difference between Hart and Mohun, and a Lord Chamberlain's warrant exactly a week later stated that Mohun was not to be paid for "the tyme he was absent from playeing." Just what happened and how long Mohun was inactive is not known.

Comments on Mohun's acting are rare and not always very descriptive. Pepys saw *Othello* on 6 February 1669 and found it "ill-acted in most parts; Mohun, which did a little surprise me, not acting Iago's part by much as well as Clun used to do. . . ." Mohun's Melantius in *The Maid's Tragedy*, especially in the 1660s and 1670s when Hart also acted, brought praise in later years from Rymer: "Both our *AEsopus* and *Roscius* are on the Stage together; Mr. *Hart* and Mr. *Mohun* are wanting in Nothing. To these we owe for what is Pleasing in every Scene wherin they appear."

After the loss by fire of their Bridges Street playhouse the King's Company moved to the Lincoln's Inn Fields Theatre, which had been vacated by the Duke's players when their new house in Dorset Garden opened in 1671. The first performance at the old tennis court theatre was on 26 February 1672, a month after the Bridges Street fire, with Charles II in the audience. *Wit Without Money* was presented, with Mohun as Valentine (Langbaine later called him "that compleat Actor" in that part) and speaker of the prologue. "The Curtaine being drawne up," stated an anonymous writer in a Sloane manuscript of the prologue, "all the Actors were discover'd on the stage in Melancholick postures, & Moone advancing before the rest speaks as follows, addressing himself chiefly to ye King." The troupe was in a melancholy position indeed. The building shares dropped in value (Mohun sold his two to John Tombes), and the company faced the expense of erecting a new playhouse or staying at Lincoln's Inn Fields. Forced to compete with the new and lavish Dorset Garden Theatre, they probably felt they had no choice but to raise money for a new building.

Until their new playhouse, Drury Lane, on the site of the Bridges Street Theatre, was ready for occupancy, the King's troupe performed at Lincoln's Inn Fields, where Mohun is known to have acted Rhodophil in *Marriage à la Mode*, Sebastiano in *The Maides Revenge*, the Duke of Mantona in *The Assignation*, and Mr Beamont in *Amboyna*. Mohun continued a sharer in the acting company, but the new building investors were, for the most part, business men and not players. The acting sharers agreed with the new group of building investors to act at Drury Lane and pay to the investors a rental which ultimately came to £5 14s. per acting day, according to Hotson.

On 26 March 1674 the new house opened with *The Beggar's Bush*; Mohun spoke a prologue by Dryden which apologized for the austerity of the new house (in comparison, evidently, with the more opulent Dorset Garden Theatre). Mohun's first known role at the new theatre was Britannicus in *Nero* on 16 May, though he very likely acted in the opening production and others that followed. He continued at Drury Lane to the end of his career. His known new parts were the title role in *Brennoralt* (according to notes in a Bodleian copy), Pinchwife in *The Country Wife*, Hannibal in *Sophonisba*, Tribultio in *Love in the Dark*, probably Acius in *Lucina's Rape* (that was the intended casting), the old Emperor in *Aureng-Zebe*, Augustus Caesar in *Gloriana*, the high priest Matthias in both parts of *The Destruction of Jerusalem*, Clytus in *The Rival Queens*, Edgar in *King Lear and Alfreda*, Ventidius in *All for Love*, the title role in *Mithridates*, Breakbond in *The Man of Newmarket*, Sir Wilding Frollick in *Trick for Trick*, Burleigh in *The Unhappy Favorite*, and Ismael in *The Loyal Brother*. (A manuscript cast in a Yale copy of *A King and No King* names Mohun as Mardonius, a role he had played for years, and the date of the cast would appear to have been 1682–83, when the two patent houses had combined into the United Company, though Mohun is thought to have retired before the union.)

As before, Mohun was involved, but we cannot always tell how deeply, in the day-to-day operation of the King's Company and its finances. On 20 March 1674 the troupe decided that the new Drury Lane Theatre, which opened six days later, needed a new addition for the storage of scenery and costumes. Mohun, who still held one and a quarter acting shares, invested £200 in the new scene house, the total cost of which, Hotson reports, came to £2040.

By 1675 the sharing actors were making little profit. In January they gave up half their profits to help pay company debts, and later some of them threatened to cease acting. The Killigrews persuaded the sharers to enter into a new agreement on 1 May 1676. According to information revealed in a 1696 law suit, the new articles provided that each whole sharer, after three months' notice, should have 5s. each acting day for life and £100 to his executors upon his death. That was in lieu of £1 12s. 4d. each acting day until a sharer's contribution of £160 was repaid. In Mohun's case, since he held one and a quarter shares, his daily fee was to have been 6s. 3d. The new arrangement also involved Thomas Killigrew giving over to his young son Charles the patent and governorship of the company. When Thomas failed to do so, on 9 September 1676 the Lord Chamberlain put the actors Hart, Mohun, and Kynaston in charge of the company as a committee of control. Soon after that Hart was made sole manager.

Though Hart replaced the trio, Mohun's name was regularly cited in connection with company affairs. For example, on 8 August 1677 he and three other leading players were ordered, for the company, to pay a debt to the scene painters Aggas and Towers; the following November a similar order concerned pay-

ment of a debt to Robert Baden, possibly for costumes; another warrant on 5 April 1678 named Hart and Mohun as defendants in a case taken to court by (Thomas?) Jolly for clothes; on 19 April Mohun and two other actors posted a £500 bond to assure that costumes would not be taken out of the theatre; about 1678 Mohun was one of the players named in a complaint against Dryden for not living up to his agreement to provide them with plays; and on 30 October 1679 Mohun was named by the Lord Chamberlain to get from Charles Killigrew an inventory of the company stock Killigrew had taken from the theatre.

Mohun was perhaps 60 years old in 1676, and the records indicate that he was not quite as active on stage as he had been, partly, we know, because of gout. The epilogue to *Love in the Dark* referred to it:

Those Blades indeed, but cripples in their art,—
Mimic his foot, but not his speaking part.

Yet his powers were still great. When Mohun played Mithridates in February 1678, said the prompter Downes, "An Eminent Poet [probably Lee] seeing him Act this . . . vented suddenly this Saying: Oh Mohun, Mohun! Thou little Man of Mettle, if I should write a 100 Plays, I'd [always] Write a Part for thy Mouth. . . ." In short, said Downes, "in all his Parts, he was most Accurate and Correct."

On 14 December 1678 Mohun wrote a letter to Secretary Williamson in connection with the King's order after the Popish Plot that all Papists should stay at least 10 miles from London and Westminster. Mohun, though he buried his offspring at St Giles in the Fields, was a Catholic:

So soon as the proclamation came forth to banish all Popish recusants from the City, I waited twice on his Majesty to know his pleasure whether I should go or stay, for if I went, the play-house must of necessity lie still, I having so great an employment in it, on which consideration his Majesty ordered me to stay and he would protect me, on which I delivered a petition to his Majesty in Council to remind him of his gracious promise, and he and the Council ordered me a license to stay in town, which is ready drawn up in the office, but being lame of the gout makes me incapable of getting it signed myself. My humble request is that you would the next Council further it with your gracious assistance and I am sure it will be done. (Transcribed by Blackburne Daniell in the *Calendar of State Papers Domestic*.)

It may be that by that time Mohun was, as J. H. Wilson suggested in his biography of the actor Goodman, stage manager of the King's troupe. He surely could not do much acting if his gout kept him from getting his petition signed.

By March 1679, when *The Ambitious Statesman* was probably performed, the prologue commented sadly on Hart (who was afflicted with the stone and gravel) and Mohun:

In our poor Play-house fallen to the ground,
The Times Neglect, and Maladies have thrown
The two great Pillars of our Play-house down.

Mohun acted little between 1679 and 1682, and when the two rival troupes were joined in the latter year, the control of the United Company was in the hands of old Duke's Company members.

In late 1682 Mohun petitioned the King for a pension:

That yo˚ pet˚ hath faithfully served yo˚ Maᵗᵉ & Father (of ever Blessed Memory) 48 yeares in yᵉ quality of an Actor, and in all yᵉ Warrs in England & Ireland & at yᵉ Seege of Dublin was desperately wounded & 13 monethes a Prisoner, and after that yo˚ pet˚ served yo˚ Maᵗᵉ in yᵉ Regmᵗ of Dixmeaᵈ in Flanders & came over with yo˚ Maᵗᵉ into England where yo˚ Sacred Pleasure was that he should Act againe, as he hath ever since vpon all Occasions continued. That it being yo˚ Maᵗᵉˢ Pleasure to reduce the two companyes into one yᵗ pet˚ is deprived of his share and quarter in yᵉ Scenes Clothes & playes (that cost about 4000ˡˡ) by Mʳ Charles Killigrew who has rented them to mʳ Davenant for a share (as yo˚ pet˚ is informed) and tells him if yo˚ pet˚ hath any right theirto he must gett it by law. And instead of a share & quarter wᶜʰ yo˚ pet˚ had formerly in yo˚ Maᵗᵉˢ Company for Acting he is now only proffered 20ˢ a day when they haue occasion to vse him, soe that they hauing not studyed Our [i.e. King's Company] Playes nor yo˚ pet˚ therein he cannot conceaue the same will amount to aboue 20ˡˡ p anº Wherefore yo˚ pet˚ most humbly prayes That yo˚ Maᵗᵉ will be graciously pleased to Order the p˚sent Company to allow him the same Conditions as Mʳ Hart and Mʳ Kinaston haue, (whos Shares were all equall before) whereby he may be enabled to support himself & 5 children And yo˚ pet˚ shall as in duty bond pray &c.

His request was granted on 23 November 1682, and on 5 December a second order stated that

Mohun should be employed and given his old parts to act.

Perhaps, as we have noted earlier, he acted in *A King and No King* in 1682–83, but proof is lacking, and no other records indicate any activity by him after the granting of his petition. Michael Mohun died at his house in Brownlow Street (now Betterton Street) and was buried at St Giles in the Fields on 11 October 1684. His widow Ann was buried there on 2 January 1702.

On 25 November 1709 the *Tatler* praised "My old friends, Hart and Mohun, the one by his natural and proper force, the other by his great skill and art, never failed to send me home full of such ideas as affected my behaviour, and made me insensibly more courteous and humane to my friends and acquaintances." But it was a comment of the actor William Mountfort that probably would have pleased Mohun most; in his dedication to Powell's *The Treacherous Brothers* in 1690 Mountfort wrote: "Heaven bless Mohun and Heaven bless Hart, the good actors that got [playwrights] their good third days; and who were consequently more substantial Patrons than the greatest name in the frontispiece of a dedication."

A portrait of Mohun, dating about 1660 and sometimes attributed to Kneller, is in the collection at Knole. A copy, engraved by E. Harding, Jr, was published as a plate to Harding's *Biographical Mirrour*, 1793; a copy by an unknown engraver was published by H. Rodd, 1822.

Moisson. *See* MORRISON.

Mojon, Mr ₍*fl.* 1791₎, *dancer.*
William Smith in *The Italian Opera in London* lists a Mr Mojon as a dancer at the new King's Theatre from 26 March to 6 June 1791.

Molbery, Mr ₍*fl.* 1782₎, *actor.*
Mr Molbery played the Lord Mayor in a single performance of *Richard III* at the Haymarket Theatre on 4 March 1782.

"Molière of His Age, The." *See* FOOTE, SAMUEL.

Molini, Signor [*fl.* 1785–1797?], *singer, acting manager, composer?*

In the Public Record Office is a transcript of salaries of King's Theatre singers under Gallini's management in which Molini is set down for the modest sum of £52 10*s*. in the 1785–86 season. His name is not found in any opera bills known to us; he must have been an obscure member of the chorus. In 1786–87, however, according to *The London Stage*, Molini shared the duties of acting manager with Badini, Carnevale, and Johnson. In a letter (in the Folger Library) dated "Sept 1794" from the singer Mme Mara to the actress Jane Pope, Molini's address was given as No 14, Hanover Street, Hanover Square.

Perhaps he was the "Sig" Molini who was the composer of *The Fife Hunt, a favourite Scotch air* and *Of noble race was Shenkin . . . Welch air*, both of which were published in *The Piano-Forte Magazine* in 1797.

Molini, Miss [*fl.* 1797–1800], *actress.*

The "young Lady" who made her first appearance on the Drury Lane stage on 17 February 1798 in the role of Miss Peggy in *The Country Girl* was identified by J. P. Kemble's notation on his playbill as Miss Molini. The *Monthly Visitor* of February 1798 reported that she had been instructed by Mrs Jordan, under whose tuition she had performed at the Richmond Theatre the previous summer. The *Monthly Mirror* of that March found her performance "regulated by a studied anxiety to be *as like* our great comic actress as possible; and if there was any native dramatic genius at all, it was trammelled and biased so as to be rendered comfortable to the model." She was described by that journal as possessing

an engaging countenance, and a figure that becomes the male attire; her voice is powerful, and not unmusical, but she has a habit of mumbling which affects her articulation; and her action has all the redundancy and awkwardness of inexperience. This lady performed once or twice last summer, at the Richmond Theatre, under the patronage of the Duke of Queensberry.

Miss Molini, again advertised only as a young lady, made her second appearance at Drury Lane the following season on 28 November 1798, as Little Pickle in *The Spoil'd Child*. The December *Monthly Mirror* regretted having to

confirm its earlier opinion: "she is the neatest figure, in male attire, we have ever beheld; and she has some theatrical talents; but, at present, this is all we are justified in stating." She repeated Little Pickle on 1 December, and acted Miss Peggy again on 21 December 1798, when her name first appeared in the bills. The last performance for which she was advertised was as Miss Peggy on 18 January 1799, but she probably played some small, unnoticed roles that season in order to earn the £3 per week (or 10*s*. per night) which the paylist indicated she received. Though she was not at Drury Lane in 1799–1800, she was paid £5 5*s*. on 25 January 1800 on account of arrears for the previous season.

"Molipitano, Claudio" [*fl.* 1751], *performer?*

At Christopher Smart's zany production called *The Old Woman's Oratory* at the Castle Tavern on 3 December 1751, "Claudio Molipitano" entertained the audience with "Candles snuffed to soft Musick." The bill did not make clear whether Molipitano was a candle snuffer or a musician or both. In any case, his name was doubtless a Smart concoction.

"Moll, Orange." *See* MEGGS, MARY.

Molloy, Mrs Francis. *See* WHEELER, ELIZA.

Molton, Mr [*fl.* 1795], *scene painter?*

A surviving paylist in the British Library (MS 29949) reveals that a Mr Molton was paid £52 10*s*. by Covent Garden Theatre in June 1795 for painting.

Monanni, Angiolo. *See* "MANZOLETTO."

Monari. *See* FABRIS MONARI.

Mönch. *See* MOENCH.

Monck. *See also* MONK.

Monck, Mr [*fl.* 1760–1770], *house servant.*

The Covent Garden Theatre accounts show payments to Mr Monck in January 1760; he received £20 on the fifth for 80 days of work, and on the twelfth he was down for a weekly salary of £1 10s. A decade later, on 5 April 1770, "Monk" was paid £2 12s. 6d. for "mending the Owl & new Spring." He was evidently a house servant working backstage.

Monck, Mr *d. 1770, organist.*

The *Gentleman's Magazine* reported that Mr Monck, organist of the King's chapel at Whitehall, died on 8 February 1770.

Monday. *See also* MUNDAY.

Monday, Mrs [*fl. 1794*], *singer.*

Doane's *Musical Directory* of 1794 listed Mrs Monday of Oxford as a soprano who sang at Ranelagh Gardens in London.

Mondini, Signor [*fl. 1755–1756*], *singer.*

On 17 March 1755 at the King's Theatre benefit for indigent musicians Signor Mondini sang "Non pensi." Dr Burney said Mondini had "a baritono voice, between a tenor and base" and was one of the singers at the opera house who "brought up the rear." Signora Mondini was slightly higher on the scale. She sang Adrastus in *L'Ipermestra* on 9 November 1754, had a vocal part in a "Concerto Spirituale" at Drury Lane on 2 April 1756 (Mondini sang in a quartet), sang a song at the annual King's Theatre benefit on 5 April, and was Decius in *Tito Manlio* at the King's on 10 April.

Mondini, Signora [*fl. 1754–1756*], *singer.* *See* MONDINI, SIGNOR.

Mondozie, Miss [*fl. 1748*], *dancer.*

Miss Mondozie danced with Nicholson between the acts at the Haymarket Theatre on 2 May 1748.

Monet or **Monette.** *See* MONNET.

Monetti, Signor [*fl. 1783–1784*], *dancer.*

Signor Monetti danced at the King's Theatre from 6 December 1783 to 3 February 1784, appearing in *The Pastimes of Terpsycore* and a pas de deux with Zuchelli.

Money, Mr [*fl. 1782*], *actor.*

The principal characters in *Love at a Venture* at the Haymarket Theatre on 21 March 1782 were taken by "performers engaged from different Theatres." One of the actors was Mr Money, but from what theatre he came the bill did not say.

Monfort. *See* MOUNTFORT.

Monger, John [*fl. 1739*], *musician.*

John Monger was one of the original subscribers to the Royal Society of Musicians when it was established on 28 August 1739.

Monk. *See also* MONCK.

Monk, Mr [*fl. 1749*], *actor.*

Mr Monk played a Recruit in *The Recruiting Officer* at Southwark on 9 January 1749.

Monk, Mrs [*fl. 1774?–1798?*], *actress.*

The Mrs Monk who acted in Birmingham in August 1774 may have been the Mrs Monk who appeared at Hammersmith from 17 June to 27 July 1795 as Mrs Gadabout in *The Lying Valet*, Cicely in *The Quaker*, Lady Randolph in *Douglas*, Deborah in *Love in a Village*, the title role in *Jane Shore*, Gimp in *Bon Ton*, Lady Sycamore in *The Maid of the Mill*, Mrs Heidelberg in *The Clandestine Marriage*, Mysis in *Midas*, the Duenna in *The Spanish Fryar*, Marcelina in *The Follies of a Day*, Mrs Hardcastle in *She Stoops to Conquer*, and the Old Lady in *Robinson Crusoe*. The same Mrs Monk, perhaps, played Miss Neville in *Know Your Own Mind* and Louisa in *No Song No Supper* on 19 October 1791 at Bristol and was at St Albans, Hertfordshire, in November 1792.

It is likely that our subject was the Mrs Monk who performed in Richardson's troupe at Bartholomew Fair in 1798. The manager said,

I had a great run of business; in fact, we were compelled to perform twenty-one times in a day, so numerous were the visitors. I cannot say much in favour of the pieces, as each audience did not fail to abuse us as they left the house; poor old Mrs Monk generally got upon the garret stairs to cool herself, and, as the spectators had to pass her in going out, she was generally saluted with many "damns!" and "you old bitch, you have taken us in!" Mrs Monk was a good-natured creature, and her only reply was, "What can you expect, gentlemen, at a fair?" Upon the whole, our performances passed off tolerably quiet.

Monlass, Mr ₁*fl. 1733–1735*₁, *actor, singer.*

Mr Monlass was first noticed in London bills on 10 December 1733, when he played Pedro in *The Wonder* at the Goodman's Fields playhouse. Through 17 May 1734 he appeared also as Metaphrastus in *The Mistake*, Diana in *The Beggar's Opera* (his wife played Mrs Peachum), the Bookseller in *The Committee*, Foigard in *The Stratagem*, Old Hob in *Flora*, a Citizen in *Julius Caesar*, Prim in *The Lover's Opera*, a Witch in *Macbeth*, an Attendant and a Grenadier in *Britannia*, and Wilful in *The Double Gallant*. In June 1734 he went over to the Haymarket Theatre to play Mouldy in *The Humours of Sir John Falstaff* and then Sir Jasper in *The Mock Doctor* and Diana in *The Beggar's Opera Tragediz'd*. *The London Stage* lists Monlass as singing at Covent Garden Theatre in 1733–34, but we could not find his name in the bills.

Monlass was again at Goodman's Fields in 1734–35, playing such new roles as an Egg Woman in *Britannia*, Bardolph in *1 Henry IV*, Mrs Fardingale in *The Funeral*, a Murderer in *Macbeth*, Argus in *Jupiter and Io*, and Tom in *The Constant Couple*. His last notice was on 5 May 1735, when he was a Bravo in *The Inconstant*. Mr and Mrs Monlass had a son who appeared at Goodman's Fields in February and March 1735.

Monlass, Mrs ₁*fl. 1733–1735*₁, *actress, singer.*

The career of Mrs Monlass paralleled that of her husband, though she played more roles of importance than he. She first appeared at Goodman's Fields Theatre, on 11 December 1733, as Inis in *The Wonder*. During the rest of the 1733–34 season she was seen as the Player Queen in *Hamlet*, Isabella in *The Mistake*, Mrs Peachum in *The Beggar's Opera*, Lucinda in *Don Quixote*, Hob's Mother in *Flora*, Lucy in *The Recruiting Officer*, Phillida in *Damon and Phillida*, Regan in *King Lear*, Altea in *Rule a Wife and Have a Wife*, and Tattleaid in *The Funeral*. In June 1734 she acted at the Haymarket Theatre, playing the Hostess in *The Humours of Sir John Falstaff*, Dorcas in *The Mock Doctor*, Mrs Stocks in *The Lottery*, Mrs Motherly in *The Provok'd Husband*, and Lady Bountiful in *The Stratagem*.

At Goodman's Fields in 1734–35 she added such new roles as Mrs Sealand in *The Conscious Lovers*, an Attendant in *Jupiter and Io* (in which her son played Cupid), Parly in *The Constant Couple*, and Jenny in *The Beggar's Opera*. Her last appearance seems to have been in *The Mistake* on 1 May 1735.

Monlass, Master ₁*fl. 1735*₁, *actor.*

Master Monlass played Cupid in *Jupiter and Io* at Goodman's Fields Theatre from 27 February to 4 March 1735. His parents also acted at that house.

Monnet, Jean Louis *1703?–1785, manager.*

Hedgcock in *Garrick and His French Friends* states that Jean Louis Monnet was born at Condrieux, on the Rhone, in 1703, though Campardon in *Les Spectacles de la Foire* dates Monnet's birth "vers 1710." Monnet was the

Harvard Theatre Collection

JEAN LOUIS MONNET
engraving by Saint-Aubin, after Cochin

son of a poor baker, but through Parisian friends he became a page in the household of the Duchesse de Berry. After his patroness died Monnet tried his hand at printing and writing, considered becoming a Trappist monk, spent some time in the Bastille because of his infamous verses and songs, and, in 1743, became Director of the failing Opéra Comique. He rebuilt its reputation by attracting to it the comedian Préville, the author and stage manager Simon Favart, the composer Rameau, the designer Boucher, and the ballet master Dupré (who brought with him the young Noverre). The Opéra Comique did so well against the Comédie Française and the Comédie Italienne that the rival houses managed to have Monnet's privilege taken away, and the Opéra Comique closed.

Monnet found a new position in Lyons, as director of the theatre there, a post he occupied in 1745–46. By 1747 he was again in Paris, and in August 1748, according to his *Mémoires*, Monnet began negotiations with John Rich, manager of Covent Garden Theatre. Rich had proposed through Owen Swiney that Monnet should form a company of French players and perform for a season in London. Monnet anticipated that the cost of the venture would be about £3000 and estimated that a year would be required to make the necessary arrangements. Monnet came to London, armed with letters of support from the Maréchal de Saxe and Lord Stafford. He conferred with Rich, who suggested that Monnet should bring over a troupe to perform from October 1748 to Lent 1749 at Lincoln's Inn Fields Theatre, alternating with an English company. Rich agreed to advance money for salaries; the expenses of the venture (and presumably the profits) would be shared by Monnet and Rich.

Monnet, though he had originally felt that a year of planning would be required, quickly wrote to several actors in France, offering them salaries and committing himself up to £1000. At a second conference with Rich it was decided that the French performers would act twice a week at Covent Garden rather than on alternating days at the old Lincoln's Inn Fields. That must have pleased Monnet, and he beckoned his players to set out for London. Later, when he asked Rich for a written contract to ensure his actors' salaries, Rich, "having consulted his friends upon this undertaking," according to *An Impartial State of the Case* (1750), "sent him word that he would not be concerned in it, for fear it might prejudice him with the public." Rich was probably right; England and France had only recently signed a peace, and anti-Gallic sentiment was still high.

Monnet applied to Garrick at Drury Lane but was turned down, and the gallant Frenchman said Garrick's refusal was "for reasons which I could not but approve; he gave me, too, advice worthy of all the uprightness and honourableness of which I have had full experience from him since then." Garrick and others suggested to Monnet that he and his troupe should perform at the Haymarket Theatre. A license was granted him by the Lord Chamberlain on 23 March 1749, and when the subscription brought in £294, Monnet felt secure in bringing over his players. They arrived in the fall of 1749.

Not only was there anti-Gallic sentiment among some Londoners, but the passage of the Licensing Act 12 years earlier had been a blow to many English players who had managed to survive by performing at the very theatre which was now closed to them but open to Monnet's foreign company. French Huguenots, in forced exile in London since the revocation of the Edict of Nantes, were also against Monnet's Catholic performers and saw an opportunity to revenge themselves. The press was also alive with stories of English actors being refused opportunities to perform in France. On 14 November 1749 Monnet's troupe opened at the Haymarket with *Le Coq du village* and *Les Amans réunis*. In the audience were many subscribers who were anxious to support the visiting actors, but there were many, too, who had no intention of allowing the performance to take place.

In his *Mémoires* Monnet told what happened. At six in the evening, by which time the galleries were crowded with French refugees, Lord "G." and 30 other gentlemen equipped with canes arrived. Lord G. and Duke "D." stationed themselves in upper boxes, where they could keep an eye on the gallery. Only three women were in the audience, two actresses and a lady of quality. When the overture began the men in the gallery began chanting "We don't want French comedians." The curtain rose, and the first performers to appear, an actor and an actress, were greeted with apples and oranges. The actress was hit in the throat by a candle. Lord G. pleaded for quiet and assured the rioters that their money would be returned if they left peacefully. When his plea fell on deaf ears he and other gentlemen went up to the gallery and imposed silence with their canes.

Soldiers with drawn swords arrived and formed a line on stage to protect the players, while a fight broke out in the pit, instigated by two Englishmen who were attached to Monnet's troupe. The two toughs managed to frighten everyone into silence and the two plays were then performed without interruption.

L'Ecole des femmes was announced for the second night. The gentlemen this time brought a group of rugged, armed river boatmen in livery and stationed them about the auditorium. Soon fighting began, with some people in the gallery throwing themselves into the pit below to avoid being struck. The actresses, with officers to protect them, took refuge in the boxes. The anti-Gallic forces were again defeated, and the show went on. The rioters did not return for the third and fourth performances.

On 22 November 1749 the troupe could not perform, because it was the birthday of the Prince of Wales; and they had to cancel the performance scheduled for the twenty-fourth, because an actor was ill. Then the Westminster parliamentary election, which went on for a month, defeated Monnet further, for one of the candidates, Lord Trentham, had supported the French players, and their presence in town became a political issue. The papers were full of the controversy. A satirical print showing Britannia nursing Rich and Garrick had her say, "Lunn & Frible are my only Theatrical Children. I will Cherish no French vagrants." Finally, to avoid more turmoil, the King ordered the Lord Chamberlain to withdraw Monnet's license.

Monnet was left with a company of 15 who now demanded their pay. He followed the advice of friends and went to debtor's prison (with one of his actresses); he was permitted the liberty of the town as long as he was with a guard, paid for by Monnet. According to a news clipping of 14 May 1750, transcribed by Latreille, Monnet was in confinement four months. He was aided financially by Lord Stafford, an unnamed member of Parliament, the Duke of Grafton (the Lord Chamberlain, who loaned him about £59), and Garrick (who arranged a benefit for Monnet at Drury Lane).

The benefit was given on 21 May 1750, the last day of the season, and the bill carried the following plea:

Mr Monnet, the innocent tho' unfortunate cause of disgusting the Public by his attempting to represent French Plays, most humbly implores their assistance, by the means of this Benefit Play, to extricate him out of his present most deplorable situation. Without such relief his Misfortunes must detain him a ruined Man in England; a severity which he is persuaded never was proposed as any part of the purpose of the most disoblig'd, or determined against his Undertaking. With this relief he hopes to be able to return to France, and promises never again to risque their favours. He most submissively hopes he shall not be the only the single instance that may seem to contradict the hitherto unimpeached GOOD NATURE and HUMANITY, which is universally acknowledged the Characteristic of the English Nation.

The receipts came to a disappointing £120. According to an account in French and English, now at the Bibliothèque National, Monnet had expenses (salaries, rental of the Haymarket, his own travel expenses and lodging, etc.) of £2157 1s. From 56 subscriptions, box office receipts from the four Haymarket performances, and a subscription raised by Mr Arthur, master of White's Chocolate House, Monnet's receipts came to £850 8s. 4d.

That account, made up after the event in France, apparently, stated that "Mr Monnet is entirely out of Pocket [£1306 12s. 8d.], besides two Years and a half of his Time spent for it." Another benefit was held for Monnet, at Covent Garden on 15 January 1751. He was able to recover at least some of his losses, but how much is not clear. Some sources suggest that Monnet returned to France about April 1750, but the newspapers in May made it sound as though he was still in England when his first benefit was given, and he may have remained for the second one. To recoup their losses, his troupe gave five performances in the spring of 1750, but Monnet himself may not have had anything to do with those presentations.

Monnet was reappointed director of the Opéra Comique (in 1752 say Campardon and Hedgcock, in 1754 says Sybil Rosenfeld in

Foreign Theatrical Companies). He held that post until 1757, after which he retired from the theatre.

During his stay in England Monnet had become a close friend of David Garrick, and after his return to France he served Garrick in a variety of ways. They exchanged letters frequently, and Garrick saved a number of his French friend's replies. They show that Monnet befriended Garrick by mollifying Frenchmen whom Garrick had offended by not replying at once to their letters, gathering information about theatrical equipment, auditioning French dancers and arranging contracts for engagements in England, showing Garrick's friends around Paris, arranging for the education of Garrick's nieces, supplying Mrs Garrick with dress materials and style books, recommending to Garrick artists, musicians, pyrotechnists, jewelers, and cooks, and serving generally as a factotum for his English friend. Clothes that Garrick had left with Monnet in Paris Monnet wore—they were a perfect fit, he said—and Monnet promised to buy Garrick a new suit on his next visit to France. It was Monnet who arranged for the ballet master Noverre to join Garrick in 1755 at Drury Lane to produce his *Chinese Festival*—which aroused another wave of anti-Gallic sentiment and was withdrawn after six performances.

Garrick wrote George Colman on 27 January 1765:

This brings me to mention the former Director of yᵉ Comic Operas, our old Friend Monet, He is yᵉ gayest man at Paris— He has got enough by his Operas to live happily, he has honorably paid all his debts that his unfortunate expedition to London brought upon him, He is greatly belov'd by the Men of Wit & Pleasure who have assisted him in collecting materials for three Volˢ of the most chosen Songs in the french language—it will be a compleet history of their Lyric poetry— He has great taste himself & he began his Collection, when he was yᵉ Manager of Operas— His Engravings for yᵉ Musick, his elegant designs exquisitely executed, with the happy choice of the poetry, will make a very great addition to yᵉ Musical Library— the songs are all now set by yᵉ best Masters here [in Paris]—pray recommend them as warmly to yʳ Friends as I most sincerely & warmly to you—

Monnet's book was *Anthologie françoise ou chansons choises, depuis le XIIIᵉ siècle jusqu'a present*,

which Garrick promoted in London with puffs in the *St James's Chronicle* and the *Public Advertiser*.

Monnet's letters, as translated by Hedgcock, show him to have been a man for all seasons, very knowledgeable about theatrical matters and blessed with a chatty, pleasant personality. For example, for Garrick he procured some lighting equipment, and on 15 June 1765, by which time Garrick had returned to London, he wrote:

. . . I will send you a reflector and two different samples of the lamp you want for the footlights at your theatre. There are two kinds of reflectors: those that are placed in a niche in the wall, and which have one wick; and those which are hung up like a chandelier, and which have five; the first, which are, I fancy, the more suitable for the illumination of your hall, cost twelve shillings and sixpence, and the others from thirty shillings up to three pounds, according to the size and the ornaments applied to them. . . . As to the lamps for lighting your stage, they are of two kinds: some are of earthenware, and in biscuit form; they have six or eight wicks, and you put oil in them; the others are of tin, in the shape of a candle, with a spring, and you put candles in them. The first are less costly, and give more light. But for them not to smell, you must use the best oil and keep the lamps very clean.

He was similarly helpful in providing Garrick with information on other technical matters.

Monnet was responsible not only for bringing Garrick and Noverre together (which led to a fiasco) but for introducing the scene designer De Loutherbourg to the London manager in 1771 (which led to some of the most important advances of the century in English technical theatre). Monnet visited London in 1766, and during his stay Garrick offered him the use of his Southampton Street house, entertained Monnet at Hampton, and took him to Bath. In 1771 Monnet lost part of his fortune (Garrick immediately offered financial help), and to recoup some of his losses published his *Mémoires*.

Monnet's last letter to Garrick was dated 4 December 1778, from Soissons, Rue St Leger. He inquired for his friend's health, gave him all the latest news from France, and conveyed Madame Monnet's compliments to the Garricks. The Englishman's health was, in fact, very poor. Garrick died the following 20 January 1779. Jean Louis Monnet died in 1785.

A portrait of Jean Monnet by C. H. Cochin was engraved by Auguste de Saint-Aubin in 1765.

Monro. *See also* MONROE and MUNRO.

Monro, Mr ₁*fl. 1794*₁, *oboist.*

Doane's *Musical Directory* of 1794 listed a Mr "Munro" of Lincoln as an oboist who played in the Handel concerts at Westminster Abbey. The oboist was very likely the father of the pianist Henry Monro. Henry provided the musical biographer Sainsbury with a brief autobiographical sketch in which he noted that he was the son of a Lincoln musician. (Grove may be incorrect in giving Henry's birthdate as 1774; that was the year the violinist Samuel Munro was born. But Henry Monro was still serving his apprenticeship in the early 1790s in London, so he, too, may have been born in 1774.)

Monro, George *c. 1700–1731, organist, harpsichordist, composer.*

Deutsch in his *Handel* conjectures that George Monro (or Monroe) was born about 1700. James Bridges, the Duke of Chandos, said that "this young genius [was] of very good family—one of the Monroes in Scotland." The Duke engaged young George as a page at Cannons in 1714, but upon discovering the boy's talent in music, he placed him under Handel and Pepusch, "& he hath been so successful in his improvement . . . that he is become, though young, a perfect master both for composition & performance on the organ & harpsichord." Monro's wages at Cannons came to £7 10s. per quarter.

In January 1723 the Duke of Chandos recommended Monro as organist for a chapel which a Mr Mitchell had built, and in 1724 he recommended the young man to the Bishop of London, suggesting that George be made organist of "the Banquetting House." At some point Monro was made organist of St Peter, Cornhill, though the registers there do not mention him. On 16 March 1722 at Hickford's Music Room Monro played harpsichord pieces for his own benefit, and he is known to have performed on the harpsichord again on 13 March 1728 at a concert at York Buildings.

In 1729 he began playing in the band at the Goodman's Fields Theatre, and there he remained until his death two years later. Several of Monro's songs were published in *Musical Miscellany* in 1731.

Monroe. *See also* MONRO and MUNRO.

Monroe, George *d. 1671, trumpeter.*

George Monroe was a trumpeter in the King's Musick and accompanied Lord Howard, ambassador to Morocco, on a trip there from 10 June 1669 to 25 August 1670. Monroe was granted £20 for the journey, supposedly over and above his regular salary as a court musician, and from his will we learn that he was to have been paid still more for his trip. Monroe drew up his will on 10 February 1671 just before his death. In it he described himself as a trumpeter to his Majesty from the parish of St Margaret, Westminster, and he requested burial in the chapel yard. His worldly goods were to be divided between his executors, John Wright and Daniell Monroe. An inventory of his estate had been made on 3 January 1671; included were Monroe's clothes, "A garnish Trumpett," "A Brasse Trumpett," and a list of debtors: "John Crowder his Maᵗˢ Trumpett in Ordinary, owes me a Pistoll of Gold," "The Serjeant Trumpett of England Scotland and Ireland, does owe me seven & Thirty pounds, for my going my Journey with the Lord Howard," "Owing to me from yᵉ Lord of Carbrow [?] for Wages . . . fforty Seaven pounds," and "Nyne Pistolls of Gold & one Jacobus in my owne Custody." Monroe signed the will with his mark. On 16 February 1671 the will was proved by his executors.

Mons, Signora ₁*fl. 1717–1719*₁, *singer.*

A benefit concert was held at Hickford's Music Room on 10 April 1717 for "Mrs" Mons, and at a second one there the following 18 December Signora Mons sang. She had a benefit at York Buildings on 27 March 1718 and another at the King's Theatre on 25 April 1719.

Monsett, Mme ₁*fl. 1792–1793*₁, *dancer.*

Mme Monsett danced at Sadler's Wells in 1792 and 1793. Her roles included a Savage Princess in *The Savages* in 1792 and America in *The Hall of Augusta* in 1793, according to the cast lists in the published versions of those entertainments.

Monsett, Peter   [*fl.* 1685], *trumpeter.*

Peter Monsett (or Mounset) marched in the coronation procession of James II on 23 April 1685, though he was not sworn a trumpeter in the King's Musick until 12 June.

Monson, Mr   [*fl.* 1670], *performer?*

A Lord Chamberlain's warrant of 11 or 12 August 1670 ordered the apprehension of Mr Monson for absenting himself from his duties (unspecified) at the Duke's Company at the Lincoln's Inn Fields playhouse.

Monson, Charles   [*fl.* 1691], *singer.*

On 8 December 1691 a livery allowance was paid to Charles Monson, a Chapel Royal chorister whose voice had broken; it was traditional to support the boys a year or two after they left the Chapel.

"Monstrous Craws, The"   [*fl.* 1787], *curiosities.*

Three South American dwarfs, two females and a male, evidently goitered Indians, were exhibited under the name of "The Monstrous Craws" in Flockton's booth at the Peckham Fair in August 1787. Sharing the booth were fantoccini, the conjuror Mr Lane, and "Sir Jeffrey Dunstan." Contemporary reports described them as no more than four feet high, each with a monstrous craw under the throat:

Their country, language, &c. are as yet unknown to mankind. It is supposed they started in some canoe from their native place (a remote quarter in South America), and being wrecked were picked up by a Spanish vessel. At that period they were each of a dark-olive complexion, but which has astonishingly, by degrees, changed to the colour of that of Europeans. They are tractable and respectful towards strangers, and of lively and merry disposition among themselves; singing and dancing in the most extraordinary way, at the will and pleasure of the company.

A small woodcut of "the Monstrous Craws" is in an extra-illustrated volume of George Daniel's *Merrie England in the Olden Time* at the Huntington Library.

Montagnana, Antonio   [*fl.* 1730–1750], *singer.*

The basso Antonio Montagnana sang in Rome in 1730, and in Turin in 1731. He made his London debut as Timagene in Handel's *Poro* on 23 November 1731 at the King's Theatre. During the rest of his first season under Handel he sang Meraspe in *Admeto*, Varo in *Ezio*, Altomaro in *Sosarme*, Sesto Furio in *Coriolano*, Lotario in *Flavio*, Haman in *Esther*, M. Fabio in *Lucio Papiro*, and Polifemo in *Acis and Galatea*. In 1732–33 at the King's he was heard in such new roles as Cesare in *Cato*, Clitho in *Alessandro*, Araspe in *Tolomeo*, Zorastro in *Orlando*, and Abinoam and the Chief Priest in *Deborah*.

At the Lincoln's Inn Fields playhouse under Porpora's direction in 1733–34 he sang Pirito in *Arianna in Nasso*, Fenicio in *Astarto*, and Turnus in *Enea*. He was at the King's again in 1734–35, where he remained through 1737–38 singing such new roles as the title parts in *Artaserse* and *Polifemo*, Toante in *Issipile*, Calcante in *Iphigenia in Aulis*, Osroa in *Adriano*, Stilicone in *Honorio*, Archelao in *Mitridate*, Arasse in *Siroe*, Artabano in *Arsace*, Mitrane in *Demetrio*, Publio in *Tito*, Marziano in *Alessandro Severo*, and Gustavo in *Faramondo*. He was mentioned by Burney as having a very deep bass; Mrs Pendarves, writing to her sister Ann Granville on 27 November 1736 said that Montagnana "roars as usual!"

He served at the royal chapel in Madrid from 1740 until his retirement in 1750.

Montagu, Henry   [*fl.* 1669], *singer.*

Henry Montagu was one of the children of the Chapel Royal, but by 8 January 1669 his voice had broken and Henry Cooke, the master of the young choristers, was delivered clothing for Henry and other boys who had left the Chapel. A warrant in the Lord Chamberlain's accounts dated 5 April 1669 indicated that Henry's mother, Sarah, was to be paid £30 annually for her son's maintenance.

Montague, Mr. *See* TALBOT, MONTAGUE.

Montague, Constantia   [*fl.* 1775–1782], *actress.*

Constantia Montague, whom Tate Wilkinson described in his *Wandering Patentee* as "of a good family at Norwich," seems to have acted at Birmingham before she sought a job from Wilkinson at Wakefield in September 1775. On her trial night at Wakefield, she played Queen Margaret and was "as wild as an untamed colt." But Wilkinson found her promising enough to engage her at Doncaster for the winter, during which season she also appeared at Hull and York. She possessed a graceful figure and a voice "uncommonly excellent." Despite bad dialect, a "not very exact ear," and a mind not "equal to the patience of much teaching," she had the potential, thought Wilkinson, of rising to the upper ranks of the profession.

Though a member of Wilkinson's company on the Yorkshire circuit until 1779 she also acted at Bath in December 1777 and at Liverpool from June 1778 through 19 October, earning at the latter city £2 per week. In 1779 she was with Glassington's troupe at the Stourbridge Fair, Cambridge. During those years, to the dismay of her manager and the discomfiture of her colleagues, she often exhibited a fiery temper. Her insolence several times brought her the disfavor of provincial audiences. "She was of uncontroulable spirit, when provoked, even with the least reason," Wilkinson related, "and when the fury was over, was easily led, full of contrition and good humour till a new breeze fanned the fire and set the billows of her mind once more raging. . . ."

On 18 June 1779 Mrs Montague made her first appearance at the Haymarket Theatre as Mrs Oakly in *The Jealous Wife*. Next day the *Gazeteer* reported her to be:

a spirited & natural actress; her voice powerful & pleasing, & her figure extremely good, though somewhat too much *en bon point* for the general line of stage characters. In Mrs Oakly she was perfectly characteristic; suspicion & jealous rage were given in very marking colours throughout the part, & she was warmly applauded, particularly on her fainting in the last act, from which, however, her recovery seemed too sudden & complete. Whatever affectation may be suppposed in the fainting, the distress & agitation is real. She is, however, in the hands of so able an instructor [Colman?], & appears to have profited so much by his advice, that we doubt not she will rank with the most favourite performers in her line.

The press continued to praise her comic abilities in subsequent performances of *The Jealous*

Wife, describing her as buxom, with a very pretty face. On 17 July 1779 she created the role of Mrs Sharp in the premiere of Jodrell's comedy *A Widow and No Widow*, which was performed a total of 11 times that summer. But criticisms of her playing of the serious role of Editha in the premiere of Mrs Cowley's tragedy *Albina, Countess of Raimond* on 31 July 1779 were especially severe. On the second night, 2 August, according to the *Morning Chronicle* next day, some young officers were talking loudly in a side box, provoking some of the audience to hiss at them. Mrs Montague, believing the hisses were directed at herself, "burst into a flood of tears & retir'd to the back of the stage in great disorder." After a moment or two she returned, curtsied, and apologized and complained "that it was surely very hard that the editor of a newspaper should take away the character of a woman, on which she depended for her bread." After some general confusion the play resumed. Mrs Montague gave a third performance as Editha on 3 August but the play was then withdrawn to allow time to train Miss Sherry in the role. When *Albina* was brought back on 9 August, Miss Sherry was Editha, and when the play was printed she, not Mrs Montague, was listed for the role.

In the *Morning Post* on 17 August 1779 a witty poem signed "Heigh-ho" praised Miss Sherry's salvation of the play and attacked "Eumenes," a critic who had written in favor of Mrs Montague. "Heigh-ho" claimed that in the green room the actress had denounced members of the audience, and threatened, "If I had the curs here, I'd sink 'em to hell." Next morning that paper printed a statement from "C. Montague" absolutely denying having used that expression.

During the winter of 1779–80 Mrs Montague was a member of Wilkinson's company at the Theatre Royal, Shakespeare Square, Edinburgh, where on 18 December 1779 she appeared as Mrs Oakly. Her roles through March 1780 included Arpasia in *Tamerlane*, Clarinda in *The Suspicious Husband*, Horatia in *The Roman Father*, the title role in *The Irish Widow*, Lady Constance in *King John*, Louisa in *Love Makes a Man*, Lydia Languish in *The Rivals*, the title role in *Merope*, Mrs Belville in *The School for Wives*, Mrs Heidelberg in *The Clandestine Marriage*, Mrs Revel in *Separate Maintenance*, Mrs Sullen in *The Beaux' Stratagem*, Queen

Elizabeth in *Richard III*, Gertrude in *Hamlet*, Veluria in *Coriolanus*, and the title role in *Zara*.

In May 1780 she returned to the York company. We last notice her at Smock Alley, Dublin, in 1780–81 and 1781–82. A letter to the press signed by Smock Alley actors on 10 May 1781 gave her initial as E., and in his *Irish Stage in the County Towns* William Clark calls her Mrs F. Montague. Wilkinson, however, reprinted a letter from her dated 17 October 1778 and signed Constantia Montague. She died, according to Wilkinson, writing in 1795, "some years ago in Ireland."

Montevolli. *See* MONTICELLI.

Montfort. *See* MOUNTFORT.

Montgomery, Mr [*fl.* 1735–1741], *singer.*

Mr Montgomery, a Mason, sang Masonic songs at the Haymarket Theatre on 4 August 1735, Covent Garden on 29 August 1738 ("in his Tyler's Habilements"), Drury Lane on 28 May 1739, and Goodman's Fields on 29 April 1741. The last occasion was a shared benefit for Montgomery and his fellow Mason the actor and singer James Excell.

Montgomery, Mr [*fl.* 1800–1810], *dancer, choreographer.*

A Mr Montgomery was performing in pantomimes at the Royal Circus by the spring of 1800. On 15 April 1800 the press congratulated the proprietors "on the rapid improvement of Mr MONTGOMERY, the clown, whose comic abilities kept the house in one continual roar of laughter and applause." The bills carried his name on 29 May 1800 as the Clown in *Harlequin Highlander*. By mid-1801 Montgomery was also composing dances, a function he served at the Royal Circus through 1807. Among the productions he choreographed were *The Fire King*, *Halloween*, and *The Eclipse* in 1801, *The Golden Farmer* and *Gonsalvo de Cordova* in 1802, *The Black Forest* in 1803, *Love and Glory* in 1804, *Cottage Courtship* in 1806, and *Werter and Charlotte* in 1807.

In 1809 Montgomery was at the Royalty Theatre in Wellclose Square, where he directed and performed in the dances *Love and Laughter* and *The Hero of Hungary* on 27 November. In the latter piece, Mrs Montgomery, announced

as from the Royal Circus, played the role of Alexina. Montgomery was at the Royal Theatre again in 1810.

Montgomery, Robert 1725–1753, *actor.*

When Robert Montgomery was admitted to Trinity College, Dublin, on 3 January 1743 he was 17 years old and thus probably born in 1725. He made his debut at the Smock Alley Theatre on 2 November 1750, according to *Faulkner's Dublin Journal*. He acted Othello on the fourteenth and Iago on the twenty-eighth, and on 15 May 1751 he made his first attempt in comedy as Young Mirabel in *The Inconstant*. Montgomery made a single appearance in London, as Iago on 12 March 1752 at Drury Lane. He acted at Smock Alley in 1751–52 and 1752–53, but he was too ill on 2 April 1753 to appear at his benefit. He died on the nineteenth. A satirical pamphlet lampooning Thomas Sheridan, *The Curtain Lecture* (1758), referred to our subject:

I'd sooner be shock'd by Montgomery's Spectre,
Than listen to your damn'd curtain lecture.

Monticelli, Angelo Maria *c.* 1710–1764?, *singer.*

The *New Grove* says that the male soprano Angelo Maria Monticelli was born in Milan about 1710–1715. Monticelli made his debut in Rome, according to Dr. Burney, in 1730. He sang in Venice in 1731 and 1732 and from 1733 to 1750 was attached to the Austrian Court at a salary of 2000 florins annually. During his tenure there he was permitted appearances elsewhere, for he sang in Milan in 1734, in Florence in 1737, and in London beginning in 1741.

He was the "Montevolli" mentioned in *The London Stage* as having been engaged to sing at the King's Theatre at a season salary of 1000 guineas. He was the company's *primo uomo* and made his London debut on 31 October 1741 in an unspecified role in the *pasticcio Alessandro in Persia*. During the 1741–42 season he also sang parts in *Penelope*, *A Musical Entertainment*, and *Meraspeo l'Olimpiade* and appeared as the title characters in *Polidoro* and *Scipione in Cartagine*.

Monticelli was again at the King's in 1742–43 and 1743–44, singing such parts as Al-

ANGELO MARIA MONTICELLI

engraving by Faber, after Casali

merin in *Mandane*, Alessandro in *Rossane*, the title characters in *Alfonso* and *Alceste*, Constante in *Rosalinda*, and Serse in *Temistocle*. He also participated in the annual benefits for indigent musicians and their families. Monticelli was away for a season but returned in 1745–46 to sing Demetrio in *Antigono* and participate in the annual charity benefit.

Of Monticelli Dr Burney said:

His voice was clear, sweet, and free from defects of every kind. He was a chaste performer, and never hazarded any difficulty which he was not certain of executing with the utmost precision. To his vocal excellence may be added the praise of a good actor; so that nothing but the recent remembrance of the gigantic talents of Farinelli, and the grand and majestic style of Senesino, could have left an English audience any thing to wish.

While in England Monticelli gained the friendship of Sir Robert Walpole. Horace Walpole on 7 July 1742 wrote, "Monticelli dines frequently with Sir Robert, which diverts me extremely: you know how low his ideas are of music and the virtuosi; he calls them all *fiddlers*."

After his London engagement Monticelli sang in Naples and Vienna. When he appeared in Naples in 1752 the impresario there, according to Heriot, was highly critical of the castrato's singing, and his voice by then must have deteriorated. Nevertheless, Monticelli continued performing and was in Dresden in 1756. He died there in 1764 (according to Grove; Heriot in *The Castrati in Opera* says 1758).

Monticelli's portrait was engraved by Faber, after Casali.

Montier. *See also* MOUNTIER.

Montier, Mrs [*fl.* 1744], *actress.*
Mrs Montier played Lady Graveairs in *The Careless Husband* in a single performance on 10 December 1744 at the James Street Theatre.

Montigny, Mons [*fl.* 1727], *actor, dancer?*
Monsieur Montigny shared a benefit with two minor actors at Lincoln's Inn Fields Theatre on 15 May 1727; the gross receipts came to a handsome £152 2s. 6d. Montigny may also have been an actor, though from his name we would guess that dancing would be a more likely specialty.

Monza, Maria [*fl.* 1729–1741], *singer.*
According to the *New Grove*, Maria Monza was the daughter of Bartolomeo Monza, who directed the Hamburg Opera in 1737–38. Maria sang in Venice from 1729 to 1731 and Prague in 1734–35; she was in Hamburg from 1736 to 1738 before being enlisted by Handel for his opera company in London. Grove dates her London debut at Lincoln's Inn Fields Theatre as 10 January 1741, when she sang Nerea in *Deidamia*, but by 21 December 1740 Mrs Pendarves had heard Signora Monza and wrote to her sister that "Her voice is between Cuzzoni's and Strada's—strong, but not harsh, her person *miserably bad*, being very low, and excessively crooked."

On 31 January 1741 at Lincoln's Inn Fields Signora Monza sang one of the additional songs in *L'allegro ed il Penseroso ed il moderato*. Dean in *Handel's Dramatic Oratorios* notes that she probably sang Filli in *Acis and Galatea* and Merab in *Saul* in 1741 as well. On 28 April 1741 she held a benefit concert at Hickford's Music Room.

Monzani, Tebaldo   *1762–1839, flutist, composer, instrument maker, music seller and publisher.*

The Italian flutist Tebaldo Monzani was born in Modena in 1762. He was living in London by 28 February 1785, on which night he played a concerto at the Haymarket Theatre. On 1 May 1785 William Napier proposed Monzani for membership in the Royal Society of Musicians, but on 5 June 1785 he was denied admission by a vote of 22 nays to 3 yeas. He was a musician in the opera at the Pantheon in 1791 and at the King's Theatre in 1795–96, 1797–98, and probably in other seasons.

Grove reports that Monzani "acquired some fame as an orchestral flutist." In 1794 Doane's *Musical Directory*, which gave his address as No 46, South Molton Street, stated he was a flutist for the opera and the Oxford Meeting of 1793. He played a Bach *concertante* with W. Parke and G. and C. Ashley at Covent Garden Theatre on 23 March 1798. On 5 February 1807 Monzani, described as a music seller of No 100, Cheapside, became a freeman of the Worshipfull Company of Musicians.

In reply to Sainsbury's request for information for his *Dictionary of Music*, Monzani wrote on 26 December 1823:

> I explain'd Previous to your last application my motives for not wanting any notice to be taken Regarding the History of my life. I now again beg to say—having retired from the Profession of music (now 20 Years) beg to Decline Complying with your Request.

In addition to his professional performances, which he gave up about 1803, Monzani had been an instrument maker and a music publisher in London for many years, issuing his own compositions and other music from his various shops. His first known address was No 10, Princes Street, Cavendish Square, in 1787 and 1788; but in 1789 and 1790 his publications were printed and sold for him by James Ball, No 1, Duke Street, Grosvenor Square. In 1792 Monzani's address was No 6, Conventry Street, corner of Coventry Court, Haymarket. Subsequent addresses were No 6, Great Marlborough Street in 1793; No 16, Down Street, Piccadilly, in 1795; No 5, Hamilton Street, Piccadilly, from 1796 to February 1798; and No 2, Pall Mall from February 1798 to early 1800.

In 1800 Monzani entered into partnership with Giambattista Cimador as Monzani & Cimador at No 2, Pall Mall to about 1803 and then at No 3, Old Bond Street (the Opera Warehouse) until 1805. (Cimador's name appeared incorrectly in the directories as Cringdon, Cumdon, and Cungdor.) After 1805, Monzani continued on his own until he became Henry Hill's partner in 1807, when the firm became Monzani & Hill, with premises at No 3, Old Bond Street until 1813; at No 24, Dover Street, to about 1819; and at No 28, Regent Street, until 1829. They had additional space at No 100, Cheapside, from about 1807 to 1814. The partnership dissolved in 1829, when Monzani seems to have retired. The business continued as Hill & Co and then Hill & Son until the stock-in-trade was sold by auction in May 1845.

Tebaldo Monzani died in London on 14 June 1839, soon after the death of his former partner, Henry Hill, the previous January. They had published a large amount of sheet music, especially Italian vocal pieces, and they had enjoyed reputations as excellent flute makers. A list of Monzani's compositions is given in the *Catalogue of Printed Music in the British Museum*. In 1801 he wrote and published *Instructions for the German Flute*.

Monzani's son, Willoughby Theobald Monzani, became a freeman of the Worshipfull Company of Musicians on 19 May 1825. He was proposed for membership in the Royal Society of Musicians on 3 July 1825 and was elected on 1 January 1826, the year in which W. N. James in *A Word or Two on the Flute* called him "perhaps the most promising performer in England." The younger Monzani was a Governor of the Royal Society of Musicians in 1827. He was permitted to be absent from the Society's annual concert at St Paul's in June 1831 because of ill health. In 1836 he was allowed to send a deputy to that concert, for on 3 April 1836 he had written a letter stating he had been in prison 12 months for debt and that his wife was pregnant. The financial relief he requested was denied because the Governors claimed that the Society could not grant assistance in such instances.

Moody, John, stage name of John Cochran   *1727–1812, actor, singer.*

The inscription on John Moody's tombstone at Barnes gave his age at the time of his death in 1812 as 85, thus placing his birth in 1727. It also stated that he was "a native of the Parish of St Clement Danes London." But contemporary memoirs, like *Secret History of the Green Rooms* (1795) and "Anthony Pasquin's" (John Williams's) *Poems* (1786), declared that the actor was born in Cork, the eldest son of a hairdresser named Cochran. Wishing to pass himself off as an Englishman, the young man changed his name to Moody and claimed that he had been born in Stanhope Street, Clare Market. The fact that Moody seems not to have made a public denial of those memoirs written in his lifetime, provides presumptive evidence that his tombstone inscription was written with some license. After following his father's trade in Tuckey's Lane, Cork, for several years, he left for the West Indies, it is said, in order to avoid conscription during the 1745 uprising.

At Kingston in Jamaica Moody joined a

JOHN MOODY
by Hardy

company of players with whom he reputedly acted Hamlet, Romeo, Lear, and other capital roles. Michael Kelly claimed in his *Reminiscences* that Moody had told him "that he worked his passage home as a sailor before the mast." Returning to England possessed with some "property of consequence," he became a principal actor in Norwich in 1758, specializing in heroes and lovers. Tate Wilkinson remembered acting Lord Townly to Moody's Manly in *The Provok'd Husband* at Portsmouth soon after the latter had returned from Jamaica. (The date was 20 June 1759; the playbill was cited in *Notes and Queries*, June 1891.) According to Wilkinson, Garrick saw Moody play Lockit in *The Beggar's Opera* at Portsmouth during that engagement and hired him at 30s. per week. But Moody had appeared in London prior to the Portsmouth engagement. On 12 January 1759, Holland being ill, Moody was given five guineas by Garrick to act Thyreus in *Antony and Cleopatra* at Drury Lane and to make his first appearance in London. That debut is substantiated by John Kemble's notation on a playbill for the date. Apparently Moody was also "the gentleman" who acted Henry VIII at Drury Lane on 22 May 1759 and whom the bills described as the gentleman making his first appearance on the stage, despite Moody's debut four months earlier. Only then followed the June appearance with Wilkinson in *The Provok'd Husband* at Portsmouth.

On 12 September 1759 the Drury Lane prompter Richard Cross entered in his diary that "one Moody, a Stroler," had been engaged. The bills for 27 September 1759 carried his name for Mopsus in *Damon and Phillida*, a role he repeated on 12 October, when he also played Seyward in *Macbeth*. After appearing as Henry VIII on 22 October and in a part in *The Rehearsal* on 30 October, Moody was on 31 October 1759 the original Kingston in *High Life below Stairs*, a role he played numerous times that season. On 12 December 1759 he created his first great Irish character, Sir Callaghan O'Brallagan in Macklin's *Love à-la-Mode*. Other roles that season included Lorenzo in *The Merchant of Venice*, Catesby in *Jane Shore*, a Clown in *Harlequin's Invasion*, Sable in *The Funeral*, Puff in *Miss in Her Teens*, a part in *Every Woman in Her Humour*, Phelim O'Blunder in *The Double Disappointment*, and the Miller in *The Miller of Mansfield*.

In 1760–61 he played Teague in *The Committee*, another of his very successful portrayals, on 29 December 1760; Moody created Captain O'Cutter in *The Jealous Wife* on February 1761, and was also seen as the English Herald in *King John*, Robin in *The Contrivances*, Foigard in *The Stratagem*, Obadiah Prim in *A Bold Stroke for a Wife*, Vulture in *Woman's a Riddle*, and an Irishman in *The Register Office*. On 24 April 1761 he delivered his specialty number, "Teddy Wolloughan's Whimsical Oratorical Description of a Man o' War and Sea Fight, with Hibernian Notes on the Whole," a sing-song rendition with which he entertained the public over many years. Next season, 1761–62, he played Cratander in *Hecuba*, the Coachman in *The Drummer*, Colonel Bully in *The Provok'd*

Civica Raccolta delle Stampe Achille Bertarelli, Castello Sforzesco, Milan

JOHN MOODY, as Jobson
engraving by Bromley, after Drummond

Wife, Carners in *1 Henry IV*, Henry VI in *Richard III*, Montague in *Romeo and Juliet*, and Quaver in *The Virgin Unmask'd*. In the summer of 1762 Moody acted at Birmingham.

Moody's fourth season at Drury Lane began well enough on 21 September 1762, when he performed Peachum in *The Beggar's Opera*, and proceeded harmlessly for several months during which he offered his regular characters and added Mouldy in *2 Henry IV*, the Lieutenant in *Richard III*, and Cob in *Every Man in His Humour*. Twenty-five January 1763, a night on which he was scheduled to act the Host in *The Two Gentlemen of Verona*, was the occasion of the "Half-Price Riot" led by the Irishman Fitzpatrick. In the uproar Moody grabbed a torch from a madman who was intent upon burning down the theatre. On the following night, responding to a demand from the Fitzpatrick faction for an apology, Moody stepped on to the stage and in the tone of a low-bred Irishman—his specialty dialect—said that "he was very sorry he had displeased them by saving their lives in putting out the fire." The irony only served to incense further the mob, who insisted that he go down on his knees to beg forgiveness. As Tom Davies tells the story in his *Life of Garrick* Moody exclaimed, "I will not, by G———," and stomped off the stage to be embraced by Garrick, who told him that as long as he was master of a guinea he would pay Moody. But the tumult was great, and the next night, to appease the audience, Garrick promised that Moody would not appear on the Drury Lane stage again while he still suffered their displeasure. Faced with the dilemma either of going out on tour or accepting Garrick's support while he did not act, Moody confronted Fitzpatrick and in a dialogue printed by Davies (as delivered to him by Moody) he compelled the mob's leader to a conciliation. In a letter to Garrick, Fitzpatrick promised that his friends would attend if Moody was reinstated. On 5 February 1763 Moody took space in the press to explain

That the impropriety of his behaviour at the Theatre was intirely owing to the confusion of mind he was under; which unhappily for him was misconstrued into disrespect; tho' nothing co'd be farther from his Thought: He therefore earnestly hopes and entreats that he may be permitted to appear before them again; as he most humbly asks their

Pardon for whatever he inadvertently said or did to incur their Displeasure.

He did not reappear, however, until 15 February 1763, when he played Kingston in *High Life below Stairs*. He acted Gage in *Phoebe* on 24 February and an unspecified role in *Sketch of a Fine Lady's Return from a Rout* on 21 March. These he followed with Captain O'Cutter, Puff, Foigard, Mouldy, and, on 3 May 1763, Stephano in *The Tempest*.

Over the years under Garrick, Moody was a serviceable actor and established a reputation as a comic Irishman, excelling in roles written especially for him, like Major O'Flaherty in Cumberland's *The West Indian*, first performed on 19 January 1771, Sir Patrick O'Neale in Garrick's *The Irish Widow* on 23 October 1772, Connolly, an Irish clerk, in Kelly's *The School for Wives* on 11 December 1773, and Mc-Cormuck in Cumberland's *A Note of Hand, or a Trip to Newmarket* on 9 February 1774. Among his numerous other roles at Drury Lane during Garrick's management were Teague in *The Twin*

Courtesy of the Garrick Club

JOHN MOODY as Teague and WILLIAM PARSONS as Obadiah, in *The Committee*

by Van der Gucht

Rivals, Ben in *Love for Love*, Simon Burley in *The Anatomist*, Vamp in *The Author*, Dervise in *Tamerlane*, Brainworm in *Every Man in His Humour*, Jobson in *The Devil to Pay*, Major Oldfox in *The Plain Dealer*, Gibby in *The Wonder*, the Watchman in *Queen Mab*, the Irishman in *The Jubilee*, Dr Cantwell in *The Hypocrite*, Gregory in *The Choleric Man*, Captain Ironsides in *The Brothers*, Machoof in *The Spleen*, and the Painter in *The Maid of the Oaks*. He created the Scottish servant Colin MacLeed in Cumberland's *The Fashionable Lover* on 20 January 1772 and Commodore Flip in Thompson's alteration of *The Fair Quaker of Deal* on 9 November 1773. Though often required to sing in some of his roles, Moody was not a trained vocalist. Apparently he was intended for the role of Mungo in Bickerstaff's opera *The Padlock*, but Charles Dibdin, who composed the music, wanted the part for himself; Dibdin therefore made the songs too difficult for Moody, and when the piece opened on 3 October 1768 Dibdin acted the role. (Moody did get to play Mungo five years later, at the Haymarket Theatre on 5 July 1773.)

Moody's salary at Drury Lane was 10*s.* per day, or £3 per week, by 1764–65, a figure he was still earning in 1766–67. By 1774–75 it had been raised to £6 per week. In letters to Garrick in 1774 and 1775 Moody expressed dissatisfaction with his salary, especially, as he wrote on 11 August 1775, when he was obliged to give up some of his roles to Yates, who in his opinion was not a better actor but had a better income. Moody reminded Garrick he had stayed with him through all of his business with "great cheerfulness" even when Yates had meanly left him.

Twice Moody obliged the Covent Garden Theatre management by acting Henry VIII there on 22 September 1773 and 15 October 1775. In the summer of 1773 he engaged with Foote at the Haymarket. According to *The London Stage* he appeared for the first time there in an unspecified role in *The Nabob* on 17 May 1773. That night, however, he acted O'Connor in the premiere of Waldron's *The Maid of Kent* at Drury Lane. Both pieces seem to have been scheduled for the first part of the bill. He did act at the Haymarket that summer Mopsus in *Damon and Phillida*, Vamp in *The Author*, O'Blunder in *The Double Disappointment*, Mrs

Loveit in *The Commissary*, Mungo in *The Pad-lock*, O'Flam in *The Bankrupt*, the Irishman in *The Register Office*, and parts in *The Maid of Bath*, *The Devil upon Two Sticks*, and *She Stoops to Conquer*. He acted summers at Bristol in 1770, 1771, 1772, 1777, and 1778; at Leeds and York in 1774; and at Liverpool in 1775 and 1776, where he earned £2 per week. On the stage of the Plymouth Theatre, on 18 July 1766, the actress Mrs Jefferson, having had a seizure in the midst of a hearty laugh during a rehearsal, died in his arms.

In the earlier part of his career Moody was a popular actor, well regarded by Churchill, who devoted ten lines to him in *The Rosciad*. Francis Gentleman in *The Theatres* (1772) wrote he "well deserves the favour of the town" in all his roles, especially "When he depicts the Irish Gentleman." As Major O'Flaherty in *The West Indian*, "he played with such judgment and masterly execution," claimed the *Theatrical Bi-ography* (1772), "as to divide applause with the author." William Hawkins in *Miscellanies in Prose and Verse* (1775) judged him "capital" in many low comedy roles, asserting one could not find a better Commodore Flip, Adam, or Vamp—"There is considerable ease and pro-priety in his manner of acting; . . . of late Mr. Moody has become no less a favourite with the boxes, than he is with the galleries." Though the prompter Hopkins wrote in his diary that Moody's first attempt at Dr Cantwell in *The Hypocrite* on 27 November 1771 was "very bad," the critic in the *Theatrical Review* was more charitable, stating that considering Moody took on the role at short notice because of King's illness it was executed with "great propriety and justice."

After Garrick's retirement in 1776 Moody remained at Drury Lane under Sheridan and Kemble through 1795–96. Among his origi-nal roles during that period were Phelim in Colman's *New Brooms* on 21 September 1776; Sir Tunbelly Clumsey in Sheridan's alteration of Vanbrugh's *A Trip to Scarborough* on 24 Feb-ruary 1777; O'Daub in Sheridan's (or Tickell's) *The Camp* on 15 October 1778; Lord Burleigh in Sheridan's *The Critic* on 30 October 1779; Dennis Dogherty in Jackman's *The Divorce* on 10 November 1781; Major O'Flaherty in Cumberland's *The Natural Son* on 22 December 1784; and Hugo in Cobb's *The Haunted Tower*

Courtesy of the Garrick Club

JOHN MOODY, as Commodore Flip
by De Wilde

(with music by Storace) on 24 November 1789. His roles in his last season, 1795–96, included MacFloggan in *The Three and the Deuce*, Sir Lucius O'Trigger in *The Rivals*, Kilmallock in *The Mountaineers*, Sir Sampson in *Love for Love*, a Witch in *Macbeth*, Sir Tunbelly Clumsey in *A Trip to Scarborough*, Adam in *As You Like It*, Gripe in *The Confederacy*, Bullock in *The Re-cruiting Officer*, John Moody in *The Provok'd Husband*, Jobson in *The Devil to Pay*, Major Oldfox in *The Plain Dealer*, the Host of the Garter in *The Merry Wives of Windsor*, and Sy-mon in *The Gentle Shepherd*. In the summer of 1793 he played a few nights at Richmond and in August 1795 at Derby. Late in 1791 Moody acted Sir Lucius O'Trigger at the Earl of Bar-

JOHN MOODY, as Stephano

by Dighton

rymore's theatre at Wargrave, and no doubt he made similar appearances in other private theatricals.

Moody's last performance at Drury Lane was as Sir Patrick O'Neale in *The Irish Widow* on 13 June 1796, the night that Dodd, playing Kecksey in the same piece, also retired from the stage. Moody's salary that season was £8 per week, an amount he had been earning at least since 1789–90. Like other Drury Lane employees, Moody had trouble getting his wages from Sheridan, and according to the 1796 edition of *A Pin Basket to the Children of Thespis* he had been discharged by Sheridan for attempting "to *enforce* the payment" of £500 due him; previous to his dismissal Moody wrote a vindictive letter to Sheridan which he circulated among his friends and threatened "to read it publicly on the hustings" at Stafford, Sheridan's constituency, unless his demands were paid. The *Monthly Mirror* in 1797 reported

that Moody had been kept on at Drury Lane as long as he had because Sheridan found it more convenient to keep him engaged than pay him off, but when Moody, sick of delay, insisted on his salary and "all evasion was fruitless" Sheridan fired him. As late as November 1800 Moody was still suing in the Court of the King's Bench for back salary. Lord Kenyon found on his behalf, praising him as "a frugal and prudent man," and that month the Drury Lane treasurer paid out £125 for "Moody's Cause" and £100 on 28 January 1801 to complete the obligation.

During his last years on the stage, critics began to accuse Moody of mugging, becoming lazy, and failing to grow as an actor. In *Thespis*, Kelly called him "mud-ey'd Moody," who gaped around the house regardless of his part, "All brass in front, and marble all in heart." The anonymous author of *The Modern Stage Exemplified* (1788) wrote:

> MOODY *devoid of spirit, humour, grace!*
> *No strong expression of his face we find;*
> *No passion marks the features of his mind.*
> *Dull, sluggish, cold insensible and tame,*
> *He gives no pleasure, and deserves no fame.*

In *A Pin Basket* Williams characterized him:

> HERE *comes lazy* MOODY—*that indolent elf*
> *Seems lost in the deep contemplation of self;*
> *A* noli me tangere *sits on each feature,*
> *Repelling the wishes of social good nature:*
> *Approaching this wight, ere your wish you rehearse,*
> *By instinct the man—clapps his hand on his purse:*
> *Go ask him his health, as—How are you, Sir, pray?*
> *He'll answer—The Stocks, Friend—is that what you say?*
> *By the Lord, man, they fell half an eighth yesterday.*
> *To laziness wedded, no passions can warm,*
> *For he sleeps like a Belgian lake in a storm;*
> *By his meanness subdu'd, his ambition is o'er,*
> *And he crawls on the stage—but to add to his store.*
> ....
> *'Tis ascertain'd easy, by plain Common Sense,*
> *He's a Swiss in the drama, and fights for the pence;*
> *No laudable motive, no love of the art,*
> *Gives force to his judgment, or warmth to his heart.*
> *He jogs the same trot he did ten years before,*
> *Contented to know—two and two will make four.*

Unknown to the Muses, and Excellence scorning.
He sighs for the stipend, and Saturday morning.
....

    When I think of the worth of this veteran
      stager,
His COMMODORE FLIP *and* HIBERNIAN MA-
      JOR,
It mads me to see that the man is contented
To sculk to his tomb by each muse unlamented.
As he knows he can charm us whenever he'll please,
'Tis a shame he gets fat and enjoys so much ease.

There was an increasing "insufferable drowsiness" in Moody's acting, wrote Hawkins, so that "lately these defects have grown to such enormity that we trust his good sense will determine him to quit a profession which, fortunately for him, has filled his coffers with the necessary means of retiring." The *Monthly Mirror* of 1797, in retrospection of his stage career, described Moody as "tall and bulky," with "large and leaden" eyes which were "as sleepy as his habit." His lethargic performance stimulated audiences to little more than a yawn to his approach and a nod at his retirement—"We believe no one had a desire to see Moody twice; he was perfectly uniform in his representations, and one part was a sample of all."

After 37 years on the London stage, during which he seldom had exhibited any ambition to extend his line or exert any creative effort, Moody lived in some comfort at Barnes Common. The press reported in August 1798 that he had also bought a house at Norwich, where he intended some day to retire. Despite his rheumatism, he kept busy with growing and selling vegetables and he retained his interest in theatrical events; he belonged to the so-called "School of Garrick," a fellowship of actors who had been the great man's colleagues. Michael Kelly, "always partial to Moody's society," praised him as a generous and entertaining man. When eight actors printed their *Statement of the Differences Subsisting Between the Proprietors and Performers of the Theatre Royal Covent Garden* in 1800 they presented him with a copy, now in the Garrick Club, which bears the inscription "To John Moody Esq; With the greatest Respect for his professional Talents, with the warmest Esteem for his private Worth; and with the sincerest Acknowledgments for his Approbation of our Endeavours to reestablish Actors in their just Rights, this book is presented . . . " During that altercation be-

tween the actors and the Covent Garden management, Moody published in the *Morning Post* and *Morning Chronicle* an open letter to Joseph G. Holman, one of the rebels, to thank him for his copy of their pamphlet:

Ten thousand thanks for your attention to a poor old actor, sequestered in this obscure corner of the Thames. You have called back my youth; but no period of Theatrical history affords such a group of honest fellows, asserting the rights of their bretheran.

Do ye want pecuniary aid? Let me be enrolled, that I may *have a slice* of the immortality that must eventually attach itself to so generous, so liberal an undertaking.

He returned to the stage for one performance at Covent Garden on 26 June 1804 to play Jobson in *The Devil to Pay* for the benefit of the Bayswater Hospital, an event announced as "his first appearance these ten years, and positively his last on any stage."

Moody had been one of the original committee of actors which had been formed on 18 May 1774 to "make such rules and orders as should . . . seem most conducive" to setting up the Drury Lane Actors Fund, and he was one of the original subscribers. He became in 1805 chairman of the Fund. In the Garrick Club is the "Memorandum Notebook" kept by him, in which he wrote on 21 December 1805, "had the Mastership of the Corporation of Actors bestowed upon me; an honor worn at my heart's core." In the thirty-two-page notebook he recorded the affairs of the Fund for seven years. Illness forced him to miss many meetings in 1806 and early 1807, and on 16 March of the latter year he wrote that Maddocks called upon him to invite him to a meeting for electing an annual committee and also had hinted that they intended to choose a master in Moody's place. The following day, 17 March 1807, Moody wrote a cordial and sentimental letter of resignation, giving his address as Lawn Place, Shepherd's Bush, and stating he could no longer carry out the responsibilities of the chair. Nevertheless, he continued in the position, and on 4 January 1811 recorded having received a letter from the Fund committee requesting his resignation, but he could not attend the meeting because he was ill. On the next to last page of the notebook he wrote "Was a rude Committee 25 March 1812 rec^d

10£ as a temporary relief." On the last page he noted that he had given Maddocks a draft containing all the amount of cash of the Fund in his hand, and on 7 April 1812 he "Resigned the common seal and Mastership to Mr. John Powel." At the age of 84 his hand was still firm.

He died on 26 December 1812, at Shepherd's Bush, according to the *Gentleman's Magazine* which gave his age as 85, or in Leicester Square, according to the *European Magazine*. Though he requested burial in St Clement's graveyard in Portugal Street—with a headstone bearing the words, "A native of this parish, and an old member of Drury Lane Theatre"—that cemetery was full; so he was interred in Barnes churchyard, with the remains of his first wife, Anne Moody, who had died on 12 May 1805 at the age of 88.

In his will made on 28 July 1808, when he gave his address as Lawn Place, Shepherd's Bush, Hammersmith, he bequeathed all he possessed, including unspecified amounts in the public funds and his freehold estate at Barnes, to his second wife Kitty Ann Moody. As executrix she proved the will on 8 January 1813. A transcript of Moody's tombstone at Barnes was printed in *Notes and Queries* on 8 May 1875:

Mrs Anne Moody
Wife of John Moody Esquire of this
Parish
Died the 12 of May 1805
Aged 88.
Here also lies the body of
Mr John Moody, a native of the
Parish of St Clement Danes London,
and an old member of
Drury Lane Theatre.
For his Memoirs see
The European Magazine
For his professional abilities
See Churchill's Rosciad.
Obit December 26th 1812
Anno aetatis 85.
Also the remains of
Kitty Ann widow of the above
Mr John Moody who died Octr 29th 1846
Aged 83.

Moody's second wife, a dancer, whom he had married at St Dionis Backchurch on 22 May 1806, was born Kitty Ann Worlock, the daughter of Simion and Elizabeth Worlock.

When she went on the stage at the age of six she adopted her mother's maiden name, Elizabeth Armstrong, and is noticed in this dictionary.

Portraits of John Moody include:

1. By unknown artist. One of 12 portraits of the "School of Garrick." In the Garrick Club (No 50c).

2. Engraved portrait by T. Hardy. Published by the engraver, 1792.

3. Engraved portrait by W. Ridley, after Spicer. Published as a plate to Parsons' *Minor Theatre*, 1794.

4. As Commodore Flip in *The Fair Quaker*. Oil by S. De Wilde. In the Garrick Club. Engraving by P. Audinet published as a plate to *Bell's British Theatre*, 1792.

5. As Foigard in *The Beaux' Stratagem*. Oil by J. Zoffany. Bought by Lord Charlemont in 1764; once owned by Henry Irving; sold at Sotheby's on 13 October 1954. Now in the possession of Arthur Richard Dufty. Shown in the Zoffany exhibition by the National Portrait Gallery at Carlton House, January-March 1977. Engraving by J. Marchi, sold by I. Wesson.

6. As the Irishman in *The Jubilee*. By unknown engraver. Not listed in the Harvard Theatre Collection catalogue; a copy is in the British Museum.

7. As the Irishman, with John Packer as Gulwell, in *The Register Office*. Oil by B. Van der Gucht. Shown at the Royal Academy in 1773 (No 298) and bought by the Earl of Bessborough. Owned by Messrs Thomas Agnew Sons in 1949 and bought from them in 1954 by the Leicester Museum and Art Gallery, where the canvas now hangs. Engraving by J. Saunders, published 1773. This picture is reproduced with our notice of John Packer.

8. As Jobson in *The Devil to Pay*. Oil by S. Drummond. In the Garrick Club (No 455). Engraving by W. Bromley, published as a plate to *European Magazine*, 1790.

9. As Major O'Flaherty, with William Parsons as Varland, in *The West Indian*. Engraving by W. Dickinson, after J. Mortimer. Published by the engraver, 1776.

10. As Major O'Flaherty. Watercolor by W. Loftis, 1789. In the Folger Shakespeare Library.

11. As Simon in *Harlequin's Invasion*. By unknown engraver. Published by Smith and Sayer, 1769.

12. As Simon. By unknown artist, on a delftware wall tile. Manchester Art Gallery.

13. As Stephano in *The Tempest*. Watercolor by Dighton. In the Harvard Theatre Collection.

14. As Teague, with William Parsons as Obadiah, in *The Committee*. Engraving by J. Collyer, after D. Dodd. Published as a plate to Lowndes *New English Theatre*, 1776.

15. As Teague. Colored drawing by J. Roberts. In the British Museum. Engraving by Walker, published as a plate to *Bell's British Theatre*, 1776. A reversed copy, by an unknown engraver, was published in the same work.

16. As Teague. Engraving by Terry. Published by Harrison & Co, 1779.

17. As Teague, with William Parsons as Obadiah. Oil by B. Van der Gucht. Exhibited at the Royal Academy in 1775. In the Garrick Club (No 33).

18. As Teague. By unknown artist. On a Delftware wall tile. Manchester Art Gallery.

19. In "The Apotheosis of Garrick." Oil by George Carter. In the Gallery of the Royal Shakespeare Theatre, Stratford-upon-Avon. Moody is one of Drury Lane performers pictured making their farewells to Garrick. Engraving by Smith and Caldwell, with a key plate, published by Carter, 1783.

Moody, Mrs John the second. See ARMSTRONG, ELIZABETH.

Moon. See also MOHUN.

Moon, Joseph ₁*fl.* 1794₁, *singer.*
Doane's *Musical Directory* of 1794 listed Joseph Moon, of No 46, Holywell Street ("Back of St. Clements"), as a bass who sang for the Handelian Society.

Moor, Mr ₁*fl.* 1775–1777₁, *doorkeeper, cheque taker.*
The Drury Lane Theatre accounts list a Mr Moor (or Moore) as the first gallery cheque taker as of 5 October 1775. He was surely the Mr Moor listed as a doorkeeper in 1776–77.

Moor, Thomas ₁*fl.* 1735–1747₁, *box bookkeeper.*
Thomas Moor (or Moore) served Drury Lane as a box bookkeeper in 1735–36, though his

benefit was held at the Lincoln's Inn Fields playhouse on 20 April 1736. He was cited in Drury Lane benefit bills from time to time through 28 April 1747, his address being given as "in the Playhouse Passage." He augmented his income, at least from May 1746 on, by running a lodging house. His wife was a sometime actress and house servant.

Moor, Mrs Thomas ₁*fl.* 1733–1742₁, *actress, ticket agent.*
Mrs Thomas Moor (or More, Moore) played Rose in *The Recruiting Officer* and Sally in *The Farmer's Son* at the Haymarket Theatre on 14 March 1733. She acted Sylvia in *The Recruiting Officer* at Southwark on 7 April 1735. Her benefit tickets were accepted at Drury Lane on 1 July 1735, and perhaps by that time she had begun serving that house as a ticket agent. Her tickets were admitted again on 28 May 1740, and on the Drury Lane bill for 24 February 1742 it was stated that "Places for the Stage [could be had] of Mrs Moor, at the Sign of the Theatre, in the Playhouse Passage."

Moore, Mr ₁*fl.* 1724–1735₁, *actor.*
The earliest notice we have found of the Dublin actor Moore dates from the 1724–25 season at Smock Alley, where he is known to have played Wilful in *The Double Gallant* and Squib in *Tunbridge Walks*. The research of the late William S. Clark shows that Moore was again (or still?) at Smock Alley in 1725–26 and performed there and at the Rainsford Street playhouse in 1732–33. That season he is known to have played Sir Sampson in *Love for Love* and Hamlet.

On 25 September 1733 Moore played Westmoreland in *1 Henry IV* to begin a two-season engagement at the Goodman's Fields Theatre in London. He was also seen as Eumenes in *The Rival Queens*, Francisco in *Hamlet*, a High Priest in *The Indian Emperor*, Metellus in *Julius Caesar*, an Attendant on Germanicus and a Grenadier in *Britannia*, Oxford in *Richard III*, and an Attendant on Jupiter in *Jupiter and Io*. Moore shared in benefits in May 1734 and May 1735. He apparently made little impression on London managers and audiences.

Chetwood in his *General History* in 1749 noted that by then Moore had died.

Moore, Mr [*fl. 1745?*], *singer.*

The *Catalogue of Printed Music in the British Museum* lists the song *Save Women and Wine*, published in 1745 (?), as sung by Mr Moore at Sadler's Wells.

Moore, Mr [*fl. 1755–1772?*], *actor.*

The Mr Moore who played Clodpole in *The Happy Gallant* at Bence's Room at Bartholomew Fair on 6 September 1755 was probably the Mr "Moor" who acted the Second King of Brentford in *The Rehearsal* at the Haymarket Theatre on 20 August 1764 and Justice Clement in *Every Man in His Humour* at the same house the following 1 September. Perhaps the same Moore played Bramville in *Venice Preserv'd* at the Haymarket on 29 October 1770 and took an unspecified part in *The Rehearsal* there on 10 and 31 August 1772.

Moore Mr [*fl. 1765–c. 1775?*], *singer, music seller?*

Wroth in *The London Pleasure Gardens* notes that a Mr Moore sang at Finch's Grotto Gardens in 1765. William Yates's song *The Lucky Escape* was published about 1770 with Moore named as the singer, again at Finch's. Perhaps our subject was the Mr Moore of No 2, Bridgewater Square, Barbican, who printed and sold *Six Easy Lessons for the Harpsichord* by Bartholomew Davis about 1775.

Moore, Mr [*fl. 1765–1777*], *dresser.*

Mr Moore was one of the men's dressers at Drury Lane Theatre who, on a paylist dated 9 February 1765, was down for 1*s*. 6*d*. daily or 9*s*. per week, a salary he was still earning in the 1776–77 season.

Moore, Mr [*fl. 1794*], *singer.*

Doane's *Musical Directory* of 1794 listed a Moore and a Moore Junior (possibly, but not necessarily, father and son) as tenors who sang in the Handelian performances at Westminster Abbey (probably in the latest ones, in 1791). The Moores were from Ilminster.

Moore, Junior, Mr [*fl. 1794*], *singer.*
See MOORE, MR [*fl. 1794*].

Moore, Master [*fl. 1754–1757*], *actor.*

Master Moore was first noticed in the bills on 5 November 1754, when he was a Fairy in *Queen Mab* at Drury Lane Theatre (though he probably played the part when the work was given the previous 31 October). He appeared as Puck in *The Fairies* on 3 February 1755 and was Captain Flash in a children's production of *Miss in Her Teens* on 28 April. He shared a benefit with two others on 3 May. Master Moore was again in the Drury Lane troupe in 1755–56, playing Cupid in *Chrononhotonthologos* on 29 April 1756.

On 17 June 1757 he played a Frenchman in *Harlequin's Frolic* at the Haymarket Theatre, and at that house the following 31 October he had an unspecified part in *The Farmer Trick'd*.

Moore, Miss [*fl. 1752*], *actress.*

At the Richmond Theatre in the summer of 1752 a Miss Moore acted Mrs Trippet in *The Lying Valet*, Lady Bountiful in *The Beaux' Stratagem*, Myrtillo in *The Provok'd Husband*, Selima in *Zara*, Betty in *The Gamester*, the Princess in *A Duke and No Duke*, and the Hostess in *Henry IV*. She shared a benefit with English on 25 September.

Moore, Anthony [*fl. 1663–1670*], *scenekeeper.*

The London Stage lists Anthony Moore, a scenekeeper, as a member of the King's Company at the Bridges Street Theatre in 1663–64, 1666–67, and 1669–70. A Lord Chamberlain's warrant cited him on 20 February 1665.

Moore, Henrietta [*fl. 1698–1730*], *actress.*

Mrs Henrietta Moore (or Moor, More) was first noticed in the bills in March 1698, when she played Widow Thoroshift in *The Pretenders* and spoke the epilogue at the Lincoln's Inn Fields Theatre. In mid-May she acted Morella in *Beauty in Distress* at the same house. The following December Mrs Moore was at Drury Lane Theatre playing Pindress in *Love and a Bottle*. A year later, on 7 November 1699, she returned to Lincoln's Inn Fields to play Cyllene in *Friendship Improved*, but on the twenty-eighth she was again at Drury Lane, acting Parly in *The Constant Couple*. We take it that her appearance at Lincoln's Inn Fields was by some special arrangement, for she seems to have been a regular member of the Drury Lane troupe under Christopher Rich in 1699–1700 and, indeed, spent most of the rest of her long career there. She completed her 1699–1700 season playing Fidelia in *The Reform'd Wife*, Juletta in *The Pilgrim*, and Melintha in *Courtship a la Mode*.

During the first decade of the eighteenth century Henrietta Moore attempted a number of new parts, among which were Honoria in *Love Makes a Man*, Combrush in *The Bath*, Flora in *She Wou'd and She Wou'd Not*, the Steward's Wife in *The Twin Rivals*, Penelope in *Tunbridge Walks*, Lady Oldmore and Gatty in *The Old Mode and the New*, Lady Graveairs in *The Careless Husband*, Silvia in *The Recruiting Officer*, Louisa in *Love Makes a Man*, Flavia in *Love à-la-Mode*, Hortensia in *Aesop*, the Widow in *The Scornful Lady*, Mrs Fantast in *Bury Fair*, Violante in *Greenwich Park*, Valeria in *The Rover*, Arabella in *The London Cuckolds*, Mrs Wellborn and Mrs Grace in *Bartholomew Fair*, Miranda in *The Tempest*, Bellemante in *The Emperor of the Moon*, Victoria in *The Fatal Marriage*, Altea in *Rule a Wife and Have a Wife*, Isabella and Teresa in *The Squire of Alsatia*, Mrs Jilt in *Epsom Wells*, Elvira in *The Spanish Fryar*, Miranda in *The Busy Body*, Arabella in *The Committee*, Mrs Foresight in *Love for Love*, Araminta in *The Confederacy*, and Belinda in *The Fair Quaker*. She seems to have been active at Drury Lane every season except 1705–6.

Having developed a respectable repertoire of good roles, Mrs Moore left Drury Lane after the 1709–10 season. She was probably the Mrs Moore who was given a benefit concert at the Two Golden Balls on 2 April 1711, after which she again disappeared from the bills. On 7 January 1715 she turned up at the new Lincoln's Inn Fields playhouse to play Belinda in *The Fair Quaker*, after which, through August, she acted Araminta in *The Confederacy*, Mrs Foresight in *Love for Love*, Teresa in *The Squire of Alsatia*, and Isabella in *The False Count*. At her benefit on 5 May 2 *Don Quixote* was performed, but the bill did not indicate what role, if any, she played. Mrs Moore returned to Lincoln's Inn Fields for the 1715–16 season to play such new roles as Mary the Buxom in 2 *Don Quixote* (perhaps she had played that the previous spring), Narcissa in *Love's Last Shift*, Emilia in *The Fond Husband*, and Julia in *The Humours of Purgatory*. On 10 October 1716 she was again at Lincoln's Inn Fields, acting Mrs Fantast in *Bury Fair*, but she shared a benefit

with Chetwood at Drury Lane on 10 May 1717 and played the Widow in *The Northern Lass* there on 24 June.

Mrs Moore remained at Drury Lane to her retirement in 1730, though until 1721–22 she seems to have carried a reduced schedule—or perhaps the company employed her backstage in some capacity. In 1717–18, for example, she was not named in the bills until her shared benefit in May 1718, and then she performed through the summer; in 1718–19 she was named for only one role (Mrs Foresight), yet she shared a benefit with Ray at the end of the season; and in 1720–21 she did not receive mention in the bills until her benefit, and then she played one role in the summer. Even from 1721–22 on she was usually named for only two or three roles per season.

Her new parts from 1717–18 through 1729–30 included Tearshift in *Love for Money*, Lady Flippant in *Love in a Wood*, Olympia in *The Bondman*, Mrs Overdo in *Bartholomew Fair*, the Aunt in *The Tender Husband*, Lady Fidget in *The Country Wife*, Lady Laycock in *The Amorous Widow*, Lady Haughty in *The Silent Woman*, Mrs Sealand in *The Conscious Lovers*, Widow Blackacre in *The Plain Dealer*, Lady Woodly in *The Man of Mode*, Goody in *The Country Wit*, Lady Darling in *The Constant Couple*, Lady Bountiful in *The Conscious Lovers*, Mrs Motherly in *The Provok'd Husband*, Lady Trap in *Love in Several Masques*, and the Mother in *The Chances* (those last five parts she acted for the first time in 1727–28; in previous seasons she had rarely tried more than one new part per season). Henrietta Moore retired from the stage in 1730.

Moore, Henry [*fl.* 1766–c. 1777], drummer.

By 1766, according to the *St James's Register*, Henry Moore had succeeded John Conquest as Drum Major General in the King's Musick. The *London Gazette* of 1–4 February 1777 reported that Moore had been succeeded by Charles Stuart.

Moore, James [*fl.* 1715–1726], musician.

The Lord Chamberlain's accounts show that James Moore (or Moor, More) replaced James Kremberg in the King's Musick on 23 September 1715 at an unspecified salary retroactive to

18 September. He was in turn replaced by Michael Christian Festing on 4 November 1726.

Moore, John [*fl. 1732*], *singer.*

John Moore sang Haman in a private performance of the oratorio *Esther* at the Crown and Anchor Tavern in the Strand on 23 February 1732. Some of the participants were professional musicians, and it is probable that Moore was a Gentleman of the Chapel Royal.

Moore, John [*fl. 1794*], *singer.*

Doane's *Musical Directory* of 1794 listed the Reverend John Moore, a tenor and minor canon of the Chapel Royal and St Paul's choirs, as a resident of No 60, Red Lion Street, Clerkenwell.

Moore, Mrs Mark *d. c. 1787, actress.*

The *Hibernian Journal* of 7 January 1774 reported that "A Young Lady" would make her stage debut that night at the Capel Street playhouse, playing Cordelia in *King Lear*. On 1 February the young lady who had played Cordelia tried the title role in *Jane Shore*, and on 9 February Mrs Moore, identified now as the lady who had played *Jane Shore*, was advertised for the part of Mrs Belville in an unspecified play. Mrs Moore came to London to play a role in *The Snuff Box* and Jessica in *The Merchant of Venice* at the Haymarket Theatre on 23 March 1775. The following summer she performed at Birmingham, and on 21 January 1784 she tried London again, playing an unspecified but principal part in *The Talisman* at the Haymarket. According to *The Memoirs and Adventures of Mark Moore* (1795), Mrs Moore died at Chelmsford about 1787. Her husband, who wrote his memoirs under the name of Signor Morini, spent some time in the Navy and from time to time earned a living as a provincial manager. He seems not to have appeared in London.

Moore, Mrs S. *See* WOOD, MISS [*fl. 1778–1792*].

Moore, Susan. *See* FAWCETT, THE FIRST MRS JOHN THE YOUNGER.

Moorehead, Alexander *d. 1803, violinist.*

Alexander Moorehead was leader of the band at Sadler's Wells when Charles Dibdin the younger opened his enterprise on Easter Monday 1800. His brother John was at that time composer to the Wells. Nothing further is known of Alexander Moorehead, except that, according to Dibdin in his *Memoirs*, he died insane, like his brother John. The notice on John in *The Dictionary of National Biography* says that Alexander died "in 1803 in a Liverpool lunatic asylum."

Moorehead, John *d. 1804, violinist, violist, composer.*

John Moorehead was born in Ireland, according to *The Thespian Dictionary* (1805). The subscription ledger of the *Irish Musical Fund* records a Mr Moorehead, probably either John or his brother Alexander, who was expelled on account of nonpayment as of 5 July 1789. According to Hodgkinson and Pogson in *The Early Manchester Theatre*, John was at the Bolton Theatre in 1793, when he was a guest at the wedding of Mr Merchant and Miss Hilliar at the Collegiate Church, Manchester, on 23 May. He played among the principals at the Three Choirs Festival at Worcester in 1794. About 1795 he was brought by Thomas John Dibdin to Sadler's Wells Theatre to play viola in the band.

The Dictionary of National Biography asserts that from 1796 to 1800 Moorehead set to music many of the entertainments performed at Sadler's Wells, among them *Alonzo and Imogene*, *Birds of a Feather*, *Sadak and Kalasrade*, *Old Fools*, and *Blankenberg*, and Allardyce Nicoll adds, the music to Charles Isaac Mungo Dibdin's *Harlequin Benedick*.

In 1798 Moorehead was also enrolled in the band at Covent Garden as violinist and occasional composer. He was first noticed in a bill of that theatre when he played with the band on 8 February 1799 a *Grand Selection of Sacred Music from the Works of Handel*. He composed for that theatre incidental music for T. J. Dibdin's farce *The Horse and the Widow*, which had its debut on 4 May 1799; songs for T. J. Dibdin's musical interlude *The Naval Pillar* on 7 October 1799; music for T. J. Dibdin's pantomime *The Volcano* on 23 December 1799; incidental music for Thomas Morton's comedy

Speed the Plough on 8 February 1800; the music to T. J. Dibdin's famous song "The Muffin Man," introduced as an entr'acte song 28 May 1800; the music for T. J. Dibdin's song "Scarce within Her Sea-Girt Reign," introduced on 5 June 1800; music for *The Dominion of Fancy* and *Il Bondocani* on 15 November 1800; music for the "historical pantomime" *La Perouse*, with Davy on 28 February 1801; music for *The Cabinet*, with Reeve, Davy, Corri, and Braham on 9 January 1802; music for *Family Quarrels*, with Braham and Reeve on 18 December 1802, and the popular overture to *Harlequin Habeas* on 27 December 1802. The British Library's manuscripts Egerton 2300 and 2301 show that in the 1799–1800 season Moorehead was paid 5*s.* per night for his services in the band and that he was paid by the job for composing: on 1 March 1800, £25 (probably for *The Cabinet*); on 16 April 1803, for "Family Quarrels & Panto £20"; and on 16 May 1803, for "Two Farmers £25."

John Moorehead also performed away from London. He played concerts on the violin in Liverpool in April and May 1801. *The Townsman* of Manchester cited an 1804 benefit shared with Chambers, in which the proceeds were £55 12*s.* Numbers of Moorehead's songs were published as having been sung at Sadler's Wells, Covent Garden, the Haymarket, and Vauxhall. Eighteen are listed in the *Catalogue of Printed Music in the British Museum.*

Charles Dibdin testified that Moorehead was a man of education. One of his close friends was the celebrated classicist Richard Porson. But a vein of dementia ran in the Moorehead family. John's brother Alexander, also a musician, died insane in a Liverpool asylum in 1803. Always eccentric, John's later productions were composed between recurrent attacks of a nervous malady which grew gradually until he began to suffer periods of outright insanity. Moorehead was a powerful man, and in one of his fits threatened Dibdin but was dissuaded from assault by a red-hot poker. He "nearly killed Mr. Goodwin, the music copyist of Covent-Garden Theatre, on some imaginary cause of offence, by striking him on the temple with a large rummer glass." Yet, when he recovered his senses he was always horrified by his actions, which were, Dibdin said, "generally directed against those who, in moments of sanity, he most valued and esteemed." Thomas

Dibdin left a vivid account of his friend's decline. Moorehead was confined for "some time . . . in Northampton-house," was released, but relapsed:

. . . at Richmond . . . he posted critical placards on the merits of contemporary composers, in the public reading-rooms, broke all the glasses and furniture in his lodgings, stopped the Duke of Queensberry's horses on Richmond Hill, and turned the carriage round, in spite of the well-applied lash of an athletic coachman; and one day, having snatched a Secretary to the Russian Embassy up in his arms, on the public walk at Richmond, and very nearly succeeded in an attempt to throw him in the Thames, poor Moorehead was committed, in a straight waistcoat, to Tothill-Fields Prison.

After his liberation from Tothill-Fields Prison, Moorehead enlisted as a sailor on board the *Monarch*, flagship of Admiral Lord Keith, who discovered his identity and made him master of his band.

One afternoon, while the ship lay in the Downs, the captain observing Moorehead more than usually depressed, gave him leave to go on shore for a day or two by way of relaxation: he called on a musical friend in Deal, who was giving a lesson, and Moorehead observed he would take a walk, and return to tea. He was never more seen alive, being found some days afterwards strangled with his handkerchief, which he had tied to the lower bar of a field gate.

Dibdin believed that "a third brother" had also died mad. (The *Thespian Dictionary's* account mentioned that "His brothers are likewise in the musical line.")

Moorland, Mr [*fl.* 1780], *actor.*
Mr Moorland played a principal but unnamed character in a single performance of *A School for Ladies* at the Haymarket Theatre on 5 April 1780.

Moose, Mrs. *See* MOSS, MRS.

Morales, Mrs Isaac. *See* WAINWRIGHT, SARAH.

Moralt, Mrs John Alvis. *See* DUSSEK, MRS JAN LADISLAV.

Mordaunt, Mr [*fl.* 1732], *actor.*

Mr Mordaunt played Sir John in *The Devil to Pay* on 31 March 1732 at the Haymarket Theatre.

More *See also* MARR, MOOR, MOORE.

More, Mr [*fl.* 1751], *actor.*

A Mr More played Gloster in *Jane Shore* on 21 August 1751 at the Richmond Theatre.

Moreau, Miss [*fl.* 1738–1747], *dancer, actress, singer.*

Miss Moreau, surely the daughter of the dancers Mr and Mrs Anthony Moreau, danced with her parents at the Aungier Street playhouse in Dublin on 14 December 1738. Since the bill did not indicate that she was making her debut, she had probably performed in public before. (The Miss Moreau listed in *The London Stage* as portraying a Grace in *The Royal Chace* at Covent Garden on 13 February 1738 was Mrs Moreau.) Miss Moreau was at Smock Alley in Dublin from 1739–40 through 1741–42 and perhaps longer (our information on Dublin theatricals in the eighteenth century is far from complete). Miss Moreau had an engagement at the Goodman's Fields Theatre in London in 1746–47, appearing there first on 21 November 1746 as Isabella in *The Stage Coach* and then acting Wheedle in *The Miser*, Rose in *The Recruiting Officer*, Honoria in *Love Makes a Man*, Lettice in *The School Boy*, Jenny Diver in *The Beggar's Opera*, Lucy in *Oroonoko*, Mademoiselle in *The Provok'd Wife*, Miss Hoyden in *The Relapse*, Clarinda in *Woman's a Riddle*, Ariel in *The Tempest*, Lucy in *The Devil to Pay*, Kitty in *The Lying Valet*, the title role in *Flora*, and Miss Biddy in *Miss in Her Teens*. At the Haymarket Theatre on 22 April 1747 she had a principal but unnamed role in *The Diversions of the Morning*, and at Bartholomew Fair on 22 August she played Colombine in *The Frolicksome Lasses*.

Sheldon's *Thomas Sheridan* reports that a Miss Moreau was advertised as making her first appearance on any stage at Smock Alley on 29 April 1751 dancing a minuet and louvre with Monsieur Moreau. That must have been a younger sister of the performer we have been following. The younger one was probably the Miss Moreau active at Smock Alley in 1751–52; she did not appear in London. Our Miss

Moreau seems not to have continued her career after August 1747.

Moreau, Anthony [*fl.* 1714–1752], *dancer, choreographer.*

Anthony Moreau (so Stockwell, in *Dublin Theatres*, cites him, from a Dublin lease in 1733) was first mentioned in London bills on 28 December 1714, when he danced between the acts at the new Lincoln's Inn Fields Theatre. He performed throughout the 1714–15 and 1715–16 seasons at that theatre in such entr'acte turns as *Harlequin and Two Punches* and a *Grand Spanish Entry*. On 10 May 1716 he shared a benefit with the treasurer Wood that brought in £105 6s. He continued dancing at Lincoln's Inn Fields through the 1718–19 season, offering from time to time new works of his own composition, such as *A New Grand Comic Dance* on 15 November 1716, an *Indian Dance* in *Mangora* on 14 December 1717, a *Grand Wedding Dance* on 4 October 1718, and a new *Spanish Dance* on 10 November 1718. He appeared regularly in entr'acte dances, many of them not given names in the bills, and he performed rarely in productions, one of his known parts being Harlequin in *The Jealous Doctor* on 29 October 1717. From July to September 1718 Moreau danced at Pinkethman's theatre in Richmond. Moreau had married one of his own pupils, Miss (sometimes Mrs) Schoolding between 3 and 13 March 1718.

In 1720–21 he performed at the Smock Alley Theatre in Dublin, and it may be that he had been there in 1719–20 as well, for we find no evidence of his having then been in London. His engagement at Smock Alley lasted until at least 1724–25, sometime after which he and Mrs Moreau went to Paris. They were advertised as making their first appearance in London since their arrival from the French capital on 1 October 1728, when they danced at Lincoln's Inn Fields. The couple stayed in London only for the 1728–29 season, with Moreau dancing between the acts, playing a Fury in *Harlequin Sorcerer*, a Frenchman in "The Triumphs of Love" at the conclusion of *Apollo and Daphne*, a Demon, Fire, and a God of the Woods in *The Rape of Proserpine*, a Mad Dancing Master in *The Humours of Bedlam*, and a Masquerader in *Italian Jealousy* and choreographing a new ballet for the benefit he shared with his wife on 19 April 1728. Receipts came to £95 6d.

In 1729–30 the Moreaus were back at Smock Alley. Records of Moreau's work in Dublin are fragmentary, but the research of the late W. S. Clark shows that Moreau danced with Madame Violante's troupe at Dame Street in 1730–31, was at Smock Alley in 1732–33 and 1734–35, and was at the Aungier Street Theatre on 5 May 1737 and remained there through the 1738–39 season. He was at Smock Alley again from 1739–40 through 1741–42; during that last season he was also at Aungier Street, where he danced through 1743–44; in 1744–45 he performed at Smock Alley and then in the United Company, for whom he is known to have danced the Miller and a Devil in *The Necromancer* on 21 March 1745; and he began the 1745–46 season at Aungier Street, but the company moved to Smock Alley on 5 December 1745.

On 2 September 1746 an unidentified clipping, transcribed by Latreille, stated that "Mons Moreau having quitted the Playhouse is removed to Founes Street near Dame Street, and will teach young Masters and Misses to dance, Tuesdays, Thursdays and Saturdays from 3 to 6 in the evening." He rejoined Smock Alley in 1747–48, however, stayed there in 1748–49, was absent for a season (unless evidence is simply missing), returned in 1750–51, and remained through 1751–52. After that, by which time he must have been well along in years, Anthony Moreau was not mentioned in theatrical documents again. Possibly he was an ancestor of the dancer Moreau who appeared at the King's Theatre, Sadler's Wells, and the Pantheon from 1805 to 1813. We assume that the Miss Moreau who danced with Mr and Mrs Moreau at the Aungier Street Theatre on 14 December 1738 and continued appearing in Ireland and England until 1747 was a daughter of Anthony and his wife. Another, presumably younger, Miss Moreau danced in Ireland in 1751 and 1752 but did not appear in London.

Moreau, Mrs Anthony, née Schoolding [*fl. c.* 1713–1749], *dancer, actress.*

The Miss (sometimes Mrs) Schoolding who married the dancer Anthony Moreau was probably the one who was first mentioned in playbills in London on 22 December 1714 as dancing at the Lincoln's Inn Fields Theatre. W. S.

Clark in *The Early Irish Stage* lists her as active in Dublin about 1713–14 before coming to London. Miss Schoolding's parents were dancers, as was her sister, and since our subject was occasionally called Mrs, the possibility of confusing her with her mother and sister is great. However, we believe she was the one who danced regularly between the acts at Lincoln's Inn Fields in 1714–15 and played Sylvia in *The Old Bachelor* on 4 January 1715, the title role in *The Fair Quaker* on 7 January, Corinna in *The Confederacy* on 8 January, and Prue in *Love for Love* on 2 February and had a solo benefit on 9 April that brought in £88 17s. 6d.. She played Phrinia in *Timon of Athens* and Mrs Chat in *The Committee* in Dublin about 1715—perhaps during the summer, when she is not known to have been performing in London.

From 1715–16 to the middle of the 1717–18 season at Lincoln's Inn Fields, cited in advertisements usually as Mrs Schoolding, she danced between the acts and played Peggy in *The London Cuckolds*, Mademoiselle in *The Provok'd Wife*, Mrs Tagg in *The Adventures of Half an Hour*, Maria in *The Artful Husband*, Mrs Townley (Colombine) in *The Jealous Doctor*, Sylvia in *The Old Bachelor*, an unnamed part in *The Fair Example*, Venus in *Mars and Venus*, the title part in *Colombine*, and Colombine in *Amadis*. She played that last part as Mrs Schoolding on 3 March 1718; when the work was repeated on 13 March she had become Mrs Moreau, wife of Anthony Moreau, her dancing teacher. During the remainder of the 1717–18 season she continued dancing entr'acte turns and played Mademoiselle in *The Provok'd Wife* and Arabella in *The Committee*. At Pinkethman's theatre in Richmond in August she danced and was seen as Arabella again and as Prue in *Love for Love*. She remained at Lincoln's Inn Fields for one more season, as did her husband, dancing regularly and playing, in addition to her earlier roles, Mrs Fancy in *The Fair Example*, Miranda in *Woman's a Riddle*, a part in *Platonic Love*, and Alicia in *'Tis Well If It Takes*. At Richmond in August and September 1719 she had a principal but unnamed part in *The Soldier's Stratagem*, after which she and her husband probably left London, perhaps for Dublin, where they appeared in 1720–21.

Mrs Moreau's parts at the Smock Alley playhouse in Dublin are only partly known: she

played Lady Quibble in *A Wife and No Wife* in
1723–24 and Rosara in *She Wou'd and She Wou'd
Not* and Lady Sadlife in *The Double Gallant* in
1724–25, and she must have been seen in
many other parts for which records have not
been found. Sometime after the spring of 1725
the Moreaus went to Paris, from which city
they were said to be when they danced on 1
October 1728 at Lincoln's Inn Fields. During
the 1728–29 season she danced in entr'acte
specialties regularly and was seen as Mademoiselle in *The Provok'd Husband*, a Pierrot Woman
in *The Necromancer*, Colombine in *Apollo and
Daphne* and a French Woman in "The Triumphs
of Love" that concluded that pantomime, Colombine in *The Rape of Proserpine*, and Hillaria
in *Tunbridge Walks*. W. S. Clark's research into
the Dublin Theatre in the eighteenth century
revealed that Mrs Moreau was at Smock Alley
in Dublin sometime in 1728–29 and there
played Megra in *Philaster*; that may well have
been in the summer of 1729 after her Lincoln's
Inn Fields engagement ended. She was at Lincoln's Inn Fields on 6 October 1729 to play
Mademoiselle in *The Provok'd Wife*, but when
the play was repeated on 16 October Mrs
Wetherilt took the part. Mrs Moreau is recorded as spending the rest of the 1729–30
season in Dublin; it is probable that she had
come to London for a visit only and was not
actually engaged at Lincoln's Inn Fields.

The Moreaus were in Madame Violante's
troupe at the Dame Street playhouse in Dublin
in 1730–31 and then back at Smock Alley the
following season. Mrs Moreau played there
through 1733–34 and we know that she appeared as Millwood in *The London Merchant* on
21 September 1731 and Rose in *The Recruiting
Officer* on 9 March 1734. She danced at Covent
Garden Theatre in 1736–37 and 1737–38
(Anthony Moreau was in Dublin those seasons). Her first appearance was as the Miller's
Wife and a Mezzetin Woman in *The Necromancer* on 22 September 1736, after which she
acted a Female in *The Rape of Proserpine*, a
Spanish Woman in *Apollo and Daphne*, her favorite part of Mademoiselle, an Amazon in
Perseus and Andromeda, a Grace in *The Royal
Chace*, and Mademoiselle D'Epingle in *The Funeral*. She also appeared in such entr'acte dances
as *French Peasant*, a *Grand Comic Dance*, *Peasant*, and a *Scots Dance*.

Mrs Moreau performed at the Aungier Street

Theatre in Dublin and at Smock Alley in 1738–
39, playing, among other parts we know not
of, Lappet in *The Miser*. She was at Smock
Alley in 1739–40 and 1740–41, at Smock
Alley and Aungier Street in 1741–42, and
then at Smock Alley and in the United Company in 1744–45, the Miller's Wife in *The
Necromancer* on 21 March 1745 being one of
her known parts. In 1748–49 she performed
at Smock Alley, but after that Mrs Moreau was
not named in any documents yet discovered.

Moreland. *See also* MORLAND.

Moreland, Mrs [*fl.* 1798–1800], *actress.*

In the Harvard Theatre Collection is a letter
from the provincial manager Tate Wilkinson
to the actor John Emery, dated 19 April 1800.
Wilkinson said that in his company at York
was a Mrs Moreland: "She seems *quite the thing.*
Says she was at Covent Garden Theatre two
years ago. last autumn at Windsor, and acted
in one play at the Haymarket last Nov^r." Perhaps Mrs Moreland was lying; *The London Stage*
does not list her, and the Haymarket was,
apparently, dark throughout the month of November 1799.

Morell, Mons [*fl.* 1729], *performer.*
On 26 and 29 May 1729 at the Haymarket
Theatre Monsieur Morell, lately arrived from
France, played "several comic and diverting
French pieces" in *The Beggar's Opera*. It is diffi-
cult from that description to tell whether Mo-
rell was an actor, singer, dancer, or instrumen-
talist.

Morella. *See* MARELLA.

Morelli, Signor [*fl.* 1800–1809], *actor,
dancer, prompter.*
Our first knowledge of Mr Morelli of Sadler's
Wells comes from one of the scattered bills of
that establishment, that of 31 May 1800, when
he had some part in *Blackenberg*. "Signor Morelli" was the Knight of Spain in Charles Dibdin's *The Old Man of the Mountains* at the Wells
sometime in 1803 and danced (also in 1803)
in *British Amazons*. Dibdin, the manager,
mentioned him in *Memoirs of Charles Dibdin the
Younger*, also as present in 1803:

We introduced also to the public, the first band of *Pandeans* [players on Pan-pipes] that ever appeared in England; who were brought to me by my Prompter, whose name was Morelli; an Italian; and to whom all the Italian Minstrels and gymnastical performers used to apply, on their arrival in England, as to a House of Call, and he brought them all, first, to me.

Morelli was still identified as the Sadler's Wells prompter when he took a benefit on 10 October 1809. He lived at that time in Spa Gardens. The Master Morelli at Sadler's Wells in 1806, the Master Morelli there in 1814–16, and the Misses Morelli there on 1 July 1816 probably were kin. So also, perhaps, was the Miss Morelli (a sister?) who danced a hornpipe when the Italian Fantoccini played Bristol in April 1781.

Morelli, Giovanni   [*fl.* 1787–1815], singer, actor, composer.

The circumstances of the birth, early life, and musical education of Giovanni Morelli are unknown. He may have been a native Floren-

Harvard Theatre Collection

GIOVANNI MORELLI

engraving by Godefroy, after Cosway

tine. Julian Marshall's vignette of Morelli in Grove repeats a story that he was running footman to Lord Cowper in Florence and was brought to England because of his remarkable bass voice.

Whatever the circumstances of his initiation to the profession, he succeeded with London audiences from his first appearance, as Bastiano Ammazzagatte in Paisiello's new comic opera *Gli schiavi per amore*, at the King's Theatre on 24 April 1787. He sang at the fourth annual Handel commemoration in June. He repeated the performance of Bastiano several times during the season, the last occasion being for his benefit on 7 June. Tickets could then be had of him at his lodgings, No 18, Oxendon Street, Haymarket. Before the end of his second season he had snatched the honors of *primo buffo caricato* away from the fine basso Andrea Morigi.

Morelli was absent from the London boards, and probably from England, from the spring of 1788 until that of 1791. But he was a popular figure almost constantly through the nineties and, though his engagements then gradually tapered off as his voice weakened, he sang on through the opening decade of the nineteenth century. He seems to have impoverished himself by unwise speculation and after 1805–6 was overshadowed by Naldi, who nevertheless, according to Smith in *The Italian Opera in London* kindly loaned him money. Morelli was in the company in the rebuilt Pantheon in 1812 when Catherine Stephens made her first appearance. But he returned to the Haymarket operas for a time in 1815.

The record of Morelli's other roles, chronologically until 1799–1800, follows: in 1787–88, at the King's, Tadeo in *Il Re Teodoro in Venezia*, Don Polidoro in *La locondiera*, Don Pancrazio Garofano in *La camariera astuta*, some principal part in *La francatana*; and in spring-summer 1791 at the Pantheon, Don Pistofolo in *La Molinarella*, and Arsenio in *La locanda*. During the oratorio season at the King's in 1792, he sang solos in *Redemption*, "Selected from the works of Handel by Dr Arnold," and in four other programs—*Grand Selections*—of the master's music, in company with a strong group which included Kelly, Reinhold, Incledon, Dignum, Mrs Bland, and Mrs Crouch. With the Drury Lane Company at the King's Theatre he participated in Bannister's benefit, singing "Non andrai farfalone amoroso" and

"Donne, donne, chi vi crede" in the musical interlude *The Festive Board*.

Thereafter, with the King's opera company, he added: in the season of 1793, an unspecified role in Paisiello's *Il barbiere di Siviglia* and solo parts in *Messiah* and more "Grand Selections"; in the season of 1793, Titta in *Le nozze di Dorina*; and in the season of 1794, Cecchino in *I contadini bizzarri*, Don Perinzonio in *Il capriccio*, Don Alfonso in *La bella pescatrice*, Uberto in *La serva padrona*, Don Fabrizio in *La Frascatana*.

In the 1794–95 season he was Pandolfo in *I zingari in Fiera*, Bonario in *La scola dei maritata*, Taddeo in *Il conte ridicolo*, and Corrado in *L'Isola del piacere*; in 1795–96, Carbonaro in *La bella Arsene*, Giorgiolone in *I traci amanti*, a principal character in *I due gobbi*, Don Gavino in *La modista raggiratrice*, an unspecified character in *Il Tesoro*, and Ali in *Zemira e Azor*; in 1796–97, Filiberto in *Il consiglio imprudente*, Doristo

Harvard Theatre Collection

GIOVANNI MORELLI
engraving by De Loutherbourg

in *L'Albero di Diana*, and Cecchino in *Le gelosie villane*; in the spring of 1798, Rusticone in *La cifra*, Tamburlano in *La sposa in Equivoco* (one act only, in a "Benefit for Voluntary Contributions for the Defense of the Country"), Don Perinzonio in *Il capriccio drammatico*, and Il Conte Robinson in *Il matrimonio segreto*; in 1798–99, a principal character in *Gli schiavi per amore* and Lanzman in *I due Suizzeri*; and, in the spring of 1800, Alberto in *I due fratelli rivali* and Pierotto Spazzacamino in *Il principe spazzacamino*.

James Boaden, in his *Memoirs of the Life of John Philip Kemble* (1825) judged that Morelli "was an actor such as the Italian stage has seldom witnessed. He was, I used to think, in his prime, quite upon a par with [Tom] King [the comedian] of Drury Lane Theatre. Like him, he was distinguished for neat articulation, and an unremitting attention to the business of the whole stage."

Evidently Morelli tried his hand at composing, though the only evidence is his name, along with the creatively more illustrious ones of Paisiello and Storace, on a playbill as a contributor to the songs and incidental music to John O'Keeffe's musical farce *The Farmer* which opened at Covent Garden on 31 November 1787.

An engraved portrait of Giovanni Morelli by J. Godefroy, said to be after R. Cosway, was published by Molinari in 1797. A caricature of Morelli by De Loutherbourg was published by W. Holland in 1790.

Morelli, John Baptist *1717?–1796, violinist, composer.*

The *Pocket Magazine* for April 1796 speaks of the death "lately" of John Baptist Morelli, identified as a composer and the leader of the band "at the Opera." The death in April is confirmed by a Burney clipping in the British Library, which adds "Aged 79." Nothing else is known about him, though he was perhaps a relative of the great basso at the King's Theatre, Giovanni Morelli.

Morello, Mr [*fl.* 1790] *puppeteer.*
See MORELLO, CHARLES.

Morello, Charles [*fl.* 1790–1798?], *puppeteer.*

The Pie Powder Court Book at the Guildhall Library shows payments of 8*s*. each on 6 September 1790 by the puppeteers Mr Morella and Charles Morella (in later years the name was always spelled Morello). The fees were for licenses to exhibit puppets at Bartholomew Fair. A Morello, perhaps Charles, also worked his puppets at the Fair in 1791, 1792, 1794, 1795, 1796, and 1798.

Moretti, Signora. *See* AMORETTI, GIUSTINA.

Morey, Master [*fl.* 1779], *dancer.*
Master Morey danced in *Richard III* at Drury Lane Theatre on 18 May 1779 and was not mentioned in the bills again.

Morgan, Mr [*fl.* 1696?–1719?], *singer, composer.*
In August 1699 *Mercurius Musicus* published "Cease, cease, cease," a song "Set by Mr. Morgan, being the last he made in Ireland." The same Mr Morgan, presumably, was the one cited in *Wit and Mirth* in 1719 as the composer of "Aurelia now one Moment lost" and as the singer of John Eccles's "Fly, fly ye lazy Hours." The Eccles song was from *The Loves of Mars and Venus*, which had been produced at the Lincoln's Inn Fields Theatre on 14 November 1696. No singer named Morgan is known to have been at that playhouse in the late seventeenth or early eighteenth century, but a Morgan composed songs for *Imposture Defeated* at Drury Lane Theatre in September 1697. The appearance of Morgan's name in the 1719 edition of *Wit and Mirth* is no proof that he was still active then. He seems not to have been the actor (Robert?) Morgan, though they may have been related.

Morgan, Mr [*fl.* 1746–1747], *singer.*
Mr Morgan sang in the chorus of *Macbeth* at Drury Lane Theatre on 7 November 1746 and subsequent dates through 1 May 1747.

Morgan, Mr [*fl.* 1776–1797?], *actor.*
Mr Morgan played Tom in *The Jealous Wife* at the Haymarket Theatre on 2 May 1776, spoke the prologue to *Richard III* at the China Hall, Rotherhithe, on 4 October 1776, and played an unspecified character in *The Reprisal* at the Haymarket on 23 February 1784. Perhaps he was the Morgan who was at Leigh on

11 February 1789, playing Hawthorn in *Love in a Village* and Lenox, a Bleeding Captain, and the Second Witch in *Macbeth*. He may also have been the Morgan in Johnson's troupe at Barking, Essex, in 1792 and the Morgan who acted in Philadelphia from 1795 to 1797.

Morgan, Dr [*fl.* 1784], *singer.*
The Reverend Dr Morgan sang bass in the Handel Memorial Concerts at Westminster Abbey and the Pantheon in May and June 1784.

"Morgan, Lady" *b.* 1756?, *dwarf.*
Morley in his *Memoirs of Bartholomew Fair* quotes a newspaper advertisement concerning the dwarf Thomas Allen:

Also MISS MORGAN, the Celebrated WINDSOR FAIRY, known in *London* and *Windsor* by the Addition of LADY MORGAN, *a Title which His Majesty was pleased to confer on her.*

This unparalleled Woman is in the 35th year of her age, and only 18 pounds weight. Her form affords a pleasing surprise, and her admirable symmetry engages attention. She was introduced to Their MAJESTIES at the *Queen's Lodge, Windsor,* on Saturday, the 4th of August, 1781 [*recte:* 1791?] by the recommendation of the late Dr. *Hunter;* when they were pleased to pronounce her the finest Display of Human Nature in *miniature* they ever saw.— But we shall say no more of these great Wonders of Nature: let those who honour them with their visits, judge for themselves.

Let others boast of stature, or of birth,
This Glorious Truth shall fill our souls with mirth:
"That we now are, and hope, for years, to sing
The SMALLEST *subjects of the* GREATEST *King!"*
☞Admittance to Ladies and Gentlemen, 1s.— Children, Half Price.
*§*In this and many other parts of the Kingdom, it is too common to show deformed persons, with various arts and deceptions, under denominations of persons in miniature, to impose on the public.

This Little Couple are, beyond contradiction, the most wonderful display of nature ever held out to the admiration of mankind.
N.B. The above Lady's mother is with her, and will attend at any Lady or Gentleman's house, if required.

Morley does not provide a date for that appearance of Lady Morgan at Bartholomew Fair, though he places the advertisement under the period 1787–1791.

Another puff, hand-dated on a copy at the Huntington Library 27 December 1791, reads:

TO BE SEEN AT THE LYCEUM, STRAND.
However, striking a curiosity may be, there is generally some difficulty in engaging the attention of the public, but even this is not the case with that graceful Couple in Miniature, Mr. THOMAS ALLEN, who is now in the seventy-fourth [recte: twenty-fourth] year of his age, and Lady MORGAN, the celebrated Windsor Fairy, who is now in the thirty-fourth year of her age, and only eighteen pounds weight. The curious of all degrees may resort to see them, being sensible that prodigies equal to these never made their appearance amongst us before, and the most penetrating have frankly declared, that neither the tongue of the most florid orator, or pen of the most ingenious writer, can describe the beauty and elegance of those phenomena of nature, and that all description must fall infinitely short of giving that satisfaction which may be obtained on a judicious inspection.
N.B. Ladies and Gentlemen waited on [in] their own houses if required.

With that advertisement was a jingle concerning the Queen asking the King to give Lady Morgan royal protection:

When George the Third with pleasure view'd
Each native symmetry endu'd,
And no one gift unseen;
When thus, with kind complacent look,
Reply'd his far-fam'd Queen

—and so on, the implication being that the little lady exhibited in the nude.
Another clipping at the Huntington, hand-dated 31 December 1791, is headed "ROYAL VISIT TO THE LYCEUM":

Their Royal Highnesses the Dukes of York and Clarence went yesterday to the Lyceum in the Strand, to see the most curious of all curiosities, the living Lilliputians, Mr. Thomas Allen and Lady Morgan. Their Royal Highnesses conversed with them for some time in the most affable and engaging manner, and expressed their surprize and approbation at the sight of these *Lusus Naturae.*—Several of the Nobility and Gentry also visited them yesterday, and were equally gratified and delighted. Indeed, they are now become the general topic of conversation, and every one is anxious to pay an early visit to these surprising dwarfs.
Mr THOMAS ALLEN, who was never before shewn to the Public, is in his 24th year, and of beautiful symmetry. Lady MORGAN, the Windsor Fairy, who was introduced to their Majesties, at the Queen's Lodge, by the late Dr. Hunter in August 1791;

when his Majesty was pleased to confer on her the above title.

We take it that 1791 is the correct year for all of the notices quoted and that Lady Morgan's birth date was about 1756. She was also exhibited at Bristol, according to an advertisement dated 2 September 1786. She and James Harris, described as midgets, were on display at Mrs Williams's, the Three Tuns, St James's Back.
A picture of Lady Morgan, with Thomas Allen, accompanies Allen's entry in the first volume of this dictionary. It was published in the *Wonderful Magazine* in November 1803.

Morgan, Master [fl. 1745], *harpsichordist.*
Morgan Junior, possibly George Morgan's son, played the harpsichord on 20 February 1745 at a benefit held by Valentine Snow at his house.

Morgan, Master [fl. 1746–1747], *actor, dancer.*
At the Goodman's Field's playhouse Master Morgan played the young Duke of York in *Richard III* on 17 December 1746, Fleance in *Macbeth* on 5 January 1747, and Robin in *The Merry Wives of Windsor* on 9 January. During the season he was frequently seen in entr'acte dances, most of them untitled. His partner was often Miss Baker, with whom he appeared in a *Peasant Dance* on 27 October 1746.

Morgan, Charles 1717–1746, *actor.*
Charles Morgan was born in 1717, the son of the actors Mr and Mrs (Robert?) Morgan. The prompter Chetwood in his *General History* said "the Son play'd Childrens Parts as soon as he could speak plain." When that was we do not know; the first record of "Young Morgan" on stage dates from 23 August 1732, when he played Spindle in *The Perjur'd Prince* at Bullock's booth at Bartholomew Fair. The Morgans were at the Smock Alley Theatre in Dublin in 1736–37, and on 11 November 1736 "C. Morgan" (Charles apparently, for no other Morgan qualifies) acted Falstaff in *The Merry Wives of Windsor*. Other roles known for him in Dublin were Lolpoop in *The Squire of Alsatia* in November 1737, a part he is known to have repeated in June 1741, Hob in *Flora*, Cimber-

ton in *The Conscious Lovers*, Launcelot Gobbo in *The Merchant of Venice*, Roderigo in *Othello*, the Captain in *Love and Loyalty*, and Faustus's Man in *The Necromancer*. Chetwood said that Morgan also acted Beau Clincher in *The Constant Couple*. On 23 August 1743 Morgan played Cimberton at the Aungier Street Theatre.

Chetwood related an accident that befell Morgan: "Mr. *Morgan* being to fly on the Back of a Witch, in the *Lancashire Witches*, thro' the Ignorance of the Workers in the Machinery, the Fly broke, and they both fell together, but thro' Providence they neither of them were much hurt. . . ." Chetwood reported that Morgan made great progress in low comedy and "gave great Hopes of Perfection, if a lingering Consumption had not taken him off in the Flower of his Age." He died, Chetwood said, in May 1745 at the age of 28; Genest corrected the year of Morgan's death to 1746. Davies said Charles Morgan was commonly called "Drib."

Morgan, E. N. *See* BONVILLE, MR.

Morgan, George ₁*fl. c. 1720–1750?*₁, *composer, singer?*

The *Catalogue of Printed Music in the British Museum* lists three songs by George Morgan, one published about 1720 and the other two dating about 1730. George Morgan was one of the original subscribers to the Royal Society of Musicians when it was organized on 28 August 1739. By 1744 Morgan was a member of the King's Musick at a salary of £40 annually, a post he held until at least 1749. Perhaps he was the Mr Morgan who was cited as the singer in the separately printed song *Advice* (1750?) by Arne, but that Morgan may have been the actor and singer Robert (?).

Morgan, George ₁*fl. 1763*₁, *violist.*

Mortimer's London Directory of 1763 listed George Morgan, of Maddox Street, as a tenor (i.e. violist) in the King's band of musicians at court.

Morgan, James ₁*fl. 1754–1772*₁, *actor, singer, dancer.*

The actor-singer James Morgan was one of two Masters Morgan in the York troupe in 1754, according to Sybil Rosenfeld's *Strolling Players*. The other one, probably his brother, was born about 1747 and had performed as early as 1752. James Morgan is known to have played *Tom Thumb* in York in 1754.

Master Morgan—presumably James—first appeared in London on 20 October 1762 at Covent Garden Theatre, playing Simple in *The Merry Wives of Windsor*. The rest of the season saw him as Aminidab in *A Bold Stroke for a Wife*, beginning on 27 December and the Page in *The Inconstant*, beginning on 1 February 1763. He continued at Covent Garden as Master Morgan to the beginning of the 1765–66 season, adding such new roles as Jessamin in *The City Wives Confederacy*, Fleance in *Macbeth*, a Drawer in *The Spanish Fryar*, and Parisatis in *The Rival Queens; or, Death of Alexander the Little*. On 15 October 1765 he was called Master Morgan in *The Apprentice*, but on the twenty-sixth he was advertised as Mr Morgan, playing Aminidab. Morgan was also a dancer, one of his turns being *Hippisley's Drunken Man*, which he danced on 7 May 1764.

Morgan continued at Covent Garden through the 1768–69 season, attempting, among other new parts, Daniel in *The Conscious Lovers*, Francis in *1 Henry IV*, a Planter in *Oroonoko*, Frank in *All in the Right*, a Watchman in *The Upholsterer*, Peter in *Romeo and Juliet*, Squire Gawky and Drudge in *Orpheus and Eurydice*, the Welsh Collier in *The Recruiting Officer*, Sideboard in *The Way to Keep Him*, Lucianus in *Hamlet*, Richard in *The Provok'd Husband*, Faustus's Man in *Harlequin Doctor Faustus*, Bardolph in *Henry V*, and Gibbet in *The Stratagem*. His daily salary as of September 1767 was 3s. 4d..

In the summer of 1768 Morgan appeared at the Haymarket Theatre as a member of Foote's company, playing Mrs Loveit (*sic*) in *The Commissary* beginning on 13 July and Dick in *The Minor* beginning on 18 July. He was probably the Mr Morgan named as the singer of *Help me each Harmonious Grove* at Sadler's Wells when the song was published in 1768. His full name appeared in the *Theatrical Monitor* on 5 November 1768. Morgan returned to the Haymarket for a single appearance as Dick in *The Minor* on 29 May 1769. He was probably the Morgan who acted at the new theatre, the White Hart in Launceston, Cornwall, in the summer of 1772. He was Douglas in *Henry IV* and had a part in the Burletta *Midas* on 5 May. On 3 June he played a Servant in *The Orphan*, and on 5 June he was Phillop in *The Brothers*.

Morgan, Mrs John the first. *See* MORTON, MARY.

Morgan, Manly [*fl.* 1727], singer.

The Lord Chamberlain issued a warrant on 30 June 1727 authorizing an allowance for Manly Morgan, one of the children of the Chapel Royal whose voice had changed.

Morgan, [Robert?] [*fl.* 1716–1759], actor, singer, dancer.

The Mr Morgan who began acting in London as early as 1716 and was still performing in the 1750s may have been Robert Morgan, who in 1753 subscribed to Aaron Hill's *Works*. His wife, Henrietta Maria Morgan, had a career that stretched from 1721 to the late 1740s and ran parallel to her husband's career for many years. They had a son, Charles, who acted when a child and whose career was cut short by consumption in 1746. There were a number of other Morgans performing in the eighteenth century in London and Dublin, but it is difficult to ascertain relationships, and, indeed, sometimes difficult to distinguish one Morgan from another.

Our Morgan seems to have been noticed first on 27 April 1716, when he originated the role of Ralph in *The Northern Heiress* at Lincoln's Inn Fields Theatre. The following 3 August he played Crapine in *The Feign'd Curtizans* at the same house. The same Morgan, presumably, played Ben in *Love for Love* at Lincoln's Inn Fields on 13 November 1719, and during the rest of the 1719–20 season appeared again as Ben and as the Mad Welshman in *The Pilgrim*. On 7 June 1720 he shared a benefit with three others.

He continued at Lincoln's Inn Fields to the fall of 1730, playing such parts as the third Witch in *Macbeth*, Abhorson in *Measure for Measure*, Aspen in *Woman's a Riddle*, a Recruit in *The Recruiting Officer*, Obadiah in *The Committee*, a Ravished Woman in *Don Quixote*, Snuffle in *Injured Love*, a Sailor in *The Fair Quaker of Deal*, Goth in *Titus Andronicus*, Dashwell in *The London Cuckolds*, Foigard in *The Stratagem*, the Gentleman Usher in *King Lear*, Setter and

Sir Joseph in *The Old Bachelor*, a Parishioner in *The Spanish Curate*, Butler in *The Drummer* (he often replaced Spiller in such parts), Antonio in *Venice Preserv'd*, Fourbin in *The Soldiers Fortune*, Sir William in *The Squire of Alsatia*, Ferret in *The Beggar's Bush*, Froth in *The Double Dealer*, Pamphlet and Mockmode in *Love and a Bottle*, Bomilcar in *Sophonisba*, Martin in *Love's Contrivance*, Jamy in *The Taming of the Shrew*, Philo in *Money the Mistress*, Blunt in *The Rover*, Sir Roger in *The Fond Husband*, Squib in *Tunbridge Walks*, Jodelet in *The Man's the Master*, Hector and the Marquis of Hazard in *The Gamester*, Hidewell in *The Spanish Wives*, Sir Morglay Thwack in *The Wits*, Brass in *The Confederacy*, Hogstye and Quaint in *Aesop*, Tyro in *The Cheats*, Ben Budge in *The Beggar's Opera*, and Simon Pure in *A Bold Stroke for a Wife*. Morgan was also advertised once as an entr'acte dancer.

His engagement at Lincoln's Inn Fields was apparently interrupted in 1728–29. On 20 November 1728 he acted a Plebeian in *Julius Caesar*, but that seems to have been his only appearance at his home theatre that season. On 25 January 1729, he shared a benefit at the Haymarket with two others at a performance of *The Beggar's Opera*. The bill did not reveal whether or not he played a role. He was back at Lincoln's Inn Fields in 1729–30, however.

He shared benefits at Lincoln's Inn Fields, at first with as many as four others but, by the end of the 1720's, with just one other performer. The records show that his benefit receipts were moderate: about £145 in 1721, £62 in 1723, £100 in 1726, and £144 in 1728. His daily salary in 1724–25 was 10s., and two years later it was apparently up to 15s. Morgan augmented his income by acting at the late summer fairs, his earliest recorded appearance being at Bartholomew Fair on 24 August 1721 as Terrible in *The Siege of Bethulia*. The following 8 September he played Ninepence in *The Noble Englishman*, a droll, at Southwark Fair. Other parts he acted at the fairs in the 1720s included Trusty in *The Unnatural Parents*. He and his wife acted at Richmond in the summer of 1730.

Morgan began the 1730–31 season at Lincoln's Inn Fields, playing through 6 November 1730. Then, on 9 November he acted Cholerick in *Love Makes a Man* at the Haymarket (his wife played Angelina). The Morgans continued at the Haymarket to 9 December. He was seen as Duretête in *The Inconstant*, Squib in *Tunbridge Walks*, Don Gulielmo in *The False Count*, Flail in *The Battle of the Poets*, and an unspecified part in *The Merry Masqueraders*.

On 14 December 1730 the Morgans moved to the Goodman's Fields Theatre to play Ben and Prue in *Love for Love*. Their engagement continued through the fall of 1733, with Morgan appearing in such new parts as Sir Francis in *The Provok'd Husband*, Bullock in *The Recruiting Officer*, the first Gravedigger in *Hamlet*, Alphonso in *The Pilgrim*, Jobson in *The Devil of a Wife*, Fondlewife in *The Old Bachelor*, Snap in *Love's Last Shift*, Obadiah in *A Bold Stroke for a Wife*, Toby in *The Cobler of Preston*, Crack in *Sir Courtly Nice*, Clincher Senior in *The Constant Couple*, Vellum in *The Drummer*, Teague in *The Committee*, Old Wilful in *The Double Gallant*, Flip in *The Fair Quaker of Deal*, Cacafogo in *Rule a Wife and Have a Wife*, the Cobler in *The Cobler's Opera*, Hannibal in *Sophonisba*, Trinculo in *The Tempest*, the Host in *The Merry Wives of Windsor*, Trappanti in *She Wou'd and She Wou'd Not*, a Carrier in *1 Henry IV*, Driver in *Oroonoko*, Mat in *The Beggar's Opera*, the Mayor in *Richard III*, Macahone in *The Stage Coach Opera*, Hellebore in *The Mock Doctor*, and Coupler in *The Relapse*. Morgan also became a popular speaker of epilogues, usually delivering them seated on an ass, in the tradition of Joe Haines and William Pinkethman.

He continued appearing at the late summer fairs, playing such parts as Rogero in *Guy, Earl of Warwick*, the title role in *Whittington*, and Toby Crab in *The Perjur'd Prince* (at Bullock's booth at Bartholomew Fair on 23 August 1732, on which date "Young Morgan," our subject's son Charles, acted Spindle—though the prompter Chetwood said the younger Morgan had begun making stage appearances as soon as he was able to talk, which would have been by 1720). Morgan and his wife also continued acting during the summers at Richmond. He played mostly his regular repertoire from the winter seasons, but in July 1731 at Richmond he acted Humphrey in *The Conscious Lovers* and in August 1732 he was seen as Peascod in *The What D'Ye Call It*. Once during his years at Goodman's Fields he put in an appearance at the Haymarket: on 28 May 1733, as Sir Francis in *The Provok'd Husband*.

Morgan left Goodman's Fields in mid-November 1733 and engaged with John Rich at the new Covent Garden Theatre, making his first appearance there on 26 November as Cholerick in *Love Makes a Man*. During the rest of the season he appeared as The Mad Englishman in *The Pilgrim*, Gripe in *The Confederacy*, Sir Joslin in *She Wou'd If She Cou'd*, Vandunck in *The Royal Merchant*, Priam in *Troilus and Cressida*, Snap in *Love's Last Shift*, a Witch in *Macbeth*, Bonniface in *The Beaux' Stratagem*, an unspecified role in *The Distress'd Wife*, Sir William in *The Squire of Alsatia*, Macahone in *The Strollers*, and Sir Jealous in *The Busy Body*.

After the 1733–34 season concluded Morgan appeared at Richmond in June as a Carrier in *1 Henry IV*, at York Buildings on 8 July as Moneses in *Tamerlane*, at a single performance of *The Busy Body* at Covent Garden on 2 September, and as Bristle the Cobler in *The Siege of Troy* at Southwark Fair on 7 September.

Morgan's 1734–35 season was spent at Covent Garden, with a few scattered appearances at Lincoln's Inn Fields. At the patent house he played a number of his old parts and added Waitwell in *The Way of the World*, Sir Jasper in *The Mock Doctor*, Pedro in *The Wonder*, Sir Soloman in *The Mock Countess*, Bolus in *The Double Gallant*, Stocks in *The Lottery*, Clodpole in *The Amorous Widow*, Charon in *Macheath in the Shades*, and Luca in *The Country House*. At Lincoln's Inn Fields he acted Badger in *Don Quixote in London*, Bullock in *The Recruiting Officer*, Snap in *Love's Last Shift*, Mat in *The Beggar's Opera*, and Don Lewis in *Love Makes a Man*.

The 1735–36 season found Morgan at the Ransford Street Theatre in Dublin, acting Vandunck and Don Lewis in November and December, and then moving to Smock Alley in 1736–37, where he acted Alexander in *The Rival Queens*. In 1737–38 he is known to have played his old role of Sir William in *The Squire of Alsatia*. He was Harlequin in *The Emperor of the Moon* in February 1739 at Aungier Street; then he acted at Smock Alley again in 1740–41.

On 18 September 1742 Morgan made his first appearance at Drury Lane Theatre in London (advertised as from Dublin) playing Sir Sampson in *Love for Love*. He remained at Drury Lane through 1744–45, playing such parts as Sir Henry in *The Tender Husband*, the Miller in *The King and the Miller of Mansfield*, Smuggler in *The Constant Couple*, Squeeze Purse in *The Wedding Day*, Ananias in *The Alchemist*, Sir Roger in *The What D'Ye Call it*, Balderdash in *The Twin Rivals*, Antonio in *Love Makes a Man*, Martin in *The Anatomist*, Nym in *The Merry Wives of Windsor*, Galoon in *The Gamester*, Alguazile in *The Wonder*, Major Rakish in *The School Boy*, Hothead in *Sir Courtly Nice*, and several of his old roles.

Presumably it was the elder Morgan who acted at Smock Alley in 1742–43, probably during the summer of 1743, and who acted Dry Boots in *The French Doctor Outwitted* at Bartholomew Fair in London on 23 August of that year. On 11 October 1743 a Morgan acted Cimberton in *The Conscious Lovers* at the Aungier Street Theatre; on the twentieth a Morgan played Sir Harry in *The Tender Husband* at Drury Lane in London. We take it that the Morgan in Dublin was our subject's son, Charles, since one man could hardly have made both appearances. And we are guessing that the elder Morgan played Sir Toby Riot in *The Prodigal* at the Haymarket Theatre on 11 October 1744.

The elder Morgan was at Goodman's Fields in London in 1745–46, playing several of his old parts—Foigard, Sir Francis, Ben, Mat, Driver, the Miller, and the Gravedigger—and he also acted, among other parts, Fondlewife in *The Old Bachelor*, Gomez in *The Spanish Fryar*, Old Laroon in *The Debauchees*, Stephano in *The Tempest*, the Commodore in *The Fair Quaker of Deal*, Woodcock in *Tunbridge Walks*, Scrub in *The Beaux' Stratagem*, and Sable in *The Funeral*. Morgan was incorrectly advertised as making his first appearance at Goodman's Fields that season, for he had played there in the early 1730s.

The summer of 1746 a Morgan was at Richmond, playing Cimberton in *The Conscious Lovers* on 4 June (a role his son played in 1743 and earlier) and then Smuggler in *The Constant Couple*, a Senator in *Othello*, Testimony in *Sir Courtly Nice*, Kite in *The Recruiting Officer*, Dr Specifick in *The Resolute Husband*, and Sir William in *The Squire of Alsatia*. That summer Morgan had a solo benefit on 2 September and shared a benefit with his wife on 15 September. Their son Charles died, according to Genest, in 1746.

In 1746–47 Morgan was again at Covent Garden, at 15s. weekly, playing some of his old roles and also one of the Kings of Brentford

in *The Rehearsal*. He was again at Richmond in the summer of 1747, but his only known roles were Puff in *Miss in Her Teens* and one of the gravediggers (presumably the first one) in *Hamlet*. He returned to Covent Garden in 1747–48, though he acted a reduced schedule in the first half of the season. He tried Sir Wilful in *The Way of the World* and Plumehearse in *Drum's Demolished*. Then he spent the summer acting at the Jacob's Wells Theatre in Bristol and, again, at Richmond and the late summer fairs in London. At Southwark on 26 September 1748 he played the title role in *Richard III*, but there is no way of telling what sort of a variation on Shakespeare that was. He sang "The Cries of Dublin" at Mrs Morgan's benefit at Southwark on 24 October 1748. He acted at the New Wells, Clerkenwell, in December 1748, playing Fainwell in *A Bold Stroke for a Wife*, Coupée in *The Virgin Unmask'd*, and Barnwell in *The London Merchant*. In January and February 1749 he was at Southwark playing Lockit in *The Beggar's Opera*, Teague in *The Committee*, and Harlequin in *The Bottle Conjurer Outdone*. Presumably he was the Morgan who played Laronneau in the French version of *The Beggar's Opera*, called *L'Opera du Gueux*, at the Haymarket Theatre beginning on 29 April 1749. He and Miss Stevens shared a benefit at the Haymarket on 26 May 1749.

Our subject was probably the Morgan who appeared as Trinculo in *The Tempest* at Bartholomew Fair on 23 August 1749 and subsequent dates and then was Squire Sapskull in *The Industrious Lovers* at Southwark Fair in September. London records of Morgan stop after that, but Dublin bills collected by the late W. S. Clark show that Morgan played at the Capel Street Theatre and at Smock Alley in 1749–50. Perhaps he was the Morgan who performed, according to Penley's *The Bath Stage*, at Bath about 1750 to 1755. He was certainly the Mr Morgan who had one-third of a benefit at Drury Lane on 24 May 1756, sharing some of the proceeds with another retired performer, Mrs Horton. Morgan made an attempt to recover some of his past when he acted Major Rakish in *The School Boy* on 27 May 1757 (his first appearance at Covent Garden Theatre in 10 years the bill said, almost correctly—he had last acted there in the spring of 1748). The performance was for his benefit and was presented by performers from both Drury Lane and Covent Garden to honor "the Oldest Actor in England." Covent Garden allowed Morgan benefit tickets in May 1758, Drury Lane gave a benefit for retired actors on 22 June 1758 that brought Morgan £21, and Covent Garden allowed him benefit tickets on 25 May 1759. After that, all trace of him disappears.

The Morgan who was an office keeper at the theatres in Dublin in 1732 and 1733–34 was very likely related to our subject; possibly he was another son.

Morgan, Mrs [Robert?], Henrietta Maria [*fl. 1721–1758*], *actress, singer.*

Henrietta Maria Morgan, whose husband's Christian name may have been Robert, was first noticed in London bills on 8 September 1721, when she played Rosara in *The Noble Englishman* at Lee's booth at Southwark Fair. The following summer in Richmond, on 23 July 1722, she acted Belinda in *Richmond Wells*, and on 1 August she appeared at the Lincoln's Inn Fields playhouse as Lavinia in *Titus Andronicus*. At the Lee-Spiller-Harper booth at Bartholomew Fair on 25 August she had an unspecified part in the droll *Darius*. A letter (now at the Folger Shakespeare Library) dated 19 October 1722 from John Rich at the Lincoln's Inn Fields Theatre to his rivals at Drury Lane announced that Rich had hired Mrs Henrietta Maria Morgan.

Mrs Morgan performed at Lincoln's Inn Fields for the rest of the decade, appearing in such new parts as Mrs Saracen in *The Compromise*, Isabella in *Like to Like*, Arsinoe in *Mariamne*, Pindress in *Love and a Bottle*, Rosalinda in *Sophonisba*, Martin's Wife in *Love's Contrivance*, Prudence in *The Amorous Widow*, Tippet in *Bath Unmask'd*, Frances in *The Female Fortune Teller*, Betty in *The Fond Husband*, Hillaria in *Tunbridge Walks*, Beatrice in *The Man's the Master*, Dorothy Fribble in *Epsom Wells*, Angelica in *The Gamester*, Orada in *The Spanish Wives*, Lucy and Lady Fidget in *The Country Wife*, Parisatis in *The Rival Queens*, Florinda in *The Rover*, Alinda in *The Pilgrim*, Rodriguez in *2 Don Quixote*, and Sophia in *Frederick*. She was not on the season roster in 1728–29, yet she shared a benefit on 13 May 1729. (Her salary had been, in 1724 at least 6s. 8d. daily.) She did not appear at Lincoln's Inn Fields in 1729–30 until 18 April 1730, when she acted Isabelle in *The Mistake*.

During the 1720s Mrs Morgan acted regularly at the late summer fairs, some of her parts being Arabella in *The Blind Beggar*, Athelia in *Valentine and Orson*, Betty Wealthy in *The Unnatural Parents*, Gossip Magpye in *Bateman*, and Mopsa in *Dorastus and Faunia*. In the summer of 1730 she and her husband acted at Richmond and then appeared at both Bartholomew and Southwark fairs.

On 9 November 1730 the Morgans acted in *Love Makes a Man* at the Haymarket Theatre, Henrietta Maria taking the role of Angelina. During the rest of the month she appeared there as Bisarre in *The Inconstant*, Hillaria in *Tunbridge Walks*, and Isabella in *The False Count*. On 9 December she had a role in *The Merry Masqueraders*, and then she made her first appearance at the Goodman's Fields playhouse on 14 December as Prue in *Love for Love*. Her winter seasons were spent at that house through 1733–34, and to her repertoire she added such parts as Lady Wronghead and Trusty in *The Provok'd Husband*, Lucy and Rose in *The Recruiting Officer*, Juletta in *The Pilgrim*, Louisa and Angelica in *Love Makes a Man*, Edging in *The Careless Husband*, Narcissa in *Love's Last Shift*, Mrs Slammekin in *The Beggar's Opera*, the Countess of Nottingham in *The Fall of the Earl of Essex*, Cherry in *The Beaux' Stratagem*, Leonora in *Sir Courtly Nice*, Hellena and Moretta in *The Rover*, Bellaria in *The Temple Beau*, Mrs Chat and Mrs Day in *The Committee*, Clarinda, Situp, and Wishwell in *The Double Gallant*, Altea in *Rule a Wife and Have a Wife*, Miranda in *The Busy Body*, Belinda and Lucy in *Tunbridge Walks*, the Countess of Rutland in *The Unhappy Favorite*, Dorinda in *The Tempest*, Monimia and Florella in *The Orphan*, Mrs Quickly in *The Merry Wives of Windsor*, Mrs Prim in *A Bold Stroke for a Wife*, Parly in *The Constant Couple*, Lucy in *The Old Bachelor*, Mrs Frail in *Love for Love*, the Hostess in *Henry IV*, Lucy in *The London Merchant*, Abigail in *The Drummer*, Fainlove in *The Tender Husband*, Mrs Sealand in *The Conscious Lovers*, Regan in *King Lear*, Tattleaid in *The Funeral*, and Inis in *The Wonder*.

Mrs Morgan continued her association with the late summer fairs, appearing in such parts as Phillis in *Guy, Earl of Warwick*, Gilflurt in *Whittington*, Hoyden in *The Perjur'd Prince*, the Nurse in *Jeptha's Rash Vow*, and the Cobler's Wife in *The Siege of Troy*. She also performed some summers at Richmond, usually playing roles from her regular repertoire but also appearing as Anne Page in *The Merry Wives of Windsor* and Phillis in *The Conscious Lovers*.

After the late summer of 1734 Mrs Morgan's name disappeared from the bills until 29 August 1735, when she acted Elvira in *Love Makes a Man* at Lincoln's Inn Fields. After that single appearance, she once again dropped from sight. On 25 May 1737 Mrs Morgan shared a benefit at the Smock Alley Theatre in Dublin, and during the 1737–38 season there she is known to have acted Isabella in *The Squire of Alsatia* and Lady Pliant in *The Double Dealer*. She was at Smock Alley again (or perhaps still) in 1740–41, one of her parts being Teresa in *The Squire of Alsatia* in June 1741. The late summer of 1746 found her again at Richmond, sharing a benefit with her husband on 15 September, but we know of no roles for her.

Mrs Morgan's appearances in the late 1740s were similarly sporadic. She played Colombine in *Harlequin Captive* at Bartholomew Fair on 24 August 1748 and Hippolita in *The Tempest* at Southwark Fair on the following 7 September, Queen Elizabeth in *Richard III* at Southwark on 26 September, Ann Lovely in *A Bold Stroke for a Wife* and Millwood in *The London Merchant* at the New Wells, Clerkenwell, in December, Mrs Peachum in *The Beggar's Opera* and Rose in *The Recruiting Officer* at Southwark in January 1749, Hippolita in *The Tempest* again at Bartholomew Fair in August, and, finally, Harriet in *The Industrious Lovers* at Southwark Fair on 7 September 1749. At Southwark on 24 October 1748 Mrs Morgan had been given a benefit at which her husband sang, but the bill did not mention any performing on her part. She had another benefit at Southwark on 18 September 1749.

Of Mrs Morgan's personal life virtually nothing is known. She was the mother of Charles Morgan, who had a promising career as an actor but died young.

Morgan, Thomas ₍*fl.* 1697–1700₎, *singer.*

"Mr. Magnus' Boy" sang Daniel Purcell's *So fair young Celia's Charms*, from *The Triumphs of Virtue*, a work presented at Drury Lane in February 1697. The song was published, with the boy's credit, in 1697. The printed song *Lovely Charmer, dearest Creature* (1700), also by Daniel

Purcell, was sung by "Magnus's boy" in *The Island Princess*. That piece was given at Drury Lane in November 1698. The British Library manuscript of *The Island Princess* reveals yet another song sung by the lad: "All the pleasure Hymen brings." Magnus's boy is there identified as Thomas Morgan. Possibly he was the son of the singer and composer Morgan (fl. 1696?–1719?).

Morgetroy, Mr ₍*fl.* 1794₎, *flutist.*

Doane's *Musical Directory* of 1794 listed Mr Morgetroy, of No 6, Blewit's Buildings, Fetter Lane, as a flutist who played for the Cecilian Society. There was a Joseph Murgatroyd who sold musical books at his premises at No 23, Chiswell Street about the time the flutist Morgetroy was active. The bookseller was in business at last from 1792 to 1797. There is no way of knowing if the two were related.

Morhall, John ₍*fl.* 1794₎, *flutist.*

Doane's *Musical Directory* of 1794 listed John Morhall, of No 6, Oat Lane, Foster Lane, as a flutist who played for the Cecilian Society.

Morichelli, Signora Anna   1759–1800, *singer, actress.*

Signora Anna Morichelli, who sang in operas at the King's Theatre in the seasons of January to July 1794, 1794–95, and 1795–96, was "geboren Bosello" in Florence in 1759 according to the *Katalog der Portrat-Sammlung der K. V. K. General Intendanz der K. K. Hoftheater* (Vienna, 1892–94). But of her lengthy continental career nothing is known.

Signora Morichelli's first part at the King's Theatre was Angelica in *Il burbero di buon cuore* on 17 May 1794, when she was said to be singing in England for the first time. On 5 June she sang for her own benefit Violante in *La Frascatana*. Her address was given on the playbill as No 127, Pall Mall, and did not change while she remained in London.

In the following season she appeared as Rachelina in *L'amore contrastato* on 6 December and several times thereafter, as Lucrezia in *I zingari in fiera* on 10 January 1795 and following as Donna Ciprigna in *La scola dei maritati* on 27 January, with several repetitions (it was postponed on 3 February because of her "sudden indisposition"), Lisetta in *Il conte ridicolo* on 14 and 18 April, Cibele in *Ati e Cibele* for

Civica Raccolta delle Stampe Achille Bertarelli, Castello Sforzesco, Milan

ANNA MORICHELLI

engraving by Zatta, after Trussarelli

her benefit on 14 May, Amelina in *L'Isola del piacere* on 26 and 28 May, a "principal character" unspecified in the second piece on 28 May, *Le nozze dei contadini spagnuoli*, Dorina in *Le nozze di Dorina* on 23 June, and some principal character (probably her old character Donna Ciprigna) in *La scola dei maritati* on her last night at the King's Theatre, 30 June 1795.

Dr Burney mentions her singing at a benefit for Haydn in May 1795. He had not liked her singing, but she had improved. Two songs as sung by her in operas are listed in the *Catalogue of Printed Music in the British Museum*.

She is called in the libretti of *Il trionfo de Clelia* (Turin, 1787) and of *L'Italiana in Londra* Anna Morichelli Bosello, and Hogan adopts that form in the index to *The London Stage*.

She is said to have died at Trieste on 30 October 1800.

In the Civica Raccolta delle Stampe, Milano, is a portrait of her engraved by F. Guasconi and one by G. Zatta, after Trussarelli, published in Venice, 1796. She was pictured

with a large group of singers in an engraving by Rainaldi, after Fedi, published in Florence between 1801 and 1807. In the Portrait Collection at the Hoftheater, Vienna, is an engraved portrait of her by Mansfield, after Kreutzinger, and a portrait of her as Violante in *La Frascatana* engraved by J. Godefroy, after L. Guttenbrun, 1796.

Moriggi and **Morighi.** *See* MORIGI.

Morigi, Andrea [*fl.* 1766–1793], *singer, actor.*

John Gordon, one of the impresarios of the opera at the King's Theatre, decided in the summer of 1766 (according to Burney's *General History of Music*) "to engage two distinct companies of singers for the performance of serious operas on Saturdays, and comic on Tuesdays . . ." during the following season. He accordingly embarked for Italy, where he hired 10 singers, among whom was Andrea Morigi (his first name furnished by the cast list of *Giannina e Bernardone*). Morigi's bass, as *primo buffo*, was heard frequently in London until the spring of 1772 when he departed, presumably for the Continent. After a nine-year absence, he returned in December 1781 and remained until 1783. There was another gap in the record in 1784, and he was absent nearly four years, from the late spring of 1788 until January 1793. He disappeared from the London record finally after 14 May 1793. At the time of his benefit on 15 May 1788 he lived at No 3, Angel Court, Windmill Street, Haymarket. His address in 1794 was listed in Doane's *Musical Directory* as No 2, Mary-le-bone Street, Golden Square. Signorina Margherita Morigi, his daughter, sang at the King's in 1782–83, 1785–86, and 1787–88.

Andrea Morigi's roles at the King's Theatre were as follows: in 1766–67, some part unspecified in *Gli stravaganti*, Tagliaferro in *La buona figliuola*, and some parts in *La buona figliuola maritata* and *Don Trastullo*; in 1767–68, probably some part in *Tigrane*, Orgontes in *Sisostri*, and some part in *Il filosofo di campagna* (at his benefit on 5 May 1768); in 1768–69, a part unstated in *Gli amanti ridicoli*; in 1769–70, Gianfriso in *Le contadini bizzarre*, Matan in *Gioas re di Giuda* (a Bach oratorio), and Gian Luigi in *Il disertore*; and in the spring season, 1771, Sibari in *Semiramide riconosciuta*, some part unspecified in *La passione*, and Soldato in *La buona figliuola*. Morigi sang at the King's Theatre on 21 February 1772 in a *Concert of Vocal and Instrumental Music* for the benefit of the "Fund for the Support of Decayed Musicians" but is not recorded in opera that spring. Very likely he was singing in concerts at taverns and gardens.

Morigi returned to the King's after his nine-year absence on 11 December 1781 to sing Patterio in Anfossi's new comic opera *I viaggiatori felici*. Thereafter that season he sang a part in *La buona figliuola* and Dottor Stoppino in *La contadina in corte*. In 1782–83, new parts he sang were Don Massimo in *Il convito*, Pasquale in *Il trionfo della costanza*, Flaterio in *I vecchi burlati*, and Orgasmo in *L'Avaro*. In the spring of 1785 he suffered an illness which helped cause the postponement of *Orfeo* but sang his old part of Patterio on 28 May. In the spring of 1786 he sang the title role in *Il marchese tulipano*, Paisiello's new comic opera, which opened on 24 January, sang in the first London performances of Salieri's *La scuola de gelosi*, as Lumaca, and was the original Caterina in C. F. Badini and Pasquale Anfossi's *L'Inglese in Italia* on 20 May, when his daughter sang as Voluntina.

In the spring of 1787 Morigi added Bernardone in *Giannina e Bernardone*, some part unspecified in *Il tutor burlato*, and Monsieur Perruque in *Gli schiava per amore*. In 1787–88, Morigi added to his repertoire Acmet in *Il rè Teodoro in Venezia*, the original Anselmo Buonvivente in *La cameriera astuta*, Stephen Storace's new comic opera, and a part unstated in *La Frascatana*, but by that time the notable bass Giovanni Morelli had supplanted him as first *buffo caricato*.

When Morigi returned to the King's Theatre on 29 January 1793 he sang some part unrevealed by the bill in *Il barbiere di Siviglia*. On 14 May he sang the role of Frappa in the first London performance of Paisiello's *I zingari in fiera*. Apparently it was his last performance there and, as far as records reveal, anywhere in England.

Morigi, Angelo   *1725–1801, violinist, composer.*

Angelo Morigi was born in 1725 in Rimini, according to E. Heron-Allen, writing in *Grove's Dictionary* (fifth edition). He was taught violin

by Giuseppi Tartini and harmony and theory by Francesco Antonio Valotti. Chappel White in the *New Grove* writes that he appeared in London in 1750. But the earliest London bill that we have found with Morigi's name on it is dated 20 May 1751. On that date Madame Francesca Cuzzoni confessed to her public in an appeal in the *General Advertiser* that she found herself "Unhappily Involved in a few Debts" and would seek to recoup at a benefit concert at Hickford's Great Room on 23 May. Angelo Morigi would play the violin, Miller the bassoon, and Bencki the violoncello while Signors Palma and Guadagni would sing.

Morigi was appointed in 1758 first violin and leader of the band of the Prince of Parma and in 1773 became director of the court music. He composed and taught. The composer Bonifazio Azioli, his pupil, published Morigi's *Trattato di contrappunto frigato* after his death at Parma on 22 January 1801.

New Grove lists a number of his compositions for violin, cello, and harpsichord, as well as six *concerti grossi* dedicated to the Infanta Donna Felipe.

Morigi, Margherita   *[fl. 1782–1788], singer, actress.*

Margherita Morigi was the daughter of the strikingly successful *buffo* Andrea Morigi and through his influence was brought on at the King's Theatre on 14 November 1782 in the part of Selene in Giovanni de Gamerra's new serious opera *Medonte*. The premiere had had to be postponed from the date of its announced opening, 12 November, "on account of Sga Morigi's not being quite recovered from a severe indisposition."

She had sung in 1781 at the Teatro di S. Moisé nella Primavera in Venice. But she was to have small success in London. Burney, in *A General History of Music*, condemned her heartily. The "expectations of the public" were not

gratified on the arrival of Signora MORIGI, daughter of the buffo caricato of that name. . . . [A]las! his long services were not sufficient to render the public partial to his daughter, who in the autumn of 1782, when she appeared in the opera of *Medonte*, astonished the audience, not by the powers she *had*, but by those she *wanted*; for it was hardly possible to account for such a singer having been recommended, or thought of, for the first woman of a serious opera, or indeed of *any* opera. She was

Civica Raccolta delle Stampe Achille Bertarelli, Castello Sforzesco, Milan

MARGHERITA MORIGI

artist unknown

not only much limited in her taste, style, and knowledge, but in total want of voice. In recitative she had not one musical tone; and in her songs the greatest efforts she made amounted to little notes at the top of her compass (F, G, and A,) on which, when she had time allowed for it, she could make something of a swell.

As if that were not judgment harsh enough, Burney concluded, ungallantly, "She was young, had a pretty figure, and, with teeth, would have been handsome."

On 18 February 1783, she was given some part unspecified in *Ifigenia in Aulide*. On 6 March she sang Aristea in *L'Olimpiade*, and that concluded her initial season.

When Signorina Morigi returned again to the King's, three years later, she had abandoned serious opera. She sang Volantina in Badini and Anfossi's new comic opera *L'Inglese in Italia*, in which her father played Caterina (*sic*). But, so far as the bills show, that was her lone performance that season. And only one other London performance by Margherita Morigi is known: that at the King's on 15 May 1788, the occasion of her father's benefit, when she had a part unspecified in *La Frascatana*.

Inasmuch as the 1786 performance was said to be "the first on any stage" one might conclude that two of Morigi's daughters are here concerned. But that claim was often made when unknown performers returned after considerable absences.

A portrait of Margherita Morigi by an unknown engraver is in the Civica Raccolta delle Stampe, Milan.

Morland. *See also* MORELAND.

Morland, Mr [*fl. 1743–1744*], *singer, actor.*

Mr Morland made his first stage appearance singing between the acts at Drury Lane Theatre on 12 December 1743. He appeared regularly as an entr'acte singer during the 1743–44 season, but only once, on 9 April 1744, did the bill give the title of the song he sang: "Britons Strike Home." Morland was also employed as an actor, appearing first as an Attendant on Hecate in *The Amorous Goddess* on 1 February 1744 and then playing Leander in *The Mock Doctor*, Quaver in *The Virgin Unmask'd*, Hillyard in *The Jovial Crew*, and Sir John Loverule in *The Devil to Pay*. Morland (sometimes Moreland) also sang songs in *The London Merchant* and *The Conscious Lovers*.

Morland, Mrs, née Westray [*fl. c. 1765–1772*], *actress.*

The "Young Gentlewoman" who played Juliet in *Romeo and Juliet* at Drury Lane on 29 October 1770 was identified by the prompter Hopkins as "Mrs. Morland from the Norwich Theatre a thin small figure too long a waste—wants power has a small impediment in her Speech she may be useful but never Capital—Pretty well receiv'd." She had been Miss Westray and had performed as early as perhaps 1765. "The Manager's Note-Book" mentioned that she accompanied the elder John Edwin and Francis G. Waldron to Manchester about that time, a trip during which their chaise overturned. *A Letter from a Gentleman in Edinburgh* to his *Friend in the Country* (1766) commented that Miss Westray was "a young female who performs here and is very beautiful. . . . [T]hough her talents in acting are not very conspicuous, yet the audiences desire to *see* her." They saw her, according to the surviving bills, as Margery Pinchwife in *The Country Wife*, Dorinda in the altered *Tempest*, and in a part unspecified in *The Clandestine Marriage*.

From 1767 to 1770 she acted at Norwich. Pinn's *Roscius* spoke of her "winning softness, and enchanting Ease." Sometime between 22 May 1769 and 10 April 1770 she married a Mr Morland, judging by notices of her in the "Committee Books" of the Norwich Theatre. On the latter date she was called, apparently in error, Mrs "McMorland" and offered half a guinea weekly for the following season should she choose to engage. She did not so choose, for the following October she made her London debut, and she acted at Drury Lane through the end of the 1771–72 season. When she arrived in London the *Town and Country Magazine* pointed out that Mrs Morland was "late Miss Westery," and the *London Chronicle* just before her appearance noted that her maiden name had been "Westrey" and not, as some publication must have had it, "Western."

After her modest success with Juliet, Mrs Morland appeared as Hero in *Much Ado about Nothing*, Bridget in *Every Man in His Humour*, Aurora in *'Tis Well It's No Worse*, Charlotte in *The Gamester*, Fanny in *The Clandestine Marriage*, Harriet in *The School for Rakes*, a Spirit in *The Institution of the Garter*, Ophelia in *Hamlet*, Sophia in *Almida*, Mrs Strickland in *The Suspicious Husband*, and Clara in *The Humours of the Turf*.

Mrs Morland was almost certainly of the provincial acting family of Westrays. She may have been the sister of Anthony Westray (d. 1789) who married Juliana Frisby on 18 September 1777 and by her had three girls later well-known in the American theatre: Juliana (Mrs William Burke Wood) 1778–1836, Eleanora (Mrs John Darley) 1780–1849, and Elizabeth Ann (Mrs William Twaits, later Mrs Thomas Clarendon Villiers) 1787–1813.

Morley, Mr ₍fl. 1785₎, *actor.*
Mr Morley played James in a single performance of *'Tis Well It's No Worse* at the Haymarket Theatre on 25 April 1785.

Morley, William ₍fl. 1680–1681₎, *treasurer.*
The London Stage lists William Morley as treasurer of the King's Company in 1680–81, when the regular treasurer James Gray was off in Edinburgh. On 11 May 1681 Morley reported that receipts fell below £10 to £3 14s. 6d. Morley is not otherwise known, and there is a possibility that the correct Christian name was Thomas, for Captain Thomas Morley (d. 1693) held four and a half shares in the Drury Lane Theatre as early as September 1677 and was frequently cited in lawsuits involving King's Company finances. Thomas Morley is not known to have been more than a sharer in the theatre building, however. If William is the correct Christian name for the company treasurer in 1680–81, he was very likely related to Thomas.

Morley, William *d. 1721, singer, composer.*
On 23 April 1685 William Morley marched in the coronation procession of James II as one of the children of the choir of Westminster. About 1710 he and John Isham published *A Collection of New Songs set to Musick*, and on 17 July 1713 Morley received a music degree from Oxford. From at least as early as 1715 he was a member of the King's Musick. He died on 29 October 1721. His will, dated 1 June 1711 but not witnessed, left to his brother Richard a total of £290 which William had in the Bank of England, in government lotteries, or in money owed him. On 20 November 1721 Dr William Croft, the organist and composer under whom Morley may have worked at Oxford, testified to the authenticity of the handwriting in the will. William's brother Richard then proved the will on 7 December.

Morphew, Mr ₍fl. c. 1717–c. 1720₎, *singer.*
Mr Morphew, a male contralto or alto, sang at Cannons about 1717–1720.

Morphew, Mr ₍fl. 1794₎, *actor.*
Mr Morphew played Crabtree in a single performance of *The School for Scandal* at Hammersmith on 24 March 1794.

Morphy. *See also* MURPHY.

Morphy, Mr ₍*fl. 1712–1725*₎, *harpist.*

On 14 May 1712 "the famous Mr Morphy" played the Irish harp at Stationers' Hall. At Mr Mayor's on 21 May 1712 a benefit concert was held for Morphy, who played on the "Silver-String'd Harp," as he had before the King of Portugal. He had another benefit on 26 April 1717 at the Corner House, Thrift Street, at which he played, among other works, a piece by Antonio Corria. At the Two Golden Balls on 7 March 1718 another benefit concert was held for him. In Durfey's *Wit and Mirth* in 1719 was printed a song called "The Bath Teasers: Or a Comical Description of the Diversions at Bath." One stanza concerned our subject:

Next Morphew the Harper with his Pigg's Face,
Lye tickling a Treble and vamping a Bass,
And all he can do 'tis but Musick's disgrace
      There's rare doings, &c.

It was one of the more vicious stanzas in the anonymous song. The last mention of Morphy so far found was a concert at Hickford's Music Room on 31 May 1725 at which he played the harp.

Morrall, Mrs *1760–1804, freak.*

At the Guildhall Library is a clipping dated 1804 reporting the sudden death at Bury of Mrs Morrall, aged 44. She had been born without arms and had been exhibited throughout the kingdom, the clipping stated. "She could cut the smallest watch-papers and devices . . . with a pair of scissors, by means of her toes. She has for many years travelled the country as a public exhibition."

Morrell. *See also* MORELL *and* MORRIL.

Morrell, Mr ₍*fl. 1798*₎, *actor.*

In the Pie Powder Court Book a comedian named Morrell was listed as performing at Bartholomew Fair in 1798. Also at the Fair that year was the puppeteer Morello, apparently not related.

Morrice. *See also* MORRIS.

Morrice, Miss ₍*fl. 1740*₎, *actress.*

Miss Morrice played the Page in *The Orphan* at Covent Garden Theatre on 7 November 1740.

Morrice, George ₍*fl. 1667–1675?*₎, *scenekeeper, actor?*

George Morrice (or Morris, but not, as in *The London Stage*, Norrice) was a scenekeeper in the King's Company in 1667–68 and for several seasons following. The Lord Chamberlain's accounts cited him on occasion, usually in connection with debts he owed. On 25 May 1671, for example, Ezekiell Lampon, merchant, went against Morrice and his fellow scenekeeper Thomas Phelps for a debt, and on 21 June 1672 Martin Powell (the actor?) sued Morrice. Two manuscript casts from the 1670s mention an actor named "Moris" or "Morris," and quite possibly Morrice the scenekeeper occasionally handled walk-ons and bit parts. Notes in a copy of *Sir Salomon*, probably concerned with a performance in Edinburgh in 1672 or later cite "Moris" as playing Ralph; in the cast were other players from the King's Company in London. Notes in a Bodleian copy of *Brennoralt*, dating about 1673–1675, cite a Morris as playing a Servant and a Soldier.

Morrice, Milbert *d. c. 1684, trumpeter.*

Keepers of the Lord Chamberlain's accounts had a difficult time with the trumpeter Milbert Morrice's name; it appeared in various combinations of Milbert, Millibert, and Milibert and Morrice, Meurs, Mears, Meares, and Myers. Our choice here is rather arbitrary and not necessarily as our subject would have preferred it. On 3 October 1660 a warrant was written and then canceled appointing Morrice a trumpeter in ordinary in the King's Musick; he had to wait until 30 November for a firm appointment. His salary was £60 annually, presumably plus livery, but he was able to augment his income considerably on trips overseas. On 9 May 1666 he was appointed to accompany Prince Rupert and the Duke of Albemarle at sea; on 1 February 1672 he was to be paid £20 for serving Lord Duras "in his Majesty's service beyond the seas," and in that instance he was the recipient of money for his fellow trumpeters and the kettledrummer; and on 18 July 1675 he was paid for accompanying the Duke of Richmond to Denmark from 29 March 1672 to 6 January 1673. The last payment had been delayed because some of the musicians involved had been overseas since 1672 and had not presented their bills; Morrice may have been one of them. A warrant dated 1 March

1681 appointed Thomas Barwell to replace Morris, but the name of Barwell was crossed out; Morrice may have retired or died, though usually when a court musician's post was vacated by his death the warrants so stated. On 13 February 1684 John Stevenson, trumpeter, was appointed to replace "Milbert Meares," deceased.

Morrigi. *See* MORIGI.

Morril, Mr [*fl.* 1747–1750], *actor.*
Mr Morril played Dumont in *Jane Shore* at Southwark Fair on 24 September 1747. He was probably the Morrel who may have acted Jeptha in *Jeptha's Rash Vow* at the same Fair on 7 and 10 September 1750 (Carr was assigned that role in some advertisements).

Morris, Mr [*fl.* 1710], *actor.*
Sybil Rosenfeld in *Strolling Players* lists a Morris, from outside London, as a member of Pinkethman's troupe at Greenwich in 1710.

Morris, Mr [*fl.* 1726–1727], *house servant?*
A Mrs Morris "from the office" was named on the free list at the Lincoln's Inn Fields Theatre in 1726–1727, according to the accounts now at Harvard. Mr Morris's son was also cited, but he seems not to have been a theatre employee. Morris was presumably one of the house servants.

Morris, Mr [*fl.* 1733–1742], *doorkeeper.*
Mr Morris shared benefits at Goodman's Fields on 16 May 1733, 13 May 1734, and 10 May 1742. At the latter benefit he was identified as one of the doorkeepers, and Master Morris, probably a relative but not his son, danced.

Morris, Mr [*fl.* 1746], *performer.*
A Mr Morris performed at Sadler's Wells in April 1746, according to bills in the Percival Collection at the British Library. He was not John Morris, though John came to London later in the year.

Morris, Mr [*fl.* 1777–1783], *actor.*
A Mr Morris had some role unspecified in *The Coquette; or, Mistakes of the Heart* at the Haymarket on 9 October 1777. A company of 16 actors put on a special performance at the Haymarket on 21 April 1782, the bill assuring the public that the "entertainments have been a long time in rehearsal," that "care has been taken . . . to have the principal parts supported by veterans." One of the group was Morris, who had a part (again unspecified) in *Love at a Venture*. On 6 May following, Morris joined a group of 13 to secure permission from the Lord Chamberlain for a performance at the Haymarket. Again, though he had a role in *The Fashionable Wife*, we are not told which one by the playbill.

Morris was listed among those whose benefit tickets would be admitted at Drury Lane on 28 May 1779, 25 May 1780, 26 May 1781, 31 May 1782, and 30 May 1783.

Morris, Mrs [*fl.* 1772?–1803?], *actress.*
A Mrs Morris was a member of a strolling company playing at Coopers' Hall in Bristol from November 1772 to April 1773. Perhaps that woman was the Mrs Morris whose benefit tickets were accepted at Covent Garden Theatre in London on 4 May 1775, 11 May 1776, and 9 May 1777. A Mrs Morris, again perhaps the same woman, played Dame Furrow in *Harlequin Teague* at the Haymarket Theatre on 18, 19, and 20 September 1782, and she was at that house again on 10 August 1784 as the Ghost of Bess Smut in *The What D'Ye Call It*. On 31 August 1785 she appeared in *Here and There and Everywhere*. Master and Miss Morris, presumably her children, were also in the cast of *The What D'Ye Call It*. Our subject may have been the female Morris listed in the Covent Garden accounts as receiving £4 weekly in 1794–95. She was named in the accounts again in 1802–3.

Morris, Master [*fl.* 1741–1746], *dancer.*
See MORRIS, JOHN [*fl.* 1723?–1762].

Morris, Master [*fl.* 1784], *actor.*
Master Morris played the Ghost of a Child Unborn in *The What D'Ye Call it* at the Haymarket Theatre on 10 August 1784.

Morris, Miss [*fl.* 1743–1746], *dancer.*
See MORRIS, JOHN [*fl.* 1723?–1762].

Morris, Miss *c. 1751–1769, actress.*

On 26 November 1768 at Covent Garden Theatre a young woman who had never appeared on any stage before played Juliet to Powell's Romeo. The prompter Hopkins identified her as Miss Morris and said she was a pupil of Mr Colman's. The prologue that introduced her, spoken by Powell, said she was "Fearful as young, and *really not Eighteen*"—which allows us to suppose she was born about 1751. According to evidence presented in the Harris-Colman litigation in 1768 Miss Morris's friends and relations were against her going on the stage, but Colman persuaded her to try. The opening night results were described in *Lloyd's Evening Post* of 28–30 November:

The managers of both theatres have of late, in order to put a stop to the Public complaint against a dearth of actors, given trials to several stage candidates that seemed to have any promising requisite. Such experiments have not proved fruitless. The most brilliant and interesting of which was the young lady's appearance on Covent Garden Theatre last night, in the character of Juliet. So great was her terror, on presenting herself for the first time before a crowded audience, that, deprived of all her powers, she fell down on the stage in a swoon. The first act in consequence, was all terror on her side, all compassion and anxiety on that of the audience. But having had time between the first and second Acts to recover from her panic, she shone forth in the Balcony Scene the most pleasing promise of a young tragic actress that has been seen for half a century past, and continued so throughout. Her person is genteel, her tone of voice insinuating, variable, and melodious; her recitation is just and sensible; very affecting in the pathetic parts; condescending, free, and polite are the familiar speeches with the Nurse. She is happily devoid of all stage whine, and tragedy Cant. The manner she has been rudimented in does great honour to her instructors, who have so judiciously prevented the so excellent actor of this verily a Shakespeare's Juliet, from being sophisticated by the studied tricks, and false ornamenting of mistaken modern and degenerate art.

In addition to Juliet, Miss Morris acted Cordelia in *King Lear* on 11 January 1769, Amelia in *The English Merchant* on 28 January, and Miss Courtney in *The Sister* on 18 February. She became ill in the spring, and at her benefit on 15 April Mrs Bellamy had to play Juliet for her. Miss Morris made over £56 after house charges, and the account books show that she

was paid £50 for her season's work—which amounted to very few performances. Though she went to the Gravel Pits in Kensington for her health, she never recovered. Miss Morris died on 1 May 1769. Wewitzer identified her as Miss Corbyn Morris, but that was certainly incorrect; she was, according to Musgrave's *Obituary*, Corbyn Morris's niece.

Morris, Miss, later Mrs Pierce [*fl. 1792–1799?*], *actress.*

The young lady who made her first appearance on any stage playing Sylvia in *The Recruiting Officer* on 14 November 1792 at Covent Garden Theatre was identified by the *European Magazine* that month as Miss Morris. The reviewer was cool: she seemed to him to be not unpromising, with a person "something embonpoint," a pleasing manner and a flexible voice, but he went no further than to say she had talent that might some day be displayed to advantage. When she tried Lady Randolph in *Douglas* on 20 December the same periodical said Miss Morris might in time play the part well, but she needed more care and study.

She apparently decided not to attempt anything further in London, and we believe she was the Miss Morris, identified as from Covent Garden Theatre in London, who was mentioned in the *Theatrical Journal* as playing Miranda in *The Busy Body* at Manchester in the summer of 1793. During the 1793–94 season Miss Morris was on the payroll at Covent Garden again, at £3 weekly, playing Hortensia Lamotte in *Fontainville Forest*, the Duchess of Orleans in *The Siege of Meaux*, Roxana in *Alexander the Great*, and the Lady in *The Sicilian Romance*. The *Thespian Magazine* noted that Miss Morris was at Liverpool in the summer of 1794.

Miss Morris was back at Covent Garden in 1794–95, her salary having been raised to £4 weekly. Some of her new characters were Ellen Holstein in *The Secret Tribunal*, Lady Capulet in *Romeo and Juliet*, the Queen in *Hamlet*, Goneril in *King Lear*, Statira in *Alexander the Great*, Lesbia in *The Comedy of Errors*, and the Countess of Rutland in *The Earl of Essex*. In 1795–96 she added Oswena in *The Days of Yore*, and in 1796–97 Mrs Ratcliffe in *The Jew*, Mrs Seymour in *Fortune's Fool*, Megra in *Philaster*, Millwood in *The London Merchant*, Marcia in *Cato*, and the Queen in *Richard III*. On 25 May 1797 the Covent Garden management allowed her to play Gertrude in *Hamlet* at Drury Lane (Mrs Powell, whose benefit it was, played Hamlet). The *Authentic Memoirs of the Green Room* said she "met with considerable applause."

John Williams in *A Pin Basket to the Children of Thespis* in 1797 was not very complimentary:

Her port is transhuman, vast, comely, and grand,
And she looks like a type of the fat o' the land.
....
There are muffins and crumpets in all her dimensions!
....
To clad her in velvets, they're surely mistaken,
It is Might aiding Strength—it is buttering bacon!
At the tone of her voice victuallers lose half their vices,
And meat, grains, and greens are reduc'd in their prices.
....
As an actress she's parts, yet with these she's absurd;
She is solemn and stately as Juno's own bird;
She's too frozen, too methodiz'd, stiffen'd, and cold.

The *Monthly Mirror* in August 1797 announced the marriage of "Mr. Pierce, an eminent fishmonger, to Miss Morris, of Covent-Garden theatre." Perhaps she retired from the stage at that point, or perhaps she was the Mrs Pierce reported by Pollock as performing in Halifax, Nova Scotia, on 15 April 1799.

Morris, Catherine, later Mrs George Colman the first [*fl.* 1777–1784], *actress, singer.*

The first theatrical notice of Catherine Morris was taken when she appeared as one of nine children—"Lilliputians"—in a revival of Garrick's *Lilliput* at the elder George Colman's Haymarket on 15 May 1777. It is not known what her age was at the time of her debut, but by the time the younger George Colman's first dramatic effort, *The Female Dramatist*, was hissed off his father's stage in August 1782, Catherine had caught the young man's eye. Efforts to distract him with a continental tour in August 1784 failed, and he flew with Miss Morris to Gretna Green, where they were married on 3 October following his return. At her insistence the ceremony was repeated on 10 November at Chelsea Church. The marriage was kept

secret until 1788. One son, George, was its fruit, but the date of his birth is not known.

By about 1795 Colman's affair with the actress Maria Gibbs was open and notorious. In a letter of 22 September 1796, Colman told Henry Woodfall, who proposed to write his biography: "Mrs. C—— and I have long been mutual plagues. A year ago we determined to separate: the proposal came first from her, and I accepted it instantly. She wished afterward to retract, but I would not." He said that he had provided her with £800 per year.

Catherine Morris's acting career was short, but fairly eventful. It ended before her marriage. Her later life is obscure and her death date unknown.

Her roles, after *Lilliput*, as she added them at the summer Haymarket, and at the Colmans' winter theatre, Covent Garden, were as follows: at the Haymarket in 1777, a Lady in *Rule a Wife and Have a Wife* and a Lilliputian in *The Fairy Tale*; at Covent Garden in 1777–78, Prince Edward in *Richard III*, some minor part in *The Rehearsal*, a Page in *The Orphan* and Edgar in *The British Heroine* (in the first London performance of John Jackson's tragedy); at the Haymarket in 1778, member of the singing chorus in *Macbeth*, and at Covent Garden in 1779–80, some part unspecified in *The Touchstone*, the Little Girl in *The Mirror; or, Harlequin Everywhere*, unassigned parts in *The Belle's Stratagem* and *The Touchstone*, Attendant Genius in *The Fête Anticipated*, Wit, singing in *An Interlude Between Plutus and Wit*, and the original Jenny in George Downing's musical prelude *The Volunteers*. When she had sung at the Haymarket as Ursula in *Falstaff's Wedding* on 27 December 1779 she had been billed "Miss Morris, who sung last season at Ranelagh."

In 1780–81, Miss Morris added Ann Page in *The Merry Wives of Windsor*, Sabrina in *Comus*, a Vocal Part in *Theodosius*, the original Julina in Charles Dibdin's comic opera *The Islanders*, Betsy Blossom in *The Deaf Lover*, and Eliza in *The Flitch of Bacon*; and in 1781–82, one of the singers in the "solemn Dirge" accompanying Juliet's funeral, Mat o' the Mint in *The Beggar's Opera* (a performance in which all parts were taken by women), a principal role, unspecified, in *The Touchstone*, Maudlin in *Poor Vulcan!*, Meriel in *The Jovial Crew*, Pleasure in *The Choice of Harlequin*, the original Cupid in Matthew Feilde's pastoral *Vertumnus and Pomona*, and Peggy Wiseacres in *The London Cuckolds*. In the summer of 1782, again at the Haymarket, she added to her repertoire a role unspecified in *The Humours of an Election*, Columbine in The *Genius of Nonsense*, Laura in *The Agreeable Surprise*, Rosina ("with additional airs") in *The Spanish Barber*, the original Nancy Johnson in Frances Burney's comedy *The East Indian*, Miss Doyley in *Who's the Dupe?*, singing in the masquerade in Act I of *Cymbeline*, a Maid of Honour in *The Life and Death of Common Sense*, Maria ("with a song") in *The Maid of the Oaks*, the original Marriet in young George Colman's musical farce *The Female Dramatist*, the wife in *The Recruiting Serjeant*, both Lucinda and Rosetta in *Love in a Village* on different nights, and Lucy in *The Beggar's Opera*.

In 1782–83 Miss Morris added Manto in *The Wishes*, Dolly Trull in *The Beggar's Opera*, Harriet in *The Devil upon Two Sticks*, Louisa in *The Discovery*, Venus in *The Golden Pippin*, a vocal part in "The Entry" in *Alexander the Great*, Marcella in *A Bold Stroke for a Husband*, Miss Mortimer in *The Chapter of Accidents*, Jenny Diver in *The Beggar's Opera*, Belinda in *The Ghost*, Victoria in *The Castle of Andalusia*, and an unspecified part in Leonard Macnally's new musical farce *Coalition*. In the summer of 1783, at the Haymarket, she took a leading place in the company, singing many of her old roles and widening her repertoire by a dozen more: Lettice in *Man and Wife*, Columbine in *Harlequin Teague*, Phoebe in *As You Like It*, Fanny in *A Friend in Need is a Friend Indeed*, a new comedy by Denis O'Bryen, Floretta in *The Quaker*, Semira in *Artaxerxes*, the original Araminta in *The Young Quaker*, John O'Keeffe's comedy, the original Maria Goodall in John Dent's farce *The Receipt Tax*, a Maid of Honour in *Chrononhotonthologos*, Mopsa in *The Sheep Shearing*, the original Miss Plumb in Charles Stuart and John O'Keeffe's musical farce *Gretna Green*, and an Italian Girl in *The Critic*, besides singing in several pastiche *Fêtes*.

Miss Morris did not return to the Covent Garden Company for the 1783–84 season (though she volunteered her services on 10 June 1784 for the prompter Wild's benefit). She was, however, active at the Haymarket in the summer of 1784, adding these parts to her repertoire: Miss Rantipole in *The Tobacconist*, the original Zaphira in Elizabeth Inchbald's afterpiece *A Mogul Tale*, Laura in *Tancred and Sigismunda*, Daphne in *Midas*, the original Alice in Thomas Holcroft's comic opera *The Noble Peasant*, Theodosia in *The Maid of the Mill*, and the Chambermaid in *The Clandestine Marriage*. After 26 September 1784 she did not perform again.

Morris, David *d. 1777, actor, singer.*
The David Morris who was the dancer and actor Joseline Shawford's son-in-law's brother (and to whom Shawford left a guinea for a mourning ring in a will of 1760) was probably also the actor who began a career at Covent Garden in 1765. The Fawcett notebook in the Folger Library furnishes the first name, David, and the death date, 1 January 1777. The name seems to be confirmed both by the occurrence of the initial D. in a letter in the *Theatrical Monitor* of 5 November 1768 signed by Morris and addressed to the Covent Garden manager and by the burial of a David Morris at the "actors' church," St Paul, Covent Garden, on 5 January 1777. (But Joseph Reed said he died at Exeter.)

Arthur Murphy's list of per diem salaries for the Covent Garden performers as of 14 September 1767 gives Morris 8s. 4d. The deposition attending the Covent Garden lawsuits of 1768–1770 shows him to have been signed to a three-year contract on 1 June 1768 for £3 9s. 8d. per week and a partial benefit. (In May 1767 his benefit, jointly with Tindal, had, after charges, paid him £88 7s. His benefits produced deficiencies in 1768 and 1769.)

Morris's first known appearance, as Kite in *The Recruiting Officer*, at Covent Garden on 2 October 1765 was advertised as his first appearance on "that stage," implying country experience. In the course of his career he added the following parts, by season: in 1765–66, Lodovico in *Othello*, Pierrot in *The Royal Chace*, Ferdinand in *The Summer's Tale*, Lepidus in *Julius Caesar*, Kent in *King Lear* and Mat o' Mint in *The Beggar's Opera*; in 1766–67, Westmorland in *Henry V*, Mowbray in *2 Henry IV*, some unspecified role in *Harlequin Doctor Faustus*, probably Sir Trusty in *Rosamond* ("Morrice"), and the Governor in *Love Makes a Man*; and in 1767–68, the Duke in *Venice Preserv'd*, Clement in *Every Man in His Humour*, Hawthorn in

Love in a Village, Williams in *Henry V*, Austria in *King John*, the Duke in *The Merchant of Venice*, Omar in *Tamerlane*, Pedro in *The Wonder*, the Major in *The Irish Fine Lady*, Giles in *The Maid of the Mill*, a Countryman in *Philaster*, Gargle in *The Apprentice*, Sackbut in *A Bold Stroke for a Wife*, Philario in *The Royal Chace*, Escalus in *Romeo and Juliet*, the Clown and Squire Gawky in *Orpheus and Eurydice*, Subtle in *The Englishman in Paris*, and the Bailiff in the premier performance of Oliver Goldsmith's comedy *The Good-Natured Man*.

In 1768–69 he added Philario in *Cymbeline*, Sir Ardolph in *The Countess of Salisbury*, Lockit in *The Beggar's Opera*, Bonniface in *The Strategem*, Miller in *Harlequin Doctor Faustus*, the original Old Nightingale in Joseph Reed's comic opera, *Tom Jones* and Downright and (on other nights) Justice Clement in *Every Man in His Humour*; in 1769–70, the original Landlord in George Colman's comedy *Man and Wife; or, the Shakespeare Jubilee*, Pierrot in *Harlequin Skeleton*, Omar in *Tamerlane*, the Yeoman in *The Rape of Proserpine*, Carbuncle in *The Country Lasses*, Balderdash in *The Twin Rivals*, Decius in *Cato*, some part in *Harlequin's Jubilee*, and Patrico in *The Jovial Crew*.

In 1770–71 Morris added Serjeant Flower in *The Clandestine Marriage*, an unspecified character in *Mother Shipton*, and J. Fungus in *The Commissary*; in 1771–72, Orcanes in *Timanthes*, the title role in *Cymbeline*, Varnish in *A Wife in the Right*, and Lord Mayor in *Richard III*; and in 1772–73, Camperius in *Henry VIII* and an original part in James Messink's new pantomine *The Pigmy Revels; or, Harlequin Sorcerer*.

When, on 24 January 1774, a company of little-known London actors and two "Young Ladies" who had not appeared before proffered a special benefit to the actor Brunsdon "from Edinburgh" at the Haymarket, one of the group was Morris. He played Sir Jealous in *The Busy Body*. On 4 April 1774 at another special benefit for the actor Kennedy at the Haymarket, Morris sang Lockit in *The Beggar's Opera* and played the Miller in *The King and the Miller of Mansfield*. On the twelfth of that month he played Biondello in *Catherine and Petruchio* at the Haymarket. But he was also acting at Covent Garden that spring (Biondello for a benefit he shared on 20 May with Mrs P. Green and

Hussey). On 28 October 1775 he repeated Hawthorn in *Love in a Village* at a benefit "for Brother Jacobs. By Particular Desire of the Masons."

David Morris is shown as the Duke, seated on the dais, in Zoffany's painting of the trial scene in *The Merchant of Venice*, with Charles Macklin as Shylock, about 1768. The painting is in the Tate Gallery; it is reproduced with Macklin's notice in this dictionary.

Morris, Dimmock ₍*fl. c.* 1715₎, *house servant.*

The Drury Lane Theatre accounts at the Folger Shakespeare Library name Dimmock (or Dymock) Morris about 1715. He seems to have been a house servant.

Morris, John ₍*fl.* 1723?–1762₎, *dancer, actor, singer.*

The prompter Chetwood in his *General History* (1749) said that John Morris was born in Ireland, played at most of the theatres in Dublin and London, was a singer, and often played Pierrot as well as Irish characters, old men, and straight parts. That combination of details encourages us to believe that most, if not all, of the citations presented here concern John Morris.

A Morris was performing at Norwich from 1723 to 1728. The next reference comes in the 1732 edition of *The Blazing Comet*, in which Morris was listed as Romondo; the work was presented at the Haymarket Theatre in London on 2 March 1732. The same Morris was probably the one who acted Mirvan in *Tamerlane* at the Goodman's Fields Theatre on 28 March and a Servant in *Harlequin's Contrivance* on 10 May. He played Robert in *The Mock Doctor* on 4 August at Tottenham Court.

Signora Violante brought a troupe to London to perform at the Haymarket in the fall of 1732; they acted *The Beggar's Opera* "after the Irish Manner," just as the company had presented it in Dublin. The piece was given on 4 September, with Morris as Peachum and Peg Woffington as Macheath. The Morris who had been acting in London since March could hardly have been with the Violante troupe in Ireland, though he may well have been acting in Dublin before his London appearances and may have rejoined the Signora's players when they came over to play *The Beggar's Opera*. At the Haymarket on 11 September Morris (sometimes Morrice) played Harlequin in *The Jealous Husband Outwitted*, and on 26 July 1733 he had an unnamed role in *The Amorous Lady*. *The London Stage* has a Morris playing the Landlord in *The Tavern Bilkers* on 3 February 1733 at Goodman's Fields and sharing a benefit there on 16 May, but those citations are probably a mistake for the younger Jubilee Dicky Norris, who was in the Goodman's Fields troupe that season. Norris was there in 1731–32 as well, which might suggest that the two references to Morris in the spring of 1732 may have been mistakes for Norris, too. Similarly, the Morris who acted Hottman in *Oroonoko* at Covent Garden Theatre on 2 August 1733 may have been our subject or Norris. *The London Stage* has Norris (and his wife) as actors at Goodman's Fields in 1733–34, but the calendar shows Morris playing Sir John in *Lady Jane Gray* on 19 September 1733 and then appearing as the Landlord in *The Tavern Bilkers*, Budge in *The Beggar's Opera*, a Grenadier in *Britannia*, and a Follower in *Diana and Acteon*. In 1734–35 at Goodman's Fields Morris was an Attendant in *Jupiter and Io* and appeared again in *Britannia*. During those two seasons the roster has Morris listed as a dancer.

A Morris worked at Covent Garden the following season, for the company accounts show him discharged on 18 November 1735 after having worked 36 days at 2s. daily. Only if he put in some of those days at the end of the previous season could he have been John, who is known to have acted Hubert in *The Royal Merchant* on 13 November 1735 at the Ransford Street Theatre in Dublin. Before the end of the 1735–36 season in Dublin John Morris moved to the Smock Alley Theatre, where on 3 April 1736 he danced a *Pierrot* and a *Wooden Shoe*. He was there again in 1736–37, one of his known characters being Pierrot in *The Hussar* on 2 May 1737. In 1737–38 he acted Termagant in *The Squire of Alsatia* on 14 January 1737, Pierrot in *The Hussar* on 7 January 1738, and Gainlove in *A Cure for a Scold* on 16 January. He was a featured entr'acte dancer on 8 May. Through 1743–44 Morris remained at Smock Alley, his discovered parts being Harlequin in *The Harlot's Progress*, Teague in *The*

Twin Rivals, Teague in *The Committee*, Justice Lovelaw in *The Mock Lawyer*, Sir John Friendly in *The Relapse*, Pierrot in *Harlequin Metamorphos'd*, Pierrot in *Harlequin's Vagaries*, Teague in *The Lancashire Witches*, Falstaff in *1 Henry IV*, Pinchwife in *The Country Wife*, Pierrot in *The Rival Sorcerers*, Maccahone in *The Stage Coach*, Macheath in *The Beggar's Opera*, Pierrot in *The Grand Sultan*, Captain O'Blunder in *The Brave Irishman*, Roderigo in *Othello*, Catesby in *Richard III*, Hecate in *Macbeth*, and Loverule in *The Devil to Pay*.

In 1744–45 John Morris was at the Capel Street Theatre in Dublin, and perhaps he was the Morris who, with Mrs Master and Miss Morris, performed in Salisbury early in 1745; on 11 March Mr Morris was the Clown to Mons Dominique's Drunken Peasant in a dance. In 1745–46 Morris began the season at Aungier Street, Dublin, but the company moved to Smock Alley in mid-season. Sheldon in *Thomas Sheridan* has Morris playing Polonius in *Hamlet* at Aungier Street on 7 November 1745, it being advertised as his first appearance (on that stage) in two years. No earlier roles at that theatre are known for him.

Morris returned to London for the 1746–47 season at £5 weekly, appearing at Covent Garden Theatre on 15 October 1746 as Teague in *The Committee* and then acting Foigard in *The Stratagem* and Teague in *The Twin Rivals*. He was again at Covent Garden in 1747–48 but not for the full season. He acted Teague in *The Committee*, Foigard, Sir Hugh in *The Merry Wives of Windsor*, Vulture in *Woman is a Riddle*, Sable in *The Funeral*, and the Mad Englishman in *The Pilgrim* (the last on 21 April 1748). He was back at Smock Alley in May.

Morris remained at Smock Alley in 1748–49, and he was there again in 1750–51; he may well have performed there in 1749–50 and 1751–52, but evidence is lacking. From 1752–53 through 1758–59 Morris acted at Drury Lane Theatre in London, appearing first on 19 September 1752 in a *Punch Dance* between the acts. The bills made little mention of him, though he is known to have performed a solo hornpipe and, with Miss Shawford, a comic dance and a minuet. He shared a benefit with three others on 14 May 1753. The evidence would suggest that by the 1750s Morris may have been past his prime and no longer admired as a singer, dancer, or actor in plays and musical pieces but still useful as an entr'-acte entertainer. In 1753–54 he participated in a *Masquerade Dance* in *The Man of Mode*, danced *The Drunken Peasant* with his friend Shawford, and offered his hornpipe.

The remainder of Morris's stay at Drury Lane followed the same pattern. He acted no named parts but was used as a specialty dancer, his hornpipe being his most popular turn. He was also seen over the years dancing in *The Running Footman* and *The Drunken Peasant*. The bills usually mentioned his name only near the end of the season, though he may have been employed in minor dancing capacities throughout the season. He turned up at the Haymarket a few times, dancing a hornpipe with Miss Durham on 22 August 1757 and subsequent dates. He was at the Crow Street Theatre in Dublin from 1759–60 through 1761–62, after which we have found no further records of John Morris as a performer. We suppose that he retired.

The Drury Lane bills of the 1750s make it clear that Morris was a friend of the dancer Shawford. In his will, dated 7 February 1760, Shawford left John Morris a guinea for a mourning ring. We do not know if Morris was still alive when the will was proved in London on 2 January 1764.

Chetwood found Morris "masterly" in several old men's parts. "He sings passingly, is esteemed a good Teague, and an excellent Pierrot. He has a Brother [Patrick, who never performed in London] of the same calling." Those remarks were made in 1749, and Chetwood presumably saw Morris when he was at his best. Mrs J[ohn?] Morris was in the Smock Alley Theatre Company in 1742–43, but of her we know little. James Morris was a dancer in Dublin in 1742, married John Rich's daughter Mary, and died in 1767; he was probably a relative of John Morris.

We have found performance records of a Mrs, Master, and Miss Morris, and though we think they may have been John Morris's wife and children, we cannot be certain. Mrs Morris was a Sea Nymph in *Neptune's Palace* on 23 August 1740 at Hallam's booth at Bartholomew Fair on 23 August 1740 and performed (as Mrs J. Morris) at the Smock Alley Theatre in Dublin in 1742–43. On 27 December 1742 a Mrs Morris danced at the New Wells, Clerkenwell;

on 12 March 1745 she sang at Salisbury (where a Mr, Master, and Miss Morris were performing); and on 4 March 1746 at Stokes Croft, Bristol, she sang at a benefit shared by Morris, Master Morris, and Miss Morris. Mr and Mrs Morris were at the Crow Street Theatre in Dublin in 1759–60.

Master Morris performed a *Scots Dance* at Drury Lane on 25 May 1741 for his first appearance on that stage. On 10 May 1742 at Goodman's Fields Theatre he danced a *Dutch Skipper*, *A Running Footman*, and *The French Peasant* at a benefit shared by Morris the doorkeeper, who may have been a relative. Master Morris offered his *Running Footman* again on 24 May at Drury Lane. He and his sister danced at Southwark Fair on 8 September 1743. Master and Miss Morris offered "Ground-Dancing" at Salisbury on 14 January 1755, according to M. E. Knapp in *Theatre Notebook*, 35, and on 28 January Master Morris was a Scotch Gentleman in *Harlequin Restored*. He shared a benefit with his father and sister at Stoke's Croft, Bristol, on 4 March 1746.

Morris, Mrs [John?] [*fl. 1740–1760*] *singer, dancer.* See MORRIS, JOHN [*fl. 1723?–1762*].

Morris, John [*fl. 1794–1822*], *lighting man, machinist, property man.*

The Drury Lane accounts for 21 July 1794 show a payment of £7 12*s.* to a Mr Morris for the lamplighter's bill. One supposes he was responsible for paying the lighting technicians on the theatre staff. He was, we believe, the John Morris who was named in the accounts as a machinist in 1810–12 and who was receiving £6 weekly as superintendent of the theatre machines in 1812–13. He had seen duty as a machinist at the Lyceum at £4 10*s.* weekly in 1811–12, and he was probably the Morris who presented an exhibition of gas lights at Sadler's Wells on 3 November 1807. Charles Dibdin the younger said in his *Memoirs* that Morris exhibited an hydraulic scene at the Wells in 1817 and worked at Vauxhall Gardens. Morris was working as a property man at the Gardens in 1822.

A John Morris, possibly our man, witnessed the will of Luffman Atterbury on 7 June 1796, as did Priscilla Morris, probably his wife.

Morris, Joseph *[fl. 1794–1815?]*, *violinist, clarinetist.*

Doane's *Musical Directory* of 1794 listed Joseph Morris of Bath as a violinist and clarinetist who performed for the New Musical Fund, presumably in London. He may have been the J. Morris of Essex who was cited in the New Musical Fund benefit bill of 1815. Two brothers named Morris were named in Domenico Dragonetti's will in May 1846; the younger received a violin and the elder a tenor (viola), and both were described as members of the orchestra at the Italian opera house in London. Perhaps Joseph Morris was one of those musicians, but there is no way of telling, and the date is long after any certain evidence of Joseph's activity.

Morris, Robert *[fl. 1768–1809]*, *scene painter.*

Robert Morris of No 19, Glanville Street, Rathbone Place, exhibited a landscape in oils at the show of the Society of Artists of Great Britain in 1777 and two drawings in 1790: *Ruins of Burrowick Chapel, Caermarthenshire*, and *Lord Vernon's House near Britton Ferry, North River*. In 1790 the artist lived in Fulham. Graves's *Dictionary* says that he exhibited here and there in London from 1768 to 1809. He was probably that Robert Morris who painted scenery at Covent Garden Theatre occasionally from, at latest, 1793 until after 1800.

Sybil Rosenfeld and Edward Croft-Murray cite the Folger Library's Covent Garden account book in *Theatre Notebook* 19 and the British Library MSS Egerton 2293–2298 to show him working at the theatre in December 1793, in 1794–95, 1798–99, and in April 1800 when, for three and a half days' work on a pantomime, he received £1 6s. 0d. He may also have been the painter Morris who worked intermittently at Covent Garden in the 1802–3 season—though that could have been either G. Morris or J. Morris, both of whom Egerton 2299 gives as painting scenery in December 1800.

Robert Morris may have been related to those painters and to Edward Morris, a painter ("decorateur") at Drury Lane from 1801 to about 1816, and John Morris, a machinist and property man at Drury Lane and Vauxhall from about 1794 to 1822. On 17 December 1767

administration of the property of Robert Morris, "Herald Painter," was granted to Ann his widow. Were these the parents of our Robert Morris? And was our Robert Morris the Morris "herald painter" who was paid £19 16s. 6d. on 29 November 1771 and seven guineas on 14 May 1774 for decorations at Covent Garden?

Morris, Willoughby Lacy. *See* LACY, WILLOUGHBY *1749–1831*

Morrison, Mr *[fl. 1725–1747]*, *ticket agent, dancer.*

Bills in the Burney Collection at the British Library for the Haymarket Theatre in January and February 1725, when a foreign company was offering French plays, carried a notice that "All Persons that want Places to be kept, or Boxes, are desired to send to Mr. Moisson, in Little Suffolk-street." As will be seen, that man was evidently Mr Morrison, who was still handling theatre tickets in 1744. He was also, we believe, the Morrison who was a minor dancer at Drury Lane Theatre in 1737–38 and 1738–39.

A benefit was held at Covent Garden playhouse on 19 January 1744 for Mrs Saunders, and tickets for it were available from Mr Morrison at the Two Golden Balls in Longacre. Morrison seems to have been an employee of Covent Garden in 1746–47, but he was dropped from the roster on 25 April 1747.

The Mrs Morrison who was active in the 1740s was perhaps Anne Morrison, née Saunders, the sister of the Mrs Saunders whose benefit tickets Mr Morrison sold. If so, then Morrison could not have been the husband of Mrs Morrison, for Margaret Saunders's will of 1743 stated that Anne Morrison was a widow. Possibly Mr Morrison was her brother-in-law.

Morrison, Mr *[fl. 1774?–1777]*, *actor.*

Perhaps the Mr Morrison who served as a supernumerary actor at Drury Lane Theatre in 1774–75 was the Morrison who played Symon in *The Gentle Shepherd* at the Haymarket Theatre on 13 October 1777.

Morrison, Master ₁*fl. 1749*₁, *dancer.*
Master Morrison made his first and apparently last stage appearance dancing *Periot's Dance* with Master Shawford at Drury Lane Theatre on 2 May 1749. He was presumably the son of (Anne?) Morrison, who was active in the 1740s.

Morrison, Miss ₁*fl. 1748–1749*₁, *house servant.*
A Miss Morrison is listed as a house servant at Covent Garden in the 1748–49 season by the Latreille transcriptions in the British Library.

Morrison, Miss ₁*fl. 1772*₁, *actress.*
Miss Morrison played an unspecified role in a single performance of *Madrigal and Trulletta* at the Haymarket Theatre on 17 September 1772.

Morrison, Anna Maria. *See* HULL, MRS THOMAS.

Morrison, ₁Anne, née Saunders?₁ ₁*fl. 1741–1751*₁, *actress.*
Mrs Morrison played Millwood in *The London Merchant* on 9 November 1741 at the James Street playhouse. She returned there on 31 May 1742 to act the Queen in *Ulysses.* She was employed at Covent Garden Theatre in 1746–47 at 7s. 6d. weekly. That theatre's accounts show that she was paid 5s. for two days on 29 September 1747 but was dropped from the roster on 21 April 1750.

It is quite possible that our subject was Mrs Anne Morrison, the sister of Miss Margaret Saunders, who, in her will dated 16 January 1743, named Anne her executrix and residuary legatee. The will noted that Anne was then a widow and that her daughter's name was Anna Maria. Anna Maria Morrison became Mrs Thomas Hull. The dancer and ticket agent Morrison, who was active in the 1740s, was perhaps our subject's brother-in-law. The Master Morrison who danced in 1749 may have been Mrs Morrison's son.

Morse, Mrs ₁*fl. 1731–1733*₁, *actress.*
The Mrs "Moss" who played Parly in *The Constant Couple* at Goodman's Fields Theatre in

11 October 1731 was probably Mrs Morse, who appeared at Lincoln's Inn Fields Theatre two nights later as Myrtilla in *The Provok'd Husband.* Mrs Morse was Penelope in *Tunbridge Walks* on 27 October following, and Jiltup in *The Fair Quaker* on 8 November. At the Haymarket Theatre on 2 March 1732 Mrs Morse was Calsine in *The Blazing Comet,* a new "Dramatic Everything" by the "mad" Samuel Johnson of Cheshire. She played the Queen in *The Spanish Fryar* there on 10 May and had some role unspecified in *The Coquet's Surrender* on 15 May. On 4 August 1732 she played both Charlotte in *The Mock Doctor* and a Country Lass in *The Metamorphosis of Harlequin* "At the Great Theatrical Booth in the Cherry-Tree Garden near the Mote" at the Tottenham Court Fair. By 22 August she had moved to the Fielding-Hippisley booth at Bartholomew Fair to assume some role in *The Envious Statesman.*

Mrs Morse returned to the Haymarket on 20 March 1733 as Charlotte and on 26 March she was Millwood in *The London Merchant.* She put on the domino of a Masquerader in *Ridotto al' Fresco* at the Griffin-Cibber-Bullock-Hallam booth on 23 August at Bartholomew Fair. She was the "Miss" Morse who played Charlot in *Oroonoko* at Drury Lane on 8 October 1733. But she was apparently not of the regular company and after playing Chloe in *Timon of Athens* at Drury Lane on 22 November she vanished from the bills.

Morse, Mary. *See* ELMY, MRS WILLIAM.

Mortellari, Mr ₁*fl. 1790–1791*₁, *trumpeter.*
A Mr Mortellari (who apparently cannot have been the composer and singing-master Michele Mortellari) played a divertimento on Clagget's patent French horn on 18 May 1790 at the Hanover Square Rooms. The piece was published in 1790. He was doubtless the same Mortellari who played trumpet for operas at the Pantheon in 1791.

Mortimer, Mr ₁*fl. 1757–1781*₁, *box office keeper, actor.*
Each May, 1757 through 1781, Mr Mortimer, a box office keeper at Drury Lane, shared a benefit with two, three, or four of his fellow house servants or minor performers. He was

himself a performer on several occasions: the First Recruit in *The Recruiting Officer* on his benefit nights, 19 May 1757 and 16 May 1758; an unspecified but surely small role in Guerini's unsuccessful pantomime *The Magician of the Mountain* on 3, 4, and 5 January 1763; and one of the Fryars in the afterpiece *The Witches* on 26 December 1771 and 22 nights thereafter.

In the company lists of 1765 and 1767 he is carried as an actor—why is not clear, since to our knowledge he was in no bills those years. He probably had a couple of walk-on parts. He was, anyway, one of two lowliest in an acting company of 54, at 2*s.* per night. He certainly received an additional, and larger, sum for tending the box office, whose keepers are not named in either list, only in 1767: "2 at £ [per week]," "3 at 15*s.*," and "1 at 12*s.*." The Folger Library Drury Lane accounts show him earning 15*s.* per week in 1776–77.

Morton, Mr ₁*fl. 1736*₁, *actor.*
At York Buildings on 26 April 1736 a company gave *The London Merchant*, with Mr Morton playing Barnwell Senior and Mrs Morton, Maria. In the farce, *The Devil to Pay*, Mrs Morton was Lady Loverule.

Morton, Mrs ₁*fl. 1736*₁, *actress. See* **MORTON, MR** ₁*fl. 1736*₁.

Morton, Mr ₁*fl. 1792–1803?*₁, *actor.*
A Mr Morton was Belville in *The Country Girl* when a pickup company performed by special license at the Haymarket Theatre on 15 October 1792, for the benefit of the actor Sims. On 23 January 1797, also at the Haymarket, a Morton was an unspecified "Principal Character" in a performance of *The Battle of Eddington*, repeated with the same cast on 10 May as a benefit under the patronage of the Prince of Wales for the families of wounded and dead in Sir John Jervis's victory over the Spanish fleet. Perhaps these performances involved the same Morton. It is more hazardous to suggest that this (or one or the other) Morton is the provincial actor who married the actress Charlotte Jane Chapman sometime in the 1780s. That individual, according to *The Secret History of the Green Room* (1790), had been born in Shrewsbury and eventually retired to business there. He may have been the Morton

who was at Chester in 1785. The *Monthly Mirror* cited a Morton managing a company on the Isle of Wight in 1797. A Morton was in the Brighton bill of 17 July 1798; one was at Weymouth in 1802; and one was at Edinburgh in January and February 1803, playing Don Pedro in *Much Ado about Nothing* and Malvoglio in *A Tale of Mystery.*

Morton, Charlotte Jane. *See* CHAPMAN, CHARLOTTE JANE.

Morton, Edward ₁*fl. 1685*₁, *singer.*
Edward Morton, a countertenor, was sworn a Gentleman of the Chapel Royal extraordinary on 12 April 1685; that designation meant that he served without a salary until a place became vacant. He marched in the place of Michael Wise among the countertenors in the coronation procession of James II on 23 April 1685, but he was not mentioned in the Lord Chamberlain's accounts after that, and it is likely that he left the Chapel.

Morton, Mary, née Dayes, later Mrs John Morgan *1756–1800, actress, singer.*
Mary Dayes was the anonymous "Young Lady" making her first appearance on "any stage" at Covent Garden Theatre on 2 May 1772, according to information given us by C. B. Hogan. She was playing Juliet opposite an equally anonymous and amateur Romeo. On 27 October 1773 the Covent Garden playbill assured the public that the "Young Lady" who was singing Lucy in *The Beggar's Opera* that evening was making her very first appearance. But John Philip Kemble noted on his copy of the playbill that the young lady was Miss Dayes. That sort of harmless misrepresentation by the playbills was frequent. It was for her the prelude to eleven successive successful seasons at Covent Garden, seasons in which she would serve frequently and in a wide variety of ways—playing secondary and tertiary parts in comedy, singing in choruses and second leads in ballad opera, and occasionally playing a primary part in farce or melodrama. We have no record of Mrs Morton's playing anywhere else.

Her recorded roles, as she added them were: in 1773–74, Lucy in *The Beggar's Opera*, Perdita ("with Sheep Shearing Ballad") in *The Winter's Tale* and unspecified roles in *The Prince* of *Agra* and in the new anonymous comedy *The South Briton*; in 1774–75, Parisatis in *Alexander the Great*, Amie in *The Jovial Crew*, the Bride in *The Druids*, Arante in Tate's *King Lear*, Cephisa in *The Distrest Mother*, Lucilla in *The Fair Penitent*, Anna in *Douglas*, Flavilla in *Theodosius*, Dorcas in *The What D'Ye Call It*, Arsino in *Cleonice*; in 1775–76, Jessica in *The Merchant of Venice*, Rhodope in *Orpheus and Eurydice*, Semira in *Artaxerxes*, Lady Blanch in *King John*, a Bacchante in *Comus*, Nancy in *Three Weeks after Marriage*, Wit in the Interlude in *Amphitryon*, Phoebe in *As You Like It* and Leonora in *The Padlock*; in 1776–77, Sabrina in *Comus*, Margery in *Love in a Village*, Pallas in *The Golden Pippin*, Clarissa in *All in the Wrong*, the original Polly in Charles Dibdin and Edward Thompson's new comic opera *The Seraglio*, Patience ("with a Song") in *Henry VIII*, Lady Bab in *High Life below Stairs*, Juno in *The Tempest*, Lady Jane in *Know Your Own Mind*, Eleanor in *The Countess of Salisbury*.

In 1777–78, she added Rose in *The Recruiting Officer*, Charlotte in *The Apprentice*, A Gypsy in James Messink and Carlo Delpini's new pantomime *The Norwood Gypsies*, Lettice in *Man and Wife*, the original Grace in Charles Dibdin's burletta *Poor Vulcan!*, and Theodosia in *The Maid of the Mill*; in 1778–79, the original Miss Tokay in Dibdin's comic opera *The Wives Revenged*, one of a Chorus of British Virgins in *Elfrida*, Betty in *The Dutiful Deception*, the original Emily in Frederick Pilon's farce *The Invasion*, Mysis in *True-Blue*, Kate in *The Cobler of Castlebury*, Teresa in *Gallic Gratitude* and Louisa in *The Duenna*; in 1779–80, Caelia in *As You Like It*, Sophia in *The Device*, Lucinda in *Love in a Village*, Fanny in *The Liverpool Prize*, Sophia in *The Deaf Lover*, the original Maria in *The Belle's Stratagem*, a comedy by Hannah Cowley, Clara in *The Duenna*, Venus in *A Fête* and Leonora in *The Padlock*; in 1780–81, Maria in *The Excise-Man*, Miss Ogle in *The Belle's Stratagem*, and Daphne in *Midas*; 1781–82, both Dolly Trull and Jenny Diver in *The Beggar's Opera*, Night in *Jupiter and Alcmena*, the original Jacquelin in Robert Jephson's tragedy *The Count of Narbonne*, Pleasure in *The Choice of Harlequin*, and Eugenia in *The London Cuckolds*; in 1782–83, Ethelinda in *King Henry II*, Clarissa in *All in the Wrong*, the Widow in *The Capricious Lady*, Charlotte in *Love-à-la-Mode*, Dorcas in *The Winter's Tale*, Shelah in *The Sham-

rock*, Egla in *The Spanish Curate*, Harriet in *The Jealous Wife*, and Dolly in *The Ghost*.

In the *Public Advertiser*'s notice for Covent Garden's performance of 2 April 1778 she had appeared as Miss Dayes; in that of 4 April and subsequently, until the end of her career at Covent Garden, she was called Mrs Morton. She was living under that name at No 15, New Crown Court, Russell Street, in May 1779 and May 1780. At some time after she left the theatre she became the first Mrs John Morgan, according to Thomas Faulkner in his *History of Brentford, Ealing and Chiswick* (1845). Faulkner gave her death date as 19 April 1800. Her husband Morgan died in 1808. They were buried at St Mary's, Ealing.

"Moscovita, La." *See* PANICHI, LUCIA.

Moseley, John [*fl. 1659–1661*], *actor.*
Though no roles are known for John Moseley (or Mosely), he "commonly Acted the Part of a Bawd and Whore," according to the prompter John Downes. Since the practice of having men play the female roles died out with the introduction of actresses on the public stage, it is not surprising that Moseley's career was short. He was a member of the Rhodes troupe at the Cockpit in Drury Lane in 1659–60 and joined Sir William Davenant's Duke's Company at Salisbury Court in 1660–61.

Moseley, John *d. 1707, instrument keeper, violinist?*
On 8 December 1690 John Moseley (or Mosley) was listed in a Lord Chamberlain's warrant as one of the court musicians who would accompany William III on a forthcoming trip to Holland. What instrument Moseley played was never mentioned in the accounts, though on 27 February 1692 he was cited as a member of the King's private music, which suggests he was a violinist. He was usually referred to as the musical instrument keeper for the King's Musick. His salary in 1699, and probably earlier as well, was £40 annually. On 8 November 1707 William Brown replaced Moseley, who had recently died.

Moseley, Robert [*fl. 1663?–1667*], *scenekeeper.*
The London Stage lists Robert Moseley as a scenekeeper in 1663–64 in the King's Com-

pany, but that may be an error for 1664–65, for a Lord Chamberlain's warrant dated 1 February 1665 is the earliest notice of Moseley's employment in the troupe. *The London Stage* has him with the company in 1666–67.

Moser, Mr [*fl. 1768*], *singer.*
Mr Moser sang Amasis in *Sesostri* at the King's Theatre on 10 March 1768.

Möser, Karl *1774–1851, violinist, conductor, composer.*
Born in Berlin on 24 January 1774, the son of an oboist in the Ziethen Hussars, Karl Möser studied under Böttcher and made his debut as a violinist on 24 April 1784. For a while he was employed at the court chapel of the Margrave of Schwedt, then he returned for further study under Karl Haak in Berlin and was appointed on 1 January 1792 a royal chamber musician. An affair with the Countess of Mark, natural daughter of the King, caused Möser's exile from Berlin in 1796. He went to Hamburg, then toured Denmark and Norway, and finally came to London to perform for Salomon. We have found no specific records of his London performances.

By 1797 he was back in Berlin at his former post, the Prussian King having died. He lived in St Petersburg from 1806 to 1811 but returned to Berlin to serve as *Konzertmeister* of the royal chapel. He promoted quartet performances in 1813, adding symphonies and overtures in 1816. In 1826 he conducted the first performance of Beethoven's Fourth Symphony. He was made royal *Kapellmeister* in 1842, and though he was pensioned he still continued presiding over the instrumental class. He composed some works, but none of importance. Möser died in Berlin on 27 January 1851.

Moses, Mr [*fl. 1686*]. *See* MOSSE, JOHN.

Moses, Mr [*fl. 1727–1732*], *house servant.*
The boxkeeper "Moss" mentioned in the Lincoln's Inn Fields accounts at Harvard as active at that house on 21 January 1727 only (probably extra help was needed) was very likely the Mr Moses who was a house servant at Goodman's Fields Theatre a few years later. Moses shared a benefit with Temple on 25 June

1730, was cited as a pit doorkeeper at his shared benefit with Sandford on 17 May 1731, and was called a gallery keeper at his solo benefit on 22 May 1732.

Moses, Mr [*fl. 1729*], *actor.*
A Mr Moses played Priuli in *Venice Preserv'd* at the Haymarket Theatre on 1 February 1729.

Moses, Mr [*fl. 1776–1782*], *acrobat.*
Mr Moses was a member of Astley's company at Birmingham on 30 December 1776 when with others he exhibited a tumbling act called "The Egyptian Pyramid or La Force D'Hercule." On 3 February 1782 Moses was in Andrews's company from London, again participating in "Egyptian Pyramids," at Coopers' Hall in King Street, Bristol. No record has been found of Moses performing in London, but he evidently worked there for both Astley and Andrews.

Moset. *See* MONSETT.

Mosley. *See* MOSELEY.

Moss. *See also* MOSES and MOSSE.

Moss, Mr [*fl. 1724–1725*], *singer.*
The London Stage lists "Young Moss" as singing at Lincoln's Inn Fields Theatre in 1724–25. Possibly he was related to the boxkeeper Moses, whose name was sometimes spelled Moss. Moses was active at Lincoln's Inn Fields as early as 1727.

Moss, Mrs. *See* MORSE, MRS.

Moss, Mary. *See also* ELMY, MRS WILLIAM.

Moss, Mary [*fl. 1775–1777*], *actress.*
A group of Scottish actors annually performed Allan Ramsay's pastoral *The Gentle Shepherd* in specially-licensed performances at the Haymarket. On 20 November 1775 the part of Peggy was taken by a "Young Lady, first appearance on any stage." On 7 October 1776, when the ritual was repeated, Peggy was "The Lady who performed it with universal Applause last February," certainly a mistake for "November." The error was repeated when, on 22 April 1777 *The Gentle Shepherd* played for

the benefit of "Mrs Moss, who performed Peggy in February and October 1776." On that occasion Mrs Moss was playing the "breeches" role of Patie "(1st appearance in that character in England)." The inference in the last statement—"in England"—would seem to cast doubt on the claim of amateurism made by the bill in her first London appearance. C. B. Hogan in his *London Stage* index identifies the lady as Mrs *Mary* Moss from evidence on the license granted her to act at the Haymarket for her benefit in 1777.

Moss, William Henry *1751–1817, actor, singer, manager.*

William Henry Moss was born in Capel Street, Dublin, and was as a child sent to England "and there engaged in an active profession," according to the brief account in *The Secret History of the Green Room* (1792). But

Harvard Theatre Collection

WILLIAM HENRY MOSS, as Midas
engraving by Brocas, after De Grifft

he "precipitately relinquished his occupation, and joined a Company of Performers at Enfield in Essex." We believe it almost certain that he was also the Moss who acted Montano in *Othello* and Puff in *Miss in Her Teens* with a company gathered to give the actor Phillips a benefit at the Haymarket on 28 March 1769. William Henry was then 18 or thereabouts.

The Secret History's writer remarked that "Mr. Moss is, we believe, known, and has distinguished himself as a Comedian in most of the Companies in Britain and Ireland" and that he had been a favorite in Edinburgh. But the chronology which we are now able to piece together shows only a small part of his restless wanderings, although we know over 180 of the roles he played. The manuscript calendar of Norma Armstrong supplies his characters in a number of the January-to-June seasons of Edinburgh's Theatre Royal, Shakespeare Square; and the notes left by W. S. Clark reveal his membership in several Irish companies, though what he played in Ireland is not recorded.

In 1772, at Edinburgh, Moss played at least two of his enormous number of roles in his varied lines of eccentrics, blunt men, foreigners, and country characters: the Old Woman in *Linco's Travels* and Sir Toby Belch in *Twelfth Night*. In 1772 he perhaps turned up again at the Haymarket in the summer company, for a prompt copy in the Library of Congress of the new (on 10 June) farce *The Cooper* gives him the part of Matthews on 12 June and, presumably, on 15, 17, 19 June, 22 and 24 July, and 19 and 31 August.

Moss was back at Edinburgh in the season of 1773, when he played: Cornwall in *King Lear*, Gibbet in *The Beaux' Stratagem*, a Gravedigger in *Hamlet*, the Physician in *The Rehearsal*, and the Watchman in *The Provok'd Wife*.

Again at Edinburgh in January 1774 and following, he played Alonzo in *The Tempest*, Cimberton in *The Conscious Lovers*, Dick in *The Lying Valet*, Don Diego in *The Padlock*, Dorus in *Cymon*, Francis in *1 Henry IV*, Justice Shallow in *The Merry Wives of Windsor*, Pedro in *The Spanish Fryar*, Perez in *The Mourning Bride*, Robin in *The Author*, Sir Jacob Jollop in *The Mayor of Garratt*, Dr Druid in *The Fashionable Lover*, Tom in *The Jealous Wife*, and unspecified parts in *The Bankrupt* and *The Maid of Bath*.

At the Haymarket in the summer of 1773 he added to his repertoire Coupée in *The Virgin*

Harvard Theatre Collection

WILLIAM HENRY MOSS, as Caleb

by Kay

Unmask'd, Corydon in *Damon and Phillida*, Jasper in *The Mock Doctor*, Sir Gregory in *Cupid's Revenge*, Transfer in *The Minor*, Gripe in *The Double Disappointment*, Wingate in *The Apprentice*, Simon in *The Commissary*, and unspecified parts in several other plays.

Moss was listed as a member of the Birmingham company in the summer of 1775. Billed as "from the Theatre Royal, Edinburgh" he returned to London on 7 October 1776 to play Kecksey in *The Irish Widow* at Covent Garden Theatre. He was identified as the prompter at the Liverpool Theatre when he signed "William Henry Moss," to a letter published in the London *Morning Chronicle* of 14 September 1776. In the 1776–77 season he was at the Fishamble Street Theatre, Dublin and, after the failure of that theatre, at Crow Street. *The Secret History* asserted that "Mr. [Charles] Macklin . . . recommended him to the Dublin Stage," and that was certainly his route of preferment there, for a letter in the Harvard Theatre Collection, dated 12 March 1777 from Leonard MacNally to Macklin observes, "Moss, whom you recommended is much liked; he has played the Miser, Hardcastle, Sneak, &c with great success. I believe him to

be a very grateful man, he speaks much of the obligation he owes you for instruction."

In the winter seasons of 1777–78, 1778–79, and 1779–80, he continued at Crow Street and each of the several summers was at Cork. In 1780–81 he played sometimes both at Crow Street and Smock Alley. He may have been touring in England in the summer and early fall of 1781, if he was the Moss who was among the miscellaneous group of actors who hired the Haymarket for a specially-licensed performance on 12 November 1781. If so, he hastened back to Ireland to play at Crow Street and Smock Alley again in the winter season of 1781–82. He was at Londonderry in the summer of 1782. In 1782 he transferred his allegiance briefly to Capel Street, Dublin, where, according to Clark's records, he was advertised as "from Drury Lane." (We have no knowledge of a Drury Lane performance that early, but even one would have constituted sufficient reason for the advertisement in any provincial manager's mind.)

Again, in 1783, Moss crossed St George's Channel and in January 1783 was on the Edinburgh roster for the first time in a decade. There his parts were: Admiral Dreadnought in *The Fair American*, Tokay in *The Wives Revenged*, Aspin in *Woman is a Riddle*, Davy in *Bon Ton*, Dip in *The Illumination of the Gladiator's Conspiracy*, Dogberry in *Much Ado about Nothing*, Don Isaac Mendoza in *The Duenna*, Filch in *The Beggar's Opera*, Clodpole in *Barnaby Brittle*, Bauldy in *The Gentle Shepherd*, Bobby Pendragon in *Which Is the Man?*, Captain Meadows in *The Deaf Lover*, General Worry in *The Rival Candidates*, Harry Humbug in *The Intriguing Footman*, Jerry Sneak in *The Mayor of Garratt*, Jobson in *The Devil to Pay*, Justice Woodcock in *Love in a Village*, Linco in *Cymon*, Lingo in *The Agreeable Surprise*, Lovegold in *The Miser*, Hardcastle in *She Stoops to Conquer*, Motley in *The Dead Alive*, Old Philpot in *The Citizen*, Probe in *The Trip to Scarborough*, Rashly in *Lord of the Manor*, a Sailor in *Robinson Crusoe*, Serjeant Slashem in *The Camp*, Sir Anthony Absolute in *The Rivals*, Sir Harry Beagle in *The Jealous Wife*, Thomas Corkscrew in *Piety in Pattens*, Touchstone in *As You Like It*, and Varland in *The West Indian*.

Moss dropped down to York to act in the summer of 1783. But he returned to a grateful Edinburgh in time for the January opening of the theatre in Shakespeare Square. That year he showed the audience Bob Acres in *The Rivals*, Cloten in *Cymbeline*, Colonel Oldboy in *Lionel and Clarissa*, Counsellor Torrington in *The School for Wives*, Croaker in *The Good-Natured Man*, a Countryman in *The Recruiting Serjeant*, Drugget in *Three Weeks after Marriage*, the Good Woman in *The Good Woman without a Head*, John in *The Election*, Launcelot Gobbo in *The Merchant of Venice*, Lazarillo in *The Fruitless Precaution*, Lingo in *Lingo's Wedding*, Lord Grizzle in *Tom Thumb the Great*, the title role in *Midas*, Pantaloon in *The Portrait*, Pedrillo in *The Castle of Andalusia*, Quitam in *The Divorce*, Sellbargain in *Hollow Fair*, Sir Harry Henpeckt in *The Receipt Tax*, Skirmish in *The Deserter*, Snip in *The Invasion of Harlequin*, Tipple in *The Flitch of Bacon*, Tony Lumpkin in *She Stoops to Conquer*, and William in *Rosina*.

In 1784–85, back Moss went to Smock Alley, where he remained through 1785–86, playing in the summer (at least a few times) at Cork in 1785 and at Waterford in 1786. On 30 October 1786 the Drury Lane playbill announced *The Miser*. "The Miser by Mr. MOSS, (From the Theatre Royal in Dublin), being his First Appearance on this Stage." The critic for the *European Magazine* found that he sustained the part with vigor and spirit, possessed a considerable degree of *vis comica*, and received great applause notwithstanding his "provincial dialect." But again, Moss failed to stick in London. By 20 November he (or his manager) was exploiting that single appearance by advertising him at Bristol as "from Drury Lane and Dublin." He apparently stayed with the Bristol-Bath company some part of the 1786–87 season.

From 1787 through 1790, Moss was to alternate between the short winter-spring season in Edinburgh and the Haymarket's summer season. (He also played once more at Drury Lane, Sharp in *The Lying Valet* on 2 October 1788.) At one or another of these theatres at this period he acted the following parts for the first time (so far as we have seen, though he probably developed many of them in his provincial wanderings): Sir James Juniper in *Summer Amusement*, Blister in *The Virgin Unmask'd*, Podesto in *The Siege of Curzolo*, Governor Harcourt in *The Chapter of Accidents*, Rorey in *Gretna Green,* Momus in *The Golden Pippin*, Sir Walter Weathercock in *The Dead Alive*, Old Clackit in

The Guardian, Bootekin in *English Readings*, Pan in *Midas*, Goodall in *The Intriguing Chambermaid*, Doctor Bartholo in *The Follies of a Day*, Justice Mittimus in *The Village Lawyer*, Trusty in *The Ghost*, Grub in *Cross Purposes*, Catchpenny in *The Suicide*, Peachum in *The Beggar's Opera*, Major Benbow in *The Flitch of Bacon*, Cranky in *The Son-in-Law*, Old Dowdle in *The Prisoner at Large*, Quirk in *Ways and Means*, the Stone Eater in *The Gnome*, Clod in *The Young Quaker*, the Agreeable Companion in *The Blade Bone*, Plainwell in *A Quarter of an Hour before Dinner*, Polonius in *Hamlet*, Watty Cockney in *The Romp*, Johnny Atkins in *A Mogul Tale*, Mr Dupely in *Two to One*, Alderman Smuggler in *The Constant Couple*, Mr Honeycomb in *Polly Honeycomb*, the Drummer in *The Battle of Hexham*, Sir Brimmer Bountiful in *Thimble's Flight from the Shopboard*, Old Philpot in *The Citizen*, Quick in *Ways and Means*, Morecraft in *Modern Breakfast*, and Mr Euston in *I'll Tell You What*.

There were also: Billy Bristle in *Hunt the Slipper*, the Butler in *The Virtuous Chambermaid*, Cobb in *He Would be a Soldier*, Darby in *The Poor Soldier*, Diggory Ducklin in *The Dramatic Phrenzy*, Doctor Last in *The Devil upon Two Sticks*, Dumps in *The Natural Son*, a Witch in *Macbeth*, Harry in *Fun upon Fun*, Harry in *The Maid of the Oaks*, Jacob in *A Chapter of Accidents*, Jerome in *The Widow's Vows*, John Moody in *The Provok'd Husband*, Justice Dorus in *Cymon*, Little John in *Robin Hood*, the Mayor in *Peeping Tom of Coventry*, Mungo in *The Padlock*, Pedrillo in *The School for Grayhounds*, Quiz in *Patrick in Prussia*, Ralph in *Maid of the Mill*, Sancho in *Like Master, Like Man*, Benjamin Dove in *The Brothers*, Sir Bernard Savage in *Fashionable Levities*, Sir Christopher Curry in *Inkle and Yarico*, Sir Fretful Plagiary in *The Critic*, Sir Barry in *High Life below Stairs*, Sir Hugh Evans in *The Merry Wives of Windsor*, Blunder in *The Honest Yorkshireman*, Corporal Trim in *Tristam Shandy*, Diggory in *All the World's a Stage*, Dr Prattle in *The Deuce Is in Him*, Don Pedro in *The Wonder*, Harry in *The Intriguing Footman*, Hodge in *Love in a Village*, Jimmy Jumps in *The Farmer*, Nicholas in *The Midnight Hour*, Humphry Gubbins in *The Tender Husband*, the Old Shepherd in *Orpheus*, Paul Prig in *The Cozeners*, Rigdum Funidos in *Chrononhotonthologos*, Roderigo in *Othello*, Sir Luke Tremor in *Such Things Are*, the Taylor in

Catherine and Petruchio, Tester in *The Suspicious Husband*, Verges in *Much Ado about Nothing*, Trinculo in *The Tempest*, Young Hob in *Hob in the Well*, Lazarillo in *The Pannel*, the Old Man in *Lethe*, Abraham in *Harlequin's Invasion*, Crabtree in *The School for Scandal*, Daniel in *The Conscious Lovers*, Bilioso in *The Doctor and the Apothecary*, Peter in *Romeo and Juliet*, and Perriwinkle in *A Bold Stroke for a Wife*.

In the summer or fall of 1790 Moss drifted back to Ireland and is traceable, in two surviving playbills, at Limerick on 8 November and 18 December 1790. He was at Limerick again on 23 February and 18 March 1791 and Cork on 26 April. During the winter seasons of 1791–92, 1792–93, and 1793–94 he performed at Crow Street. On 13 June and 2 July 1792 and 3 July 1793 he acted at Kilkenny and at Waterford on 30 September 1793.

He may have been the Moss who managed at Dumfries in Scotland in 1805 and later at Whitehaven. Francis Courtney Wemyss in his memoirs recalled encountering Moss managing a ragged company of strollers at Falkirk in 1814.

The manager Murray gave Moss a benefit on the last night of the Edinburgh season, 20 May 1815. J. C. Dibdin wrote that "by this time" he was "a confirmed invalid in the City Hospital." He died at Edinburgh on 11 January 1817, according to the *Gentleman's Magazine* of that month.

William Henry Moss was married by 1784, when his wife was first noticed on the Edinburgh roster. Norma Armstrong's calendar shows Mrs Moss in the short winter season in 1784, 1787, and 1790. Also in 1790, in November and December she was at Limerick, in February and March 1791 at Limerick, and April 1791 at Cork, and in September and October 1793 at Galway, all according to W. S. Clark. No trace of her is found again until the Edinburgh season of 1814. She returned in 1815, 1816, 1817, and 1818. Her recoverable roles at Edinburgh were: in 1784, Antonia in *The Chances*; in 1787, Mrs Dangle in *The Critic*; 1790, Betsy Blossom in *The Deaf Lover*, the Chambermaid in *The Jealous Wife*, Columbine in *The Chaplet*, a Singing Witch in *Macbeth*, Tiffany in *Which is the Man*; in 1815, Jannette in *For England, Ho!*; in 1816, the Rich Sister in *The Forty Thieves*; in 1817, Lady Bull in *Harlequin Wittington*; in 1818, Attendant in

The Youthful Days of Frederick the Great, Bianca in *The Cabinet*, Flora in *The Hunter of the Alps*, Jenny in *The Way to Keep Him*, a Maid in *The Belles' Stratagem*, Mrs Enfield in *The Falls of Clyde*, Mrs Ledger in *The Road to Ruin*, Mrs Millefleur in *The Young Quaker*, and Plumante in *Tom Thumb the Great*. She did not act in London.

A portrait of William Henry Moss as Caleb in *He Would Be a Soldier* was engraved by J. Kay in 1787. A pen-and-wash drawing by William Sadler, done in 1777, of Moss as Lovegold in *The Miser* is in the Huntington Library; an engraving was also issued. A portrait of Moss in the title role in *Midas* was engraved by H. Brocas, after De Grifft. An anonymous portrait of him as Midas was published with a memoir in the *Hibernian Magazine*, May 1794.

Mosse, Mrs [*fl. 1702–1706*],   *dancer.*

At Drury Lane Theatre on 8 December 1702 there was dancing between the acts "by a Devonshire Girl never seen on the Stage before, who performs a *Genteel Round* to the Harp alone; an Irish Humour, *The Whip of Dunboyne*, with her Master; another genteel dance; a Highland *Lilt* with her Master; and *A Country Farmer's Daughter*, all in Natural Habits." The identity of the "Devonshire Girl," as the bills after that called her, is not certain, but it seems most likely that she was the Mrs Mosse (or Moss) who performed many of the same dances two years later, after references to the Devonshire Girl waned. The dancer's master was Mr Claxton, who was in 1704 identified as the dancing master of Mrs Mosse.

The Devonshire Girl continued offering the dances named in her initial bill during the remainder of the 1702–3 season and added a dance in imitation of Mlle Subligny. The bill on 30 April 1703 explained that "the *Devonshire Girl*, being now upon her Return to the City of Exeter, will perform three several Dances, particularly her last New Entry in Imitation of *Mademoiselle Subligni*, and the *Whip of* Duboyne by Mr. Claxton *her* Master, being the last time of their Performance till Winter." She was regarded highly enough that in a proposal for a new performing company about 1703 (previously thought to date from 1707) the "Devonshire girle" was listed as a dancer at £20 per year.

She was back at Drury Lane for the 1703–4

season, occasionally appearing with Claxton, and on 30 March 1704 there was offered an *Indian Tambour* "by the two Devonshire Girls and a little Boy." The identity of the second girl is not known. One of the last notices of the Devonshire Girl was on 16 August 1704, when she danced a *Harlequin Man and Woman* with "Laforest" and, solo, a *Quaker's Dance* and *Country Farmer's Daughter*. On the following 20 October at Drury Lane the *Country Farmer's Daughter* and *Highland Lilt* were danced by Mrs Mosse, and Claxton, her dancing master, danced the *Whip of Dunboyn*. Thereafter Mrs Mosse danced between the acts regularly in 1704–5 and 1705–6, and there were no further references to the Devonshire Girl. Possibly she was related to the Restoration violinist John Mosse.

Mosse, John [*fl.* 1662–1686], *violinist, bass viol player, organist, composer.*

The Mr Mosse who failed in 1662 to answer a summons by the Corporation of Music and was ordered apprehended by warrant of the Lord Chamberlain on 28 June 1669 for "teaching, practising and executing music in companies or otherwise, without the approbation or lycence of the Marshall and Corporation of musick" was very likely the composer and court musician John Mosse (or Moss). Perhaps, since in a later document Mosse was called "Moses," the Mr Moses who owned a 30′ by 20′ plot of land on Bedford Street south of King Street (as shown on Lacy's map of St Paul, Covent Garden, parish in 1673) was also John Mosse. He taught music at Christ's Hospital in 1674 and 1675.

John was listed on a livery warrant of 1674 as due £16 2s. 6d. as a member of the King's Musick; he was cited as replacing John Jenkins. That information was noted again on Michaelmas 1675 on a document at the Public Record Office quoted in Zimmerman's *Purcell*. Yet a Lord Chamberlain's warrant dated 19 April 1678 stated that John Mosse was to replace John Jenkins in the King's private music (the band of 24 violins), as though John had not already been in the court musical establishment. After that Mosse was regularly mentioned in livery warrants, and one, in 1683, indicated that he was then still owed livery allowances from 1679 through 1682, and another, dated 25 February 1686, noted that he

had not been paid for 1679 through 1684. On 21 September 1686 James II tried to make amends and directed that Mosse be paid £96 15s. in arrears from a new tax on tobacco and sugar. The last notice of Mosse was dated 30 September 1686, when he had others judged the organ-playing ability of candidates for organist at St Katherine Kree. That would certainly suggest that Mosse was also an accomplished organist. Grove notes that some of Mosse's dances are in *Musicke's Recreation* (1669), and some keyboard pieces are in *Musicke's Hand-Maide* (1663) and *Melothesia* (1673). Mosse's *Lessons for the Base-Viol* were published in 1671.

Mosses. *See* MOSES.

Mossop, Henry 1729?–1774, *actor, manager.*

Henry Mossop was born in Dublin in 1729, according to his friends, the actor-critic Francis Gentleman and the poet Samuel Whyte.

Courtesy of the National Gallery of Ireland

HENRY MOSSOP

artist unknown

That date perhaps is more valid than the claim in the *Gentleman's Magazine's* obituary notice in December 1774 that he was in his forty-second year at the time of his death or the statement in Randall Davies's history of *Chelsea Old Church* and Faulkner's *Historical Description of Chelsea* that he died at the age of 43. Mossop's father was the Reverend John Mossop, M.A. of Trinity College, who on 10 August 1737 became prebend of Kilmeen, Tuam, where he died on 15 May 1759.

When the Reverend John Mossop took up his assignment at Tuam, young Henry remained in Dublin with his uncle, a bookseller. After attending a grammar school in Digges Street he entered Trinity College with intentions of becoming a clergyman. Lysons in his *Environs* stated that Mossop was encouraged by an uncle to leave Ireland for London, and when his expectations of becoming his uncle's heir were disappointed he decided to become an actor. He was rejected by Garrick and Rich, both of whom advised him against taking up acting; however, through the influence of Francis Gentleman, an old schoolmate, Mossop was engaged by Thomas Sheridan at the Smock Alley Theatre in Dublin.

Advertised as "a gentleman of this Country, who never yet appeared on any Stage," Mossop made his debut at Smock Alley as Zanga in *The Revenge* on 30 November 1749 (not 28 November as stated in *The Dictionary of National Biography*). Benjamin Victor in his *Original Letters* described Mossop as "a wild awkward youth, that had never taken the business and propriety of acting in consideration." From Quin, upon whom he had modeled his portrayal of Zanga, Mossop had adopted "the faults instead of the beauties." Mossop's second role was Othello to Macklin's Iago on 13 December. Though announced for Cassius in *Julius Caesar* on 23 December 1749 he became too ill to play that night and did not appear in the part until 8 January 1750. His other roles that season included Gloster in *Jane Shore*, Polydore in *The Orphan*, Ribemont in *Edward the Black Prince*, Orestes in *The Distrest Mother*, Bajazet in *Tamerlane*, and the title role in *Comus*. On 31 March 1750 he acted Othello to Sheridan's Iago, and played King John on 4 April and Macbeth on 23 May 1750. In a letter to Riley Towers on 13 January 1750 Lord Orrery wrote from Dublin to describe Mossop as

A good person, manly, but no carriage; his action wild, ranting irregular but still improving after he has once gone through a part. Voice sweet & strong, but he imitates Quin too much, especially in modelling his voice, that it commonly sounds hard & untuneable. Diggs is an actor, Mossop will be one.

The next season at Smock Alley Mossop acted Aboan in *Oroonoko*, Marcian in *Theodosius*, Torrismond in *The Spanish Fryar*, Pembroke in *Lady Jane Gray*, Hotspur in 1 *Henry IV*, and Sempronius in *Cato*. When he played Richard III for the first time at his benefit on 13 March 1751 he appeared "unaccountably dressed . . . in white satin puckered," prompting Sheridan's gibe that the costume gave him "a most coxcombly appearance." When the remark reached his ears the next morning, Mossop, who had a staccato delivery, confronted the manager: "Mr. *She-ri-dan*, I hear you said I dressed Richard like a *Cox-comb*: that is an *af-front*; you wear a sword, pull it out of the *scab-bord*; I'll draw mine, and thrust it into your *bo-dy*." That story is told in an *Historical View of the Irish Stage* (1788–1794) by Robert Hitchcock, who incorrectly placed Mossop's playing of Richard III in the previous season and claimed that Sheridan merely smiled at Mossop's explosion and the contretemps passed. But that quarrel may have been the one which caused Mossop to abandon his Smock Alley engagement suddenly in the middle of March 1751.

It was perhaps on the recommendation of Lord Orrery that Mossop was engaged by Garrick for the 1751–52 season. His debut at Drury Lane Theatre occurred on 26 September 1751, as Richard III. The prompter Cross wrote in his diary that night: "the house was crowded in ten minutes, he was receiv'd with great applause, but happening to crack towards the end a few hiss'd, but were overpowered by the Claps—he is very young has been upon ye Irish Stage but two years—his performance was so well, that we cou'd find no want but—Garrick." When Mossop repeated Richard the next night he "play'd easier & preserv'd his Voice, great Applause." Thomas Davies thought that Richard III was a wise choice for Mossop's London debut, for in that role the awkwardness of his manner was disguised. Mossop was more a powerful speaker than a pleasing actor, possessed of a strong and harmonious voice which could range from the lowest note to the highest pitch, indeed a voice "the most comprehensive" Davies ever heard. That opinion was shared by Tate Wilkinson, who in his *Memoirs* wrote that Mossop owned "the most melodious clear voice I ever heard."

Mossop's next part at Drury Lane was Zanga in *The Revenge* on 10 October 1751. That role came to be regarded by most critics, including Davies, as his masterpiece. In that first Drury Lane season he also appeared as Bajazet in *Tamerlane* (on 4 November 1751 when Cross wrote "Mr Mossop did Bajazet—Oh"), Horatio in *The Fair Penitent*, Theseus in *Phaedra and Hippolitus*, Orestes in *The Distrest Mother*, Macbeth (on 28 January 1752, and Cross reported "much hissing when given out again"), Pembroke in *Lady Jane Gray*, and Wolsey in *Henry VIII*. He acted Othello for his benefit on 12 March 1752 when tickets were available at his lodgings in Southampton Street, Covent Garden.

Over the next three seasons Mossop excelled at Drury Lane in parts of turbulence and rage, marked by regal tyranny and sententious grav-

Harvard Theatre Collection

HENRY MOSSOP, as Bajazet

artist unknown

ity. With all his defects, thought Davies, Mossop was after only Garrick and Barry "the most valuable actor on the stage." Among his new parts in 1752–53 were Pierre in *Venice Preserv'd*, Dorox in *Don Sebastian, King of Portugal*, Lewson in the premiere of Moore's *The Gamester* on 7 February 1753, and the original Perseus in Young's *The Brothers* on 3 March 1753. When he acted Pierre on 28 October 1752, to Garrick's Jaffeir and Mrs Bellamy's Belvidera, his awkwardness worked to his great advantage. John Hill pointed out the portrayal as an excellent example of "playing which appears natural, because it is divested of all pomp and ceremony." According to Davies, Mossop owed much to Quin in the passages of sentimental gravity, though Quin never had displayed the gallantry shown by Mossop in his third-act scene with the conspirators, a gallantry "as striking as it was unexpected." In his *History of the Scottish Stage* (1793) John Jackson, having seen Barry and Garrick play both Pierre and Jaffeir, claimed that Mossop had "raised the character of *Pierre* beyond all reach, and left any Jaffeir I ever saw with him at a distance."

Mossop's performances that season were reviewed in *A General View of the Stage* (1753), wherein he was described as an actor who understood his author "perfectly well" and owned one of the finest voices in the world. In *The Present State of the Stage* (1753), Theophilus Cibber called him "extremely just & spirited" as Pierre and "masterly" as Richard III; "his Person is far from being a bad one; but he hurts it by his Action, which . . . wants modelling." Encouraged that Mossop had learned to control his left hand, which he used to shake about so much, Cibber expressed great hopes for the young performer's continuing industry and improvement. Mossop took his benefit that season as Othello on 2 April 1753, at which time he lodged at Newton's Warehouse, Tavistock Street, his abode until the summer of 1755.

When Mossop acted Richard III early in the 1753–54 season Arthur Murphy in *Gray's Inn Journal* of 29 September 1753, praised him for pleasing a splendid and numerous audience and for his great improvement. His performance of Pierre in late October, reported Murphy, was full of "Gallantry and heroic Ardor." That season Mossop added to his Drury Lane repertoire Shore in *Jane Shore*, King John in

King John, and Osman in *Zara* (for his benefit on 25 March 1754). He created the original characters of Aenobarbus in Glover's *Boadicia* on 1 December 1753, Appius in Crisp's *Virginius* on 25 February 1754, and Phorbus in Whitehead's *Creusa* on 20 April 1754. In 1754–55 he played Coriolanus, the Duke in *Measure for Measure*, and the original Barbarossa in Brown's *Barbarossa* on 17 December 1754.

On 13 September 1755 the prompter Cross recorded in his diary, "Mr Mossop left us." He had accepted an advantageous offer from Victor and Sowden (the Smock Alley managers while Sheridan was spending two years in London) to act in Dublin. Hitchcock reported that Mossop had engaged at terms which included one-third of the profits, after a nightly charge of £40, for acting once a week for a total of 24 nights. Mossop's desertion of Drury Lane caused some hard feelings between him and Garrick, but on 16 October 1755 Garrick wrote to the Marquis of Huntington in Dublin recommending Mossop ("who has great Merit both as a Man & as an Actor") to the attention of his noble friend. There "was a little Misunderstanding between Us," wrote Garrick, "but upon an Eclaircissement, We were both most Sorry that other engagements had hinder'd Us from being togeather." For his reappearance at Smock Alley Mossop acted Achmet in *Barbarossa*, a curious choice, since he was unsuited for that role, while the title role was regarded as among his finest portrayals. In his first 18 nights of acting, Mossop drew £2000 into the box office coffers, according to a letter written by Victor in February 1756, but an illness which plagued him throughout the rest of the season frustrated the management's expectations of improving the theatre's perilous financial situation. Mossop himself, however, managed to earn between £800 and £900.

Subsequently Mossop reengaged at Drury Lane, returning on 21 September 1756 as Richard III. As the playbill for his benefit on 26 March 1757 indicated, he also had resumed lodging at Newton's Warehouse in Tavistock Street. That season he appeared as Maskwell in *The Double Dealer*, Osmyn in *The Mourning Bride*, Aletes in *Creusa*, and the title role in *Cato*. His new London roles in 1757–58 included Prospero in *The Tempest*, Young Bevil in *The Conscious Lovers*, Publius in *The Roman Father*, Hamlet, Hastings in *Jane Shore*, and the

original Agis in Hume's new tragedy *Agis* on 21 February 1758. The *Theatrical Review* of 1757 praised his understanding, voice, and appearance as major assets, but also noted several liabilities, like harsh, sharp, unnatural transitions, an "uncouth expression of impatience," a habit of turning his back and walking away from other characters at the end of his speeches, and a fondness for "certain favorite gestures and motions, which, being repeated, threw a sameness in most of the characters he acts."

Mossop, indeed, did not fare well at the hands of the critics in 1757, especially in regard to his acting of genteel or comic roles. That year *The Theatrical Examiner* examined him at length:

Mr. M——p has acquired some reputation as an actor;—it is very happy for him, that he is indulged with a greater degree of favour from many than I can possibly bestow on him; for which he is in so small measure obliged to his countrymen, who were determined to carry a point in his support. His person is neither good or utterly bad, but is rendered less agreeable by a stoop, and awkward use of his arms: his voice is fine, yet with that I must confess him the most void of feeling, of any man I ever yet heard; but what is still more surprising, he speaks highly judicious: yet it rather appears the work of labour than nature. I shall begin with a remark or two on his Comus,—where is the glee? the heartfelt voluptuous sense of jollity and mirth expressed? 'tis true, his countenance carries a forced smile!—but he gives not the image of *Laughter holding both his sides,—but one of Laughter set aside:*—why does he sit *statue-fixed* as the lady, while the songs and dances are decreed to excite her attention? would it make him seem less in earnest, if he would venture to address her in dumb shew, and seemingly endeavour to draw her attention . . . ? Horatio in the Fair Penitent, is neither a bully or a country schoolmaster; Mr. M——p! he is a gentleman, a friend, and a man of strict honour: and these sort of folks are not without feeling and elegance. . . . Your Zanga will remind me of the more masterly strokes of Quin and Sheridan.

Arthur Murphy saw Mossop's first attempt at Young Bevil in *The Conscious Lovers* on 26 November 1757 and wrote a long essay in the next *Morning Chronicle*:

I must own I went that Night to the Play with some Prejudices; I had always entertained a Notion that though Mr. Mossop's Person was far from ungenteel, his Behaviour and Deportment on the Stage never had that graceful unconstrained Freedom which is annexed to our Idea of a Man of Fashion; moreover methinks I had observed that he had partly received from Nature, partly contracted through too great a Habit of Tragick Parts of a certain Cast, a kind of cloudy Countenance, a morose Lowering of the Brows and Eyelids, which could never suit the Openness of Generosity, the constituent Quality in Bevil's Character; but what seemed to me most incompatible with that Part, and indeed with any Part in Comedy, was the Stiffness of his Voice, which though it may sometimes and perforce be, as it were, cracked and broke to the strong Purposes of Tragedy, can never be bent to the soft Pliancy, to the nice Inflections and gentle Changes of the Tones which characterise the Comic Dialogue.

All those Prejudices did I carry with me, and brought them home as entire, as absolute as ever; and I found myself more and more confirmed in my Opinion, that Mr. Mossop was never intended by Nature for a Theatrical Wooer, but much less in Comedy, than in Tragedy. . . . As to the Scenes of another Kind, where a plain unimpassioned, but nice and judicious Delivery was required, such as most of his scenes with Sir John, with Humphrey, and with Myrtle, but more particularly the beautiful scene of the Duel, it is but mere Justice to say that his Performance of them was excellent, and such as we might expect it from an Actor of his Parts and Understanding. But even then I could not but lament to see him lose Part of the Merit of his *Vocal* Delivery, by unnatural Position of his Arms, which seemed to be foreign to his Body, by the aukward and unmeaning Motions of his Hands, which he continually busied in buttoning and unbuttoning his Waistcoat, in short, by the Stiffness of his whole Deportment and Person.

To his repertoire in 1758–59 Mossop added the Elder Wou'dbe in *The Twin Rivals*, Caled in *The Siege of Damascus*, and characters in *Aesop* and *The Ambitious Step-Mother*. On 21 April 1759 he was the original Etan in the premiere of Murphy's *The Orphan of China*. His performance of Hamlet on 23 May 1759 proved to be his last appearance at Drury Lane. Though he was announced in the bills for Osmyn in *The Mourning Bride* on 29 May 1759, his father's death prevented Mossop's playing, and Smith was borrowed from Covent Garden to act the role that night. The *London Chronicle* of 29–31 May 1759 claimed Mossop inherited from his father an estate worth £200 a year. That year he was the object of a vitriolic attack by Edward Purdom in *A Letter to David Garrick on opening the Theatre* (misdated 1769), for which

an apology was subsequently issued. Purdom called Mossop "as wretched a performer as ever graced a stage," who played with harsh and unnatural elocution and ungainly gestures. Other observers, such as the author of *An Essay on the Present State of the Theatre* (1760), noted that Mossop lacked "art" and tended to show the same face "without any variety or alteration." But Purdom's charge that he lacked any understanding of his characters—"He is the same unmeaning bellower in them all"—was unkind and exaggerated. Despite his faults of execution, Mossop's awareness of a role's dynamics and an author's intent was praised by most critics.

In the fall of 1759 Mossop quit Drury Lane and engaged with Barry and Woodward at the Crow Street Theatre, Dublin. Despite Garrick's encouraging him and casting him in roles for which he was best suited, the vain and ill-tempered Mossop had been unduly influenced by the flattery of Fitzpatrick, Garrick's enemy, who claimed that the manager was deliberately keeping the actor in an inferior rank. At Dublin he was well received and added to his repertoire Ventidius, Iago, and Kitely. Stricken by the urge to manage, on 4 May 1760 he leased the Smock Alley and Aungier Street theatres from the proprietors.

The terms found in the Registry of Deeds in Dublin called for the lease to begin on 1 October 1760 for the period of Mossop's life or 21 years, at a yearly rate of £100. Fearing the competition, Barry and Woodward had offered him £1000 per year (and two benefits), a very advantageous proposition which, as it turned out, he was foolish to reject. The Dublin press announced on 7 June 1760 that Mossop had executed the lease, had engaged Brown, Sparks, and Sowden for the ensuing season, and was soon to set out for London to recruit more performers. He had begun a destructive rivalry which would seriously injure the welfare of the Irish stage and leave him ruined in health and fortune.

The Smock Alley Theatre opened under Mossop's management on 17 November 1760—after the period of mourning for George II had been completed—with a production of *Venice Preserv'd*, in which Mossop acted Pierre, Digges Jaffeir, and Mrs Bellamy Belvidera. With the assistance of Mrs Abington, Tom King, Sam Reddish, and Tate Wilkinson, Mossop held his own in the competition between the two houses for several seasons. The same pieces were often foolishly offered at both theatres on the same evening. On 7 February 1762 Dr Thomas Wilson wrote to Samuel Derrick at Bath: "Mossop has succeeded tolerably well, not indeed in proportion to his own Merit, or the Strength of his Company, but yet he is gaining ground— And this winter will produce him a good deal of Money, and a vast accession of Theatrical Reputation." Indeed, Mossop's engagement of an Italian opera company temporarily forestalled the inevitable. About that time appeared *An Epistle to Henry Mossop*, a pamphlet criticizing his allowing equilibrists, fire-eaters, animal acts, and other low acts on his stage but praising his "amazing" powers in the characters of Richard III and Zanga.

In 1763 Mossop began to think about giving up the struggle. Barry and Woodward had proved powerful opposition, and as Mossop's fortunes declined his players began to revolt. "Their weekly salaries," reported the *Theatrical Biography* (1772), "became first to be curtailed, which brought on large arrears . . . so that his corps hourly went over to the enemy." On 17 March 1763 he advised George Garrick that he needed more time to settle his difficult affairs in Ireland, and he could not return to Drury Lane until next season. He asked the Garricks to keep the correspondence a secret, and promised to send the money he owed David from the first receipts that would come into his house from the performances of Charles Holland, who would soon arrive in Dublin. After Holland's arrival, however, Mossop again wrote to ask David for an extension of a few months on the debt because business had been bad. Ned Shuter had broken an agreement with him and still had £50 of Mossop's money in his possession; Mossop had begun a suit against Shuter. Mossop told Garrick he could not join Drury Lane for the ensuing season but would see him in London about 15 August.

In 1762–63 the combined receipts at both Smock Alley and Crow Street were insufficient to meet the expenses of one theatre. Salaries were either severely reduced or simply not paid, forcing the actors into impoverished conditions. The money that Mossop did not spend on litigation he squandered in gambling. On 10 March 1764 he mortgaged the Smock Alley and Aungier Street theatres to John Wingfield

Courtesy of the Garrick Club

HENRY MOSSOP
by Hone

Pollard, and on 6 June 1765 he mortgaged again to the Reverend Thomas Wilson.

Mossop held on in Dublin until the spring of 1771. Despite the perilous financial situation, Mossop remained a great stage favorite, adding to his repertoire Zamti in *The Orphan of China*, Leon in *Rule a Wife and Have a Wife*, Carlos in *Like Master Like Man*, Archer in *The Stratagem*, Belcour in *The West Indian*, and many more characters. Upon Barry's retirement in 1767 Mossop took over both theatres and held a monopoly in Dublin. On 7 December 1767 he appeared as Richard III at Crow Street, where he played under Barry's patent. He took the company to Wexford in the summer of 1766 and to Cork in the summers of 1768 and 1769.

Late in 1770 he gave up Crow Street with its title of Theatre Royal to William Dawson, who the previous season at the Capel Street Theatre had met him head-on in a competition for the public and had won. After some difficulty obtaining a license from the Lord Mayor, Mossop tried to play out the season at Smock Alley, but by the spring he was broken in health. On 28 March 1771, Dawson wrote from Dublin to Charles Macklin, "Mossop is Pronounced out of Danger by his Physicians but they say he will not be able to Play for twelve Months to Come." Mossop was unable to appear at his benefit on 17 April 1771.

In fact, he never again appeared on the stage. He left for London, presumably in search of recruits, leaving the management to Thomas Ryder. Garrick had thoughts of hiring him, writing to John Moody on 6 June 1771, "do you imagine that Mossop would be of Service to Drury? . . . did you See him, hear him & Understand him?" On 6 September 1771 the press announced that Mossop was preparing to leave London to return to Dublin, having satisfied his Irish creditors with a proposal to give them all the profits, except two guineas a week on which he intended to subsist. The proprietors generously offered him three guineas. Mossop was invested "with full power to carry over some of the best performers he can pick up on this side of the water." A few days later, on 9 September 1771, a press report denied a rumor that Mossop's problems were not resolved, stating that while it was true that he "had the Misfortune last season to be afflicted with a dangerous and malignant Fever, which prevented him from appearing upon the Stage for some months," and the loss was nearly £1500, no meeting of creditors had been proposed, and he had been offered for his property more than double the amount of his debts. However, on the eve of his departure for Ireland in November 1771 he was arrested for debt. In Dublin James Wilder implored public support in the *Dublin Journal* of 14–17 December 1771 for his Smock Alley benefit to save all his possessions from being attached by the sheriff because he had been foolish enough to underwrite one of Mossop's debts.

Upon being declared a bankrupt in January 1772 Mossop was released from the King's Bench. But in May 1772 the *Dublin Journal* reported "A few days ago, a celebrated Tragedian, Mossop, removed to his new apartments in the rules of the Fleet." Pride prevented his application to Garrick, for, he said, Garrick knew he was in London. The dissenting minister David Williams in an abusive pamphlet entitled *A Letter to David Garrick, Esq., on his Conduct as Principal Manager and Actor at Drury-Lane*, published in March 1772, unwisely suggested that Garrick's powers were on the decline and that Mossop's talents were needed at Drury Lane. Garrick, of course, was not persuaded. Mossop tried for a job at Covent Garden but failed when Mrs Barry—wife of his Dublin rival—refused to act with him. In the

Forster Collection at the Victoria and Albert Museum is a letter—signed "Menander," but in the hand of the Reverend David Williams—intended for the printer of "Owen's Chronicle or the Westminster Journal." Therein Williams again attacked Garrick on Mossop's behalf, explaining that his physician had advised the actor to seek a warmer climate:

But he is neither so far in a Decline, nor at such a distance but he will readily obey the call of the publick & appear for their entertainment. Indeed Mr Garrick's being the *Broker* in this transaction, & Mr Mossop's talents being commodities of a sort which he does not chuse to deal in, the public may be disappointed, & be insulted one winter more with Raree-shews. . . . You may be assured then that if Mr Mossop does not appear on any stage, it is owing to the *great Roscius*, who not only hates a rival, but must have no one near him to share in the least in the regard of the publick. . . .

A notation in one of the Winston manuscripts, dated 18 March 1772, states that Mossop had been "engag'd for Haymarket for tragedy," but no such engagement materialized. Mossop left for the Continent with a friend named Edward Smith, stopping a while in Paris and then settling down in southern France by 1773. The trip failed to benefit Mossop, and after a year abroad he returned to London emaciated and mentally debilitated. Charles Lee Lewes in his *Memoirs* described Mossop's self-starvation. He died in the Strand on 27 December 1774 in great poverty; it was said his only possessions were 4½d. in his pocket and a broken heart. He was buried in Chelsea churchyard on 1 January 1775, attended by Robert Baddeley, James Aickin, and Johnson, the Drury Lane under-prompter. The *Public Advertiser* of 4 January reported his funeral and claimed that Mossop had not been able to bring himself to borrow from friends, but that a few days before his death he had sent to borrow of a maternal uncle at the Inner Temple, worth £40,000, who denied him. Supposedly Garrick offered to pay the funeral expenses but the shamed uncle refused the gesture and paid them himself.

On his deathbed Mossop had sent Garrick a play he had written, bequeathing it to Garrick in hopes that a production would pay his creditors. When Mossop had been declared bankrupt two years earlier, his chief creditor listed was Garrick, to whom he owned £200. On 28

December 1774, the day after Mossop died, Garrick wrote Colman to tell him that he had not yet read the play, but that a friend had and had reported that it was without humor. Apparently the play was neither acted nor printed. On 8 January 1775 Garrick wrote to the Reverend David Williams that Williams's account of Mossop's final days had greatly disturbed him; "had I known his distress I shou'd most certainly have reliev'd it—he was too great a Credit to our Profession, not to have done all in our Power to have made him *easy* at least, if not happy."

Little is known of Mossop's personal life, and we find no mention of a wife or legitimate children. He lived for a time with Sarah Ford, sometimes described as an actress (though we find no evidence). By her he had a daughter, Harriet Ann Ford, about 1754, who first appeared at Drury Lane, as a child, in November 1762. By that time Sarah Ford was living with the author-manager George Colman the elder, whom she married in 1767. A rumor that Mossop had married "the elder Amici," a singer, in Dublin was denied by Dr Thomas Wilson in a letter to Samuel Derrick at Bath on 27 March 1762: "I believe neither of them ever

Harvard Theatre Collection

HENRY MOSSOP, as Zanga

artist unknown

dream'd of marriage or anything tending toward marriage. But the Malice of the Town will embrace the slightest occasion for the propogating of a false report." Presumably Wilson was referring to the sister-in-law of Sga Anna Lucia De Amicis, wife of Domenico De Amicis.

The death of Elizabeth Mossop, said to have been the sister of the actor, was reported in the *Freeman's Journal* on 20 January 1808; her age was given as 59, which if correct would place her birth in 1748 or 1749, some 20 years after Henry Mossop's and in the late years of their father's life. One William Henry Mossop, described in a *Gentleman's Magazine* obituary as a nephew of the actor, died in 1788. The medallist William Mossop (1751–1804) was also related to the actor; he had been born the son of a Roman Catholic named Browne, whose widow subsequently married a W. Mossop and changed her son's name to Mossop so he could be admitted to the Dublin Bluecoat School, a Protestant academy. The nineteenth-century actor George Mossop (d. 1850), who was the second husband of the actress Louisa Lane (later Mrs John Drew), was not related to Henry Mossop, so far as we have been able to determine.

John Bernard wrote that Henry Mossop "though intelligent & clever, was stern, proud, fiery, and commanding," a man sensitive to his rights and protective of his personal dignity. One night in September 1769 when playing at Cork Mossop alienated an army officer, who jumped on the stage and attacked him with such fury that the actor had to draw his sword and wound the officer in the side. Mossop lost money gambling and he sought fashionable society when he might better have mustered his personal and financial resources for his professional obligations. Ryan in his *Table Talk* claimed that Mossop, hoping to mend his broken fortunes "by the chance of a die, or by the turn of a card," often left his theatre with £100 only to return home, after a night of gambling, with "an aching head and heart." For someone who knew the art of flattery so well, he was strangely prone to listen to bad advisors. He cultivated what Oxberry called "a mysterious grandeur" and as the result of being involved in considerable litigation he had acquired "a great many legal technicalities in conversation."

The desperate state of Mossop's finances at

Smock Alley spawned a number of anecdotes about his stinginess and avarice. George Parker claimed that he was hired as an actor by bribing Mossop with a pair of silk stockings worth 18 shillings. "The Great Man, as they called him," wrote Parker in his *Society and Manners*, "was certainly for pride and arrogance the most extraordinary character the world ever produced. . . . The only object of this hero was to *stand alone*, as he phrased it." If he acted Othello he did not expect the audience had come to see Shakespeare's play but vainly supposed he was "the sole object of their attention."

But even Parker, who was hardly fond of Mossop, agreed that as an actor he was, in most respects, at the top of his profession. Cooke, Macklin's biographer, described Mossop as of middle size, "tolerably well formed, with a face of much expression, and an eye that evidently marked a proud and independent mind." Macklin thought him "well enough adapted to the general line of parts which he chose" but criticized him for "too great a mechanism in his action and delivery." Mossop was sometimes ridiculed—because of the frequent placing of his left hand on his hip and extending his right—as a "teapot" actor; others labeled him "the Distiller of Syllable" because of his weighty manner of forcing out syllables. Churchill treated him with severity in *The Rosciad*:

> *Mossop, attach'd to military plan,*
> *Still keeps his eye fix'd on his right-hand man,*
> *Whilst the mouth measures words with seeming skill,*
> *The right hand labours, and the left lies still;*
> *For he resolves on scripture grounds to go,*
> *"What the right doth let not the left hand know";*
> *With studied impropriety of speech,*
> *He soars beyond the hacknied critic's reach.*
> To epithets allots emphatic state,
> *Whilst principals, ungraced, like lackeys wait;*
> *Conjunction, preposition, adverb join*
> *To stamp new vigour on the nervous line;*
> *In monosyllables his thunders roll,*
> He, she, it, and we, ye, they, fright the soul.

Yet what disturbed one critic impressed another. In a "Rosciad"-like poem called *The Mirror* (1790), in which the old actors were conjured up, we read:

> *See Mossop appears, though ungraceful his mien,*

> *A better performer scarce ever was seen.*
> *His tones were so deep comprehensive and clear*
> *They harrowed each heart while they filled every ear*
> *The turbulent passions he nobly expressed*
> *And stormed the fierce feelings which live in the breast.*

When Mossop played roles which best suited his natural bent he was superb, as in the fiery and savage Caled in *The Siege of Damascus* and the unrelenting villain Perseus in *The Brothers*. His Richard III was excelled only by Garrick's, claimed Davies; "he has justly conceived the character in every situation . . . he seems to know the real drift of Richard in every speech of designing villainy, or of artful hypocrisy." In his *Dramatic Censor* in 1770 Francis Gentleman provided an extensive and balanced account of Mossop's characterizations. Gentleman noted the faults others had generally recognized but concluded that Mossop "in point of literary knowledge, and strong natural parts, stands very high in the theatrical list." (Davies, indeed, placed him only lower than Garrick and Barry.) As Zanga, wrote Gentleman, Mossop "most certainly stands in this part alone"; as Cassius he "shewed much power but very little nature"; as Hotspur he had the suitable power, but he lacked "ease" and displayed too much "sameness"; as Cato he was guilty of shameless oratory and "emphasis hunting," but he was the best Sempronius in that play "within our knowledge." His faults became his assets as Lord Townly in *The Provok'd Husband*:

haughty as a bashaw [pasha-type popular in "Turkish" tragedies], vulgar as a stage-coachman, boisterous as a tavern-keeper, and awkward as a country dancing-master; pumping up every sentence from the bottom of the stomach; stalking backward and forward, like a Jack-tar on the quarter-deck, and clenching his fists, as if Lady Townly was every moment to feel the effects of them.

As King John, reported Gentleman, he

deserves our warmest praise, and we are happy to give it to him. That stiffness and premeditate method which, in other characters, took off from his great powers and good conception, being less visible in King John. The rays of glowing merit here broke upon us unclouded and dazzling; where the author's genius soared aloft, he kept pace with equal wing; where Shakespeare flagged, he bore him up.

Despite his penchant for gambling and society, Mossop was a hard-working actor. According to O'Keefe, he marked his copy of his role with detailed notes about facial expression, the action of his eyebrows, and the projection of his underlip; each speech had its own spot on the stage. In 1799 the *Monthly Mirror* published Mossop's directions for his acting of Wolsey's soliloquy in Act III, scene ii, of *Henry VIII*, which begins "*Eye upwards, surprize, and peevish.*" These directions are reprinted and discussed by Antony Coleman in *Theatre Notebook*, 35. An analysis of Mossop's acting is provided by Bertram Joseph in *The Tragic Actor*.

Portraits of Henry Mossop include:

1. By Thomas Hickey. Chalk drawing. In the National Gallery of Ireland.

2. By Nathaniel Hone. Oil in the Garrick Club (No 42).

3. By J. H. Mortimer. Drawing, location unknown. An engraving by W. Ridley "from an original drawing by Mortimer, in the Possession of W. T. Lewis, Esq." was published as a plate to the *Monthly Mirror*, September 1799.

4. By unknown artist. Oil in the National Gallery of Ireland.

5. By unknown engraver. Bust, oval in rectangle, name on base. Published as a plate to *Gentleman's and London Magazine*, Dublin, February 1775. Reproduced by La Tourette Stockwell, in *Dublin Theatres* (1938).

6. As Bajazet in *Tamerlane*. By unknown engraver. Printed for E. Jackson, London. Several other impressions were issued.

7. As Osmyn in *The Mourning Bride*. By unknown engraver. Published as a plate to *Hibernian Magazine*, February 1775.

8. As Zanga in *The Revenge*. By unknown engraver. Published as a plate to an edition of the play, by Wenman 1777.

Mosticelli. *See* MONTICELLI.

"Mother Shipton." *See* COLMAN, GEORGE *1732–1794.*

Motini. *See* MOLINI.

Motley. *See also* MORLEY.

Motley, Mr [*fl.* 1675], *dancer.*
Mr Motley danced in the court masque *Calisto* on 15 February 1675.

Mott, Mr [*fl.* 1788–1791], *house servant?*
On 24 May 1788, 12 June 1790, and 14 June 1791 the benefit tickets of Mr Mott, probably a house servant, were admitted at Covent Garden Theatre.

Motte *See* LAMOTTE.

Mottett. *See* MOFFETT.

Motteux, Mrs [*fl.* 1731–1744], *actress.*
Mrs Motteux (or Motteaux) was listed as acting the Lady in Tony Aston's *The Fool's Opera* in the 1731 edition of that work. At Southwark Fair on 8 September 1743 she played the Widow in *The Blind Beggar of Bethnal Green* and on 22 March 1744 (not 1743 as Leo Hughes has it in *A Century of English Farce*) she was again with Aston. On that date she was given a benefit at the Trumpet in Sheer Lane, Temple Bar, and played the Widow in a scene from *The Plain Dealer*. In 1744 she was styled Widow Motteux.

Moudet or **Moudette.** *See* MAUDET.

Mouggi. *See* MORIGI.

Moulcer, Master *b. 1789, equestrian, actor.*
The bill for Astley's Amphitheatre for 15 June 1793 listed Master Moulcer, age four, as one of the equestrians. On one bill that season his name was spelled "Moulder," but Moulcer was used on most bills, and when he played Envy in *Harlequin Invincible* on 22 August 1795 that spelling persisted.

Moulds, John [*fl.* 1784–1798?], *singer, composer.*
The *Catalogue of Printed Music in the British Museum* lists a large number of works by John Moulds which were published between 1784 and 1800. Most of them were popular songs sung at Ranelagh, Vauxhall, or the Lyceum, and some were sung by Moulds himself. He was a countertenor and sang in the Handel Memorial Concerts at Westminster Abbey and the Pantheon in May and June 1784. Doane's *Musical Directory* in 1794 gave Moulds's ad-

dress as Islington. *A Sailor's Soul, or Sympathetic Fred* was published about 1798 and called "the last Composition of the Celebrated late Mr. J. Moulds."

Mounsell. *See* FARREN, MRS WILLIAM, and MANSEL.

Mounset. *See* MONSETT.

Mount, Mrs ₍*fl. 1744*₎, *actress, singer.*
The "Queen of Hungary's Company of Comedians," led by the eccentric Charlotte Charke, performed *The Beggar's Opera* on 26 December 1744 at the Haymarket Theatre. A Mrs Mount played Mrs Peachum.

Mountain, D. ₍*fl. 1799*₎, *trumpeter.*
A Mr D. Mountain, a member of the Royal Society of Musicians, was directed by the Society to play trumpet in the Society's charity concert for the clergy at St Paul's Cathedral in May 1799. He is not otherwise recorded.

Mountain, Henry *d. 1794, violinist, music publisher.*
Notes left by W. S. Clark place Henry Mountain as violinist in the Smock Alley Theatre band in Dublin 1749–50. In 1751, according to Frank Kidsar in Grove, he was in the band at the Dublin Rotunda. Ita Hogan in *Anglo-Irish Music, 1780–1830*, said that he "performed at Concerts from 1751." Clark found him in the Crow Street Theatre's band in 1759–60. Kidson wrote that for 20 years, 1765–1785, he was leader of the Dublin City Music. He was publisher of single songs extracted from popular operas and, about 1785, edited and published *The Gentleman's Catch Book*, dedicated to the Hibernian Catch Club. He lived before 1785 at No 20, Whitefriar Street, Dublin, but around 1790 removed to No 44, Grafton Street. Clark reported his death date as 15 November 1794.

Doane's *Musical Directory* (1794) listed a Mountain, "violin," from Dublin, who had played in the "grand performances" in Westminster Abbey, i.e., one or several of the Handel Commemorations which were held annually from 1784 through 1787 and again in 1791. We believe that violinist to have been Henry Mountain, for his son John is separately listed by Doane.

Mountain, John *b. 1766, violinist, violist, pianist.*
John Mountain (not "Joseph," as in *Grove's Dictionary*, 5th edition, and elsewhere) was born in Dublin, the son of the Irish violinist and music publisher Henry Mountain. John came to Liverpool around 1785, when he was about 19. By the time he was 20, when, according to Oxberry, he was "leader of the band at the Concert-hall and theatre," he had met the rising young provincial actress and singer Rosemond Wilkinson (not "Sarah," as in Grove), then 18. In the summer of 1786, she left the Yorkshire circuit for London to take up an engagement at Covent Garden Theatre. John Mountain followed, and they were married, on 5 June 1787, according to the London *Morning Chronicle*. Oxberry thought that the marriage angered her relations. It certainly produced many quarrels between the principals, but also one son, in 1791. It endured with faithfulness on both sides, despite the quarrels and the greater celebrity of Mrs Mountain's talents.

John Mountain's career can now only be glimpsed. It was important, but miscellaneous, and much of it was conducted outside the theatre, in London and provincial places for which surviving records are scarce. By 2 March 1788, when he was recommended for membership in the Royal Society of Musicians by the violinist Anthony Shaw, he had been engaged in the Covent Garden band, according to Shaw's formal allegation, and was "a Married Man, has no children . . . Plays the violin and tenor [viola]." Whether he played in the Covent Garden pit band or simply assisted in the oratorios for the first few seasons in uncertain. He remained a fixture there until well into the nineteenth century. By 1790 he had found also a long-term relationship with Vauxhall Gardens where, according to Cudworth, he played 44 concertos on the violin in 1791. He began to be billed as "leader" in 1793. Mrs Mountain began singing there in 1794 and very shortly she became a featured attraction.

Mrs Mountain accepted engagements at Crow Street Theatre, Dublin, in the summers of 1789, 1790, and 1793, and it is likely that John accompanied her all three summers. W. S. Clark recorded a bill of summer, 1790, on which appear Mrs Mountain and "Mountain Jr." (certainly to distinguish John from his fa-

ther Henry). In London, Mountain played in
the quartet of the Anacreontic Society and in
the band of the Philharmonic Society and he
led the band at the Fantoccini Theatre in Savile
Row in 1791.

John Mountain's name occurs a few times in
the Minute Books of the Royal Society of Musicians. He was on the list to play the violin at
the Society's charity concerts at St Paul's Cathedral in May of 1789, 1790, and 1791. He
was proposed as a Governor of the Society in
June 1792. Porter in his *History of the Theatres
of Brighton*, cited him as residing at Hampstead
in 1824 and conducting the band at Brighton
Theatre on 18 September 1824. Mountain was
still alive in 1841, when administration of his
wife's property was granted him.

Mountain, Mrs John, Rosemond, née Wilkinson *c. 1768–1841, singer, actress.*

Rosemond Wilkinson was the daughter of
Mr Wilkinson, who performed on the slack-
wire and tightrope (and also fashioned theatrical wigs and dressed hair), and his wife, a
minor actress and dresser. Rosemond was apparently the sister of Caroline, Frederick, and
George Wilkinson—all performers—and perhaps the niece of the celebrated rope dancer
and performer on the musical glasses, Isabella
Wilkinson. Tate Wilkinson, the quixotic York
circuit manager, seemed to establish the latter
relationship in his *Wandering Patentee* (1795),
while at the same time denying his own connection with that family:

[Rosemond] was then and is now, by many, believed to be my daughter, merely from the accident
of her first appearance at Covent-Garden Theatre
being announced, *Miss Wilkinson*, from the Theatre-Royal, York; not that I need blush, but be
proud of my progeny, as she is a lady of great merit
and genius.

Her parents may have been playing at Sadler's Wells at the time of her birth, as some
accounts assert (Sadler's Wells was almost a
home to various members of the family later).
It may also be true, as some early sources state,
that she was named "Rosoman[d]" in compliment to her parents' employer, the proprietor
of the Wells, Thomas Rosoman (sometimes
Rosamond). *The Dictionary of National Biography* calls her Rosoman, while Grove gives her

ROSEMOND MOUNTAIN
engraving by Ridley

first name—on what authority we know not—
as "Sarah" but adds, "also known as Rosoman
and sometimes as Sophia." The baptismal entry
for a son at St Paul, Covent Garden, 8 May
1791, gives her Christian name as "Rosemond," and so she appears to have understood
it to be, for she always signed herself "Rose."

Rose Wilkinson was said to have played
some slight characters at the Haymarket in the
summer of 1782 or earlier. But in his sketch
of her in *Dramatic Biography* (1825) Oxberry,
who knew her well, gave her first named character as Madame Hazard in a burletta called
Mount Parnassus, at the Royal Circus on 4 November 1782. She had been trained for the role
by Charles Dibdin, who later, in his memoirs,
wrote proudly, "Miss Decamp, Mrs. Mountain, and Mrs. Bland, are deservedly favourites
as singers, merely because I took care they
should be taught nothing more than correctness, expression, and an unaffected pronunciation of the words; the infallible and only way
to perfect a singer."

Those early performances attracted the enthralled attention of audiences and were continued for several years, with some changes, as *The Fairy World*. During 1782 and 1783, Rose "remained at [the Circus in] St. George's Fields, where she was a great favourite, and where she received two guineas a week, a pretty considerable remuneration . . . for one of her tender years." It was considerable indeed, and presaged her even more considerable earning ability as an adult. The only bill of that period which we have seen gives her some character unspecified in an opera called *The Cestus* on 18 October 1783.

Evidently about January 1784, her parents lost their foothold at the Circus, and there followed for Rose a long period of wandering "with her father, mother, brother, &c.," wrote Oxberry. Their engagements gradually diminished and Rose found herself largely responsible for her aging parents. In the fall of 1784, her brother Frederick being at Hull on Tate Wilkinson's circuit, she and her parents went to visit him and while there made application on Rose's behalf to the manager. They were refused, but the country player Buck (stage name of Reginald Bucknall) hired her to enliven his benefit. She played Patty in *The Maid of the Mill* and afterward delivered George Alexander Stevens's *Lecture on Heads*. Wilkinson remembered his astonishment at the abilities she displayed:

Harvard Theatre Collection

ROSEMOND MOUNTAIN
engraving by Eudes, after Dujardin (after Buck)

in point of speaking, deportment, singing, humour not void of discrimination, I do honestly confess and profess, that I have seldom witnessed such a performance at so early an age; for I do not believe she was more than fifteen, and in every part of the difficult task she had to sustain, I do not think but a London audience would have joined in my humble opinion, that her merit was undoubted, and not only gave promise but a great deal . . .

Wilkinson's company was "loaded, and [his] lady singers," among them Dora Jordan, were "tenacious," so Rose did not achieve a place in the regular company. But after a second such triumph, playing Rosetta in *Love in a Village* for Inchbald's benefit, Miss Wilkinson was engaged ". . . as one of the fraternity *without the kiss*," that is, without a contract. Tate Wilkinson pressed her into service at his own benefit 21 December 1784, when she acted Stella in *Robin Hood*. By then he "judged it necessary,

as she had secured public esteem, and as she was really in want . . . to give her a benefit, which was on the 31st of December, 'Lionel and Clarissa.'" Tate Wilkinson acted Oldboy, Mrs Jordan generously volunteered to assume breeches as Lionel, and Rose Wilkinson was Clarissa and repeated her *Lecture*. From that point she acted regularly on the Yorkshire circuit, the "only novelty" Tate could produce to his audiences that year, except for Signor Scaglioni's dancing dogs. "Miss Wilkinson that season improved mightily." She was also accepted by the company and judged "*very pleasing and promising*" by the eminent London actors the Richard Yateses.

By the time of the closing of the winter season at York and the opening of the summer season at Leeds in 1785, Rose had become something of a pet of the old manager. And when his "great treasure" Dora Jordan left him for London after one of their recurrent tiffs, his "little treasure" Rose inherited the older actress's roles, attempting first the title role in *The Poor Soldier* at Wakefield and Doncaster races in 1785:

It is true that she did not sport a leg *like the Jordan*, neither was her person so tall, but she was then a delightful pretty girl, and made a smart little soldier: She was received with raptures, and gave that farce a new run for the ensuing winter [1785–86] seasons at Hull and York. The first night she made her effort in that character at Doncaster, I supped with my true friend, General St. Leger and a party of gentlemen, at Stanuel's Hotel, when every one of the party after requested I would receive a guinea from each . . . my own guinea being added . . . This was presented as a compliment for the great pleasure she had afforded so immediately after the loss of Mrs Jordan.

By the end of the winter season of 1785–86 news of Miss Wilkinson's talent had circulated widely, and she had received an attractive offer from the Liverpool management for the summer of 1786, and from Thomas Harris, the Covent Garden proprietor, a contract for the 1786–87 and the two following seasons, at a rising scale of £5, £6 and £7 a week. She had been making 18s. a week at York.

From her Yorkshire conquest, Rose moved on to a successful summer at Liverpool, where

Courtesy of the Garrick Club

ROSEMOND MOUNTAIN
by Romney

her benefit cleared £68 11s. There John Mountain, the twenty-year-old violinist who led the theatre band, capitulated to her charm. He soon followed Rose to London, and on 5 June 1787, despite the opposition of her relatives, they were married. Her ascent to metropolitan fame was, after her first London season, under his name. Likely enough, much of it was due to his assistance, for though he is a somewhat shadowy figure, he was evidently a fine musician and probably continued the training which Dibdin had initiated. Certainly he accompanied her in many concert programs at public halls and gardens, and for a long time was in the Covent Garden band, for some of that time as leader.

On 4 October 1786, advertised as from the Theatre Royal, York, Rose made her Covent Garden debut as Fidelia in *The Foundling* and also played Leonora in *The Padlock*. Her fortunes were to be tied principally to Covent Garden for the following decade. She played constantly at the theatre in all seasons from 1786–87 through 1791–92 (rising from £5 to £7 per week in 1788–89, and then for some reason falling back to £6). She sometimes acted away from London during that period: Richmond occasionally in the fall of 1788, Crow Street Theatre, Dublin, in the summers of 1789 and 1790, and Liverpool in September 1791 and July 1792.

After acting at Covent Garden on 26 September 1792 she quarreled with Harris when he stopped her salary during a brief illness, and went back to Crow Street, Dublin for the 1792–93 season. She and Harris were reconciled by correspondence, and in the spring she returned by way of Liverpool and York. At York on 12 May she fell from a fractious horse and broke her arm. Her benefit on the fourteenth went off as scheduled, she advertising that she would "sing the song of Sweet Echo behind the scenes which she hope[d would] be accepted as the only effort her present situation admit[ted] of."

From 1793–94 through 1795–96 she earned £6 per week and in 1796–97 and 1797–98, £7. After that season, when she quarreled again with Harris over salary (her pique seems to have been justified) she left London to act for the Bath-Bristol Company. The move seems to have been in large part dictated by her desire to be taught by the composer and teacher Venanzio Rauzzini, who had retired to Bath. After an absence of two years from acting, during which time she spent some months touring in England and Ireland, she returned to London. Ignoring fresh overtures from Harris, Mrs Mountain signed on with Kemble at Drury Lane. She was at Birmingham for four nights from 4 June 1800 (her first appearances there) and then moved on for a long summer at the Haymarket before taking up her duties as a principal singing actress at Drury Lane. She was at that house from 1800–1801 through 1807–8, with the company when it removed to the Lyceum in 1809–10 and 1810–11, came back with it to the new Drury Lane in 1812–13, and retired on 4 May 1815. During that time her salary rose from £9 in 1800 to £15

Harvard Theatre Collection

ROSEMOND MOUNTAIN, as Varietta
by De Wilde

by 1805–6 and sank back to £10 from 1812–13 through 1814–15. During her later years she made occasional forays outside London singing songs and speaking a monologue written especially for her by the comic actor Andrew Cherry entitled *The Lyric Novelist, or Life Epitomized.* Panormo, later a celebrated pianist, but then a pupil of John Mountain's, accompanied her in the presentation, which had "unprecedented success" in provincial towns. She was, for instance, at Edinburgh in some parts of the summers of 1804, 1807, and 1808, at both Capel Street Theatre, Dublin, and the Manchester Theatre in the summer of 1805, and in January and February 1815 at Bristol. Oxberry remembered that she and her husband had, around 1807, emulated Michael Kelly and Mrs Crouch by holding concerts at their house in Russell Street, Bloomsbury, where Kelly, Naldi, Braham, Madame Storace, and others "combined to render this species of amusement the best that has ever been presented in this country."

Throughout her whole career Mrs Mountain accepted concert engagements and sang in oratorios and from 1793 to 1798 was a much-acclaimed singer of popular ballads at Vauxhall Gardens, where her husband was leader of the band. Numerous sentimental, patriotic, and comic songs were published "as sung by" Mrs Mountain at the theatres and pleasure gardens.

A list of Rose Mountain's roles in London through 1799–1800 (many, no doubt previously acted in the country) would include: at Covent Garden, in 1786–87 (as Miss Wilkinson), Fidelia in *The Foundling,* Leonora in *The Padlock,* Norah in *The Poor Soldier,* Victoria in *The Castle of Andalusia,* Nysa in *Midas,* Miss Neville in *Know Your Own Mind,* Angelina in *Love Makes a Man,* Aurelia in *Such Things Are,* Maria in *Love and War,* Lucinda in *The Conscious Lovers,* a Pastoral Nymph in *Comus,* Louisa in *The Deserter,* Annette in *Annette and Lubin,* Eliza in *Nina,* Harriet in *The Miser,* Charlotte in *Bonds Without Judgment,* and Sylvia in *Cymon;* in 1787–88 (as Mrs Mountain), Dorinda in *The Beaux' Stratagem,* Luciana in *The Comedy of Errors,* Maria in *The Maid of the Oaks,* Clarinda in *Robin Hood,* Louisa in *The Duenna,* Rosa in *Fontainebleau,* Norah in *Love in a Camp,* Patrick (for her benefit: "first and only time") in *The Poor Soldier,* and Selima in *The Nunnery;* in 1788–89, Louisa in *The Farmer,* Semira in

Artaxerxes, Jessica in *The Merchant of Venice*, Narcissa in *Inkle and Yarico*, Laura in *Tancred and Sigismunda*, Silvia in *The Old Bachelor*, Peggy in *Marian*, Harriott in *St George's Day*, Gillian in *The Quaker*, Huncamunca in *Tom Thumb*, Donna Anna in *Don Juan*, Allen O'Dale (for her benefit: "for that night only") in *Robin Hood*, Louisa in *Perseverance*; in 1789–90, Jenny in *The Highland Reel*, Angelica in *The Constant Couple*, Carlos in *The Duenna*, Sally in *Thomas and Sally*, Clarissa in *All in the Wrong*, a Shepherdess (with songs) in *Harlequin's Chaplet*, Mrs Applejack in *The Czar*, Miss Leeson in *The School for Wives*, Jenny in *The Two Misers*, the Wife in *The Recruiting Serjeant*, the original Landlady in James Byrne's musical entertainment *Nootka Sound*, and Mrs Tokay in *The Wives Revenged*.

In 1790–91 Rose Mountain added Caelia in *As You Like It*, a Female Indian in the first performances of J. C. Cross's musical interlude *A Divertissement*, Isabinda in *The Busy Body*, Rose in *Rose and Colin*, the original Scotch Girl (Jeannet) in Richard Wilson's musical entertainment *The Union*, William ("first time and for that night only," for her benefit) in *Rosina*, and Orra in *Tippoo Saib*; in 1791–92, one of the Peasantry in *Oscar and Malvina*, James Byrn's new ballet pantomime, Ceristantia in *The Crusade*, the original Nelly in Robert Merry's comic opera *The Magician No Conjuror*, Cupid in *Orpheus and Eurydice*, one of the Genii in *Zelma; or the Will O' the Wisp*, Jeremiah Meyer and William Hayley's new melodrama, Maria in *Just in Time*, Venus in *The Golden Pippin*, Perdita in *The Winter's Tale*, and Diana in *Lionel and Clarissa*; in 1793–94, the original Maria in John O'Keeffe's comedy *The World in a Village*, Emily in *The Woodman*, Philidel in James Wilde's new pantomime *Harlequin and Faustus*, Adelais in *The Midnight Wanderers*, Clara in *Hartford Bridge*, Sophia in *The Road to Ruin*, Mary in The *Sprigs of Laurel*, Julia in *The Travellers in Switzerland*, Harriet in *The Jealous Wife*, Ellen Woodbine in *Netley Abbey*, Nancy in *True Blue*, Stella in *Robin Hood*, Angelina in *Love Makes a Man*, the original Alinda in the melodrama *The Sicilian Romance*, by Henry Siddons, and Wilhelmina in *The Waterman*; and in 1794–95, the original Clara Sedley in *The Rage!*, a comedy by Frederick Reynolds, the original Louisa Bowers in William Pearce's musical farce *Arrived at Portsmouth*, Ophelia in

Hamlet, the original Constantia in *The Mysteries of the Castle*, a melodrama by Miles Peter Andrews, Annette in *British Fortitude and Hibernian Friendship*, and Patty in *The Maid of the Mill*.

In 1795–96 she added to her repertoire Sally Flounce in *The Bank Note*, Jenny in *Lord Mayor's Day*, Cowslip in *The Agreeable Surprise*, a Villager in *The Battle of Hexham*, Dorcas in *The Winter's Tale*, Martha in Pearce's new pantomime *Merry Sherwood*, Kitty Barleycorn in *The London Hermit*, the original Virtue in the anonymous pantomime *Harlequin's Treasure*, Shelah in O'Keeffe's new comic opera *The Lad of the Hills*, Rachel in *Zorinski*, Patty in *The Witch of the Wood*, and Catalina in *The Castle of Andalusia*; in 1796–97, Marianne in *The Dramatist*, the original Louisa in *Bantry Bay*, a musical entertainment by George N. Reynolds, the original Agnes in *Raymond and Agnes*, Charles Farley's melodramatic pantomime, Isabel in *The Italian Villagers*, Laura in *Lock and Key*, Emma in *Peeping Tom*, Kate in *The Village Fête*, and Adriana in *Diamond Cut Diamond*, a comic opera written by James Hook especially for her benefit night; and in 1797–98, the original Donna Leonora in J. C. Cross's musical farce *An Escape into Prison*, the original Rose Sydney in Thomas Morton's comedy *Secrets Worth Knowing*, Blanche in *Joan of Arc*, Hero in *Much Ado about Nothing*, the original Lady Charlotte Fairfield in Henry Heartwell's comic opera *Reformed in Time*, and Eliza in *The Flitch of Bacon*.

After the absence of two years from the dramatic boards described above, she took a summer engagement at the Haymarket Theatre in 1800, adding to her repertoire Ellen in *Sighs*, Madelon in *The Surrender of Calais*, Laura in *The Agreeable Surprise*, the original Quashee's Wife in Farley's celebrated pantomime *Obi; or Three-Finger'd Jack*, Rosina in *The Castle of Sorrento*, Betsy Blossom in *The Deaf Lover* and the original Leonora in Joseph George Holman's comic opera, *What a Blunder!*

When in the fall of 1800 Mrs Mountain shifted her allegiance to Drury Lane, her singing was said to have been vastly improved by her lessons with Rauzzini. She opened her campaign with Polly in *The Beggar's Opera*. Among the roles she added from then until the end of her career, at Drury Lane and the Haymarket, were Caroline Dormer in *The Heir-at-Law*, Janetta in *False and True*, Araminta in

The Young Quaker, Rachel in *Zorinski*, Rosina in *The Spanish Barber*, Mrs Belmont in *The Castle of Sorrento*, Agnes in *The Mountaineers*, Yarico in *Inkle and Yarico*, Lauretta in *The Maniac*, Margaretta in *No Song, No Supper*, Lady Elenor in *The Haunted Tower*, the title role in *Lodoiska*, Katherine in *The Siege of Belgrade*, Victoria in *The Castle of Andalusia*, Maud in *Peeping Tom*, Cecilia in *Who's to Have Her?*, Emily in *The Bee Hive*, Julian in *The Peasant Boy*, Floretta in *The Cabinet*, Juliana in *Up All Night*, Lady Gayland in *False Alarms*, Jennet in *Virginia*, Cicely in *The Veteran Tar*, Eugenia in *The Wife of Two Husbands*, Marianne in *Deaf and Dumb*, Frederika in *Hero of the North*, Clotilde in *Youth, Love, and Folly*, Celinda in *The Travellers*, Lady Northland in *The Fortune Teller*, Orilla in *Adelmorn*, Antonia in *The Gypsy Prince*, Daphne in *Midas*, Rosa in *The Dart*, Carline in *The Young Hussar*, Leila in *Kaïs*, Zelma in *The Jew of Mogadore*, Rachel in *The Circassian Bride*, Juliana in *Up All Night*, Adelnai in *The Russian Impostor*, Annette in *Safe and Sound*, Miss Selwyn in *M. P.*, and Lodina in *The Americans*.

Oxberry in *Dramatic Biography* (1825) testified that "A whisper has never fanned the fair fame of Mrs. Mountain," praised her for "artless, elegant manners," "amiable simplicity," and "unaffected urbanity," and spoke of her smile of "playful serenity". The *Monthly Mirror* correspondent in October 1798 commended her "correct ear and good taste [which] would render her valuable to any theatre." Williams, in *A Pin Basket to the Children of Thespis* (1797) remembered her early shyness:

> *In the rays of her virgin timidity basking,*
> *Her heart seems to fear what her wishes are asking:*
> *When she warbles her sonnets with rapture and skill,*
> *'Tis an instance where Nature has triumph'd over will.*

A fellow performer, F. G. Waldron, thought her "A pretty singer with an engaging regularity of features, and easy deportment. There is a melancholy lack of spirit through the whole of her acting." In her later years she became corpulent but seems never to have lost her prettiness.

Rose and John Mountain had one child, a son, baptized at St Paul, Covent Garden on 8

May 1791. In London they lived successively at No 91, Bow Street, Covent Garden in 1791, No 33, Tavistock Court in 1794, No 6, York Street, Covent Garden in 1795, No 28, Maiden Lane in 1797, Tavistock Street in 1812, and Hampstead in 1824. Rose died at their house, No 5, Hammersmith Terrace, on 3 July 1841. On 5 August administration of the property (unspecified) of "Rosoman Mountain late of Hammersmith" was granted to "John Mountain esq. the lawful husband."

Portraits of Mrs Mountain include:

1. By Samuel De Wilde. Watercolor in the Harvard Theatre Collection.

2. By "S. G.," 1806. Miniature on ivory in the National Portrait Gallery (No 760).

3. By George Romney. Sketch in oil. In the Garrick Club (No 428).

4. Engraved portrait by T. Cheeseman, after A. Buck. Published by W. Holland, 1804. A copy, engraved by Eudes, after Dujardin, was also published.

5. Engraved portrait by J. Hopwood, after "J. C." Published by Vernor, Hood & Sharpe, 1811.

6. Engraved portrait by K. Mackenzie, after R. Dighton. Published as a plate to *Thespian Dictionary*, 1805; also published as a plate to *The Myrtle and the Vine*, 1800.

7. Engraved portrait by W. Ridley. Published as a plate to the *Monthly Mirror*, 1797.

8. As Clara in *The Rage*. Engraving by C. Turner, after J. Masquerier, 1804. A copy, engraved by Rogers, after Masquerier, was published as a plate to Oxberry's *Dramatic Biography*, 1825.

9. As Daphne in *Midas*. Engraving by J. Alais. Published by J. Roach, 1802.

10. As Fidelia in *The Foundling*. Engraving by T. Trotter, after De Wilde. Published as a plate to *Bell's British Library*, 1792.

11. As Matilda in *Richard Coeur de Lion*. Watercolor by De Wilde. In the Garrick Club (No 61d). Engraving by Schiavonetti published as a plate to Cawthorn's *Minor British Theatre*, 1806.

12. As Peggy in *The Gentle Shepherd*. Engraving by J. Alais. Published by J. Roach, 1809.

13. As Varietta in *The Masquerade*. Watercolor by De Wilde, 1808. In the Harvard Theatre Collection.

A portrait by M. A. Shee of an actress as

Ophelia was once labeled "Mrs Mountain," but the identification was changed to "Miss Lee" after it was bought by Henry Clay Folger in the Leverhulme sale at Anderson Galleries, 17–19 February 1926. The Folger Library sold it to the American Shakespeare Festival Theatre, Stratford, Connecticut, in February 1962, but it seems to be no longer in that collection. It was not, however, listed in the sale of that theatre's pictures at Sotheby Parke Bernet, New York, in January 1977.

Mountain, Joseph. *See* MOUNTAIN, JOHN.

Mountford, John [*fl.* 1776–1785], *carpenter*.

Egerton manuscript 2279 in the British Library cited a Mr Mountford as head carpenter at Covent Garden Theatre on 26 October 1776. He was surely John Mountford, who was master carpenter, according to the Lord Chamberlain's accounts, from 1783 to 1785 at the King's Theatre.

Mountfort, Mr [*fl.* 1728?–1729], *actor, singer?*

A Mr Mountfort played an unnamed character in *Hunter* at Fielding's booth at Bartholomew Fair on 23 August 1729. Perhaps he was the Mr Mountfort whose name was mentioned in the advertisement for a concert at York Buildings on 12 April 1728, but the bill said "several favourite Ballads by Mr Mountfort," which could mean that a Mr Mountfort sang them or that they were composed by a Mr Mountfort, perhaps the actor William. Possibly the 1729 reference is an error for the Mrs Mountfort who was active at the time.

Mountfort, Mrs [*fl.* 1728–1731], *actress, singer, dancer*.

Mrs Mountfort (or Monfort) performed at the Haymarket Theatre in 1728–29, achieving her first notice in the playbills on 14 November 1728, when she played the Page in *The Orphan*. Since that role was often taken by children, it is probable that Mrs Mountfort was quite petite. During the rest of the season she offered entr'acte songs and appeared as Flora in *The Lottery*, Henrietta in *Don Carlos*, Polly in *The Beggar's Opera*, Rose in *The Recruiting Officer*, a Grace, Aurora, and a Nymph in *The Humours of Harlequin*, an unnamed part in *The*

Royal Captives, Seringo in *Hurlothrumbo*, Phebe in *The Beggar's Wedding*, and the title part in *Flora*. *The London Stage* lists her as playing Phillida in *Damon and Phillida* on 16 August 1729 at Drury Lane, but that must be an error for the Haymarket. Mrs Mountfort concluded her busy season at the late summer fairs, singing and acting at booths run by Fielding and Reynolds.

The London Stage lists both a Mrs and Miss Mountfort at the Goodman's Fields playhouse in 1729–30, the latter a dancer, but there was only Mrs Mountfort, who sang, danced, and acted. She opened her season as Rose in *The Recruiting Officer* on 31 October 1729 and then repeated some of her old parts but played a number of new ones: Prue in *Love for Love*, Penelope in *Tunbridge Walks*, Lucy in *Oroonoko*, Cherry in *The Stratagem*, Sylvia in *The Old Bachelor*, Betty in *The Gamester*, Leonora in *The Spanish Fryar*, Scentwell in *The Busy Body*, Lucilla in *The Fair Penitent*, and Anne Page in *The Merry Wives of Windsor*. With members of the Goodman's Fields troupe she acted Lady Friendly in *Mad Tom of Bedlam* at Tottenham Court on 1 August 1730 and subsequent dates through 19 August, then she played the Genius of England in *Wat Tyler and Jack Straw* at Bartholomew Fair on 31 August.

Mrs Mountfort was at Goodman's Fields again in 1730–31, at least for the first half of the season, and there she added to her repertoire such parts as Jenny in *The Provok'd Husband*, a Spirit and Lettice in *The Devil of a Wife*, Lucy in *The Beggar's Opera*, the title part in *Phebe*, Jaculine in *The Royal Merchant*, Clara in *Rule a Wife and Have a Wife*, the title part in *The Fashionable Lady*, Gypsey in *The Stratagem*, Margery in *The Wedding*, and Myrtilla in *The Provok'd Husband*. After those three years of promising activity Mrs Mountfort seems to have left the London stage. Her relationship, if any, to Susanna Mountfort of earlier in the century is not known.

Mountfort, Susanna 1690–1720, *actress*.

Susanna Mountfort, the daughter of the performers William and Susanna Percival Mountfort, was born on 27 April 1690 and christened at St Giles in the Fields on 11 May. Her father was murdered in December 1692, and her mother married the actor John Verbruggen in January 1694. By about 1703, when a document was drawn up entitled "Establishm^t of ye Company," young Susanna Mountfort was an actress herself, listed at £30 at the bottom of the list of women in the proposed company.

At Court on 28 February 1704 "Mrs" Mountfort played Betty in *Sir Solomon Single* in a successful production by the Lincoln's Inn Fields troupe under Thomas Betterton. The following 26 June at the theatre "Miss" Mountfort played Damaris in *The Amorous Widow*. She began the 1704–5 season at Lincoln's Inn Fields playing Betty Frisk in *Sir Mannerly Shallow* on 16 October 1704 for her shared benefit with Miss Evans. On 4 December she was Angelica in *The Biter* (again called "Mrs" Mountfort, though she was only 14). The scanty records of the early years of the eighteenth century do not show whether Susanna completed the season or not; in June 1705, however, she changed her allegiance to Drury Lane.

For her first appearance at her new house she played Betty in *Sir Solomon Single* and spoke the epilogue. Once again she was called "Mrs Mountfort," and that was her usual styling during the rest of her career.

On 16 June 1705 at Drury Lane Susanna played a part originally acted by her mother: Madam Bernard in *The Country House*. In 1705–6 Mrs Mountfort acted the full season at Drury Lane, appearing as Estifania in *Rule a Wife and Have a Wife*, the little Thief in *The Night Walker*, Berynthia in *Hampstead Heath*, Ophelia in *Hamlet*, Ruth in *The Committee*, and Rose in *The Recruiting Officer*. She was given a solo benefit on 28 March 1706. Hippolita in *The Tempest* seems to have been her only new role in 1706–7 (when she was again called Miss Mountfort on some bills), and in 1707–8 she is known to have tried only one new part, the title role in *The Northern Lass*. After that season her name disappeared from London playbills for several years.

When she was mentioned again it was as Ophelia at Drury Lane on 4 October 1712, opposite the Hamlet of Robert Wilks. In the cast as the Ghost was Barton Booth. At some point after that date she and Booth began an affair. The story goes that Susan had an annuity of £300 given her on the condition that she should not marry. Booth proposed marriage, but she evidently did not want to lose her annuity, so they settled for living together for

a few years. They jointly bought a lottery ticket in 1714 that, according to Doran, won £5000; they had agreed to share and share alike, but Mrs Mountfort kept the money. When the couple dissolved their relationship about 1718, Booth returned £3200 which he had kept in trust for Susan, but her next lover, Edward Minshull, squandered it.

Meanwhile Mrs Mountfort had kept up a regular winter acting schedule at Drury Lane, attempting such new parts as Teresa in *The Squire of Alsatia*, Gatty in *She Wou'd If She Cou'd*, the title role in *The Fair Quaker of Deal*, Belinda in *The Old Bachelor*, Clarinda in *The Double Gallant*, Charlotte in *The Female Advocates*, Belvedira in *The Humours of the Army*, Florinda in *The Wife of Bath*, Arabella in *The Wife's Relief*, Aurelia in *The Apparition*, Harriet in *The Man of Mode*, Florimel in *Marriage à la Mode*, Elvira in *Love Makes a Man*, Flora in *The Country Lasses*, Lady Brumpton in *The Funeral*, Dorinda in *The Beaux' Stratagem*, Hypolita in *She Wou'd and She Wou'd Not*, Lady Graveairs in *The Careless Husband*, Mrs Conquest in *The Lady's Last Stake*, Hellena in *The Rover*, Lady Dunce in *The Soldier's Fortune*, Aspatia in *The Maid's Tragedy*, Narcissa in *Love's Last Shift*, and Fidelia in *The Play is the Plot*.

On 21 October 1718 Susan made her first appearance at the new Lincoln's Inn Fields Theatre as the title character in *The Fair Quaker of Deal*, but that was the last role known for her. The story that she went insane when her friend Hester Santlow married Barton Booth in July 1719 may be true, though Susan had so willingly taken up with Minshull after she broke off her relationship with Booth that it seems unlikely that the marriage of her best female friend and her former lover would have been the sole cause of her madness. But that is the story, as told in *Theatres and Theatricals*:

THIS lady, who was the identical fair on whom Gay founded his celebrated ballad of *Black-eyed Susan*, was an actress of considerable fame, and was one of the contemporaries of Cibber. After her retirement from the stage, love, and the ingratitude of a bosom friend, deprived her of her senses, and she was placed in a receptacle for lunatics. One day, during a lucid interval, she asked her attendant what play was to be performed that evening; and was told it was *Hamlet*. In this tragedy, whilst on the stage, she had been received with rapture, in *Ophelia*. The recollection struck her, and, with that cunning which is so often allied to insanity, she eluded the care of the keepers, and got to the theatre, where she concealed herself, until the scene in which *Ophelia* enters in her insane state; she then pushed on the stage, before the lady [Mrs Booth?] who had performed the previous part of the character could come on, and exhibited a more perfect presentation of madness than the utmost exertions of mimic art could effect; she was in truth *Ophelia* herself, to the amazement of the performers and astonishment of the audience.

Nature having made this last effort, her vital powers failed her. On going off, she exclaimed, "It is all over!" She was immediately conveyed back to her late place of security; and a few days after,—

"Like a lilly dropping, she hung her head, and died."

George Anne Bellamy told a similar story, saying it came to her from Colley Cibber; in it Susanna Mountfort was not placed in any rigorous confinement but at her house. But the rest of the story was almost verbatim.

Mist's reported on 7 May 1720 that Susanna Mountfort had died on 3 May.

Mountfort, William   *c. 1664–1692, actor, singer, dancer, playwright.*

William Mountfort was born about 1664, the son, according to a sketch of his life prefacing the edition of his *Six Plays* in 1720, of Captain Mountfort, a gentleman of good family from Staffordshire. The actor's modern biographer, Albert Borgman, could find no certain evidence of Captain Mountfort, though there were a number of Mountforts in that shire. Young William spent his early years in Staffordshire; he was "a Person of a great deal of good Nature, and perfectly well bred: He well understood Musick, could sing very agreeable, and he Danc'd finely," the 1720 account said. Those were some of the accomplishments he brought with him to London in the 1670s, talents admirably suited to performing.

Mountfort had not been trained for any employment, but he was attracted to the theatre when he came to London and by 28 May 1678 had become a member of the Duke's Company at the Dorset Garden playhouse; on that date "Young Mumford" played the Boy in *The Counterfeits*. He had doubtless been acting unnamed parts before that, and following his first billing he probably continued acting roles that were not named in cast lists. The next notice of him

came in 1680 (in January, argues Robert Hume; in late June states *The London Stage*), when he was Jack the Barber's boy in *The Revenge*. His name that time, too, was spelled "Mumford." Then after two years we find his name in the bills again, for Corso in *The Duke of Guise*, with the new United Company at Drury Lane in December 1682. He was still relegated to small parts, but he and his fellow actor Carlisle had by the union of the King's and Duke's companies in 1682 "grown to the Maturity of good Actors" in the judgment of the prompter John Downes.

With the United Company, usually at Drury Lane but sometimes at their second playhouse in Dorset Garden, Mountfort played increasingly important roles during the years that followed: Hartwell in *Dame Dobson*, Metellus Cimber in *Julius Caesar*, "Mephostophilis" in *Doctor Faustus* (according to a British Library manuscript cast dating about 1682–1685), Master Tallboy and the Lawyer in *The Jovial Crew*, Nonsense in *The Northern Lass*, Jack Daw in *The Silent Woman*, the title role in *Sir Courtly Nice* (on 9 May 1685, his first really important part, and in a highly successful production), Alexander in *The Rival Queens*, Don Lopez in *The Libertine*, Don Charmante in *The Emperor of the Moon*, Pymero in *The Island Princess*, Dorenalus in *The Injur'd Lovers*, Lyonel in *A Fool's Preferment* (in which he sang "If thou wilt give me back my love"), Belfond Junior in *The Squire of Alsatia*, Young Wealthy in *The Fortune Hunters*, Wildish in *Bury Fair*, Charles IX in *The Massacre of Paris*, Don Antonio in *Don Sebastian*, Silvio in *Successful Strangers*, Menaphon in *The Treacherous Brothers*, Richmond in *Richard III*, Raymond Mounchensey in *The Merry Devil of Edmonton*, Hormidas in *Distress'd Innocence*, Lord Mountacute in *Edward III* (given to Mountfort by Bancroft; performed in November 1690), probably Willmore in *The Rover*, Cesario in *Alphonso*, Sir William Rant in *The Scowrers*, Ricardo in *The Mistakes*, Jack Amorous in *Love for Money*, the title role in *Bussy D'Ambois*, Young Reveller in *Greenwich Park*, Craftmore in *Win Her and Take Her*, Friendall in *The Wive's Excuse*, Sir Philip Freewit in *The Marriage-Hater Match'd*, Cleanthes in *Cleomenes*, and Asdrubel in *Regulus*.

A number of other roles were played or probably played by Mountfort, though we have no dates for them (and, consequently, they are not all listed in *The London Stage*). For example, Colley Cibber later said that Mountfort played Sparkish in *The Country Wife*, and that was certainly a role well-suited to his talents. Manuscript casts in a Folger Shakespeare Library copy of *The Plain Dealer* have Mountfort down for Novel in one cast and Lord Plausible in another. Montague Summers said that after Charles Hart retired Mountfort played Palamede in *Marriage à la Mode* and that Mountfort acted Celadon in *Secret Love*, another Hart role. Summers also stated that, according to a manuscript cast, Mountfort acted Lycias in *Valentinian*, but he did not cite the source of his information.

In addition to his many significant roles, Mountfort became a popular United Company speaker (and sometimes writer) of epilogues. His playwriting career was modest and moderately successful, for he performed in most of his works. His *Injur'd Lovers* was played at Drury Lane, probably in February 1688, *Successful Strangers* in January 1690, and *Greenwich Park* in mid-April 1691. He also wrote a farce, *The Life and Death of Doctor Faustus*, but if he acted in it we have no evidence to tell us what part he may have played. The work is listed in *The London Stage* under 13 March 1697, but Robert Hume has shown that the premiere was probably in the spring of 1688, when Mountfort was still alive and a few years after he had himself acted in the original Marlowe piece.

The account of his life in 1720 noted that Mountfort's

Company was desir'd by Persons of the best Figure and Fashion, whom he was sure to Entertain, at the same time he Improv'd from them. His great Ambition off the Stage as well as upon it, was to render himself acceptable to the Town. . . . He was very graceful in his Person, and for Vivacity, equal'd the greatest Comedian of his Time [Anthony Leigh].

Indeed, Mountfort rendered himself so agreeable that for a time in 1686 (before or after his marriage in July?) he withdrew from the stage and lived with the family of Lord Chancellor Jefferies. The *Memoirs of Sir John Reresby* contain a description of an entertainment at Jefferies's house on 18 January 1686:

After dinner the Chancellor, having drunke smartly at table (which was his custome) called for one Monfort, a gentleman of his that had been a comedian, an excellent mimick, and to divert the

company, as he called it, made him give us a caus, that is, plead before him in a feigned action, where he acted all the principal lawyers of the age, in their tone of voice, and action or gesture of body; and thus ridiculed not only the lawyers, but the law itself. This, I confesse, was very diverting, but not soe prudent as I thought for soe eminent a man in soe great a station of the lawe . . .

Reresby's saying the Chancellor allowed Mountfort to go too far may have been correct in more ways than one. In *Poems on Affairs of State* (IV, 72) is quoted a scandalous verse:

> There's a story of late
> That the Chancellor's mate
> Has been f——d and been f——d by player
>   Mountfort;
> Which though false, yet's as true,
> My Lord gave him his due,
> For he had a small tilt at his bum for it.

And *A Poem on the Deponents*, celebrating the birth of the Prince of Wales on 10 June 1688, referred also to the Chancellor having been cuckolded: "he wears horns that were by Mountfort made—"

The actor's association with the Lord Chancellor and his circle of luminaries in high society, law, and politics probably gave Mountfort useful examples in the parts he acted. Matthew Prior in *Upon the Poets* wrote

> *Mountfort how fit for Politicks and Law*
> *That play'd so well Sir Courtly and Jack Daw.*

The prompter Downes said that "Sir Courtly was so nicely Perform'd, that not any succeeding, but Mr. Cyber has Equall'd him."

Our most complete description of Mountfort's acting, and the highest praise for his foppish characters, came from Colley Cibber himself, who excelled in the very same line. Cibber was just beginning his career when Mountfort was at the peak of his:

Of Person he was tall, well made, fair, and of an agreeable Aspect: His Voice clear, full, and melodious: In Tragedy he was the most affecting Lover within my Memory: His Addresses had a resistless Recommendation from the very Tone of his Voice, which gave his Words such Softness that, as *Dryden* says,—*Like Flakes of feather'd Snow,/They melted as they fell*! [from *The Spanish Fryar*]. All this he particularly verify'd in that Scene of *Alexander*, where the Hero throws himself at the Feet of *Statira* for Pardon of his past Infidelities. There we saw the Great, the Tender, the Penitent, the Despairing, the Transported, and the Amiable, in the highest Perfection. In Comedy he gave the truest Life to what we call the *Fine Gentleman*; his Spirit shone brighter for being polish'd with Decency: In Scenes of Gaiety he never broke into the Regard that was due to the Presence of equal or superior Characters, tho' inferior Actors play'd them; he fill'd the Stage, not by elbowing and crossing it before others, or disconcerting their Action, but by surpassing them in true masterly Touches of Nature. He never laugh'd at his own Jest, unless the Point of his Raillery upon another requir'd it.—He had a particular Talent in giving Life to *bons Mots* and *Repartees*: The Wit of the Poet seem'd always to come from him *extempore*, and sharpen'd into more Wit from his brilliant manner of delivering it; he had himself a good Share of it, or what is equal to it, so lively a Pleasantness of Humour, that when either of these fell into his Hands upon the Stage, he wantoned with them to the highest delight of his Auditors. The *agreeable* was so natural to him, that even in that dissolute Character of the Rover he seem'd to wash off the Guilt from Vice, and gave it Charms and Merit. For tho' it may be a Reproach to the Poet to draw such Characters not only unpunish'd but rewarded, the Actor may still be allow'd his due Praise in his excellent Performance. And this is a Distinction which, when this Comedy was acted at *Whitehall*, King *William's* Queen *Mary* was pleas'd to make in favor of *Monfort*, notwithstanding her Disapprobation of the Play. He had, besides all this, a Variety in his Genius which few capital Actors have shewn, or perhaps have thought it any Addition to their Merit to arrive at; he could entirely change himself; could at once throw off the man of Sense for the brisk, vain, rude, and lively Coxcomb, the false, flashy Pretender to Wit, and the Dupe of his own Sufficiency: Of this he gave a delightful Instance in the Character of *Sparkish* in *Wycherly's Country Wife*. In that of *Sir Courtly Nice* his Excellence was still greater: There his whole Man, Voice, Mien, and Gesture was no longer *Monfort*, but another Person. There, the insipid, soft Civility, the elegant and formal Mien, the drawling Delicacy of Voice, the stately Flatness of his Address and the empty Eminence of his Attitudes were so nicely observ'd and guarded by him, that he had not been an entire Master of Nature had he not kept his Judgment, as it were, a Centinel upon himself, not to admit the least Likeness of what he us'd to be to enter into any Part of his Performance, he could not possibly have so completely finish'd it.

Cibber said he himself learned how to play those characters by using Mountfort as an example. What Cibber lacked that Mountfort had, was a fine voice: "he sung a clear Counter-tenour, and had a melodious, warbling Throat, which could not but set off the last Scene of Sir *Courtly* with an uncommon Happiness. . . ."

William Mountfort married the budding actress Susanna Percival at St Giles in the Fields on 2 July 1686. Borgman notes that in the Allegations for Marriage Licenses Mountfort was noted as from the parish of St Martin-in-the-Fields and a bachelor 22 years old; Miss Percival was from the parish of St Giles and a spinster 19 years of age, marrying with the consent of her parents. Her father was a minor actor. In the prologue to his first play, *The Injured Lovers* in 1688, Mountfort said

> Jo Hayns's *Fate is now become my share,*
> *For I'm a* Poet, Married, *and a* Player:
> *The Greatest of these* Curses *is the* First;
> *As for the latter* two, *I know the* worst;
> *But how you mean to deal with me to* Day,
> *Or how you'l* Massacre *my harmless* Play,
> *I must confess distracts me every* Way
> . . . .
> *I never Writ till* Love *first touch'd my* Brain,
> *And surely* Love *will now* Loves *Cause Maintain,*
> *Besides my* Natural Love *to Write again.*

The account of Mountfort's life in 1720 stated that when he died he "left two Daughters; one whereof is an excellent Actress, but she has lately quitted the Stage." That actress was Susanna, who called herself throughout most of her career Mrs Mountfort, even though she apparently never married. She is separately noticed in this dictionary. Her birth record, which Borgman stated he could not locate, we have found in the registers of St Giles in the Fields: Susanna, the daughter of William "Mountford," gentleman, and his wife Susanna, was born on 27 April 1690 and christened the following 11 May. Another child of William and Susanna Mountfort was born after William died; she was christened Mary on 27 April 1693 at St Clement Danes.

The Mountforts had other children. Borgman notes that "Elizabeth Mumford of William Mumford gent and Susanna uxor" was baptized at St Clement Danes on 22 March 1692 and buried on the thirtieth. We find also that their son Edward was born on 1 April 1691 and baptized four days later at St Giles in the Fields; he died in infancy and was buried on 3 May. Borgman notes that *The Stage Veteran* said Mountfort had an illegitimate child by a lady of high rank and that the child was brought up by Mrs Mountfort as her own. That child (sex not specified) was said to have been alive in 1730. Mrs William Mountfort's acting career was mostly as Mrs John Verbruggen, and she is entered in this work under that name.

Mountfort served very briefly in the army. In mid-October 1689 he spoke a prologue "after he came from the Army, and Acted on the stage," a note on the separately printed prologue stated. And in addition to his own plays, Mountfort had a hand in others. Settle in his dedication to *Distressed Innocence* (performed at Drury Lane in late October 1690) said he was indebted to Mountfort "for the last Scene of my Play which he was so kind to write for me." Joseph Harris, in the preface to *The Mistakes* (mid-December 1690 at Drury Lane) said that Mountfort wrote one scene in the fifth act. And Mountfort wrote occasional prologues and epilogues and some music. Thorp in *Songs from the Restoration Theatre* notes that Mountfort wrote "Bonny Jockey now with Clasping and Kissing," "Rise bonny Kate," and an overture and eight tunes for strings which may have been used in the theatre (the last are at Christ Church Library).

The promising career of William Mountfort was cut short in 1692. On 10 December Narcissus Luttrell reported:

Last night Lord Mohun [age 15], captain Hill [probably about 20, though then reported to have been about 18] of collonel Earles regiment and others pursued Mountfort the actor from the playhouse to his lodgings in Norfolk Street, where one kist him while Hill run him thro' the belly: they ran away, but his lordship was this morning seized and committed to prison. Mountfort died of his wounds this afternoon. The quarrell was about Bracegirdle the actresse, whom they would have trapan'd away, but Mountfort prevented it, wherefore they murthered him thus.

The report, as will be seen, was almost correct. On his deathbed Mountfort drew his will. He described himself as of the parish of St Clement Danes (he must recently have changed from St Giles). He left his entire estate to his wife Susanna in trust for her, their daughter Susanna, and the unborn child Mrs Mountfort was then carrying, share and share alike. Luttrell stated that Mountfort was buried on Tuesday night, 13 December, at St Clement's with 1000 people present; some of the Whitehall choristers and the King's organist [Purcell, presumably] provided the music.

Richard Hill escaped. Mohun was tried by the House of Lords, and all the details of the murder of Mountfort and the events leading up to it were brought out and published in 1693 in *The Tryal of Charles Lord Mohun*. Mountfort's death caused a great stir and elicited at least two poems. One, *A Tragical Song on Mr. Wil. Montfort, The Famous Actor Unfortunately Kill'd* was to be sung to the tune of "Mary live Long." It went, in part:

> *His Name still will last*
> > *In Court Town or Country,*
> *By Cits, or the Gentry,*
> > *Till Ages are past*
> *For Acts on the stage;*
> > *For in playing a Part,*
> *He excells the fam'd* Hart,
> > *Or* Moon *that's dead too,*
> *Nay, no one thats living.*
> *Can* Mountfort *out-do.*
>
> *His Carriage was such,*
> > *In all Conversation,*
> *To be free from Passion,*
> > *And never thought much*
> *To oblige any one;*
> > *From a Lord to a Cit,*
> *He was free with his VVit,*
> > *And Courteous withal:*
> *But now alas Killing,*
> *But now alas Killing,*
> *Is us'd all in all.*

The other was Tom Brown's *The Ladies Lamentation for their Adonis: Or, an Elegy on the Death of Mr. Mountford the Player*. It too was a song, to be sung to the tune of "Packington's Pound." Typical was the first stanza:

> *Poor* Mountford *is gone, and the Ladies do all*
> *Break their Hearts for this Beau, as they did for*
> > *D'Val,*
> *And they the two Brats for this Tragedy damn,*
> *At* Kensington-Court, *and the Court of* Bantam.
> > *They all vow and swear,*
> > *That if any Peer,*
> *Shou'd acquit the young Lord, he shou'd pay very*
> > *dear;*
> *Now will they be pleas'd with him, who on Throne*
> > *is,*
> *If he do's not his Part, to revenge their* Adonis.

The poem went on to warn all and sundry that an acquittal would not be acceptable to the town, even though Mountfort once "Did banter the lawful King of this Nation" and was "a base and unmannerly Whig. . . ."

Those poems came out before the trial began in January 1693. *The Player's Tragedy*, a novel, was published that year. In it Mountfort was thinly disguised as the character Monfredo, who was described as "Handsom, cou'd Sing, Dance, and Play on the Musick, had a Manly presence, and yet a soft Effeminacy in his face, that cou'd not but render him agreeable to the wanton dalliances of the Fair." Acting had given him "a forward and bold Assurance, both in Love, and Conversation; he knew his whole stock of Wit." Monfredo wrote some plays, captured the heart of Bracilla (Anne Bracegirdle the actress), and aroused the jealousy of Montano (Captain Hill), who killed him.

Mohun was indicted before he faced his peers in the House of Lords. He had, the indictment read, been present when Captain Hill ran Mountfort through and "was Aiding, Abetting Assisting and Comforting . . . Hill; and thereupon we do say, he is Guilty of this Murder. . . ." The Attorney General's opening presentation at the five-day trial sketched in the background of the case: Hill had made "Addresses of Courtship" to the actress Anne Bracegirdle, had been rebuffed, and declared in a rage that Mountfort stood in his way. Hill and Mohun got together and plotted to abduct Mrs Bracegirdle (that portion of the story is presented in more detail in her entry). Despite the fact that they had hired a small band of soldiers to help with the abduction, Hill and Mohun were unsuccessful, and Mrs Bracegirdle ended up safe within her house in Howard Street. Foiled, Hill and Mohun paced up and down the street outside, swords drawn, and determined to take out their revenge on Mountfort should he approach or should he be seen going toward his house in Norfolk Street nearby.

Word was sent to Mrs Mountfort to warn her husband—wherever he was—not to come home, but Mountfort could not be found. Then, as the Attorney General stated it:

The Witnesses will inform your Lordships, that as Mr. *Mountford*, about 12 a Clock, was coming Home, my Lord *Mohun* met him, and saluted him.

Mr. *Mountford* said, My Lord *Mohun*, What does your Lordship do here at this time of Night? And my Lord made answer, He supposed Mr. *Mountford* had been sent for. No, says *Mountford*, I came by chance. My Lord said to him again, I suppose you have heard about the Lady. Mr. *Mountford* answered, I hope my Wife had given your Lordship no Offence. No, says my Lord *Mohun*, It's Mrs. *Bracegirdle* I mean, To this, the Reply of Mr. *Mountford* was, Mrs. *Bracegirdle* is no concern of mine, but I hope your Lordship does not countenance any ill Action of Mr. *Hill*.

Upon this *Hill* came up to them, and said to my Lord, it was not a time to discourse of those Matters; and as my Lord continued to talk with *Mountford*, *Hill* struck *Mountford* first, and in a manner, at the same instant made a Pass at him, and run him clean through the Body, and this before Mr. *Mountford's* Sword was drawn. Immediately upon this there was a Cry of Murder, and the Watch came with what haste they could, and took my Lord *Mohun*, but *Hill* was fled; when my Lord was taken, his Sword was not drawn.

In the trial proper, Mrs Browne, at whose house Anne Bracegirdle lodged, testified that she had gone out to prevent Mountfort coming up the street to the Browne house, for he clearly was not heading toward his own home in the neighboring street. But though she tried to speak to him as he came up the street, he did not hear and went to speak to Lord Mohun. She was asked at the trial if it appeared that Mountfort was going to his own house or hers, and she testified that it looked "As if he was coming to mine."

The actor George Powell, a friend of Mountfort, testified that Hill had threatened to be revenged on Mountfort, for he was convinced that it was Mountfort who stood between him and Anne Bracegirdle. ". . . I am resolved to have the Blood of *Mountford*," Hill had said to Powell. Powell was not at the scene of the murder, but he came to Mountfort's house soon after:

I saw him lying upon the Parlor Floor [he testified], and afterward saw him laid to Bed, and sate up all Night with him, and about four a Clock in the Morning I asked Mr. *Mountford* how the thing happened. He told me Captain *Hill* killed him basely; I asked him if his Sword was drawn; Yes, says he, but it was after I had received my Wound, for whilst my Lord *Mohun* talked to me *Hill* run me through.

Several witnesses provided similar evidence that Hill had done the threatening and the killing, and that Mohun had been an accessory but not actively involved in the actual murder.

Mountfort, after he was run through, apparently managed to stagger to his own house himself. Mrs Page, who had been sent by Mrs Bracegirdle to the Mountfort house to have Mrs Mountfort send out a (second) search for her husband to warn him to stay where he was or come home with a guard, was at Mountfort's house when the murder was committed. She testified: ". . . I heard Murder cry'd out; immediately I open'd Mr. *Mountford's* Door, and he came in, and fell with his Arms about my Neck to support himself, I suppose, and he said Hill had Murder'd him. *I* helped him as far as the Parlor Door, and there down he fell." Mr Bancroft, a "chirurgeon," was called to attend Mountfort. He found that the sword had been thrust through Mountfort's body and

out by his Back-bone, behind his left Side. *I* told him what he must expect, that he was a Dead Man. *I* attended him that Night, till about Four a Clock in the Morning, and then *I* took my leave of him, and went home: About Eight a Clock in the Morning *I* came thither again, and met Mr. *Hobbs* there, and he was of the same Opinion. He lived till about One, and then he Died.

Bancroft questioned Mountfort about the scuffle, and Mountfort stated that Mohun had "*offered me no Violence . . .*" Lord Mohun was declared not guilty of the murder. Borgman's *The Life and Death of William Mountfort* contains many more details of the case.

Mrs Mountfort, according to what Luttrell heard, appealed the verdict, but when Mohun heard of it he pleaded with the Lords to have the appeal set aside; as it turned out no actual appeal had been brought, so the Lords dismissed the matter. Mohun, who had a poor reputation to begin with, appears to have had a fair trial, and to have received a just verdict. After a short life filled with violent acts, he died in a duel with the fourth Duke of Hamilton in 1712. Hill escaped first to the Isle of Wight and then to Scotland. He was reported to have surrendered himself at St Germain in 1694, but that must have been just a rumor, for he was back in service by 1697. He appealed for a pardon from Queen Anne, pleading his youthfulness at the time of the murder.

He probably was pardoned, though evidence is lacking. Borgman thinks he was the Captain Hill who was recommended for a commission in the "New Levies" in 1706. The Hill who was killed five years after the murder (in September 1697) in a tavern brawl near Charing Cross was not Richard Hill but Captain William Hill and he was killed by none other than Lord Mohun; for that murder Mohun was indicted and imprisoned, but pardoned. (In our notice of Anne Bracegirdle we incorrectly followed the earlier report that Richard Hill was the Hill killed in the 1697 tavern brawl.)

In *The Music in English Drama*, Manifold suggests that perhaps Mountfort was the "Mumford" who contributed to the "Small Collection of Flute Tunes" appended to John Carr's *Vinculum Societatis*, 1687–1691.

Mountfort, Mrs William. *See* VERBRUGGEN, MRS JOHN.

Mountier, Thomas [*fl. 1719–1740*], *singer, actor.*

The Dictionary of National Biography states that the tenor Thomas Mountier was lay vicar and, from 1719 to 1732, preceptor of the choristers of Chichester Cathedral. His post there was declared vacant on 12 May 1732, but by that time young Mountier had moved to London. On 2 April 1731 there had been advertised a forthcoming concert at the Haymarket Theatre: "At the request of great numbers of gentlemen and ladies, for the benefit of Thomas Mountier, the Chichester boy (who sang at Mr. Smith's concert at the Theatre in Lincoln's Inn Fields), at the New Theatre in the Haymarket, on 6 May 1731, a concert." Mountier sang at Geminiani's concerts at Hickford's Music Room in November 1732 and in concerts at Lincoln's Inn Fields playhouse in March 1732. He sang in both Italian and English at Hickford's on 27 March and in April 1732. On 17 May he made his first appearance in a character, singing Acis in *Acis and Galatea* at the Haymarket, when that work was first presented "in a theatrical way" with scenes and machines.

At the Haymarket in 1732–33 Mountier sang Phoebus and later Neptune in *Britannia* and the King in *The Opera of Operas*. He per-

formed at Drury Lane in 1733–34, making his
first appearance there on 7 November 1733 as
Noddle in *The Opera of Operas*, then he played
Mercury, Apollo, and Signor Treblini in *Cupid
and Psyche*, a Sea God in *Cephalus and Procris*,
Milcha in *The Tempest*, and a Shepherd in *Love
and Glory* (*Britannia*). Both Grove and the *DNB*
have Mountier singing Adelberto in *Ottone* in
1733, but when that opera was revived at the
King's Theatre on 13 November 1733 the role
was sung by Signor Scalzi. Deutsch in his *Handel* lists Scalzi, yet under the date of 6 May
1732 he, too, states that Mountier sang Adelberto in 1733, so our subject may have done
so at one of the performances.

Mountier was not cited in bills again until
19 March 1740, when he sang at Hickford's
Music Room for Valentine Snow's benefit. In
1740 Mountier was admitted to the Royal
Society of Musicians, according to Deutsch.

"Moustache" [fl. 1784–1785], performing dog.

J. F. Reynolds in his *Life and Times* remembered going to Sadler's Wells to see the trained
dogs of Signor Scaglioni act in *The Deserter* in
1784, with "Moustache" playing the title role:

I see him now, in his little uniform, military boots,
with smart musket and helmet, cheering and inspiring his fellow soldiers, to follow him up the
scaling ladders, and storm the fort. . . . At the
moment, when the gallant assailants seemed secure
of victory, a retreat was sounded, and Moustache
and his adherents [were] seen receding from the
repulse, rushing down the ladders, and then staggering towards the lamps in a state of panic and
dismay. . . .

The attraction brought a clear profit to Sadler's
Wells of over £7000. Dog lovers will be sorry
to hear that the maneuvre was accomplished
by starving the dogs and putting food on the
other side of the ramparts, and then whipping
and threatening the dogs back. Scaglioni took
his dogs in 1785 to York, where the storming
of the fort drew great applause. The troupe
also appeared in Dublin, Manchester, and Liverpool.

Mowat, Miss [fl. 1760–1761], actress.

A "Young Gentlewoman who never appeared before" played the title role in *Jane Shore*
at Covent Garden Theatre on 24 January 1760

and is identified by the theatre's cash book in
the Folger Library as Miss Mowat. She repeated the part on 28 January and 13 February.
On 6 March she was Harriet Partlet in the
farce, *The Spirit of Contradiction*, and on 30
April was allowed to try Juliet in *Romeo and
Juliet* for her benefit, at which she realized £79
11s. after house charges. (The cash book on
this occasion called her, incorrectly, "Manet.")

On 3 January 1761 Miss Mowat appeared at
Drury Lane for the first time, again anonymously—but identified by the prompter Hopkins in his diary. She played the Countess of
Rutland in *The Earl of Essex*, which was three
times repeated. On 23 April she was Belvidera
in *Venice Preserv'd* and on 30 April Desdemona
in *Othello*, and then disappeared. She seems not
to have seized the opportunities repeatedly furnished by those leading roles.

Moyer, Mr [fl. 1783–1785], house servant.

The Lord Chamberlain's accounts show that
Mr Moyer was a boxkeeper and a lobby keeper
at the King's Theatre from 1783 to 1785.

Moyle, Mr [fl. 1796–1802], house servant?

The Drury Lane accounts show that a Mr
Moyle (?) was added to the paylist at 4s. 2d.
(daily, presumably) on 31 December 1796. He
was last mentioned on 11 December 1802.
Since the spelling of his name is uncertain and
could be phonetic, perhaps he was the Mr
Miles who was cited in the accounts for a payment of 2s. 4d. on 19 November 1801.

Moyle, Mrs [fl. 1681–1682], actress.

Mrs Moyle played Millicent in *Sir Barnaby
Whigg* in the summer of 1681 (argues Robert
Hume; *The London Stage* gives late October)
with the King's Company at Drury Lane. On
18 July 1682 she spoke an epilogue at Oxford.
Possibly Mrs Moyle should be identified as Mrs
Miles, who acted with the United Company
from 1689 to 1692.

Moylin, Mons [fl. 1718–1719], actor.

In the French company playing at Lincoln's
Inn Fields and the King's Theatre from 7 November 1718 to 19 March 1719 were Francisque Moylin, his wife, presumably his brother

Simon, and Moylin junior, who on 13 January 1719 acted Damis in Moliere's *Tartuffe*. The junior Moylin was perhaps Simon's son.

Moylin, Francisque, called "Francisque" [*fl. 1715–1751*], *actor, manager, dancer, acrobat.*

The actor-manager Francisque Moylin, commonly referred to as "Francisque," is thought by J. Fransen in *Les comediens français en Hollande* to have been the father of the actor-manager Jean Francisque, with whom our subject has sometimes been confused. Campardon in *Les Spectacles de la foire* notes that after performing in the provinces, Francisque Moylin came to Paris to appear at the St Germain Fair as Pellegrin in 1715. He then joined the company of St Edme, and at the St Germain Fair in 1718 he performed with remnants of Madame Baron's troupe.

Moylin formed a troupe, made up chiefly of relatives, to perform in London in 1718–19. He was engaged by the harlequin-manager John Rich at Lincoln's Inn Fields Theatre, where Moylin's group began performing on 7 November 1718, advertised as "lately arriv'd from the Theatre Royal in Paris"—which may or may not have been true. The company offered *La Foire de St Germain* for the benefit of John Rich and his brother and brought in gross receipts of over £157. The troupe's stay was supposed to have been brief, but they were so successful, especially with the aristocracy (who could understand French) that they remained through 19 March 1719, transferring to the King's Theatre on 11 February to complete their engagement. The French players attracted good crowds, made Rich richer, caught the fancy of the royal family, and received a gift from George I of 100 guineas. Moylin's programs consisted of French and Italian plays, the latter containing improvised scenes in the manner of *commedia dell' arte* troupes, though all plays were scripted or partly scripted. The works were embellished with entr'acte songs, dances, and tumbling. Offerings included *La Fausse Coquette*, *Le Maitre etourdi* (Moliere's *Etourdi*, supposedly), *Le Tombeau du maître Andre*, *Arlequin Laron, juge et grand prevost*, *La Baguette de Vulcain*, *Colombine avocat, pour et contre*, *Les Deux Arlequins*, *Colombine fille sçavante*, *Les Chinois*, *La Retour de la foire*, *Harlequin l'homme a bonne fortune*, *Les Pasquinades Italiennes*, *Le Tar-*

tuffe and *George Dandin* by Moliere, and *Pierot maitre valet et l'opera de campagne*.

Members of the troupe were not often named in the bills but included Moylin's wife (née Sallé, sister of Marie Sallé the dancer; she and Moylin were married in Paris in 1718, according to Fuchs's *Lexique*), Simon Moylin (Moylin's brother), Moylin Junior (Jean Francisque?), Moylin's sister and her husband (Michael Cochois), Mme Moylin's niece and nephew, and the child dancers, Marie Sallé and her brother. There appears to be some confusion about the relationships of some of the company members; Sybil Rosenfeld in her *Foreign Theatrical Companies*, following Fuchs, states that Moylin's wife was the sister of Marie Sallé; Emmett Avery in his article on "Foreign Performers" in *Philological Quarterly* in 1937 makes Moylin and his wife the uncle and aunt of the Sallé children. The French performers were occasionally joined by members of Rich's English company in entr'acte turns. Francisque Moylin was the harlequin of the troupe (sometimes performing without a mask) and spoke occasional prologues. He can be credited with bringing to Londoners the first performances of Molière in the original French.

Moylin was given a benefit on 8 January 1719, when he played the lead in *Arlequin esprit folet*; on 13 January he played the title role in *Tartuffe*; and on 27 January he was Baron in Doisson's *Le Baron de la crasse*. On 9 May 1720 at the King's Theatre Moylin appeared with De Grimbergue's company as Harlequin in Molière's "Le Tourdy." He was hailed as "the famous Monsieur Francisque, who had the Honour to be so much Applauded last Year." During the rest of May he was the harlequin in *La Fausse coquette*, *La Foire St Germain*, *Le Dragon de Moscovy*, and *Les Bains de la porte de St Bernard*. At his benefit on 31 May he performed tumbling between the acts and probably played in *Les Deux Arlequins*. Mary Countess Cowper found it a "most dismal Performance. No Wonder People are Slaves who can entertain themselves with such stuff." In the *Theatre*, Steele also voiced strong disapproval of the French visitors.

Moylin's company played at the St Germain Fair in 1720 and 1721 and at the St Laurent Fair in 1721. Briefly in 1721 Moylin was allowed to operate an opéra comique company in Paris.

De Grimbergue's company had returned to London in the winter of 1720–21, playing at the Haymarket; it was the main showplace for French troupes from that time forward and was often called the French Theatre. The company acted from 29 December 1720 to the end of January 1721. In addition to acting in *Tartuffe* and other works, Moylin presented what was apparently a solo turn called *The Hat* on 2 February 1721. He made "a Speech to the Audience on a Matter of Consequence" on 14 February; perhaps it had something to do with his supposedly refusing to act on 17 February, causing De Grimbergue to dismiss the audience. On 20 February the manager softened the report and said that Moylin had been ill and unable to appear. Moylin was given a benefit on 20 March, but by 18 April a new harlequin was in the troupe, Moylin having left.

After 1721 Francisque Moylin's travels are sometimes difficult to trace. He was at the fairs in Paris in 1722, after which, according to Campardon, he left for the provinces; Dacier in *Une Danseuse de l'opera* has him leaving Paris in 1724. Moylin was in Bordeaux in January 1731, where he lost all his belongings in a theatre fire; he was also in Dijon in 1731, according to Fuchs. On 14 November 1731 Moylin appeared as a rope dancer and acrobat in Grenoble. He headed a troupe in Nancy in 1732 and one in Rouen in February 1733. Fuchs traces him to Amiens after February. *The London Stage* lists "Francisque" as a member of Theophilus Cibber's rebel troupe at the Haymarket Theatre in London in the spring of 1734, playing Harlequin in *The Burgomaster Trick'd*. (He was probably not the "Arlequin en Chien" who had played the Marquis De Fresco in *The Harlot's Progress* at Drury Lane on 31 March 1733 and continued appearing in that part as late as the fall of 1733.) Moylin was the head of a company at Brussels in 1734, according to Fuchs, drawn there, perhaps, by (his son?) Jean Francisque, who was active in Holland the previous year.

On 26 October 1734 Moylin and his company opened an engagement at the Haymarket Theatre in London which lasted until 3 June 1735; the players also appeared at the Goodman's Fields Theatre on 23 May and 4 June 1735. About 116 performances were given,

often at the command of the royal family. In the troupe, again, were some of Moylin's relatives: his wife, his brother-in-law Cochois, and Master Francis Cochois. The troupe was a full one, including boxkeepers, scenekeepers, and a wardrobe master. Francisque appeared as the harlequin in a number of works: *Harlequin Hulla, L'Embarras des richesses, Harlequin Sauvage, Arlequin gardien du fleuve d'Oubly, Timon le misanthrope,* and *Arlequin balourd.* He was also Tartuffe, the Baron in *Le Baron de la crasse,* Don Pedro in *Inès de Castro,* Dr Panciasse in *Le Mariage forcé,* Viscount Jodelet in *Les Precieuses ridicules,* Azarias in *Athalia,* Dame Alison in *Le Carillon de maitre Gerval Gervaise et Dame Alison,* and two characters in *La Fausse Coquette*: Arlequin Intriguant and La Fausse coquette. Moylin was probably the Professor and Harlequin in *Isabelle fille capitaine et Arlequin sergeant* and Bailly de Challiot in *Agnès de Challiot*; on those occasions the actor was cited not as Francisque but as Arlequin.

The reception of the French strollers was mixed, though the season was evidently successful. A letter from a "True Briton" in the *Grub Street Journal* on 13 March 1735 stated that the quality of the French fare was no higher than English players offered; he said that at a coffee house he met one of the French performers, who claimed that the company acted plays in London "with the greatest applause, which, if we attempted at home, we should be stoned off the stage." Aaron Hill in *The Prompter* on 24 December 1734 rather liked the French-speaking harlequin and wished that the dumb English harlequins would speak; he admired the skill in mime that the French players displayed. He was speaking of Moylin; English managers, he suggested, should

transplant into their *Pantomimes*, such of the *French* Harlequin's *Gestures*, and *Tours*, as are exprest in dumb Shew in the French Theatre.—This besides the Novelty of it in ours, will render Mr. *Francisque* so *common*, that it will be no charity to see him: And thus the Edge of Curiosity once worn off, and *Harlequin* WELL TRANSLATED, our Theatres will be protected from Foreign Invasion, and the *English* still maintain their *Right* of *diverting an* English *Audience.*

"General" Moylin, Hill said, "has shown himself not only an able *Actor* at the Head of his little *Corps* but a most consummate Politician, by forbearing to attack his too powerful OPPO-SITE [John Rich] and ceasing his Hostilities the Nights the other *takes the Field*." He concluded that "Ev'ry *Body must own*, the French Harlequin *is infinitely more entertaining than the* English *one*." But Hill did not appreciate the ridicule of the English in Moylin's production of *Le François à Londres*.

The Abbé Prévost in *Le Pour et le contre*, No 87, claimed that Moylin had earned 6000 *écus* since his arrival in England, a measure of his popularity with London audiences. Prévost described one of Moylin's comic turns. He disguised himself as a lady of quality and sat in one of the stage boxes, toying with the advances of some of the gentlemen nearby. When the curtain rose, the "lady" asked loudly why the play had begun so late; an actor, pretending surprise, said that the company's harlequin could not be found. The lady protested that she would never come to the theatre again if Harlequin did not appear. The actors made excuses, but the lady finally leaped onto the stage and offered to fill the part herself.

After the successful 1734–35 season Moylin and his company returned to the Continent. They were at Nancy in February 1736 and at Avignon in July. In 1738 Moylin's players were at Amiens in February and Avignon in June, after which they went to Paris.

On 4 October 1738 the *Daily Advertiser* in London reported that Moylin and a company of 70 had arrived to play at the Haymarket, a house closed to English troupes by the Licensing Act of 1737. "It seems to be a little unnatural that French Strollers should have a Superior Privilege to those of our own Country," a reporter commented, and, indeed, the visit created a fever of anti-Gallic sentiment. The French troupe was led, according to Sybil Rosenfeld, by "Francisque junior, younger brother of Francisque, and Lesage junior." Our subject's younger brother was Simon Moylin, who in later years was a harlequin, but when the troupe opened with *L'Embarras des richesses* on 9 October the harlequin was advertised as "Moylin Françisque." We take it that our subject was the performer in question, possibly working under the leadership of his younger brother and Lesage, yet the newspapers in November again referred to the co-manager as Moylin Francisque. There is the possibility that, in the face of the riots caused by the French performance on 9 October, the elder Moylin took over the management.

In his *History of the Theatres* Benjamin Victor described the wild opening night:

People went early to the Theatre, as a crouded House was certain. I was there, in the Centre of the Pit; where I soon perceived that we were visited by two Westminster Justices, Deveil and Manning. The Leaders, that had the Conduct of the Opposition, were known to be there; one of whom called aloud for the Song in Praise of English Roast Beef, which was accordingly sung in the Gallery by a Person prepared for that Purpose; and the whole House besides joining in the Chorus, saluted the Close with three Huzzas! This, Justice Deveil was pleased to say, was a Riot; upon which Disputes commenced directly, which were carried on with some Degree of Decency on both Sides. The Justice at first informed us, "That he was come there as a Magistrate to maintain the King's Authority; that Colonel Pulteney, with a full Company of the Guards, were without, to support him in the Execution of his Office; that it was the King's Command the Play should be acted; and that the obstructing it was opposing the King's Authority; and if that was done, he must read the Proclamation; after which all Offenders would be secured directly by the Guards in waiting." To all these most arbitrary Threatnings, this Abuse of his Majesty's Name, the Reply was to the following Effect:—"That the Audience had a legal Right to shew their Dislike to any Play or Actor; that the common Laws of the Land were nothing but common Custom, and the antient Usuage of the People; that the Judicature of the Pit had been acknowledged and acquiesced to, Time immemorial; and as the present Set of Actors were to take their Fate from the Public, they were free to receive them as they pleased."

By this Time the Hour of Six drew near; and the French and Spanish Embassadors, with their Ladies; the late Lord and Lady Gage; and Sir T——— R———, a Commissioner of the Excise, all appeared in the Stage Box together! At that Instant the Curtain drew up, and discovered the Actors standing between two Files of Grenadiers, with their Bayonets fixed, and resting on their Firelocks. There was a Sight! enough to animate the coldest Briton. At this the whole Pit rose, and unanimously turned to the Justices, who sat in the Middle of it, to demand the Reason of such arbitrary Proceedings? The Justices either knew nothing of the Soldiers being placed there, or thought it safest to declare so. At that Declaration, they demanded of Justice

Deveil (who had owned himself the commanding Officer in the Affair) to order them off the Stage. He did so immediately, and they disappeared. Then began the Serenade; not only Catcalls, but all the various portable Instruments, that could make a disagreeable Noise, were brought up on this Occasion, which were continually tuning in all Parts of the House; and as an Attempt to speaking was ridiculous, the Actors retired, and they opened with a grand Dance of twelve Men and twelve Women; but even that was prepared for; and they were directly saluted with a Bushel or two of Peas, which made their Capering very unsafe. After this they attempted to open the Comedy; but had the Actor the Voice of Thunder, it would have been lost in the confused Sounds from a thousand various Instruments. Here, at the waving Deviel's Hand, all was silent, and (standing up on his Seat) he made a Proposal to the House to this Effect:—"That if they persisted in the Opposition, he must read the Proclamation; that if they would permit the Play to go on, and to be acted through that Night, he would promise, (on his Honour) to lay their Dislikes, and Resentment to the Actors, before the King, and he doubted not but a speedy End would be put to their acting." The Answer to this Proposal was very short, and very expressive. "No Treaties, No Treaties!" At this the Justice called for Candles to read the Proclamation, and ordered the Guards to be in Readiness; but a Gentleman seizing Mr Deveil's Hand, stretched out for the Candle, begged of him to consider what he was going to do, for his own Sake, for ours, for the King's! that he saw the unanimous Resolution of the House; and that the Appearance of Soldiers in the Pit would throw us all into a Tumult, which must end with the Lives of many. This earnest Remonstrance made the Justice turn pale and passive. At this Pause the Actors made a second Attempt to go on, and the Uproar revived; which continuing some Time, the Embassadors and their Ladies left their Box, which occasioned a universal Huzza from the whole House! and after calling out some Time for the Falling of the Curtain, down it fell.

The French troupe did not try to perform again.

The managers made an appeal in the *Daily Post* on 8 November 1738:

The Case of the FRENCH COMEDIANS. Whereas we, Moylin Francisque and John Baptist le Sage, were in England in the Month of February last, and having then obtained leave to bring over a French Company of Comedians, for to represent the same in the Little Theatre in the Hay-Market this Season; we, for that Purpose, returned into France, and collected together the best Company that were to be had; being wholly ignorant of any

Affairs transacted in England relating to the Regulation of the Stage, and not in the least doubting but that the Company would meet with the same Encouragement as heretofore, made us engage with several Performers abroad, at very great Expences, to come into England; and the Night the said Company were to have acted, they met with such an Obstruction from the Audience, that a Stop was put to the Performance, and the said Company discontinued, and laid aside all Thoughts of making the least Attempt, since the same was not agreeable to the Publick. Notwithstanding we the said Undertakers, by the Contracts we made, have been obliged to pay to each Performer the same Monies hitherto, and liable to the same Obligations for the Remainder of this whole Season, as if the Company had performed the whole Time, and have besides expended large Sums of Money, and contracted several Debts here, which we are not in Circumstances to pay: So that we are obliged to lay our Case before the Publick, in hopes that they will be so indulgent as to permit us to perform three Nights only in one of the Patent Theatres, so as to enable us to discharge those Debts we have contracted here, and we will then humbly take our Leaves, and return to France, with grateful Acknowledgement for the Favour done to us. Suffolk-street, Nov. 6, 1738.

The *Evening Post* of 18 November stated that £600 was collected for the French players, over £300 coming from the court. But no foreign troupes visited London again until 1745.

We have supposed that Francisque Moylin was the Moylin chiefly involved in the disastrous event of October 1738, though the performer-manager in question may have been his brother Simon, calling himself Francisque. Fuchs indicates that Simon Moylin, Lesage, and Godar, had a company at Gand in December 1738, whereas Fuchs lists no activity for Francisque Moylin between June 1738 at Avignon and 1739 at Toulouse. Moylin performed at Bordeaux from May 1739 to June 1740. He made his debut as Harlequin at the Comédie Italienne in Paris in 1739 or 1740. References after 1740, as recorded by Fuchs, indicate that both Simon and Francisque Moylin continued active during the 1740's, but sometimes one cannot be sure which performer was being cited. One of them was in Marseille in 1747; Francisque was at Dijon from 18 December 1750 to 2 April 1751; a Moylin, dancer, performed at Strasbourg in 1752–53, but he may have been Simon's son. Fuchs believes that the brothers Moylin left the theatre about 1750.

Moylin, Mme Francisque ₍*fl. 1718–1735*₎, *actress.*

The harlequin-manager Francisque Moylin married Mlle Sallé in Paris in 1718, according to Fuchs's *Lexique*. She was the sister of the dancer Marie Sallé (though some sources say Marie Sallé was the neice of Moylin). Mme Moylin was in her husband's troupe in London, playing at Lincoln's Inn Fields Theatre and the King's Theatre from 7 November 1718 to 19 March 1719. On 13 January 1719 she acted Elmire in Molière's *Tartuffe* at Lincoln's Inn Fields. She probably acted with her husband's company over the years, but her next certain citation came on 20 November 1734, when she again played Elmire at the Haymarket. (She was probably not the "Mlle Arlequin en Chien" who played the Marchioness de Fresco in *Ridotto Al'Fresco* on 23 August and 4 September at Bartholomew Fair.) At the Haymarket in December 1734 Mme Moylin acted Armille in *Sampson Judge of Israel* and was the Colombine in *Arlequin balourd* and in *La Fille capitaine et Arlequin son sergeant.* At the Goodman's Fields playhouse on 23 May 1735 she acted Mlle Midas in *L'Embarras de richesses*.

Moylin, Simon ₍*fl. 1718–1756*₎, *actor, manager.*

Simon Moylin, the younger brother of the actor-manager Francisque Moylin, was married by 1718, according to Fuchs's *Lexique*; his wife played *amorosa* roles at the Comédie Italienne. Simon was in Francisque's troupe in England in 1718–19 and is known to have acted Valère in *Tartuffe* at Lincoln's Inn Fields Theatre on 13 January 1719. He was advertised as Moylin, Sr, which suggests that the Moylin, Jr, who acted Damis, may have been his son.

Some references in the records to a Moylin (or Moilin, Moulin), or to a Francisque, could refer to either Francisque or Simon Moylin. The certain references to Simon are recorded by Fuchs as follows: he led a troupe at Grenoble on 6 July 1733; had a child christened at Lyon on 12 October 1734; with Lesage and Godar led a company at Gand on 18 December 1738 and Rameaux in 1739; was at Bordeaux in 1739; with Lesage managed a troupe at Douai, Gand, and Amiens in 1741; made his debut as Harlequin at the Comédie Italienne on 23 August 1741; led a company at Gre-

noble in July 1744; had a child baptized at Lyon on 3 March 1746; left the stage about 1750; and was in retirement at Toulouse in 1756.

There is some question whether the Francisque Moylin who, with Jean Baptiste Lesage, led a troupe to London in the fall of 1738 was Simon or Francisque Moylin. Sybil Rosenfeld in *Foreign Theatrical Companies* cites the co-manager as Simon, yet the newspaper references to him are to "Moylin Francisque" and we have guessed in our entry for Francisque Moylin that though Simon may have been in charge of the company when it came to London in September 1738, his elder brother Francisque may have taken over when the troupe ran into problems with anti-Gallic sentiment.

Moylin, Mme Simon ₍*fl. 1718–1719*₎, *actress.*

Mme Simon Moylin played *amorosa* parts at the Comédie Italienne in Paris and was married to Moylin by 1718. She and her husband came to London in the fall of 1718 with a troupe managed by Simon's brother Francisque. Mme Moylin is known to have played Marianne in *Tartuffe* at Lincoln's Inn Fields Theatre on 13 January 1719. Playing Damis, Marianne's brother, was Moylin junior, apparently Mme Moylin's son.

Moyse, Miss ₍*fl. c. 1765*₎, *singer.*

According to Wroth's *The London Pleasure Gardens*, Miss Moyse sang at Finch's Grotto Gardens about 1765.

Mozart, Maria Anna *1751–1829, pianist, composer.*

Maria Anna Mozart (Walburga Ignatia completes her baptismal name) was born in Salzburg on 30 or 31 July 1751, daughter of the musician Leopold Mozart and his wife Anna Maria Pertl Mozart. "Nannerl," as the child Maria Anna was called, received early musical instruction from her father and showed an aptitude not far inferior to that of the genius Wolfgang Amadeus, her brother. In January 1762 Leopold Mozart and his two prodigies went to Munich to perform and, in September following, to Vienna.

From June 1763 until late November 1766 the little musical family toured Europe, performing before enthralled audiences of kings

Harvard Theatre Collection

MARIA ANNA MOZART

woodcut after Koch

and commoners in most of the important cultural centers of northern Europe. For 15 months they were in England, arriving in May 1764. In London they gave four concerts—at Spring Gardens, at Ranelagh, at the Haymarket Theatre, and at Hickford's Room—and were received at court. After the winter theatrical season of 1764–65 ended, the family traveled to Canterbury for a short visit with Horace Mann and then, on 1 August 1765, embarked from Dover to resume their continental tour. In 1767 Nannerl went again to perform in Vienna with her father and brother. After 1769 she played no more in public.

On 23 August 1784 she married Johann Baptist von Berchtold zu Sonnenburg (1736–1801) of Gilgen, by whom she had three children: Leopold Alois Pantaleon, Jeanette, and Maria Babette. She returned to Salzburg after her husband's death in 1801. She lived an uneventful life there and gradually sank into

comparative poverty. She was entirely blind after 1825. Maria Anna Mozart died in Salzburg on 29 October 1829 and was buried there, at St Peter's Abbey.

Maria Anna Mozart is pictured with her brother and father in a scene engraved by J. B. Delafosse, after L. C. Carmontelle, published 1764 with the legend, "Leopold Mozart Père de Marianne Mozart, Virtuose âgée de onze ans et de J. G. Wolfgang Mozart, Compositeur et Mâitre de Musique âgé de sept ans." In the picture, Maria Anna is singing. There is a woodcut of her, after a portrait by Karl Koch.

Mozart, Wolfgang Amadeus *1756–1791, composer, instrumentalist.*

Wolfgang Amadeus Mozart was born in a house in the Getreidegasse in Salzburg on 27

The Louvre, Collection Rothschild

Leopold Mozart, WOLFGANG AMADEUS MOZART, and MARIA ANNA MOZART

engraving by Delafosse, after Carmontelle

January 1756, the seventh and last child of the violinist and composer Leopold Mozart and his wife, née Anna Maria Pertl. (The baptismal name Joannes Chrysostomus Wolfgangus Theophilus was never used.) All of Wolfgang's siblings except his gifted elder sister Maria Anna died in infancy.

Mozart's astonishing musical precocity began to be manifested in his compositions when he was five years old, and he was by then also fairly proficient on several keyboard instruments. He made his first public appearance in a musical theatrical performance at Salzburg University in 1761. He traveled with his father and sister to Munich in January 1762. There the children played the harpsichord before the Elector of Bavaria.

For the 15 years following—and to some extent to the end of his life—Mozart's story is one of restless journeying. His father considered early travel and performance both good business and an essential part of a young musician's education. In September 1762 Leopold and his two children left Salzburg for Vienna by way of Passau and Linz. They remained in Vienna for three months, appearing twice before the Empress Maria Theresia, and returned to Salzburg in January 1763. From 9 June 1763 through 30 November 1766—some forty months—they were again away from home, this time on a wide swing through northern Europe—to Munich, Augsburg, Ludwigsburg, Schwetzingen, Mainz, Frankfurt, Koblenz, Aachen, Brussels, and on to Paris, where they remained for five months and charmed Louis XV with their playing.

In April 1764 the trio crossed to England, where they stayed for 15 months. Their first lodgings were at the house of a "Mr Couzin hare cutter" in Cecil Court, St Martin's Lane, according to the *Survey of London*. They were received at court, where George III devised cunning tests for young Wolfgang, obliging him to play difficult and unfamiliar pieces at sight. The child passed the tests with easy grace and excited further admiration with a brief recital on the organ. He accompanied a flutist and then the Queen as she sang. He capped the performance with some brilliant improvisations. Later, Daines Barrington, an amateur of science, subjected Mozart to his own battery of rigorous tests (and presented his amazing results in the Royal Society's *Phil-*

osophical Transactions in 1770). Wolfgang struck up close friendships with the Queen's music master, Johann Christian Bach, and with the singers Tenducci and Manzuoli.

The first public concert by Wolfgang and Nannerl his sister in London was given in the Great Room at Spring Gardens, St James Park, on 5 June 1764. Admission was half a guinea. In the advertisement the children were termed by their father "prodigies of Nature," and the response of the public to their recital on harpsichord and organ was enthusiastic. The receipts, said to be over 100 guineas, principally benefited the Mozarts; some of the other musicians who assisted—the vocalists Signora Cremonini and Signor Quilici, the violinist Barthélemon, and the 'cellist Cirri—refused their shares.

The Mozarts devoted the proceeds of their second concert, at Ranelagh Gardens on 29 June, to charity. The newsbill in the *Public Advertiser*, quoted by Mollie Sands in *Invitation to Ranelagh*, promised that

in the course of the Evening's Entertainments, the celebrated and astonishing Master MOZART, lately arrived, a Child of 7 years of Age [he was actually eight and a half], will perform several fine select pieces of his own Composition on the Harpsichord and on the Organ, which has already given the highest Pleasure, Delight and Surprize to the greatest Judges of Music in England or Italy, and is justly esteemed the most extraordinary Prodigy, and most amazing Genius that has appeared in any age.

The ages of both children were routinely lowered by a year or more in the advertisements for their engagements.

In July, the children's father, Leopold, took cold returning late from a private concert and became seriously ill. The family moved from the smoky city to the house of a Dr Randall at Five-fields in Chelsea. Forced to desist from practice on an instrument because his father needed quiet, Mozart there composed his first two symphonies. Shortly after the recovery of Leopold the family moved back to town, to the house of a Mr Williamson in Thrift Street, Soho. On 25 October 1764 they were again invited to play at court. Leopold had six of Wolfgang's sonatas engraved, dedicating them to the Queen, who sent him 50 guineas.

A third concert for the benefit of the children, still called "prodigies of Nature," was held at the Haymarket Theatre on 21 February 1765. The bill proclaimed "All the overtures will be from the compositions of these astonishing composers," but it is impossible to apportion different selections to individual Mozarts, for it is not known what they played. The final concert in London was at Hickford's Great Room in Brewer Street, on 13 May 1765. The children there played a sonata by Wolfgang, written for four hands, a practice then brand-new.

But by mid-May the novelty of the marvelous children had somewhat faded, and Leopold had begun to insert advertisements in newspapers inviting the public to private sessions with his youngsters at home and, later, at the Swan and Hoop in Cornhill. That scheme did not take, however. A visit of the family to the British Museum produced a commemorative four-part motet by Wolfgang—his only vocal piece written for English words. On 24 July 1765 the family left London. After a brief visit with Horace Mann at Canterbury they proceeded to Dover and, on 1 August, sailed for Calais. No member of the family ever returned to England.

Details of Mozart's illustrious continental career, his relationships with his father, sister, and patrons, with Haydn and other musicians, and with his wife are fully and authoritatively set forth by Stanley Sadie in the *New Grove*. Mozart's marriage with the soprano Costanza Weber, contracted against his family's wishes, was solemnized on 4 August 1782. It was a troubled one emotionally and financially. It produced six children, only two of whom survived to maturity: Carl Thomas Mozart (1784–1858) and Franz Xaver Wolfgang Mozart (1791–1844).

Wolfgang Amadeus Mozart's production was enormous and of a wider range—concertos, operas, symphonies, sonatas, fantasies, masses, canons, country dances, fugues—and of higher general quality than that of any other great composer. His work was often, also, produced under the most unpropitious circumstances.

Mozart died at Vienna after a brief illness, on 5 December 1791. He was buried, according to the contemporary Viennese custom, in a mass grave in St Marx churchyard outside the city.

Mozart's portrait was painted and engraved

Royal College of Music

WOLFGANG AMADEUS MOZART

statue by Barrias

by many artists. Especially interesting is an engraving by J. B. Delafosse, after L. C. Carmontelle, published 1764, in which Mozart, age seven, plays the harpsichord, his sister Maria Anna, age eleven, sings, and his father plays the violin. A canvas by an unknown artist, said to contain portraits of Mozart and his father, is at the Royal College of Music; but Deutsch suggests that the sitters are not the Mozarts. A life-size statue of Mozart as a child, tuning his violin, by Barrias is also at the Royal College of Music. A small figure of Mozart as a child by Grégoire has recently been stolen from the Royal Academy of Music.

Moze, Henry *d. 1787, organist, composer.*

Henry Moze wrote the overture to *The Witches* about 1770. The work was revived by Garrick at Drury Lane on 26 December 1771. Moze was organist of St Anne, Soho, the collegiate church of St Katherine near the Tower, and the German church in the Savoy. He died, the *European Magazine* reported, on 21 December 1787.

Mozeen, Thomas *1720?–1768, actor, dancer, playwright, song writer.*

Thomas Mozeen was of French parentage but born in England, according to early memoirs. (Gilliland incorrectly gave his Christian name as William.) A photocopy of a manuscript which we find not always reliable, now in the Folger Shakespeare Library, places his birth in 1720. Under the sponsorship of Dr Henry Sacheverall, Mozeen was reputedly bred to the bar, but turned to the stage, perhaps playing in the provinces before he made his first appearance as Stanley in *Richard III* on 27 December 1742 with a company managed by Theophilus Cibber at Lincoln's Inn Fields Theatre. He acted Freeman in *The Stratagem* the next night and was also seen that season as Sharper in *The Old Bachelor*, Albany in *King Lear*, Pacolet in *Bickerstaff's Unburied Dead*, Rossano in *The Fair Penitent*, Dumain Sr in *All's Well that End's Well*, Charles in *The Non-Juror*, Ratcliff in *Jane Shore*, the Player in *The Beggar's Opera*, and Clerimont in *The Miser*. The following season found him at Covent Garden, where he first appeared on 10 October 1743 as Beau Trippet in *The Lying Valet* and subsequently acted Robert in *The Mock Doctor* and Mirvan in *Tamerlane*.

After playing the summer at the Jacob's Wells Theatre in Bristol, Mozeen returned to London in the fall of 1744 to join Cibber's company at the Haymarket, where he acted Cassio in *Othello* on 22 September 1744 and then Worthy in *The Recruiting Officer*, Paris in *Romeo and Juliet*, the Lieutenant in *Love in a Low Life*, Freeman in *The Prodigal*, and Pylades in *The Distrest Mother*. His last performance that season at the Haymarket was as Paris on 17 December 1744, and then in mid-season he was engaged at

Drury Lane, where he made his debut on 20 February 1745 as Pembroke in *King John*, a role he played throughout the remainder of the season. He also acted there Norfolk in *Richard III*, Montano in *Othello*, a role in *Tancred and Sigismunda* at its premiere on 18 March 1745, Clitander in *The Quacks*, Lothario in *The Fair Penitent*, and Valentine in *Love for Love*. Among his supporting roles at Drury Lane over the next three seasons were Young Larson in *The Debauchees*, Sussex in *Lady Jane Gray*, Basil in *The Stage Coach*, Young Fashion in *The Relapse*, a character in *Albumazar*, Oliver in *As You Like It*, and Antonio in *The Tempest*. On 5 November 1745 a new song titled "The Subscription" written by Mozeen and set by Arne was sung by Lowe and was received, according to the press, "with universal applause."

Sometime between 25 April and 19 May 1746 Mozeen married Miss Edwards, an actress at Drury Lane, who on the latter date was advertised in the role of Miranda in *The Tempest* as Mrs Mozeen.

During the years of his first engagement at Drury Lane Mozeen also began his long association with Bristol in the summers. He acted regularly at the Jacob's Wells Theatre there in 1745 and 1746, when he was advertised for such roles as Lord Morelove in *The Careless Husband*, Lord Bellguard in *Sir Courtly Nice*, Cassio in *Othello*, Charles in *The Non-Juror*, Vizard in *The Constant Couple*, Altamont in *The Fair Penitent*, Bassanio in *The Merchant of Venice*, and Careless in *The Double Dealer*, roles a cut slightly above his accustomed London assignments.

Sheridan engaged the Mozeens for Smock Alley, Dublin, in 1748–49. Mozeen's only known roles there were Montano in *Othello* and Granger in *The Refusal*, though Chetwood thought him an actor of promise, with a genteel education and a good voice and understanding. Mrs Mozeen, who made her Smock Alley debut on 3 October 1748, as Celia in *As You Like It*, seems to have made a greater impression on Dublin audiences. She remained in Dublin the next season while Mozeen returned to Drury Lane in the fall of 1750.

After his reappearance at Drury Lane on 15 September 1750 as Young Fashion in *The Relapse*, Mozeen remained regularly engaged at that theatre for 14 seasons, during which he continued to be relegated to secondary and tertiary roles. These modest assignments included, among many others, Catesby in *Jane Shore*, Perez in *The Mourning Bride*, Valentine in *Twelfth Night*, Benvolio in *Romeo and Juliet*, Worthy in *The Recruiting Officer*, Don Pedro in *Much Ado about Nothing*, Jack Stanmore in *Oroonoko*, Sebastian in *The Tempest*, Hortensio in *Catherine and Petruchio*, Cob in *Every Man in his Humour*, Tom in *High Life below Stairs*, Waitwell in *The Way of the World*, and Blunt in *The London Merchant*.

After the 1763–64 season Mozeen was no longer associated with Drury Lane. He returned to London to act Bardolph in *2 Henry IV* at Covent Garden Theatre on 6 October 1766 and then seems to have been engaged at Norwich in the summer of 1767. In 1767–68 he joined the Covent Garden company, with a salary of 3s. 6d. per day, appearing on 16 September 1767 as Elliot in *Venice Preserv'd*. He acted Blunt in *The London Merchant* on 26 October, Cob in *Every Man in His Humour* on 24 November, and Gratiano in *Othello* on 5 December. He died on 28 March 1768, before the season ended.

Mozeen's wife, who pursued an independent career after 1750, acted in the provinces, mainly in Ireland, until at least 1773. Their son acted at Belfast in September 1768, but he did not appear in London.

In a manuscript notation on a copy of *Young Scarron* at the Folger Shakespeare Library, Mozeen is said to have been the author of that play which narrates the summer expedition of some London players. Published at London in 1752 *Young Scarron* proves to be an imitation of Scarron's *Le Roman Comique*. It seems never to have been performed in London, though the manuscript cast provided in the Folger copy suggests it was introduced in the provinces. For a benefit Mozeen shared with others at Drury Lane on 21 May 1759 his two-act farce *The Heiress; or, The Antigallican*, was introduced for its only performance. The prompter Cross found it an indifferent piece. It was published in 1762 in Mozeen's *A Collection of Miscellaneous Essays in Verse*, which included excerpts from the play in prose and selections of pieces for Sadler's Wells Theatre and other places. Among these were the plan of a pantomime called *Harlequin Deserter*, intended for Sadler's Wells, and *Frolics in May*, an interlude of dancing and singing. Also included in the collection was the song *The Kilruddery Hunt*, which he wrote with Owen Bray in Ireland. Tate Wilkinson credits Mozeen with the new song introduced by Beard in a revival of Shadwell's *The Fair Quaker of Deal* at Drury Lane on 7 October 1755, a production in which Mozeen appeared as one of the dancing sailors. He also furnished the words for the song "The Blooming Maid," sung by Mrs Hooper in London about 1760. Some of Mozeen's lyrics were published in *The Lyrical Pacquet, containing most of the Favourite Songs performed for Three Seasons past at Sadler's Wells*, printed in 1764. *Fables in Verse* by Mozeen, dedicated to Richard Grenville Temple, Viscount Cobham, appeared in two volumes in 1765. The stage recitation *Bucks have at ye all* has also been credited to Mozeen. That popular monologue was introduced by Tom King at Drury Lane on 29 March 1760; the manuscript of the specialty is in the Larpent Collection at the Huntington Library. Some of his prologues and epilogues were spoken at the Jacob's Wells Theatre in Bristol, where he returned in 1752, 1754, from 1756 through 1764, in 1766, and probably in the intervening years as well.

Mozeen, Mrs Thomas [Mary?], née Edwards [fl. 1724?–1773], *singer, actress.*

It is possible that the young singer Miss Edwards, who married the actor Thomas Mozeen in 1746, was Mary Edwards, daughter of the singer Thomas Edwards, noticed in volume 5 of this dictionary. If so, then she had been born by 18 June 1724, when Thomas Edwards drew his will and bequeathed £1000 in trust for the benefit of his children Mary and Thomas. The elder Thomas Edwards's will was proved on 28 August 1730.

On 19 November 1737 the pantomime *The Burgomaster Trick'd* was performed at Drury Lane Theatre by "Lilliputians," a group of Leviez's young dancing students, among whom appeared Miss Edwards as one of the Country Lasses. Despite a number of performances in *The Burgomaster Trick'd*, when Miss Edwards acted Margerina in *The Dragon of Wantley* on 16 May 1738, the bills announced it was to be her first time on any stage. That summer on 23 August she played the same role when the Drury Lane "Lilliputian Company" presented *The Dragon of Wantley* in Hallam's booth at the George Inn Yard during Bartholomew Fair.

At Drury Lane on 30 October 1738 Miss Edwards acted Glowworm in *Robin Goodfellow*, a pantomime that was repeated numerous times that season. She played the Page in Arne's opera *Rosamond* on 8 March 1740; in the title role was Kitty Clive, under whose care Miss Edwards "sprung up," Chetwood reported in his *General History of the Stage* (1749). At Mrs Clive's benefit on 17 March 1740, Miss Edwards sang "Would you taste the noon-tide air," a song from *Comus*, which she repeated several times that season. She played Milcha (with the original songs) in *The Tempest* on 14 May.

In the fall of 1740 she reappeared in performances of *Robin Goodfellow* at Drury Lane. More significantly, she sang Clomiri in the premiere of Handel's *Hymen* at Lincoln's Inn Fields Theatre on 22 November 1740, and on 10 January 1741 at the same place sang Achille in the premiere of that composer's *Deidamia*. It is suggested by Deutsch that Miss Edwards sang the soprano songs of Cloris and Eurilla in Handel's *Acis and Galatea* on 28 February 1741; she may also have sung a soprano part in *L'allegro* on 31 January. Back at Drury Lane on 14 March 1741 for Mrs Clive's benefit, she sang favorite airs from *L'allegro*. On 24 March she again played the Page in *Rosamond* and on 24 April 1741 she sang for the benefit of Harper and Raftor.

Miss Edwards's Drury Lane appearances in 1741–42 seem to have been limited to singing in Italian and English for Mrs Clive's benefit on 8 March and a performance as Juno in Arne's *The Judgment of Paris* on 12 March 1742. In 1742–43 she played Sabrina in *Comus* for Mrs Clive's benefit on 8 March 1743 and sang on 14 March and 6 May at Drury Lane. That season she sang as a Philistine Woman in the first presentation of Handel's *Samson* at Covent Garden Theatre on 18 February 1743, and she may have sung at that theatre a month later, on 23 March, when the first London performance of the *Messiah* was offered.

Next Miss Edwards was an occasional performer at Covent Garden for several seasons, making her acting debut there, as Jessica in *The Merchant of Venice*, on 14 March 1744. With Mrs Clive she sang "My faith and truth," a duet from *Samson*, on 2 April 1744, a selection they repeated on 28 April. At the Crown and Anchor Tavern in the Strand on 21 March

1744, Miss Edwards sang with Mrs Clive, Beard, and Savage in De Fesch's new serenata, *Love and Friendship*. In 1744–45 she sang for Mills's benefit at the Haymarket on 11 December, and at Covent Garden she performed a similar service for Mrs Clive's benefit on 14 March 1745, sang in Lampe's *Joseph* on 3 April, offered a duet with Beard on 20 April, and played Polly in *The Beggar's Opera* for the first time on 29 May 1745, for a benefit she shared with Raftor.

In 1745–46 Miss Edwards was engaged at Drury Lane, and her acting appearances became more frequent, beginning on 30 November 1745 as Polly. She also played Miranda in *The Tempest*, Corinna in *The Confederacy*, Amoret in *Harlequin Incendiary*, Flavia in *The Comical Lovers*, Miranda in *The She Gallant*, Martha in *The Scornful Lady*, Isabel in *The Double Disappointment*, Jessica in *The Merchant of Venice*, Sabrina in *Comus*, Clorinda in *Love and Friendship*, Desdemona in *Othello*, a role in *The Jovial Crew* (for her benefit on 15 April 1746), Ariadne in *The Sea Voyage*, and the Goddess Hecate in *The Amorous Goddess*. It was in the last-named piece on 25 April 1746 (when she also acted Martha in *The Scornful Lady*) that she was last advertised as Miss Edwards. She seems not to have played for several weeks, and then on 19 May 1746, having married the actor Thomas Mozeen in the interim, she acted Miranda in *The Tempest*, now billed as Mrs Mozeen.

Soon after, the Mozeens left London to play the summer at Jacob's Wells Theatre in Bristol. She sang there for the first time on 2 June 1746, advertised as Mrs Mozeen, late Miss Edwards. She entertained with songs frequently but seems not to have acted until 29 August, when she played Jessica in *The Merchant of Venice*. She was Phillida in *The Double Dealer* on 1 September.

Their Bristol season over on 5 September 1746, the Mozeens returned to Drury Lane, where in 1746–47 Mrs Mozeen added to her repertoire a vocal role in *Macbeth*, Miss Jenny in *The Provok'd Husband*, Araminta in *The Confederacy*, the title role in *Flora*, and Mauxalinda in *The Dragon of Wantley*. These roles, with the addition of Peggy in *The King and the Miller of Mansfield* were her staples in 1747–48 as well. Her performance as Peggy on 2 May 1748 proved to be her last appearance in London, for Garrick, who had become manager at the beginning of that season, did not reengage her or her husband.

Sheridan took them on in 1748–49 at Smock Alley, Dublin, where she made her debut as Celia in *As You Like It* on 3 October 1748 and was seen for two seasons in a number of roles, among which were Polly in *The Beggar's Opera*, Fidelia in *The Foundling*, Lady Percy in *1 Henry IV*, Blanch in *King John*, Jessica in *The Merchant of Venice*, Rose in *The Recruiting Officer*, and Mrs Fainall in *The Way of the World*. On 13 February 1749 she acted Juliet, the first time of her "attempting a Character in Tragedy." On 26 April 1749 she played Maria in *The London Merchant*, and on 27 November 1750 Ophelia. Chetwood praised her assets, including a charming manner and voice, but indicated that her "innate Modesty" handicapped her as an actress. She blushed at the least suggestive joke, "to such a degree," wrote Wilkinson, "as to give the beholder pain for an offence not intended." But, as Joseph Knight wrote cryptically in Thomas Mozeen's notice in *The Dictionary of National Biography*, her bashfulness "was accompanied by no very keen scruples as to her conduct, which was irregular enough to induce Mrs. Clive to withdraw her support."

Though her husband was engaged regularly in London from 1750–51 almost until his death in 1768, Mrs Mozeen passed the rest of her career in the provinces, appearing with the Bath company between 1750 and 1754, then at Belfast from 1754 until she went to Edinburgh in 1758, where she played regularly to 1765. Boswell and Gentleman in their *View of the Edinburgh Theatre* (1759) found her Imoinda in *Oroonoko* "very Delicate and pretty" and her gentle Ophelia "pleasing," but regretted to state that "although we have received much Pleasure from her Singing, in which she greatly excels, yet she has always a Lifelessness and Insipidity about her, that renders her an indifferent Actress." She also acted at Norwich in 1767, perhaps with her husband.

After her husband's death on 28 March 1768, Mrs Mozeen spent the rest of her career, it seems, in Ireland; she was in Parker's company at Belfast in 1768–69; at Newry and Kilkenny also in 1769; at Belfast again in 1772; and at Dublin in 1773, after which time we lose her trace. Her son acted at Belfast in September 1768, but he did not appear in London.

Mozeen, William. *See* MOZEEN, THOMAS.

Mozi, Signor [*fl.* 1767], *singer.*
Sylas Neville heard Signor and Signora Mozi sing at Ranelagh Gardens in 1767.

Mozi, Signora [*fl.* 1767], *singer. See* MOZI, SIGNOR.

Mozon, Mlle [*fl.* 1786–1791], *dancer.*
Mlle Mozon was first noticed in the bills on 24 January 1786 when she danced with Marie Vestris and the two Mlles Simonet, at the King's Theatre in a new *Divertissement Serieux* and a new *Divertissement Villageois*. Those pieces were repeated throughout the season. On 18 February she appeared as Thetis in *Acis and Galatea*. She danced the Mother of Melide in the London premiere of *Le Premier navigateur*, a ballet originally by Gardel but now prepared by Vestris, on 23 March. She performed in D'Egville's new ballet *L'Amour Jardinier* on 1 April. For her benefit on 27 April 1786, when tickets were available from her at No 234, Piccadilly, she offered a pas seul, a pas de quartre with Vestris, Fabiani, and Mlle Baccelli, and *La Provençale* in the new ballet *La Fête Marine*. On 23 May she danced in Giroux's *Les Deux solitaires*.

At the King's again in 1786–87 Mlle Mozon danced in a number of similar ballets. She was not noticed in the bills for several seasons until 26 March 1791, when she danced in *Orpheus and Eurydice*. That season at the King's she also appeared as a Slave in *La Mort d'Hercule*, Bergère Thesalienne in *L'Amadriade*, a country woman in *La Fête du seigneur*, and, for her benefit on 26 May 1761 (when she lived at No 32, St Martin Street, Leicester Fields), a role in *Les Folies d'Espagne*, a pas de trois with the younger Vestris and Mlle Hilligsberg, and a pas de deux with Joubert. Her last London performance we notice was on 28 June 1791 in *La Fête du seigneur*.

Mucklow. *See also* MUTLOW.

Mucklow, Mary. *See* WOOD, MRS CHARLES.

Muffett, Master [*fl.* 1786], *singer.*
At the Windsor Castle Inn, King Street, Hammersmith, on 10 July 1786 Master Muf-

fett made his first appearance in public, singing "Sweet Poll of Plymouth" after Act I of *The Heiress*.

Mugleton, Mr [*fl.* 1728], *boxkeeper.*

The account books for Lincoln's Inn Fields Theatre at Harvard show that for the 24 April 1728 benefit of Hall and Mrs Egleton, Mr Mugleton (or Mugleston) and (Mrs?) S. Mugleton worked as boxkeepers. They were evidently hired for that performance only.

Mugleton, [**Mrs?**] **S.** [*fl.* 1728], *boxkeeper. See* MUGLETON, MR.

Muilment, Michael *d. 1747, dancer.*

Michael Muilment, advertised as "lately arrived from Paris," made his first appearance on the English stage on 18 November 1736 dancing at Drury Lane Theatre. During the rest of the 1736–37 season and until his death in 1747 Muilment's name appeared frequently in the Drury Lane bills as an entr'acte dancer and for parts in masques and pantomimes. His initial season was fairly typical. He appeared in many entr'acte dances that were not given titles, and he usually danced alone. But some dances he was in had names: a *Turkish Dance* with several others, a *Serious Dance* (solo), and a *Dance of Winds* in *The Tempest* with others. His one pantomime part was an Ethiopian in *The Fall of Phaeton*, which he danced first on 7 December 1736. On 28 April 1737 he shared a benefit with Miss Mann.

In the seasons that followed he continued appearing regularly as a soloist and in such entr'acte pieces as a *Grand Ballet*, an *Aethiopian Dance*, a *Moors Dance*, *Les Jardiniers Suédois*, *Shepherds and Shepherdesses*, an allemande with Mlle Chateauneuf, *Pastor Fido*, a *Grand Dance*, and a *Shepherd's Dance*, and he danced in *The Tempest* and *Comus*. The parts he took included Apollo in *Mars and Venus*, a Sea God in *Harlequin Shipwrecked*, Cupid in *The Fortune Tellers*, Thyrsis and Apollo in *The Rural Sports*, a Shepherd in *The Amorous Goddess*.

The benefit bills show that Muilment was living at the Dial and Crown in Castle Street, beside Cranbourn Alley, in April 1739. A year later, when his scholar Master Giller made his first appearance, Muilment was next door to the Golden Star in Greek Street, Soho. By April 1744 he had lodgings next door to Old Slaughter's Coffee House in St Martin's Lane, and by 1746 he was living at (or making tickets available at) the Angel in King Street, Covent Garden.

Muilment's season at Drury Lane in 1741–42 was very light, and he was not there at all in 1742–43. Possibly he returned to France for a visit, but in the summer of 1743 he was at the Aungier Street Theatre in Dublin, advertised on 16 June as just arrived from England. He returned to Drury Lane full time in 1743–44 and continued dancing there to within a month of his death on 2 June 1747 (according to reports in the *General Advertiser* and the Burney papers at the British Library; *The London Stage*, without citing its sources, quotes some newspaper report on 2 June: "Yesterday died Mr Muilment, a Famous Dancer, who has given great entertainment to the town at both theatres; and was much esteem'd by all who knew him personally"). The bills do not show Muilment to have appeared at Covent Garden (the other patent house), though he may well have done so.

On 23 June 1747 administration of the estate of "Michael Mullement" of the parish of St Paul, Covent Garden, was granted to his widow Mary. Muilment (for that was the way his surname regularly appeared on the bills for years) was not buried at St Paul, Covent Garden, though he lived in that parish.

Mulcaster, Robert [*fl.* 1794–1805], *violist, bass player, horn player.*

Doane's *Musical Directory* of 1794 listed Robert Mulcaster Junior, of St Martin-le-Grand, as a performer on the viola, bass, and horn who played for the New Musical Fund, the Handelian Society, and in the oratorios at Westminster Abbey and Drury Lane. He was still a subscriber to the New Musical Fund in 1805.

Mullart, Mr [*fl.* 1757–1758], *See* MULLART, SUSANNA.

Mullart, Susanna, later Mrs Evans *b. 1735, actress.*

Susanna Mullart was baptized at St Paul, Covent Garden, on 5 April 1735, the daughter of the performers William and Elizabeth Mullart. Susanna made her first appearance on any stage at Covent Garden Theatre on 23 May 1740 as Tom Thumb in *The Tragedy of Tragedies*. The occasion was her father's benefit. She acted Tom Thumb again on 7 April 1741, at which time she was on the Covent Garden payroll at 5*s*. daily. On 22 August at Bartholomew Fair she was a Page in *The Modern Pimp*. She tried Falstaff's Page in *2 Henry IV* at Covent Garden on 7 May 1742. After those isolated appearances she was not advertised again until the summer of 1743, when she acted at Jacob's Wells Theatre in Bristol; she was paid 2*s*. for each performance. On 6 February 1746 she played the Page in *The Man of Mode* at Covent Garden, after which she returned to Bristol for the summer session.

Back at Covent Garden in 1746–47 she acted two other juvenile roles, the Page in *The Orphan* and the Duke of York in *Richard III*. Through the middle of the 1761–62 season at Covent Garden Miss Mullart continued performing, gradually moving from children's parts to more mature roles: Robin in *The Merry Wives of Windsor*, Princess Elizabeth in *Vertue Betray'd*, Prince Arthur in *King John*, Fleance in *Macbeth*, Sukey Tawdry in *The Beggar's Opera*, Peggy in *The London Cuckolds*, Mademoiselle in *The Funeral*, an Amazon in *Perseus and Andromeda*, Priss in *The Lying Valet*, Iras in *All for Love*, Phoebe in *As You Like It*, Clara in *The Cheats of Scapin*, Dorcas in *The Sheep Shearing*, Betty in *Flora*, Jessica in *The Merchant of Venice*, Lucinda in *The Conscious Lovers*, a Beggar Woman in *The Jovial Crew*, and Betty in *A Bold Stroke for a Wife*.

She continued performing at Bristol during the summers through 1748 at 2*s*. 6*d*. nightly. At Covent Garden her salary had dropped to 3*s*. 4*d*. daily by 22 September 1760. Miss Mullart was at Liverpool for a time in 1760. In the middle of the 1761–62 season she suddenly began calling herself Mrs Evans. A manuscript note by the prompter Hopkins on 28 December 1761 explained: "Miss Susan Mullart, since called Mrs. Evans. It is said that Mr. Ridout very artfully seduced her, and that Proofs of their Intimacy appearing, Miss Mullart assumed the name of Mrs. Evans, and gave out that she had been privately married." Evidently she was undecided what to call herself in 1761. *The London Stage* shows that on 2 and 20 April and on 30 December she was advertised as Mrs Evans, yet between 16 September

and 28 December she was cited as Miss Mullart. From January 1762 through November 1774 she was advertised as Mrs Evans (the Mr Evans listed in *The London Stage* as playing a Beggarwoman in *The Jovial Crew* on 1 November 1774 was surely Mrs Evans).

As Mrs Evans she continued in the same roles as earlier, adding such new ones as Simple in *The Merry Wives of Windsor*, Philotis in *The Frenchify'd Lady Never in Paris*, Mrs Vixen in *The Beggar's Opera*, Flametta in *A Duke and No Duke*, Corinna in *The Citizen*, a Barmaid in *The Fair Quaker of Deal*, Charlotte in *The Apprentice*, Peggy in *The Miller of Mansfield*, Wheedle in *The Miser*, and Honoria in *Love Makes a Man*. After November 1774 Susanna Evans seems to have left the stage. She was left 10 guineas in the will of the actress Elizabeth Bennett, which was signed on 24 August 1791 and proved the following 20 September.

Mullart, William *d. 1742. actor, singer.*

The first London appearance of William Mullart may have been at Bartholomew Fair on 23 August 1729, when he acted Holofernes in *The Seige of Bethulia*. He repeated the role at Southwark Fair on 15 September and also played Chaunter in *The Beggar's Wedding*. In 1729–30 he performed regularly at the Haymarket Theatre, appearing first as Rovewell in *Love and Revenge* on 12 November 1729. He then played Chaunter again, Mopsus in *Damon and Phillida*, the title part in *Hurlothrumbo*, a role in *The Village Opera*, Alvarez in *Fatal Love*, Sullen and Aimwell in *The Stratagem*, a part in *The Cheshire Comicks*, Lucy in *The Metamorphosis of the Beggar's Opera*, Loadum in *The Half Pay Officers*, Luckless in *The Author's Farce*, Pyrrhus in *The Rival Father*, King Arthur in *Tom Thumb*, Ramble in *Rape upon Rape*, Brabantio in *Othello*, and Lothario in *The Fair Penitent*.

At Tottenham Court on 1 August 1730 Mullart was the Rum Duke in *The Rum Duke and the Queer Duke*; at Bartholomew Fair on 22 August he had the title role in *Scipio's Triumph*; and at Southwark Fair on 9 September he played Achmet in *Amurath*.

Mullart was again at the Haymarket in 1730–31, acting such new characters as the Governor in *Love Makes a Man*, Carlos in *The False Count*, Clerimont in *The Generous Freemason*, Tom in *The Jealous Taylor*, Manly in *The Provok'd Husband*, Scandal in *Love for Love*, Robin in *The*

Welch Opera, and Mortimer in *The Fall of Mortimer*. On 21 July 1731, when he was playing Mortimer, the constables came to the theatre with a warrant to arrest the players because of some political allusions that had been added to the text, but, according to a clipping transcribed by Latreille, all escaped. That season Mullart shared a benefit with his wife on 19 May 1731.

Mullart made appearances at Bartholomew and Southwark fairs in August and September 1731, appearing as the Emperor in *Guy, Earl of Warwick*, Sir John in *The Devil to Pay*, and Factor in *Whittington*. He and his wife had engagements at Drury Lane Theatre in 1731–32, though Mullart's name did not appear in casts until 1 January 1732, when he acted the Second Buyer in *The Lottery*. Then he played Porter in *The Modern Husband*, Drawcansir in *The Rehearsal*, Arthur in *The Tragedy of Tragedies*, a Servant in *The Devil to Pay*, Captain Bilkum in *The Covent Garden Tragedy*, James in *The Mock Doctor*, and Lockit in *The Beggar's Opera*. He returned to Bartholomew Fair in August to take an unnamed role in *The Envious Statesman*.

He remained at Drury Lane through the 1733–34 season, adding to his repertoire such parts as Dervise in *Tamerlane*, the Shoemaker in *The Relapse*, the Shoemaker in *The Man of Mode*, a Watchman in *The Provok'd Wife*, Wrangle in *Betty*, Alonzo in *Rule a Wife and Have a Wife*, Bubbleboy and the Lawyer in *The Miser*, Justice Mittimus in *The Harlot's Progress*, Snap in *The Imaginary Cuckolds*, Leontine in *Theodosius*, Amor in *Damon and Daphne*, Whisper in *The Busy Body*, Roger in *Aesop*, Jobson in *The Devil to Pay*, the Mayor in *Richard III*, Bullock in *The Recruiting Officer*, an Italian Bravo in *Cephalus and Procris*, Gonzalo and a Waterman in *The Tempest*, Sancho in *Love Makes a Man*, Toby in *The Livery Rake*, an Old Woman in *Cupid and Psyche*, Gripe in *The Confederacy*, and Campeius in *Henry VIII*.

The summer of 1733 found Mullart at Covent Garden Theatre. He played Vulcan in *Momus Turn'd Fabulist* on 26 June, Maherbal in *Sophonisba* on 6 July, Truncheon in *The Stage Mutineers* on 27 June, Grimbald in *The Fancy'd Queen* on 14 August, and Tarquin in *The Tuscan Treaty* on 20 August. In the middle of his stay there he went over to the Haymarket, on 26 July, to act a part in *The Amorous Lady*. At

Bartholomew Fair in August he played Lysimachus in *Love and Jealousy*. Similarly, between March and August 1734 Mullart made isolated appearances elsewhere: at Drury Lane on 30 March as Bernard in *The Country House*, at the Haymarket on 5 April as Sancho in *Don Quixote in England*, at Lincoln's Inn Fields Theatre on 15 April (when he also acted at Drury Lane) as James in *The Miser* (he was in the mainpiece at one house and the afterpiece at the other), at Lincoln's Inn Fields on 9 and 23 May as Cacafogo in *Rule a Wife and Have a Wife* and Lockit in *The Beggar's Opera* respectively, at the Haymarket on 16 and 21 August as Bonniface in *The Beaux' Stratagem* and Sancho in *Don Quixote in England* respectively, and at Bartholomew Fair on 24 August and 2 September as the Boatswain's Mate in *The Barren Island*.

For the 1734–35 season Mullart switched to John Rich's troupe at Covent Garden, and there he remained until his death in 1742, making, as before, occasional appearances elsewhere. Some of his new parts at Covent Garden were the Second Gravedigger in *Hamlet* (for his first appearance on 18 September 1734), Sly in *Love's Last Shift*, Mat in *The Beggar's Opera*, Doodle in *The London Cuckolds*, Woodcock in *Tunbridge Walks*, Quack in *The Country Wife*, a Carrier in *1 Henry IV*, Old Hob in *Flora*, Wilful in *The Double Gallant*, a Savoyard in *The Rape of Proserpine*, Poundage in *The Provok'd Husband*, Sir Roger in *The Fond Husband*, Sir Peter in *The Amorous Widow*, Petulant in *The Plain Dealer*, Sir Thomas in *The Gamester*, Bluff in *The Old Bachelor*, Hackum in *The Squire of Alsatia*, Antonio in *Love Makes a Man*, Kite in *The Recruiting Officer*, Vandunk in *The Royal Merchant*, Sir Joslin in *She Wou'd if She Cou'd*, a Witch in *Macbeth*, Caius in *The Merry Wives of Windsor*, Driver in *Oroonoko*, Sir Tunbelly in *The Relapse*, Swagger in *The Funeral*, Morecraft in *The Scornful Lady*, Ajax in *Achilles*, Abel in *The Committee*, Austria in *King John*, Blunder in *The Honest Yorkshireman*, Humphrey in *The Conscious Lovers*, Bulcalf in *2 Henry IV*, Bates in *Henry V*, Carbuncle in *The Country Lasses*, Jolt in *The Stage Coach*, Harry in *The Mock Doctor*, Felix in *The Mistake*, Balderdash in *The Twin Rivals*, the Constable in *The Constant Couple*, Sassafras in *Greenwich Park*, the Player King in *Hamlet*, Lopez in *The Pilgrim*, and Sir Harry in *The Tender Husband*.

At Lincoln's Inn Fields between 1 October

1734 and 26 June 1737 Mullart was seen in such parts as Sancho Panza in *Don Quixote in England*, Kite in *The Recruiting Officer*, Sly in *Love's Last Shift*, Barnwell in *The London Merchant*, the title part in *Squire Basinghall*, Cokes in *Bartholomew Fair*, Poundage in *The Provok'd Husband*, Sir Jealous in *The Busy Body*, Possum in *Three Hours after Marriage*, and Sir Christopher Swash in *The Woman Captain*.

At Bartholomew Fair on 23 August 1736 and 22 August 1741 he acted Grey Goose in *The Modern Pimp*. *The London Stage* has him playing Duart in *Love Makes a Man* at Goodman's Fields on 18 November 1740, but he is also listed for Harry in *The Mock Doctor* and Humphrey in *The Conscious Lovers* at Covent Garden that evening. At least one of those billings must be in error; perhaps it was the bill for Goodman's Fields, for Duart was not Mullart's usual role in *Love Makes a Man*.

There is also some confusion in *The London Stage* concerning Mullart's last appearance. Reed in his "Notitia Dramatica" quotes a newspaper notice dated 24 September 1742 saying "Mr Mullart of Cov: Garden Theatre Died." The Player King in *Hamlet* at Covent Garden on 20 May 1742 should have been his last performance, and Latreille noted that Mullart's name disappeared from the bills after 1741–42. Yet *The London Stage* has Mullart playing Pistol in *The Merry Wives of Windsor* at Covent Garden on 27 January, 22 February, and 22 March 1743. Caius was Mullart's usual role in that comedy; James played Pistol in the 1741–42 season and again in 1743–44, so the references to Mullart in the spring of 1743 are surely mistakes.

Little else is known of Mullart. He and his wife had a daughter Susanna (b. 1735) who acted from 1740 through 1774. The Mullarts are known to have lived in Crown Court, Russell Street, Covent Garden in 1736, and they were both paid £86 for the 1735–36 season. Mullart's salary at Covent Garden in 1740–41 was 5s. daily. Mrs. Mullart died in 1745 leaving two orphan children, one presumably being Susanna. They were given a charity benefit at Covent Garden on 15 April 1749.

Mullart, Mrs William, Elizabeth *d.*
1745, actress, singer.

Elizabeth Mullart, the wife of the actor William Mullart, was first noticed in London casts when she played Bellamira in *Love and Revenge* at the Haymarket Theatre on 12 November 1729. During the rest of the 1729–30 season she was seen as Mrs Chaunter in *The Beggar's Wedding*, Cadamore in *Hurlothrumbo*, a major character in *The Village Opera*, Ismena in *Fatal Love*, Mrs Sullen in *The Stratagem*, a part in *The Cheshire Comics*, Lockit in *The Metamorphosis of the Beggar's Opera*, Jane in *Half Pay Officers*, the Goddess of Nonsense in *The Author's Farce*, Polyxena in *The Rival Father*, Queen Dollalolla and Mrs Moneywood in *Tom Thumb*, Hilaret in *Rape Upon Rape* (and she spoke the epilogue), Emilia in *Othello*, and Calista in *The Fair Penitent*. On 1 August 1730 at Tottenham Court Mrs Mullart was in *The Rum Duke and the Queer Duke* and played the Goddess of Nonsense in *Punch's Oratory*. At Bartholomew Fair three weeks later she was Almeyda in *Scipio's Triumph*, and on 4 September at that Fair she played Dollalolla in *Tom Thumb*.

She was again at the Haymarket in 1730–31, adding to her repertoire such characters as Tippet in *The Beggar's Wedding*, Elvira in *Love Makes a Man*, Oriana in *The Inconstant*, Belinda in *Tunbridge Walks*, Julia in *The False Count*, Desdemona in *Othello*, Elvira in *The Spanish Fryar*, Lady Townly in *The Provok'd Husband*, Angelica in *Love for Love*, Susan in *The Welch Opera*, and Isabella in *The Fall of Mortimer* (and she spoke the epilogue). She was at both Bartholomew and Southwark fairs in August and September 1731, playing the Empress in *Guy, Earl of Warwick*, Lady Loverule in *The Devil to Pay*, and Mrs Grace in *Whittington*.

From 30 March 1732 through the 1733–34 season Mrs Mullart was a member of the Drury Lane company. Her first part was Mrs Day in *The Committee*, after which she was seen in such new roles as Amaryllis in *The Rehearsal*, Lady Lurewell in *The Devil to Pay*, Stormandra in *The Covent Garden Tragedy*, Mrs Peachum in *The Beggar's Opera*, Dol Common in *The Alchemist*, the Nurse in *The Relapse*, Goody Stubble in *Betty*, Silvia in *The Double Gallant*, Charlotte in *The Mock Doctor*, Lady Wishfort in *The Way of the World*, Wheedle in *The Miser*, Honoria in *Love Makes a Man*, Lady Darling in *The Constant Couple*, Isabella in *The Conscious Lovers*, Patch in *The Busy Body*, Mrs Fruitful in *Aesop*, the Duchess of York in *Richard III*, Lucy in *The Recruiting Officer*, the Countess of Nottingham in *The Unhappy Favorite*, Aurora in *Cephalus and Procris*, Melissa in *Timon of Athens*, Pulcheria in *Theodosius*, Widow Lackit in *Oroonoko*, and Lady Graveairs in *The Careless Husband*.

Mrs Mullart performed at Bartholomew Fair in August of 1732, 1733, and 1734, and she made isolated appearances at Covent Garden, the Haymarket, and Lincoln's Inn Fields. At Covent Garden on 6 July 1733 she acted Rezembe in *Sophonisba* and Lady Loverule in *The Devil to Pay*; on 26 July she had a part in *The Amorous Lady* at the Haymarket; and she donned men's clothes to act Aruns in *The Tuscan Treaty* at Covent Garden on 20 August. At Lincoln's Inn Fields Mrs Mullart played Wheedle in *The Miser* on 15 April 1734 and Lady Manlove in *The School Boy* and Mrs Peachum in *The Beggar's Opera* on 23 May; at the Haymarket she appeared as Dorinda in *The Beaux' Stratagem* on 16 August. According to *The London Stage*, on 2 September 1734 she played Mrs Sullen in *The Beaux' Stratagem* at Hampstead and also appeared at Bartholomew Fair as Maria in *Don John*, possibly Clarinda in *The Barren Island*, and the Farrier's Wife in *The Farrier Nick'd*. On 1 October at Lincoln's Inn Fields she was Dorothea in *Don Quixote in England*.

Mrs Mullart joined John Rich's troupe in the fall of 1734, appearing first at Covent Garden on 7 October as Lady Wishfort in *The Way of the World*. At Covent Garden in 1735–36 Mrs Mullart was earning £86, for which she acted 172 days. Except for some performances with other groups, she remained at Covent Garden until her death in 1745. Some of her new parts were Widow Blackacre in *The Plain Dealer*, Flora in *The Wonder*, Wishwell in *The Double Gallant*, Jenny in *The Beggar's Opera*, Lady Laycock in *The Amorous Widow*, Abigail in *The Drummer*, Sysigambis in *The Rival Queens*, Mlle D'Epingle in *The Funeral*, Mrs Quickly in *The Merry Wives of Windsor*, Lady Plyant in *The Double Dealer*, Cleone in *The Distrest Mother*, Lady Fidget and Alithea in *The Country Wife*, Goneril and Regan in *King Lear*, Lady Woudbe in *Volpone*, Abigail in *The Scornful Lady*, Mrs Amlet in *The Confederacy*, Lady Faulconbridge in *King John*, Margaret in *Much Ado about Nothing*, Jenny in *The Fair Quaker of Deal*, Altea in *Rule a Wife and Have a Wife*, Trusty in *The Provok'd Husband*, Lucy in *The Old Bachelor*, the Hostess in *Henry V*, Moll Buxom in *Don Quixote*, Dolly in *The Stage Coach*, Millwood in *The London Merchant*, Huncamunca in *The Tragedy of Tragedies*, the Player Queen in *Hamlet*, Leonora in *The Mourning Bride*, Moretta in *The Rover*, and Francisca in *Measure for Measure*. Her last appearance at Covent Garden seems to have been on 28 March 1745, when she acted Mrs Peachum in *The Beggar's Opera*.

During her years at Covent Garden Mrs Mullart made appearances elsewhere. From 11 July through 5 September 1735 she acted at Lincoln's Inn Fields, appearing as Dorcas in *The Mock Doctor*, Darneit in *Squire Basinghall*, Fanny Wellplot in *Politicks on Both Sides*, Lavinia in *Caius Marius*, Loveit in *Bartholomew Fair*, Louisa in *Love Makes a Man*, Lucy in *The Beggar's Opera*, Colombine in *The Carnival*, and some of her old roles. She was seen at that house again on 2 April 1736 as Widow Lackit in *Oroonoko*, on 18 October 1736 as Lady Fidget in *The Country Wife*, and in June 1737 as Mrs Peachum in *The Beggar's Opera*, Sarsnet in *Three Hours after Marriage*, and Melinda in *The Recruiting Officer*. At Bartholomew Fair on 22 August 1741 she acted the lead in *Fair Rosamond*. In February 1743 at Southwark Mrs Mullart played Angelica in *Love for Love*, Miranda in *The Busy Body* and Hob's Mother in *Flora*. In the summer of 1743 she performed at the Jacob's Wells Theatre in Bristol. At May Fair in June 1744 she acted Peggy in *The Miller of Mansfield*, Lady Betty in *The Careless Husband*, and some of her old roles.

Her husband William Mullart died in 1742. Elizabeth Mullart died in May 1745; she was buried at Greenwich on the fourteenth.

Several entries in the registers of St Paul, Covent Garden, concern a William and Elizabeth Mullart, and since many performers belonged to that church, one is tempted to accept the references as being to our subject and her husband. But the baptismal notices sometimes suggest birth dates for children of William and Elizabeth Mullart that do not fit with Mrs Mullart's acting schedule. On 30 October 1732 Elizabeth, daughter of William and Elizabeth Mullart, was baptized. Our actress had been busy performing at Drury Lane throughout August and on 19 September; then she did not act until 7 November; her schedule would have allowed for the birth of a child, perhaps in mid-October. A daughter Christiana was baptized on 13 February 1733, only three and a half months after the baptism of the Mullarts' daughter Elizabeth. Were there two different

Mullart families, or were either Elizabeth or Christiana not infants when they were christened? If our actress was the mother of Christiana, she could have given birth to a child shortly before 13 February 1733, for though she had a busy acting schedule from 7 November 1732 through May 1733, she had time off between 20 December 1732 and 9 January 1733. Christiana Mullart was buried on 1 September 1735. The actress Elizabeth Mullart had performed regularly in August and, indeed, acted on 2 September.

On 10 March 1735 John, the son of William Mullart (no wife mentioned) was buried. On 5 April 1735 Susanna, the daughter of William and Elizabeth Mullart was christened. The actress Elizabeth Mullart did not perform between mid-February and 7 April. Augusta, the daughter of William Mullart, was buried on 11 April 1740. The actress Mrs Mullart did not perform between 27 March and 16 April. William Mullart was cited as being from the parish of St Martin-in-the-Fields.

Though it is conceivable that the Mullarts who were performers were in fact the Mullarts cited in the parish registers, more evidence is needed to make a certain identification.

Mullement. *See* MUILMENT.

Mullens, Mr ₁*fl. 1781–1782*₁, *scene painter.*
The Drury Lane treasurer's book at the Folger Shakespeare Library cites Mr Mullens as assistant painter at that theatre from February 1781 to March 1782.

Müller *See also* MILLER..

Muller, Mr ₁*fl. 1767*₁, *musician.*
Mr Muller was on the payroll at Covent Garden Theatre as of 14 September 1767 at a daily salary of 5s. He was listed as a member of the orchestra.

Müller, Christian Friedrich *1752–1809, violinist, composer.*
According to van der Straeten in his *History of the Violin*, Christian Friedrich Müller was born in Rheinsberg on 29 December 1752 (Grove does not list him in the large Müller family of string players). Müller was a pupil of

Salomon and served for a while in the chapel of Prince Henry of Prussia. He toured in 1778 with Madame Mara, and at some point lured Caroline Friderike Walther, a singer, away from her husband and married her. They performed in Stockholm; then, in 1782, says van der Straeten, they appeared in England, though we have found no specific performance dates for them in London. In 1783 they returned to Stockholm for a ten-year engagement. Müller's wife left him in the 1790s; she went to Copenhagen and he remained in Stockholm. Christian visited St Petersburg in 1801 and then returned to Stockholm, where he died in 1809. He composed a number of violin solos.

Müller, Frau Christian Friedrich, formerly Caroline Friderike Walther ₁*fl. 1778–c. 1795*₁, *singer. See* MÜLLER, CHRISTIAN.

Mullet. *See* MULLART.

Mulliner, Mr ₁*fl. 1754*₁, *actor.*
Mr Mulliner played the Clown in an *Aethiopian Concert* at the Haymarket Theatre on 28 November 1754. He shared a benefit there on 9 December.

Mullins. *See* MULLENS.

Mumfert. *See* MOUNTFORT.

Mumford, Miss ₁*fl. 1734*₁, *actress.*
Miss Mumford played Nell in a single performance of *The Miser* at the James Street playhouse on 29 May 1734.

Mumford, Daniel ₁*fl. 1794–1805*₁, *singer?*
Doane's *Musical Directory* of 1794 listed Daniel Mumford, of Greville Street, Brook's Market, Holborn, as an alto (singer?) who performed for the New Musical Fund, Handelian Society, and in the oratorios at Westminster Abbey and Drury Lane. Mumford was a member of the Court of Assistants of the New Musical Fund in 1805.

Mumford, Francis ₁*fl. 1794–1805*₁, *violinist, violist.*
Doane's *Musical Directory* of 1794 listed Francis Mumford of Bath as a violinist and

violist who played for the New Musical Fund. He was still a subscriber to the New Musical Fund in 1805.

Mumfort. *See* MOUNTFORT.

Munck, Mr ₍*fl. 1758*₎, *singer.*
Mr Munck sang in the *Messiah* at the Chapel of the Foundling Hospital on 27 April 1758 for 10s. 6d. Possibly he should be identified as the organist Monck.

Munday, Mr ₍*fl. 1794–1811*₎, *door-keeper.*
In the Drury Lane accounts Mr Munday (or Monday, Mundy) was cited as a stage door-keeper as early as 14 April 1794. On that date he and Beaumont were paid £1 16s. for twelve nights. Munday was last mentioned in the books in 1810–11.

Munday, Mrs. *See* MAHON, MISS.

Munden, Joseph Shepherd *1758–1832*, *actor, singer, manager.*
Joseph Shepherd Munden was born in 1758 in Brook's Market, Leather Lane, Holborn, where his father was a poulterer. His mother, Alice Munden, was still alive when Joseph made his will in 1810, but his father died when our subject was a small lad. At the age of 12 Munden was placed with an apothecary. Soon after, however, his good penmanship commended him for a position with an attorney in New Inn, and subsequently he was apprenticed to Mr Druce, a law stationer at Staples Inn Gate. It was said that Munden's affectations of gentility vexed Druce, so Munden quit that position and went to work for a lawyer in the Borough, with whom he remained for about a year. In his manuscript additions to Roach's *Green Room* (1796) in the British Library, Reed claimed that Druce had told him on 29 May 1800 that Munden had been his apprentice, "but he gave up his indentures on his neglecting his business."

Contemporary memoirs of Munden vary in the details of his earliest theatrical activities in the provinces. His first venture on the stage came either at Rochdale or Liverpool about 1775. Evidently he spent about two years at

Harvard Theatre Collection

JOSEPH S. MUNDEN
engraving by S. W. Reynolds, after Opie

the latter city, acting supernumerary roles for 18 d. per week and supporting himself otherwise as a scrivener in the office of the town clerk. He played with strollers at Rochdale, Chester, Leatherhead, Wallingford, Windsor, and Colnbrook, and no doubt in other places, before moving on to London.

Munden's first appearance on the London stage seems to have occurred on 11 January 1779 at the Haymarket Theatre, a night when that theatre was taken over by a group of actors from the north for specially-licensed performances of *The Gentle Shepherd* and *The Students*. Munden's name appeared for the role of Andrew in the latter piece. He was not seen again in London until the next autumn, when he returned to the Haymarket on 13 October 1779 to act Sir Philip Modelove in *A Bold Stroke for a Wife* and a character in *The She Gallant* for a specially-licensed benefit for Massey. His subsequent roles at the Haymarket that season included a part in *The Touchstone of Invention*, a piece altered by John Brownsmith from Otway's *The Soldier's Fortune*, on 18 October, Bardolph in *Falstaff's Wedding* and Staytape in *The Rival Milliners* on 27 December, Timothy in *The Modish Wife* and Caveat in *Wit's Last Stake* on 3 January 1780, and Andrew in *The Students* on 17 January 1780.

After those appearances at the Haymarket, Munden receded into the provinces for a decade. He was at Canterbury in 1780 under Hurst, acting the original Faddle in Mrs Burgess's comedy *The Oaks; or, The Beauties of Canterbury*. After playing some of the southern towns he went north to join the Austin and Whitlock Company, with whom he performed at Newcastle, Lancaster, Preston, Whitehaven, Sheffield, Manchester, and other places. When Austin retired in 1789, Munden obtained his share and joined Whitlock in the management of the company's circuit. That year they opened a new theatre royal in Moseley Street, Newcastle upon Tyne, which was built for about £6800 by subscription of a hundred people. Munden tired of management within 15 months and disposed of his moiety to his partner Whitlock.

During his ten years in the provinces Munden developed a reputation in leading comic business, so upon Edwin's death in 1790 he was engaged at Covent Garden Theatre, at a salary of £6 per week. In London, Munden first lived in Portugal Street, Clare Market, and then in Catherine Street, the Strand.

Munden made his Covent Garden debut on 2 December 1790, as Sir Francis Gripe in *The Busy Body* and Jemmy Jumps in *The Farmer*. The critic "Anthony Pasquin" compared him unfavorably with Quick and with Edwin, the recently deceased burletta favorite, quipping that he equaled "Neither the Quick nor the dead." Munden's debut, nevertheless, was successful. The *World* of 3 December reported his person "rather under the middle size, his figure good, his voice powerful and melodious, and his articulation the clearest and most rapid we ever witnessed." The *Gazetteer* of that date was pleased that "Without the aid of grimace or buffoonery, he gave all the effect to the part that the author intended, and in his general stile of playing he seems to have studied nature more than any living model."

After several repetitions as Jemmy Jumps, Munden's next character was Don Louis in *Love Makes a Man* on 10 December 1790. Subse-

quently that season he was seen as Meadows in *The Deaf Lover*, Quidnunc in *The Upholsterer*, the original Samuel Sheepy in Holcroft's *The School for Arrogance* on 4 February 1791, Lazarillo in *Two Strings to Your Bow*, the original Frank in O'Keeffe's *Modern Antiques* on 14 March 1791, Lovell in *High Life below Stairs*, the original Ephraim Smooth in O'Keeffe's *Wild Oats* on 16 April 1791, Cassander in *Alexander the Little*, Pedrillo in *The Castle of Andalusia*, Sir David Drowsey in *The Dreamer Awake*, Tipple in *The Flitch of Bacon*, Young Quiz in *The Union*, an unspecified character in *Primrose Green*, a Countryman in *The Cottage Maid*, and Camillo in *Double Falsehood*. For his benefit on 19 May 1791, when tickets could be had of Munden at No 8, Portsmouth Street, Lincoln's Inn Fields, he acted Darly in *Love in a Camp* and Caleb in *He Wou'd be a Soldier*; tickets receipts were £334 17s.

Munden returned to Covent Garden in 1791–92, still earning £6 per week, and added to his expanding repertoire Ennui in *The Dramatist*, Sir Troubadour in *The Crusade*, a Witch in *Macbeth*, a Pedlar in *Oscar and Malvina*, Lord Jargon in *Notoriety*, Sebastian in *The Midnight Hour*, a Carrier in *1 Henry IV*, Lopez in *Lover's Quarrels*, Mustapha in *A Day in Turkey*, Tipy Bob in *Blue-Beard*, Grub in *The Magician No Conjuror*, Sam Stern in *The Positive Man*, Proteus in *The Mermaid*, Nicholas in *Fashionable Levities*, Old Shepherd in *A Peep behind the Curtain*, Darif in *Zelma*, Aircastle in *The Cozeners*, Closefist in *The Intrigues of a Morning*, Taylor in *Catherine and Petruchio*, and a character in *A Cure for a Coxcomb*. He made an especially good impression as Old Dornton in the premiere of Holcroft's comedy *The Road to Ruin* on 18 February 1792, a role he accepted with some reluctance because Silkey, his original assignment, was taken over by Quick. He acted David in *The Rivals* on 2 May 1792. For his benefit on 10 May (when tickets were available from him at No 15, Catherine Street, and he profited by £415, less £105 house charges), Munden acted Stave in the premiere of Hurlstone's comic opera *Just in Time* and also played Meadows in *The Deaf Lover*. That season he also participated in some private theatricals at Wargrave.

The author of *The Children of Thespis* in 1792 observed that the actor's worth at Covent Garden was not yet appreciated:

Yet eventual honors shall make this wight dear,
What PALMER's *at* Drury *shall* MUNDEN *be here;*
More general talents were scarce ever seen,
T'embellish th'eccentric—the solemn—the mean.
His Deaf Love's *a chief, with the best should be*
        class'd,
His Dornton's *a feat that's been seldom surpassed.*

After playing at Edinburgh and Liverpool in the summer of 1792, Munden began his third season at Covent Garden by acting Dornton in *The Road to Ruin*, a role that served as a favorite throughout his career, on 17 September 1792. On 5 November he played Polonius for the first time, and the *Morning Herald* commended him for rescuing the character "from the buffoonery" by which it had traditionally been disgraced. That part also became one of his finest, later drawing from Byron the remark that Polonius would die with Munden as Lady Macbeth had died with Mrs Siddons. Among his many characters that season were Sir Anthony Absolute in *The Rivals* on 7 November 1792, Don Jerome in *The Duenna* on 22 December, and Hardcastle in *She Stoops to Conquer* on 2 January 1793. When Follett became injured and could not play Clodpole the Clown in the premiere of *Harlequin's Museum; or, Mother Shipton Triumphant* on 20 December 1792, Munden substituted for him (though Follett's name appeared in the bills), thereby, according to the *Thespian Magazine* of February 1793, "giving the Public an additional proof of the versatility of his talents." By 26 December, however, Follett was sufficiently recovered, so Munden was relegated to Punch, a principal vocal character, for the numerous performances of that pantomime during the remainder of the season. At the time of his benefit on 3 May 1793 his address was No 6, Frith Street, Soho, a street inhabited by many performers. That night, when gross receipts were a substantial £448 17s. 6d., Munden appeared as Dornton, Lazarillo in *Two Strings to Your Bow*, and Robin Redhead in the first performance of *To Arms; or, The British Recruit*, a musical interlude by Hurlstone.

That year, 1793, several of Shield's songs were published as sung by Munden, including *A Glass is good and a Lass is good, Gad a merch* (from *The Farmer*); the latter was printed in the *Hibernian Magazine* in July 1793. The *Thespian Magazine* reported that Munden made his debut at Manchester on 12 July 1793, but that report must be erroneous, for the actor seems still to have been in Ireland, which he had set out for on 31 May 1793. He proved very successful at the Crow Street Theatre, Dublin, in June and July. On 6 September 1793 he was acting at Cork, whence he made a hasty return to London to appear as Ephraim Smooth in *Wild Oats* and Peregrine Forrester in *Hartford Bridge* on 16 September, the opening night of the season at Covent Garden.

Except for his frequent summer tours into the provinces and occasional appearances at the Haymarket Theatre, Munden remained at Covent Garden until 1811, appearing in over 200 (perhaps even 300) roles, including principals in numerous pieces by Colman, Reynolds, Morton, and other concocters of light entertainment. Among those roles in which he was seen before the turn of the century were Peachum in *The Beggar's Opera*, Skirmish in *The Deserter*, Russet in *The Jealous Husband*, Arthur in *Tom Thumb*, Flush in *The Rage*, Piccaroon in *Arrived at Portsmouth*, Dromio of Syracuse in *The Comedy of Errors*, the Town Clerk in *Much Ado about Nothing*, Oakland in *Netley Abbey*, Cimberton in *The Conscious Lovers*, Valoury in *The Mysteries of the Castle*, Sir Francis Wronghead in *The Provok'd Husband*, Antonio in *The Follies of a Day*, Thomas in *The Irish Widow*, Nipperkin in *The Rival Soldiers*, Jobson in *The Devil to Pay*, Autolicus in *The Winter's Tale*, Squire Tallyho in *Fontainbleau*, Zarno in *Zorinski*, Frost in *The Irishman in London*, Lord Scratch in *The Dramatist*, Sir Charles Clackit in *The Guardian*, Jeremy Maythorn in *The Italian Villagers*, Sir Peter Teazle in *The School for Scandal*, Sir Harry Sycamore in *The Maid of the Mill*, Scrub in *The Beaux' Stratagem*, Justice Clement in *Every Man in his Humour*, Dogberry in *Much Ado about Nothing*, Lovel in *High Life below Stairs*, Colonel Oldboy in *Lionel and Clarissa*, Chillingo in *Ramah Droog*, Sir Fretful Plagiary in *The Critic*, and Sir Walter Waring in *The Woodman*.

Among Munden's original roles at Covent Garden during that period were Mr Craig Campbell in Holcroft's *Love's Frailties* on 5 February 1794, Mr Sidney in Bate's *The Travellers in Switzerland* on 22 February 1794, Sir Hans Burgess in O'Keeffe's *Life's Vagaries* on 19 March 1795, Project in Reynolds's *Speculation* on 7 November 1795, Caustic in Morton's *The Way to Get Married* on 23 January 1796, Brummagem in Hoare's *Lock and Key* on 2 February 1796, Old Testy in Holman's *Abroad and at Home* on 19 November 1796, Old Rapid in Morton's *A Cure for the Heart-Ache* on 10 January 1797, Sir William Dorrillon in Mrs Inchbald's *Wives As They Were and Maids As They Are* on 4 March 1797, Obadiah in Knight's *The Honest Thieves* on 9 May 1797, Simon Single in Cumberland's *False Impressions* on 23 November 1797, Undermine in Morton's *Secrets Worth Knowing* on 11 January 1798, Verdun the Butler in Mrs Inchbald's *Lover's Vows* on 11 October 1798, Oakworth in Holman's *The Votary of Wealth* on 12 January 1799, Worry in Reynolds's *The Management* on 31 October 1799, Crack in Knight's *The Turnpike Gate* on 14 November 1799, Wolf in Cumberland's *Joanna* on 16 January 1800, Sir Abel Hardy in Morton's *Speed the Plough* on 8 February 1800, and Dominique in Cobb's *Paul and Virginia* on 1 May 1800. During the 1790s Munden joined some of his fellow actors in private theatricals sponsored by the nobility. He appeared as Sir Anthony Absolute in *The Rivals* for the Earl of Barrymore at Wargrave on 30 January 1792 and as Peregrine Forester in *Hartford Bridge* he sang the "Traveller's Song" at the Margravine of Anspach's theatre in Brandenburgh House on 21 March 1796.

By 1795–96 Munden's salary, which had been £6 per week was raised to £10, and in 1797–98 it was raised again to £12, the level at which it remained through 1802–3. By the spring of 1795 he had moved a few doors along Frith Street to No 12. In April 1796 benefit tickets could be had from him at No 77, the Corner of Longacre, and also at Prospect Place, Kentish Town. In May 1797 he lived at No 16, Clement's Inn, an address he retained at least through April 1800. His summer engagements included Chester and Richmond, Surrey, in 1795, Cork and Limerick in 1796, and Birmingham in 1797 and 1799.

Munden's first summer engagement at the Haymarket Theatre was in 1797, when he made his debut there as Captain Meadows in *The Deaf Lover* and Frost in *The Irishman in London* on 15 June. That summer he was also seen as Dawdle in *The Prisoner at Large*, Tony Lumpkin in *She Stoops to Conquer*, Lazarillo in *Two Strings to Your Bow*, Obadiah in *The Honest Thieves*, Brummagem in *Lock and Key*, Governor Harcourt in *The Chapter of Accidents*, Nipperkin

in *The Rival Soldiers*, Zarno in *Zorinski*, Tipple in *The Flitch of Bacon*, Clod in *The Young Quaker*, and Corney in *The Beggar on Horseback*. On 15 April 1797 he created the role of Zekiel Homespun in the premiere of Colman's *The Heir at Law*. He returned to the Haymarket in the summer of 1798 to play many of the same roles, to which he added a character in *Blue Devils*, Colonel Oldboy in *Lionel and Clarissa*, Shenkin in *Cambro-Britains*, Darby in *The Poor Soldier*, and the four roles now very much associated with him: Jemmy Jumps in *The Farmer*, Count Benini in *False and True*, Old Dornton in *The Road to Ruin*, and Polonius in *Hamlet*. On 7 September 1798 he sang "The United

Courtesy of the Garrick Club

JOSEPH S. MUNDEN, as Peregrine
by De Wilde

Englishmen" in a musical interlude called *An Olla Podrida*.

Though most of Munden's repertory was confined to roles in pieces of little lasting consequence, by the end of the century he had acquired a reputation as an actor of considerable merit. His lively imagination, mimetic powers, and a "wonder-working face" greatly enhanced the trivial roles, for he played in a style called by Boaden "broad and voluptuous." In his *Candid and Impartial Strictures on the Performers* in 1795, F. G. Waldron agreed that Munden was a performer with first-rate abilities, but claimed that he had been raised too high:

His figure is vulgar and heavy, and from its apparent strength, destroys the effect of his endeavours to give us an idea of the feeble, decrepid old man, or of the airy, fantastic coxcomb. His action is hard and deficient in variety. His voice strong, and face expressive, but he is too fond of grimace, and in almost every thing he performs, outsteps the modesty of nature. We see less of this in his clowns than in any other cast of parts.

On the other hand, Bellamy in *The London Theatres* reported that Munden had developed sterling powers that enriched the higher scenes of comedy and praised especially the actor's expert abilities in portraying the dress, look, and speech of decrepitude. His style was so distinct that:

For dressing CHARACTER *he bears a name,*
Nor will it be forgotten, or put by, —
The Munden cut, *when Munden's day is past.*

Munden's acting of Sir Francis Wronghead in *The Provok'd Husband* was called by the *Morning Herald* on 29 September 1798 "a very pleasing display of comicality," though Munden should have contented himself "with what was set down by the author, without introducing his own common place allusions to the fashions of the present day." In *The Dramatic Censor* (1800) Thomas Dutton ranked Munden's personation of Old Dornton in *The Road to Ruin* as among his best performances, proclaiming it "real acting" of a kind that prior to his appearance in that character in 1792 "was supposed to be altogether foreign to his line and sphere."

In 1800 Munden was one of the eight leading actors at Covent Garden who entered into a public controversy with the management over

financial terms and issued *A Statement of the differences subsisting between the proprietors and the performers of the Theatre-Royal, Covent-Garden.* The actors' appeal to the Lord Chamberlain was rejected. According to Dutton, in 1799–1800 Munden's total remuneration, including net benefit receipts, had been £868 6*s*.; the account books show gross ticket sales of £565 0*s*. 6*d*. on 22 April 1800, Munden's benefit, and his salary that season was £12 per week.

After playing the summer of 1800 at the Crow Street Theatre in Dublin, and also at Birmingham, Chester, and elsewhere, Munden returned to Covent Garden, where he remained for another 11 seasons as a firmly established audience favorite. In 1800–1801 his salary was still £12 per week; the following season it was raised to £14, and in 1805–6 it became £17. His annual benefit receipts were substantial, averaging about £600. In 1805–6, for example, he received £603 in benefit tickets and signed a Covent Garden pay sheet (in the Harvard Theatre Collection) for £522 10*s*. in salary for the season. His new roles included Old Liberal in T. Dibdin's *School for Prejudice* on 3 January 1801, Sir Robert Bramble in Colman's *The Poor Gentleman* on 11 February 1801, General Tarragon in Morton's *The School of Reform* on 15 January 1805, Lord Danberry in Mrs Inchbald's *To Marry or not to Marry* on 16 February 1805, Torrent in Colman's *Who Wants a Guinea* on 18 April 1805, the Count of Rosenheim in Diamond's *Adrian and Orrila* on 15 November 1806, Diaper in Tobin's *The School for Authors* on 3 December 1808, and Heartwell in Holman's *Gazette Extraordinary* on 23 April 1811.

During the first decade of the nineteenth century Munden continued to make frequent summer excursions to provincial theatres. He was at Weymouth, Southampton, and Dublin in 1801. An Irish playgoer's journal extolled Munden's comic virtuosity at Dublin that July; one night he "exerted himself . . . to such degree that Huddart & Coyne who had parts in the same scene, could not resist their inclination to laughter & ran together off the stage." At the end of that summer, before beginning his Covent Garden season, Munden acted Sir Robert Bramble in *The Poor Gentleman* at the Haymarket on 7 September 1801 for Mrs Gibbs's benefit, his first appearance there in two years. He played at York in August 1802

Courtesy of the Garrick Club

JOSEPH S. MUNDEN, as Verdun
by De Wilde

and at Preston in early September. In 1803 he was again in Dublin and almost lost his life when his ship was wrecked on the voyage back to England. In 1804 he appeared at Edinburgh from March through July in a repertoire of his best-known roles. Dublin saw him again in July 1808. Other engagements included Bristol, Bath, and Brighton in 1809.

A quarrel with the management over money led to Munden's departure from Covent Garden after 1810–11, and except for a benefit he never again entered that theatre. He acted Casimere in Colman's *The Quadrupeds of Quedlinburgh* at the Haymarket on 26 July 1811 and also appeared there in 1812. The years 1811 to 1813, however, he passed mainly out of London, attracted by large amounts of money at Newcastle, Rochdale, Chester, Manchester, Glasgow, and Edinburgh. About that time Munden, who had been somewhat of an indulgent and hospitable man, a martyr to gout and a secretary of the Beefsteak Club, began

to exhibit an uncharacteristic stinginess, which later evolved into miserliness.

In the autumn of 1813 Munden engaged at Drury Lane Theatre, where he spent the final years of his career, earning a steady £20 per week. His first appearance at that theatre was as Sir Abel Handy in *Speed the Plough* on 4 October 1813. On 11 March 1815 he played the original Old Dozey in T. Dibdin's *Past Ten O'Clock and a Rainy Night*, a role that ranked among his greatest. The last of his trivial new roles at Drury Lane was General Van in Knight's *Veteran; or, The Farmer's Son* on 23 February 1822. A Drury Lane casting book dating from about 1815 (now at the Folger Shakespeare Library) lists 31 characters in Munden's active repertoire at the time, all in farce, light comedy, or musical pieces (except for a Witch in *Macbeth*, a role, however, traditionally played in a comic vein). His assignments in musical plays offered no extraordinary challenge to his tenor voice.

Recurring illnesses forced Munden's retirement after about 50 years on the boards. His farewell performance at Drury Lane occurred on 31 May 1824, when he acted Sir Robert Bramble and Old Dozey and recited a farewell address. A letter (in the Huntington Library) from Mary Sibella Novello to Leigh Hunt records an amusing incident on that night:

Munden has taken his leave of the Stage & the Public much to our regret as he never played finer than this season—he sent 2 tickets to Mr Lamb with his thanks for the very handsome manner in which he had spoken of him—Mr and Miss L. went & were seated in the orchestra boxes with a gay party, when between the acts, Munden [thrust?] out his hand, & head, & with one of his grimaces presented a vulgar pot of porter, which made all the fine folks shrink in confusion, but C. L. stretched forth his arms & seized the . . . beverage, & . . . quaffed a long draught. . . .

According to Charles and Mary Cowden Clarke's *Recollections of Writers*, it was Mary Lamb who coined the pun, which had sometimes been attributed to her brother, "Sic transit gloria *Munden*." Mary Lamb recollected:

The very look, the very gesture, the whole bearing of Munden first in the pathetic character of the gentleman-father, next in the farce-character of the village cobbler, remain impressed upon the brain of her who witnessed them as if I beheld but yes-

Harvard Theatre Collection

JOSEPH S. MUNDEN, as Kit Sly

by G. Cruikshank

terday. The tipsy lunge with which he rolled up to the table whereon stood that tempting brown jug, the leer of mingled slyness and attempted unconcernedness with which he slid out his furtive thought to the audience—"Some gentleman has left his ale!" then with an unctous smack of his lips, jovial and anticipating, adding, "And some other gentleman will drink it"—all stand present to fancy vivid and unforgotten.

For the next eight years Munden lived as something of a recluse, nursed by his second wife, at No 2, Bernard Street, Russell Square, having moved from Kentish Town, St Pancras, before 1820. (When living at Kentish Town, it had been his custom to drink the water at Bagnigge Wells three times a week.) Severe financial losses from high-risk investments in real estate troubled his final years and probably

contributed to his death. He declined many invitations to act again; one of his replies to such an offer is preserved, undated, in the Harvard Theatre Collection:

I reced yours, and felt much flatter'd by your request that I shou'd once more appear on the boards of Drury Lane Theatre; But having taken leave of the Public in so marked a manner when I quitted, it is impossible, consistently, to put on the Sock again, added to which, I have such frequent attacks of Gout, that no dependence cou'd be placed upon me; I have been confin'd these last six weeks, and unable to quit my bed.

Indeed, after the death of his favorite daughter, his spirit was much broken and he seldom left his bed.

In January 1832 Munden suffered "under the derangement of the bowels," from which disorder, despite the efforts of his physicians Dr Roots and Dr Bright, he died at his house in Bernard Street, Russell Square, on 6 February 1832 at the age of 74, and was buried in the vaults at St George, Bloomsbury.

In his earlier years Munden had lived for some time with Mary Jones, an actress who in the 1780s performed as Mrs Munden in the provinces, particularly at Newcastle and Chester. By her he had four daughters. In 1789 she deserted Munden to marry the actor John Hodgkinson at Bath; soon after, Hodgkinson ran off to America with Miss Brett to become an important figure in the development of the early American theatre. Mary Hodgkinson continued to perform in the provinces (though she seems never to have appeared in London) until her death at Tiverton, Bath, about 8 October 1792.

Munden, meanwhile, had married the actress Frances Butler on 20 October 1789 at the parish church of St Oswald, Chester. Five years Munden's senior, she was reputed to be a lineal descendant of William Wollaston (1660–1724), the author of *Religion of Nature Delineated*, and she was a near relative of William Hyde Wollaston (1766–1828), an eminent chemist. Her father was a gentleman of property—one of his estates was near Lutterworth in Leicestershire—so she, indeed, had "some claims to social position," as *The Dictionary of National Biography* put it. As Miss Butler she had made her debut at Lewes on 28 July 1785 in the role of Louisa Dudley in *The West Indian*, and then she played in provincial theatres on the circuit managed by Munden. Upon her marriage to him she retired from the stage, but she accompanied him when he came to London for his debut at Covent Garden in 1790.

In his will drawn on 12 February 1810, Munden left his wife Frances inadequately provided for, considering the large amounts of money he had earned from the stage. She was to receive 20 guineas immediately at his death, along with any household effects, furniture, and linen she might desire but not exceeding £100 in value. Munden allowed her to keep her own clothes and jewels. He directed that his estate be sold and that the sums be invested in the Society for Equitable Assurance on Lives and Survivorship to provide equal annuities of £125 to his wife and to his mother Alice Munden. To his son (probably by Frances Butler Munden), then second mate on the *Sir William Pultoney*, an East Indiaman, he bequeathed £200, half to be paid six months after Munden's death, the other half after two years. The balance of the proceeds from his divested estate were to be divided in five equal parts to his four daughters (by Mary Jones): Esther Greenwood, Mary Munden, Ellen Munden, and Alice Munden, and to another son (by Frances Munden), then a minor. Esther Greenwood's share was to be reduced by £500, the amount which had been advanced to her as her marriage portion.

Specific birth dates of Munden's daughters by name are not known to us, but the *Newcastle Chronicle* on 15 April 1786 reported three daughters had been born by that date: one on 10 April 1784, another in 1785, and the third on 10 April 1786. In one of several codicils, on 24 April 1826, his daughter Ellen Munden Wilbraham having lately died (evidently in childbirth), Munden settled an annuity of the interest on £500 on his unnamed granddaughter, who at the age of 21 would receive the principal. On 26 November 1830 he added a bequest of £500 to Thomas Somerset, of Eastwick, Wiltshire, "who intermarried with my daughter Alice now deceased."

Munden's will was proved at London on 22 February 1832 by his widow Frances Munden. She died on 20 September 1837, aged 83, at Islington, and was buried with the remains of her husband at St George, Bloomsbury. In her will drawn on 29 February 1832, she left all

her property of every description to her son Thomas Shepherd Munden, who as sole executor proved the will at London on 13 December 1837. Thomas Shepherd Munden, author of a biography of his father, died at Islington in July 1850, at the age of 50.

In person Munden had large blue eyes, a short physique, and a profile described by Leigh Hunt in 1807 as having "something close, carping, and even severe in it; but it was redeemed by his front face, which was handsome for one so old, and singularly pliable about the eyes and brows." Hunt compared Munden's features to "the reflection of a man's face in a ruffled stream, they undergo a perpetual undulation of grin." Most of the force of his action, Hunt thought, consisted "in two or three ludicrous gestures and an innumerable variety of as fanciful contortions of countenance as ever threw women into hysterics."

Much of Munden's acting consisted of mugging and caricaturing. Indeed, Hazlitt believed him to indulge too much in grimace, and to be a caricaturist in comparison to Liston. Hazlitt reported that Northcote had called Munden an "excellent but an artificial actor." In his *Dramatic Censor* (1800) Dutton claimed that Munden and others like him, who had developed the taste for "caricatures," were responsible for the "debauched taste of the town," yet later in the same publication he praised him as a technician in his line; Morton's *Speed the Plough* owed its success to such acting, and "the irresistible drollery of MUNDEN, whose peculiarity of manner constitutes the life and soul of the piece." Dutton thought he sang humorous songs well, and as Old Croaker in *The Good-Natured Man* he "literally set the house in a roar." In praising his portrayal of Polonius, the *Monthly Mirror* in January 1804 stated, "but Munden can be something else than a *low*-comedian, if he please; & he will make you laugh at one time, in Scrub; and at another call forth tears, in spite of you, as Old Dornton." He had a clear field, after the departure of Parsons, in his excellence in old men, and most critics could think of nothing finer than his Old Dozey.

It is through Charles Lamb's *Essays of Elia* ("On the Acting of Munden," "Munden's Farewell," and "The Death of Munden") that the comedian's merits are best known. Lamb proclaimed that in the grand grotesque of farce,

Munden stood out "as single and unaccompanied as Hogarth." Such fine actors as Farley, Knight, and Liston had but one face each, while, in Lamb's words:

Munden has none that you can properly pin down and call *his*. When you think he has exhausted his battery of looks . . . suddenly he sprouts out an entirely new set of features, like Hydra. He is not one, but legion; not so much a comedian as a company. If his name could be multiplied like his countenance, it might fill a playbill. He, and he alone, literally *makes faces*. . . .

Lamb thought Munden could *"do* anything." He was not an actor, believed Lamb, "but something better." As Old Foresight in *Love for Love*,

. . . he dropped the old man, the doater—which makes the character—but he substituted for it a moonstruck character, a perfection abstraction from this earth, that looked as if he had newly come down from the planets. *Now, that* is not what I call *acting*. . . . He was only a wonderful man, exerting his vivid impressions through the agency of the stage. . . .

Upon Munden's retirement Lamb exclaimed: "The regular playgoers ought to put on mourning, for the king of broad comedy is dead to the drama! Alas! Munden is no more!— give sorrow vent."

Notices about Munden and appreciations of his acting appeared in numerous periodicals and books that were published during his lifetime and shortly after his death. Many of these are preserved in an extra-illustrated volume (II, Nos 4 and 5) of Matthews and Hutton's *Actors and Actresses* in the Harvard Theatre Collection. In 1844, his son Thomas Shepherd Munden published the *Memoirs of Joseph Shepherd Munden, Comedian*, in which further details of his career may be read.

Portraits of Joseph Shepherd Munden include:

1. By George Clint. In the National Portrait Gallery (No 1283). Engraving by T. Lupton, 1822.

2. By George Dance, drawing in pencil. Sold at Christie's on 1 July 1898 (No 96) and now in the National Portrait Gallery (No 1149). Engraving by W. Daniell, published by the engraver, 1814.

3. By Samuel De Wilde, watercolor drawing. In the Garrick Club (No 559B).

4. By S. Drummond. In the Garrick Club (No 433).

5. By J. P. Knight. In the Garrick Club (No 342), from the bequest of Rudolph Glover, 1897.

6. By James Lonsdale, charcoal drawing. In the Garrick Club (No 141), presented by the artist's son in 1852.

7. By John Opie, c. 1801. In the Garrick Club (No 405). Engraving by S. W. Reynolds, published by the engraver 1804.

8. By M. A. Shee. In the Garrick Club (No 481), presented by W. C. Macready in 1842. Engraving by W. Ridley published in Bellamy's *Picturesque Magazine*, 1793; reprinted as a plate to *European Magazine*, 1796.

9. By W. Wood, a miniature. Present location unknown. Engraving by W. Ridley published as a plate to *Monthly Mirror*, February 1799.

10. By unknown artist. One of nine silhouettes on paper. In the Garrick Club (No 494D). Perhaps this is the portrait credited to Turmeau by *The Dictionary of National Biography*.

11. By unknown artist. In a four-panel painting, with Anna Maria Crouch, Charles Lee Lewes, and Dorothy Jordan. In the possession of the Earl of Munster.

12. By E. H. Bailey, 1825. Bust for Drury Lane Theatre.

13. Engraved portrait by J. Condé. Published as a plate to *Thespian Magazine*, 1792.

14. Engraved portrait by Mackenzie, after R. Dighton. Published as a plate to *The Myrtle and the Vine* (vol. III), 1800; reprinted as a plate to *Thespian Dictionary*, 1805.

15. Engraved portrait by W. Ridley, after De Wilde. Published as a plate to *General Magazine and Impartial Review*, 1791.

16. Engraved portrait by W. Ridley, after Edridge.

17. By unknown artist. Lithograph with the title "Old Joey."

18. As Sir Abel Hardy in *Speed the Plough*. By unknown engraver. Published by Harrison, 1800.

19. As Autolycus in *The Winter's Tale*. Watercolor by S. De Wilde, dated 30 October 1808. In the Garrick Club (No 45B). Engraving by W. Bond published as a plate to *Theatrical Inquisitor*, June 1813.

20. As Autolycus. Watercolor by S. De Wilde. In the Garrick Club (No 484), similar

to item above. Presented by Sir Arthur Wing Pinero in 1929.

21. As Autolycus. By S. De Wilde, exhibited at the Royal Academy in 1809 (No 399). Presumably a painting, present location unknown, and not either of the above watercolors by De Wilde.

22. As Baillie in *The Maid and the Magpie*. By unknown engraver, published as a "penny plain" by W. West.

23. As Crop in *Blue-Beard*. By unknown engraver, published as a plate to *Attic Miscellany*, 1792; reprinted as a plate to *Charlton House Magazine*.

24. As Dozey in *Past Ten O'Clock*. By unknown engraver, published by Hodgson & Co, 1823.

25. As Sir Francis Gripe in *The Busy Body*. By S. De Wilde. Present location unknown. Engravings by Wray and Thornthwaite were published as plates to *Bell's British Library*, 1791; an engraving by an unknown engraver was published as a plate to *British Drama*, 1817.

26. As Sir Francis Gripe. Engraving by J. Rogers, after Kennerley. Published as a plate to Oxberry's *Dramatic Biography*, 1825.

27. As Sir Francis Gripe. Attributed to T. Wageman. In the Players Club, New York. An engraving by J. Hopwood was published as a plate to Oxberry's *New English Drama*, 1819, and one by J. Cook was published as a plate to Munden's *Memoirs*, 1844.

28. As General Bastion in *We Fly By Night*. Engraving by R. Page.

29. As Jemmy Jumps in *The Farmer*. Etching by unknown engraver.

30. As Jemmy Jumps. Stipple by unknown engraver. Published in *Hibernian Magazine*, July 1793.

31. As Jemmy Jumps. By unknown engraver. Published by W. Wellings, 1790.

32. As Justice Woodcock in *Love in a Village*. Engraving by R. Page. Published as a plate to *The Drama*, 1824.

33. As Justice Woodcock. Engraving by R. Page. Published as a plate to *British Stage*, November 1821.

34. As Kit Sly in *The Cobler of Preston*. Engraving by G. Cruikshank. Published as a plate to *British Stage*, November 1817.

35. As Sir Matthew Maxim in *Five Thousand*

Courtesy of the Garrick Club

JOSEPH S. MUNDEN
by Drummond

a Year. Engraving by R. Dighton. Published on a music sheet by Longman, Clementi & Co.

36. As Old Brummagem, with Edward Knight as Ralph, Mrs Orger as Fanny, and Miss Cubitt as Laura, in *Lock and Key*. Canvas by George Clint, exhibited at the Royal Academy, 1821 (No 273). In the Garrick Club. Engraving by T. Lupton, 1824.

37. As Old Rapid, with Bannister as Young Rapid, and two other actors, in *A Cure for the Heart-Ache*. By unknown engraver. Scarce print in Harvard Theatre Collection, undated.

38. As Peachum, with William Dowton as Lockit, in *The Beggar's Opera*. Oil by Robert Smirke. In the possession of J. O. Flatter in 1960. A photograph of the painting appeared in *Theatre Notebook*, 14.

39. As Peregrine Forester in *Hartford Bridge*. Oil by S. De Wilde. In the Garrick Club (No 123).

40. As Polonius in *Hamlet*. Watercolor by W. Loftis, 1793. In the Folger Shakespeare Library.

41. As Polonius. By unknown engraver.

Published as a plate to *Mirror of the Stage*, 1823.

42. As Project, with John Quick as Alderman Arable and William T. Lewis as Tanjore, in *Speculation*. By Johann Zoffany. In the Garrick Club (No 104).

43. As Verdun in *Lover's Vows*. Oil by S. De Wilde, exhibited at the Royal Academy, 1799, and included in the Harris sale of 1819. Now in the Garrick Club.

44. As Verdun. Engraving by R. Dighton. Published by Dighton, 1798.

45. As a character in George Clint's large painting of a scene from *A New Way to Pay Old Debts*. The painting also features William Oxberry and Edmund Kean, but it is not based on an actual performance, because the artist includes himself, the engraver Thomas Lupton, and several other non-performers, in the tradition of G. H. Harlow's painting of the trial scene in *Henry VIII*. Exhibited at the Royal Academy in 1820, and presented in 1889 by Henry Irving to the Garrick Club (No 465).

46. As an unspecified character. Watercolor by S. De Wilde, showing Munden in frock coat, tricot hat, with an envelope in his pocket. In the Harvard Theatre Collection.

Munfer. *See* MOUNTFORT.

Munford, Mr [*fl.* 1799–1800], *musician*.

The Covent Garden accounts show that Mr Munford played in the band there in 1799–1800 for 5*s*. nightly.

Munfort. *See* MOUNTFORT.

Munier, Mr. *See* MUNIER, MRS.

Munier, Mrs [*fl.* 1759], *actress*.

The London Stage lists a Mr Munier in the Drury Lane roster for 1759–60, but the only mention of that name in the calendar of performances is for Mrs Munier, who was added to the cast of *Fortunatus* on 19 November 1759 and performed in that work again on 20 and 23 November.

Munro. *See also* MONRO and MONROE.

Munro, Mr [*fl.* 1734], *house servant?*

Mr Munro's benefit tickets were admitted at Drury Lane Theatre on 21 May 1734. Perhaps he was one of the house servants.

Munro, Robert [*fl.* 1774–1800], *oboist, flutist, clarinetist*.

The London Stage is, we believe, incorrect in naming the oboist Munro of the 1790s Henry and identifying him as the Henry Monro listed in *Grove's Dictionary of Music and Musicians* (fifth edition) as an organist born in Lincoln in 1774. The London oboist was listed in Doane's *Musical Directory* of 1794 as Robert Munro, of Waller Row, St George's Fields. Doane said Munro was proficient on the oboe, flute, and clarinet, was a member of the Royal Society of Musicians and the band of the Third Regiment of Guards and had participated in the oratorios at Covent Garden Theatre. In May and June 1784, according to Dr Burney, a Mr Munro had played oboe in the Handel Memorial Concerts at Westminster Abbey and the Pantheon, and the Minute Books of the Royal Society of Musicians listed a Monro as oboist in the St Paul's Concert on 10 and 12 May 1791. Munro played in the oratorio band at Covent Garden from February 1792 to February 1800.

Robert Munro was the father of the string instrumentalist Samuel Munro. The registers of St Margaret, Westminster, show that Samuel, the son of Robert and Lucia Ann Munro, was christened on 5 June 1774.

Munro, Samuel 1774–1820, *violinist, violist*.

Samuel Munro, the son of Robert and Lucia Ann Munro, was born on 18 May 1774 and christened at St Margeret, Westminster, on 5 June. Doane's *Musical Directory* in 1794 listed "Munroe" Junior as a violist who had played in the Handel performances at Westminster Abbey. His address was that of his father: Waller Row, St George's Fields. On 2 August 1795 Robert Munro recommended his son for membership in the Royal Society of Musicians, noting that Samuel was proficient on the violin, viola, and harpsichord and had engagements at Covent Garden Theatre and Vauxhall Gardens. Samuel was unanimously elected to membership on 1 November.

In February 1796 and each year through

1800 Samuel played in the oratorios at Covent Garden, and from May 1796 on he was a regular participant in the annual St Paul's Concert. The Covent Garden accounts listed a "Monro" in the band there in 1799–1800 at 6s. 8d. nightly, and we take that reference to concern Samuel.

On 21 April 1808 at St Marylebone, Samuel Munro married Susan Court, who was pregnant, of the parish of St Mary, Dover. The Stephen Court who witnessed the marriage was probably Susan's father. After his marriage Munro gave up his musical career in London and moved to Dover. The registers of St Mary's show the baptism of Samuel Court Munro, son of Samuel and Susanna, on 24 July 1808. The couple had a son George, who was christened on 20 June 1811, and a son Henry, christened on 7 August 1816.

Despite his removal from London, Samuel Munro continued paying his subscription to the Royal Society of Musicians until his death in early 1820. On 5 February of that year administration of the estate of Samuel Munro, late of Winchester Street in the parish of Allhallows in the Wall, London, was granted to his widow Susanna. The estate was worth less than £300. The following day Mrs Munro was recommended for financial aid from the Royal Society of Musicians. We do not know when the Munros had moved back to London.

Mrs Munro and her three boys were granted a full allowance (amount unspecified) from the Society, and the Governors also granted £12 to cover Samuel Munro's funeral expenses. Mrs Munro returned to Dover, for in February 1823 the Society granted her permission (and a fee, presumably) to apprentice her son Samuel to a Dover linen draper, Mr W. Standon. In May 1825 young George Munro was also apprenticed to Standon, but a year later Mrs Munro removed her son from Standon because the business did not agree with the boy's health. She apprenticed him instead to a butcher and grazier.

The third son, Henry, was apprenticed in 1830 to Mr Elwin, a grocer and tallow chandler of Dartford. Of George Munro we hear no more, but the masters of both Samuel and Henry attested in 1830 and 1837 respectively that the boys had done well. The Royal Society of Musicians awarded each young man a present of £10.

Munroe or **Munrow.** *See* MONROE.

Munto, John [*fl.* 1790–1800], *singer, actor.*

John Munto was one of the singers in *Arthur* at the Royalty Theatre on 5 April 1790. He may have remained a member of the Royalty company for several years, for when he traveled to America to join the Old American Company while it was playing at Philadelphia in 1794 he was advertised as "from Goodman's Fields," the location of the Royalty Theatre in London. Munto was performing at the Southwark Theatre, Philadelphia, by 25 June 1794 and remained there until December of that year. His first known role was Lounge in *The Fair Quaker* on 26 September 1794. He made his debut at the John Street Theatre in New York, according to William Dunlap, as Eustace in *Love in a Village.*

Chiefly a singing actor, Munto (and his wife) played "in the South," probably at Charleston, for about a year before returning to the John Street Theatre in February 1796. He was a member of Hodgkinson's company at Boston's Haymarket Theatre in the summer of 1797, having also been with Hodgkinson at Hartford in that and the previous summer. At the Federal Street Theatre in Boston in November 1798 Munto was earning $10 per week. In 1799–1800 he was at the same theatre under the management of Giles L. Barrett. In the summer of 1800 he performed at the Boston Haymarket; thereafter he fell into obscurity.

Muraile. *See* DUMIRAIL.

Murch, Mr [*fl.* 1799–1820], *doorkeeper.*

The Drury Lane Theatre accounts show a doorkeeper named Murch from December 1799 through the season of 1819–20. His weekly salary at the beginning of his tenure was £2 2s., but by the end he was down to a paltry 15s. Occasionally he was called the stage doorkeeper.

Murden, Mr [*fl.* 1760?–1772], *actor.*

The Murden who trouped with Durravan's company on the Derby circuit from about 25 April through 7 July 1760 was probably the actor of that name who played some minor part unspecified in *The Mayor of Garratt* at the

Haymarket Theatre on 20 June 1763. He was Rackett in *The Englishman Return'd from Paris* on 5 and 22 August. He played Gibbet in *The Beaux' Stratagem* on 5 September and also took some role in the farce of that night, *The Contented Cuckold*. He finished his summer at the Haymarket on 7 September as Don Duart in *Love Makes a Man*. On 11 November he returned to Derby and played in that company through early February 1764.

Murden secured a trial at Covent Garden early in 1765, playing Tim Shacklefigure in *The Country Lasses* on 17 January and Spinner in *The Male Coquette* on 21 January. No other parts are recorded, but he must have done something to earn the benefit tickets he shared with Mrs Godwin on 9 May 1765.

In 1766 Murden had a busy summer, acting both for Foote at the Haymarket (1 July through 6 August) and for Barry at the King's Theatre (nearly every night through 11 September). He added the following roles: Justice in *The Lying Valet*, unspecified parts in *The Orators* and *The Cheats of Scapin*, Sir Jacob Jollup in *The Mayor of Garratt*, Sir Jasper Wilding in *The Citizen*, Gratiano in *Othello*, Eliot in *Venice Preserv'd*, Montague in *Romeo and Juliet*, Burgundy in *King Lear*, James in *The Provok'd Husband*, and Sir John in *The Conscious Lovers*.

After that flurry of activity Murden left London. But he seems to have had a provincial career of some duration. The Committee Books of the Norwich Theatre bear the notation of 25 May 1771: "Ordered That Mr Griffith engage Mr & Mrs Murden for the ensuing Season." He was in Tate Wilkinson's company on the York circuit in 1771 and 1772, making his debut at Hull on 1 November 1771.

On 18 July 1772 Murden played Perriwinkle in *A Bold Stroke for a Wife* at Edinburgh's Theatre Royal, Shakespeare Square. On 20 July he was Touchstone in *As You Like It* and on 21 July Sir Andrew Aguecheek in *Twelfth Night*. After that date Murden drops from the record, but Mrs Murden played Miss Fuzz in *A Peep behind the Curtain* on 17 and 19 April 1773 at Edinburgh and in 1774–75 was in Whitley's company at Derby.

Murgetroyd, Miss [*fl.* 1748–1750], actress.

Miss Murgetroyd (or Murgatroyd) performed at Drury Lane for two seasons, achieving her first notice in the bills on 26 December 1748, when she was Bellemonte in *The Emperor of the Moon*. After that she appeared as Betty Doxy in *The Beggar's Opera*, Prudentia in *A Duke and No Duke*, an unnamed character in *The Rehearsal*, and Louisa in *Edward the Black Prince*. Her last appearance seems to have been in *The Rehearsal* on 14 February 1750.

Murphin, Mr [*fl.* 1760s–1772], singer.

In the Rendel manuscript notes on Southwark at the Folger Shakespeare Library Mr Murphin is listed as singing at Finch's Grotto Gardens, George Street, St George's Fields, Southwark, sometime between 1760 and 1769. Wroth in *The London Pleasure Gardens* notes that Murphin was at Finch's about 1771. There on 17 August 1772 he sang the part of a Soldier in *The Ephesian Matron*.

Murphy. *See also* MORPHY.

Murphy, Mr [*fl.* 1792], actor.

A Mr Murphy played Planter in *Inkle and Yarico* in a pickup company at the Crown Inn in Islington on 16 January 1792.

Murphy, Mr [*fl.* 1798–1799], piper.

Mr Murphy played the Union Pipes as part of a performance of *Oscar and Malvina* at Covent Garden Theatre on 5 May 1798. On 28 May following, he returned and played a solo, accompanied by John Michael Weippert on the harp. On 21 July following, he performed an overture at the Haymarket Theatre with Weippert and C. Jones on pedal harps. When Thomas John Dibdin's elaborate pantomime *The Magic Oak* was brought forth at Covent Garden on 29 January 1799 there was a "*Medley Overture* on the Union Pipes and Pedal Harp by Murphy and Weippert." The pair teamed for the last time at Covent Garden on 2 March in Reeve's overture to *Oscar and Malvina*.

Murphy, Arthur 1727–1805, playwright, actor, essayist.

Arthur Murphy was born in the house of his maternal uncle Arthur French at Clooniquin, Roscommon, Ireland on 27 December 1727. He was the younger surviving child of Richard Murphy, a Dublin merchant, and his wife Jane French. After her husband was lost in the At-

Courtesy of the National Gallery of Ireland

ARTHUR MURPHY
by N. Dance

lantic in 1729 while on a business journey to North America, Mrs Murphy lived with Arthur and his elder brother James at St George's Quay, Dublin. In 1735 the family moved to London, where Arthur remained for a brief time before being sent in 1736 to live at Boulogne with Mrs Arthur Plunkett, his mother's sister. In 1738, under the name of Arthur French, he matriculated at the English College of St Omer, a Jesuit monastery. After six years of studies there, during which he distinguished himself as a student of classics and was graduated in July 1744, he rejoined his mother at London. Another maternal uncle, Jeffrey French, M.P., steered him toward a career in commerce, sending him to Webster's Academy for the study of accounting.

While living with his mother for three years in York Buildings in the Strand, Murphy read widely in literature and became acquainted with the stimulating company that frequented the coffeehouses and theatres. Through his brother James he came to know, among other lively personalities, the actor William Havard, the playwright Samuel Foote, and the writers

Christopher Smart and Henry Fielding. In August 1747 his uncle sent Murphy to Cork to serve as clerk to the merchant Edmund Harrold. There he remained for almost two years until April 1749, when declining to sail to Jamaica to look after Jeffrey French's interests, he entered the London banking house of Ironside and Belchier in Lombard Street.

By the end of 1751 Murphy had left commerce for journalism. He is characterized by his recent biographer Robert D. Spector (*Arthur Murphy*, 1979) as "a man capable of social mobility, quick to take advantage of opportunities that would further his career," and possessed with sufficient facility and charm to "turn potentially disasterous circumstances to success." He would need such attributes to weather the storms that lay ahead on his theatrical and literary voyage.

Some scholars have conjectured that Murphy was a staff writer for Fielding's *Covent Garden Journal* in 1752, and it is also possible that he was the author of an attack in May 1752 on John Hill in a pamphlet entitled *Libertina sine Conflictu; or, a True Narrative of the Untimely Death of Doctor Atall*.

Adopting the pseudonym Charles Ranger, from the popular character in Hoadley's comedy *The Suspicious Husband*, Murphy from 21 October 1752 contributed 49 weekly essays to the *Gray's Inn Journal* in the *Craftsman*, and then on 29 September 1753 began the independent publication of the *Gray's Inn Journal*, which ran for 52 weekly numbers until 21 September 1754. No copies of the *Craftsman* have survived, but at the end of 1754 the 52 new numbers of the *Gray's Inn Journal* were collected and reprinted as a single folio volume, and in 1756 Murphy published a two-volume edition of 104 numbers, which probably included those he had written for the *Craftsman*. In these essays modeled on the *Spectator*, Murphy ranged over a variety of literary and social topics, the most important of which are those on drama and acting, evidently written in opposition to John Hill's newspaper column, "The Inspector."

Disappointed by not having received an expected legacy at the death of his uncle, and £300 in debt, Murphy had to terminate publication of the *Gray's Inn Journal* in September 1754. In *The Life of Arthur Murphy, Esq.*, published in 1811, the biographer Jesse Foot prints some of Murphy's autobiographical notes in which Samuel Foote—"my intimate friend and chief adviser"—was credited with turning him to the stage. Murphy wrote that he appeared at Covent Garden Theatre as Othello in the autumn of 1754. But it seems probable that he had appeared as an actor at least a year earlier, as a member of the company playing at Richmond in the summer of 1753. An actor named Murphy, very likely Arthur, acted Foigard in *The Beaux' Stratagem* at Richmond on 24 July 1753, and there on 25 August he played the Old Man in *Lethe*.

Murphy wrote a new prologue, spoken by Foote at a performance of that playwright's *The Knights* at Drury Lane Theatre on 12 February 1754. About that time he offered an early draft of his first play *The Apprentice* (then called *The Young Apprentice*) to Garrick, who declined to produce it. Murphy was also preparing for his London acting debut with puffs in the *Entertainer*, written by himself. In that paper on 3 September 1754 it was announced that "the tragedy of Othello will be performed at Covent-Garden Theatre, with the addition of a young gentleman, who has already display'd his admirable genius and capacity to the world," with the presumptuous promise that the portrayal would "leave no room to regret the loss of Mr. Barry," who had engaged to play at Dublin that season. On 24 September the *Entertainer* reported further that "A brilliant wit will appear some time next month" as Othello.

At Covent Garden on 18 October 1754, announced as "a Gentleman who never appeared on any stage before," Murphy acted Othello to Ryan's Iago and Mrs Bellamy's Desdemona. Mrs Hamilton as Emilia spoke the prologue, written by Murphy, in which it was said of him,

> He copies no man—of what Shakespeare drew
> His humble sense he offers to your view.

Of his debut the *Entertainer* wrote on 22 October:

This evening the ingenious author of the Grays-Inn Journal, appeared for the first time in the character of Othello . . . [and] gave a convincing proof that he is perfectly acquainted with the various passions that influence the human heart, and has entered into the very meaning of Shakespeare.— The contest between *love and jealousy*, when he lays hold of the treacherous Iago, is perfectly pictured

Harvard Theatre Collection

ARTHUR MURPHY
engraving by Condé, after Poole

by him; and this passage, together with his posture, when Aemilia knocks without, truly deserve the greatest applause.

According to Tate Wilkinson, Murphy acted Othello with good judgment but without power sufficient for great effect. He repeated the part on 18 and 21 October, and again on 15 November when the bills identified him by name. On 23 November 1754 he acted Jaffeir in *Venice Preserv'd*, with Thomas Sheridan as Pierre and Mrs Bellamy as Belvidera. On that night, according to the story in the *Daily Advertiser* of 27 November, a well-dressed man who sat in the gallery threw his wig at Murphy, an action which so irritated the audience "that they call'd out to have him flung over." The guards escorted the fellow from the theatre, "but he afterwards came into one of the Front Boxes, and was carried out a second Time."

Murphy played Jaffeir again on 26 November, and Othello once more on 5 December. In a notice to the press on 16 December 1754, sent from Tavistock Row, Murphy denied the "invidious insinuation" abroad that he was again engaged in writing for the journals, declaring that since relinquishing the *Gray's Inn Journal* he had not been the author of "a single line in any Paper Whatever." Though not called upon by the management of Covent Garden "to appear frequently as an Actor," nevertheless, he was, he claimed, "so attentive to the business he has undertaken that he cannot spare time for the avocation of a periodical writer."

The remainder of Murphy's performances during his debut season at Covent Garden included Othello on 24 January 1755, Zamor in Hill's *Alzira* on 18 March (with alterations made by Murphy at the request of Mrs Bellamy, for her benefit) and 20 March, Young Bevil in *The Conscious Lovers* for Sparks's benefit on 22 March, Archer in *The Stratagem* for Theophilus Cibber's benefit on 2 April, and Hamlet for his own benefit on 4 April 1755. He acted Jaffeir again on 5 April, and then appeared as Richard III on 17 April, Biron in *The Fatal Marriage* on 18 April, repeated Jaffeir on 29 April, played Macbeth on 5 May, and repeated Othello on 8 May.

The following season Murphy was engaged by Garrick, whom he had frequently praised in the *Gray's Inn Journal*, and he first appeared at Drury Lane Theatre on 20 September 1755 as Osmyn in *The Mourning Bride*. The prompter Cross wrote in his diary that night, "Mr Murphy from Covent Garden did Osmyn. Indiff—tho' great applause." After repeating Osmyn on 30 September and 21 October, Murphy played the title role in *The Earl of Essex* on 24 and 25 October and Bajazet in *Tamerlane* on 4 November. His other roles were Richard III on 8 December 1755, Barbarossa on 23 December, and Horatio in *The Fair Penitent* on 12 January 1756.

Murphy's first play, *The Apprentice*, a farce in two acts, was brought on at Drury Lane on 2 January 1756, with a prologue written by Garrick and spoken by Woodward and an epilogue delivered by Kitty Clive. Murphy did not act in the play, which was well supported by Woodward as Dick. The philistine character of Wingate, acted by Yates, was modeled on Jeffrey French, Murphy's recently deceased uncle. Employing "humours" characters, Murphy's first

effort, described by Spector as a "blend of Restoration comedy of manners and Augustan satire," was received with applause for 16 performances. Murphy claimed to have cleared "within a trifle of 800 l" at his benefits. The accounts show gross receipts of £220, £130, and £140 for the third, sixth, and ninth nights, ordinarily the author's benefits; but only 12 January 1756, the eighth night, was specified in the bills for Murphy's benefit, at which gross receipts of £200 were taken. He continued to revise *The Apprentice* throughout the season; on 15 March 1756 it was played with "Additions to the Spouting Club," and then on 26 April it was acted with an additional scene.

Soon after the appearance of *The Apprentice*, Murphy published *The Spouter; or the Triple Revenge*. Never intended for production, and published anonymously, perhaps with Garrick's encouragement, this farce consisted of transparent mockeries of John Rich, John Hill, Theophilus Cibber, Foote, and Garrick himself. The attack on Foote, who had recently been his friend and benefactor, was provoked by that author's betrayal. In the summer of 1755 Murphy had prepared a sequel to Foote's *The Englishman in Paris* (which had been first acted at Covent Garden on 24 March 1753), and had confided many of its details to the approving Foote, who then stole the material to bring out with haste his own *The Englishman Return'd from Paris* at Covent Garden on 3 February 1756. Two months later Murphy's *The Englishman from Paris* was acted at Drury Lane on 3 April 1756, for the author's benefit (gross receipts £240) and, according to Cross, "went off well." Murphy's farce, however, was not played again and was not printed until the manuscript in the Newberry Library was published by Simon Trefman in 1969 (Augustan Reprint Society, No 137).

In the summer of 1756 Murphy carried on negotiations with Garrick about terms for the following season. Murphy began to express doubts about the manager's good faith, a theme he often returned to in alluding to their relations over the years. On 16 June 1756 the manager wrote: "If therefore You think it not incompatible with yr Ease & Reputation to be in our Company (wch from yr Conversation we had reason to hope) & will be contented with a Cast of Characters (of ye kind we mention to You) Mr Lacy & I are well inclin'd to Enter into another Engagement with You." Murphy was disturbed about the return of Mossop to the Drury Lane Company, but Garrick explained that Murphy could not "have suppl'd ye Characters" which Mossop was fit for, "with Credit to Yrself & Us." Whatever the reason, Murphy was not reengaged at Drury Lane. In his autobiographical notes he explained that the profits from his plays the previous season, after paying off his debts, left him with about £400 in his pocket, "and with that sum I determined to quit the dramatic line." Sometime in 1756, however, he wrote *The Foundling*, a comedy not acted and now lost.

In 1756 Murphy began publishing the *Test*, a weekly paper in opposition to Owen Ruffhead's the *Contest*. The *Test* supported the politics of Henry Fox, later Lord Holland. It appeared in 35 numbers between 6 November 1756 and 9 July 1757. Murphy also contributed to Johnson's *Literary Magazine*. In 1756 he applied to enter as a student of the Middle Temple but was refused because he had been an actor. But Lord Mansfield was induced by Lord Holland to secure Murphy's admission to Lincoln's Inn. He was called to the bar on 21 June 1762.

Though Murphy had turned to the law, evidently for security and respectability, his interest in the theatre remained strong. In 1757 he wrote his first draft of *The Orphan of China*, and beginning in that year and running to the end of 1758 he contributed about 50 essays to the "Theatre" column in Dodsley's *London Chronicle*, described by Howard Dunbar in *The Dramatic Career of Arthur Murphy* (1956) as "informed, fair, sometimes brilliant criticism." These essays, concerned with current productions, in the words of Spector "introduced a new mode of criticism, going beyond customary plot summary to acute evaluation of production."

In 1758 he resumed his own dramatic career, when on 30 March his farce *The Upholsterer; or, What News?*, owing debts to the *Tatler* and Fielding's *Coffee House Politician*, was produced at Drury Lane for Mossop's benefit. Garrick played the role of Pamphlet, but the play succeeded indifferently. The following season Murphy's first tragedy, *The Orphan of China*, based on Voltaire's *Orphelin de la Chine*, was first acted at Drury Lane on 21 April 1759 (and had been published a few weeks earlier on

3 April). Bolstered by an all-star cast, including Garrick as Zamti, Mossop as Etan, Holland as Hamet, and Mrs Yates as Mandane, and with new scenery and costumes, the tragedy, according to Cross, "went off with great applause." But the success had been bought at the price of a major quarrel with Garrick. For some time Murphy had been unable to commit Garrick to a definite production date. He accused the manager of maneuvering in a nefarious manner to slip out of his agreement to play the piece. The premiere set for 25 February 1759 was postponed to 10 March, and then to 21 April, much to Murphy's irritation. Neither man acted with credit in the dispute over the postponement, but the facts were more on Garrick's side, for he did not receive the completed script until 23 January, and on 18 February it was still being altered and cut. Mrs Cibber became ill during rehearsals and had to be replaced by Mrs Yates—actually Murphy had been rehearsing the latter secretly—and at the height of the season, Oram, one of the theatre's best scene painters, died.

Author and manager patched up their differences, and in the next season, on 24 January 1760, two pieces by Murphy were produced at Drury Lane: *The Desert Island*, a three-act dramatic poem in imitation of Metastasio, and *The Way to Keep Him*, a three-act comedy. The latter play was enlarged to five acts and brought out again at Drury Lane on 10 January 1761. The three and five-act versions of *The Way to Keep Him* were published in 1760 and 1761, respectively.

In the summer of 1761 Murphy joined a reconciled Foote in partnership and rented Drury Lane Theatre, where they offered 23 performances. Among them were Murphy's comedy *All in the Wrong*, played on 15 June, and his farces *The Old Maid* and *The Citizen*, both acted on 2 July.

Over the remaining 40 years of the century nine new plays by Murphy were produced on the London stage, most of them before the end of the 1770s. *No One's Enemy But His Own*, a three-act comedy version of Voltaire's *L'Indiscret*, appeared unsuccessfully at Covent Garden on 9 January 1764, along with Murphy's two-act comedy *What We Must All Come To* (inspired by the *Guardian*, No 173). The plays were victimized by the supporters of John Wilks, and the hissing of the latter prevented completion of the performance. Published that year, *No One's Enemy But His Own* later was shortened to two acts for performance at Covent Garden on 26 October 1774. *What We Must All Come To* was converted to a musical farce, with airs by Hook, and was performed as *Marriage à la Mode* on 22 April 1767. The play was again revived as *Three Weeks after Marriage* at Covent Garden on 30 March 1776, when it was successful and became a frequently played repertory piece. His two-act farce *The Choice* appeared at Covent Garden on 23 March 1765 (not 23 February 1764 as given in *The Dictionary of National Biography*). At the same house on 10 January 1767 was acted *The School for Guardians*, a comedy taken from three plays by Molière (principally *L'Ecole des Femmes*); subsequently it was altered by Thomas Hull into a comic opera called *Love Finds the Way*, performed at Covent Garden on 18 November 1777.

Perhaps in an effort to secure a more estimable reputation and some lasting fame, Murphy then turned to the tragic genre. His previous effort in that line had been the successful *The Orphan of China* in 1759, and he had fared less well with the tragicomedy *The Desert Island* in 1760. After suffering setbacks with recent comedies at Covent Garden, Murphy re-allied with Garrick, their long-standing alienation having been terminated through the good services of the playwright Isaac Bickerstaffe. Murphy's *Zenobia*, an adaptation of Crébillon's *Rhadamiste et Zénobie*, opened at Drury Lane on 27 February 1768 and proved to be one of the superior heroic tragedies of its day. Murphy's benefits totaled £687, less house charges of £220. Four years later, on 26 February 1772, *The Grecian Daughter*, his best-known tragedy, was given a first-rate performance by Garrick's excellent company. On 23 January 1772, when rehearsals were about to begin, Murphy wrote to Garrick: "Were the play to be got up at another playhouse, I should think it absolutely necessary to attend rehearsals, but when you are willing to undertake the trouble, the anxiety of an author may be natural, but it is superfluous." Murphy's fair opinion of Garrick could alter with the wind. In the preface to the published *Zenobia* he had effusively expressed his gratitude for the manager's preparation of that piece. But during the preparation of *The Way to Keep Him* in 1760 Murphy

had written acidly that he thought plays were brought into the green room for rehearsal, not for the purpose of treating the author "as if he were going to school." The remark was provoked by Garrick's insisting on revisions in order to make Lovemore, the role he was to play, more attractive.

The Grecian Daughter was, as Hopkins wrote in his prompter's diary, "very carefully got up & well perform'd, & receiv'd uncommon applause." The tragedy was accorded high praise in the *Oxford Magazine* in March 1772. Murphy's benefits brought him £600. The leading roles of Evander and Euphrasia were admirably played by Spranger and Ann Barry, the latter's performance being accounted among her very best. Later Euphrasia became one of Mrs Siddons's great portrayals; Mrs Piozzi thought her interpretation the noblest example of womanhood and the play "unquestionably" the best modern tragedy.

Despite their success with *The Grecian Daughter*, Murphy and Garrick quarreled once more, this time over the Tragedy *Alzuma*. Murphy had written it in 1762, but political inferences perhaps caused Garrick's coolness toward it and delayed its production. Murphy did not help his cause when he wrote a satirical piece called *Hamlet with Alterations*, a parody of Garrick's alteration of *Hamlet* that had been produced at Drury Lane on 18 December 1772. Murphy's parody was not intended for production, and it was not published in his day, but the manuscript evidently had been seen by some people who brought reports to Garrick. *Hamlet with Alterations* was published in Jesse Foot's biography of Murphy in 1811.

Again on the outs with Garrick, Murphy finally gave his *Alzuma* to Colman at Covent Garden, where it was first performed on 23 February 1773. Colman also subjected Murphy to some play-doctoring, but in the advertisement to the published edition that year Murphy pointedly observed that for the first time in his life he had no reason to feel disgust at the internal occurrences of a theatre. Garrick's judgment, however, was vindicated, for *Alzuma*, suffering from bad casting and staging, though not an outright failure, was coldly received. Murphy's benefits amounted to only £270.

In the advertisement to the printed text of *Alzuma*, Murphy announced his intention to withdraw from writing for the stage in order to devote his time to his legal profession. That resolution was weakened, however, by a paper war with George Steevens, editor and scholar, which erupted in 1773 over the latter's attacks on *Alzuma* in the *Morning Chronicle*. Murphy contributed a prologue to Jephson's *Braganza* at Drury Lane on 17 February 1775, in which he attacked sentimental comedy. Again he satirized sentimental comedy in *News from Parnassus*, a witty dramatic prelude commissioned by Covent Garden to open the season on 23 September 1776. Therein Murphy also complimented Garrick, who had retired at the end of the previous season, so some reconciliation either had taken place or was wished for by Murphy. That December Murphy also successfully defended Foote against charges of sexual perversion brought by his footman at the instigation of the editor William Jackson.

Murphy enjoyed another success with the production of *Know Your Own Mind* at Covent Garden on 22 February 1777. Though the last of his comedies to be presented, Murphy had written the first draft by 1760. One quarrel had caused Murphy to withdraw it from Garrick's consideration in September 1767, and another had caused him to withdraw a revised version late in 1772. Yet Garrick provided the epilogue for the production in 1777. Though handicapped by some inferior acting, *Know Your Own Mind* was given 18 performances before the end of the season and Murphy earned over £600 at his benefits. Murphy had based the piece on Destouche's *L'Irrésolu* and possibly had also borrowed from Foote's *A Trip to Calais*. In turn, *Know Your Own Mind* provided some situations and characters, especially the inspiration for Joseph Surface, for Sheridan's *The School for Scandal*, produced the same season, at Drury Lane on 8 May 1777. These borrowings from Murphy by Sheridan are reviewed in *The Dramatic Career of Arthur Murphy*, where Dunbar writes that Sheridan's play "is the first in wit; of that there can be no question, though the margin is less than one might imagine." While Sheridan's has the wit "of give and take and naturally has more sparkle," Murphy's has wit also. Moreover, Dunbar finds the plot of *Know Your Own Mind* to be "better constructed and integrated," and the female characters to be superior to those in Sheridan's more famous comedy.

On 6 November 1777 Murphy's alteration (with additions) of his *The Orphan of China* appeared at Covent Garden. The *London Chronicle* next day printed a detailed synopsis of Murphy's reworked tragedy.

During the remainder of his life, Murphy occupied himself with his law practice (until he retired from the bar in 1788) and with editing, translating, and writing essays and biographies. He also held several political appointments. His tragedy *The Rival Sisters*, which had been published in his collected *Works* in 1786, was adapted for presentation on the stage at the King's Theatre on 18 March 1793. Staged by Kemble, with Mrs Siddons in the leading role, it was acted six times, the last of Murphy's works to be produced. Subsequently he wrote at least two tragedies, an opera, and part of a comedy, but refused to submit them for production because of his dissatisfaction with the state of the stage. His *Arminius*, a political tragedy condemning the French Revolution, was published by him in 1798 but was not acted.

As a dramatist who had enjoyed a long and prominent career, Murphy was often called upon to offer advice or assistance to other writers, including William Dodd, John Delap, and Fanny Burney. He served as literary advisor to John Palmer's short-lived Royalty Theatre venture in 1787, writing an occasional address for the opening on 20 June, and providing two prologues and a dramatic satire, *A Tale From Baker's Chronicle*. A mock tragedy called *Almirina*, written for the Royalty, has been sometimes attributed to Murphy but probably was by Isaac Jackman. Murphy also supplied prologues and epilogues for various plays.

Other literary productions by Murphy include *A Poetical Epistle to Samuel Johnson* (1760); *An Ode to the Naiads of Fleet Ditch*, an answer to Churchill's *Rosciad*, in which he calls Churchill a "literary pickpocket" and generally insults him in sometimes clever, and sometimes merely scatalogical, language, in 1761; The *Examiner*, in which he answered Maculloch's *The Murphiad*, in 1761; a translation into verse of Beckford's *A Letter from a Right Honourable Person and the Answer to it* (1761); *A Letter from the anonymous author of the Letters Versified to the anonymous writer of the Monitor* (1761); *An Essay on the Life and Genius of Henry Fielding*, in Murphy's edition of Fielding's *Works*

(1762); *The Auditor*, periodical essays from 15 July 1762 to 16 May 1763 in which he supported Lord Bute; contributions to the *Monthly Review* in 1786 and to the *Gentleman's Magazine* in 1787; *Seventeen Hundred and Ninety One*, imitated from Juvenal's thirteenth satire, dedicated to Johnson's memory (1791); *An Essay on the Life and Genius of Samuel Johnson*, published separately and as an introduction to Murphy's edition of Johnson's works (1792); a four-volume translation of *Works of Cornelius Tacitus* (1793); a translation of Sallust's *The History of Cataline's Conspiracy; with the Four Orations of Cicero*, brought out under the pseudonym George Frederick Sydney (1795); *The Bees*, a translation from Vaniere's *Praedium Rusticum* (1799); and a translation into Latin of Addison's *Epistle to Lord Halifax* (1799). Murphy's translation of Sallust was edited by Thomas Moore and published in 1807, and his translation of Vida's Latin poem, *The Game of Chess*, was published in 1876.

Among the most important of Murphy's writings was his publication in 1801, in two volumes, of *The Life of David Garrick*. In 1786 Murphy collected and published his own works up to that time, in seven volumes.

In 1758 Murphy had written a farce called *The Rout*, which was not acted and which occasioned yet another quarrel with Garrick because on 20 December of that year the manager brought out a new play by John Hill, with the same title. In February 1761 Murphy received £120 in advance from Garrick for three plays: *The Citizen*, *The Embarrassment*, and *The Humourist*. The latter two were not acted. In the sale of Murphy's effects in December 1805 were three manuscripts, which, according to Jesse Foot, were in his hand: *The Heroic Sisters*, a tragedy; *The Duke of Florence*, a tragedy; and *The Gardener of Sidon*, a musical drama. Three other plays, *The Graces*, *The Comical Fellow*, and *The Tender Wife*, were sold at that time and seem to have been by him. Another drama called *Prometheus; or, The World Display'd* may also have been his.

In 1788 Murphy retired from the bar and sold his chamber in Lincoln's Inn for 2000 guineas. His clients had included Sir Patrick Blake (divorce), Captain Baillie, the Lt Gov of Green Hospital (in a case for libel brought by Lord Sandwich), members of the Thrale family, Lord Montford, Baron Rodney, and Charles Macklin. Having been appointed by Lord Loughborough as a commissioner of bankrupts in 1765, he served until he resigned in February 1778, and then again held the position from 1795 to 1805. In 1779 he had been appointed Recorder of Sudbury, a post he filled until his resignation in 1789.

Murphy's plays and practice had brought him a considerable income. He had also inherited from Mrs James Plunkett (from the estate of Jeffrey French) a bequest of West Indian slaves, whom he sold for £1000. Another legacy of £2000 came from Mrs Ford, a relative. Nevertheless he remained in financial distress for some time. He spent large sums in attempts to publish his various translations. He also seems to have lived beyond his means, enjoying good food and the good society in which he was much respected. Johnson, it was said in Maxwell's *Collectanea*, "very much loved him." Murphy became a member of Johnson's Essex Head Club in December 1783, and he was also an intimate of the Prince of Wales and of Samuel Rogers.

About 1788 he moved from Brentwood to Chiswick, and in the 1790s he lived in a house in the westernmost end of Hammersmith Terrace. Financial circumstances forced him to sell the Hammersmith house in 1799; he moved to Brompton and, in 1800, to No 14, Queen's Row, Knightsbridge. A debt of £500 was forgiven by Thomas Coutts, the banker to whom he had dedicated his biography of Garrick. On 5 January 1803, at the instigation of Henry Addington, George III granted Murphy a pension of £200 per year, thereby allowing him to live the remaining several years of his life with some dignity. But by then he was failing in health and mind. He died at his house in Knightsbridge on 18 June 1805, at the age of 77, and was buried, as he had requested, in St Paul's, Hammersmith, where an epitaph was placed by Jesse Foot.

Though he was never married, Murphy lived for some time with the actress Ann Elliot, who was his protégée and played the original Maria in his *The Citizen* at the Haymarket in July 1761. About 1766 he gave her up to the Duke of Cumberland. Yet, as *Thraliana* claimed, Murphy's "heart was exhausted of Love by Miss Elliot," and they remained friends until her death in 1769. He declined her bequest of most of her money, but he served as one of the executors of her estate and proved her will on 15 July 1769.

Murphy's elder brother James Murphy, born in Dublin in September 1725, was educated at Westminster School and entered the Middle Temple. Soon after being called to the bar he changed his name and adopted the surname French. Occasionally he wrote for his brother's *Gray's Inn Journal*, and he authored two plays, *The Brothers* and *The Conjuror; or, The Enchanted Garden*, neither of which was acted or published; the manuscripts were sold with Arthur Murphy's library in 1805. James Murphy went to Jamaica on his uncle's business in 1758 and died at Kingston soon after on 5 January 1759.

The biography of Arthur Murphy published in 1811 by Jesse Foot (but evidently actually written by William Combe) was founded on Murphy's papers, including an autobiographical sketch. He has also been well served by three modern biographers to whom this notice is much indebted: Howard K. Dunbar, *The Dramatic Career of Arthur Murphy* (1946); John P. Emery, *Arthur Murphy: An Eminent Dramatist of the Eighteenth Century* (1946); and Robert D. Spector, *Arthur Murphy* (1979). Those biographies offer considerable and valuable discussions of his plays. Murphy has also been the subject of numerous articles in learned journals. *The Way to Keep Him and Five Other Plays*, edited by J. P. Emery, was published in 1956. Arthur Sherbo has edited *New Essays by Arthur Murphy* (1968), and Matthew Grace has edited *The Lives of Henry Fielding and Samuel Johnson, together with essays from the Gray's-Inn Journal* (1968). In the Folger Shakespeare Library is Murphy's "Common Place Book," a manuscript of 525 pages containing descriptions of many of his contemporaries; it is described, in part, by J. H. Caskey in "Arthur Murphy's Commonplace Book," *Studies in Philology* 37 (1940).

Murphy was a well-built man, with an oval face of fair complexion but marked with the smallpox.

Portraits of Arthur Murphy include:

1. By Nathaniel Dance. Oil on canvas, in the National Portrait Gallery (No 10). A similar portrait by Dance is in the National Gallery of Ireland (No 939). Engravings by T. Cook, published by Cadell as a plate to Murphy's collected works, 1786; by W. Ridley, published as a plate to *European Magazine*, 1805; by N. Ward, published by Thompson, 1805; by Neagle, published by Stockdale, 1811; by P. Condé, published as a plate to J. Foot's *Life of Arthur Murphy*, 1811; by J. Romney, after Brighty, published by Dyer, 1817; and by Hall, published as a plate to *Biographical Magazine*, 1820.

2. By N. Dance. Location unknown. Engraving by E. Scriven, after J. Jackson, published as a plate to *Contemporary Portraits*, 1815.

3. By Joshua Reynolds. Location unknown. According to Howard Dunbar, Murphy sat for Reynolds in 1779.

4. Engraving by P. Condé. At age 72. From a wax model by T. R. Poole, 1799. Published as a plate to Foot's *Life of Arthur Murphy*, 1811.

5. Engraving by W. Ridley, after S. Drummond. Published as a plate to the *Monthly Mirror*, 1798.

6. Engraving by E. Scriven, from a marble bust by P. Turnerelli.

7. By unknown engraver. Published in *Town and Country Magazine*, XX, 1788.

Murray. *See also* **MURRY**.

Murray, Mr [*fl.* 1772], *actor*.

A Mr Murray acted Bauldy in *The Gentle Shepherd*, for the benefit of Lauder's widow, at the Haymarket Theatre on 21 December 1772.

Murray, Mr [*fl.* 1781–1797], *actor*.

A Mr Murray appeared at the Crown Inn, Islington, on 5 April 1781 as Ernesto in *The Orphan* and gave two specialty monologues: *A Dissertation on Macaronies* and *Abel Drugger's Descripton of a Fête Champêtre*. At the Haymarket on 9 February 1784 a Mr Murray played the female role of Madge in a curious performance of *The Gentle Shepherd*; that piece was repeated on 24 January 1785, but with Murray as Bauldy. A playbill for the Windsor Castle Inn, King Street, Hammersmith, on 17 June 1785 contains a Murray's name for Frederick in *The Wonder*; but one copy of that bill (now in the New York Public Library for the Performing Arts at Lincoln Center) bears a hand deletion of his name, with Mr Francis's substituted. Mr Murray was a member of the company at Richmond, Surrey, in the summer of 1785.

At the Haymarket on 12 December 1791 a Mr Murray took a benefit; his name did not appear in the bills for a role, but Lady Randolph in *Douglas* was played by Mrs Murray. A similar circumstance prevailed at that theatre on 26 December 1792, when again Murray had a benefit and Mrs Murray acted Lady Randolph.

On 4 December 1797 a Mr Murray acted Young Wilding in *The Citizen* at the Haymarket.

Murray, Mrs ₍*fl.* *1791–1792*₎. *See also* WHEELER, ELIZA.

Murray, Mrs ₍*fl.* *1791–1792*₎, *actress*.
A Mrs Murray acted Lady Randolph in *Douglas* at the Haymarket Theatre on 12 December 1791, for the benefit of a Mr Murray, presumably her husband, whose name did not appear in the bills for a role that night. Mrs Murray played Emilia in *Othello* at the Haymarket on 6 February 1792, and on 26 December 1792 she again appeared there as Lady Randolph, for Mr Murray's benefit. This actress seems not to have been either Mrs Charles Murray the second (fl. 1770–1799) or Eliza Wheeler (d. 1794) who acted as Mrs Murray for a while in 1791–1792; those women were primarily comic and singing actresses, respectively.

Murray, Alexander ₍*fl.* *1672–1705?*₎, *wardrobe keeper*.
The London Stage lists Alexander Murray as a member of the King's Company in 1672–73. The Lord Chamberlain's accounts named him as "Tyreman" and wardrobe keeper on 13 June 1673. Perhaps he was the Alexander Murray whose wife Alice was buried at St Paul, Covent Garden, on 14 December 1705, though the name was not uncommon. An Alexander Murray from St Giles in the Fields was buried at St Paul, Covent Garden, on 18 October 1716; he may have been related to our subject.

Murray, Andrew ₍*fl.* *1800*₎, *actor, manager*.
A license to act plays and entertainments at the Haymarket Theatre was granted to Andrew Murray on 12 May 1800. *The London Stage*, however, records no performances at the Haymarket subsequent to that license until

Colman opened his regular summer season on 13 June 1800. Possibly Andrew Murray was the actor of that surname who played occasionally at London in the 1780s and 1790s.

Murray, Charles *1754–1821*, *actor, playwright*.
Charles Murray was born at Cheshunt, Hertfordshire, in 1754. He was the son of Sir John Murray, baronet (1718–1777), of Broughton, who in the rebellion of 1745 was secretary to the Pretender and was subsequently arraigned for high treason but was pardoned by the King. He is noticed in *The Dictionary of National Biography*. Our subject was the eldest of six children by Sir John Murray's second wife, a Miss Webb, a young Quaker

Harvard Theatre Collection

CHARLES MURRAY

engraving by Chapman

whom Murray had found in a provincial English boarding school. Charles had three half-brothers, sons of his father's first wife Margaret Ferguson: David, who inherited the baronetcy and became a naval officer; Robert, who succeeded to the title upon David's death in 1791 without issue; and Thomas, who became a lieutenant general.

Young Charles Murray was given an excellent classical education under his father's direction and was sent to France to acquire fluency in the language. He studied pharmacy and some surgery under a physician in London, and was a surgeon's mate in service which took him on several voyages into the Mediterranean.

After leaving the sea service in 1773, Murray performed in a private theatre. That amateur experience was in Liverpool, according to the *Biographia Dramatica*; but J. Austin's note on a playbill in the British Library indicates it was at Chester, and that he had used the name Raymur to save his family embarrassment. His success encouraged him to apply for a position with Younger, then manager at Liverpool. Though Younger had no vacancy he recommended Murray to Wilkinson at York. On 21 April 1773 at York, for Gay's benefit, nineteen-year-old Murray, using the name Raymur, made his professional debut as Carlos in Cibber's *Love Makes a Man; or, The Fop's Fortune*. In his *Wandering Patentee*, Wilkinson described Murray's success under difficult circumstances:

Within five or six days of a Mr. Gay's benefit night . . . he for some reason . . . wanted "The Fop's Fortune," but we had not any *Carlos*: It was what we on the stage term *twenty lengths*, a part very considerable, and difficult cramp study; and I dare aver Mr. Raymur had never read the play, nor seen it: However, without hesitation, he with joy to get on the stage, accepted the character, and actually performed it literally perfect, and was received as a good actor from that night. . . .

The young "Raymur" continued to prove a quick and apt study and soon became a "useful performer," as Wilkinson put it, on the York circuit. But in a tavern at Wakefield in September 1776, he quarreled with another drinker over what he conceived to be a slur on his profession. The next night at the theatre a party appeared to shut up the place because of the actor's behavior at the tavern unless he

came forward to confess and apologize. Murray refused, thus forcing Wilkinson reluctantly to dismiss him.

In 1777, Murray was stationed under Griffiths at Norwich, where he resumed his real name and increased his reputation over the next eight years. A number of references to Murray appear in the *Committee Books* of the Norwich Theatre, usually in connection with advances or payments on notes. On 28 May 1778 he was advanced 15 guineas. His application for a loan of £50 was refused on 28 November 1780. His first wife was also a member of the company. Their combined salary in 1777–78 was a very modest £1 16s. per week; on 28 May 1779 it was advanced to £2 6s. 6d. On 29 January 1780 the *Norwich Chronicle* reported that Mrs Murray had died on 21 January, at the age of 21.

By 1782 Murray was living with the Norwich actress Anne Payne (née Acres); she was the wife of the actor Jonathan Payne, from whom she had become estranged after 1776. Payne did not die, it seems, until 1784, so whether or not Murray and Ann Payne ever married is not clear. She acted as Mrs Murray on the Norwich and York circuits until 1785.

While at Norwich, Murray wrote several pieces for the stage. His farce *The Experiment* was played at Norwich on 10 May 1779 and was published there that year. The manuscript is in the Larpent Collection at the Huntington Library. He has also been credited with the authorship of *The New Maid of the Oaks*, said to have been acted at Norwich and published there in 1778, but this bad tragedy is assigned by the *Biographia Dramatica* to one "Ahab Salem."

In the autumn of 1785, having been offered excellent terms, Murray and his wife joined the company at Bath, where on 8 October he made his first appearance as Sir Giles Overreach in *A New Way to Pay Old Debts*. On 3 December 1785 he was the original Albert in Reynolds's *Werter*. During his first season at Bath and Bristol he also acted Clifford in *The Heiress*, Evander in *The Grecian Daughter*, Oakly in *The Jealous Wife*, Pierre in *Venice Preserv'd* Macbeth, Shylock, Iago, Iachimo, and other characters. According to Genest, the Murrays did not sell a single ticket when they appeared for their benefit as Gibbet and Cherry in *The Beaux' Stratagem*.

But over the next 11 seasons Murray became a favorite at Bath and Bristol. According to *Farley's Bristol Journal* of 15 October 1796, "he was heard with applause and attention on stage, respected in private, and his benefits were always crouded." Among his best roles were Adam in *As You Like It*, Sir Peter Teazle in *The School for Scandal*, Old Dornton in *The Road to Ruin*, and King John. The Murrays also played occasionally in other provincial cities, appearing at Swansea in August 1789, Wexford in 1789, and at Crow Street, Dublin, from 1791 to 1794.

Having received an engagement at Covent Garden Theatre for the 1796–97 season at £9 per week, Murray took his farewell benefit at Bristol as Polixenes and his daughter Harriet

Courtesy of the Garrick Club

CHARLES MURRAY, as Tobias
by De Wilde

appeared as Perdita in *Florizel and Perdita*. In his address Murray made the usual protestations of friendship and expressed his reluctance to leave Bristol. The *Monthly Mirror* of August 1796 described Murray as "a man of cultivated genius and understanding, who in every character was respectable, and in some particular lines unrivalled." The *Authentic Memoirs of the Green Room* (1799) claimed that while at Bath Murray had received instruction from John Henderson, and "frequently reminded us of his master," but Henderson had died in November 1785 in London, only a few months after Murray had arrived at Bath.

Murray's first appearance at Covent Garden was on 30 September 1796 as Shylock in *The Merchant of Venice* and Bagatelle in *The Poor Soldier*. The reviews were mixed, as the critics proffered general praise to him for his acting but observed that the role of Shylock was not suitable to display his talents to proper advantage. The *Monthly Mirror* found his delivery "manly and sensible, and his articulation perfectly distinct," but complained of "a drawl in his recitation" that tended to produce "langour and inattention." The writer in *How Do You Do* on 8 October 1796 noted the same defect. Murray's action also was described as deficient in majesty or grace. His face was amiable and interesting but lacked strong expression. His figure was heavy—he appeared to be about 45 years of age (he was 42)—and though his voice had little range it was "sweeter and better modulated in the *level*," than perhaps that of any other actor on the stage. Despite his shortcomings, he was in the judgment of the *Monthly Mirror* better suited for the roles of older tragic figures (Shylock aside) like Lear, Old Norval, or Evander "than any actor we ever remember to have seen."

The other roles in which Murray appeared during his first season at Covent Garden included Alcanor in *Mahomet*, Henry in *1 Henry IV*, Iago in *Othello*, Old Norval in *Douglas*, Monsieur Grand Pas in the premiere of Holman's *Abroad and at Home* on 19 November 1796, the King in *Philaster*, Mr Heartly in *The Guardian*, Lusignan in *Zara*, Strickland in *The Suspicious Husband*, Thoroughgood in *The London Merchant*, Dr Caius in *The Merry Wives of Windsor*, Sir Hubert Stanley in *A Cure for the Heart-Ache*, Justice in the premiere of Reynolds's musical entertainment *Bantry Bay* on

18 February 1797, the Duke of Urbino in the premiere of Hoare's comic opera *Italian Villagers* on 25 April 1797, Sir Thomas Severn in *The Tatler*, Stukely in *The Gamester*, Mr Ordeal in *The Fashionable Levities*, Sempronius in *Cato*, Sir George Touchwood in *The Belle's Stratagem*, Sidney in *The Man of the World*, Lord Norland in *Every One Has His Fault*, Scandal in *Love for Love*, and Moody in *The Country Girl*. Murray also played one night at Drury Lane, appearing on 29 May 1797 for the indisposed Thomas King as Sir Peter Teazle in *The School for Scandal*, with Mrs Jordan as Lady Teazle, for the latter's benefit. Sir Peter, according to the *Monthly Mirror*, "was a part well suited to Murray, who excels in the still and the pathetic." He was especially impressive in the screen scene. In his *Pin Basket to the Children of Thespis* (1797), John Williams was not so complimentary to Murray, calling him a "ridiculous oaf" who never should have left Bath.

After an engagement at Birmingham in the summer of 1797, Murray returned to Covent Garden for his second season, again at £9 per week, to become a very busy actor, mainly in his walk of old men. Among his many new roles in 1797–98 were the Ghost in *Hamlet*, Stockwell in *The West Indian*, Gloster in *Jane Shore*, and Acasto in *The Orphan*. On 2 October 1797, Holman being ill, Murray filled in as Richard III and, according to the October *Monthly Mirror*, delighted "with the originality of his conception and the subtilty of his discrimination." His voice, however, failed from the beginning—"The house is too large for his powers." On 20 November he acted King Lear for the first time in London (having first played the role at Bath on 21 February 1788). On 23 November he was the original Sir Oliver Montrath in Cumberland's *False Impressions* and on 13 February 1798 the original Doctor Gosterman in Holcroft's *He's Much to Blame*. At his benefit on 12 May 1798 Murray acted the Englishman in *Voluntary Contributions* and Polixenes in *Florizel and Perdita*—with his daughter Harriet making her London debut as Perdita. Tickets were available from Murray at No 77, Longacre, and gross receipts were £198 17s.

During 1798 Murray enjoyed a better press, at least from T. Harral in his *Monody on the Death of Palmer*, who pointed out that he was a "chaste actor" of unequaled quality:

When you see Murray on the boards you see a gentleman: no stage tricks, no studied attitude, no affected tone; but all is happy, easy nature. . . . Murray pleases only the discerning few. . . . Murray is allowed to be the first Shylock of the day. In genteel comedy he is all that can be wished. Yet possessed of all these excellencies, Murray will never acquire universal popularity. But he does more—he deserves it.

After playing at Bristol in the summer of 1798, Murray began his third season at Covent Garden with a salary raised to £10 per week. On 11 October 1798 he was the original Baron Wildenheim in Mrs Inchbald's *Lovers' Vows*, on 23 November he played Specific in the first London performance of T. J. Dibdin's *The Jew and the Doctor*, and on 12 January 1799 he was the original Cleveland in Holman's *The Votary of Wealth*. For his benefit on 10 May 1799 he acted Friar Lawrence, and his daughter Harriet played Juliet. The same evening, Mrs Murray—who seems to have been in retirement for several years—made her first appearance as Jacintha in *Lovers' Quarrels*. Murray's receipts were £263, less house charges, and his address was still No 77, Longacre. The Murrays engaged at Liverpool in the summer of 1799.

In 1799–1800 at Covent Garden, he was praised by Thomas Dutton in *The Dramatic Censor* for his acting Strickland in *The Suspicious Husband* on 8 January 1800 as "The very character which the author designed":

He evinced a command of countenance which spoke the part, if we may be allowed the paradox, without words. A dramatic writer need never wish to have a more accurate exposition of his ideas. To uncommon justness of conception, Mr. MURRAY joins equal powers of expression; he is, beyond controversy, the very first declaimer the stage of Covent-garden can boast.

Murray's original roles that season included the Hermit in Cumberland's *Joanna* on 16 January 1800 and Morrington in Morton's *Speed the Plough* on 8 February.

Murray continued to act at Covent Garden through 1816–1817. On 3 May 1817 he played Alvarez in the premiere of *Apostate*. He also appeared in the farewell performances of John Philip Kemble, ending with *Coriolanus* on 23 June 1817. His failing health and infirmities were unkindly commented upon in the *Monthly Mirror* of February 1817. Murray took his own

CHARLES MURRAY, as Heartly
engraving by Maddocks, after De Wilde

farewell at Covent Garden on 17 July 1817 as
Brabantio to Young's Othello, Booth's Iago,
and Miss O'Neill's Desdemona.

Drawing £70 per year from the Covent Garden Fund, Murray lived for a while at No 4,
Tufton Street, Westminster, and, in 1818, at
No 24, Maiden Lane, Covent Garden. Some
of his time was passed assisting his son, William Henry Murray, in obtaining licenses from
John Larpent for performances of plays in
Edinburgh. Threatened by paralysis, the elder
Murray soon retired to Edinburgh to be near
his children. He died there on 8 November
1821.

Murray's chief characters—of interesting old
men in tragedy and comedy—were represented with a special dignity. His portrayal of
Eustace Saint Pierre in *The Surrender of Calais*

was notable, reported the *Peep into Paris* (1794),
for the glowing warmth revealed in "The rough
patriot, the brave undaunted citizen, and the
feeling parent. . . ." Murray was a pleasant
man, it seems, who, in the words of the author
of *The Festival of Wit* (1806), was "notorious
for dealing in the marvellous, telling a very
strange and improbable story." On 15 October
1796 *Farley's Bristol Journal* described him as
"just and exemplary in all his dealings: his
demeanor in private life is truly commendable,
and his conduct behind the scenes secure him
the affection of every individual—Of all the
men who have so long been held in public
admiration, Charles Murray is the most humble, being destitute of every particle of pride,
vanity, and affectation."

Murray's second wife, Ann Murray, the former Mrs Payne, had evidently retired from the
stage by the turn of the century. The date of
her death is unknown to us. Information on
Murray's children by her is in her notice. The
Monthly Mirror of October 1801 reported the
death of "the eldest son of Mr. Murray, of
Covent Garden theatre, of the yellow fever," at
Surinam; that child was perhaps by Murray's
first wife, who died in 1780.

Portraits of Charles Murray include:

1. Engraved portrait by J. Chapman, from
a painting. Published as a plate to *Thespian
Dictionary*, 1802; another impression in same
publication, 1805.

2. As Baron Wildenheim in *Lovers' Vows*,
Painting by Gainsborough Dupont. In the
Garrick Club (No 472).

3. As Baron Wildenheim. Painting by Sir
John Watson Gordon, a free copy after Dupont. In the Garrick Club (No 573).

4. As Demetrius in *The Brothers*. Engraving
by W. Leney. Published as a plate to *Bell's
British Theatre*, 1797.

5. As Heartly in *The Guardian*. Engraving
by Maddocks, after De Wilde. Published as a
plate to *Minor British Theatre*, 1805.

6. As Tobias in *The Stranger*. Watercolor
drawing by De Wilde, 1815. In the Garrick
Club (No 65E)

**Murray, Mrs Charles the second, Ann,
née Acres, earlier Mrs Jonathan Payne**
[*fl.* 1770–1799], *actress, dancer, singer.*
The actress who was born Ann Acres was by
February 1770 the wife of the actor Jonathan

Payne, and in that month they were in a troupe playing in Glasgow. The following autumn, Mr and Mrs Payne were engaged as dancers.

The Paynes came to London on 18 September 1772 to play Young Meadows and Lucinda in a performance of *Love in a Village* at the Haymarket Theatre. They returned north and together they remained members of the companies at Norwich and York until 1776, after which year their careers did not run parallel. Payne was to be found in the south, mainly at Bath and Bristol, until his death on 18 December 1784. Mrs Payne, however, evidently estranged from her husband, remained in the north, mainly at Norwich. She acted at the New Theatre in Derby in September 1775 and at Richmond, Surrey, in June 1778 (when Payne was also there), and again at Derby in December 1779.

In 1781, Mrs Payne was earning £1 5s. per week as a member of the Norwich company. Sometime soon after, in 1782 it seems, she began to call herself Mrs Murray, having become the second wife of the Norwich actor Charles Murray, whose first wife, also a Norwich performer, had died at the age of 21 in January 1780. It is not clear that Ann Payne was legally married to Murray at this time, because Jonathan Payne, from whom she was estranged, did not die until 1784.

Mrs Murray acted with Charles Murray on the Norwich and York circuit until 1785, and then they became familiar performers at Bath and Bristol for over a decade. She also acted at Brighton in 1786. She was probably the Mrs Murray who was at Limerick in November 1790 and March 1791, at Cork in the summer of 1791, and at Crow Street, Dublin, also in that latter year. At Mrs Murray's benefit in Bath on 19 May 1796, her daughter Harriet played the Fine Lady in *Lethe* and her husband spoke a farewell. The receipts of £64 were disappointing.

Though her husband began a successful and long engagement at Covent Garden Theatre in September 1796, Mrs Murray made only one appearance there. On 10 May 1799 she acted Jacintha in *Lovers' Quarrels*, for her husband's benefit. That night Murray played Friar Lawrence in *Romeo and Juliet*, and their daughter Harriet Murray (later Mrs Henry Siddons) appeared as Juliet. Her engagement with her husband at Liverpool in the summer of 1799

is the last record we have of Mrs Murray, though she may have lived on in retirement for some years.

The *Norwich Chronicle* of 21 February 1784 had referred to Mrs Murray as "the Thalia of Norwich" and remarked on her "truly comic face."

By her former marriage to Jonathan Payne, Ann Murray had a son who acted at York in 1776. A daughter called Miss Payne married the actor William Noble at Newcastle on 6 March 1803 (the *Gentleman's Magazine* identified her as the daughter of Mrs Charles Murray, "by a former husband"); as Mrs Noble, she acted with her husband at Norwich from 1804 to 1806, and in the latter year became a chorus singer in the summer company at the Haymarket Theatre.

At least three of Ann Murray's children were sired by Charles Murray. Maria Murray appeared as Titania in *A Midsummer Night's Dream* at Bath on 11 March 1794, for her father's benefit. She subsequently became the first wife of the actor and author Joseph Leathley Cowell (1792–1863) and the mother of the scene painter Joe Cowell, the actor William Cowell, and the singer Samuel Houghton Cowell. Another of Charles and Ann Murray's daughters, Harriet Murray, born in 1783, acted as a child at Bath and made her first appearance at Covent Garden as Perdita in *The Winter's Tale* on 12 May 1798; in 1802 she married the actor Henry Siddons (the son of the famous Sarah Siddons); she is noticed in this dictionary under her married name. Charles and Ann Murray's son, William Henry Murray, born in 1790, played modest roles at Covent Garden in the first decade of the nineteenth century and then managed at Edinburgh for many years; he is noticed in *The Dictionary of National Biography*. Also, the *Monthly Mirror* of October 1801 reported the death at Surinam, from yellow fever, of the eldest son of Charles Murray; but that child may have been the issue of Murray's first marriage.

Murray, Harriet. *See* SIDDONS, MRS HENRY.

Murray, John   *d. 1687?, actor?*

The *London Stage* lists John Murray as a member of the King's Company in 1668–69 and 1669–70. The Lord Chamberlain's accounts cited Murray as a member of the troupe's staff on 12 January 1669. Perhaps he was the John Murray who was buried at St Paul, Covent Garden, on 23 February 1687.

Murray, William ₍*fl.* 1674?–1695?₎, *treasurer.*

The Lord Chamberlain's accounts named William Murray as a member of the King's Company as of 9 November 1675. In a court case in 1695, analyzed by Leslie Hotson in *The Commonwealth and Restoration Stage*, William Murray testified to the activities of the company in 1681–82, when Charles Killigrew was at law with Richard Kent and the troupe was taking money out of Kent's share of the rent to the tune of £150 or £200. Murray, the company treasurer, also testified that the actor Philip Griffin carried off some of the troupe's costumes. How long Murray served as company treasurer is not known, but the records suggest that he may have held the post as early as 1674 and perhaps also worked as the United Company's treasurer from 1682 to 1695. *The London Stage* does not list Murray.

Murry. *See also* MURRAY.

Murry, Mr ₍*fl.* 1749₎, *actor.*

A Mr Murry acted Brazen in *The Recruiting Officer* on 9 January 1749 at a booth in Southwark.

"Musardo, Signor" ₍*fl.* 1754₎, *actor?*

"Mrs Midnight" (Christopher Smart) put on an entertainment called *Sack Posset* at the Haymarket Theatre on 10 September 1754; among other things presented was "Mad Tom by Sg Musardo." Musardo may have been a performer's real name—if the performer was a human being and not, perhaps, a trained animal—but it is more likely that it was a pseudonym, of the sort that Smart often gave his performers.

"Muscovita, La." *See* PANICHI, LUCIA.

Musgrave, Mrs ₍*fl.* 1774–1778₎, *actress.*

Mrs Musgrave (or Musgrove) acted at Drury Lane Theatre from 1774–75 to her retirement in 1778, according to the accounts, though she seems not to have been named in any bills. Her salary in 1776–77 was £1 weekly. She had

subscribed 10*s.* 6*d.* to the Drury Lane Fund in 1775.

"Musical Child, The." *See also* CROTCH, WILLIAM.

"Musical Child, The" *b.* 1782, *pianist, mandolin player.*

The bill at Astley's Amphitheatre on 6 June 1785 advertised the appearance of "The Musical Child," a toddler only 36 months old from Newcastle upon Tyne who played the pianoforte. The prodigy had, the bill boasted, "the judgment of the most professed theorist in Music, and is allowed by all ranks of persons, to be the most astonishing natural production that ever made its appearance in the known world." The bill for 21 July called the infant "a great phenomenon." After frequent appearances in the summer of 1785 the tiny mite was brought back in 1786, and the bill for 24 July called the musical child "the best mandoline player in the world." There were many other appearances, not described in detail, but one supposes that the child performed on both the piano and the mandolin during the season.

The prodigy was not heard again at Astley's until 1793, during which year its appearances were also recorded at the Royal Circus. On 8 April and again on 24 October the pantomime *Maternal Affection* concluded with a concerto "led" by the musical child. There is no certainty that the child in 1793 was the same as the one in the 1780s, nor can we be sure whether the prodigy was a girl or a boy.

"Musical Small Coal Man, The." *See* BRITTON, THOMAS.

Mussini, Nicolò ₍*fl.* 1790₎, *singer.*

From 27 February to 10 July 1790 the tenor Nicolò Mussini sang in London; except for the last date, when he was at Covent Garden Theatre, all of his appearances were at the Haymarket Theatre. He was first heard as Conte in *La villanella rapita*, then he sang an unnamed character in the first act of *La buona figliuola*, Demofoonte in *L'usurpator innocente*, a part in *Andromaca*, and, at Covent Garden, a part in *Le generosità d'Alessandro*.

Mussolini, Signor [fl. 1773], *mandolin and guitar player.*

On 27 April 1773 Signor Mussolini made his first appearance in public at Covent Garden Theatre playing a concerto on the double mandolin and royal guitar and accompanying a young gentlewoman in a song.

Mussulmo, Mahomet Achmed Vizaro [fl. 1747], *equilibrist.*

At Bartholomew Fair on 22 August 1747 at Hussey's booth equilibres on the slack rope were performed by Mahomet Achmed Vizaro Mussulmo, who had recently arrived from Constantinople.

Mutlow, Master [fl. 1790?], *singer.*

The *Catalogue of Printed Music in the British Museum* cites two songs by Hayes, *Anna's Bower* and *Lovely Polly*, both published about 1790 and both sung by Master Mutlow (Mucklow?).

Muzioli, Signor [fl. 1763], *dancer.*

Signor Muzioli made his first appearance on an English stage on 8 March 1763 when he danced a new comic piece called *The Tyrolese* at Covent Garden Theatre.

Myer, John *d. c. 1683, violinist.*

In Foster's *London Marriages* we find that on 7 December 1660 Jervas Price of Westminster, gentleman, received a license to marry Martha Mayer, spinster, daughter of John Mayer of St Peter, Paul's Wharf. Though the spelling is different, the father of the bride may have been the Restoration court violinist John Myer (whose name turned up as Myre and Mayer in the Lord Chamberlain's accounts on occasion). Jervas Price, the groom, was certainly Gervase Price, who became the King's Sergeant Trumpeter.

John Myer was appointed a musician in ordinary for the violin in the King's Musick on 14 November 1662, but the warrant noted that he had to serve without fee until a salaried post was vacated. That must have happened before 10 July 1665, when John was noted as a member of the King's band of 24 violins under John Banister. His annual salary in 1668 was £4 10s. 10d., plus livery, and he augmented his income whenever he accompanied the King out of London, as he did in May and June 1670, when he went to Dover. The Lord

Chamberlain's accounts show that beginning 28 May 1668 he had been receiving the salary previously paid William Youckney, who had died. Youckney's mother petitioned on 21 May 1672 for half of that salary—there must have been some agreement dating from 1668 that Myer would pay her a portion. John's salary was stopped in July until his debt to Mrs Youckney was paid, but it was begun again in January 1673 and then once more cut to half in July. Myer may have been the victim of delinquent livery payments, as were most of the court musicians, and if he was in financial straits, he may have tried to renege on his payments to Youckney's mother.

A July 1674 warrant directed that Myer, among others, should practice at the theatre in Whitehall under Monsieur Cambert and prepare to attend the King at Windsor for the remainder of the summer. On 15 February 1675 Myer played violin in the court masque *Calisto*; he went once more to Windsor in the summers of 1675 and 1678. Myer was in financial trouble again in February 1680, when he had to assign part of his salary to a creditor. Henry Heale was appointed to replace John Myer, deceased, on 26 February 1683. Usually such replacements were made very soon after the death of a court musician.

Myers. *See also* MEYERS and MORRICE.

Myers, Thomas [fl. 1794], *singer.*

Doane's *Musical Directory* of 1794 listed Thomas Myers, of Ferry Street, near Lambeth Church, as a bass who sang for the Chapel Royal, but was no longer a member of that organization. Myers belonged to the Academy of Ancient Music, sang at the Oxford Meeting in 1793, and participated in the oratorios at Covent Garden Theatre and Westminster Abbey.

Myners, Miss. *See* MINORS, SYBILLA.

Mynet. *See* MYNITT.

Mynitt, William *b. 1710, actor, singer.*

In his *A General History of the Stage* (1749) William Rufus Chetwood inserted a thumbnail sketch of William Mynitt which instructs us that he was born of good family at Weobly, Hertfordshire, in 1710, was early sent to London to be apprenticed, and deserted business for the stage. Oddly, instead of the usual heroic attempts of debutants he selected Polonius and gained such applause that "he resolv'd to put on the Sock, with which he walked an easy Pace in the right Road to perfection."

That first trial, wrote Chetwood, was "at the Theatre in the Hay-Market (commonly call'd the French House)." Afterwards Mynitt went to the Bath company, where he gave good satisfaction and where "persons of Distinction" promised to recommend him to one of the established theatres in London. But instead, Mynitt joined a company going to Ireland.

None of that progression is recoverable in other records preserved today. The first performance by Mynitt shown by surviving bills was when he played Faction in Britannia, a "New English Opera" by Thomas Lediard and John Frederick Lampe, at the Haymarket on 16 November 1732. He played thereafter that season Dick in The Farmer's Son, the Country Squire (Guardian to Colombine) in Love Runs All Dangers, Leander in The Mock Doctor, and Doodle in The Opera of Operas. Those were Mynitt's only recorded London appearances.

The following fifteen years of his history are dark except for one brief gleam, and even after that little detail is known. Company rosters compiled from Dublin bills and newspaper notices by W. S. Clark show that Mynitt was at Smock Alley Theatre in 1743–44, at Capel Street in 1746–47, and back at Smock Alley in 1747–48. Not recorded in 1749–50, Mynitt was at Smock Alley every season from 1750–51 to 1758–59, and at Crow Street 1759–60 and 1761–62. In addition, Clark discovered him at Cork on 13 September 1756 and 8 May 1757. He was at Edinburgh in April and May 1758. He was at Cork on 14 August and 20 September 1758, 25 July and 30 September 1760, 27 October 1762, 14 September 1764, and 26 September 1765. C. B. Hogan tells us that Mynitt was back in Dublin for the season of 1764–65. Mynitt was still alive on 2 June 1768, for Faulkner's Dublin Journal proclaimed a "ticket night" for him then.

Mynitt was married by 1743, when Mrs Mynitt's name began appearing in Smock Alley playbills. Chetwood, who never saw her act, was nevertheless able to testify to her "amiable person and excellent voice." She seems to have been a capable actress whose career closely paralleled her husband's as to place and theatre. She did, however, play in Edinburgh in the winter season of 1757–58, seemingly without her husband. James C. Dibdin's Annals (1888) cited an announcement, dated 26 November 1757, that her chaise had overturned and her face had been painfully bruised. Nevertheless, that evening the redoubtable lady played Estifania in Rule a Wife and Have a Wife. James Dibdin called her specialty "old women," and said she sang Mrs Peachum in The Beggar's Opera and acted the Nurse in Romeo and Juliet. Norma Armstrong, in her calendar of Edinburgh performances, cites neither of those parts, but gives her unspecified roles in Agis and The Male Coquette, Doll Common in The Alchemist, Queen Gertrude in Hamlet, and Zara in The Mourning Bride. She never played in London, so far as we know. She died early in January 1761, according to Faulkner's Dublin Journal. It is not known when William Mynitt died.

The Mynitts had at least one child, who, as Master Mynitt, acted at Smock Alley every season from 1750–51 through 1755–56, at least. On 7 May 1755 he spoke "a piece" on the occasion of his parents' benefit and on 31 March 1756 he played a solo on the violin. Faulkner's Dublin Journal of 13 July 1756 mourned the passing of "his early theatrical genius" on 9 July.

Mynns, Mr ₍fl. 1696–1733₎, actor.

The part of Gypsy and the epilogue to Love's a Jest at Lincoln's Inn Fields Theatre in June 1696 were taken by Mr Mynns, whose name can be found variously spelled: Mins, Minn, Minns, Mynn. The strolling player Tony Aston spoke of touring with John Coysh, Thomas Doggett, a Mr Booker, and Mynns, probably in 1696–97 in Norwich and neighboring towns.

No sign can be found of Mynns in London until 27 November 1704, when Christopher Rich complained that the venturers who were preparing to open the new Queen's Theatre in the Haymarket were trying to lure Mynns away from Drury Lane. But records are very sparse for the early years of the century, and it is quite possible that Mynns had been acting in London for some time. He is known to have played Antonio in The Cares of Love at the Lincoln's Inn Fields playhouse on 1 August 1705, and in 1705–6 he proved the truth of Rich's concern, for he was a member of the Queen's Theatre troupe. There he acted Clip in *The Confederacy*, Polydamas in *Ulysses*, Damerature in *The Faithful General*, and Beron in *The Revolution in Sweden*. He shared a benefit with two others on 30 April 1706 and played Kent in *King Lear* on 30 November. After that we find no record of him until 4 January 1707, when he played the Merchant in *Wit Without Money* at the Queen's. The following 9 May 1707 he shared a benefit with two others. After that season he seems to have left the London stage.

W. S. Clark in *The Early Irish Stage* lists "Minns" in Dublin about 1714, and Chetwood in his *General History* in 1749 said that "Minns" about 1715 played Mirvan in *Tamerlane* and the second Committeeman in *The Committee*. After that we can find no references to our subject until 31 January 1723 at the Haymarket Theatre, when "Minns" played Nennius in *Bonduca*. Then in 13 February he acted Priuli in *The Orphan* at the same house and on 14 March was Sullen in *The Stratagem*.

Mynns acted at Norwich in 1728 but seems not to have performed in London again until 7 November 1729, when he appeared at the Goodman's Fields playhouse as Catesby in *Jane Shore*. He continued to the end of 1729–30, playing Alphonso in *The Spanish Fryar*, the Governor in *Oroonoko*, Sir Walter in *The Unhappy Favorite*, Tradelove in *A Bold Stroke for a Wife*, Vainlove in *The Old Bachelor*, Priuli in *Venice Preserv'd*, and Dugard in *The Inconstant*, Old Constant in *The Man's Bewitch'd*, Old Hob in *Flora*, Clerimont in *The Cobler of Preston*, and a Sailor in *The Fair Quaker*.

Again his name dropped from the bills until 28 September 1731, when he played Tradelove again at Southwark for Timothy Fielding. Perhaps he was at the Haymarket Theatre for the full 1731–32 season, but his name was not in the bills until 16 February 1732. On that date he acted Thrifty in *The Cheats of Scapin*, after which he played Plenty in *The Blazing Comet*, Tradelove once more, Ballance in *The Recruiting Officer*, Acasto in *The Orphan*, and Alphonso in *The Spanish Fryar*. He was gone almost a year, returning to the Haymarket on 19 March 1733 to act Sullen in *The Beaux' Stratagem*; a month later he played Ballance in *The Recruiting Officer*. He was doubtless the "Minns" who played Bomilcar in *Sophonisba* at Covent Garden on 6 July 1733, his last known London role.

His relationship, if any, to Mrs Mynns the booth operator of the Restoration and early eighteenth century is not known.

Mynns, Mrs   *d. 1717, booth operator.*

Though 1703 is the earliest year in which we have a record of Mrs Mynns operating a booth at the late summer fairs, her daughter, Elizabeth Leigh, had been active theatrically as early as 1681 with the playwright Elkanah Settle. As of 1687 Miss Leigh was a spinster, so one supposes that Leigh was the name of Mrs Mynns's first husband. Her second husband may have been the actor Mynns who was busy from 1696 to 1733, but there is no evidence to prove a relationship.

Montague Summers in his *Bibliography of Restoration Drama* claimed, without supplying proof, that Mrs Mynns presented Settle's *The Siege of Troy* in booths at Bartholomew and Southwark fairs in August and September 1703. She certainly produced that work at Bartholomew Fair in 1707, for the edition of that date names her booth and describes the elaborate scenes and machines she used. On 5 May 1708 Mrs Mynns put on an entertainment at Epsom. The *Daily Courant* of 3 May had announced that "at the new Cock-Pit, will be Acted Variety of Tragedies and Comedies by that Company of Players who perform'd the Siege of Troy with so much Applause last Bartholomew Fair, and who had had the Honour for several Years to play at Windsor for the Entertainment of the Nobility, being by long Travel together able to act near Fifty Plays perfect." The next notice we find of Mrs Mynns's activity comes from the *Daily Courant* of 2 September 1715, which advertised her productions of *The Siege of Troy* and *Bateman* at Southwark Fair.

The *Weekly Journal or British Gazetteer* on 4 January 1718 reported that

On Monday last [30 December 1717] was Interr'd the famous Mrs Mynns, who had for so many Years constantly kept a Booth in Bartholomew and Southwark Fair. She was a Woman of a very Masculine Temper, and govern'd the Legions under her Power with great Justice and exactness. . . . She has left three or four Thousand Pounds behind her.

Mead's Journal on 11 January augmented that report by noting that her actors who played "Caesar or Alexander have sometimes been content to put up a Box of the Ear from her."

Most of her fortune, that periodical reported, was "given to her Daughter; but as her Husband is Living, 'tis expected he wil set aside any Will." More on that evidently estranged marriage is not known.

How long Mrs Mynns's daughter Elizabeth worked with her is not known, though she was said by Summers to have been in the business when Settle was a salaried droll-writer and actor as late as 1716. She seems not to have continued the fair-booth operation after her mother's death, and it may well be that Mr Mynns prevented her from coming into her full inheritance. But a Mrs "Lee" was active in the 1720s at the fairs and was described on 28 August 1724 as a daughter of Mrs "Minns."

She planned to surpass even her mother, she announced, in a production of *The Siege of Troy*. That Mrs Lee is known to have been Hannah, not Elizabeth; she may have been Elizabeth's younger sister, and the altered spelling of her name may have been by choice, or she could well have married a Mr Lee. In 1735 Hannah Lee, calling herself a widow, pleaded against the proposed licensing act, and said that the company run by her mother years before had been the "nursery" of such actors as Mrs Bowtell and Mr Booth.

Myres. *See* MEYER.

Myres. *See* MAYERS, MEYERS, MORRIS.

= N =

"N. N., Signor" [*fl.* *1760–1761?*], *singer.*

On 25 August 1760 Signora Mattei announced that a Signor "N. N." would sing third man in the burlettas during the forthcoming season at the King's Theatre. Perhaps he did, but the bills for the 1760–61 season mentioned no one with those initials.

"N. N., Mons" [*fl.* *1776*], *dancer.*

On 9 January 1776 a Monsieur "N. N." danced at the King's Theatre in *Les Evenemens imprevues* and *La Generosité de Scipion*. He continued appearing through 13 February, but the bills did not reveal his full name.

Nackwood, Mr [*fl.* *1783*], *musician.*

The Lord Chamberlain's accounts show that a Mr Nackwood was a musician at the King's Theatre in 1783.

Nailer. *See* NAYLOR.

Naish, Mr [*fl.* *1688*], *singer?*

The Lord Chamberlain issued a warrant in December 1688 to pay Mr Naish, one of the Gentlemen of the Chapel Royal—and possibly a singer—for attendance at Windsor from 25 July to 19 September 1688. Naish received 6s. riding charges for his travel plus 1s. 6d. daily during his stay at Windsor. Possibly he was—or was related to—Robert Nash, who was a musician active in 1672, but there is not sufficient evidence to make an identification.

Namora. *See* LE NAMORA.

"Nan." *See* BRACEGIRDLE, ANNE, and CATLEY, ANN.

Nanfan, Master [*fl.* *1737–1741*], *dancer, actor.*

Master Nanfan was perhaps the son of the actor Nanfan who played Iago in *Othello* at the Rainsford Street playhouse in Dublin on 14 May 1735 but who is not known to have performed in London. Master Nanfan (or Nansan) shared a benefit with four others at the Lincoln's Inn Fields Theatre on 7 May 1737, when *The Honest Yorkshireman* was presented by "Capt. Gulliver's Company of Lilliputians." As a member of the troupe at the Goodman's Fields playhouse in 1740–41 Master Nanfan played Cupid in *King Arthur* beginning on 19 February 1741, and he was used as an entr'acte dancer. The following 22 August he acted Sydrophal in *Thamas Kouli Kan* at Bartholomew Fair.

Nansan. *See* NANFAN.

Napier, William *c.* *1741–1812, violinist, violist, composer, music publisher.*

William Napier was born about 1741. Little is known about his parentage, early life, or education. Possibly he was related to Dr Archibald Napier, whose daughter Mary Ann married the musician Samuel Arnold in 1771. By 1757–58 he was employed as a violinist in the band of the Canongate Theatre in Edinburgh. Napier settled in London by 1765, the year he became a member of the Royal Society of Musicians. On 8 January 1766 at St Paul, Covent Garden, he married Jane Stewart. The license granted by the Bishop of London specified that he was a bachelor, age 24, of St Martin-in-the-Fields, and that she was above the age of 21.

In the 1780s Napier was leader of the band at Ranelagh Gardens. He led the violas in the Handel Memorial Concerts at Westminster Abbey and the Pantheon in May and June 1784. For playing in the concerts of the Academy of Ancient Music in 1787–88 he was paid 13 guineas. A concert for his benefit was given at the Pantheon on 17 June 1789. In 1794 Doane's *Musical Directory* listed him as a member of the Royal Society of Musicians and a player in the Professional Concerts, the Concerts of the Academy of Ancient Music, and the Handelian concerts at Westminster Abbey. In February 1795 he was a violist in the Covent Garden oratorios.

Napier was also for many years an enterprising publisher and seller of music operating from a shop at No 474, the Strand, corner of Lancaster Court, from about 1772 to March 1791. During his last months at that address he suffered financial reverses and bankruptcy. On 5 December 1790 he informed the Governors of the Royal Society of Musicians that his goods had been taken in execution, that he was confined to the King's Bench, and that his wife and children were in extreme distress. The Governors granted him £8 14*s.* for that month. On 6 February 1791, still in the King's Bench, and confined to his bed with gout, he again begged relief for his wife and *eleven* children, five of them under the age of 14. That month the Governors responded with the usual allowance, but on 7 March 1791 they ordered the allowance discontinued, inasmuch as Napier was now liberated and in good health.

Upon his release, Napier ventured again into publishing, at No 49, Great Queen Street. In order to help Napier become reestablished, Haydn arranged a book of Scottish songs with accompaniment for pianoforte, violin, and violoncello. It sold so well that Napier could pay him £50; and for a subsequent book Haydn received £100. The caricaturist Gillray started his career in Napier's shop, and the musician George Smart also was once in his employ.

About 1800 Napier moved his business to No 8, Lisle Street, Leicester Square, in 1809 to Princess Street, Leicester Square. By the latter year his business was lagging again and his health declining. On 3 April 1808, upon an application from Napier which showed his income as £37 per annum, the Royal Society of Musicians granted ten guineas for medical assistance and £2 15*s.* per month for subsistence. In response to another representation of grave ill health, he was granted five guineas for medical aid on 2 September 1810. Grants of similar amounts were made on 6 May 1811, 4 August 1811, and 5 January 1812. In a letter to the Society on 4 August 1811, written

from Mr Bonsall's, cabinet maker in London Road, St George's Fields, Napier explained his plight:

The long and severe illness which I experienced at the beginning of the year occasioned me to contract a larger debt with the apothecary than the allowance which the Society was so kind as to send me could discharge and as I am to leave this place in the course of three weeks, I will be pressed for what remains.

Napier's death at Somerston on 31 July 1812, in his seventy-second year, was reported in the *Scot's Magazine* for August 1812: "He was distinguished for his musicall skill; and for the beautiful selections of Scotch ballads which he edited. For many years he belonged to his Majesty's band, and to the professional Concert; but he was obliged to retire on account of the gout in his hands, to which he became a victim."

On 2 August 1812 the Royal Society of Musicians paid £5 to discharge Napier's medical expenses and £8 to cover the costs of his funeral. Nothing is known by us of his wife or any of the 11 children he claimed to have fathered by 1791. Perhaps one of them was William Napier, late of Southampton and 1st Lieutenant on the H.M.S. *St George*, the administration of whose estate (less than £100) was granted to his widow Mary Napier on 27 February 1812.

Napier published a number of instrumental works, and he held the copyright to the popular ballad operas *Rosina* and *The Maid of the Mill*. Among his best-known publications was *A Selection of Original Scottish Songs*, three volumes issued between 1790 and 1794 with frontispieces by Bartolozzi. "Guglielmo Napier" is the imprint of *Sei Divertimenti per due violini . . . d℈ Luigi Borghi. Op III*ᵃ, about 1780. In 1784 Napier instituted a circulating musical library. About 1785 Napier sold some of his plates, copyrights, and a stock of books to Joseph Dale for £450.

"Napoleon of Wych Street, The Little." *See* ELLISTON, ROBERT WILLIAM.

Napp. *See* KNAPP.

Nares, James *1715–1783, organist, composer.*

James Nares was born at Stanwell, Middlesex, in 1715 and was baptized there on 19 April of that year. He was the elder son of George Nares of Albany, Oxfordshire, steward to the Earl of Abingdon. James's younger brother was Sir George Nares (1716–1786), a justice of the Court of Common Pleas. As a chorister in the Chapel Royal James was instructed by Gates, Croft, and Pepusch. He served for a while as deputy organist, under the younger Francis Piggott, at St George's Chapel, Windsor, until at the age of 20 he became in August 1735 organist of York Minster, a position to which he was formally appointed on 8 November 1735. After over 20 years he left York, where he had composed services and anthems, to succeed Greene as composer and organist to the Chapel Royal on 13 January 1756. The following year he became Doctor of Music at Cambridge.

Nares succeeded Gates as Master of the Children of the Chapel Royal in October 1757. In

Harvard Theatre Collection

JAMES NARES

engraving by Ward, after Engleheart

1763 *Mortimer's London Directory* listed his address in James Street, Westminster, the location of the Chapel Royal. He won a prize at the Catch Club in 1770 for his glee "To all Lovers of Harmony."

On at least one occasion Nares brought his choristers to sing in a theatrical production, Dibdin's masque *The Institution of the Garter*, a spectacle that opened at Drury Lane on 28 October 1771 and ran for a number of nights. On 12 November 1771 the Drury Lane treasurer paid "Dr Nares and Mr Cooke's Boys in the *Garter* 12 nights (11th inst. inclusive) £36."

Nares resigned his duties as Master of the Children of the Chapel Royal on 1 July 1780 and was succeeded by Edmund Ayrton, a close friend and former pupil. Another pupil, Samuel Arnold, succeeded Nares as organist of the Chapel Royal at his teacher's death. Also among Nares's pupils were John Crosdill, John and Matthew Camidge, John Holder, William Carnaby, and John Stafford Smith.

Nares died on 10 February 1783, leaving a widow, two sons, and two daughters. He was buried in the vault of St Margaret, Westminster. In his will drawn on 1 November 1782—"in the 68th year of my Age"—he left his wife Jane all his real and personal estate, provided she did not marry again, and made provisions for passing the legacy to his children. To his daughter Jane he bequeathed his Worcester Bridge securities and a house rented to a Mr Just. Son Robert was left a house a Mr Tibbs rented and Nares's own house. Daughter Mary received the Tontine annuities in her name and the mortgage on William Lord's house. And son William was left all Nares's stock and annuities in three per cent consols and the Tontine. The balance of his estate was to be divided among the children, but since Robert had received an expensive education, £500 was to be deducted from his share; and since William and Mary owned £100 in the Irish Tontine, he left an additional £100 to his daughter Jane. He also stipulated that "If I die suddenly without any accident I desire I may be opened." His brother Justice George Nares and his friend William Ayrton, the named executors, proved the will on 25 February 1783.

Sainsbury judged Nares "a studious and sound musician," whose writings demonstrated that he had been "endowed with a very considerable share both of genius and learning in his profession." Nares's glee for four voices and a canon are in manuscript in the Euing Collection at Glasgow University. Among his published compositions were: *A Collection of Catches, Canons and Glees* (1775?); *Six Fugues with Introductory Voluntary's for the Organ or Harpsichord* (1775?); *Three Lessons for the Harpsichord with a Sonata in Score for the Harpsichord or Organ* (1759?); *Il Principio or a Regular Introduction to playing on the Harpsichord or Organ* (1760?); *The Royal Pastoral, a Dramatic Ode*, a full score (1769); various collections of psalms, hymns, catches, and glees; and various lessons for the harpsichord. Several of his services and anthems were published in Page's *Harmonia sacra*, Arnold's *Cathedral Music*, and Stevens's *Sacred Music*. Some catches and rounds were included in Warren's collections. *A Morning & Evening Service . . . Together with Six Anthems in Score* by Nares was published posthumously in 1788; that publication also contained a brief memoir of his life by his son Robert Nares (1753–1829), who became an eminent philologist and manuscript librarian at the British Museum. An appreciation of Nares's compositions is given in the *New Grove Dictionary*.

Nares's portrait was painted by John Hoppner, who had been a Chapel Royal chorister under him. The location of the canvas is unknown, but an engraving by W. Ward, of a copy by G. Engleheart, was published as frontispiece to Nares's *A Morning and Evening Service*, 1788. A similar portrait of Nares, stippled by T. Hardy, was published as a plate to the *European Magazine*, 1795.

Narici, Bernardo [*fl. 1678–1679*], actor.

Bernardo Narici was one of the members of the Duke of Modena's Company. That troupe performed six times in London between November 1678 and mid-February 1679, with Narici playing the *amoroso* Orazio.

Narr. *See* MARR.

"Nasaquitine, Don John de" [*fl. 1749*], performer?

On 16 January 1749 a large audience gathered at the Haymarket Theatre, lured by advertisements promising an extraordinary performance by one who would put himself inside an ordinary bottle. The "Bottle Conjuror"

(William Nicholls) did not appear, of course, and the audience rioted. The *General Advertiser* on 27 January carried the following notice:

Don John de Nasaquitine, sworn brother and champion to the man that was to have jumped into the bottle . . . hereby invites all such as were then disappointed to repair to the theatre on Monday the 30th, and that shall be exhibited to them which never was before, nor ever will be hereafter seen. All such as shall swear upon the Book of Wisdom that they paid for seeing the Bottle man, will be admitted gratis; the rest at Gotham prices.

There is no record of a performance at any London theatre on 30 January (it was a traditional day of observance of the death of Charles I and the theatres always closed), but whoever was parading under the pseudonym of Don John de Nasaquitine may have provided some kind of entertainment somewhere.

"Nash, Madame de la." *See* FIELDING, HENRY.

Nash, Miss [*fl. 1782*], actress.

A Miss Nash was one of the four Tailors' Ladies in the pantomime *The Taylors* at a specially-licensed performance at the Haymarket Theatre on 25 November 1782.

Nash, John [*fl. 1670–1677*], rope dancer, manager.

The Lord Chamberlain ordered the apprehension of John Nash on 29 August 1670 for presenting dumb shows, rope dances, and the like. A strolling performer, Nash was in Edinburgh in 1677 and applied for permission to perform. In the *Extracts from The Records of the Burgh of Edinburgh* is a record of the reply of 23 November:

The council upon a petitione given in be John Nash roap dancer craving libertie and permission for erecting ane stage within the tinnes court oposit to the tron and to put up volting roaps therein for the acting of his shews . . . hes herby liberty to take from each persone that sahll desyreto see the saids playes thrie shilling scots money and no more . . .

The information on the Edinburgh activity of Nash was presented in *Theatre Notebook* 22 by Terence Tobin.

Nash, Joseph *d. 1793, actor.*

The first known notice of the actor Nash later identifiable as Joseph Nash was on the Drury Lane playbill for 31 December 1776. He walked on as the Messenger in *The Way of the World*. The following night he played—or perhaps only sat—as one of five Justices in the pantomime *Harlequin's Invasion*, very popular that season. He remained at Drury Lane, much employed in similar service, but adding only the following to his repertoire: in 1777–78, Peto in *1 Henry IV*, an Officer in *Twelfth Night*, Nym in *The Merry Wives of Windsor*; in 1778–79, a part unspecified in *The Wonders of Derbyshire* and a Drawer in *The Gamester*; in 1779–80, the Fat Cook in *Queen Mab* and a "Principal Character" in *The Genii*; in 1780–81 unspecified roles in *The Camp* and *The Lord of the Manor*; and in 1781–82, an unspecified role in *Lun's Ghost*. Nash played at Richmond, Surrey, in the summer of 1777.

When a special benefit was arranged at the Haymarket Theatre for Griffiths, "formerly of Drury Lane Theatre," on 6 March 1786, Nash played Dervise in *Tamerlane the Great*. He seems to have joined the small company at the Windsor Inn, Hammersmith, in the summer of 1786. But many of those playbills are lost and we know only that he played Major O'Flaherty in *The Natural Son* on 5 August 1786.

James Winston's transcription of the accounts of the Drury Lane Fund, now at the Folger Library, shows that Joseph Nash subscribed the usual 10s. 6d. in 1777, "claimed" benefits in November 1792, and died in February 1793.

Nash, Robert *[fl. 1672], musician.*

The Lord Chamberlain ordered the apprehension of Robert Nash and others on 2 October 1672; they were all men who tried to "teach, practise and exercise music without lycence of the Marshall and Corporation of Musick."

Illustrations

SCENES AND MACHINES

INSIDE OF THE DUKES THEATRE
in Lincoln's Inn Fields .
as it appeared in the reign of King Charles II.

This view represents the stage of the above Theatre, and its very elegant frontispiece, during the perform-
ance of a scene from Elkannah Settle's Empress of Morocco. *The Theatre itself was deserted twelve*
years after its foundation, for the one in Dorset Gardens; *being found too small and incommodious*
for the company that visited it. Part of it was discovered by the late fire in "Bear Yard". Its size
must have been extremely small, compared with our present Theatres.

The stage of the Dorset Garden Theatre (1673)

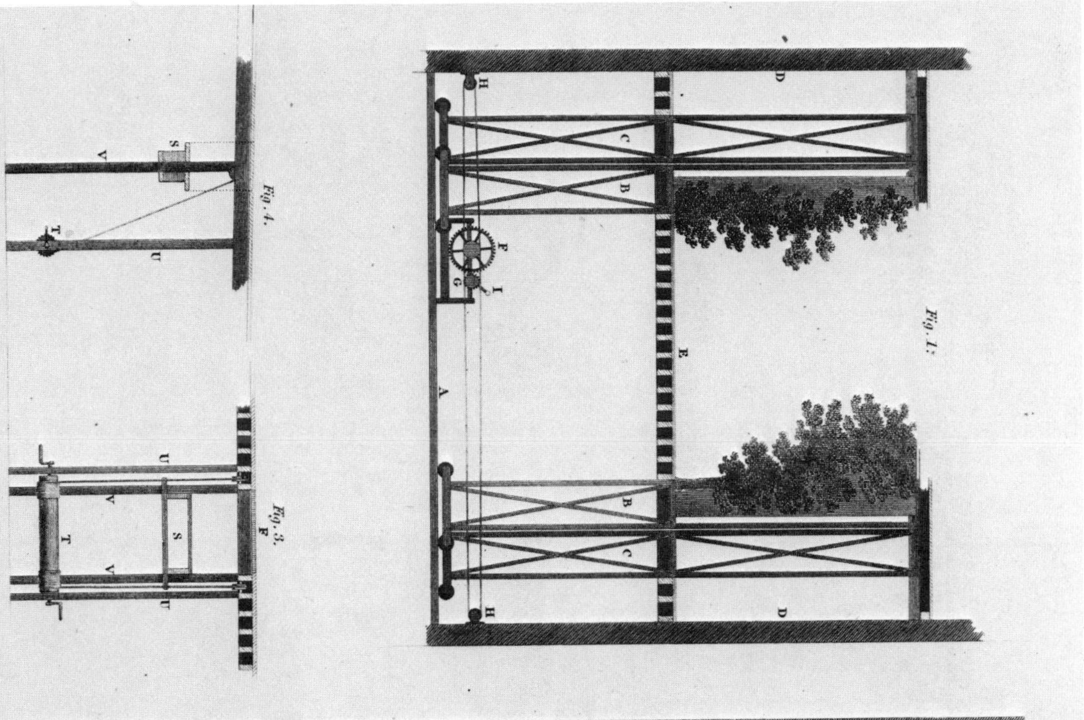

Fig. 4.

Fig. 3.

Fig. 1.

Fig. 2.

Fig. 1.

from *Rees' Cyclopedia (1803–1811)*

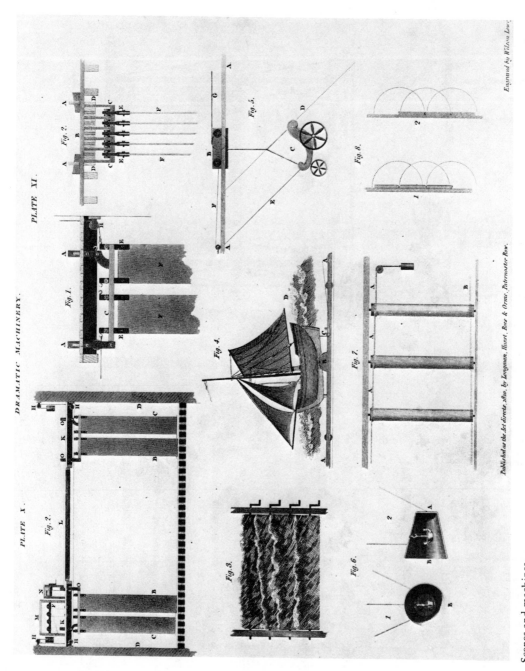

420

DRAMATIC MACHINERY.

PLATE XI.

PLATE X.

Engraved by Wilson Lowry.

Published as the Act directs, 1811, by Longman, Hurst, Rees & Orme, Paternoster Row.

Fig. 1.

Fig. 2.

Fig. 3.

Fig. 4.

Fig. 5.

Fig. 6.

Fig. 7.

Fig. 8.

Scenes and machines
from Rees' Cyclopedia (1803–1811)

421

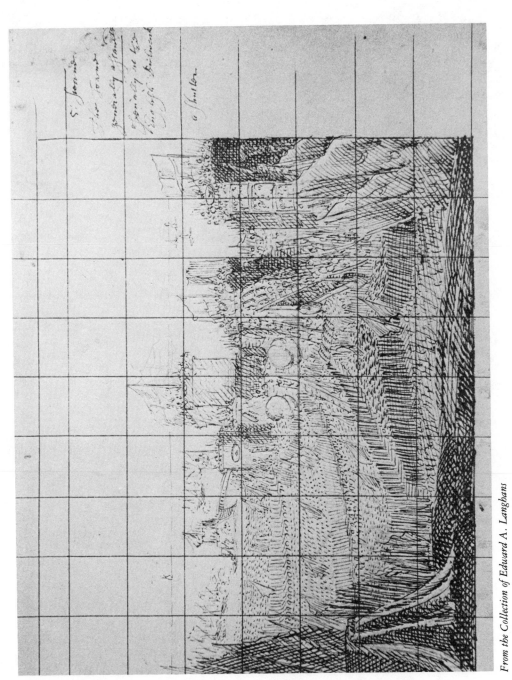

From the Collection of Edward A. Langhans

Scene design by Webb for *The Siege of Rhodes* (1656)

422

Scene design, probably for the King's Theatre

Stage setting at the Royalty Theatre (1785–1787)

from Wilkinson's Londina Illustrata (1825)

Harvard Theatre Collection

The Sadler's Wells stage, fitted with a water tank (1815)

425

Courtesy of the Leicestershire Libraries and Information Service

Scene design by Capon for *Richard III*